Los Angeles

written and researched by

JD Dickey

www.roughguides.com

Introduction to
Los Angeles

A maddening collection of freeways and beaches, fast-food joints and theme parks, seedy suburbs and high-gloss neighborhoods, Los Angeles is California's biggest and most stimulating city – though an unconventional one by any standard. Indeed, LA's character is so shifting and elusive – understandable "only dimly, and in flashes," according to F. Scott Fitzgerald – that the city might be freely dismissed by many outsiders if it weren't so central to the world's mass culture. Its multiple personalities and lack of any unifying design make it seem at first neither approachable, nor perhaps even enjoyable; but once the free-spirited chaos of the place takes hold, you'll be hard-pressed to resist.

Made up of scores of distinct municipalities, LA is a model for modern city development, having traded urban centralization for suburban sprawl and high-rise corporate towers for strip malls. It gets more than ample opportunity to show off its wares because of its stature as global entertainment center, which paints a picture of a sunny and glamorous place like no other. It is certainly unique, an unpredictable and addictive assault on the senses, where mud-wrestling venues and porn cinemas stand next door to chic boutiques and trendy restaurants, the whole of it under constant threat of the next earthquake, flood, or natural disaster.

Despite this uniqueness, LA has much in common with other major US cities. With the largest combined port in the country (and biggest in the world outside of China), LA is a center for transpacific trade and a dominant **financial hub** in its own right. Meanwhile, LA's **social gaps** are

Fact file

- The **population** of the city of Los Angeles is 3.7 million, with another 5.8 million elsewhere in LA County, and 2.8 million in Orange County. Add to this another 4 million from surrounding counties, and Southern California is the second most populous region in the United States, fourth in the Western Hemisphere, and ninth in the world.

- Some one hundred **languages** are spoken among LA's schoolchildren, whose families emigrated here from nearly 150 countries. More than half the population is Hispanic, and the remainder includes significant numbers of Vietnamese, Russians, Koreans, Filipinos, Chinese and Iranians, as well as English expatriates, who number some 360,000 in LA County alone.

- The **Olympics** were held in the city in 1932 and 1984, with respective profits of $50 and $300 million.

- **Famous dishes** invented in LA include the cheeseburger, hot fudge sundae, French dip sandwich and Caesar salad.

- Of the more than two thousand varieties of **palm tree** in Southern California (most of them planted between the world wars), only one type is native to the region — the California Palm.

quite broad, and there appears to be no end in sight for the nasty racial divisions broadcast to the world during the 1992 riots. Not a simple matter of black versus white, LA's unparalleled diversity means

Los Angeles is California's biggest and most stimulating city – though an unconventional one by any standard

that more languages are spoken here than in any other US city, even as some residents – especially white suburbanites – cordon themselves off from one another in gated communities.

Unlike more conventional cities, LA does not reward an attraction-oriented itinerary, going from one museum or official exhibit to the next. While there are world-class institutions here – the Getty Center foremost among them – the sights

that are most worth seeing tend to be separated by vast distances, and you'll doubtless spend most of your time on the freeway if you try to see them all. Instead, LA is perhaps best experienced as the locals do, by way of its innovative restaurants and dynamic nightlife, funky shopping strips and colorful boardwalks. Surprisingly for such a huge place, many of these places are concentrated in fairly compact neighborhoods, such as Venice and Old Pasadena, where you can often leave your car in a parking lot or just take public transit to get there. Outside the central city, LA can be surprisingly relaxing as well, whether you're lounging on a deserted beach, taking an island tour of Santa Catalina, or skiing in the eastern mountains.

What to see

Most of the city of Los Angeles lies in a flat basin, contained within and around the Santa Monica, San Gabriel, Santa Ana and Verdugo mountains, and hemmed in by the Pacific Ocean to the west – a geography best appreciated from the crest of the Hollywood Hills, where on any given night you're likely to see the city lights spread out before you in a seemingly perfect, and endless, illuminated grid. Though ideal for hosting a vast network of freeways, the landscape also features undulating hills, coastal bluffs, mountain ranges and rocky canyons, places that are variously home to shopping malls, theme parks and fancy homes, not to mention impressive museums and rugged parks.

The Googie style

Named after a Hollywood coffee shop, the term "Googie" refers to a particularly exuberant style of postwar design, first used in roadside diners and notable for its array of eye-catching decor – boomerang curves, plate-glass windows, Formica countertops, and cantilevered

roofs. The outdoor signs are especially characteristic, using colorful neon in a variety of outlandish, Space Age shapes – starbursts, amoebas, atoms, and even flying saucers. Although many of the eateries, motels, bowling alleys, and gas stations built in this style have been demolished or remodeled, there are still enough worthwhile Googie examples in LA that you can take a tour of them (see p.35), or check them out online at Ⓦ www.roadsidepeek.com or Ⓦ www.spaceagecity.com.

Starting in the center of the region, the hub of LA's political and financial life is Downtown, and yet within this fairly compact area you'll also encounter modern art museums, bustling immigrant enclaves, old moviehouses and, of course, a growing collection of skyscrapers. On the whole, though, the district is missing the sort of vibrant nightlife and inherent excitement that often characterizes the more tourist-friendly zones of the Westside.

Just west of Downtown, the loosely defined district of **Mid–Wilshire**, built around the commercial strip of Wilshire Boulevard, is where you'll find some of LA's best Art Deco architecture, along with the colourful shopping strip of Melrose Avenue, but most

Stargazing in LA

If you really want to catch a glimpse of the glitterati in LA, you can do much better than riding around on a tour bus staring at the locked gates outside the homes of the rich and famous — and paying a bundle for the privilege. In fact, with a minimum of preparation, you can quickly find yourself

within sight of your favorite movie hero, TV star or media celebrity (ie, someone famous for just being famous).

One of the best methods is to drop by Hollywood's Motion Picture Production Office (see p.100) and pick up a list of the daily production shoots around town, and sneak a peek at the big names from the sidelines. To catch the stars while they're playing instead of working, the city's trendiest bars and clubs are the places to go (check the *LA Times'* weekly entertainment section, Calendar Live), as are the celebrity-oriented restaurants listed in the box on p.268. If you do get the chance to approach a celebrity, consider the circumstances: they're much less likely to blow you off in full public view, especially in the company of a reporter or press agent, than they are if you have the temerity to invade their privacy at a back-room dining booth or on the Stairmaster at an upscale gym.

visitors head first to the renowned neighborhood north of here, **Hollywood**. Despite its longstanding patina of grime, the district is still an essential stop for tourists, its faded allure surviving in grand movie palaces like the Chinese Theatre and the ever-popular "Walk of Fame." To the west, trendy **West Hollywood** is the place for designer boutiques, elite galleries and pricey restaurants, while north of Hollywood proper, the Hollywood Hills are dotted

with stylish cliff-hanging mansions, and are perhaps best known for massive Griffith Park, location of LA's famed observatory.

West of here, in the heart of the city's Westside, **Beverly Hills** and **West LA** are where visitors often base themselves, keeping close to the all-out glitz of Rodeo Drive or Westwood's movie theaters and affordable shops. In the latter district, there's also the picturesque UCLA campus, and further west, in the Sepulveda corridor, LA's showpiece, the Getty Center. Less hyped is **Culver City**, to the south, where you'll find a few small-scale museums and an abundance of experimental architecture.

Traffic and smog

Whatever you may have heard about LA's more dangerous side, it's more likely you'll only face the typical pitfalls of traffic and smog. The latter, while still virulent, has slowly improved in recent years, with LA briefly ceding its ranking as the most polluted place in America to Houston, Texas. Gridlock can also be avoided to an extent, as many neighborhoods are surprisingly compact and can be seen on foot, but you'll still likely need a car to jump around from place to place, or to see any semblance of the city sprawl. Driving on LA's myriad freeways can be a challenge, but as long as you don't try to emulate some of the crazier local motorists, you should have few problems. Whatever your transportation plan, make sure to budget plenty of time for your travels. While on the best of days, you can travel from Santa Monica to Downtown LA in twenty minutes by freeway, most likely it will take twice that, or more than seventy minutes on side streets.

The coastal cities of **Santa Monica** and **Venice**, known for their piers, amusement parks, and surfers, give LA its popular seaside image. These low-scaled beach communities attract different sets of residents – well-heeled yuppies and aging pensioners in Santa Monica, and struggling artists and well-off bohemians in Venice. Although both areas offer a fairly diverse mix of offbeat shops and quirky modern homes, most visitors prefer to stick to the comfy confines of the Third Street Promenade, Santa Monica Pier, and Venice Boardwalk.

Well off the path of most tourists and dogged by crime, **South Central** and **East LA** hold a few scattered but notable sights like historic architecture and important cultural institutions, while well to the south, the largely residential and industrial **South Bay** and **LA Harbor** feature some attrac-

tive oceanside scenery, plus a few unpretentious beachfront towns, including the port cities of San Pedro and Long Beach. Not far away, at the southwestern edge of LA, the Palos Verdes Peninsula offers breathtaking ocean vistas amid some of LA's priciest real estate.

The sprawling suburbs of the **San Gabriel** and **San Fernando valleys**, east and north of the Hollywood Hills, have become increasingly popular for dining, shopping, and a range of cultural activities, from Burbank's working movie studios and Glendale's famed Forest Lawn cemetery to the historic town of Pasadena. More appealing to nature lovers, however, are the areas around **Malibu** and the **Santa Monica Mountains**, where the many state and regional parks are ideal for exploring on foot, or by car along the scenic Mulholland Highway. Nearby, the exclusive enclave of Pacific Palisades holds a few architectural highlights, while the city of Malibu to the north is a celebrity haven whose beaches are famously difficult, though not impossible, to access.

More accessible beach options abound in **Orange County**, though the area is better known for sights like Knott's Berry Farm and Disneyland. The most distant attractions will take you almost halfway to San Diego, where you can chase the swallows of Mission San Juan Capistrano or take a peek at Nixon's old haunt of San Clemente.

When to go

Los Angeles holds several types of warm **climate zones**, including desert, semi-arid and Mediterranean areas, and differences in temperature between constituent cities can be great: for example, Pasadena is ten to fifteen degrees hotter on average than Santa Monica, which can resemble a maritime climate at times. In general, toasty air and sunny skies reign: summer and fall months are fairly warm and dry; winter and spring periods are cooler and wetter, but still quite warm.

Due to the geography of the LA basin, the city sometimes suffers from high levels of smog, worst during a few summer months in the eastern parts of the region. Torrential rainstorms occur during the winter months, and disastrous fires and mudslides affect hillside neighborhoods across the city with unsettling frequency.

Average temperatures and rainfall

	Jan	Feb	Mar	Apr	May	June	July	Aug	Sept	Oct	Nov	Dec
Max °F	65	66	68	71	73	77	83	82	81	77	73	68
Min °F	47	48	49	53	55	60	63	63	60	57	53	49
Max °C	18	19	20	22	23	25	28	28	27	25	23	20
Min °C	8	9	9	12	13	16	17	17	16	14	12	9

19

things not to miss

It's not possible to see everything that Los Angeles has to offer in one trip — and we don't suggest you try. What follows is a selective and subjective taste of the city's highlights: dynamic restaurants and bars, striking architecture, glamorous shopping districts and relaxed beach towns. They're arranged in five color-coded categories to help you find the very best things to see, do and experience. All entries have a page reference to take you straight into the Guide, where you can find out more.

01 Third Street Promenade Page **134** • Sooner or later, all visitors to LA visit this Santa Monica pedestrian mall for its people watching, swinging nightlife and fine dining options.

02 Getty Center Page **122** • High above West LA, this celebrated arts center holds an impressive art collection, but it's equally noteworthy for its sleek modern design.

03 Hanging out on the Venice Boardwalk Page **138** • Despite the hordes of tourists, this free-spirited strip is still a fun way to get a feel for Southern California's beach life, especially on rollerblades.

04 Gamble House Page **183** • This beautifully preserved Craftsman-style house is one of Pasadena's gems, with alluring architectural details both inside and out.

06 Bradbury Building Page **63** • Atmospherically shot in movies from *Citizen Kane* to *Blade Runner*, this office building features a gorgeous lobby containing some of the best-preserved Victorian decor around.

05 Griffith Park Page **91** • You could easily spend an afternoon rambling along the trails of the nation's largest municipal park, making your way up to the famed observatory for its panoramic views of the city.

07 Shopping on Melrose Avenue Page **86** • For a look at LA's quirky side, head to this eclectic shopping strip – one of the only places in the city where you'll find designer boutiques mixed in with racy novelty stores and oddball retailers.

09 Musso and Frank Grill
Page **98** • The quintessential Hollywood watering hole – dark, moody and serious about their cocktails. Celebrities have been hanging out here since Hollywood's golden age.

08 The Viper Room Page **109** •
A Sunset Strip mainstay and one of the best spots in LA to catch live rock, punk, and metal.

11 Queen Mary Page **171** • Soak up the Art Deco details aboard the sumptuous *Queen Mary*, the site of a spectacular fireworks show on Independence Day.

10 Greystone Mansion Page **115** • He may have been a ruthless oil baron, but Edward Doheny left behind an elegant manor in Beverly Hills, surrounded by manicured lawns.

12 **The Chinese Theatre** Page 99 • A cherished relic of the 1920s, preserving Hollywood's golden age in its Art Deco interior and in the celebrity hand- and footprints pressed into the pavement outside.

13 **Watts Towers** Page 154 • These spiny towers built from cast-off glass and pottery are a welcome sight in South Central LA, where their graceful silhouettes lend an otherworldly touch.

14 **Museum of Contemporary Art (MOCA)** Page 65 • If the Pop Art and photography inside don't tempt you, the building itself no doubt will – a whimsical design set against a backdrop of gleaming Downtown skyscrapers.

15 **Canter's Deli** Page 250 • A slice of old Los Angeles, with enormous sandwiches served to you by brassy waitresses. At night, catch the live music and vaudeville-style acts in the adjoining "Kibbitz Room" bar.

16 Cruising Sunset Boulevard Page **101** • The Strip has long been a choice LA place to hang out in, jammed with groovy bars and clubs, swanky hotels, offbeat boutiques and towering billboards.

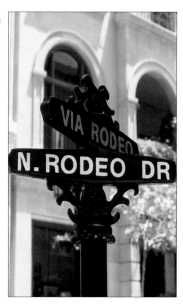

17 **Golden Triangle/Rodeo Drive** Page **113** • Mostly fun for window-shopping, this immaculately kept shopping district features all the high-end retailers, from Gucci to Armani.

18 **Disneyland** Page **210** • Much more than a theme park, the "Magic Kingdom" is a carefully planned resort where you can eat, sleep and take a spin on the family-oriented rides without ever leaving its gates.

19 **Malibu Creek State Park** Page **207** • Terrific camping and hiking opportunities abound in this expansive park tucked away in the Santa Monica Mountains, its vistas strikingly familiar from movies and TV.

Contents

Using this Rough Guide

We've tried to make this Rough Guide a good read and easy to use. The book is divided into six main sections, and you should be able to find whatever you want in one of them.

Front section

The front color section offers a quick tour of Los Angeles. The **introduction** aims to give you a feel for the city, with suggestions on where to go. We also tell you what the weather is like and include a basic fact file. Next, our author rounds up his favorite aspects of Los Angeles in the **things not to miss section** – whether it's great food, amazing sights or a special activity. Right after this comes the Rough Guide's full **contents** list.

Basics

The Basics section covers all the **pre-departure** nitty-gritty to help you plan your trip and the practicalities you'll want to know once there. This is where to find out about money and costs, Internet access, transportation, car rental, local media – in fact just about every piece of **general practical information** you might need.

The City

This is the heart of the Rough Guide, divided into user-friendly chapters, each of which covers a specific area. Every chapter contains an **introduction** that helps you to decide where to go, followed by an extensive tour of the sights, all plotted on a neighborhood map.

Listings

Listings contain all the consumer information needed to make the most of your stay, with chapters on **accommodation**, places to **eat** and **drink**, **live music** and **culture** venues, **shopping**, **sports** and **festivals**.

Contexts

Read Contexts to get a deeper understanding of what makes Los Angeles tick. We include a brief **history**, plus a look at the city's film industry, along with a detailed section that reviews numerous **books and films** relating to the city.

Index + small print

Apart from a **full index**, which includes maps as well as places, this section covers publishing information, credits and acknowledgments, and also has our contact details in case you want to send in updates and corrections to the book – or suggestions as to how we might improve it.

Color maps

The back color section contains eight detailed maps and plans to help you explore the city up close and locate every place recommended in the guide.

Map and chapter list

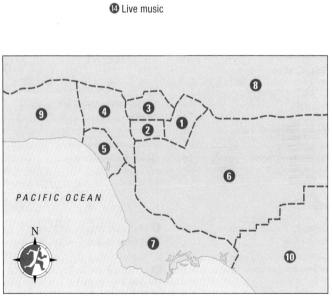

▼ Santa Catalina Island

PACIFIC OCEAN

N

Contents

Contexts 353

Index + small print 395

Color maps at back of book

1. Regional bus routes
2. Los Angeles region
3. Central LA
4. Downtown LA

5. Hollywood
6. West Hollywood and the Miracle Mile
7. The Westside
8. Santa Monica and Venice

Map symbols

maps are listed in the full index using colored text

⬛80⬛	Interstate	✕	Airport
30	US Highway	Ⓜ	Metrorail station
1	Highway	◉	Hotel
= = =	Road under construction	◼	Restaurant
= = = = =	Pedestrianized road	🗼	Lighthouse
⚏⚏⚏	Steps	⌃⌃⌃	Mountain range
– – – –	Walkway	⋎	Marshland
■■■	Railway	ⓘ	Information center
— —	Ferry route	■	Building
■–■–■	International border	⊞	Church
■ ■ ■	State border	⊞	Cemetery
— — —	Chapter division boundary	▢	Park/National or State Park
———	River	▢	Beach

Basics

Basics

Getting there

Unless you are coming from nearby on the West Coast, the quickest way to Los Angeles is to fly to Los Angeles International Airport or Orange County's John Wayne International (see p.26 for specific details).

Airfares always depend on the **season**, with the **highest** being around June to the end of August and around Christmas; you'll get the best prices during the **low season**, mid-January to the end of February, and October to the end of November (excluding Christmas and New Year when prices are hiked up and seats are at a premium); **shoulder seasons** cover the rest of the year. You might make major savings by shifting your departure date by a week – or even a day. Note also that flying on weekends ordinarily adds around $30–40 to the round-trip fare; price ranges quoted below assume midweek travel.

While it's worth calling the airlines directly to inquire about their fares, you'll save yourself a lot of time, and often cut costs, by going through a **specialist flight agent** – either a **consolidator**, who buys up blocks of tickets from the airlines and sells them at a discount, or a **discount agent** who, in addition to dealing with discounted flights, may also offer special student and youth fares and a range of other travel-related services such as rail passes, car rental, tours and the like. Bear in mind, though, that changing your plans can be costly. Some agents specialize in **charter flights**, which may be cheaper than anything available on a scheduled flight, but again departure dates are fixed and withdrawal penalties are high: be sure to check the refund policy. If you travel a lot, **discount travel clubs** are another option – the annual membership fee may be worth it for benefits such as cut-price air tickets and car rental. For Los Angeles, you may even find it cheaper to pick up a bargain **package deal** from one of the tour operators listed below and then find your own accommodation when you get there. A further possibility is to see if you can arrange a **courier flight**, although you'll need a flexible schedule, and preferably be traveling alone with very little luggage. In return for shepherding a parcel through customs, you can expect to get a deeply discounted ticket. You'll probably also be restricted in the duration of your stay.

If the US is only one stop on a longer journey, you might want to consider buying a **Round-the-World (RTW)** ticket. Some travel agents can sell you an "off-the-shelf" RTW ticket that will have you touching down in about half a dozen cities (Los Angeles is on many itineraries); others will have to assemble one for you, which can be tailored to your needs but is apt to be more expensive.

Overseas travelers should also keep in mind that all of the major American airlines offer air passes for flights within the US. These must be bought in advance, and usually require that you reach the US with the same airline. All the deals are broadly similar, involving the purchase of at least three coupons, each valid for a flight of any duration within the US.

Online booking agents and general travel sites

Many airlines and discount travel websites offer you the opportunity to book your tickets online, cutting out the costs of agents and middlemen. Good deals can often be found through discount or auction sites, as well as through the airlines' own websites.

ⓦ **travel.yahoo.com** Incorporates a lot of Rough Guides material in its coverage of destination countries and cities across the world, with information about places to eat, sleep and so on.

ⓦ **www.cheapflights.com** Bookings from the UK and Ireland only (for US, ⓦ www.cheapflight.com; for Canada, ⓦ www.cheapflights.ca; for Australia, ⓦ www.cheapflights.com.au). Flight deals, travel agents, plus links to other travel sites.

ⓦ **www.cheaptickets.com** Discount flight specialists (US only).

⊛**www.etn.nl/discount.htm** A hub of consolidator and discount agent Web links, maintained by the nonprofit European Travel Network.

⊛**www.expedia.com** Discount airfares, all-airline search engine and daily deals.

⊛**www.flyaow.com** Online air travel info and reservations only.

⊛**www.gaytravel.com** Gay-oriented online travel agent, offering accommodation, cruises, tours and more.

⊛**www.geocities.com/thavery2000** Has an extensive list of airline toll-free numbers (from the US) and websites.

⊛**www.hotwire.com** Bookings from the US only. Last-minute savings of up to forty percent on regular published fares. Travelers must be at least 18 and there are no refunds, transfers or changes allowed. Log-in required.

⊛**www.lastminute.com** Offers good last-minute holiday package and flight-only deals.

⊛**www.priceline.com** Name-your-own-price website that has deals at around forty percent off standard fares. You cannot specify flight times (although you do specify dates) and the tickets are nonrefundable, nontransferable and nonchangeable.

⊛**www.skyauction.com** Bookings from the US only. Auctions tickets and travel packages using a "second bid" scheme. The best strategy is to bid the maximum you're willing to pay, since if you win you'll pay just enough to beat the runner-up regardless of your maximum bid.

⊛**www.smilinjack.com/airlines.htm** Lists an up-to-date compilation of airline website addresses.

⊛**www.travelocity.com** Destination guides, hot Web fares and best deals for car hire, accommodation and lodging as well as fares. Provides access to the travel agent system SABRE, the most comprehensive central reservations system in the US.

⊛**www.travelshop.com.au** Australian website offering discounted flights, packages, insurance and online bookings.

Flights and other approaches from the US and Canada

As the major hub for domestic and international travel on the West Coast, LA is well served by air, rail and road networks. The best means of getting to LA from most places in North America is to fly, as many airlines offer daily service to LA from across the US and Canada. Rail travel is a distant second, with few options save for Amtrak, the nation's ailing train system. The cheapest and most cost-effective way is to go by bus, but it's also the least comfortable and the most time-consuming. And of course, you could follow the lead of millions of tourists and simply drive to LA.

By plane

The most convenient airport for domestic arrivals into LA is **Los Angeles International Airport**, known as "LAX." Most flights into LA use LAX, but if you're arriving from elsewhere in the US or Mexico, you can land at one of the **smaller airports** in the LA area – at John Wayne Airport in Orange County, Long Beach, Burbank, Van Nuys or Ontario (nearly thirty miles east of Downtown LA).

As airlines tend to match each other's prices, there's generally little difference in their quoted fares; however, with many companies experiencing economic troubles in recent years, week-to-week prices can vary dramatically, with some financially strapped airlines reducing their flight schedules and range of bargains, and tacking on stiff fees for meal service and nonstop routes.

The cheapest round-trip prices from New York generally start at around $230, or $200 from Chicago, $500 from Miami, and $450 from Toronto or Montréal. Flights from major US air hubs, such as Denver, Atlanta and Chicago, will often cost you less than shorter trips from smaller airports closer to LA, unless you're flying on a **regional carrier**, in which case you can expect to pay much less – in some cases less than $100 roundtrip from western US cities.

What makes more difference than your choice of carrier are the conditions governing the ticket: whether it is fully refundable, the time and day, and, most importantly, the **time of year** you travel. Least expensive is a low-season midweek flight, booked and purchased at least three weeks in advance. Some no-frills carriers can often provide good value as well, notably Southwest Airlines, Jet Blue, National, American Trans Air and Frontier.

Travelers **from Canada** may find that, with less competition on these routes, fares are somewhat higher – typically US$100–200 –

than flights originating in the US. You may often find that it's worth getting to a US city first and flying on to LA from there.

Airlines

Air Canada ☎1-888/247-2262, 🌐www.aircanada.ca

Alaska Airlines ☎1-800/252-7522, 🌐www.alaska-air.com

America West Airlines ☎1-800/235-9292, 🌐www.americawest.com

American Airlines ☎1-800/433-7300, 🌐www.aa.com

American Trans Air ☎1-800/225-2995, 🌐www.ata.com

Continental Airlines domestic ☎1-800/523-3273, international ☎1-800/231-0856, 🌐www.continental.com

Delta Air Lines domestic ☎1-800/221-1212, international ☎1-800/241-4141, 🌐www.delta.com

Frontier ☎1-888/241-7821, 🌐www.frontierairlines.com

Hawaiian Airlines ☎1-800/367-5320, 🌐www.hawaiianair.com

Horizon Air ☎1-800/547-9308, 🌐www.horizonair.com

JetBlue ☎1-800/538-2583, 🌐www.jetblue.com. Through Long Beach Airport only.

Northwest/KLM Airlines domestic ☎1-800/225-2525, international ☎1-800/447-4747, 🌐www.nwa.com or www.klm.com

Reno Air ☎1-800/433-7300, 🌐www.aa.com. Part of American Airlines.

Southwest Airlines ☎1-800/435-9792, 🌐www.southwest.com

United Airlines domestic ☎1-800/241-6522, international ☎1-800/538-2929, 🌐www.ual.com

US Airways domestic ☎1-800/428-4322, international ☎1-800/622-1015, 🌐www.usair.com

Discount travel agents

Air Brokers International ☎1-800/883-3273, 🌐www.airbrokers.com. Consolidator and specialist in round-the-world tickets.

Airtech ☎212/219-7000, 🌐www.airtech.com. Standby seat broker; also deals in consolidator fares and courier flights.

Airtreks.com ☎1-877/AIRTREKS or 415/912-5600, 🌐www.airtreks.com. Features an interactive database that lets you build and price your own round-the-world itinerary.

Council Travel ☎1-800/2COUNCIL,

🌐www.counciltravel.com. Nationwide organization that mostly specializes in student/budget travel. Flights from the US only. Owned by STA Travel.

Educational Travel Center ☎1-800/747-5551 or 608/256-5551, 🌐www.edtrav.com. Student/youth discount agent.

Skylink US ☎1-800/247-6659 or 212/573-8980, Canada ☎1-800/759-5465, 🌐www.skylinkus.com. Consolidator.

STA Travel ☎1-800/781-4040, 🌐www.sta-travel.com. Worldwide specialists in independent travel; also student IDs, travel insurance, car rental, rail passes, etc.

TFI Tours ☎1-800/745-8000 or 212/736-1140, 🌐www.lowestairprice.com. Consolidator.

Travac ☎1-800/TRAV-800, 🌐www.thetravelsite.com. Consolidator and charter broker.

Travelers Advantage ☎1-877/259-2691, 🌐www.travelersadvantage.com. Discount travel club; annual membership fee required (currently $1 for 3 months' trial).

Travel Avenue ☎1-800/333-3335, 🌐www.travelavenue.com. Full-service travel agent that offers discounts in the form of rebates.

Travel Cuts Canada ☎1-800/667-2887, US ☎1-866/246-9762, 🌐www.travelcuts.com. Canadian student-travel organization.

Worldtek Travel ☎1-800/243-1723, 🌐www.worldtek.com. Discount travel agency for worldwide travel.

Package tours

Booked **in the US**, a typical three-night jaunt to Los Angeles – including round-trip flight plus three-star room-only accommodation – starts at about $400 per person from the West Coast or about $600 from the East Coast. Add an additional $150–200 or so to upgrade to a four-star hotel.

AmeriCan Adventures/TrekAmerica ☎1-800/873-5872, 🌐www.americanadventures.com. Seven- to 25-day sports and sightseeing trips along the West Coast, from $500 to $1200.

American Express Vacations ☎1-800/241-1700, 🌐www.americanexpress.com/travel. Flights, hotels, last-minute specials and specialty tours.

Collette Vacations ☎1-800/340-5158, 🌐www.collettevacations.com. Packages range from two-night LA visits ($200) to thirteen-day trips up and down the West Coast ($2300).

Contiki Holidays ☎1-888/CONTIKI, 🌐www.contiki.com. Youth-oriented sightseeing and national park trips, with six and ten-day treks from LA for $575 to $975.

Globus Journeys ☎1-866/755-8581, ⊛www.globusjourneys.com. Options include five-day LA visits for the Rose Parade ($1300) to elaborate thirteen-day treks to national parks and West Coast cities ($2300).

Suntrek ☎1-800/SUNTREK, ⊛www.suntrek.com. One- to thirteen-week trips through California and the rest of the US, from $400 to $5400.

United Vacations ☎1-888/854-3899, ⊛www.unitedvacations.com. Chain and boutique hotel accommodation, car rental and other options for LA visits, plus various Disneyland packages.

By train

If you don't want to fly, the national passenger rail line – **Amtrak** (☎1-800/USA-RAIL, ⊛www.amtrak.com) – is a leisurely but expensive option. Although financially precarious for years (with a near shutdown in summer 2002), the company has managed to keep running – though rarely ever on time. Expect constant delays if you're traveling by rail, and the trains themselves vary in style, amenities and speed, so it can be worth checking ahead on the type of train that services your route.

To arrive by way of the Midwest and Southwest, ride on the **Southwest Chief**, which begins in Chicago and travels through Kansas City, Albuquerque and Flagstaff before reaching LA (Las Vegas is connected by bus line to this route through Needles, California). The **Sunset Limited** covers more of the South and the Southwest, taking you from central Florida through New Orleans, Houston and Tucson, and arriving in LA via Palm Springs and Pomona. A shorter but memorable route is the **Coast Starlight**, which runs between Seattle and San Diego and passes some of the most appealing scenery anywhere, from coastal whale-watching between San Luis Obispo and Santa Barbara, to an evening trip around Mount Shasta, to a journey through the wooded terrain of the Pacific Northwest. The shortest route of all, the **Pacific Surfliner**, connects San Diego to San Luis Obispo, with LA roughly on the mid-point of the journey.

One-way cross-country fares can be as low as $175 during the offseason, or as high as twice that much during peak periods. Internet users can take advantage of **online discounts** of up to 70 percent, including round-trip tickets to cities like St Louis for $250, though such fares are offered irregularly. While Amtrak's basic fares are good value, the cost rises quickly if you want to travel more comfortably. **Sleeping compartments**, which include small toilets and showers, start at around $100 for one

Amtrak rail passes

	15-day (June–Aug)	15-day (Sept–May)	30-day (June–Aug)	30-day (Sept–May)
Far West	$245	$190	$320	$250
West	$325	$200	$405	$270
Coastal	—	—	$285	$235
National	$440	$295	$550	$385

Outside the US, Amtrak rail passes are available at the following locations:

Australia Asia Pacific Travel Marketing, St David's Hall, 17 Arthur St, Surry Hills, Sydney ☎612/9319 6624, ⊛www.aptms.com.au

Ireland USIT, 19/21 Aston Quay, O'Connell Bridge, Dublin ☎01/602 1600, ⊛www.usitworld.com

New Zealand Walshes World, Ding Wall Building, 87 Queen St, Auckland ☎09/379 3708, or from almost any travel agent.

UK Destination Group, 14 Greville St, London EC1N 8SB ☎020/7400 7045, ⊛www.destination-group.com

or two people, but can climb as high as $400, depending on the class of compartment, number of nights, season and so on, but all include three meals per day.

Amtrak also offers package deals combining hotels, rental cars and other services for American travelers, as well as rail passes. The "**Explore North America**" 30-day rail pass includes Canadian routes on VIA Rail (☎1-888/842-7245, ⊛www.viarail.ca) and costs $675 for summer travel and $475 during the offseason.

Overseas travelers can choose from four **rail passes** that include the LA area, each valid for fifteen or thirty days. The most useful of these are the 30-day **Coastal Pass** ($285 peak, $235 offseason), permitting unlimited rail travel on the East and West coasts – but not in between the two – and the **California Pass**, perhaps the best deal, allowing you three weeks on the rails across the state ($159) or one week of travel in Southern California ($99). Passes must be purchased before your trip at travel agents, or at Amtrak stations in the US, on production of a passport issued outside the US or Canada.

By bus

Bus travel is a slow, often agonizing way to get to LA, and in the end you won't really save that much money. **Greyhound** (☎1-800/231-2222, ⊛www.greyhound.com) is the sole long-distance operator servicing LA, and will cost you around $200 round-trip, paid at least seven days in advance, from major cities like New York, Chicago and Miami. The main reason to take Greyhound is if you're planning to visit other places en route; the company's **Ameripass** is good for unlimited travel within a set time: 7 days of travel costs $200; 15 days, $300; 30 days, $389; and 60 days, $549; passes for overseas travelers run about ten percent less. Passes are valid from the date of purchase, so it's a bad idea to buy them in advance; overseas visitors, however, can buy Ameripasses before leaving home, and passes will be validated at the start of the trip.

Alternatively, AmeriCan Adventures provides a **US Bus Pass** (☎617/984-1556,

⊛www.americanadventures.com) that allows unlimited travel on special buses that ply fixed routes through parts of the US, including a 19-day cross-country trip that includes stops in New York City, Washington DC, Nashville, New Orleans, the Grand Canyon, Las Vegas and Los Angeles; tickets range from $875 to $1100. Shorter passes are valid for a set number of consecutive days, usually from one to two weeks, and involve overnight stays at campgrounds and inexpensive hotels, with costs around $50 per day. Prices are somewhat higher if you want to keep your start date and departure point open.

An alternative to long-distance bus travel is the colorful **Green Tortoise** line, whose buses come complete with bunks, foam cushions, coolers and sound systems, and who offer a handful of routes to get you to Southern California. In late summer (Aug–Oct), they also cross the country between New York and San Francisco; there's also a Greyhound connection for LA travelers at Bakersfield in California. These trips amount to mini-tours of the country, taking around a dozen days (for between $470–500), not including contributions to the food fund ($120–130), and allowing plenty of stops for hiking, river-rafting and hot springs. Other Green Tortoise trips include excursions to major national parks (in 16 days for $629), month-long journeys to Alaska ($1500, or $700 for two weeks), 15-

day winter trips to Costa Rica and Nicaragua ($600) or Mexico City ($540), and three-day jaunts to Yosemite ($130) and Death Valley ($150). For details, call ☎1-800/TORTOISE or visit ⌘www.greentortoise.com

By car

Obviously, for a city built on concrete and asphalt, LA is the perfect place to reach **by car**, and although there are numerous freeways within the region to hasten your trip (see "City transportation," p.31), there are really only three main routes outside Southern California that can quickly get you to the metropolis: **US Interstate 5**, the busy north–south corridor that connects LA to Mexico and Canada through the West Coast; **I-10**, a transcontinental east–west route that begins in Jacksonville, Florida, and ends in Santa Monica, where it becomes the northbound Pacific Coast Highway; and **I-15**, running along a mostly deserted stretch of desert before it reaches Las Vegas and drops down into LA's eastern San Gabriel Valley. Another option is **US Highway 101**, the famed coastal route that takes you along cliffs overhanging the Pacific Ocean and terminates in Downtown LA, after traveling through the San Fernando Valley and Hollywood, where it is known as the "Hollywood Freeway." If traveling on Hwy-101 north of LA, you can expect almost double the travel time as on Interstate 5, which goes in the same general direction.

If you don't have a car or don't trust the one you have, one option worth considering is a **driveaway**. Certain companies, operating in most major cities, are paid to find drivers to take a customer's car from one place to another. The company will normally pay for your insurance and one tank of gas; after that, you'll be expected to drive along the most direct route and to average 400 miles a day. Companies are keen to hire overseas travelers, but you'll need to be at least 21 and be willing to put down a $350 deposit, which you can get back once you've returned the car in good condition. Look under "Automobile transporters and driveaways" in the *Yellow Pages* for more information.

Unless you're planning to spend all your time in relatively compact Downtown,

Beverly Hills or Santa Monica, a car will be absolutely necessary. **Renting a car** is the usual story of phoning one of the major companies – Avis, Hertz, Budget, etc (see box below), of which Thrifty tends to be the cheapest. Most companies have offices at airports, and addresses and phone numbers are comprehensively documented in the *Yellow Pages*.

Also worth looking into are **fly-drive deals**, which offer bargain-rate and sometimes free car rental with purchase of an airline ticket. They usually work out to be less than renting on the spot and are especially good value if you intend to do a lot of driving.

Car rental companies

Ace ☎1-800/243-3443, ⌘www.acerentacar.com
Advantage ☎1-800/777-5500, ⌘www.arac.com
Alamo ☎1-800/462-5266, ⌘www.goalamo.com
Avis ☎1-800/331-1212, ⌘www.avis.com
Budget ☎1-800/527-0700, ⌘www.budgetrentacar.com
Dollar ☎1-800/800-4000, ⌘www.dollar.com
Enterprise ☎1-800/325-8007, ⌘www.enterprise.com
Fox Rent-a-Car ☎1-800/225-4369, ⌘foxrentacar.com. California only.
Hertz ☎1-800/654-3131, in Canada ☎1-800/263-0600, ⌘www.hertz.com
National ☎1-800/328-4567, ⌘www.nationalcar.com
Payless ☎1-800/729-5377, ⌘www.paylesscarrental.com
Thrifty ☎1-800/847-4389, ⌘www.thrifty.com

Flights from the UK and Ireland

There are daily **nonstop flights** to LA **from London Heathrow** with Air New Zealand, American Airlines, British Airways, United Airlines and Virgin Atlantic. Although you can fly to the US from any of the regional airports, the only nonstop flights from the UK to Los Angeles are from London (around 11 hours). Tailwinds ensure that return flights are always an hour or two shorter than outward journeys. Because of the time difference between Britain and the West Coast (eight hours most of the year), flights usually leave Britain mid-morning, while flights back from the US tend to arrive in Britain early in the morning. Most other airlines serving LA, including Continental, Delta and KLM/Northwest, fly **from London Gatwick** via their respective American or European hubs. These flights take an extra two to five hours each way, depending on how long you have to wait for the connection.

Return fares to Los Angeles can cost around £470 between July and August and at Christmas, falling to £280 in winter. Prices are for departures from London and Manchester and do not include airport tax of £40–50.

The travel ads in the weekend papers and on the holiday pages of ITV's *Teletext* give an idea of what's available; in London, scour *Time Out* and the *Evening Standard*. Giveaway magazines aimed at young travelers, like *TNT*, are also useful resources.

There are no nonstop flights from Ireland to LA, though British Airways and Aer Lingus offer service from Dublin (14–17hr), usually with a stopover in Chicago, New York or London, regardless of ticket price. The cheapest flights – if you're under 26 or a student – are available from USIT. Student-only round-trip fares range from €450 to €680. Ordinary Apex fares are only marginally higher.

For an overview of the various offers, and unofficially discounted tickets, go straight to agents specializing in low-cost flights. Especially if you're under 26 or a student, they may be able to knock up to thirty percent off the regular Apex fares. The same agents also offer cut-price seats on **charter flights**. These are particularly good value if you're traveling from a UK city other than London, although they tend to be limited to the summer season and restricted to so-called "holiday destinations," with fixed departure and return dates. Brochures are available in most high-street travel agents; otherwise, contact the specialists direct.

Standby deals, which involve open-ended tickets that you pay for and then decide your travel dates later – if there's room on the plane – are few and far between, and don't give great savings: in general you're better off with an **Apex** ticket. The conditions on these are pretty standard whoever you fly with – seats must be purchased seven days or more in advance, and you must stay for at least one Saturday night; tickets are normally valid for up to six months. Some airlines also offer less expensive **Super-Apex** tickets of two types: the first are around £150 cheaper than an ordinary Apex but must be bought 21 days in advance and require a minimum stay of seven days and a maximum stay of one month; while the second cost about £100 less than an Apex, must be purchased fourteen days in advance and require a minimum stay of a week and a maximum of two months. Such tickets are usually nonrefundable or nonchangeable. **"Open-jaw"** tickets can be a good idea, allowing you to fly into LA, for example, and back from San Francisco for little or no extra charge; fares are calculated by halving the return fares to each destination and adding the two figures together. This makes a convenient option for those who want a fly-drive holiday.

If you've got some time, or want to see more of the US, it's often possible to **stop over** in another city – New York especially – and fly on from there for little more than the cost of a direct flight to Los Angeles. Also, with increased competition on the London–Los Angeles route, thanks to Virgin Atlantic among others and price wars between US carriers, the cost of a connecting flight from LA to San Francisco has been brought down to as low as £40. Many airlines also offer **air passes**, which allow foreign travelers to fly between a set number of US cities for one discounted price.

While not as common as they used to be, **courier flights** are still an option for those on a very tight budget. Courier firms offer discounted rates (as low as £200 return to the West Coast) in return for delivering a package. There'll be someone to check you in and to meet you at your destination, which minimizes any red-tape hassle. However, you'll have to travel light, with only a cabin-bag, and accept tight restrictions on travel dates. For phone numbers, check the *Yellow Pages*, as these businesses come and go.

Packages

Packages – fly-drive, flight/accommodation deals and guided tours (or a combination of all three) – can work out cheaper than arranging the same trip yourself, especially for a short stay. The obvious drawbacks are the loss of flexibility and the fact that most operators use hotels in the mid-range bracket, but there is a wide variety of options to choose from. High-street travel agents have plenty of brochures and information detailing the various combinations.

Fly-drive deals, which give cut-rate (sometimes free) car rental when buying a transatlantic ticket, always work out cheaper than renting on the spot and give especially great value if you intend to do a lot of driving. On the other hand, you'll probably have to pay more for the flight than if you booked it through a discount agent. Competition between airlines and tour operators means that it's well worth phoning to check on special promotions. Watch out for hidden extras, such as local taxes and "**drop-off**" charges, which can be as much as a week's rental, and Collision Damage Waiver insurance. Remember, too, that while you can drive in the States with a British license, there can be problems renting vehicles if you're under 25. For more car-rental and driveaway details, see p.14.

There are plenty of specialist **touring and adventure packages** that include transportation, accommodation, food and a guide. These work best if you're planning on seeing more of California than just Los Angeles, though many companies offer specific city-breaks as well. Some of the more adventurous carry small groups around on minibuses and use a combination of budget hotels and campgrounds (equipment, except a sleeping bag, is provided). Most also have a food kitty of around £25 per week, with many meals cooked and eaten communally, although there's plenty of time to leave the group and explore your own interests.

There's no end of combined **flight and accommodation deals** to Los Angeles, and although you can often do things cheaper independently, you won't be able to do the *same* things cheaper – in fact, the equivalent room booked separately will normally be a lot more expensive – and you can leave the organizational hassles to someone else. Discount agents can set up basic packages for just over £500 each. A handful of tour operators (see opposite) offer more deluxe packages: a week in LA plus a round-trip

ticket should run you anywhere from £700–1000.

Airlines

Aer Lingus ☎01/886 8844, ⊛www.aerlingus.ie
Delta ☎01/676 8080 or 1-800/768 080, ⊛www.delta.com
Air New Zealand ☎020/8741 2299, ⊛www.airnz.co.uk
American Airlines ☎0845/7789 789 or 020/8572 5555, ⊛www.aa.com
British Airways ☎0845/773 3377, ⊛www.ba.com
Continental ☎0800/776 464, ⊛www.flycontinental.com
Delta ☎0800/414 767, ⊛www.delta.com
KLM/Northwest ☎0870/507 4074, ⊛www.klmuk.com
United Airlines ☎0845/844 4777, ⊛www.unitedairlines.co.uk
Virgin Atlantic ☎01293/747 747, ⊛www.virgin
-atlantic.com

Tour operators

Airtours UK ☎0870/238 7788, ⊛www.uk.mytravel.com. Large tour company offering trips worldwide.
AmeriCan Adventures UK ☎01295/756 200, ⊛www.americanadventures.com. Small-group camping adventure trips throughout the US and Canada.
American Holidays Belfast ☎028/9023 8762, Dublin ☎01/433 1009, ⊛www.american
-holidays.com. Specialists in travel to the US and Canada.
Bales Worldwide UK ☎0870/241 3208, ⊛www.balesworldwide.com. Family-owned company offering high-quality escorted tours, as well as tailor-made itineraries.
British Airways Holidays ☎0870/442 3820, ⊛www.baholidays.co.uk. Using British Airways and other quality international airlines, offers an exhaustive range of package and tailor-made holidays around the world.
Discover the World UK ☎01737/218 800, ⊛www.discover-the-world.co.uk. Well-established wildlife holiday specialist, with groups led by naturalists to Europe, the Americas, Africa and Asia. Popular whale- and dolphin-watching holidays. Fly-drives available.
Europa Travel UK ☎028/9062 3211, ⊛www.europatravel.com. Belfast-based operator offering sports and leisure packages, with round-trip fares to LA from €600.

Martin Randall Travel UK ☏ 020/8742 3355, ⓦ www.martinrandall.com. Small-group cultural tours: experts on art, archeology or music lead travelers in Europe, USA, the Middle East and North Africa.

North America Travel Service UK ☏ 0207/938 3737, ⓦ www.americatravelservice.com. Tailor-made flights, accommodation, car hire and so on. Branches in London, Nottingham, Manchester, and North and South Yorkshire.

Premier Holidays UK ☏ 0870/889 0850, ⓦ www.premierholidays.co.uk. Flight-plus-accommodation deals throughout California.

Thomas Cook UK ☏ 0870/5666 222, ⓦ www.thomascook.co.uk. Long-established one-stop 24-hour travel agency for package holidays or scheduled flights, with bureaux de change issuing Thomas Cook travelers' cheques, travel insurance and car rental.

Top Deck Travel UK ☏ 020/7244 8000, ⓦ www.topdecktravel.co.uk. Agents for numerous adventure-touring specialists.

Travelpack UK ☏ 08705/747101, ⓦ www.travelpack.co.uk. Escorted tours and tailor-made holidays throughout California.

Trek America UK ☏ 01295/256 777, ⓦ www.trekamerica.com. Touring-adventure holidays.

United Vacations UK ☏ 0870/606 2222, ⓦ www.unitedvacations.co.uk. City breaks, tailor-made trips and fly-drives.

Up & Away UK ☏ 020/8289 5050. Tailor-made holidays and fly-drives to Los Angeles and California national parks.

Virgin Holidays UK ☏ 0870/220 2788, ⓦ www.virginholidays.co.uk. Packages to a wide range of California destinations.

Flight and travel agents

Bridge the World UK ☏ 0870/444 7474, ⓦ www.bridgetheworld.com. Specializing in round-the-world tickets, with good deals aimed at backpackers.

Destination Group UK ☏ 020/7400 7045, ⓦ www.destination-group.com. Good discount airfares, as well as Far East and US packages.

Flightbookers UK ☏ 0870/010 7000, ⓦ www.ebookers.com. Low fares on an extensive selection of scheduled flights.

Flynow UK ☏ 0870/444 0045, ⓦ www.flynow.com. Large range of discounted tickets.

North South Travel UK ☏ 01245/608 291, ⓦ www.northsouthtravel.co.uk. Friendly, competitive travel agency, offering discounted fares worldwide – profits are used to support projects in the developing world, especially the promotion of sustainable tourism.

Premier Travel Northern Ireland ☏ 028/7126 3333, ⓦ www.premiertravel.uk.com. Discount flight specialists.

STA Travel UK ☏ 0870/1600 599, ⓦ www.statravel.co.uk. Worldwide specialists in low-cost flights and tours for students and those under 26, though other customers welcome.

Top Deck UK ☏ 020/7244 8000, ⓦ www.topdecktravel.co.uk. Long-established agent dealing in discount flights.

Trailfinders UK ☏ 020/7628 7628, ⓦ www.trailfinders.co.uk, Republic of Ireland ☏ 01/677 7888, ⓦ www.trailfinders.ie. One of the best-informed and most efficient agents for independent travelers; produces a very useful quarterly magazine worth scrutinizing for round-the-world routes.

Travel Bag UK ☏ 0870/890 1456, ⓦ www.travelbag.co.uk. Discount flights to Australia, New Zealand, the US and the Far East.

Travel Cuts UK ☏ 020/7255 2082 or 7255 1944, ⓦ www.travelcuts.co.uk. Canadian company specializing in budget, student and youth travel, and round-the-world tickets.

usit NOW Republic of Ireland ☏ 01/602 1600, Northern Ireland ☏ 028/9032 7111, ⓦ www.usitnow.ie. Student and youth specialists for flights and trains.

Getting there from Australia and New Zealand

Los Angeles is the main point of entry in the US for flights from Australia or New Zealand, so there are plenty of direct flights from those countries – though there is very little price difference between airlines. If you travel to LA via Asia, you may well have to stop over for the night, but there is a nonstop service too, via the Pacific. Air passes and round-the-world tickets can be good value if you're planning on covering more ground than just Los Angeles.

Airfares are seasonal, and the differences can add up to as much as A\$465/NZ\$500. Tickets purchased direct from the airlines are often more expensive than an RTW ticket. **Travel agents** offer the best deals on fares and have the latest information on limited special offers, such as free stopovers and fly-drive accommodation packages. Flight Centre and STA Travel (which offer fare reductions for ISIC card holders and under-26s) generally offer the lowest fares. Seat availability on most international flights out of Australia and New Zealand is often limited, so it's best to book at least several weeks ahead.

The travel time between Auckland or Sydney and LA is 12–14 hours on a nonstop flight – though some flights do allow for stopovers in Honolulu and a number of the South Pacific islands.

Traveling **from Australia**, fares to Los Angeles from eastern capitals cost much the same; from Perth they're about A$400 more. There are **daily nonstop** flights from Sydney to LA on United Airlines and Qantas for around A$1300 in low season. Similar rates apply for stopping over in New Zealand via Auckland, or in Honolulu, Fiji, Tonga or Papeete, generally starting at A$1250. The best deal for flying via Asia is on JAL during low season (A$1450), which includes a night's stopover accommodation in Tokyo in the fare, while fares on Korean Air, via Seoul, start at around A$1500. If you don't want to spend the night, Cathay Pacific and Singapore Airlines can get you there for around A$2100, via a transfer in either Hong Kong or Singapore.

From New Zealand, the best deals are out of **Auckland** (add about NZ$150–300 for Christchurch and Wellington departures) on American Airlines, which flies nonstop to LA or via Honolulu for around NZ$1900 in low season, $2600 in high. Meanwhile, Air New Zealand and Qantas, both flying via Sydney, start around NZ$1900. JAL offers the best fares via Asia, starting at NZ$1850/2200 for low and high seasons, with a transfer or stopover in Tokyo, while Korean Air via Seoul costs from NZ$2000.

Round-the-world and air passes

If you plan to visit LA as part of a world trip, a **round-the-world** (**RTW**) ticket offers the best value for the money. The most US-oriented are the fourteen airlines (among them Air New Zealand and Lufthansa) making up the "Star Alliance" network (for more details, call through individual carriers or visit ⊛www.star-alliance.com) which offers a minimum of

three and up to fifteen stopovers worldwide, with a total trip length from ten days to a year. An alternative option includes the eight carriers of the "One World Alliance" (such as Qantas, American Airlines and British Airways; ⊛www.oneworldalliance.com), which bases its rates on travel to and within the six major continents, allowing two to six possible stopovers per each continent. Costs for both plans can be as low as A/NZ$150 per segment, with the total cost for low-season fares around A$2300/NZ$2700 and high-season rates at A$3500/NZ$3800.

If you plan to visit other destinations in the US besides LA, there are a number of good-value air, train and bus passes that can be booked before you leave. For instance, various **coupon deals** are available with your international ticket for discounted flights within the US. A minimum purchase of three coupons usually applies. For example, American Airlines' Coupon Pass costs US$350 for the first three coupons, and between US$60 and $100 for each additional one (maximum of ten total). If you prefer to travel overland, **Amtrak** and **Greyhound Ameripass** offer myriad routes and destinations throughout the US (see pp.12–14).

Packages

A variety of **package holidays** to Los Angeles are available to travelers from Australia and New Zealand, but few include international flights. Occasionally Qantas or Air New Zealand, in conjunction with wholesalers, offers flight-accommodation packages to LA, but most are for land travel only. Adventure World, Creative Holidays and Insight offer four- to eight-night city stays, which include hotel accommodation in Downtown LA, Beverly Hills, Hollywood or Anaheim, tours of LA's famous haunts and homes, and passes to Hollywood's Universal Studios and Disneyland. These can be booked through most travel agents; before you book, ask about any special conditions or hidden costs that may apply, as full refunds on package holidays are uncommon.

In addition, a number of operators specialize in overland **adventure trips and sight-**

seeing tours from LA, including AmeriCan Adventures (☎617/984-1556, ⓦwww.americanadventures.com), whose ten-day round-trip "Californian Cooler" includes sightseeing tours of LA, San Francisco, Las Vegas and Santa Barbara, plus Disneyland passes, admission to the Grand Canyon and Yosemite national parks, and wine tasting to boot; it costs about A\$935/NZ\$1000 and includes a mix of hotel rooms and camping. Trek America (☎1-800/221-0596, ⓦwww.trekamerica.com) offers a fourteen-day LA-to-Seattle "Pacific Crest" trip, starting with Disneyland and the movie studios, then heading to Big Sur, to Yosemite, San Francisco and the coastal range up to Mount Rainier and Olympic national parks; prices start from A\$1476/NZ\$1590, with a similar mix of accommodation.

Airlines

Air New Zealand Australia ☎13 24 76, New Zealand ☎09/357 3000, ⓦwww.airnz.com
Air Pacific Australia ☎1-800/230 150, New Zealand ☎0800/800 178, ⓦwww.airpacific.com
America West Airlines Australia ☎02/9267 2138 or 1300/364 757, New Zealand ☎0800/866 000, ⓦwww.americawest.com
American Airlines Australia ☎1300/650 747, New Zealand ☎09/309 9159, ⓦwww.aa.com
Cathay Pacific Australia ☎13 17 47 or 1300/653 077, New Zealand ☎09/379 0861 or 0508/800 454, ⓦwww.cathaypacific.com
Continental Airlines Australia ☎1300/361 400, New Zealand ☎09/308 3350, ⓦwww.flycontinental.com
Delta Air Lines Australia ☎02/9251 3211 or 1800/500 992, New Zealand ☎09/379 3370, ⓦwww.delta-airlines.com
Japan Airlines Australia ☎02/9272 1111, New Zealand ☎09/379 9906, ⓦwww.japanair.com
KLM/Northwest Airlines Australia ☎1300/303 747, ⓦwww.klm.com/au_en, New Zealand ☎09/309 1782, ⓦwww.klm.com/nz_en
Korean Air Australia ☎02/9262 6000, New Zealand ☎09/914 2000, ⓦwww.koreanair.com.au
Qantas Australia ☎13 13 13, ⓦwww.qantas.com.au, New Zealand ☎09/357 8900, ⓦwww.qantas.co.nz
Singapore Airlines Australia ☎13 10 11, New Zealand ☎09/303 2129, ⓦwww.singaporeair.com
United Airlines Australia ☎13 17 77, ⓦwww.unitedairlines.com.au, New Zealand ☎09/379 3800 or 0800/508 648, ⓦwww.unitedairlines.co.nz. Daily to LA from Sydney and Melbourne, either direct or via Honolulu.
Virgin Atlantic Airways Australia ☎02/9244 2747, New Zealand ☎09/308 3377, ⓦwww.virgin-atlantic.com

Travel agents

Anywhere Travel Australia ☎02/9663 0411, ⓦwww.anywheretravel.com.au
Budget Travel New Zealand ☎0800/808 480, ⓦwww.budgettravel.co.nz
Flight Centre Australia ☎13 31 33 or 02/9235 3522, ⓦwww.flightcentre.com.au, New Zealand ☎0800 243 544 or 09/358 4310, ⓦwww.flightcentre.co.nz
New Zealand Destinations Unlimited New Zealand ☎09/414 1685 ⓦwww.holiday.co.nz
Northern Gateway Australia ☎1-800/174 800, ⓦwww.northerngateway.com.au
STA Travel Australia ☎1300/733 035, ⓦwww.statravel.com.au, New Zealand ☎0508/782 872, ⓦwww.statravel.co.nz
Student Uni Travel Australia ☎02/9232 8444, ⓦwww.sut.com.au, New Zealand ☎09/300 8266, ⓦwww.sut.co.nz
Thomas Cook Australia: Sydney ☎02/9231 2877, Melbourne ☎03/9282 0222; New Zealand ☎09/307 0555, ⓦwww.thomascook.com
Trailfinders Australia ☎02/9247 7666, ⓦwww.trailfinders.com.au
Travel.com.au Australia ☎02/9249 5444 or 1300/130 482, ⓦwww.travel.com.au
YHA Travel Australia: Sydney ☎02/9261 1111, Melbourne ☎03/9670 9611, Brisbane ☎07/3236 1680, ⓦwww.yha.com.au

Specialist agents and operators

Adventure World Australia ☎02/8913 0755, ⓦwww.adventureworld.com.au, New Zealand ☎09/524 5118, ⓦwww.adventureworld.co.nz. Agents for a vast array of international adventure travel companies that operate trips to every continent, and include visits to LA, Disneyland and Las Vegas.
Canada & America Travel Specialists Australia ☎02/9922 4600, ⓦwww.canada-americatravel.com.au. Wholesalers of Greyhound Ameripasses, plus flights and accommodation in North America. Covers Southern California as well as nearby US national parks.
Creative Holidays ⓦwww.creativeholidays.com.au. Packages to New York, San Francisco, Disneyland and Hawaii, and trips to West LA tourist attractions.

Silke's Travel Australia ☎1-800/807 860 or 02/8347 2000, ⊛www.silkes.com.au. Gay and lesbian specialist travel agent, helping provide US accommodation and air transit, to destinations including California.

Surf Travel Co Australia ☎02/9527 4722 or 1-800/687 873, New Zealand ☎09/473 8388, ⊛www.surftravel.com.au. Packages and advice for catching waves or snow through the whole Pacific region.

Sydney International Travel Centre ☎02/9299 8000 or 1-800/251 911, ⊛www.sydneytravel

.com.au. US flights, accommodation, city stays and car rental. Includes packages to LA and Disneyland from A$1500–2100.

Viatour Australia ☎02/8219 5400, ⊛www.viator.com. Bookings with hundreds of travel suppliers worldwide, including tours of LA movie studios and major attractions.

Wiltrans Australia ☎02/9255 0899 or 1-800/251 174. Five-star all-inclusive and escorted sightseeing holidays of California, leaving from Los Angeles.

Entry requirements

Under the Visa Waiver Scheme, designed to speed up lengthy entry require-ments, citizens of the UK, Ireland, Australia, New Zealand, most Western European countries, as well as Andorra, Argentina, Brunei, Iceland, Japan, Singapore, Slovenia and Uruguay visiting the United States for a period of less than ninety days only need an onward or return ticket, a full passport and a visa waiver form. (For visitors from the UK, "British Citizen" must be listed on the passport, otherwise the Scheme does not apply.) The visa waiver form will be provided by your travel agency or by the airline during check-in or on the plane, and must be presented to immigration on arrival. The same form covers entry across the land borders with Canada and Mexico. However, those eligible for the Scheme must apply for a visa if they intend to work, study or stay in the country for more than ninety days.

Prospective visitors from parts of the world not mentioned above require a valid pass-port and a **nonimmigrant visitor's visa** (US$100) for a maximum ninety-day stay. How you obtain a visa depends on what country you're in and your status when you apply, so telephone the nearest embassy or consulate (see opposite). More information can be found at ⊛travel.state.gov /visa_services.html.

Australian and **New Zealand** passport holders staying less than ninety days do not require a visa, provided they arrive on a commercial flight with an onward or return ticket. For longer stays, US multiple-entry visas cost the local equivalent of US$50. You'll need an application form, available

from the US visa information service (☎1-902/262 682), one signed passport photo and your passport, and either send it by post or personally lodge it at one of the American embassies or consulates. For postal applications in Australia, payment can be made at any post office; you'll also need to include the receipt of payment and an SAE. Processing takes about ten working days for postal applications; personal lodge-ments usually take two days – but check with the consulate first.

For a brief excursion into the US, **Canadian citizens** do not necessarily need even a passport – just some form of ID, but for a trip as far as California, you should really have a passport with you. If you plan to stay for more than ninety days you'll need a visa, too. Bear in mind that if you cross into the US in your car, trunks and passenger compartments are subject to spot searches by US Customs personnel. Remember too, that without the proper paperwork, Canadians are legally barred from seeking employment in the US.

US embassies and consulates

For a more complete list around the world, check ⓦusembassy.state.gov. Details of foreign consulates in LA are given in "Directory," p.351.

Australia Moonbah Place, Yarralumla, Canberra, ACT ☏02/6214 5600, ⓦusembassy -australia.state.gov/embassy; 553 St Kilda Rd, Melbourne ☏03/9526 5900; 16 St George's Terrace, 13th Floor, Perth ☏08/9231 9400 or 08/9202 1224; MLC Centre, Level 59, 19–29 Martin Place, Sydney ☏02/9373 9200

Canada 490 Sussex Drive, Ottawa, ON K1P 5T1 ☏613/238-5335, ⓦwww.usembassycanada.gov; 615 Macleod Trail SE, Room 1000, Calgary, AB T2G 4T8 ☏900/451-2778; Suite 904, Purdy's Wharf Tower II, 1969 Upper Water St, Halifax, NS B3J 3R7 ☏902/429-2485; 1155 St Alexandre St, Montréal, PQ H2Z 1Z2 ☏514/398-9695; 2 Place Terrasse Dufferin, CP 939, Québec City, PQ G1R 4T9 ☏418/692-2095; 360 University Ave, Toronto, ON M5G 1S4 ☏416/595-1700, ⓦwww.usconsulatetoronto.ca; 1095 W Pender St, Vancouver, BC V6E 2M6 ☏604/685-4311

Ireland 42 Elgin Rd, Ballsbridge, Dublin 4 ☏01/668-7122, ⓦwww.usembassy.ie

New Zealand 29 Fitzherbert Terrace, Thorndon, Wellington ☏04/462 6000, ⓦwww.usembassy.org.nz; 3rd Floor, Citibank Building, 23 Customs St, Auckland ☏09/303 2724 or Non-Immigrant Visas, Private Bag 92022, Auckland 1

UK 24 Grosvenor Square, London W1A 1AE ☏020/7499 9000, visa hotline ☏09068/200 290, ⓦwww.usembassy.org.uk; 3 Regent Terrace, Edinburgh EH7 5BW ☏0131/556 8315; Queens House, 14 Queen St, Belfast BT1 6EQ ☏028/9032 8239

Insurance

Though not compulsory, travel insurance is *essential* for foreign travelers. The US has no national health system, and you can lose an arm and a leg (so to speak) having even minor medical treatment. Before paying for a new policy, however, it's worth checking whether you are already covered; this is recommended for US residents as well. Some all-risks home insurance policies may cover your possessions when overseas, and many private medical schemes include cover when abroad. In Canada, provincial health plans usually provide partial cover for medical mishaps overseas, while holders of official student/teacher/youth cards in Canada and the US are entitled to meager accident coverage and hospital in-patient benefits. Students will often find that their student health coverage extends during the vacations and for one term beyond the date of last enrolment.

After exhausting the possibilities above, you might want to contact a specialist travel insurance company, or consider the travel insurance deal we offer (see box overleaf). A typical travel insurance policy usually provides cover for the loss of baggage, tickets and – up to a certain limit – cash or cheques, as well as cancellation or curtailment of your journey. Most of them exclude so-called dangerous sports unless an extra premium is paid: in the US, this can mean scuba-diving, whitewater rafting and windsurfing, though probably not kayaking. Many policies can be chopped and changed to

Rough Guides travel insurance

Rough Guides offers its own travel insurance, customized for readers by a leading UK broker and backed by a Lloyd's underwriter. It's available for anyone, of any nationality and any age, traveling anywhere in the world.

There are two main Rough Guide insurance plans: **Essential**, for basic, no-frills cover; and **Premier** – with more generous and extensive benefits. Alternatively, you can take out **annual multi-trip insurance**, which covers you for any number of trips throughout the year (with a maximum of 60 days for any one trip). Unlike many policies, the Rough Guides schemes are calculated by the day, so if you're traveling for 27 days rather than a month, that's all you pay for. If you intend to be away for the whole year, the Adventurer policy will cover you for 365 days. Each plan can be supplemented with a "Hazardous Activities Premium" if you plan to indulge in sports considered dangerous, such as skiing, scuba-diving or trekking.

For a policy quote, call the Rough Guide Insurance Line: US toll-free ☎1-866/220 5588, UK freefone ☎0800/015 0906, or, if you're calling from elsewhere ☎+44 1243/621 046. Alternatively, get an online quote or buy online at ⊚www.roughguidesinsurance.com

exclude coverage you don't need – for example, sickness and accident benefits can often be excluded or included at will. If you do take medical coverage, ascertain whether benefits will be paid as treatment proceeds or only after return home, and whether there is a 24-hour medical emergency number. When securing baggage cover, make sure that the per-article limit – typically under £500 – will cover your most valuable possession. If you need to make a claim, you should keep receipts for medicines and medical treatment, and in the event you have anything stolen, you must obtain an official statement from the police.

Information, websites and maps

The best way to get free information and maps about LA is to write or call any of its constituent cities' visitors bureaus. These promotional offices will send you copious material on their respective areas, including glossy promos advertising the top hotels and restaurants, lists of various sights and, occasionally, a simple map or two. However, in a region like LA, there are numerous ways to get lost, so you're better off investing a few extra dollars in a detailed map book, just so you stay on the right boulevards and freeways.

Information

The **Los Angeles Convention and Visitors Bureau** (LACVB) is the main source of **information** about the city, with offices Downtown and in Hollywood. Independent offices in smaller LA cities also offer valuable material, which relate more to their own specific attractions and less to the area in general. For information on Southern California, as well as the entire state, call or write to the **California Office of Tourism**, 801 K St, Suite 1600, Sacramento, CA 95814-3520, ☎1-800/GO-CALIF or 916/322-2881, ⊚www.visitcalifornia.com; or visit the office's own LA welcome center at 8500 Beverly Blvd, Suite 150, Mid-Wilshire ☏310/854-7616. Australian and UK travelers can also contact the Office of Tourism's representatives abroad: in Australia, get in touch with Integra Tourism Marketing, Level 5, 68 Alfred St, Milsons Point, Sydney ☏02/9959 9427; in the UK, McCluskey and Associates, 50 Sulivan Rd, London ☏020/7371 8900.

As well, you can pick up free **promotional material** like simple maps, hotel and restaurant pamphlets, and magazine-sized city guides at small kiosks across the city, or at stands in most hotels.

Visitors bureaus

Downtown LACVB, 685 S Figueroa St (Mon–Fri 8am–5pm, Sat 8.30am–5pm) ☏213/689-8822, ⊛www.lacvb.com

Hollywood LACVB, 6541 Hollywood Blvd (Mon–Sat 9am–5pm) ☏323/689-2222 or 1-800/228-2452, ⊛www.lacvb.com

Beverly Hills 239 S Beverly Drive ☏310/248-1015, ⊛www.beverlyhillscvb.com

Santa Monica 1400 Ocean Ave ☏310/393-7593, ⊛www.santamonica.com

Long Beach 1 World Trade Center, Suite 300 ☏562/436-3645, ⊛www.visitlongbeach.com

Anaheim near Disneyland at 800 W Katella Ave ☏714/999-8999, ⊛www.anaheimoc.org

Websites

You can obtain plenty of information about LA, whether you're planning your trip or already in the city and checking to see what's on in the clubs, from the **Internet**. LA's role as a center for commercial entertainment makes it the subject of some interesting and offbeat **websites** devoted to Hollywood and LA's movie culture. Besides these, there are sites with information on city hotels, restaurants and clubs, as well as quirkier pages devoted to unusual architecture or celebrity murders. Selected sites are listed below.

ArtScene ⊛artscenecal.com/index.html. Copious listing of galleries and museums in Southern California, broken down by geography.

@LA ⊛www.at-la.com. Extensive listing of sights, products and services in the LA region, from laundromats to theme parks to windsurfing.

Calendar Live ⊛www.calendarlive.com. The most comprehensive daily listing of all the city's entertainment options, broken down by

neighborhood, cost and other features. Updated regularly by the *LA Times*.

California Surf Report ⊛www.surfscene.net/surf/index.html. The latest surfing news for the Southern California counties of Los Angeles and Ventura, plus related stories and photos.

Citysearch LA ⊛losangeles.citysearch.com. The LA site of a nationwide listings guide for major US cities, somewhat useful for navigating the metropolis, though not as frequently updated as other listings websites.

Club LA ⊛www.clubLA.com. Searchable lists and reviews of trendy bars, dance clubs and comedy spots, plus fashion advice and gossip tidbits. The LA page of the club-hopping site ⊛www.clubplanet .com.

E! Online ⊛www.eonline.com. Breathlessly gossipy and visually appealing site, with a wealth of tabloid features, pages of star profiles and movie reviews.

Intercot West: Disneyland Inside and Out ⊛www.intercotwest.com. Good source of news, information and advice about the Mouse House in Anaheim, from getting good rates on tickets to avoiding the worst lines at the best rides.

LA Grim Society ⊛www.grimsociety.com. Surprisingly cheerful look at the books, movies and events relating to death in LA, past and present, with the expected focus on celebrity deaths and murder sites. Infrequently updated, though.

LA Nocturne ⊛www.nocturne.com. Reviews of pool halls, diners and clubs, plus books and movies that explore the dark side of LA, and LA after dark.

Los Angeles Conservancy ⊛www.laconservancy.org. A great place to begin exploring the wealth of classic architecture in Downtown and other parts of the city (the Conservancy itself offers periodic tours as well – see p.35). An excellent related site, ⊛www.modcom .org, covers more Pop-oriented architecture from the mid-twentieth century.

Los Angeles County Museum of Art ⊛www.lacma.org. Besides offering an online tour of the museum's exhibitions and permanent collection, this site gives a rundown on movie programs at the Bing Theatre ($3 matinees of Hollywood classics) and music concerts in the museum's forecourt.

Murals of LA ⊛www.usc.edu/isd/archives/la /pubart/LA_murals. Excellent listing by neighborhood of the many murals across the city – from resplendent Madonnas in East LA to Botticelli's Venus in Venice – accompanied by photos.

Roadside Peek ⊛www.roadsidepeek.com. Easily the best and most entertaining site about Southern California's Pop architecture (as well as select parts in the rest of the US), focusing on such subjects as "googie" diners, retro-bowling alleys, neon signs,

Route 66 motels and buildings shaped like donuts and dinosaurs.

Rock and Roll Road Map
🌐 www.rockandrollroadmap.com. Visit the sites that made local, and national, music history in the LA area.

Seeing Stars 🌐 www.seeing-stars.com.
As the name says, this site is your comprehensive guide to tracking down celebrities wherever they hide out, from obvious places like hotels and restaurants to lesser-known spots like churches, beaches and the schools they attended. Also offers a good assortment of pages detailing movie palaces, film memorabilia and almost anything connected with the Hollywood district.

Southern California Earthquake Map
🌐 www.crustal.ucsb.edu/scec/webquakes.
Disturbing (but interesting) "up-to-the-minute" map showing the regional sites of the last 500 or so quakes picked up by local seismographs, plus informative earthquake links.

Union Station: Los Angeles Rail Transit
🌐 www.westworld.com/~elson/larail. Fares, schedules, system maps and other practical information about the subways, trains and light-rail options available in LA, along with history and trivia about the Angel's Flight funicular railway.

Virtual Hollywood Walking Tour
🌐 www.historicla.com/hollywood/index.html. Wander through movie history online by way of Hollywood Boulevard and learn about the famous sights and surroundings of this faded, but still colorful, stretch.

Yesterland 🌐 www.yesterland.com. A guide to long-lost Disneyland attractions, including such favorites as the Main Street Electrical Parade, the PeopleMover and the legendary House of the Future, which once boasted that "the floors on which you are walking, the gently sloping walls around you, and even the ceilings are made of plastics."

Maps

Generally speaking, the **maps** in this book will be sufficient in helping you find your way around the main parts of town and their key attractions, with the exception of the Hollywood Hills, whose serpentine passages and switchbacks require highly detailed maps to navigate (and even then, with difficulty). For a folding map, try Gousha Publications' *Los Angeles City Map* ($2.95), or for a pocket-sized, laminated map, try *Streetwise Los Angeles* ($4.95) – both are available in many bookstores.

For a much more **detailed view** of the city, Thomas Brothers Publishing has the hefty, spiral-bound *Thomas Guide to Los Angeles*

and Orange Counties ($31.95), sold at most bookstores. Published yearly for counties across Southern California, the Thomas guides are the best maps available for regional travel, especially for venturing beyond the easily accessed parts of the city into more unfamiliar territory – like the northern deserts, eastern suburbs or the Hollywood Hills. If you're staying for several weeks, consider purchasing one if you're traveling anywhere outside central LA. If you're interested in highly detailed views of **rural terrain**, as well as the urban layout, consider DeLorme's large-format *Atlas and Gazetteer of Southern and Central California* ($19.95, last updated in 2000), which best shows national forests, parkland, hiking trails, and minor dirt and gravel roads. The colorful *Benchmark California Road and Recreation Atlas* ($24.95, published 2002) is also excellent for showing the same features, costing a bit more but revised more regularly as well.

Rand McNally operates a chain of comprehensive **travel stores** across the country. For locations, call ☎ 1-800/234-0679 or check 🌐 www.randmcnally.com. The branch in the Westside's Century City Mall (10250 Santa Monica Blvd, Century City ☎ 1-800/333-0136 or 310/556-2202) is one of the company's better stores. If you happen to be a member, the Automobile Club of Southern California, 2601 S Figueroa St, south of Downtown (☎ 213/741-3686, 🌐 www.aaa-calif.com), hands out free maps, guides and other information to member motorists and even bicyclists; while the national office of the AAA also provides maps and assistance to its members, as well as to British members of the AA and RAC, and Canadian members of the CAA (☎ 1-800/222-4357, 🌐 www.aaa.com).

LA-area travel bookshops can be found under "Shopping," p.332.

Map and travel book outlets

In Australia and New Zealand

Auckland Map Centre 1A Wyndham St, Auckland ☎ 09/309 7725
Hema Maps Australia: 25 McKechnie Drive, Eight Mile Plains, Queensland 4113 ☎ 07/3340 0000; New Zealand: Unit D 24, Ra Ora Drive, East Tamaki, Auckland ☎ 09/273 6459, 🌐 www.hemamaps.com

Map Land 372 Little Bourke St, Melbourne, Victoria 3000 ☎03/9670 4383, ⊛www.mapland.com.au

Map World 371 Pitt St, Sydney, NSW 2000 ☎02/9261 3601, ⊛www.mapworld.net.au

Mapworks 184 Keilor Rd, North Essendon, Victoria 3041 ☎03/9379 7533, ⊛www.mapworks.com.au

Melbourne Map Centre 259 High St, Kew, Victoria 3101 ☎03/9853 3526, ⊛www.melbmap.com.au

Specialty Maps 58 Albert St, Auckland ☎09/307 2217

Travel Bookshop Shop 3, 175 Liverpool St, Sydney, NSW 2000 ☎02/9261 8200

World Wide Maps & Guides 187 George St, Brisbane, Queensland 4001 ☎07/3221 4330, ⊛www.worldwidemaps.com.au

In the UK and Ireland

Blackwell's Map and Travel Shop 53 Broad St, Oxford OX1 3BQ ☎01865/792 792; 100 Charing Cross Rd, London WC2H 0JG ☎020/7292 5100, ⊛bookshop.blackwell.co.uk

Daunt Books 83 Marylebone High St, London W1M 3DE ☎020/7224 2295; 193 Haverstock Hill, NW3 4QL ☎020/7794 4006

Easons Bookshop 40 O'Connell St, Dublin 1 ☎01/858 3881, ⊛www.eason.ie

Heffers Map Centre 20 Trinity St, Cambridge CB2 1TJ ☎01865/333 536, ⊛www.heffers.co.uk

Hereford Map Centre 24–25 Church St, Hereford HR1 2LR ☎01432/266 322, ⊛www.users.globalnet.co.uk/~mapped

Hodges Figgis Bookshop 56–58 Dawson St, Dublin 2 ☎01/677 4754

James Thin Ltd 53–62 South Bridge, Edinburgh EH1 1YS ☎0131/622 8222

John Smith and Sons 57–61 St Vincent St, Glasgow G2 5TB ☎0141/221 7472, ⊛www.johnsmith.co.uk

The Map Shop 30a Belvoir St, Leicester LE1 6QH ☎0116/247 1400, ⊛www.mapshopleicester.co.uk

National Map Centre 20–22 Caxton St, London SW1H 0QU ☎020/7222 2466, ⊛www.mapstore.co.uk

Newcastle Map Centre 55 Grey St, Newcastle-upon-Tyne NE1 6EF ☎0191/261 5622

Ordnance Survey Ireland Phoenix Park, Dublin 8 ☎01/802 5300, ⊛www.osi.ie

Ordnance Survey of Northern Ireland Colby House, Stranmillis Court, Belfast BT9 5BJ ☎028/9025 5755, ⊛www.osni.gov.uk

Stanfords 12–14 Long Acre, London WC2E 9LP ☎020/7836 1321; 29 Corn St, Bristol BS1 1HT ☎0117/929 9966, ⊛www.stanfords.co.uk

The Travel Bookshop 13–15 Blenheim Crescent, London W11 2EE ☎020/7229 5260, ⊛www.thetravelbookshop.co.uk

Waterstone's Queens Bldg, 8 Royal Ave, Belfast BT1 1DA ☎028/9024 7355; 69 Patrick St, Cork ☎021/276 522, ⊛www.waterstones.co.uk

In the US and Canada

ADC Map & Travel Center 1636 I St NW, Washington, DC 20006 ☎1-800/544-2659, ⊛www.adcmap.com

Adventurous Traveler.com US ☎1-800/282-3963, ⊛adventuroustraveler.com

Book Passage 51 Tamal Vista Blvd, Corte Madera, CA 94925 ☎415/999-7909, ⊛www.bookpassage.com

Complete Traveler 199 Madison Ave, New York, NY 10016 ☎212/685-9007 and 3207 Fillmore St, San Francisco, CA 92123 ☎415/923-1511

Distant Lands 56 S Raymond Ave, Pasadena, CA 91105 ☎626/449-3220, ⊛www.distantlands.com

Elliot Bay Book Company 101 S Main St, Seattle, WA 98104 ☎1-800/962-5311, ⊛www.elliotbaybook.com

Globe Corner Bookstore 28 Church St, Cambridge, MA 02138 ☎1-800/358-6013, ⊛www.globercorner.com

International Travel Maps and Books 530 W Broadway, Vancouver BC V5Y 1P8 ☎604/879-3621, ⊛www.itmb.com

Map Link 30 S La Petera Lane #5, Santa Barbara, CA 93117 ☎805/692-6777, ⊛catalog.maplink.co

Open Air Books and Maps 25 Toronto St, Toronto ON M5C 2R1 ☎416/363-0719

Phileas Fogg's Books & Maps #87 Stanford Shopping Center, Palo Alto, CA 94304 ☎1-800/533-FOGG

Powells Travel Books 701 SW Sixth Ave, Portland, OR 97204 ☎503/228-1108, ⊛www.powells.com

Rand McNally US ☎1-800/333-0136, ⊛www.randmcnally.com. Around thirty stores across the US; dial ext 2111 or check the website for the nearest location.

Savvy Traveler 301 S Michigan Ave, Chicago, IL 60604 ☎312/913-9800, ⊛www.thesavvytraveller.com

Sierra Club Bookstore 6014 College Ave, Oakland, CA 94618 ☎510/658-7470, ⊛www.sanfranciscobay.sierraclub.org.

Travel Books & Language Center 4337 Wisconsin Ave NW, Washington, DC 20814 ☎1-800/220-2665, ⊛www.ambook.org/bookstore/travelbks

The Travel Bug Bookstore 2667 W Broadway, Vancouver BC V6K 2G2 ☎604/737-1122, ⊛www.swifty.com/tbug

Ulysses Travel Bookshop 101 Yorkville Ave, Toronto ON M5R 1C1 ☎1-800/268-4395

World of Maps 1235 Wellington St, Ottawa, ON K1Y 3A3 ☎1-800/214-8524, ⊛www.worldofmaps.com

Arrival

Depending on how you travel, arriving in LA can place you at any number of locations scattered across the city – from the train and bus stations Downtown to the main air terminal by the ocean to the freeways coming in from all directions. The length of your journey will ultimately depend on the state of traffic on the freeway and boulevards.

By air

Most people arrive in Los Angeles **by air**. Many domestic flights and also European flights touch down at Los Angeles International Airport (☎310/646-5252), known as **LAX**, sixteen miles southwest of Downtown along the ocean. If you're on a tight budget, and not planning to rent a car, the cheapest way to reach your destination is to take the free **"C" shuttle bus** (not "A" or "B," which serve the parking lots), running 24 hours a day from each terminal, to the LAX Transit Center at Vicksburg Avenue and 96th Street, just east of Sepulveda Boulevard. From here, local **buses** (MTA and others) leave for different parts of LA – see "City transportation," starting on p.32 for more on this, as well as car rental.

The most convenient way into town is to ride a minibus service such as **LAX Chequer Shuttle** (☎1-800/545-7745) or **SuperShuttle** (☎1-800/554-3146 or 310/782-6600), which run to Downtown, Hollywood, West LA, Santa Monica and most other Westside destinations (the SuperShuttle also goes to Long Beach and Disneyland) and deliver you to your door; most have flashing signs on their fronts advertising their general destination. If you're heading to Santa Monica or the South Bay, another possibility is **Coast Shuttle** (☎310/417-3988). Fares vary depending on your destination, but are generally around $25–30. The shuttles run around the clock from outside the baggage claim areas, and you probably won't have to wait more than fifteen to twenty minutes; pay the fare when you board.

Taxis from the airport are always expensive: expect to pay at least $25 to Downtown and West LA, $30 to Hollywood, and $90 to Disneyland. Unlicensed taxi operators may approach you and offer flat fares to your destination, but such offers are best avoided. Don't even consider using the **Metro** system to get to your destination from LAX. The nearest light-rail train, the Green Line, stops miles from the airport, and the overall journey involves three time-consuming transfers (very difficult with luggage) before you even arrive Downtown. Other destinations are completely inaccessible by rail.

While the vast majority of flights into LA use LAX, if you're arriving from elsewhere in the US, or Mexico, you may land at one of the several other **international airports** in the LA region – at Burbank, Long Beach, Ontario or Orange County's John Wayne International Airport. These are similarly well served by car-rental firms. If you want to use public transportation, phone the MTA Regional Information Network (Mon–Fri 6am–7pm, Sat 8am–6pm; ☎1-800/COM-MUTE or 213/626-4455, outside LA ☎1-800/2LA-RIDE, ⬡www.mta.net) on arrival and tell them where you are and where you want to go, and they'll advise you on the best mass-transit route.

By train

Arriving in LA by **train**, you'll disembark at Union Station (☎213/624-0171), on the north side of Downtown at 800 N Alameda St. (You can also connect to regional bus lines next door at Gateway Transit Center.) Union Station is the hub for three main rail lines: **Metrorail**, the subway and light-rail system (see p.32), **Metrolink**, a commuter rail line servicing distant suburbs (see p.32), and **Amtrak** (☎1-

800/USA-RAIL, @www.amtrak.com), whose long-distance trains also stop at outlying stations in the LA area.

Amtrak departures

From Los Angeles to:

Anaheim	10 daily	45min
Fullerton (for Disneyland)	10 daily	35min
Las Vegas	1 daily	10hr 30min
Oxnard	5 daily	1hr 37min
Palm Springs	2 daily	2hr 40min
Sacramento	1 daily	14hr
San Bernardino	1 daily	2hr
San Diego	10 daily	2hr 50min
San Francisco	3 daily	9–12hr (with required bus connections)
San Juan Capistrano	10 daily	1hr 17min
Santa Barbara	5 daily	2hr 45min
Tucson	2 daily	10hr
Ventura	4 daily	1hr 50min

By bus

The main **Greyhound** bus terminal, at 1716 E Seventh St (☏213/629-8401, @www .greyhound.com), is in a seedy section of Downtown – though access is restricted to ticket holders and it's safe enough inside. There are other Greyhound terminals elsewhere in LA handling fewer services: in Hollywood at 1715 N Cahuenga Blvd (☏323/466-6384); Pasadena at 645 E Walnut St (☏626/792-5116); North Hollywood at 11225 Magnolia Blvd (☏818/761-5119); Long Beach at 1498 Long Beach Blvd (☏562/218-3011); and Anaheim at 101 W Winston Rd (☏714/999-1256). Only the Downtown terminal is open around the clock.

Greyhound departures

From Los Angeles to:

Las Vegas	20 daily	5–7hr
Palm Springs	10 daily	3–4hr
Phoenix	12 daily	7–9hr
Portland	7 daily	23hr
Salt Lake City	3 daily	16hr
San Diego	30 daily	3hr
San Francisco	17 daily	8–12hr
Seattle	7 daily	27hr
Tijuana, Mexico	16 daily	3hr 30min
Tucson	10 daily	10–12hr

By car

The main routes by **car** into LA are the interstate highways, all of which pass through Downtown. From the east, I-10, the **San Bernardino** Freeway, curves south of Downtown then heads to the Westside and the coast, where it's called the **Santa Monica** Freeway. US-60, the **Pomona** Freeway, parallels I-10 through the eastern suburbs, providing a less hair-raising interchange than I-10 when it reaches Downtown. The **Foothill** Freeway, I-210 (supplanting Route 66), mainly serves the San Gabriel Valley; while the **Golden State** freeway, or I-5, is the chief north–south access corridor, with the **San Diego** freeway, I-405, used commonly as a Westside alternative.

Alternative routes into the city include US-101, the scenic route from San Francisco known as the **Ventura** freeway, which cuts across the San Fernando Valley and Hollywood into Downtown. Hwy-1 follows the entire coast of California and links up with US-101 in Ventura County, but once in LA it's known as **Pacific Coast Highway** (PCH), and uses surface streets through Santa Monica, the South Bay and Orange County.

Phones, mail and email

Like most major US cities, LA has an excellent communications infrastructure, with all manner of high-tech links to the rest of the country and the world. Although some areas are better hooked up than others – the Westside, for example – most communication services are more than adequate throughout the region, especially telephone service and e-mail, though not the US mail, which is predictably slow and prone to misplacing letters and packages.

Telephones

Los Angeles has about half a dozen area codes (listed below), which you needn't dial if you're calling from within a given area code. A **local call** on a public phone usually costs 50¢. Outside the immediate calling zone, you'll have to dial a 1, plus the area code, then the telephone number, and you'll be charged a bit more than local calls, depending on where you're calling from and dialing to. For detailed information about calls, area codes and rates in the LA area, consult the front of the telephone directory (*White Pages*).

In general, calling from your **hotel room** will cost considerably more than if you use a public phone. Hotels often charge a connection fee of at least $1 for all calls, even if they're local or toll-free, and international calls will cost a small fortune. While an increasing number of public phones accept **credit cards**, these can incur astronomical charges for long-distance service, including a high "connection fee" that can bump charges up to as much as $7 a minute.

Long-distance and international calls dialed direct are most expensive during daylight hours (7am–6pm), with evening charges slightly reduced (6–11pm) and early morning hours cheapest of all (11pm–7am). Detailed rates are listed at the front of the local *White Pages*.

Many major hotels, government agencies and car rental firms have **toll-free numbers** that are recognizable by their ☎1-800 or ☎1-888 prefixes. Some of these numbers are meant to be accessed nationally, others only within the state of California – dialing is the only way to find out. Numbers with a ☎1-900 prefix are **toll calls**, typically sports information

lines, psychic hotlines and phone-sex centers, and will cost you a variable, though consistently high, fee for just a few minutes of use.

Calling home from the US

For foreign visitors, one of the most convenient ways of phoning home from abroad is via a **telephone charge card**, available from your phone company back home. Using access codes for the country you are in and a PIN number, you can make calls from most hotel, public and private phones that will bill to your own account. The benefit of calling cards is mainly one of convenience, as the rates can't compete with discounted off-peak times many local companies offer. Since most major charge cards are free to obtain, however, it's certainly worth getting one at least for emergencies; contact your phone company for more details.

In **Canada**, AT&T, MCI, Sprint, Canada Direct and other North American long-distance companies all enable their customers to make calling-card calls while abroad, billed to their home number. Call your company's customer service line to find out if they provide service from the US, and if so, what the toll-free access code is.

In **the UK and Ireland,** it's possible to obtain a free **BT Chargecard** (☎0800/800 838), from which all calls from overseas can be charged to your quarterly domestic account. To use these cards in the US, or to make a **collect call** (to "reverse the charges") using a BT operator, contact the carrier: AT&T ☎1-800/445-5667; MCI ☎1-800/444-2162; or Sprint ☎1-800/800-0008. To avoid the international operator fee, BT credit-card calls can be made directly using

Useful telephone numbers

Emergencies ☎911 for fire, police or ambulance
Police ☎213/625-3311
Sheriff ☎213/526-5541
Operator ☎0
Local directory information ☎411
Long-distance directory information
☎1 +area code/555-1212
Directory assistance for toll-free numbers
☎1-800/555-1212

International calls to Los Angeles:
Dial your country's international access code + 1 for the US + LA area code + phone number
International calls from Los Angeles:
Dial ☎011 + country code + phone number
Country codes: Australia ☎61, Ireland ☎353, New Zealand ☎64, United Kingdom ☎44. For all other codes, dial ☎0 for the operator or check the front of the local *White Pages*.

an automated system: AT&T ☎1-800/445-5688; MCI ☎1-800/854-4826; or Sprint ☎1-800/825-4904. AT&T (dial ☎0800/890-011, then 1-888/641-6123 when you hear the AT&T prompt to be transferred to the Florida Call Center, free 24 hours) has the Global Calling Card; while **NTL** (☎0500/100 505) issues its own Global Calling Card, which can be used in more than sixty countries abroad, though the fees cannot be charged to a normal phone bill.

To call **Australia and New Zealand** from overseas, telephone charge cards such as Telstra Telecard or Optus Calling Card in Australia and Telecom NZ's Calling Card can be used to make calls abroad, which are charged back to a domestic account or credit card. Apply to Telstra (☎1-800/038 000), Optus (☎1-300/300 937) or Telecom NZ (☎04/801 9000).

An alternative to telephone charge cards is cheap **pre-paid phone cards** offering cut-rate calls to virtually anywhere in the world. Various stores in LA sell them: look for signs posted in shop windows advertising rates.

LA area codes

LA is divided into long-distance telephone districts, each with its own **area code**:

213	Downtown
310	West Hollywood, Beverly Hills, West LA, Westwood, Santa Monica, Venice, Malibu, South Bay, San Pedro
323	Mid-Wilshire, Hollywood, South Central LA, East LA
562	Long Beach, Whittier, Southeast LA
626	Pasadena, Arcadia, San Gabriel Valley
714	Northern Orange County – Anaheim, Garden Grove, Huntington Beach
805	Santa Clarita, Lancaster, northern deserts
818	Burbank, Glendale, San Fernando Valley
909	Pomona, Inland Empire
949	Southern Orange County – Costa Mesa, Newport and Laguna beaches

Mobile phones

If you want to use your cell phone, you'll need to check with your phone provider if it will work abroad, and what the call charges are. Unless you have a tri-band phone, it is unlikely that a mobile bought for use outside the US will work inside the States and vice versa, with many only working within the region designated by the area code in the phone number, ie 212, 310 etc. If you're lucky enough to have a phone that works Stateside, you'll have to inform your phone provider before going abroad to get international access switched on. You may get charged extra for this and you're also likely to be charged extra for incoming calls when abroad, as the people calling you will be paying the usual rate. If you want to retrieve messages while you're away, you'll have to ask your provider for a new access code, as your home one is unlikely to work abroad.

Tri-band phones will automatically switch to the US frequency, but these can be pricey, so you may want to rent a phone if you're traveling to the US. For further information about using your phone abroad, check out ⓦwww.telecomsadvice.org.uk/features /using_your_mobile_abroad.

Mail

Post offices are usually open Monday through Friday, from 9am to 5pm, although some are open on Saturday from 9am to noon or 1pm.

Ordinary mail sent within the US costs 37¢ (at press time) for letters weighing up to an ounce, while standard postcards cost 23¢. For anywhere outside the US, airmail letters weighing up to an ounce cost 80¢; postcards and aerogrammes 70¢. Airmail between the US and Europe, for instance, may take a week and 12–14 days to Australia and New Zealand. Drop mail off at any post office or in the blue **mail boxes** you'll find on street corners throughout LA.

You can have mail sent to you c/o **General Delivery** (known elsewhere as **poste restante**), Los Angeles, CA 90012. Letters will end up at the main post office in Downtown LA, next to Union Station (☏213/617-4405 or 1-800/275-8777), which will hold mail for thirty days before returning it to the sender – so make sure the envelope has a return address. You can pick up general delivery mail from the main post office Monday to Friday, 8am to 3pm.

If you want to send **packages** overseas from LA, check the front of telephone directories for packaging requirements. Bear in mind that you'll need to fill in a green **customs declaration form**, which is available from post offices. International parcel **rates** for items weighing less than a pound run from $5 to $16, depending on the package's size and destination, and how quickly you want it to arrive.

Email

Email is often the cheapest and most convenient way to keep in touch. **Cybercafés** are found throughout LA, including @Coffee, 7200 Melrose Ave ☏323/930-1122; CyberJava, 7080 Hollywood Blvd, Hollywood ☏323/466-5600, ⓦwww .cyberjava.com; and The World Café, 2820 Main St, Santa Monica ☏310/392-1661, ⓦwww.worldcafe.la.com. Additionally, many public libraries have computers that provide free Internet access (notably the Central Library in Downtown LA, see p.68, and the Beverly Hills Public Library, see p.114), usually for Web surfing or for accessing the library database.

If neither of these options fit the bill, or if you just need a fast machine with assorted peripherals, then find a commercial photocopying and printing shop (look under "Copying" in the *Yellow Pages*). They'll charge around 25¢ a minute for use of their computers, but you're guaranteed fast access. Most upscale hotels also offer email and Internet access – though at a steep price.

City transportation

The only certainty when it comes to getting around LA is that wherever and however you're going, you should allow plenty of time to get there. Obviously, this is partly due to the sheer size of the city, but the tangle of freeways and the gridlock common during rush hour can make car trips lengthy undertakings – and with most local buses stopping on every corner, bus travel is hardly a speedy alternative.

Driving and car rental

The best way to get around LA is to **drive**. All the major **car rental** firms have branches throughout the city (simply look in the phone book for the nearest office), and most have their main office close to LAX, linked to each terminal by a free shuttle bus. A number of smaller rental companies specialize in everything from Gremlins to Bentleys, though cost savings are often minimal and the service a bit more erratic than with the major chains. For a list of car rental firms, see p.14.

Parking is a particular problem Downtown, along Melrose Avenue's trendy Westside shopping streets, and in Beverly Hills and Westwood. Anywhere else is less troublesome, but watch out for restrictions – some lampposts boast as many as four placards listing dos and don'ts. Sometimes it's better to shell out $5 for valet parking than get stuck with a $30 ticket for parking in a residential zone.

LA's freeways

Despite traffic being bumper-to-bumper much of the time, the **freeways** are the only way to cover long distances quickly; with over 250 miles of asphalt and twenty major routes, the LA freeway system is the largest in the world, carrying up to 5 million cars a day.

The system, however, can be confusing, especially since each stretch can have two or three names (often derived from its eventual destination, however far away) as well as a number. Out of an eye-popping, four-level interchange known as "The Stack," four major freeways fan out from Downtown: the Hollywood Freeway (a section of US-101) heads northwest through Hollywood into the

San Fernando Valley; the Santa Monica Freeway (I-10) runs south of Mid-Wilshire and West LA to Santa Monica; the Harbor Freeway (I-110) goes south to San Pedro – heading northeast it's called the Pasadena Freeway; and the Santa Ana Freeway (I-5) passes Disneyland and continues south through Orange County – north of Downtown it's called the Golden State Freeway. **Other freeways** include the San Diego Freeway (I-405), which roughly follows the coast through West LA and the South Bay; the Ventura Freeway (Hwy-134), which links Burbank, Glendale and Pasadena to US-101 in the San Fernando Valley; the Long Beach Freeway (I-710), a truck-heavy route connecting East LA and Long Beach; and limited routes like Hwy-2, which serves the San Gabriel Valley, and Hwy-90, which runs through Marina del Rey. For **shorter journeys**, especially between Hollywood and West LA, the wide avenues and boulevards are a better option (sometimes the only one), not least because you get to see more of the city.

Freeway driving strategies

Visitors exploring most places between Hollywood and the coast can side-step LA's notorious **freeways**, as almost all the traveling can be done on surface streets. However, those headed to more far-flung parts of LA will find them unavoidable. Although LA freeway travel presents its own unique challenges, keeping a few things in mind will go some way toward reducing the time you spend in gridlock. For one, city drivers are not good at handling **inclement weather**, and your travel time will surely double during even a drizzle. The huge network of highways also creates its own unpredictable logic

31

– often, traffic will slow down to a crawl for no apparent reason, with the cause sometimes miles away. Furthermore, alternate route planning is critical, especially when traveling to Orange County, because **gridlock** can occur at any time of the day. To assist your planning, AM news radio stations (see p.47) provide frequent **traffic updates** identifying where the nasty tie-ups are.

The **busiest roads** are Highway 101 and the 405 freeway, with particularly hellish confluences at the Downtown "stack" and the section of the 405 at the 10 freeway, the busiest junction in LA – and the entire US. Individual roads present their own difficulties, including the 101 south through Universal City, where you only have a few yards to accelerate from a dead stop to 55mph, or the antiquated 110 freeway in Highland Park, where exit-ramp speeds suddenly drop to 5mph. At the LA River, transferring from the south 5 to the south 110 is a hair-raising merge around the base of a cliff, while following the 10 freeway through East LA plunges you briefly, and chaotically, into the confusion of Interstate 5. Finally, tractor-trailer trucks, or "big rigs," are a constant sight throughout LA County, but are almost ubiquitous on the Terminal Island Expressway, a short road near the harbor, and on the Long Beach Freeway, or 710, which offers the added pitfalls of frighteningly narrow lanes and uneven, rutted asphalt.

Public transportation

The bulk of LA's public transportation is run by the LA County Metropolitan Transit Authority (**MTA** or "**Metro**"), which is still sometimes abbreviated to its old name, the RTD (Rapid Transit District). Its massive **Gateway Transit Center**, to the east of Union Station on Vignes Street, serves commuters traveling by Metrorail, light rail, commuter rail, Amtrak and the regional bus systems. The Center comprises **Patsaouras Transit Plaza**, from where buses depart, the glass-domed **East Portal**, which leads to train connections, and the 26-story **Gateway Tower**, which has an MTA customer service office on the ground floor.

Metrorail and Metrolink

Shackled by political and financial troubles, LA's **Metrorail** subway and light-rail system is very limited and only involves three lines. The underground **Red Line** stretches from the Transit Center through Hollywood and Universal City before terminating at Lankershim and Chandler boulevards in the Valley's North Hollywood district. Of more use to residents than visitors, the **Green Line** runs between industrial El Segundo and colorless Norwalk along the middle of the Century Freeway. Tantalizingly close to LAX, in practical terms the line is absolutely useless if you are in a hurry. Currently the most complete route, the **Blue Line** leaves Downtown and heads above-ground through South Central LA to Long Beach; in the opposite direction, an extension of the Blue Line (also known as the **Gold Line**; ⓦwww.metrogoldline.org) is slated to open in July 2003, connecting Downtown with Pasadena and Sierra Madre by way of northeastern LA districts like Highland Park.

Fares on all journeys are $1.35 one way, with transfers valid for one hour available for 25¢. Peak-hour trains run at five- to six-minute intervals, at other times every ten to fifteen minutes. Don't bring refreshments on the trains – the fine is $250.

MTA offices and information

For **MTA route and transfer information**, phone ☎1-800/COMMUTE or 213/626-4455 (Mon–Fri 7.30am–3.30pm); be prepared to wait, and be ready to give precise details of where you are and where you want to go. Otherwise, you can check out the MTA website at ⓦwww.mta.net or go in person to Downtown's Gateway Transit Center, Chavez Avenue at Vignes Street (Mon–Fri 6am–6.30pm), or to three other centrally located offices: in Downtown at 515 S Flower St, on level C of Arco Plaza (Mon–Fri 7.30am–3.30pm); Mid-Wilshire at 5301 Wilshire Blvd (Mon–Fri 9am–5pm); or Hollywood at 6249 Hollywood Blvd (Mon–Fri 10am–6pm).

Other forms of rail transit mainly serve more distant parts of the city. **Amtrak** connects to points in Ventura, Riverside and Orange counties and beyond (see p.27), and **Metrolink** commuter trains primarily link cities in Orange, Ventura, Riverside and San Bernardino counties with Downtown LA on weekdays. Although casual visitors may find the service useful for reaching the outlying areas of the San Fernando Valley, the system does reach as far as Oceanside in San Diego County, from where you can connect to that region's transit system and avoid the freeways altogether. One-way fares on Metrolink range from $3–10, depending on when you're traveling (most routes operate daily during business hours) and how far you're going. For information on specific routes and schedules, call ☏1-800/371-LINK or visit ⊛www.metrolinktrains.com.

Buses

Carless Angelenos not lucky enough to live near a train route are most at ease with **buses**. Although initially bewildering, the MTA bus network is quite simple: the main routes run east–west (eg between Downtown and the coast) and north–south (eg between Downtown and the South Bay). Establishing the best transfer point can be difficult if you need to change buses, but with a bit of planning you should have few real problems – though you should always allow plenty of time.

Free area **brochures** are available from MTA offices (see box), and you can pick up diagrams and timetables for individual bus routes, as well as regional bus maps showing larger sections of the city. Buses on the major arteries between Downtown and the coast run roughly every fifteen minutes between 5am and 2am, while other routes, and the **all-night services** along the major thoroughfares, are less frequent, usually every thirty minutes or hourly. At night be careful not to get stranded Downtown waiting for connecting buses, and avoid isolated routes in risky areas.

The standard **single fare** is $1.35, except for night routes (9pm–5am), when the cost is only 75¢; **transfers**, which can be used in one direction within the time marked on the ticket (usually three hours), cost 25¢ more; **express buses** (a limited commuter service),

and any others using a freeway, are usually $1.85, but can be as much as $3.85, depending on the length of your trip and the number of "zones" that you pass through, as shown on station maps. Put exact fare (coins and/or bills) into the slot when boarding. If you're staying in LA a while, you can save some money with a **weekly** or **monthly pass** ($11/$42, with monthly student passes for $30), which also get you discounts at select shops and travel agents, or a **semi-monthly pass** (good for two weeks), which sells for $21 – all are available at MTA offices.

There are also mini **DASH** buses, which operate under the LA Department of Transportation, or LADOT (dial area code 213, 310, 323 or 818, then ☏808-2273, or visit ⊛www.ladottransit.com), and charge a flat fare of 25¢. Six routes run through Downtown every five to ten minutes between 6.30am and 6pm on weekdays, and every fifteen to twenty minutes between 10am and 5pm on Saturdays and Sundays. Other DASH routes travel widely throughout the city, including the Mid-Wilshire area, Pacific Palisades, Venice and several sections of South Central LA, usually every fifteen to thirty minutes on weekdays, more erratically on Saturdays, and not at all on Sundays.

Other **local bus services** include Orange County's OCTD lines (☏714/636-7433, ⊛www.octa.net), Long Beach's LBTD (☏562/591-2301, ⊛www.lbtransit.org), Culver City's bus network (☏310/253-6500, ⊛www.culvercity.org/depts_bus.html) and Santa Monica's Big Blue Buses (☏310/451-5444, ⊛www.bigbluebus.com).

Bus routes

MTA's **bus routes** fall into six categories, as outlined below. Whatever bus you're on, if traveling alone, especially at night, sit up front near the driver.

#1–99 Local routes to and from Downtown.
#100–299 Local routes to other areas.
#300–399 Limited-stop routes (usually rush hour only).
#400–499 Express routes to and from Downtown.
#500–599 Express routes for other areas.
#600–699 Special service routes (for sports events and the like).

Major LA bus services

From LAX to:
Downtown #42, #439
Long Beach #232
San Fernando Valley/Getty Center #561
San Pedro #225
Watts Towers #117
West Hollywood #220 (for Hollywood change to #4 along Santa Monica Boulevard)

To and from Downtown:
Along Hollywood Blvd #1
Along Sunset Blvd #2, #3, #302
Along Santa Monica Blvd #4, #304
Along Melrose Ave #10, #11
Along Wilshire Blvd #20, #21, #22, #320

From Downtown to:
Burbank Studios #96
East LA #68
Exposition Park #38, #81
Forest Lawn Cemetery, Glendale #90, #91
Huntington Library #79, #379
Long Beach #60
Manhattan Beach, Hermosa Beach, Redondo Beach #439
Orange County, Knott's Berry Farm, Disneyland #460
Palos Verdes #444
Pasadena #401, #402
San Fernando Valley #424, #425
San Pedro #445, #446, #447 (transfer to DASH #142 for Santa Catalina ferry)
Santa Monica #20, #22, #320, #322, #434
Venice #33 #333, #436

Taxis

You can find **taxis** at most transportation terminals and major hotels. Otherwise you'll have to phone ahead – among the more reliable companies are Independent Cab Co (☎1-800/521-8294), LA Taxi (☎1-800/200-1085) and United Independent Taxi (☎1-800/411-0303). The meter begins at $2, then adds $1.60 for each mile, with a $2.50 surcharge if you're picked up at LAX: the driver won't know every street in LA but will know the major ones; ask for the nearest junction and give directions from there.

Bikes

Bicycling in LA may sound perverse, but in some areas it can be one of the better ways of getting around. Beachside bike paths run between Santa Monica and Redondo Beach, and from Long Beach to Newport Beach, and there are equally enjoyable inland routes, notably around Griffith Park and the grand mansions of Pasadena (the LA River route, however, is best avoided, as it's littered with broken glass and you run the risk of being mugged, or worse). For maps and information, contact the AAA, 2601 S Figueroa St (Mon–Fri 9am–5pm; ☎213/741-3686, ⊛www.aaa-calif.com), or the LA Department of Transportation, known as CalTrans, at 120 S Spring St (Mon–Fri 8am–5pm; ☎213/897-3656, ⊛www.dot.ca.gov).

The best place to **rent a bike** for the beaches is on Washington Street around Venice Pier, where numerous outlets include Spokes 'n' Stuff, which has branches at 4175 Admiralty Way (☎310/306-3332) and 1700 Ocean Ave (☎310/395-4748); in summer bike-rental stands line the beach. Prices range from $10 a day for a junker to $20 or more a day for a mountain bike. For similar prices, many beachside stores also rent **roller skates** and **rollerblades**. More information on cycling and rollerblading can be found in "Sports and outdoor activities," p.309.

City tours

One quick and easy way to see something of LA is from the window of a tour bus. Guided bus tours vary greatly in cost and quality, with the mainstream operators taking busloads of tourists around the major sights and only worth considering if you're pushed for time – none covers anything that you couldn't see for yourself for less money. Specialist tours, tailored to suit particular interests, usually take smaller groups and are often a better value, while studio tours of film and TV production areas are covered on day-trips by most of the mainstream operators, though again you'll save money by showing up independently.

Mainstream tours

By far the most popular of the mainstream tours is the half-day **"stars' homes"** – usually including the Farmers Market, Sunset Strip, Rodeo Drive, the Hollywood Bowl and Chinese Theatre, but the "stars' homes" themselves are often no more than the gates of long-forgotten celebrities. These tours are typically the most visible to newcomers, and the area around the Chinese Theatre is usually thick with tourists queuing for their tickets. Other programs include detours around the Westside at night, to the beach areas, the *Queen Mary*, day-long excursions to Disneyland, and shopping trips into Mexico and Tijuana. Most of these can be taken at a reduced cost by staying at one of the major hostels (see "Accommodation," p.223), which offer special package trips that are often more affordable, and fun, than the usual variety.

Outside of the hostels, tour packages start at around $30 per person; you'll find a slew of leaflets in hotel lobbies and visitor centers. You can make reservations at (and be picked up from) most hotels; otherwise contact one of the following booking offices:

Casablanca Tours 6362 Hollywood Blvd ☎323/461-0156, 🌐www.casablancatours.com
Hollywood Fantasy Tours 6671 Hollywood Blvd ☎323/469-8184
Starline Tours 6925 Hollywood Blvd ☎323/463-3333, 🌐www.starlinetours.com

Specialist tours

The **specialist tours** listed below generally cost $30 or more per person. For more sug-

gestions, pick up the free *LA Visitors Guide* from hotels and visitor centers.

Black LA Tours ☎323/750-9267. Tours of notable places in African-American history, like Central Avenue, and black-oriented museums and galleries, as well as periodic trips to Allensworth, California's first all-black community, located in central California. Prices vary.

The California Native 6701 W 87th Place ☎1-800/926-1140 or 310/642-1140, 🌐www.calnative .com. Sea kayaking and adventure hikes, with tours of uninhabited islands off the California coast for $195 and up.

Googie Tours ☎323/980-3480. Pilgrimages to Southern California's remaining space-age glass and formica diners, quirky cocktail lounges, classic fast-food joints and other gems of pop architecture. $40.

Haunted Hearse Tours PO Box 461145, Hollywood ☎323/782-9652. Two-and-a-half hours in the back of a Cadillac hearse, pausing at the scene of many, though by no means all, of the eventful deaths, scandals, perverted sex acts and drugs orgies that have tainted Hollywood and West LA. $40.

Heli USA 16303 Waterman Drive, Van Nuys ☎1-877/TO-FLY-LA or 818/994-1445, 🌐www.toflyla.com. Sweeping helicopter views of the main parts of LA, including day or night tours. Half-hour trips between Downtown and the Westside start at $129, while a full-hour tour that also takes in the coast costs $100 more.

LA Bike Tours 6729 Hollywood Blvd, Hollywood ☎323/466-5890 or 1-888/775-BIKE, 🌐www.labiketours.com. Two-wheeled sightseeing tours of major city attractions like the Getty Center and the Golden Triangle in Beverly Hills, lasting from 90min to a full day. Bike and helmet included, plus lunch. $50–95.

LA Conservancy Tours ☎213/623-CITY, 🌐laconservancy.org. Excellent walking tours around

Downtown, taking in Art Deco movie palaces, once-opulent financial monuments and architectural gems like the Bradbury Building. Tours are every Saturday, leaving the *Biltmore Hotel* on Olive Street at 10am (reservations required; $8). The Conservancy also runs tours of historic neighborhoods around town as well as Pop-architecture treasures from the mid-twentieth century.

Neon Cruises 501 W Olympic Blvd, Downtown ☎213/489-9918, ⓦwww.neonmona.org/cruise.html. Three-hour-long, eye-popping evening tours of LA's best neon art, led once a month on Saturdays by the Museum of Neon Art. These very popular tours often book up months in advance. $45.

Off 'n' Running Tours 1129 Cardiff Ave, West LA ☎310/246-1418. Offbeat four- to six-mile jogging tours of the stars' homes, plus jaunts around Beverly Hills and West LA. $50.

SPARC tours: the Murals of LA 685 Venice Blvd, Venice ☎310/822-9560, ⓦwww.sparcmurals.org. Public art is alive and well in LA, and these thoroughly enlightening tours of the "mural capital of the world" are worth a look. Two-hour mural tours ($400) are personalized to your interests and sometimes include discussions with the artists.

Studio tours

For some small insight into how a film or TV show is made, or just to admire the special effects, there are guided tours at Warner Bros Studios ($33; ⓦwww.burbank.com/warner_bros_tour.shtml), NBC-TV Studios ($7) and Universal Studios ($45; ⓦwww.universalstudioshollywood.com), all in or near Burbank; see p.191. (Paramount studio tours in Hollywood have been suspended until further notice, due to security concerns.) If you want to be part of a studio **audience**, the street just outside the Chinese Theatre is the major solicitation spot: TV company reps regularly hand out free tickets, and they'll bus you to the studio and back. All you have to do is be willing to laugh and clap on cue.

Opening hours, public holidays and festivals

The opening hours of specific attractions – including museums, theme parks, public offices and homes open for tours – are given throughout the guide, with phone numbers for those sights that are open irregularly, closed until further notice, or require a reservation to visit. It's always worth checking ahead, especially if you're planning to visit attractions far from central LA.

Opening hours

As a general rule, most **museums** are open Tuesday through Saturday, from 10am until 5 or 6pm, though a select few stay open until 7 or 8pm. Those that don't tend to stay open late one evening a week – usually Thursday, when ticket prices are sometimes reduced. Government **offices**, including post offices, are open during regular business hours, typically 8 or 9am until 5pm, Monday through Friday. Most stores are open daily from 10am and close at 5 or 6pm, while specialty stores can be more erratic, usually opening and closing later in the day (from noon to 2pm until 8 to 10pm) and remaining shuttered for two days of the week. **Malls** tend to be open from 10am until 7 or 8pm daily, though individual stores may close before the mall does.

While many diners stay open around the clock, the more typical **restaurants** open daily around 11am or noon for lunch and close at 9 or 10pm. Places that serve breakfast, however, open early between 6 to 8am and serve lunch later, closing in the early or mid-afternoon. Dance and live-music **clubs** often won't open until 9 or 10pm (or even later, in some cases), and many will serve liquor until 2am and then either close for the night or stay open until dawn without serving booze. **Bars** that close at 2am may reopen as early as 6am to grab bleary-eyed customers in need of a liquid breakfast.

Finally, the big-name **theme parks** are open throughout the year, usually daily during summer, from 9 or 10am until 10 or 11pm, and with reduced hours during the offseason (ie Mon–Fri 10am–6pm, Sat & Sun 9am–9pm). The two exceptions are **Disneyland**, which generally has longer hours throughout the year, and **water parks**, which are often accessible during the summer only.

Public holidays and festivals

On the **national public holidays** listed below, banks, government offices and many museums are liable to be closed all day. Small stores, as well as some restaurants and clubs, are usually closed as well, but shopping malls, supermarkets, and department and chain stores increasingly remain open, regardless of the holiday. Most parks, beaches and cemeteries stay open during holidays, as do theme parks, which draw some of their biggest crowds during such times.

The LA region hosts a wide variety of **festivals** during the year; the highlights are described in "Listings," p.320. Most of LA may hold parades, set off fireworks and indulge in general merriment for New Year's Day, the Fourth of July, Halloween and the assorted Christmas light shows. LA has no equivalent to New York's Thanksgiving parade, and is rather subdued except for the chaotic spectacle at the local shopping malls, marking the beginning of the Christmas buying season – a four-week shopping orgy that is perhaps LA's biggest festival of all.

Official national holidays

January
New Year's Day
3rd Monday: Dr Martin Luther King Jr's birthday
February
3rd Monday: Presidents' Day
May
Last Monday: Memorial Day
July
4: Independence Day
September
1st Monday: Labor Day
October
2nd Monday: Columbus Day
November
11: Veterans Day
Last Thursday: Thanksgiving
December
25: Christmas

Costs, money and banks

Like other parts of the country, LA's economy has cooled off in recent years, and to the visitor it's likely to be pleasantly affordable. With a minimum of effort you can find plenty of bargains and reasonably priced goods and services, though of course you won't lack for choice should you want to splurge at one of the city's swankier restaurants or trendy bars.

Average costs

Accommodation is likely to be your biggest single expense in LA: adequate lodging is rarely available for less than $40, although hostels will of course be cheaper. A more reasonable room will run anywhere from

$50–90, with fancier hotels costing much more – upwards of $400 in some cases. **Camping** in LA is an alternative, but only if you're staying in more isolated areas like San Clemente, where you can get into a campground for around $15–20 per night (see "Accommodation," p.223).

Unlike accommodation, prices for good **food** range widely, as do the types of places that serve it, from hot-dog stands to chic restaurants. You could get by on as little as $15 a day, but realistically you should aim for around $40 – and remember, too, that LA has plenty of great spots for a splurge. Beyond restaurants, the city has many **bars**, **clubs** and **live music venues** to suit all tastes and wallets.

In terms of **transportation**, your best bet is probably to rent a car from any of the rental outlets around the airport, especially if you're traveling with a group. Regional distances are huge, and if you're headed anywhere beyond central LA, or more specifically beyond the Westside, you'll undoubtedly find many of the **public transit** choices to be time-consuming hassles. US gas prices, moreover, are still relatively cheap compared to those in the rest of the world and especially Europe.

Added to the cost of most items you purchase is an 8.25 percent **sales tax.** Additionally, many municipalities tack on a **hotel tax** of around 14 percent, which can drive up accommodation costs dramatically.

Finally, you should figure in costs for **tipping** into your travel budget. Expect to pay about 15 percent to waiters in restaurants (unless the service is truly wretched), 20 percent in upscale establishments. About the same amount should be added to taxi fares – and round them up to the nearest 50¢ or dollar. A hotel porter should get $1 per bag; chambermaids $1–2 a day; and valet attendants $1.

For attractions in the main part of the *Guide*, prices are quoted for adults, with children's rates listed only if they are more than a few dollars less; at some spots, kids get in for half-price, or for free if they're under 8. The city also has a few free attractions for everyone as well, but these are mostly historical and cultural monuments like adobes and old railroad stations – with the major exception of the Getty Center (though parking is $5).

Banks and ATMs

With an **ATM card**, you'll be able to withdraw cash just about anywhere in LA, though you'll be charged $2 for using a different bank's network. Foreign cash-dispensing cards linked to international networks, such as Plus or Cirrus (see box), are also widely accepted – ask your home bank or credit company which branches you can use. To find the location of the nearest ATM in LA, call: **Amex** ☎1-800/CASH-NOW; **Cirrus** ☎1-800/4-CIRRUS; **The Exchange** ☎1-800/237-ATMS; or **Plus** ☎1-800/843-7587. Make sure you have a personal identification number (PIN) that's designed to work overseas.

Bank hours are generally from 9am to 4pm or 5pm Monday to Thursday, and from 10am to 6pm on Friday. For banking services – especially currency exchange – outside normal business hours and on weekends, try major hotels or Thomas Cook outlets (see "Directory", p.351).

Travelers' checks

US **travelers' checks** are the safest way for overseas visitors to carry money, and the better-known travelers' checks, such as those issued by American Express and Visa, are treated as cash in most shops. The usual fee for travelers' check sales is one or two percent, though this fee may be waived if you buy the checks through your home bank. It pays to get a selection of denominations. Keep the purchase agreement and a record of check serial numbers safe and separate from the checks themselves. In the event that checks are lost or stolen, the issuing company will expect you to report the loss immediately (see p.42 for emergency numbers). Most companies claim to replace lost or stolen checks within 24 hours.

Credit and debit cards

Credit cards are the most widely accepted form of payment for major hotels, restaurants and retailers, even though some smaller merchants still do not accept them. You'll be asked to show a credit card when renting a car, bike, windsurfer or other such

Money: a note for foreign travelers

Generally speaking, one pound sterling will buy $1.40–1.70; one Canadian or Australian dollar is worth 55–70¢; one New Zealand dollar equals 50–70¢; and one euro is equivalent to $1.

US currency comes in bills of $1, $5, $10, $20, $50 and $100, plus various larger (and rarer) denominations – all are the same size and the same green color, so check bills carefully. The dollar is made up of 100 cents with coins of 1 cent (known as a penny), 5 cents (a nickel), 10 cents (a dime) and 25 cents (a quarter). Quarters are most useful for buses, vending machines, parking meters and telephones, so always carry plenty.

item, or to start a "tab" at hotels for incidental charges; in any case, you can always pay the bill in cash when you return the item or check out of your room. Most major credit cards issued by foreign banks are honored in the US. Visa, MasterCard, American Express and Diners Club are the most widely used.

Credit cards can also come in handy as a backup source of funds, and they can save on exchange-rate commissions. Make sure you have a **personal identification number**, or PIN, that's designed to work overseas. Remember that all cash advances are treated as loans, with interest accruing daily from the date of withdrawal (there may be a transaction fee on top of this).

If your credit cards are stolen, you'll need to provide information on where and when you made your last transactions, and the specific numbers of the cards (emergency numbers are given below).

Wiring money

Having money wired from home using one of the companies listed below is never convenient or cheap, and should be considered a last resort. It's also possible to have money wired directly from a bank in your home country to a bank in the US, even though this is somewhat less reliable as it involves two separate institutions. If you choose this option, the person making the transfer will include the address of the branch bank where you want to pick up the money, and the address and telex number of the bank to which the funds are being sent. Money wired this way will take two working days to arrive.

The quickest way to have money wired to you is to have someone take the cash to the nearest **American Express Moneygram** office (☎1-800/543-4080; also available at participating Thomas Cook branches) and have it instantaneously wired to you, minus a ten-percent commission that varies according to the amount sent – the entire process should take no longer than ten minutes. For similar, if slightly pricier, services, **Western Union** has offices throughout LA (information at ☎1-800/325-6000 in the US; ☎0800/833 833 in the UK; and ☎1-800/649 565 in Australia, ☜www.westernunion.com), with credit card payments subject to an additional $10 fee.

International Money Transfers can be made from any bank in Australia and New Zealand to a nominated bank abroad; fees run around A$25/NZ$30, but be warned – the whole process can take anywhere from a couple of days to several months. If you desperately need money, wire services are faster, but about twice as expensive.

If you have a few days' leeway, sending a postal **money order**, exchangeable at any post office through the mail, is a cheaper option. The equivalent for foreign travelers is the **international money order**, for which you need to allow up to seven days in international air mail before arrival. An ordinary **check** sent from overseas takes two or three weeks to clear.

Crime and personal safety

Much of LA's reputation for crime is somewhat overblown, helped in large part by Hollywood stereotypes of rampant muggings and frequent drive-by shootings. In reality, members of the notorious LA gangs, for instance, tend to target each other rather than tourists, and many – though not all – violent crimes can be avoided by steering clear of rough neighborhoods.

Most places in LA, from Downtown to the coast, are fairly nonthreatening during the daytime, especially in the major tourist zones, while the number of safe spots diminishes at night. Much of **Downtown**, west of Skid Row at least, is walkable during the morning and afternoon hours, while at night you should stay in your hotel room if you're staying here – the area closes up after dark anyway. **Mid-Wilshire** should be treated like Downtown, with special care given to the dicey Temple-Beaudry, Pico-Union and Westlake neighborhoods, and the area both south of Wilshire and east of La Brea Avenue. **Hollywood** is best explored on foot, and is, while dodgy in some places, a prime spot for after-hours dancing and drinking, if you don't mind a few prostitutes and petty thugs in your midst. **West Hollywood** is a busy, dynamic and generally safe place throughout the day and night, especially along the Sunset Strip, as are most **West LA** areas from Beverly Hills to Santa Monica. Most of **South Central LA** should only be visited during the day, with some areas like Compton off-limits at all times to unaccustomed visitors.

Further out, you should have few problems in the major tourist areas – Burbank, Pasadena, coastal Long Beach, Malibu, coastal Orange County. There are some scattered places where the street gangs are particularly visible – large sections of Southeast and East LA, North Long Beach, Pacoima in the San Fernando Valley, and Orange County towns like Santa Ana – and the attractions therein should be approached with caution.

Mugging and theft

If you're unlucky enough to get **mugged**, hand over your money, and afterwards find a phone and dial ☎911 for the police. LA criminals tend to be well-armed, and you're likely to risk being shot – or getting someone else shot – if you try to resist. Moreover, since drugs are a major motivation in many robberies, and criminals are often drunk or high when committing their crimes, trying to predict what the mugger will do is pointless.

Of course, **prevention** is always the best solution, and you can avoid many problems by simply steering clear of neighborhoods that look dangerous, especially at night. Deserted areas should be avoided in the evening, as should places where the residents watch visitors suspiciously or with

Breaking the law

Whether intentionally or not, foreign visitors may find themselves **breaking US laws** on occasion. Aside from **speeding** or **parking violations**, one of the most common ways visitors bring trouble on themselves is through **jaywalking**, or crossing the road against red lights or away from intersections. Fines can be stiff, and the police will most assuredly not take sympathy on you if you mumble that you "didn't think it was illegal."

   Drinking laws provide another source of irritation to visitors, particularly as the law prohibits drinking liquor, wine or beer in most public spaces like parks and beaches, and liquor is officially off-limits to anyone under 21.

hostility. If you find yourself in a rough neighborhood, especially on foot, do everything possible to avoid looking confused or terrified – such behavior will mark you as a target. When walking, carry the bulk of your cash, and all of your credit cards, in a **hidden place** separate from a token sum of cash you can use to "buy off" the mugger. Fifty dollars or so, easily accessible on your person, should be an adequate sum to send the criminal hunting for his next victim; almost all violent lawbreakers are male. After the crime occurs, immediately report it to the police so you can later attempt to recover your loss from an insurance provider – unlikely, but worth a try. Also, keep **emergency numbers** for credit cards and travelers' checks handy, so they can be canceled after the crime occurs.

One prime spot to be mugged is at an **ATM** outside the tourist areas, where you're likely to be told to make the maximum withdrawal and hand it over. Needless to say, you should treat ATM use with the strictest caution and not worry about looking paranoid – LA residents have gotten used to viewing the machines as nocturnal invitations for street crime. Aside from having a friend "spot" for you, keeping watch for any interlopers in the vicinity while you grab your cash, your best choice is to use the automatic tellers available at major hotels and entertainment areas, where it's more difficult for muggers to get away with robbing customers. But remember, even if you don't get mugged, there are all kinds of thieves who specialize in peering over your shoulder when you enter your PIN number and then pickpocketing your wallet later.

If you manage to **lose your passport**, call your country's consulate listed in the "Directory" (p.351) and pick up or have sent to you an application form, which you must submit with a notarized photocopy of your ID and a $30 reissuing fee. Because the process of issuing a new passport can take up to six weeks, you should also spend an extra $10 to have the consulate telex record departments back home.

Finally, a few **simple rules** are worth remembering: don't flash money around, leave your wallet open or count money in public; don't constantly peer at maps or guide books (or gawk up at tall buildings)

while on the street; don't look panicked, even if you are; and at night, make sure you walk on the edge of the sidewalk nearest the street, so you can dash toward the road if a confrontation occurs.

Women's safety

A woman traveling alone is not as conspicuous a target in LA as she might be in other American metropolises, but common sense still applies. As a rule, women (or men, for that matter) should **never hitchhike** anywhere in the city alone. This mode of travel leaves you open to every thug and would-be rapist motoring down the highway; if you're driving, avoid hitchhikers just as steadfastly. If you can, try not to travel at night by **public transportation**, especially in the city's dodgier parts – South Central, Boyle Heights, the barrios east of Downtown LA, and so on. If this is your only means of transit, sit as close to the bus driver as possible. Also on the danger list is **walking** through desolate, unlit streets at night; you're better off taking cabs to your destination, if even for just a few blocks. If you don't appear confused, scared or drunk, and project a serious or wary countenance instead, your chances of attack may be lessened.

If you listen to the advice of locals, and stick to safer parts of town, going into **bars** and **clubs** should pose no problems, as women's privacy is often respected, especially in dance and rock clubs. However, sexual harassment is more common for single women in country-and-western clubs, and the bars of East LA are very male-oriented and should be strictly avoided, as should those in Southeast and South Central LA. If in doubt, Westside bars and clubs are usually safe choices, and gay and lesbian bars are generally trouble-free alternatives.

Should your **vehicle break down** on the road, don't stand by it waiting for assistance. Instead, flag down a police car – the worse the neighborhood, the fewer of them you'll see – or go to the nearest store, hotel or restaurant and call for the police or a tow truck. If disaster strikes, **rape counseling services** are available throughout the city, and can be accessed through the local sheriff's office, which can make arrangements for personal help and counseling.

Emergency numbers for lost cards and checks

American Express cards ☎1-800/528-4800,
ⓦ www.americanexpress.com
American Express checks ☎1-800/221-7282
Citicorp checks ☎1-800/645-6556,
ⓦ www.citicorp.com
Diners Club ☎1-800/234-6377,
ⓦ www.dinersclub.com
Discover ☎1-800/DISCOVER,

ⓦ www.discovercard.com
MasterCard ☎1-800/826-2181,
ⓦ www.mastercard.com
Thomas Cook/MasterCard checks
☎1-800/223-9920,
ⓦ www.travelex.com or
ⓦ www.thomascook.co.uk
Visa cards ☎1-800/847-2911,
ⓦ www.visa.com
Visa checks ☎1-800/227-6811

Hotel room theft

To avoid being the victim of a **hotel room theft** – a more frequent problem for lower-end establishments, though even the elite hotels are not immune from it – lock your valuables in the room **safe** when you leave (or in the hotel safe, for that matter) and always keep doors locked with chains as well as bolts when you're in the room. Don't open the door to suspicious individuals, and if a visitor claims to be a hotel representative, phone the front desk to make sure of it.

Car crime and safety

Crimes committed against tourists driving **rental cars** have made headlines in the last decade, but there are certain precautions you can take to keep yourself safe. In major urban areas like LA, any car you rent should have nothing on it – such as a special license plate – to distinguish it as a rental car. When driving, under no circumstances should you stop in unlit or deserted urban areas, and especially not if someone is waving at you and claiming there's something wrong with your vehicle. Similarly, if you are "accidentally" rammed by the driver behind you, do not stop immediately but instead drive on to the nearest well-lit and busy spot and phone the police at ☎911. Keep doors locked and windows never more than slightly open. Do not open your door or window if someone

approaches on the pretext of asking directions. Hide valuables out of sight, either in the trunk or the glove compartment (any valuables you don't need for your journey should be left in your hotel safe).

Should a relatively uncommon **"carjacking"** occur, in which you're asked to hand over your car at gunpoint, flee the vehicle as quickly as possible and get away from the scene, then call the police. There is absolutely no reason why you should die for the sake of an automobile – even in LA.

If your car **breaks down** at night while on a boulevard or major street, activate the emergency flashers to signal a police officer for assistance, or, if possible during the day, find the nearest phone book and call for a tow truck. Should you be forced to stop your car on a **freeway**, pull over to the right shoulder of the highway – never the left, as countless motorists have been killed by oncoming traffic – and activate your flashers. Wait for assistance either in your vehicle while strapped in by a seat belt or on a safe embankment nearby. If necessary, you can use one of the **"call boxes"** found every half-mile or so along freeways in LA. No matter the situation, never do "on the spot" repair work to your vehicle beside an LA highway; numerous would-be mechanics have been killed in recent years while adjusting engines, fixing headlights and changing flat tires.

Travelers with disabilities

Travelers with mobility challenges or physical disabilities will find LA, along with the US in general, more amenable to their needs than many places in the world. Because of the passage of the 1990 Americans with Disabilities Act, or ADA, all public buildings must be wheelchair-accessible and have suitable toilets (though the US Supreme Court has limited the reach of the ADA in recent years to exclude certain work-related disorders and personal injuries). Accordingly, the city has sloped curbs at most street corners, subways have elevator access, and city buses have lifts, along with space and handgrips for wheelchair users. Most hotels and restaurants, especially those built within the last decade, also have adequate accommodations for wheelchairs, though movie theaters have been slower to change their ways, and in some venues you may end up stuck near the front row with a skewed view of the screen or parked in an alcove off to the side.

Planning your trip

American **airlines** must by law accommodate those with disabilities, some of them even allowing attendants of those with serious conditions to accompany them on the trip for a reduced fare. Similarly, almost every **Amtrak train** includes one or more cars with accommodation for disabled passengers, along with wheelchair assistance at train platforms, adapted on-board seating, free travel for guide dogs, and fifteen percent discounts on fares, with 24 hours' advance notice. Passengers with hearing impairment can get information by calling ☎1-800/523-6590 or checking out ✆www.amtrak.com.

However, traveling by **Greyhound** and **Amtrak Thruway** service is often problematic. Buses are not equipped with platforms for wheelchairs, though intercity carriers are required by law to provide assistance with boarding, and disabled passengers may be able to get priority seating. Those unable to travel alone, and in possession of a doctor's certificate, may receive two-for-one fares to bring a companion along. Call Greyhound's ADA customer assistance line for more information (☎1-800/752-4841, ✆www.greyhound.com).

The city's major **car rental** firms provide vehicles with hand controls for drivers with leg or spinal disabilities, though these are typically available only on the pricier models. The American Automobile Association

(☎213/741-3686, ✆www.aaa-calif.com) produces the *Handicapped Driver's Mobility Guide*, and **parking regulations** for disabled motorists are now uniform: licenses for the disabled must carry a three-inch-square international access symbol, and placards bearing this symbol must be hung from the car's rearview mirror (blue colors signify permanent disability, while red signifies a temporary condition of up to six months). Additionally, self-service gas stations are required to provide **full service** to disabled motorists at self-service prices.

Disabled access

The major hotel and motel chains are the best bet for accessible **accommodation**. At the higher end of the scale, *Embassy Suites* (voice ☎1-800/362-2779, TDD 1-800/458-4708, ✆www.embassysuites.com) has been working to comply with new standards of access that meet or, in some cases, exceed ADA requirements, involving building new facilities, retrofitting older hotels and providing special training to all employees. To a somewhat lesser degree, the same is true of *Hyatt Hotels* (voice ☎1-800/233-1234, TDD ☎1-800/228-9548, ✆www.hyatt.com) and the other big hoteliers in town.

Citizens or permanent residents of the US who have been "medically determined to be blind or permanently disabled" can obtain the **Golden Access Passport** (✆www.nps.gov

/fees_passes.htm), a free lifetime pass to federally operated parks, monuments, historic sites and recreation areas that charge admission fees. The pass must be picked up in person, from the sites described, and it also provides a 50 percent discount on fees charged at facilities for camping, boat launching and parking. The **Golden Bear Pass**, also free to the disabled, offers similar benefits for California state-run parks, beaches and historic sites that charge admission fees (@www.parks.ca.gov for details).

Many US **tour companies** cater to disabled travelers or specialize in organizing **group tours**. The California Office of Tourism (℡1-800/TO-CALIF, @gocalif.ca.gov) can provide you with a list of such companies, or you can contact the National Tour Association, 546 E Main St, Lexington, KY 40508 (℡1-800/682-8886, @www.ntaonline .com), an informational and advocacy group that can put you in touch with operators whose tours match your needs.

Information for disabled travelers

ACROD Australian Council for Rehabilitation of the Disabled PO Box 60, Curtin, ACT 2605 ℡02/6282 4333, @www.acrod.org.au. Provides lists of travel agencies and tour operators for people with disabilities.

Barrier-Free Travel 36 Wheatley St, North Bellingen, NSW 2454 ℡02/6655 1733. Disabled travel-access information, for a fee.

Disabled Persons Assembly Level 4, Wellington Trade Centre, 173–175 Victoria St, Wellington ℡04/801 9100, @www.dpa.org.nz. Resource center with lists of travel agencies and tour operators.

In the UK and Ireland

Access Travel 6, The Hillock, Astley, Lancashire M29 7GW ℡01942/888 844, ℱ01942/891 811, @www.access-travel.co.uk. A range of services, from consumer protection to car hire and adapted vehicles.

All Go Here ℡01923/840 463, @www .everybody.co.uk. Provides information on accommodation suitable for disabled travelers throughout the UK, including Northern Ireland.

Holiday Care Service 2nd Floor, Imperial Buildings, Victoria Road, Horley, Surrey RH6 7PZ ℡01293/774 535, ℱ01293/784 647, Minicom ℡01293/776 943, @www.holidaycare.org.uk. Offers free lists of accessible accommodation in the US and other destinations. Information on financial help for holidays available.

Irish Wheelchair Association Blackheath Drive, Clontarf, Dublin 3 ℡01/818 6400, @www.iwa.ie. Useful information provided about traveling abroad with a wheelchair.

Mencap Holiday Services Optium House, Clippers Quay, Salford Quays, Manchester M52 2XP ℡0161/888 1200, @www.mencap.org.uk. Provides information on holiday travel for the disabled, including an annual guide.

RADAR Royal Association for Disability and Rehabilitation 12 City Forum, 250 City Rd, London EC1V 8AF ℡020/7250 3222, Minicom ℡020/7250 4119, @www.radar.org.uk. General information and advice on holidays and travel.

Tripscope The Vassall Centre, Gill Avenue, Bristol BS16 2QQ ℡08457/585 641, ℱ0117/939 7736, @www.tripscope.org.uk. Registered charity providing a national telephone information service offering free advice on UK and international transport for those with mobility problems.

Access-Able PO Box 1796, Wheat Ridge, CO 80034 ℡303/232-2979, @www.access-able.com. General information service and network that assists travelers with disabilities by putting them in contact with other people with similar conditions.

California Office of Tourism 801 K St, Suite 1600, Sacramento, CA 95814-3520 ℡1-800/GO-CALIF or 916/322-2881, @www.visitcalifornia .com. Publishes a free, two-hundred-page *Travel Planning Guide* that lists disabled facilities for state accommodations and attractions.

Directions Unlimited 720 N Bedford Rd, Bedford Hills, NY 10507 ℡1-800/533-5343 or 914/241-1700. Tour operator with customized tours for people with disabilities.

Easy Access Travel 5386 Arlington Ave, Riverside, CA 92504 ℡1-800/920-8989. Travel consulting services with comprehensive tour packages.

Mobility International USA PO Box 10767, Eugene, OR 97440 ℡541/343-1284, @www.miusa.org. Answers travel questions and operates an exchange program for the disabled. Annual membership ($35) includes quarterly newsletter.

Moss Rehabilitation Hospital 1200 W Tabor Rd, Philadelphia, PA 19141-3099 ℡215/456-9900,

TDD ☎215/456-9602, ⊛www.einstein.edu/aehn/moss_rehab.html. Institutional telephone information and referral service.

Society for Accessible Travel and Hospitality (SATH) 347 Fifth Ave, #610, New York, NY 10016 ☎212/447-7284, ⊛www.sath.org. Nonprofit travel-industry group that answers travel-related queries.

Twin Peaks Press Box 129, Vancouver, WA 98666-0129 ☎360/694-2462, ⊛home.pacifier.com/~twinpeak. Publishes the *Directory of Travel Agencies for the Disabled*, listing more than 370 agencies worldwide, as well as *Travel for the Disabled*.

Wheels Up! ☎1-888/38-WHEELS, ⊛www.wheelsup.com. Online service that provides discounted air fares, tour and cruise prices for disabled travelers, and publishes a free monthly newsletter.

The media

Although LA's local press has a deserved reputation for sensationalism, known for its helicopter pursuits of police chases and constant celebrity gossip, you can still find good regional and national media outlets, though fewer for international news. With the growth of cable TV, there are more television viewing choices than ever, though the quality has only marginally improved. Area radio stations, however, can occasionally supply information and entertainment that you can't get from other sources.

Newspapers and magazines

For such a large city, LA supports surprisingly few daily **newspapers**. At the top of the list is the *Los Angeles Times* (35¢; ⊛www.latimes.com), the most widely read newspaper in Southern California, and probably the top paper in the Western US, available at news boxes and dealers throughout town. Friday's "Calendar" section is an essential source for **entertainment** and **cultural listings** (with much of the information also available online at ⊛www.calendarlive.com). Upscale hotels often distribute the newspaper to your door for free, along with a copy of the *New York Times* or *Wall Street Journal,* though less frequently. However, most **other major newspapers**, whether domestic or foreign, tend to be found mainly at city and university libraries, and a few large magazine stands.

As far as other dailies go, the *Los Angeles Daily News* (⊛www.dailynews.com) is more conservative than the *LA Times*, with a near-militant San Fernando Valley slant; while *La Opinion* (⊛www.laopinion.com) is one of the country's major Spanish-language newspapers, and has a large readership in LA. The *Orange County Register* (⊛www.ocregister .com), a right-of-center paper, is mainly found in its namesake macro-suburb and offers little for LA readers. Smaller weekly papers include such names as the *Watts Times*, *Downtown News* and *Los Angeles Independent*, each focusing on more local concerns within a particular district or community.

There are a few good **alternative weeklies,** most notably the free *LA Weekly* (⊛www.laweekly.com), affiliated with New York's *Village Voice* and found at libraries and retailers everywhere, providing engaging investigative journalism and copious entertainment listings. The *OC Weekly* (⊛www.ocweekly.com), the liberal Orange County counterpart of the *LA Weekly*, is a fine alternative source.

Every community of any size has at least a

few **free newspapers** that cater to the local scene, with some also providing specialist coverage of interests ranging from cycling to business investment. Like the *LA Weekly*, many of these are also good sources for **listings** for bars, restaurants and nightlife within their areas. Both the USC and UCLA campuses have libraries carrying recent **overseas newspapers**, while day-old English and European papers are on sale in Hollywood at *Universal News Agency*, 1645 N Las Palmas Ave (daily 7am–midnight), and the 24-hour *World Book and News*, 1652 N Cahuenga Blvd.

LA has a few style-conscious magazines, foremost among them the monthly *Los Angeles* magazine ($2.95; ☜lamag.com), packed with gossipy news and profiles of local movers and shakers, as well as reviews of the city's trendiest restaurants and clubs. There are also dozens of less mainstream publications – including *Spunk* and *The Edge* – focusing on LA's diverse gay and lesbian culture and nightclubs. As for free magazines, the touristy *Where LA* (☜www.wherela.com) is a monthly public-relations magazine found in many hotel rooms, and has both glossy reviews and more straightforward listings.

Television

LA network **television** generally offers a steady diet of talk shows, sitcoms, soap operas and game shows, with some Spanish-language and Asian stations on the UHF portion of the dial. An ad-free alternative to the standard fare is KCET, on UHF channel 28 (☜www.kcet.org), LA's public television station and one of the nation's top producers of educational programs.

Most motel and hotel rooms are hooked up to some form of **cable TV**, though the number of channels available to guests depends on where you stay. See the daily papers for channels, schedules and times. Most cable stations are actually no better than the big broadcast networks, though some of the specialized channels are interesting. **Cable News Network (CNN)** and **Headline News** both have round-the-clock news, with **Fox News** providing a right-wing slant on the day's events. **ESPN** is your best bet for all kinds of sports, **MTV** for youth-

oriented music videos and programming, and **VH-1** for Baby Boomer sounds. **Home Box Office (HBO)** and **Showtime** present big-budget Hollywood flicks and excellent TV shows such as "The Sopranos," while **American Movie Classics (AMC)** and the superior **Turner Classic Movies** take their programming from the Golden Age of cinema.

Many major **sporting events** are transmitted on a pay-per-view basis, and watching an event like a heavyweight boxing match will set you back at least $50, billed directly to your motel room. Most hotels and motels also offer a choice of **recent movies** that have just finished their theatrical runs, at around $8–10 per film.

Broadcast television stations

KCBS CBS affiliate on channel 2
KNBC NBC on channel 4
KTLA WB on channel 5
KABC ABC on channel 7
KCAL Unaffiliated on channel 9
KTTV Fox on channel 11
KCOP UPN network on channel 13
KCET PBS on channel 28 UHF
KMEX Spanish-language Univision on channel 34 UHF

Radio

Radio stations are even more abundant than broadcast TV stations, and the majority stick to mainstream commercial formats – usually rigidly programmed by huge corporations. **AM stations** are best for news, traffic reports and talk radio, while **FM stations**, particularly the federally- and subscriber-funded **public** and **college stations** found between 88 and 92 FM, broadcast diverse programming, from bizarre underground rock to obscure local theater. Of these stations, **KCRW** (89.9) has some of the most diverse programming in LA, from public affairs to dance music, which at night can be anything from trance, dub and trip-hop to ambient (listen live from your computer at ☜www.kcrw.org).

LA also has a range of decent **specialist music stations** – classical, jazz and so on – as well as a sizeable number of **Spanish-language stations**.

Local AM stations

KFI 640 Tub-thumping talk radio, mostly with a far-right slant.

KFWB 980 Frequent local news, plus talk shows.

KNX 1070 News with half-hourly sports reports.

KXTA 1150 Sports and talk.

Local FM stations

KLON 88.1 Blues and jazz.

KXLU 88.9 Underground hip-hop and Saturday-night interviews with performers.

KPCC 89.3 Jazz and blues concerts, plus arts-related talk radio. Nationally funded public radio station (NPR affiliate).

KCRW 89.9 One of the country's better NPR affiliates, with new music, transatlantic imports and world news.

KPFK 90.7 Lively opinions, news and music, from lefty political activists. Nationally funded public radio station (Pacifica affiliate).

KUSC 91.5 Classical, jazz and world music.

KCBS 93.1 "The Arrow": classic rock tunes.

KZLA 93.9 Popular country hits.

KLOS 95.5 Album rock.

KLSX 97.1 Talk radio, shock jocks, including Howard Stern.

KSSE 97.5 Latino pop favorites and salsa.

KKBT 100.3 "The Beat": soul, R&B and hip-hop.

KRTH 101.1 "K-Earth": nothing but oldies, advertised incessantly around town.

KIIS 102.7 Top 40 pop hits.

KBIG 104.3 Pop and dance, with some disco sprinkled in.

KMZT 105.1 "K-Mozart": Mainline classical music.

KPWR 106 "K-Power": Hip-hop and R&B with some Latin pop.

KROQ 106.7 Hard rock with a touch of grunge.

BASICS | The media

The City

The City

Downtown LA

O ne of the most enduring myths about Los Angeles is that it has never had any kind of urban center, and is merely an endless series of flat, disconnected suburbs. While modern LA is to many the epitome of postmodern sprawl, historically **DOWNTOWN LA** was, until the early twentieth century, the social and cultural hub of the region, where the masses could come to be entertained and enlightened by the city's governing elite – bankers, real-estate mavens, politicians and various other self-appointed power brokers. Not surprisingly, though, with the advent of the automobile, Angelenos have been moving in all directions away from their ostensible city center, paving over orange groves and beanfields in their continuous march outward. Today, despite the serviceable array of skyscrapers on display, Downtown isn't a true center for much of anything beyond finance: the old money hides in cloistered spots like Pasadena, the new money resides firmly on the Westside – along with most of LA's cultural attractions – and most of the middle and working classes have long since escaped Downtown's crumbling Victorian homes, or been forced out when most of them were destroyed by dubious urban-renewal schemes.

Still, for all its failings, Downtown can be an enjoyable place to visit, with a smattering of refurbished adobes and grand old movie palaces, some modern museums and a few interesting corporate towers. It's only fairly recently that Downtown has become vertical at all. Until 1960, **City Hall** was, at 28 stories, the town's tallest structure, but from the 1960s to the end of the 1980s, LA saw a building boom spurred on largely by foreign capital (notably from Canadian real-estate companies and, later, Japanese investment firms) that replaced the creaky Victorians atop Bunker Hill with glass curtain–walls and Brutalist concrete monsters. Inevitably, the boom faded during LA's near-depression during the early 1990s, but in recent years, the area has made a slow recovery. To many, the monumental construction of Disney Hall is a symbol of Downtown's long-awaited rebirth.

Although the gleaming modernity of Bunker Hill is immediately tempting, a trip Downtown is best experienced beginning at **the Plaza**, the original nineteenth-century town site and now the remodeled focus of a cleaned-up district known as "**El Pueblo de Los Angeles**," which also holds the historic, if over-commercialized, **Olvera Street**. To the south, LA's **Civic Center** is an almost shamefully bland seat of local government, enlivened only by the classic form of City Hall and a scant few other structures.

Further south stand the antique facades along **Spring Street** and **Broadway**. Since their heyday in the 1920s as the respective financial and cultural axes of the city, the two streets have changed considerably. Broadway is still a thriving commercial area, but now has a Hispanic character, with T-shirt

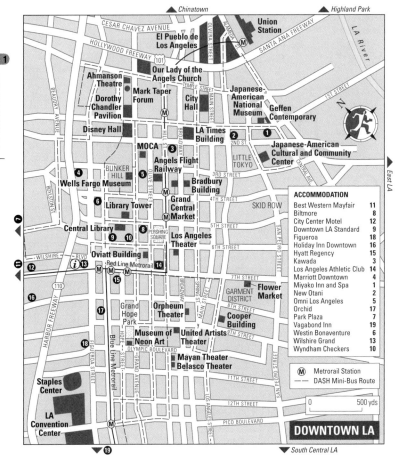

DOWNTOWN LA

ACCOMMODATION	
Best Western Mayfair	11
Biltmore	8
City Center Motel	12
Downtown LA Standard	9
Figueroa	18
Holiday Inn Downtown	16
Hyatt Regency	15
Kawada	3
Los Angeles Athletic Club	14
Marriott Downtown	4
Miyako Inn and Spa	1
New Otani	2
Omni Los Angeles	5
Orchid	17
Park Plaza	7
Vagabond Inn	19
Westin Bonaventure	6
Wilshire Grand	13
Wyndham Checkers	10

Ⓜ Metrorail Station
--- DASH Mini-Bus Route

0 ____ 500 yds

stands and fast-food vendors lining its corridor, and many of its once-grand movie palaces now host to fiery evangelist churches, hectic swap meets or the occasional Hollywood action flicks. Spring Street, on the other hand, presents a bleaker picture: the decline of banking and financial services spelled doom for the strip, though a smattering of the once-grand Neoclassical buildings have now been renovated into funky artist lofts and community theaters.

Replacing Spring Street as LA's main financial zone, **Bunker Hill** has, despite its colossal cache of new development, rather limited charms – mainly upscale museums and modernist architecture. North and east of Downtown, **Chinatown** and **Little Tokyo** are interesting mostly for their predictable wealth of ethnic restaurants, though neither is really a vital cultural center – the city's newly arrived Asian residents migrate toward livelier and more authentic places like Monterey Park and Gardena. Central American immigrants, by contrast, often end up in **Westlake**, west of Downtown, comprising the bulk of the population in the busy, and sometimes dangerous, **MacArthur Park** and **Echo Park** areas. To the northeast, the **Southwest Museum**, **Lummis**

House and **Heritage Square** offer more sedate trips through local culture and history.

Finally, sealing off Downtown from the spiderweb of freeways to the east, the **LA River** is a bleak concrete channel designed for flood control and, not surprisingly, the forbidding setting for assorted TV shows and Hollywood action flicks.

Downtown can easily be seen in a day, and if your feet get tired you can hop aboard the **DASH buses** that run every five to ten minutes to major tourist destinations in the downtown area (look for the silver-signed bus stops). The area is also the hub of the MTA networks and easily accessible by public transportation. Parking in lots is expensive on weekdays ($5–10 per hour), but on weekends is more affordable (a flat $3–8); street parking is a good alternative, except on Bunker Hill, where the meters cost at least $2 per hour.

Some history

For well over two hundred years, the center of Downtown LA has been slowly shifting. Spaniards constructed the first town site, the Plaza District, in 1781, but the tract was soon destroyed by fire and rebuilt further southeast in 1818, to the present site of El Pueblo de Los Angeles. Encompassing the historic Pico House and Plaza Church, the district was the focus of commercial activity during the Mexican years of rule and the early American period.

By the end of the nineteenth century, however, the city's commercial hub had relocated to Broadway, thick with department stores and vaudeville theaters, while Spring Street had become the financial center. The Plaza was left to decay until the 1920s, when renovation projects slowly brought the area back, this time as a tourist center. Meanwhile, Broadway and Spring were still enjoying their prosperity, and, along with City Hall, completed in 1928, were the most visible emblems of LA's emerging metropolis – by then numbering over a million people in its city limits and over two million in the surrounding LA County.

Although the Civic Center is still LA's seat of government, its financial and cultural counterparts have since relocated to the south. Cold War–era urban renewal projects shoved the city center six blocks to the west and doomed the great boulevards in the process. Bunker Hill replaced Spring Street in the 1960s as Downtown's financial nucleus, thanks to a drastic facelift engineered by LA's much-despised mega-bureaucracy, the **Community Redevelopment Agency (CRA)**. While Spring Street's financial center re-emerged on the western side of Downtown, nothing so far has re-created Broadway's buzzing entertainment zone. The Museum of Contemporary Art, plunked down at the top of the hill in the 1980s, was one attempt to draw back the crowds, as was the placement of nearby "high culture" facilities such as the Mark Taper Forum, Dorothy Chandler Pavilion and Ahmanson Theater – all of which have failed miserably in resurrecting the social vitality that once existed along Broadway. For most visitors, the new center of Downtown may be brimming with eye-catching art and architecture, but it is absolutely bereft of anything else.

The Plaza District

Because so much of LA's architectural heritage has been destroyed, it is perhaps surprising that **the Plaza** still exists. In the early 1920s, city planners wanted to demolish it to make way for a larger, even more imposing Civic Center. Luckily, the area was saved by its 1953 designation as **El Pueblo de Los Angeles State Historic Park**, 845 N Alameda St (daily 9am–5pm; free; ☎213/628-2381, ⓦwww.ci.la.ca.us/ELP). Comprising twenty-seven buildings, including eleven open to the public, the park is an essential stop on any historical journey through LA, and is also the site of numerous community celebrations, including the boisterous Cinco de Mayo party (see p.321).

In the immediate vicinity of the Plaza, **Union Station** and the adjacent **Gateway Transit Center** provide hubs for the train and bus activity throughout the region, while just north sits the latest version of LA's rather uninspiring **Chinatown**.

The Plaza and Olvera Street

Within El Pueblo de Los Angeles Historic Park, the former center of LA – the square known as **the Plaza** – was in 1870 reconstructed into the circular design just off North Los Angeles Street. However, the true focus of the early settlement was the *zanja madre*, or "mother ditch," which ran from the then-wild Los Angeles River through what is now **Olvera Street**. The canal was used for domestic and agricultural purposes as early as 1781; in the 1870s, pioneering hydrologist **William Mulholland** had an early job "ditch-digging" on the watercourse, moving up to water superintendent in eight short years. Then, just as now, *aqua* was serious business, and it's no accident that a key route like Olvera Street follows the path of an antique irrigation ditch.

Although open to pedestrian traffic (daily 10am–7pm; free; ⓦwww.olverastreet.com), Olvera Street has been closed since 1930 to automobiles; you can

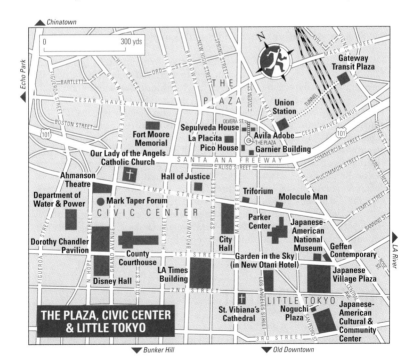

THE PLAZA, CIVIC CENTER & LITTLE TOKYO

trace the original path of the *zanja madre* by a series of marked bricks throughout. The street's re-emergence was the work of one **Christine Sterling**, who, with help from the city government, tore down the slum she found here in 1926 and created much of what you see today, incorporating some of the salvageable historic structures. For the next twenty years, she organized fiestas and worked to popularize the city's Mexican heritage while living in the early nineteenth-century **Avila Adobe** at 10 Olvera St – touted as the oldest structure in Los Angeles, although almost entirely rebuilt out of reinforced concrete following the 1971 Sylmar earthquake. Inside the house are two **museums** (daily 9am–5pm; free): one featuring an idealized view of pueblo-era domestic life; the other, across the landscaped courtyard, telling the sanitized official version of how the LA authorities connived to secure a water supply for the city (for the real story, see box on p.189, or watch the fairly accurate Hollywood version in the film *Chinatown*).

Across the street, the **Sepulveda House** (Mon–Sat 10am–3pm; closed on holidays; free; ☎213/628-1274) is a quaint 1887 Eastlake Victorian structure that serves as the park's visitor center and has rooms highlighting different periods in Mexican-American cultural history, along with an informative free film (Mon–Sat 11am & 2pm) on the history of LA. For a more detailed look at the pueblo, there are also free **guided walking tours** (on the hour Tues–Sat 10am–1pm) from the information booth at 130 Paseo de la Plaza.

Just west of the Plaza, the Catholic Plaza Church, or **La Placita**, is a small adobe structure with a gabled roof that has long served as a sanctuary for illegal Central American refugees. From 1861 to 1923 the building was remodeled or reconstructed four different times and still evokes a sense of the city's Mexican heritage, even though very little remains from the original church. To the south, the red-brick **Old Plaza Firehouse** (Tues–Sun 10am–3pm; free) was only operational for thirteen years, beginning in 1884, subsequently becoming a saloon, lodging house and pool hall before attaining museum status in 1960. If you like old firefighting equipment, this is definitely the place for you.

Along with its Mexican heritage, the pueblo also features the remnants of Chinese, Italian and even French settlements, represented in various culturally themed buildings. Two historic structures remain closed to the public: the handsome Mission-style **Pico House** was once the home of the last Mexican governor of California, Pio Pico, and LA's most luxurious hotel when it opened in 1870, is closed, while the **Merced Theater** next door was LA's first indoor theater. The **Old Masonic Hall** next door (Tues–Fri 10am–3pm; free) was the first of its kind in the city when built in 1858 and still holds the occasional Freemason meeting, as well as a cache of club artifacts such as swords, compasses and jewels.

Close by, LA's original settlement of Chinese immigrants was centered on the **Garnier Building**, an 1850 brick-and-stone structure that is slated to re-open in 2003 as the **Chinese American Museum** (information at ☎213/626-5240, ⓦ www.camla.org), with exhibits devoted to the local history of Chinese settlement and culture.

Lastly, three blocks west, at the junction of Sunset Boulevard and Hill Street, the **Fort Moore Pioneer Memorial** is a series of bas reliefs depicting early LA political and social figures who provided "for its citizens water and power for life and energy," an inscription written on the interior wall of what has been described as "the most spectacular man-made waterfall in the United States": an 80-foot-wide, 50-foot-high wall of water serving as a colossal monument to the city's aqueous needs. Not surprisingly, it was shut off more than twenty years ago.

Union Station and around

The Mission-style **Union Station**, across from the Plaza on Alameda Street, is an impressive, if underused, architectural landmark that was once the focus of much hostility from both the railroad companies, who originally viewed a centralized rail terminus as a threat to their oligarchy, and members of the local Chinese community, many of whom were forcibly evicted from the site when the station was constructed there in the 1930s. Today, despite rail travel's precipitous decline in the US, and the crippling of the national rail system – Amtrak – by budget cuts and mismanagement, the terminus remains one of the city's best-preserved monuments to the golden age of railways, replete with grand arches, a high clock tower, Spanish-tiled roof and Art Deco motifs such as geometric designs and Streamline Moderne lettering. And while it's no longer the heart of the region's transit system, the station continues to serve as the confluence for Amtrak, Metrolink and Metroline commuter trains, as well as the occasional shooting location for all kinds of Hollywood movies – most memorably in *Blade Runner*, as the gloomy, atmospheric police station.

Less glamorous is the **Gateway Transit Center**, connected to Union Station via a tunnel below the train tracks. Serving as a regional hub for bus lines, the center comprises three distinct parts: the **Gateway Tower**, an unappealing 26-story building with a customer service center on its ground floor; the **Patsaouras Transit Plaza**, which is the bus mall itself, decorated with insipid public art and worth avoiding at night; and, under a glass ceiling, the **East Portal**, a light and airy space marred by an Orwellian-looking mural supposedly celebrating LA's ethnic diversity.

There's nothing much to see beyond here, just the largest municipal **jail** in the US – where actors like Robert Downey Jr have cooled their heels – and the similarly imposing **Metropolitan Detention Center**, with its razor wire-style decor.

Chinatown

If you visit LA's **CHINATOWN** expecting to see the bustling affair you'll find in a number of other US cities, you will be sadly disappointed. Located between North Broadway and North Hill streets, this enclave is rather small and hemmed in by wide thoroughfares, a maze of ersatz-Chinese architecture and narrow, pedestrian alleys with names like Bamboo Lane – quite different from the district of old, and not particularly authentic. What is now Chinatown was established here by the late 1930s following its residents' abrupt relocation to make way for Union Station. The old Chinatown was home to many newly arrived Chinese in the late nineteenth century, impoverished laborers who endured wretched social conditions and were racial targets as well. While many cities, such as Burbank and Pasadena, evicted Chinese immigrants or kept them from buying land, the downtown area was set aside to enforce official LA segregation.

For a truer sense of contemporary Chinese culture, visit **Alhambra** and **Monterey Park**, both lively ethnic suburbs located several miles east of Downtown. Indeed, unless it's Chinese New Year, when there's a parade of dragons and firework celebrations, there's little point in turning up here except to eat in one of the restaurants (for dining recommendations, see p.259).

Civic Center

Marked by City Hall's great white pillar, the **Civic Center** is the focus of government for the city and county of LA, with various state and federal entities also occupying space in the district. Bounded on the east and west by San Pedro and Figueroa streets and on the north and south by the Hollywood Freeway and First Street, this unexciting hive of bureaucracy offers only a few interesting cultural and architectural sights. Even in the face of this, LA's political bigwigs have spent significant time and money vainly trying to pump some life into the area, resulting in the strange scene of desperate homeless people wandering in an often-deserted landscape of spartan modern architecture and ugly public artworks.

City Hall and around

One exception to the dreariness is **City Hall**, 200 N Spring St, known popularly as *Dragnet's* imposing symbol of civic virtue and as the Daily Planet office in the original *Superman* series. The building is a hodgepodge of styles: from its classical temple base rises a sleek modern tower crowned with a miniature version of the Mausoleum at Halicarnassus – one of the ancient Seven Wonders of the World. You can get a look at the building's grand marble arches and columns during a **free tour** that includes its 28th-story 360° observation deck (daily 10am & 11am; reserve at ℡213/485-4423, 🅦www.lacityhall.org).

Northeast of City Hall, at 310 N Main St, the **Children's Museum** is temporarily closed, due to reopen near the Geffen Contemporary in 2004 (information at ℡213/687-8801, 🅦www.childrensmuseumla.org). At the corner of Main and Temple, the unavoidable **Triforium** is a 1975 public art monstrosity decorated with shafts of colored glass and long-silent loudspeakers strategically placed between massive concrete legs – which all but ruins the surrounding **Fletcher Bowron Square**, dedicated to LA's pioneering reform mayor who cleaned up City Hall after his predecessor, Frank Shaw, was booted from office in a 1938 corruption scandal. More compelling is the public artwork **Molecule Man**, 255 E Temple St, sculptor Jonathan Borofsky's perforated figures supposedly illustrating the watery composition of the human body, though some critics see them as bullet-riddled bodies – a jab at the adjacent **Parker Center**, headquarters of the LAPD.

Just to the south, near Spring and First streets, the concrete and glass **Times-Mirror Complex** houses the production facilities for the *Los Angeles Times*, the West Coast's biggest newspaper. Built in the colossal PWA Moderne style in the mid-1930s, and given a drab expansion in 1973, the building supplanted an earlier version, closer to Broadway, that was bombed, rebuilt, then torn down. Take one of its free **public tours** (Mon–Fri 11.15am; ℡213/237-5757, 🅦www.latimes.com) if you're interested in seeing how the paper operates.

Civic Center West

The municipal buildings in the **Civic Center West** are largely functional, though not entirely without interest. The **Department of Water and Power Building**, at the corner of Hope and First streets, is a modern structure that casts an appealing glow at night with its narrow horizontal bands of light, though its array of fountains have been turned off to conserve water. Nearby is the 1925 **Hall of Justice**, Broadway and Temple streets, famous for the

The LA Times family dynasty

The *Los Angeles Times* began life in 1881 as the mouthpiece for **Harrison Gray Otis**, the arch-conservative publisher whose virulently anti-labor opinions and actions led him to be called the most "unfair enemy of trades unionism on the North American continent." Tensions he fostered with unions and leftists turned violent in 1910, when the original Times building was bombed. After the explosion, Otis not only rebuilt the structure, but he emerged even stronger and more powerful than ever, when partial blame was assigned to his political nemesis Job Harriman (for defending the accused, and later convicted, bombers in court and in public), who otherwise would have become the city's first and only Socialist mayor. Having already kept the Southern Pacific Railroad from monopolizing development of the LA Harbor, Otis also engineered public support for the giant construction projects that stole water from Northern California's Owens Valley water and carried it to LA, or more precisely, to the San Fernando Valley, where he and other investors made a fortune in shady real-estate deals. Roman Polanski's film *Chinatown* memorably chronicles the chicanery of these powerful figures.

The *LA Times* directly reflected Otis's sharp opinions and, when he died in 1917, his legacy was passed to his son-in-law, **Harry Chandler**, who maintained the paper's fight against unions and political reform until his death in 1941. With a personal fortune worth up to a billion dollars, much of it from San Fernando Valley real estate, Chandler was a plutocrat and mayoral kingmaker who usually got his way with city politicians, controlling them much like his father-in-law had. His one great defeat was the 1937 election of reformist mayor Fletcher Bowron.

In 1960, the paper changed course dramatically with the ascension of Harry's son Otis to the publishing throne. Through his progressive efforts, the *LA Times* finally rejected its provincial conservatism and became nationally recognized for its journalistic quality. In later decades, with the demise of rivals like William Randolph Hearst's once-powerful *Los Angeles Herald-Tribune*, the *Times* would nearly monopolize local journalism and emerge as an international news organization, with bureaus around the world. More recently, however, the paper was gobbled up in a media mega-merger by the *Chicago Tribune*, which is now running the presses in LA.

turbulent trial of the Manson Family and a compelling counterpart to City Hall, with high granite columns typifying the late-Beaux Arts style of the time.

Further west, LA has lumped together its three leading music and theater venues – the Dorothy Chandler Pavilion, Ahmanson Theatre and Mark Taper Forum – in the **Music Center**, north of First Street at 135 Grand Ave, an ugly concrete plaza with a notable lack of visitors outside of performances (see "Performing arts and film," p.294). Seeking an anchor for social activity in the Downtown area, LA took a chance on a 1987 design by pioneering architect Frank Gehry, a forerunner of the Guggenheim Bilbao in Spain. The long-awaited **Disney Hall** is finally on track to become LA's most notable example of contemporary architecture, a 2300-seat acoustic showpiece whose titanium exterior will resemble something akin to colossal broken eggshells. The entire complex is due to open in the fall of 2003, inaugurating the upcoming season of the LA Philharmonic, which will make this venue its new home (for the latest update, check out ⓦ www.disneyhall.org).

A block away from Disney Hall is LA's other widely anticipated colossus, the recently opened **Our Lady of the Angels** Catholic church, 555 W Temple St (tours Mon–Fri 1 & 3pm, Sat 11.30am & 2pm, Sun 11.30am & 2.30pm; free; ⓣ213/680-5200, ⓦ www.olacathedral.org). The $200-million centerpiece of the local archdiocese, this is a truly massive structure in its own right – eleven stories tall and capable of holding three thousand people – and solidly built of concrete. Dressed in an unattractive shade of ochre, the church's fortress-like exterior suggests a huge parking lot or prison. Still, the interior is the undeniable highlight, with its grand marble altar and giant bronze doors, tapestries of saints and ultra-thin alabaster screens for diffusing light, plus $30 million worth of art and furnishings laid out in a space longer than a football field.

Little Tokyo and around

Southeast of the Civic Center, **LITTLE TOKYO** is a more vital ethnic center than nearby Chinatown – if not quite a flourishing residential neighborhood – full of smart shops and restaurants, well-heeled visitors, and a handful of business and cultural institutions. The area, bound by First and Third streets north and south, and Central Avenue and San Pedro Street east and west, was originally named in 1908, and was home to 30,000 Japanese immigrants before they were forcibly removed to internment camps in 1942. Decades later, while the district has returned to prominence, most Japanese Americans now live well outside the area.

Little Tokyo is best explored on foot, starting at the **Japanese American Cultural and Community Center**, 244 S San Pedro St (Ⓦ www.jaccc.org), reached via the gentle contours and heavy basalt rocks of **Noguchi Plaza**, designed by sculptor Isamu Noguchi, who grew up in nearby Boyle Heights. Inside the center, the **Doizaki Gallery** (Tues–Fri noon–5pm, Sat & Sun 11am–4pm; free) shows traditional and contemporary Japanese drawing and calligraphy, along with costumes, sculptures and other associated art forms. Also on the premises is the **Japan America Theater**, which hosts cultural events such as Kabuki theater, as well as more contemporary plays. Improbably shoe-horned between the two and easy to miss, the stunning **James Irvine Garden**, with a 170-foot stream running along its sloping hillside, is a cultural treasure. Although named after its biggest financial contributor, it really owes its existence to the efforts of two hundred Japanese-American volunteers who gave up their Sundays to carve the space out of a flat lot, turning it into the "garden of the clear stream" and making the area seem a world away from LA's outside expanse of asphalt and concrete. Nearby, the more authentically Japanese **Garden in the Sky**, 120 S Los Angeles St, located on the *New Otani Hotel*'s third-floor terrace, uses local materials native to Japan. This half-acre strolling garden, or *shuyu*, works the skyline into the setting – a technique known as "borrowed scenery" – allowing you to contemplate the grandeur of City Hall during your walk around the premises.

The most active part of Little Tokyo is **Japanese Village Plaza**, an outdoor mall near First Street and Central Avenue that is lined with sushi bars, numerous upscale retailers and Zen rock gardens. Adjacent to the plaza is the area's most familiar symbol: the **Fire Tower**, a small canopy sitting atop slender wooden beams. Across First Street, the **Japanese American National Museum** (Tues–Sun 10am–5pm, Thurs closes at 8pm; $6; Ⓣ 213/625-0414, Ⓦ www.janm.org), housed in a former Buddhist temple constructed in 1925, focuses on local *Issei* pioneers and the period of Japanese internment during World War II. Amid the genealogies and assorted curios are some compelling portraits of community leaders.

Just beyond the borders of Little Tokyo is the **Geffen Contemporary**, Central Avenue at First Street (same hours and website as MOCA, to which a ticket entitles same-day admission). Occupying an old city warehouse and police garage, the Frank Gehry–designed museum was initially opened in 1983 as overflow space for the main facility on Bunker Hill, but its success has been such that it was kept on as an alternative exhibition space to its more mainstream sibling.

Further east, not far from the LA River, more intriguing art exhibits are often on display in the **Freight Depot** of the Southern California Institute of Architecture, 960 E Third St (daily 10am-6pm; free; ⓦ www.sciarc.edu), which occupies the 1907 former train depot of the famed Atchison, Topeka and Santa Fe Railroad. Now devoting its huge horizontal spaces to architectural instruction, the depot's public gallery hosts all manner of quirky and avant-garde exhibits by its students and faculty, from the high-tech computer models of bizarre futuristic structures to massive installations that riddle the gallery with Escher-like stairways, catwalks, pipes and ladders.

West of Little Tokyo, **St Vibiana's Cathedral**, 114 E Second St, is a modest replica of Barcelona's church of San Miguel del Mar, with a simple white Italianate design. For years the regional seat of the Catholic Church, as well as a sanctuary for recently arrived Latin American immigrants, the 1871 cathedral fell on tough times after it was damaged in the 1994 Northridge earthquake and the archdiocese abandoned it to build Our Lady of the Angels further west (see p.58). Saved from demolition, plans are afoot to convert the church into "Vibiana Place," home to a performing arts center, hotel, library and artist lofts.

Old Downtown

Spring Street and Broadway form the axes of **Old Downtown**, a once-thriving district that has lost some of its charm over the years. While Spring Street is partially deserted, its Neoclassical facades looming over street people and a few curious tourists, a growing number of new galleries and lofts hint at the area's potential for redevelopment. To the east, the **Garment District** and **Flower Market** more than make up for Spring Street's lack of mercantile energy, while paralleling Spring to the west, Broadway buzzes with colorful street life, though its character has changed, too: whereas movie palaces and fine restaurants once drew white middle-class crowds, its current swap meets and bargain discounters now draw working-class Hispanics.

Spring Street

Formerly comprising the "Wall Street of the West," the imperious banking and commercial buildings of **Spring Street** no longer serve their original functions, almost all of them victims of Downtown's financial relocation to Bunker Hill. Still, for those with an interest in LA history, or with a nose for sniffing out the area's slowly emerging arts scene, Spring Street may offer a few worthwhile attractions (many of which are viewable on LA Conservancy tours of the old strip; see p.35). South from the Civic Center, begin your wanderings at peaceful **Biddy Mason Park**, 333 S Spring St, which commemorates a former midwife and slave who won her freedom in an 1855 legal challenge. The small memorial provides a timeline of her life, from when she was purchased for $250, on the property that is now the park, to when she became one of the founders of the local First African Methodist Episcopal Church.

Less than a block away, at no. 408, the 1904 Braly Block is home to the **Continental Building**, which was LA's first "skyscraper," though it only

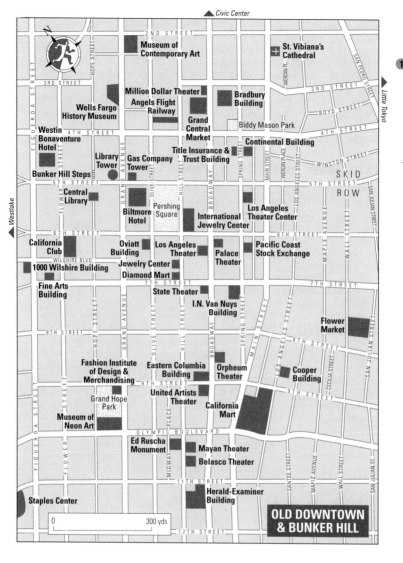

▲ Civic Center

Museum of
Contemporary Art

St. Vibiana's
Cathedral

Little Tokyo ▶

Million Dollar Theater
Angels Flight
Railway

Wells Fargo
History Museum

Bradbury
Building

Grand
Central
Market

Biddy Mason Park

Westin
Bonaventure
Hotel

Title Insurance &
Trust Building

Continental Building

Library
Tower

Gas Company
Tower

Bunker Hill Steps

SKID
ROW

Westlake ▲

Central
Library

Pershing
Square

Biltmore
Hotel

International
Jewelry Center

Los Angeles
Theater Center

California
Club

Oviatt
Building

Los Angeles
Theater

Palace
Theater

Pacific Coast
Stock Exchange

1000 Wilshire Building

Jewelry Center

Diamond Mart

Fine Arts
Building

State Theater

I.N. Van Nuys
Building

Flower
Market

Fashion Institute
of Design &
Merchandising

Eastern Columbia
Building

Orpheum
Theater

Cooper
Building

Grand Hope
Park

United Artists
Theater

Museum of
Neon Art

California
Mart

Ed Ruscha
Monument

Mayan Theater

Belasco Theater

Staples Center

Herald-Examiner
Building

OLD DOWNTOWN
& BUNKER HILL

0   300 yds

boasts twelve stories. Now converted into artist lofts and yuppie apartments,
the imposing structure – like those adjacent to it - represents LA's latest
attempt to breathe life into an urban dead zone. Nearby, at no. 433, the **Title
Insurance and Trust Company** houses municipal agencies as well as the LA
Design Center, an uneven collection of art dealers and jewelry merchants
(open to the public), featuring an appealing Art Deco design in the Zigzag style
of the late 1920s. Also remodeled, the **Security Trust and Savings Bank**, no.
514, was reincarnated in the mid-1980s as the Los Angeles Theater Center,
home to four small theaters that present intermittent productions. Further

south, the one-time **Pacific Coast Stock Exchange**, no. 618, bears an inscription stating that it was "created for the economic welfare of the community, state and nation." Ironically, the Moderne colossus was completed in 1930 – the first full year of the Great Depression. These days, the exchange functions as a weekend disco for Bunker Hill yuppies (called, appropriately enough, *Stock Exchange*; see "Bars, coffeehouses and clubs," p.278). Nearby, at Spring Street's intersection with Seventh Street, the 1910 **I.N. Van Nuys Building** celebrates one of the city's early titans, a San Fernando Valley land baron and wheat farmer, in grand Beaux Arts style, with ornamental Ionic columns and white terracotta walls adorning the old office space.

Skid Row and the Garment District

A good portion of LA's homeless population, estimated at anywhere between 60,000 and 180,000, can be found on **Skid Row**, which begins just south of Little Tokyo and continues down past Seventh Street, at its seediest along Fifth Street between San Pedro and Los Angeles streets – a stretch known as "the Nickel." Unless you're looking for exceptionally gritty inspiration – as artsy folk like the Doors (who posed in these parts for the cover of their *Morrison Hotel* album) and Charles Bukowski have before – you're best off skipping Skid Row entirely. However, those daring enough can take a tour of the **Union Rescue Mission**, 545 S San Pedro St (☎213/347-6300), for a grim, up-close view of LA's dispossessed.

If Skid Row is precisely the kind of place visitors to Downtown LA would most like to avoid, the **Garment District** (or, euphemistically, the "Fashion District"; ☎213/488-1153, Ⓦwww.fashiondistrict.org), further south, is one of the area's most appealing attractions, with twenty square blocks of clothing manufacturers and fabric discounters selling everything from cut-rate designer suits to exquisite silk and velvet draperies. The biggest retailer here, the **California Mart**, at Ninth and Los Angeles streets, fills three million square feet and seemingly has just as many visitors, while the **Cooper Building**, just across Los Angeles Street, offers designer merchandise at bargain prices; indeed, most shrewd Angelenos avoid the high-priced Westside boutiques and head to this district to do their clothes buying. To plunge into the shopping experience at its most colorful and chaotic, the area along Maple Avenue between Sixth and Ninth streets is a good place to begin your excursion, with many businesses (often run by first-generation immigrant families) selling bolts of serviceable fabrics for as little as $2 per yard. Keep in mind, however, that street parking is meager and traffic maddening. Nearby, at the atmospheric early-morning **Flower Market**, 766 Wall St (Mon, Wed & Fri 8am–noon, Tues & Thurs 6–11am, Sat 6am–noon; ☎213/627-3696, Ⓦwww.laflowerdistrict.com), you can buy wholesale flowers for a fraction of the high prices elsewhere.

Broadway

Long ago the commercial nucleus of Los Angeles, **Broadway** is now a striking mix of historic architecture and frenetic activity. Its blocks from Second to Ninth streets make up the busiest commercial strip in the western US, and, despite rapid cultural and demographic changes, the street retains a measure of its old exciting character and appeal.

An instructive place to begin exploring the strip's former color is at its southern end, with the **Herald-Examiner Building**, 1111 S Broadway, a grand

Mission-style edifice occupying a city block and featuring blue-and-yellow domes and ground-level arcades. The building was first home to William Randolph Hearst's *Los Angeles Examiner*, the progressive counterpart of the *Los Angeles Times*, which grew to have the widest afternoon circulation of any daily in the country. After it merged with Hearst's *Herald-Express*, though, trouble soon began, and the paper eventually went out of business in 1989. Although the building is currently closed to the public, it frequently hosts movie crews because of its opulent setting – fitting, considering that Orson Welles had the news magnate and the building in mind when he directed his thinly veiled critique of Hearst, *Citizen Kane.*

One block to the west, the Theater District begins at 1040 S Hill St, where the wild **Mayan Theater** is a stunning remnant of the pre-Columbian revival, its ornamental design, including sculpted reliefs of Aztec gods and bright paintings of dragons and birds, every bit as outlandish as its Chinese Theatre counterpart in Hollywood. The building is still in use, though as a dance club called, aptly, the *Mayan* (see p.285). The neighboring **Belasco Theater**, 1050 S Hill St, has similar brash appeal, with a Spanish Baroque design and a bright green color, though its partially restored interior is only open to film crews as a shooting location.

Nearby, the **United Artists Theater**, 929 S Broadway, is a 1927 Spanish Gothic movie palace with a lobby designed after a church nave. Appropriately, the theater is now the site of the Gene Scott Ministry and known as University Cathedral. A block away, stuck amidst the theaters, is the Art Deco **Eastern Columbia Building**, 849 S Broadway, with terracotta walls of gold and aquamarine, a giant clock face, and sleek dark piers on its roof, all essential viewing for anyone remotely interested in 1920s architecture. Further along, at no.744, the **Globe Theater** is a Beaux Arts design that has been clumsily converted into a flea market. The street continues with a rash of old moviehouses, some of which still show movies today. The two best remaining theaters, though, are the **Orpheum**, no. 842, a monumental French Renaissance palace of grand staircases and chandeliers, and the **Los Angeles**, no. 615, built in ninety days for the world premiere of Charlie Chaplin's *City Lights* in 1931. Inside the plush lobby, marble columns support an intricate mosaic ceiling, while the 1800-seat auditorium is enveloped by trompe l'oeil murals and lighting effects. Both can be seen on LA Conservancy tours (see p.35), but only the Orpheum is open throughout the year.

Finally, the **Million Dollar Theater**, no. 307, has appeared in numerous Hollywood movies and is renowned for its whimsical terracotta facade, mixing buffalo heads with bald eagles. The former moviehouse, now used for church services, was built in 1906 by theater magnate Sid Grauman, who went on to build the Egyptian and Chinese theaters in Hollywood (see pp.98 & 99). Across the street, the 1893 **Bradbury Building**, no. 304, has perhaps the finest atrium of any structure in the city, each level of its glazed-brick court adorned in wrought-iron railings and open-cage elevators, all atmospherically lit by a skylight. The lobby, which is as far as the public can go, should be recognizable to most from films such as *Citizen Kane* and *Blade Runner.*

As you exit on Third Street, the broadly ethnic **Grand Central Market**, between Third and Fourth, provides a good taste of modern Broadway – everything from apples and oranges to pickled pig's feet and sheep's brains.

Pershing Square and around

The city's oldest park, the uninspiring but unavoidable **Pershing Square**, acts as a buffer between Bunker Hill and Old Downtown. Constructed in 1866 and known variously as Public Square, City Park, La Plaza Abaja and St Vincent's Park, it was renamed for the last time in 1918, in honor of World War I general **John Pershing**. By the 1960s, the place had deteriorated considerably, and decades of efforts to revitalize the park have done little to improve the place, now a haven for the homeless and other street people. The lone highlight is the square's bright purple campanile, towering as it does over charmless concrete benches and a dearth of grass and other plants.

The buildings around the square hold more visual appeal, including the **Biltmore Hotel**, on the west side of the park, its three brick towers rising from a Renaissance Revival arcade along Olive Street. Inside, the grand old lobby has an intricately painted Spanish-beamed ceiling that you can admire over a pricey glass of wine, and if you don't mind paying a top-dollar rate, the hotel's accommodation is also outstanding (p.225). To the east, the **International Jewelry Center** holds more than six hundred jewelers – the majority of them offering competitive prices on gold, diamonds, and other precious stones and metals. If this doesn't satisfy your passion for pricey shopping, try the other **Jewelry Center**, 629 S Hill St, a green Art Deco gem, or the **Diamond Mart**, at the corner of Seventh and Hill streets, which occupies the former Pantages Theater, maintaining its Hollywood look with its own wraparound marquee.

At 617 S Olive St, the Art Deco **Oviatt Building** is another sumptuous survivor that recalls the vibrant nature of Old Downtown in vivid color. The ground floor once housed LA's most elegant haberdashery, catering to dapper types such as Clark Gable and John Barrymore, but has since been converted into the *Cicada* restaurant (see p.260). The building's elevators, which open onto the street-level exterior lobby, feature hand-carved oak paneling designed and fashioned by elegant Parisian craftsman René Lalique. Equally striking is the intricate 1928 design of the building's exterior, especially its grand sign and clock high above.

Bunker Hill and around

Developed as middle-class residential property in the 1870s, **Bunker Hill** was an upscale neighborhood for just a few decades; by the 1940s it was little more than a collection of fleabag dives and crumbling Victorian mansions, providing the seedy film noir backdrop for detective films such as the apocalyptic 1955 Mike Hammer movie *Kiss Me Deadly*. With its middle class having long since moved to new, outlying suburbs, in the 1960s the whole thing was plowed asunder, and Bunker Hill became the nucleus for Downtown's massive redevelopment as a high-rise corporate enclave.

The best way to approach Bunker Hill's **Financial District** is on the **Angels Flight Railway**, a funicular originally banished from the hillside along with the residents it once served. In the last decade, the two orange-and-black train cars have been brought out of storage to be resurrected as an old-fashioned transit line – this time for tourists. You can board the train just north of the intersection of Hill and Fourth streets for a quarter, though an **escalator** at the corner of Olive and Fourth streets will give you the same views of the city for free.

Penetrating the fortress of Bunker Hill

One of the first things newcomers to Downtown LA realize is how truly unpleasant it is to walk around **Bunker Hill**, filled with as many obstacles as physically possible – freeway access ramps, giant boulevards without sidewalks, walled-off corporate landscapes and even signs prohibiting pedestrians. Mike Davis, LA's pre-eminent chronicler of official wickedness, posited after the 1992 riots that politicians, architects and businessmen had conspired to keep the masses away from Bunker Hill by constructing it as a veritable **fortress**, with automatically controlled security doors and private guards as the modern equivalent of moats and mercenaries. And that it worked perfectly according to plan when the riots came, with the crowds focusing their rage elsewhere, far away from the banking towers and elite institutions at the top of the hallowed hill.

The reality may be less conspiratorial, but is almost as disturbing. Like most of LA's city planners throughout the twentieth century, the forces behind Bunker Hill probably never even considered creating a pedestrian-friendly space Downtown and simply followed the logic of much late-modern design: bigger is better, impersonal is ideal and cars are always king – a formula that, unfortunately, still persists in much of LA's municipal planning.

Still, there are a few **remedies** for dealing with Bunker Hill's layout if you're on foot. The first is to explore the area from the north or south – via Flower and Hope streets and Grand Avenue. Because of poor planning and a greater incline, the east and west sides of the hill are its most "fortified" and difficult to navigate. But if you are coming from the east, the Angels Flight Railway (see above) or a nearby escalator at Fourth and Olive streets are among the few good choices. If coming from the west, try Fifth Street, as the east–west streets to the north are among the most inaccessible to pedestrians. Motorists should also realize that while Bunker Hill was made expressly for their driving pleasure, it was not made for convenient, or cheap, parking. Find a lot below the hill and hike up the incline from there, or be prepared to cough up $2 in quarters per hour of street parking. If coming via the Red Line subway, exit at the Pershing Square stop and walk a block north to the base of Angels Flight, where you can hop on the funicular for a ride to the top. Finally, resist the temptation to walk under the hill by way of the Third Street Tunnel; despite its gleaming appearance in films like *Blade Runner*, it remains quite dangerous, even deadly, to careless pedestrians.

The Museum of Contemporary Art

The largest and most ambitious development in the district is the **California Plaza** on Grand Avenue, a billion-dollar complex of offices and luxury condos centering on the **Museum of Contemporary Art (MOCA)** (Tues–Sun 11am–5pm, Thurs 11am–8pm; $8, students $5, free Thurs 5–8pm; ☎213/626-6222, ⓦwww.moca.org). Built in 1986 and designed by showman architect **Arata Isozaki** as a "small village in the valley of the skyscrapers," it justifies a look for the building alone, its playful red pyramids a welcome splash of color among the dour skyscrapers. A barrel-vaulted entrance pavilion on Grand Avenue opens onto an outdoor sculpture plaza, and stairs lead down from the upper plaza to the smaller courtyard, between the café and the main entrance to the galleries.

Bankrolled by the high-rollers of LA's art world as a showpiece for Downtown culture (and, cynics say, to raise the value of the works they loan for display), MOCA devotes much of its gallery to temporary exhibitions, and the bulk of the permanent collection is mid-century American, particularly

△ Angels Flight Railway

from the Abstract Expressionist period, including pieces by Franz Kline and Mark Rothko, as well as an important Jackson Pollock work, his imposing, hypnotic *Number Three*, plus ten of Sam Francis's vivid splashes of color. You'll also find plenty of Pop Art, from Claes Oldenburg's papier-mâché representations of hamburgers and gaudy fast foods, Andy Warhol's print-ad black telephone, and Robert Rauschenberg's *Coca-Cola Plan*, a battered old cabinet containing three soda bottles and angelic wings tacked onto the sides. Jasper Johns' well-known *Map* is also here, a blotchy diagram of US states.

Unfortunately, there are few singularly great pieces among the established names, and most of the compelling ideas are expressed amid the paintings and sculpture of the newer stars of the art world – Alexis Smith's quirky assemblages, Martin Puryear's anthropomorphic wooden sculptures, Lari Pittman's spooky, sexualized silhouettes. The museum is also strong on photography, and features the two-thousand-print collection of New York dealer Robert Freidhaus, exhibiting the work of Diane Arbus, Larry Clark, Robert Frank, Lee Friedlander, John Pfahl and Garry Winograd, as well as a few choice, and thoroughly disturbing, images by Cindy Sherman.

The theater on the lower floor of MOCA hosts some bizarre multimedia shows and performances, as well as the more standard lectures and seminars (☎213/621-2766 for details). If you're here on a Thursday evening in summer, entry is free, and concerts, usually jazz or classical and also free, are performed outdoors under the red pyramids. At other times, a ticket to MOCA also entitles you to same-day entrance to the Geffen Contemporary (see p.59), the museum's exhibition space on the east side of Downtown.

Around MOCA

If you've overdosed on the rigors of modern art, a welcome tonic is the **Wells Fargo History Museum**, just down the street at 333 S Grand Ave (Mon–Fri 9am–5pm; free). Located at the base of the Wells Fargo Center, the museum displays an old stagecoach, mining equipment, antiques, photographs, a two-pound chunk of gold, a re-created assay office from the nineteenth century and a simulated stagecoach journey from St Louis to San Francisco.

A block away, the shining glass tubes of the **Westin Bonaventure Hotel** have become one of LA's most unusual landmarks. The only LA building by modernist architect John Portman, best known for Atlanta's Peachtree Plaza, the structure doubles as a shopping mall and office complex – an M.C. Escher–style labyrinth of spiraling ramps and balconies that's disorientating enough that you'll need to consult a color-coded map every twenty yards or so. Make sure to take a ride in the hotel's famed glass elevators that run up and down the building's exterior (famously showcased in Clint Eastwood's *In the Line of Fire*), giving expansive views over much of Downtown and beyond. (For a review of the hotel, see p.225.)

From the hotel's rotating skyline bar, the *Bona Vista*, you'll get a bird's-eye view of Bunker Hill's skyline, which has a few standouts, including the **Gas Company Tower**, 555 W Fifth St, a stunning modern high-rise whose crown symbolizes a blue natural-gas flame on its side, and the **1000 Wilshire Building**, one of Downtown's few postmodern creations with ridiculously oversized windows, sitting right off the 110 freeway.

The biggest of the skyscrapers, though, is the cylindrical **Library Tower**, at Grand Avenue and Fifth Street, designed by I.M. Pei's firm and, at 73 stories, the tallest building west of the Mississippi. In exchange for planning permission and air rights, the developers of the tower agreed to pay some fifty million dollars toward the restoration of the neighboring **Richard J. Riordan Central Library** (Mon & Thurs–Sat 10am–5.30pm, Sun 1–5pm; ☏213/228-7000, ⓦwww.lapl.org/central). Despite its small size, the library remains a marvel nonetheless; a colossal atrium seems to appear out of nowhere after you step off the escalators to the upper floors, while the gardens outside make for a pleasant stroll among the fountains and whimsical animal sculptures. The concrete walls and piers of the lower floors, enlivened by Lee Laurie's figurative sculptures symbolizing the "Virtues of Philosophy" and the "Arts," form a pedestal for the squat central tower, which is topped by a multi-colored pyramid roof. Across Fifth Street, Lawrence Halprin's huge **Bunker Hill Steps**, supposedly modeled after the Spanish Steps in Rome, curve up Bunker Hill between a series of terraces with uneventful outdoor cafés and boutiques, and ultimately end at the **Source Figure**, one of sculptor Robert Graham's small, creepy nudes, at the top. If you don't feel like walking, the Steps also feature a less appealing escalator.

On the downslope, a reminder of old LA sits at Sixth and Flower streets. **The California Club**, an exclusive men's social club, was a favorite spot for the Committee of 25, an informal grouping of local politicians and businessmen who decided important city issues behind the club's (still) closed doors. Just over a block away, the more welcoming **Fine Arts Building**, 811 W Seventh St, is notable for its bold arches, Romanesque styling and an eye-catching lobby where you'll find medieval carvings and weird art exhibits under gloomy lighting.

Finally, the peripheral attractions in the area include two of artist Kent Twitchell's massive murals. The first, **Harbor Freeway Overture**, decorates the side of a parking lot and is visible from the northbound 110 freeway at Seventh Street. In it, members of the LA Chamber Orchestra stare relentlessly out at the traffic, with the mural sponsor, and CEO of Mitsubishi, hiding somewhere among the musicians. Several blocks to the southeast, at 1031 S Hill St, Twitchell's **Ed Ruscha Monument** was the piece that first brought the muralist to fame, showing the quintessential California artist Ruscha looming high above a parking lot, with the blank expression and rigid pose of Frankenstein's monster.

South of Bunker Hill

In the immediate vicinity of the Ruscha mural, the blocks south of Bunker Hill present a handful of attractions that are worth a look if you're in the area. Serene **Grand Hope Park**, a grassy public space between Grand Avenue and Hope Street, just south of Ninth Street, was designed by Lawrence Halprin, and features a red-and-yellow clock tower, wooden canopies and concave fountains with gilt mosaics. The park is popular with visitors to the neighboring **Museum of Neon Art**, 501 W Olympic Blvd (Wed–Sat 11am–5pm, Sun noon–5pm; $5; ☏213/489-9918, ⓦwww.neonmona.org), which is recognizable by the adulterated visage of Mona Lisa smiling through blue-and-yellow neon squiggles. The museum's small exhibition space showcases contemporary neon designs and a range of strange kinetic art, plus some great old neon theater signs – notably the sweeping, streamlined lettering of the Melrose Theater – and runs monthly bus tours of LA's best neon sights (see p.36). Across the park, the **Fashion Institute of Design and Merchandising**, 919 S Grand Ave (11am–4pm Tues–Sat; free; call for information at ☏213/624-1200, ⓦwww.fidm.com), trains would-be designers and marketers, throwing the periodic fashion exhibition, with items drawn from its collection of ten thousand pieces of costume and apparel. While the French gowns, Russian jewels and shoe art sometimes on display are appealing, the real highlight is the annual **"Art of Motion Picture Costume Design"** show that runs between mid-February and April – roughly Oscar time – providing a look at colorful outfits from the golden age of cinema up to the present, from Elizabeth Taylor's Cleopatra garb to Austin Powers' retro-1960s outfits.

Finally, the **Staples Center**, 865 S Figueroa St (☎213/624-3100, ⓦwww.staplescenter.com), is another conspicuous attempt to bring the crowds back to the central city. Home to both of LA's basketball teams, the three-time champion Lakers and the ever-dismal Clippers (see p.310 to catch a game), the complex is unavoidable for mainstream music and sports.

Around Downtown

Just west of the Harbor Freeway, the **Temple–Beaudry** and **Pico-Union** barrios are home to thousands of newly arrived immigrants from Central America, areas more depressed in many ways than the noted ghettos of South Central LA (but just as open to municipal scandal as anywhere else in LA; see box p.20). They should generally be avoided at night, and **MacArthur Park** and the **Westlake** neighborhood along Wilshire Boulevard, despite the appeal of their faded Victorian architecture, should only be viewed by car – petty theft and drug dealing are rampant. North of Westlake, **Echo Park** is another immigrant center, but, like **Angelino Heights** to its east, is safer and surprisingly picturesque. Further east is car-friendly **Elysian Park**, a green space that surrounds **Dodger Stadium**. Finally, **Highland Park**, northeast of Downtown, has some decent museums, none very far from the stark concrete channel of the **LA River**.

Westlake and MacArthur Park

Westlake is the tumultuous focus of much immigration to the city, thronged with Panamanians, Hondurans, Salvadorans and other recent arrivals waiting for American citizenship or trying to avoid deportation by the much-despised agents of the Immigration and Naturalization Service. The activity centers on the intersection of **Wilshire and Alvarado**, where street vendors hawk their wares in front of busy swap meets, overlooked by the classy sign for the departed **Westlake Theater**, 638 Alvarado St, now overlooking a grubby flea market.

Across Alvarado Street, **MacArthur Park** was originally developed in the 1890s when its surrounding area was a suburb of Los Angeles; these days it's busy with drug dealing and gang activity. Although the Red Line subway passes under the park, you're best off traveling during the day and not venturing up to the surface. To the south, **Bonnie Brae Street** and **Alvarado Terrace** still have a number of quaint Victorian dwellings, such as the striking mix of Queen Anne and French chateau styles at 1036 S Bonnie Brae St. The one functional museum of note in the area is the **Grier-Musser Museum**, 403 S Bonnie Brae St (Wed–Fri noon–4pm, Sat 11am–4pm; $6, kids $3; ☎213/413-1814, ⓦhome.attbi.com/~gmuseum), offering a glimpse of the luxurious furnishings and stylish architecture of the nineteenth century, when this now-decrepit neighborhood was a pleasant middle-class suburb, and the local Victorian homes boasted copious Gothic turrets, gingerbread detailing and Italianate windows.

The Rampart scandal

LA's down-at-the-heels **Temple-Beaudry** – the barrio immediately west of Bunker Hill – has recently been the scene of one of LA's most egregious police scandals, centered around the **Rampart Division** of the LAPD, which patrols the neighborhood's dilapidated, dangerous streets. With memories of Rodney King still fresh eight years after the LA riots, a new round of racial strife erupted over the allegations that a team of LA cops operating out of Rampart had throughout the 1990s routinely fabricated evidence against innocent people, framing them outright, stealing drugs from dealers and reselling them, and even shot suspects in cold blood and covered up their crimes. Many of these charges came from the testimony of one-time LAPD officer **Rafael Perez**, whose prosecution, and subsequent plea bargain, for stealing cocaine from a police evidence room, first brought this shocking scandal to light.

Indeed, the police officers involved, part of elite anti-gang "**CRASH units**," were accused of behaving more like a Central American death squad than a legitimate urban peace force – or, as the *LA Times* put it, "an organized criminal subculture." Despite these accusations, most of the alleged perpetrators ultimately walked away from the charges, the momentum for their conviction either dissipating by a lack of social outrage or a lack of interest on the part of the local district attorney. Unfortunately, it is this very apathy, the tacit acceptance of such behavior on the part of local police, and by implication their political leaders, that has historically led to new cycles of anger and despair in the inner city, and cataclysmic riots in later decades.

Echo Park and Angelino Heights

About a mile north of Westlake along Glendale Boulevard, **Echo Park**, a tranquil arrangement of lotuses and palm trees set around an idyllic lake, was the setting for several scenes in Roman Polanski's film *Chinatown*, notably a palm tree-laden island reachable by a red footbridge and an assortment of row- and paddleboats, which you can still rent from vendors located along Echo Park Boulevard. In the large, white **Angelus Temple** on the northern side of the lake, the evangelist **Aimee Semple McPherson** used to preach fire and brimstone sermons to some five thousand people, with thousands more listening in on the radio. The first in a long line of media evangelists, "Sister Aimee" died in 1944, but the building is still used for services by her Four Square Gospel ministry, which dunks converts in its huge water tank during mass baptisms.

Just east of Echo Park on a hill overlooking the city, **Angelino Heights** was LA's first suburb, laid out in the flush of a property boom at the end of the 1880s and connected by streetcar to Downtown. Although the boom soon went bust, the elaborate houses that were built here, especially along **Carroll Avenue**, have survived and been restored as reminders of the optimism and energy of the city's early years. There's a dozen or so in all, and most repay a look for their catalog of late-Victorian details – wraparound verandas, turrets and pediments, set oddly against the Downtown skyline and occasionally used in ads for paint, among other things. One, with a weird pyramid roof, was even used as the set for the haunted house in Michael Jackson's *Thriller* video. The best of the lot is the **Sessions House**, no. 1330, a Queen Anne masterpiece with Moorish detail, decorative glass and a circular "moon window." The neighborhood has been decreed a "Historic Preservation Overlay Zone" – about as close as LA gets to an official designation of preservation – one of several that you can periodically tour through the LA Conservancy (for more on this, see p.35 in Basics).

Elysian and Highland parks

Two miles north of the Civic Center, quiet **Elysian Park** was laid out in 1886 and has been shrinking ever since. The LA Police Academy first took a chunk of the park for its training facility; later, the Pasadena Freeway sliced off another section. Finally, after city bureaucrats booted a good number of poor tenants from the land, **Dodger Stadium** was constructed in the early 1960s to host the games of the transplanted Brooklyn baseball team, the LA Dodgers, and the park became a fraction of its former self. However, even crisscrossed by winding roads, it's still worth a look, especially for its awe-inspiring views of the metropolis – when the smog doesn't intercede. **Angels Point**, on the upper western rim of the park, is your best vantage point, marked by an abstract sculpture with a palm tree growing out of its center.

Beside the freeway, a mile from Elysian Park, Highland Park is one of several neighborhoods north of Downtown that has established a surprising beachhead for the arts in a once-dilapidated part of the city (see box below). It was also the very first district annexed to LA, in 1895. Twelve years later, it became home to the **Southwest Museum** (Tues–Sat 10am–5pm; $6, $4 students; ☎323/221-2164, ⓦwww.southwestmuseum.org), the oldest museum in LA. Its name is a bit deceptive: there are in fact displays of Native American artifacts from all over North America, from pre-Columbian pottery and coastal Chumash rock art to a full-sized Cheyenne tepee. The museum also hosts traveling exhibitions, as well as some worthwhile lectures, films and performances, and its Braun Research Library has a superlative collection of recordings and photographs of Native Americans from the Bering Strait to Mexico. On the way out, there's a small gift shop where you can sift through Navajo rugs, kachina dolls and turquoise jewelry, plus an extensive selection of books and specialist publications. Nearby, the museum administers **Casa de Adobe**, 4603 N Figueroa St, a 1917 re-creation of a Mexican hacienda with a small museum inside detailing LA history into the nineteenth century. Currently closed for seismic renovation, the Casa is only open for special events (call ☎213/221-2163 for more information).

Just down the road, at 200 E Ave 43, the **Lummis House** (Fri–Sun noon–4pm; free; ☎323/222-0546, ⓦwww.socalhistory.org) is the well-preserved home of Charles F. Lummis, the city librarian who was at the heart of LA's nineteenth-century boom. An early champion of civil rights for Native Americans, and one who worked to save and preserve many of the missions, Lummis built his home as a cultural center of turn-of-the-century Los Angeles, where the literati of the day would meet to discuss poetry and the art and architecture of the Southwest. He built the house in an ad hoc mixture of Mission and Medieval styles, naming it "El Alisal" after the many large sycamore trees that shade the gardens, and constructing the thick walls out of rounded granite boulders taken from the nearby riverbed, and the beams over the living room of old telephone poles. The solid wooden front doors are similarly built to last, reinforced with iron and weighing tons, while the plaster-and-tile interior features rustic, hand-cut timber ceilings and home-made furniture.

Across the Pasadena Freeway, **Heritage Square**, 3800 Homer St (grounds open Fri–Sun noon–5pm, tours on the hour Sat & Sun noon–3pm; $5; ☎626/449-0193, ⓦwww.heritagesquare.org), is an outdoor museum – critics call it an architectural "petting zoo" – featuring a jumble of Victorian structures collected from different places in the city, most transported from Bunker Hill after the 1960s urban renewal campaign there. The strip uncomfortably sites a railway station next to an octagonal house next to a Methodist church, and

Art in post-industrial LA

Although neighborhoods like West Hollywood, Venice and Santa Monica grab most of the attention for attracting artists, in recent years the leading edge of LA's art movement has been located much further east, in the neighborhoods of **northeast Los Angeles**, which have increasingly drawn some of the city's most interesting and enterprising painters, sculptors and architects, most of them underground. Setting up homes in districts like **Highland Park, Eagle Rock, Mount Washington** and **Lincoln Heights**, these artists have done much to revitalize a previously dilapidated, industrial section of LA. While there is no one center where artists reside or work, there are a few highlights that are definitely worth a look.

A good place to start is **The Brewery**, north of Downtown at 2100 N Main St (information at ☎213/694-2911, ⊛www.oversight.com), a renovated 1920s complex that's gone from brewing suds to exhibiting designers and architects in a variety of galleries and art annexes that are open to the public. Most prominent in the complex is Michael Rotundi's striking **Carlson-Reges Residence**, a converted electrical utility building, noteworthy for its jagged architecture and post-industrial decor. (It's not open to the public, but is viewable from outside.) Other worthwhile sites include the **Judson Gallery for Contemporary and Traditional Art**, in Highland Park at 200 S Ave 66 (Tues–Fri 10am–4pm, Sat noon–4pm; free; ☎323/255-0131, ⊛www.judsonstudios.com), which displays contemporary stained glass, along with periodic exhibitions in a variety of media, and **Gallery Figueroa**, also in Highland Park at 1611 N Figueroa St (Fri–Sun noon–6pm; free; ☎323/258-5939, ⊛www.galleryfigueroa.com), where the wide-ranging shows include everything from photography and etchings to murals.

To learn more about northeast LA's art scene, check out the websites of the community-oriented **Northeast LA Network** (⊛www.nelanet.org) and the more comprehensive **Arroyo Arts Collective** (☎323/850-8566, ⊛www.ArroyoArtsCollective.org), which also organizes an annual November **Discovery Tour** of some of the best and quirkiest of the area's galleries and private studios.

although the buildings are interesting enough, the adjacent freeway makes this a less than ideal spot to imagine a Victorian world of buggies and gingerbread.

The LA River

"A beautiful, limpid little stream with willows on its banks" is how water tzar William Mulholland once described the **LA River**, the long gutter that serves as Downtown's eastern border. While the river may have often been tranquil, it was also quite volatile, periodically flooding neighboring communities until, in 1938, a typically drastic solution was imposed: its muddy bottom was turned into cement and its earthy contours became a hard, flat basin. The river mutated into a flood channel, which it remains, snaking through the city for 58 miles. Although some of the northern sections of the river (mainly through the western San Fernando Valley) have been re-seeded with foliage, efforts to return the Downtown stretch to its natural state have met with much bureaucratic resistance. Still, the fight continues, with groups like Friends of the LA River (☎1-800/LA-RIVER, ⊛www.folar.org) arguing for the restoration of the watercourse's old natural contours. To learn more about the character of the waterway and the potential for resurrecting its much-abused ecosystem, you can stop by the idyllic **Los Angeles River Center and Gardens**, 570 W Ave 26 (free entry; ☎323/221-8900 ext 301), for its informative "living river" exhibit. The center itself, set amid copious greenery and fountains, is home to various environmental and preservation groups.

Throughout Downtown, you're not allowed to poke around the river, but you can view it by driving across several Downtown bridges – designed in various revival styles, from Gothic to Baroque – or by renting movies. The empty riverbed has been used in numerous films, notably *Grease*, in which the channel hosts a wild drag race, and the *Terminator* series, in which cyborgs run amok in its bleak setting.

Mid-Wilshire

The ethnically diverse territory of **MID-WILSHIRE** takes in the general area around **Wilshire Boulevard** between Downtown and Beverly Hills, running roughly parallel to Hollywood to the north. Often bypassed by visitors, the area is one of LA's best bets for revisiting the architecture of the twentieth century, having escaped much of the redevelopment that has drastically transformed the more famous parts of town. Because Wilshire was the principal route of LA's first major suburban expansion in the 1920s, when the middle class began migrating west along the expanding strip – you can literally take a chronological tour of LA history simply by driving west from Downtown along it, from the Art Deco piles of its eastern end, to the auto-centric precinct of the mid-century Miracle Mile, to today's upscale department stores and modern superstructures of the Westside.

A true multicultural pathway, the Wilshire corridor groups together communities of middle-income Asians, old-money whites, working-class African Americans and diverse groups of Hispanics within a few miles of each other. Although the area was one of the hardest hit during the 1992 riots, **Koreatown** has, in the decade since, experienced renewed growth with a slew of modernist office towers and three-story malls. To the west, just north of Wilshire Boulevard, many of the old Anglo-Saxon estates in places like **Hancock Park** visually recall their 1920s heyday, and are now populated by a mix of Asians, Jews and African Americans.

Further along Wilshire, the **Miracle Mile** shopping strip has recently stopped its gradual decline, and boasts enough interesting Art Deco architecture to make a visit worthwhile. The western side of the strip, moreover, has been rejuvenated by the creation of **Museum Row**, a collection of institutions celebrating everything from the city's tar-soaked fossils to its worldly art, and, inevitably, its car worship. **Fairfax Avenue**, west of Museum Row, takes you through the human hive of the **Farmers Market** to the heart of the city's Jewish population. Further west, the **Third Street** shopping district, along with **La Brea Avenue**, is where the hip and trendy buy the latest designer clothes, eat in the smartest cafés, and hobnob with other would-be bohemians. These same activities occur more conspicuously on the celebrated **Melrose Avenue**, bordering the southern edge of Hollywood, though its lower-end junk stores and quirky boutiques are sadly being edged out in favor of blander designer shops. Fittingly perhaps, the western edge of Mid-Wilshire is marked by an imposing symbol of mass consumerism, the concrete monstrosity of the **Beverly Center**, looming over everything in sight.

Wilshire Boulevard

Named for oil magnate and socialist H. Gaylord Wilshire, a unique individual even for LA (see box, p.5), **Wilshire Boulevard** runs from Downtown to Beverly Hills and Santa Monica, but is at its most visually striking from Vermont to Fairfax avenues. This stretch of road was for many decades LA's prime shopping strip, until the same middle class that supported this "linear city" in the 1920s and 1930s disappeared for good in the 1970s and 1980s. These days, the storefronts along the boulevard have lost their tenants, but continue to serve as beacons of a faded era, when Zigzag and Streamline Moderne architecture were the rage and designers built apartment blocks to resemble Egyptian temples and French castles.

East of Vermont, surrounding grim **Lafayette Park**, are a few excellent examples of these early styles. The Romanesque **Park Plaza Hotel**, 607 S Park View St, is adorned by intricately crafted sculptures on the front and sides of the building, and features an exquisite marble lobby (see p.226); and the **First Congregational Church**, 540 S Commonwealth Ave, is a 1930 English Gothic cathedral known for its huge set of pipe organs and, appropriately, its annual Bach Festival (information at ☎213/385-1345, 🌐 www.fccla.org). The best example of the period-revival styles may be the historic **Granada Buildings**, 672 S Lafayette Park Place, a shopping and residential complex posing as a charming Spanish Colonial village.

Better still is the **Bullocks Wilshire** department store, 3050 Wilshire Blvd, an early Art Deco piece and the most complete and unaltered example of late-1920s architecture in the city, with a terracotta base and dazzling oxidized copper tower. Built in 1928, in what was then a suburban beanfield, it was the first department store in LA outside Downtown, and the first to construct its main entrance, a porte-cochère entry for cars, at the back of the structure adjacent to the parking lot – pandering to the automobile in a way that was to become the norm. The era's obsession with modernization and transportation extended to the inside, where murals and mosaics featured planes and ocean liners abuzz with activity. Badly vandalized during the 1992 riots, the store subsequently closed, but the building has since reopened as the law library of adjacent **Southwestern University**, which offers periodic "Tea and Tour" events that let you get a glimpse of the store's faded opulence (information at ☎213/738-8240).

The **Ambassador Hotel**, just west of Vermont Avenue at 3400 Wilshire Blvd, is another landmark of the boulevard's golden age. From the early 1920s to the late 1940s, when the hotel was the winter home of transient Hollywood celebrities, its *Cocoanut Grove* club was a favorite LA nightspot, attracting singers and musicians like Bing Crosby and Duke Ellington on stage. The large ballroom also hosted some of the early Academy Award ceremonies, and appeared in the first two versions of *A Star is Born* – though the hotel's most notorious event occurred on June 5, 1968, when **Bobby Kennedy** was fatally shot in the hotel kitchen as he tried to avoid the press after winning the California presidential primary. Though the building has since been converted into a film location and is now closed to the public, its present owners – LA's school district – have been debating its future use as a school facility (for the latest news, check out 🌐 theambassadorhotel.com). Across the street, another of LA's landmarks has been bizarrely re-sited. The **Brown Derby** restaurant, once the city's prime example of programmatic architecture (or buildings shaped like objects – in this case, a hat), has now been relocated to the roof of a minimall, where a coat of orange paint and redecorating have made it all but unrecognizable.

A few blocks west, the strikingly modern **St Basil's Roman Catholic Church**, 3611 Wilshire Blvd, was once the seat of the Church in Los Angeles (now residing Downtown at Our Lady of the Angels; see p.58), and is still LA's foremost example of contemporary ecclesiastical architecture, dating from 1969, with twelve looming concrete columns interspersed with colored-glass sculptures, resplendent teak altars and pews, and a ceiling decorated with over two thousand twisted aluminum tubes. Somewhat more traditional, the lustrous mosaics, marble and gold of the Byzantine **Wilshire Boulevard Temple**, nearby at no. 3633, are appropriately stunning. At the corner of Wilshire and Western Avenue, you can find one of LA's great Art Deco monuments: the **Wiltern Theater**, a former movie palace featuring a bluish Zigzag Moderne facade and narrow windows that make the building seem larger than it actually is. Not to be missed is the theater's dazzling interior, notable for its opulent sunburst motifs and grand Art Deco columns and friezes. Known as the Warner Bros Western Theater upon its completion in 1930, the building was nearly demolished in the 1980s until local conservationists stepped in; it has since been converted into a concert hall (see p.290), and you'll need a ticket for an up-close look inside.

Decades ago, countless **neon signs** used to illuminate the bustling blocks of the Wilshire corridor, some of which still survive. City re-development money has helped to relight a few, though the repair list is quite long and most landlords cannot afford the upkeep and electric cost that the signs require – especially since many now sparkle atop abandoned buildings and other crumbling heaps. Because there's no guarantee that these signs will be lit when you arrive for a look, neon lovers may want to hedge their bets by viewing them in the daylight. Notable examples of this signage include the elegant **Gaylord**, 3355 Wilshire Blvd, the stylishly Art Deco **Asbury**, 2505 W Sixth St, and the gentle cursive of the **Los Altos Hotel**, 4121 Wilshire Blvd. The Museum of Neon

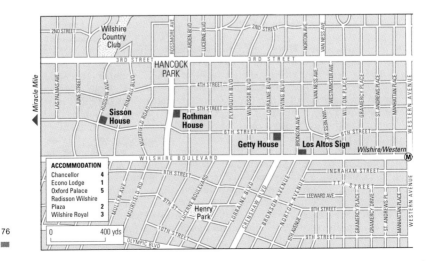

Henry Gaylord Wilshire

Aline Barnsdall, the 1920s heiress who commissioned Frank Lloyd Wright to build her Hollyhock House in Hollywood (see p.89), was not the only socialist who became rich thanks to overflowing oil profits. Decades before, **Henry Gaylord Wilshire** gained his notoriety from the petroleum industry (also making a fortune selling an electrical device that claimed to restore graying hair to its original color), and like Barnsdall was a scion of a family dynasty, as well as an entrepreneur. By the time he was 30, in the 1880s, he had already come to California and founded the Orange County town of Fullerton. Shortly thereafter, he became heavily involved in progressive causes and took up the Socialist banner in two unsuccessful runs for Congress, losing both in New York and California. These defeats did not deter his frenetic activity, however, and before long he was in London hanging out with members of the Fabian Society, as well as a then-unknown George Bernard Shaw. The turn of the century found him back in LA, this time buying up chunks of land from Pasadena to Santa Monica, including some of the Westlake neighborhood a few miles west of Downtown, site of now-decrepit MacArthur Park. Although Wilshire is often credited with creating the eponymous boulevard, the strip had actually been a wagon trail well before the Spanish had begun to settle in the area and had by Wilshire's time become known as the "**Old Road**," though it was actually little more than an uneven dirt path. The oil baron soon developed the street and the property around it, eventually helping the boulevard to connect Downtown with the ocean and creating one of the city's biggest thoroughfares in the process. Wilshire, though, had worse luck than the street he named. After another failed congressional attempt, he lost much of his money in foolhardy investments, managing to drop a cool $3 million. Still, he survived long enough to see his beloved route become one of the city's most important boulevards, a role that it holds to this day.

Art in Downtown LA offers monthly tours of these, and many other historic signs in the region (see p.36 for details).

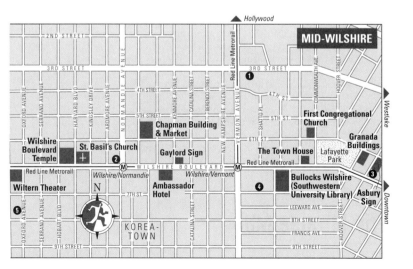

Koreatown

To get a good look at LA's cultural diversity, head south to Olympic Boulevard, between Vermont and Western avenues, to find the center of **KOREATOWN**, the largest concentration of Koreans outside Korea (some 100,000 people) and five times bigger than touristy Chinatown and Little Tokyo combined. Unlike the latter, Koreatown is an active residential and commercial district, noticeably lacking the low-rise buildings and mom-and-pop stores that fit the stereotype of ethnic enclaves elsewhere: the district is loaded with glossy modern buildings and huge, multistory mini-malls that contain several of the city's better restaurants, especially for Korean barbecue (see "Restaurants and cafés," p.263).

Except for dining, you'll probably not linger too long in Koreatown: there simply aren't enough key destinations to make a lengthy trip here worthwhile. A good place to start any visit, however, is the **Korean Cultural Center**, 5505 Wilshire Blvd (Mon–Fri 9am–5pm, Sat 10am–1pm; free; T 323/936-7141, W www.kccla.org), where you can browse through the museum's photographs, antiques and craftwork, and check out the rotating exhibits in the art gallery.

Hancock Park and around

Further west, Wilshire passes through the sloping, tree-lined neighborhood of **Hancock Park**, named after yet another oil magnate, G. Allan Hancock, who developed this expansive parcel of real estate in the 1920s as an elite suburb. The area has managed to retain its charm thanks to its well-preserved Historic Revival architecture, especially the restored 1920 **Getty House**, 605 S Irving at Sixth Street, the mayor's official residence and something of an architectural oddity, its green-and-cream Tudor design bucking the stereotype of the mayoral mansion. The house is open periodically for free tours (check W www .gettyhouse.org for details), but can be readily appreciated from the street. As for the name, J. Paul Getty himself didn't reside here – his oil company owned it, along with the surrounding blocks, before donating it to the city in 1975.

There are plenty of other lovely houses, mock-Tudor and otherwise, in the neighborhood, though none, unfortunately, are open to the public. Still, you can check out some grand exteriors, such as Paul R. Williams' magnificent **Rothman House**, 541 Rossmore Ave, a half-timbered Tudor jewel, and further west, a bizarre example of Medieval Norman, the **Sisson House**, Hudson Avenue at Sixth Street, featuring a gloomy facade and three-story tower.

Bordering Hancock Park to the west and Wilshire Boulevard to the north, the Mid-Wilshire blocks of **La Brea Avenue** have emerged as one of the city's trendier shopping districts, with weekend visitors coming to sample the edgy galleries, hip boutiques and restaurants, and antique furniture dealers. As a more relaxed, though similarly well-heeled, alternative, **Larchmont Boulevard** also has its share of high-end shops and restaurants, located just around Beverly Boulevard, on the northern edge of Hancock Park.

The Miracle Mile

Like so many of LA's iconic districts, the **Miracle Mile**, along Wilshire

Boulevard between La Brea and Fairfax avenues, was created by a property developer, in this case A.W. Ross, who realized the growing importance of the city's auto culture and quickly began developing this stretch of road in 1921. Though it never became LA's version of Fifth Avenue as Ross thought it would be, the Miracle Mile was quite a successful enterprise in its time, luring big-name department stores like Coulter's, Desmond's, Orbach's and May Company to the then-fringes of the city. (These retail operations, like the Bullocks Wilshire store to the east, had their main entrances in rear parking lots to please their car-driving customers.) Inevitably, the westward suburban shift that helped create the Miracle Mile also doomed it, and by the 1970s the area had fallen into decline, its vivid Art Deco designs left to fade and crumble after its department stores had moved away. In recent years, however, the strip has experienced a minor commercial upturn, with the arrival of celebrity-owned nightclubs like the *Conga Room* (see p.285), several stylish galleries, and a smattering of offices for movie producers and agents. Despite this, you'll have to look pretty hard at these Moderne piles – and ignore the encroaching office supply and supermarket chains – to envision this shopping strip in its glory days. If you're really interested in taking in all the history and architecture, the Los Angeles Art Deco Society will happily assist you, offering **walking tours** of the strip on the third Saturday of every month beginning at 10am ($10; reserve at ⓣ310/659-3326, ⓦwww.adsla.org).

The route begins in earnest with the **Security Pacific Bank Building**, just east of La Brea Avenue at 5209 Wilshire Blvd, which gives you a small hint of what LA's greatest Art Deco structure, the **Richfield Building** Downtown, must have looked like before it was summarily destroyed in 1968.

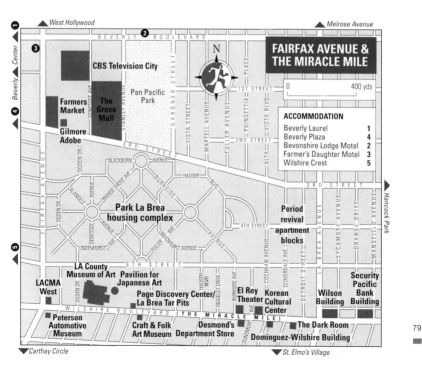

Both the original, and the current black-and-gold version, were designed by the firm of Morgan, Walls and Clements, perhaps LA's greatest purveyor of Art Deco and Historic Revival styles (see box, below). Just past this is the **Wilson Building**, 5217 Wilshire Blvd, a grand Zigzag tower known for the colossal neon beer ad on its roof, and the former **Dark Room**, no. 5370, a Streamline Moderne retail shop with a facade shaped like a huge camera, now transformed into a Cuban restaurant. Another Art Deco classic is the former home of **Desmond's Department Store**, no. 5514, with its bold Moderne tower and wraparound corners, which has been partially restored. The most vibrant classic Deco building may be the **El Rey Theater**, no. 5519, a thriving concert venue (see p.285) with its sleek king's head and flashy neon marquee, unmistakable amid the modern concrete boxes. Just to the north, a series of **period revival apartment blocks**, between Burnside and La Brea avenues around Sixth Street, manages to impress with wild 1920s and 1930s styling, everything from French chateaux to Hansel-and-Gretel cottages to pop-Baroque confections, many of them preserved with their original designs. Looming in the background to the north, the giant **Park La Brea** housing complex is a collection of mid-range postwar apartment units that more closely resembles a high-rise housing project.

LA's greatest unknown architects

Frank Lloyd Wright's forays into pre-Columbian styles in 1920s Los Angeles are well known, as are Rudolf Schindler's and Richard Neutra's early modernist efforts. However, the firm of **Morgan, Walls and Clements** had equal, if not greater, success in the age of Art Deco, even though its name is now largely forgotten.

The most conspicuous works of Octavius Morgan, J.A. Walls and Stiles O. Clements were the beloved Art Deco movie palaces that have survived the years and re-emerged as shrines to the golden age of Hollywood. The old Warner Bros Western Theater, now called the **Wiltern** (see p.76), was a triumph of the Zigzag Moderne style that was saved from the wrecking ball by community activism in the 1980s. Other of the firm's theaters, such as the **El Capitan** (p.100), have survived through massive renovation, or by being converted into nightclubs, as in the pre-Columbian fantasy of the **Mayan Theater** (p.63). While much of the architects' work has been preserved, some of their designs have been left to rot or remodeled beyond recognition, as in Downtown's former **Pantages Theater**, 534 S Broadway, now a jewelry shop, and **Globe Theater**, 744 S Broadway, a grim swap meet. Moviehouses aside, the firm's best work included a variety of commercial buildings throughout Mid-Wilshire and Hollywood in a range of styles, from the Spanish Churrigueresque of the former **Hollywood Chamber of Commerce**, on Sunset Boulevard at Hudson Avenue, to the monumental Assyrian design of the Samson Tyre and Rubber Company, now **The Citadel** shopping complex – an ersatz temple stranded alongside a busy freeway. Besides being skilled in period-revival architecture, Morgan, Walls and Clements also produced superb early Beaux Arts designs, as in Downtown's **I.N. Van Nuys building** (p.62), and the Streamline Moderne, shown best in the radiant pylon of the **KFL Building**, 133 N Vermont Ave, and the sleek and towering **Owl Drug Company**, 6380 Hollywood Blvd (now the Julian Medical Building). Perhaps their most impressive remaining structure is the Spanish Colonial **Chapman Building and Market**, at Sixth Street and Alexandria Avenue, a fanciful creation occupying a full city block and hiding an interior courtyard with assorted clubs and restaurants.

Although many of the firm's extant structures are closed to the public, their Andalusian-styled **Adamson House** in Malibu, Pacific Coast Highway at Serra Road (p.204), is not, offering the best chance to see what made their romantic escapist designs of the period so appealing to the architecture world.

Museum Row

As you continue west, the fading Art Deco monuments of the Miracle Mile give way to the cultural behemoths of **Museum Row**, the city's designated arts center. The museums begin at **La Brea Tar Pits**, Wilshire at Curson Avenue, where a large pool of smelly tar (*la brea* in Spanish) surrounds full-sized models of mastodons struggling to free themselves from the grimy muck, a re-creation of prehistoric times when such creatures tried to drink from the thin layer of water covering the tar in the pits, only to become entrapped. Millions of bones belonging to the animals (and one set of human bones) have been found here and reconstructed in the adjacent **George C. Page Museum**, 5801 Wilshire Blvd (Mon–Fri 9.30am–5pm, weekends open at 10am; $6, students $3.50; ☏323/934-7243, ⓦwww.tarpits.org), a Westside branch of the Natural History Museum in Exposition Park (see p.150). Besides watching researchers clean and categorize the bones of recent finds behind glass, you can also examine the mounted remains of many early or extinct creatures, including bison, saber-toothed tigers and giant ground sloths, their skeletons stained brown from the goo. More contemporary visitors attracted to the tar have included oil drillers, who for years pumped the liquid black gold from the ground and created an industry as endemic to Southern California as the movie business. In fact, it was a petroleum geologist, **William Orcutt**, who found the modern world's first saber-toothed tiger skull here in 1916, and an oil magnate, G. Allan Hancock, who in the same year donated this property to the county (not far from his later Hancock Park property development; see p.78). Outside, tar still seeps through the grass, but most of it oozes behind chain-link fences.

Across the street, the **Craft and Folk Art Museum**, 5814 Wilshire Blvd (Wed–Sun 11am–5pm; $3.50) has a small selection of handmade objects – rugs, pottery, clothing and the like – often with a multicultural twist, and it's worth a look if you're in the area. The fairly limited gallery space also hosts a few rotating exhibitions, among them pottery bowls and vases designed by Picasso, international carnival costumes and local examples of "low-rider" bicycles.

Further west, at the intersection of Fairfax Avenue, the **Petersen Automotive Museum**, 6060 Wilshire Blvd (Tues–Sun 10am–6pm, Fri until 9pm; $10, parking $6; ☏323/930-2277, ⓦwww.petersen.org), has enough mint-condition classic models to gratify even the staunchest autophobe. Spread over the museum's three floors are cars of all makes and kinds, from sleek luxury models to the splashiest muscle cars, including special exhibits that offer such curiosities as the "Stone Age" prop vehicle used in the movie *The Flintstones* and art cars designed like fish, guitars and high-heeled shoes. On the ground floor, an asphalt path leads you on a winding trek through the city's vehicular past, heading past dioramas of LA car worship past and present – from the reconstruction of a Streamline Moderne gas station to a mock-1950s car-hop diner to a 1960s hot-rod body shop in a suburban garage. Although the crude early-twentieth-century flivvers and wooden-track-racing roadsters are definite highlights, the museum's most memorable exhibit is its re-creation of the *Dog Café*, a departed LA landmark of roadside pop architecture shaped like a giant bulldog smoking a pipe.

The Los Angeles County Museum of Art

On the west side of the La Brea Tar Pits, the **LA County Museum of Art**, or **LACMA**, 5905 Wilshire Blvd (Mon, Tues & Thurs noon–8pm, Fri noon–9pm, Sat & Sun 11am–8pm; $7, students $5; ⓣ323/857-6000, ⓦwww.lacma.org), occupies an ugly cluster of beige-and-green blocks that were plopped down along the Miracle Mile in 1965. The much-derided complex will close in late 2004 to undergo a massive reconstruction under the guiding hand of Dutch architect Rem Koolhaas, who has planned a showcase structure for LA's art unlike anything else in town – built on stilts and roofed over with a translucent plastic tent. The only buildings left will be the Japanese Pavilion and LACMA West, which will also be the only parts of the museum open during the reconstruction. In the meantime, make sure to check out its wide-ranging stock of art, some of which are among the best in the world and justify a lengthy visit.

LACMA is enormous, and there's no way you could see it all at once: you're best off either focusing on the contemporary art and traveling exhibitions in the **Anderson Building** or diving into the fine selection of world art in the **Ahmanson Building**. And if you arrive on a Tuesday before 1pm, check out the schedule of classic Warner Bros films playing in the **Leo S. Bing Theater**, where you can see anything from a film noir to a screwball comedy for only $3.

The Ahmanson Building

Upon entering the **Ahmanson Building** on the first floor, you'll encounter the museum's surprisingly spotty collection of **American art**, highlighted by a few interesting paintings by the likes of John Singleton Copley (the regal *Portrait of a Lady*) and Winslow Homer (the dusty realism of the *Cotton Pickers*). Better is the impressive but limited assortment of American and Western **furniture**, including chairs and bureaus from the Federal period, rough-hewn Craftsman designs and machine-molded 1950s plastic seats. Also on the first floor, across the atrium, is a selection of Central and South American art, the highlight of which is the **Fearing Collection**, consisting of funeral masks and sculpted guardian figures from the early civilizations of pre-Columbian Mexico.

Below the first floor, on a small lower level, is the museum's growing collection of **Chinese and Korean Art**, of primary interest for its ancient lacquer-ware trays, hanging scrolls, bronze drinking vessels, glazed stone bowls and jade figurines all covering nearly seven thousand years of East Asian history. Outside, in the museum forecourt, the **B. Gerald Cantor Sculpture Garden** is noteworthy for its cast of characters from Rodin's *Gates of Hell*, as well as his towering *Balzac*, staring out at the passing traffic on Wilshire Boulevard.

The central attractions of the second floor are undoubtedly the **European art rooms**, which begin with a good overview of Greek and Roman art and continue into the medieval era with religious sculptures, notably a series of stone carvings of the Passion cycle. The Renaissance and Mannerist eras are represented by compelling works such as Veronese's *Two Allegories of Navigation*, great Mannerist figures filling the frame from an imposing low angle; El Greco's *The Apostle Saint Andrew*, an uncommonly reserved portrait; and Titian's *Portrait of Giacomo Dolfin*, a carefully tinted study by the great colorist. Northern European painters are well represented by Hans Holbein's small, resplendent *Portrait of a Young Woman with White Coif*, a number of Frans Hals' pictures of cheerful burghers, and Rembrandt's probing *Portrait of Marten Looten*.

In adjacent galleries are Georges de la Tour's *Magdalen with Smoking Flame*, a chiaroscuro work of a girl ruminating by candlelight while holding an ominous skull; Jean-Jacques Feuchère's wickedly grotesque bronze sculpture, *Satan*; and an excellent cache of Rodin's smaller works. Elsewhere are some lesser works by Degas, Gauguin, Renoir and the like, as well as the dramatic prints and drawings of the **Robert Gore Rifkind Center for German Expressionist Studies**, which includes a library of magazines and tracts from Weimar Germany. Rounding out the second floor are a few rooms containing ancient **Egyptian and Persian** sculptures and icons, including bronze figures and stone reliefs of Egyptian deities dating back to 3000 BC.

The third floor is most interesting for its **South and Southeast Asian and Islamic Art**, notably the selection of richly detailed sculptures of Buddha in copper and polychromed wood, watercolor images of Tibetan monks inlaid with gold, and a pantheon of Hindu gods carved in stone, copper and marble. The adjacent **costume and textile gallery** presents a wide assortment of fabrics and clothing from many different eras and cultures – including ancient Persian rugs, embroidered Jacobean gauntlets made of gold and silk, kimonos from feudal Japan and nineteenth-century New England quilts – but really draws the crowds with occasional shows on Hollywood costume design, featuring elegant gowns and outlandish headpieces from the likes of studio legends Edith Head and Adrian.

The Anderson Building

Contemporary art is showcased in the ugly **Anderson Building**, a giant concrete cube that abuts Wilshire Boulevard with a huge, sheer wall, and the adjoining **modern sculpture garden**, a largely ignored selection of uninspired

The people vs Ed Kienholz

Long before Robert Mapplethorpe and Andres Serrano stirred up controversy in the art world, **Ed Kienholz** was making waves with his *Back Seat Dodge '38*. Now sitting on the second floor of the LA County Museum of Art, Kienholz's work consists of a broken-down old Dodge with faded blue paint and dim headlights sitting on an artificial grass mat surrounded by empty beer bottles. An open door reveals two wire-mesh bodies, their grubby clothes ripped and torn, intertwined in an act of sexual frenzy and looking thoroughly decomposed. Ominous, crackly music adds to the sordid effect. Now recognized as a triumph of early social protest art, Kienholz's piece was called many other things upon its debut in the mid-1960s – indecent, morally depraved, pornographic.

LA County Supervisor Kenneth Hahn was one of the loudest voices to vilify both Kienholz and the museum for exhibiting the work, calling for the museum to be shut down unless it was removed. The battle that ensued was resolved with an appropriately ridiculous solution: the piece would be left in the gallery, but its car door would have to be closed most of the time, and opened only infrequently by a museum guard stationed nearby. Both Kienholz and Hahn moved on from the fight relatively unscathed: Hahn became a local legend for securing support for rapid transit, building Martin Luther King Jr General Hospital, creating the freeway emergency "call box" system and funding sports complexes (he had earlier successfully lured the Dodgers away from Brooklyn); Kienholz went on to establish an international reputation for daring assemblage art, becoming especially influential in Europe, though largely unheralded in his native country.

Appropriately, Kienholz carried his fixation with cars to the grave. When he was buried in 1994, in a strangely modern version of an Egyptian funeral rite, his wife drove him and his possessions down into the grave, burying him along with his favorite car – a Packard.

works around a stagnant pond. Luckily, the Anderson Building's other exhibits have a better reputation than its exterior art and architecture.

Rotating exhibitions are presented on the ground floor, while on the second and third floors, American and international **modernist art** are the focus; among the more prominent pieces of twentieth-century art on display are works by Picasso, Magritte, and abstract expressionists like Mark Rothko and Franz Kline. Less celebrated, but just as appealing, is Mariko Mori's hypnotic video presentation *Miko No Inori*, in which the platinum-blonde artist stares at the viewer with ice-blue eyes, manipulating a glowing orb to a hushed and haunting soundtrack. Also fascinating are Bill Viola's *Slowly Turning Narrative*, a huge, rotating projection screen displaying discordant images, and Ed Kienholz's *Back Seat Dodge '38*, looking just as perverse as it did in the 1960s when it caused political outrage (see box, overleaf). On a similar note, Michael McMillen's multimedia assemblage *Central Meridian* is a creepy walk-in garage, decorated with occult symbols and other mysterious ornaments, that showcases an old beater propped up on blocks and eerily lit by red neon under its chassis.

Pavilion for Japanese Art

On the north side of LACMA, adjacent to the tar pits, is the **Pavilion for Japanese Art**, easily the most effective building in the museum complex with its striking design – a traditional-modern hybrid by maverick architect Bruce Goff, modeled after traditional *shoji* screens to filter varying levels and qualities of light through to the interior. Displays of delicately painted screens and scrolls, and elegant ceramics and lacquerware are arranged beside a gradually sloping ramp that starts at the entrance and meanders down through the building, until it reaches a small, ground-floor waterfall that trickles pleasantly in the near-silence of the gallery.

LACMA West

LACMA continues on to the western end of Museum Row (and the Miracle Mile), inside the former May Company department store at Fairfax Avenue. Built in 1934 as a great westward leap over other local department stores, the building – whose eye-catching facade brings to mind an oversized perfume bottle – is home to **LACMA West** (same hours and entrance fee as the other LACMA buildings), an annex shared by LACMA and its partner, the Southwest Museum (see p.71). When this annex isn't hosting blockbuster art shows, a special gallery usually displays a good selection of experimental works, along with historic and contemporary pieces by Native American artists. The main draw for many families, though, is the special kid-friendly gallery, a giant playpen of sorts with pieces made to be jumped on, toyed with and laughed at.

South of Wilshire

A few blocks southwest of Wilshire, around San Vicente Boulevard, the period-revival architecture of **Carthay Circle**, a 1920s property development, is one of LA's best spots to see classic Spanish Colonial homes. A few more blocks to the south, **South Carthay** preserves plenty of 1920s and 1930s Historic Revival styles, and also has the added benefit of being one of the region's few protected architectural areas, known officially as a Historic Preservation Overlay Zone (and toured periodically by the LA Conservancy; see p.35). On the western edge of the neighborhood, the attractive **Center for Motion Picture Study**, 333 S La Cienega Blvd (Mon & Tues, Thurs & Fri 10am–6pm;

☎310/247-3000, Ⓦwww.oscars.org/mhl), houses the Margaret Herrick Library, whose voluminous and noncirculating collection includes books on actors, filmmaking and festivals, as well as screenplays, film production photographs and etchings. Formerly the home of the Beverly Hills Water Department, it was given a 1988 renovation by the Academy of Motion Picture Arts and Sciences, though its original spirit was kept intact – a municipal shrine to water, designed to look like a Spanish Colonial church.

A mile from Wilshire down La Brea Avenue, **St Elmo's Village**, 4836 St Elmo Drive (☎323/931-3409, Ⓦwww.stelmovillage.org), is a community arts project now thirty years old, worth a look for its colorful murals and sculptures. It's now also the site of the **Festival of the Art of Survival**, an annual celebration of folk and popular art and music held each Memorial Day.

Fairfax Avenue and around

Just beyond Museum Row, **Fairfax Avenue**, between Santa Monica and Wilshire boulevards, is the backbone of the city's Jewish culture, full of temples, yeshivas, kosher butcher shops and delicatessens. There's little in the way of sights, but it's a refreshingly vibrant neighborhood, easily explored on foot.

At Fairfax's junction with Third Street are the ramshackle buildings and white-clapboard tower of the **Farmers Market** (June–Sept Mon–Fri 9am–9pm, Sat 9am–8pm, Sun 10am–7pm; Oct–May Mon–Sat 9am–6.30pm, Sun 10am–5pm; free; ☎323/933-9211, Ⓦwww.farmersmarketla.com), created in the 1930s in an act of civic boosterism to highlight the region's agrarian heritage, much of which was being paved over at the time to make way for new suburbs. Inside the market is a bustling warren of food stalls and produce stands, popular with locals and out-of-towners to the point where it now sees 40,000 visitors daily. This growth has helped fund a monstrous new mall next door: **The Grove**, a three-level, $100-million complex that has taken over much of the market's parking lot. Also on the Farmers Market property is the 1852 **Gilmore Adobe**, named for the company that approved the Grove's creation (it also owns the other buildings). One of the oldest structures in LA, the adobe was once surrounded by a dairy farm, but has since been converted into private corporate offices.

Just north, **CBS Television City** is a thoroughly contemporary, sprawling black cube – and something of an architectural eyesore – but also a worthwhile destination if you're in town to sit in a TV-show audience for a sitcom or game show (call ☎323/852-2624 for more information). To the east on Third Street, Pan Pacific Park is one of the Westside's best green spaces, though it was once known for its striking Art Deco auditorium (since demolished).

West of the Farmers Market, the **Third Street** shopping district, running from La Jolla Avenue to La Cienega Boulevard, is another of LA's trendy retail zones, though with a bit less flash than most. Although there are numerous good antique stores, restaurants and coffee shops, most visitors are actually drawn by the huge shopping mall nearby – the imposing **Beverly Center**, Third Street at La Cienega Boulevard, a hideous brown-plaster fortress bedecked with giant fashion ads that serves as the nexus of much weekend activity for area teenagers.

Much more appealing is the small enclave of Streamline Moderne designs west of the mall at **Kings Road and First Street**. The best examples are the apartment building at **8360 First St**, with its sloping contours and aerodynamic design, and the private residence at **127 S Kings Rd**, dwellings that give you a fair idea of what many buildings in prewar LA looked like, namely beached ocean liners.

Melrose Avenue

The unofficial border between Mid-Wilshire and Hollywood, **Melrose Avenue** is, outside of Rodeo Drive, LA's most famous shopping strip. Running south of Hollywood starting at Hoover Street in Silver Lake, Melrose becomes liveliest west of La Brea Avenue, where it shifts from being a grimy, down-at-the-heels traffic corridor to a busy shopping zone with a wide range of independent retailers and chains. In its heyday, Melrose was an eccentric world of its own, a seedy district of junk emporiums, perverse novelty stores, tarot-card readers and fetish lingerie dealers with an air of anarchic creativity. Recently, though, a crush of designer boutiques, salons and restaurants has been gaining ground at the expense of the older, quirkier tenants, diluting the strip's funky allure and making it more of a touristy, homogenized place. As for parking, you won't find it easily on the avenue itself, but free spots exist on the side streets a block or two north and south of Melrose – as always, though, check the signs for parking restrictions.

The west end of Melrose becomes noticeably mainstream, and beyond Fairfax Avenue the street turns self-consciously chic and pricey until it reaches West Hollywood, where its color and vitality dissolve into an uninspiring stretch of elite boutiques and most of the window-shoppers also vanish.

Hollywood and West Hollywood

HOLLYWOOD is the birthplace of the modern movie business and one of the city's prime tourist attractions, epitomizing the LA dream of glamour, money and overnight success. Its seediness, however, is also legendary. Nathanael West memorably captured its dark side in his 1938 novel *The Day of the Locust*, Raymond Chandler made a career out of telling bleak stories of its violence and corruption, and more contemporary authors like James Ellroy have mined its depraved character in lurid detail. Nonetheless, these pejorative aspects have only served to enhance its romantic appeal and to keep the visitors coming.

Although you'd never believe it these days, Hollywood started life as a **temperance colony**, created to be a sober, God-fearing alternative to raunchy Downtown LA, eight miles away by rough country road. Purchased and named by a pair of devout Methodists in 1887, the district remained autonomous until 1911, when residents were forced, in return for a regular water supply, to affiliate their city to LA as a suburb. The film industry, meanwhile, gathering momentum on the East Coast, needed a place with guaranteed sunshine, cheap labor, diverse scenery, and most importantly, enough distance to dodge Thomas Edison's patent trust, which tried to restrict film-making nationwide. Southern California was the perfect spot. A few offices affiliated to Eastern film companies started appearing Downtown in 1906 and the first true studios opened in nearby Silver Lake, but independent hopefuls soon discovered the cheaper rents in Hollywood (for the full story, see "The rise of hollywood," p.365). Of considerable influence was **Thomas Ince**, a producer who set up shop here and established a production studio that would become a template for later film-making companies. While Hollywood soon vaulted to domestic economic success, its international dominance was only assured after the two world wars crippled Europe's vibrant film industry.

This dominion lasted until the 1950s, when government antitrust actions, television, and revitalized European competition damaged the movie industry, and by the 1960s large-scale financial flight further weakened LA's film business. In recent years, even the industrial companies involved in motion pictures – support facilities for editing, lighting and props – have been underbid by outside competitors based in North Carolina, Toronto and Vancouver, B.C., and shooting locations have migrated to those areas, mainly because of lower taxes and cheaper labor. While offices for big-name producers, directors, actors and agents are still based in LA, all of the major studios, except for Paramount, have long since moved from Hollywood to digs in Burbank, Culver City and elsewhere.

Although the district has been hobbled by the departure of the studios, tourism revenues have helped to make up some of the economic loss, and city redevelopment schemes are always in the works – including the massive Hollywood and Highland mall (see p.99), new site of the Academy Awards. While Hollywood may never be totally sanitized, most of its denizens – rock musicians, struggling writers, club-hoppers and petty criminals – prefer it to stay that way.

The far eastern boundary of Hollywood begins just beyond Echo Park at **Silver Lake**, initial home of the movie studios and now a center for Latin American immigrants and a well-established gay community. To the north, **Los Feliz** was home in the 1920s to many of the residences of Hollywood bigwigs. Nowadays, it's a charming mixed-income community with a few examples of notable architecture on its northern side. Further north lies **Griffith Park**, the site of LA's famed **observatory**, among other less well-known institutions.

The district's main drag is, of course, **Hollywood Boulevard**, which is still, despite its seediness, essential viewing – the basis for much LA myth and lore, epitomized by the ever-popular **Walk of Fame**. This street and its southern neighbor, **Sunset Boulevard**, were the central axes of the golden age of Hollywood, from the 1920s through the early 1950s, when the stars lived in exclusive homes in the **Hollywood Hills**, high above the boulevards. In recent decades, the economic core of the area has migrated west and now resides in **WEST HOLLYWOOD**, actually a separate city, attracting a diverse mix of gays and lesbians, pensioners, bohemians and a fast-growing community of Russian immigrants. Youthful poseurs and music lovers congregate on the legendary **Sunset Strip**, a traffic corridor loaded with nightclubs, bars and huge billboards.

Silver Lake and Los Feliz

As the original home of the region's film studios, **Silver Lake** and **Los Feliz** are fitting places to begin a tour of Hollywood. Unfortunately, Silver Lake's movieland heritage survives in only a few dusty pockets, and it's more noteworthy now for its striking views of the city and fine modern architecture. Los Feliz has preserved slightly more of its history and maintains a number of landmark buildings, thanks to the financial wherewithal of its richer residents, and remains a pleasantly low-key area with less of the pretension found in the Hollywood Hills to the west.

Silver Lake

Strictly as a body of water, **SILVER LAKE** is not a pretty sight – little more than a utilitarian reservoir, built in 1907, just before the area around it briefly became LA's movie capital. The neighborhood that bears the same name, however, features a number of fine homes and sweeping views of the LA basin. Divided into the wealthier sections in the hills and the poorer, mainly Hispanic parts near Sunset Boulevard, Silver Lake also has sizeable white and Latino gay populations, and the overall combination gives the area a certain vitality, especially evident in the area's varied bars and clubs, where you're apt to come across anything from old-fashioned cocktail lounges to free-wheeling drag shows.

Silver Lake's hills rise around the reservoir, and from the aptly-named **Apex Street** to the east, wealthy residents are afforded great views of the city, which you can get too, if you don't mind driving up the precipitously steep incline to reach the top. The hills to the west are peppered with prime examples of modernist homes by the likes of Gregory Ain, Richard Neutra, R.M. Schindler and Harwell Harris. One bravura example of mid-twentieth-century design is John Lautner's **Silvertop House**, 2138 Micheltorena St (best viewed from 2100 Redcliff Drive), an eye-catching design with projecting roofs and balconies, wraparound glass windows and sweeping concrete curves.

The general area around the intersection of **Sunset and Silver Lake boulevards** is the dynamic heart of the neighborhood, crowded with grubby-chic dance clubs, dingy bars, art studios, offbeat shops and a range of cheap restaurants. It's a fun, chaotic place to hang out in, and the best time to come is during the **Sunset Junction Street Fair** in August, a bohemian carnival known for its loud music, ethnic food and funky clothing stalls, which draws everyone from aging hippies with their families to pierced and tattooed youth looking for a little raucous amusement.

Silver Lake is bordered to the east by an area once known as **EDENDALE**, another early home to movie studios. Most of the district's history has been paved over or altered beyond recognition, but you could wander over to 930 Vendome St, right near a long stairway where Laurel and Hardy tried to move a grand piano up its incline in the 1932 film *The Music Box*.

Los Feliz

Named after nineteenth-century soldier and landowner José Feliz, **LOS FELIZ** is a mixed-class neighborhood with large numbers of Hispanic and gay residents, though it was once home to the glittering mansions of movie stars and studio bosses, a legacy that has left it with no small amount of eye-opening architecture.

Just northwest of Silver Lake and occupying a prime perch below Griffith Park, the district numbered among its 1920s denizens Cecil B. DeMille, W.C. Fields and Walt Disney. Early movie companies with facilities in the area included the current **KCET Studios**, 4401 Sunset Blvd, which was constructed in 1912 and is Hollywood's oldest film studio in continuous use, and the old **Vitagraph Studios**, 4151 Prospect Ave, which has since become the **ABC Television Center**. In recent months, however, most of the network's operations have departed to Burbank and the sound stages are mainly used for taping soap operas like *General Hospital* (call ☎310/557-7777 for free tickets). Melodrama junkies may also want to pass by 4616 Greenwood Place, the actual apartment complex that was used as the exterior of TV's *Melrose Place*.

More atmospheric is the **Vista Theater**, at the convergence of Sunset and Hollywood boulevards, a lovely, quasi-Egyptian renovated moviehouse. Across the street, film pioneer **D.W. Griffith** constructed his Babylonian set for the 1916 film **Intolerance**, complete with elephant statues, hanging gardens and super-sized pillars, none of it around today. A stripped-down "re-creation" of the set is now the centerpiece of the giant Hollywood and Highland mall in Central Hollywood (see p.99).

Just after the original movie set's destruction, Frank Lloyd Wright began con-

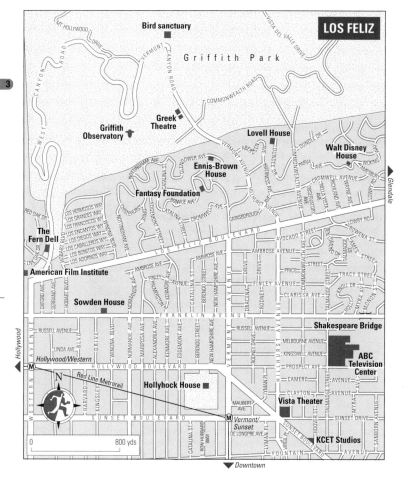

structing his first LA house up the road, on a picturesque hillside overlooking the city. The 1921 **Hollyhock House**, 4800 Hollywood Blvd, was named for the flower whose pattern is faintly discernable in the upright geometric shafts projecting from the roofline, and was supervised by Wright's student, Rudolf Schindler, later one of LA's pre-eminent architects. Covered with Mayan motifs that resemble early Art Deco designs, the bizarre building was obviously too much for its oil heiress owner, Aline Barnsdall, who lived here only for a short time before donating both the house and the surrounding land to the city for use as a cultural center. Known as **Barnsdall Art Park**, the grounds are now home to the **Barnsdall Arts Center** and the **Junior Arts Center**, which show off local art in their galleries. The entire park is currently closed for remodeling, but is due to reopen in 2003 (call ☎213/473-8434 for the latest update).

Further into the residential heart of Los Feliz, the **Shakespeare Bridge** on

Franklin Avenue near St George Street, a 1925 charmer with turrets, leads toward the **Walt Disney House**, 4053 Woking Way, an oversized cartoon cottage, perched imperiously on a high slope. Further into the hills, Richard Neutra's **Lovell House**, 4616 Dundee Drive, is a stack of blindingly white concrete slabs balanced on delicate stilts that looks quite contemporary for a 1929 building. One of LA's landmarks of early modernism, the house was used to striking effect in the film *L.A. Confidential*. More garish are the **Sowden House**, 5121 Franklin Ave, a pink box with concrete "jaws" designed by Frank Lloyd Wright's son Lloyd, and the **Ennis-Brown House**, 2655 Glendower Ave, the elder Wright's own design overlooking the Los Feliz hillside, a fascinating experiment built from hundreds of bulky concrete blocks to look like a monumental Mayan temple – one of four similar Wright oddities in LA. The house's imposing, pre-Columbian appearance has added atmosphere to over thirty movies, from Vincent Price's *The House on Haunted Hill* to *Blade Runner* and, unlike most of the area's homes, which are well-guarded fortresses, this private residence is open to the public throughout the year for ninety-minute tours (Tues, Thurs & Sat 11am, 1pm & 3pm; $15; reserve at (☎323/660-0607).

Not far away, at 2495 Glendower Ave, the **Fantasy Foundation** (Sat by appointment only; free; ☎323/MOON-FAN) boasts a truly amazing hoard of more than 300,000 items of horror, fantasy and sci-fi memorabilia. Forrest J. Ackerman, former editor of *Famous Monsters of Filmland* magazine and winner of science fiction's first Hugo award, has filled eighteen rooms of his "Ackermansion" with such delights as the robot from *Metropolis*, the facial molds of Boris Karloff, Bela Lugosi and Lon Chaney, the Creature from the Black Lagoon costume, and the fake breasts worn by Jane Fonda in *Barbarella*.

Griffith Park

Griffith Park (daily 5am–10.30pm, mountain roads close at dusk), north of Los Feliz, is the nation's largest municipal park, a sprawling combination of gentle greenery and rugged mountain slopes acquired by mining millionaire **Griffith J. Griffith** in 1884. Almost immediately, Griffith wanted to be rid of it, but could find no buyers and, in 1896, deeded the space to the city for public recreation. With its picture-postcard vistas and striking silhouette, it has since become a standard field trip for grade-school kids and a requisite stop for anyone taking a trip through Hollywood. Above the landscaped flat sections, where the crowds gather to picnic, play sports or visit the fixed attractions, the hillsides are rough and wild, marked only by foot and bridle paths, leading into appealingly unspoiled terrain that gives great views over the LA basin and out towards the ocean. Bear in mind, though, that while the park is safe by day, its reputation for violence after dark is well founded.

In its five square miles, the park contains 53 miles of **trails** and many opportunities for exploring its natural beauty. Near the entrance to the park off of Los Feliz Boulevard, Fern Dell Drive leads into the **Fern Dell**, a bucolic glade of ferns that acts as a border between the park to the east and an exclusive neighborhood to the west. Along Canyon Drive to the northwest, a hiking trail leads past a rock quarry to the lush **azalea gardens**, tucked away in a little-traveled section of the park. Further north, the **Sunset Ranch**, 3400 N Beachwood

Drive, provides Friday evening horse rides through the area for $40, including dinner (reserve at ☎ 323/469-5450, 🌐 www.sunsetranchhollywood.com), and the **LA Equestrian Center**, just across the LA River, offers horse rentals for $20 per hour or evening rides for $40, with a barbecue as well (☎818/840-8401).

If you'd rather just view the park's animals, there's a **bird sanctuary** on Vermont Canyon Road (daily during daylight hours; free), set within a modest wooded canyon, though as the birds aren't in captivity you might not see them. Caged animals, meanwhile, are plentiful in the **LA Zoo**, 5333 Zoo Drive (daily 10am–5pm; $8.25, kids $3.25; ☎323/644-6400, 🌐www .lazoo.org), one of the biggest zoos in the country and home to more than 1600 creatures, divided by continent, with pens representing various parts of the world. Despite the zoological inventory and layout, it's crammed and dismal, especially compared to its San Diego counterpart, two hours south. The park also has a **recreation center**, Los Feliz Boulevard at Riverside Drive, offering a swimming pool and various indoor and outdoor sports, and a **ranger station**, 4400 Crystal Springs Rd, that has information and maps on hiking paths (see box opposite). Bicycles can also be rented throughout the year from Spokes 'N Stuff behind the ranger station (weekends during daylight hours; $6 per hour; ☎323/662-6573).

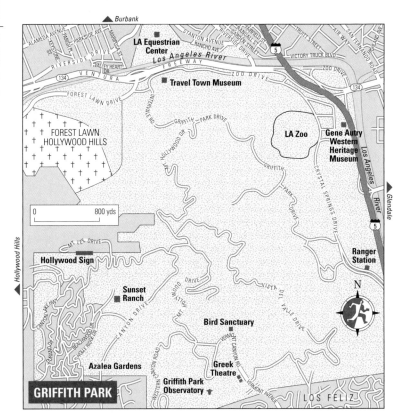

The steeper parts of Griffith Park, which blend into the foothills of the Santa Monica Mountains, offers a variety of **hiking trails**. You can get maps from the ranger station, at 4400 Crystal Springs Rd (daily during daylight hours; ℡323/662-6573) – also the starting point for guided hikes and atmospheric evening hikes, held whenever there's a full moon. The rangers also have maps for drivers that detail the best vantage points for views over the whole of Los Angeles, including the highest place in the park – the summit of Mount Hollywood.

The Griffith Observatory and around

The **Griffith Observatory** is unquestionably one of LA's monuments, a domed Art Deco shrine to science and a favorite shooting location for Hollywood film-makers, but it got off to a less than auspicious start. Just after the turn of the twentieth century, Griffith J. Griffith offered $700,000 to the city to build the observatory and theater on the parkland he had previously donated. The city declined, principally because "the Colonel," as he was known, had just been released from California's San Quentin Prison for trying to murder his wife – a 1903 incident in which Griffith, drunk and convinced that his wife was orchestrating a papal conspiracy, shot Mary Griffith through the eye. Although convicted of attempted murder, Griffith only spent a year in prison, and it wasn't until 1919, after his death, that LA finally took his money and later built the observatory and theater.

The observatory, finished in 1935, is perhaps most familiar from its use as a backdrop in *Rebel Without a Cause* and numerous sci-fi flicks, ranging from *The Amazing Colossal Man* to *The Terminator*. One of the city's most enjoyable spots, the observatory is currently closed for renovation until the spring of 2005. In the meantime, a "satellite facility" is promised on the north side of Griffith Park; find out more about this, and the renovation, by calling ℡323/664-1191 or visiting ⓦwww.griffithobs.org.

Not far away is the **Greek Theatre**, an open-air amphitheater (supposedly designed by Griffith himself) that seats nearly five thousand beneath its Greek-style columns – though if you're not going in for a show (the Greek is a venue for big-name rock, jazz and country music concerts during the summer), you'll see just the bland exterior. Opposite the park entrance, on the corner of Riverside Drive and Los Feliz Boulevard, is the grand **William Mulholland Memorial Fountain**, a tribute to the water engineer credited with building the aqueduct that gave the city its first reliable supply of water in 1913, a feat that's part of a long saga laced with scandal and corruption (see p.189).

Griffith Park's museums and cemetery

On the north side of the park, two **museums** compete for visitors' attention, with varying degrees of success. The most worthwhile is undoubtedly the **Gene Autry Western Heritage Museum**, near the junction of the Ventura and Golden State freeways at 4700 Western Heritage Way (Tues–Sun 10am–5pm, Thurs closes at 8pm; $7.50, students $5; ℡323/667-2000, ⓦwww.autry-museum.org), bearing the name of the "singing cowboy" who cut over six hundred discs from 1929 and was the star of Hollywood Westerns during the 1930s and 1940s as well as his own TV show in the 1950s. Autry fans hoping for a shrine to the man who penned the immortal "That

△ Mann's Chinese Theatre

Silver-Haired Daddy of Mine," are in for a surprise, however: the **collection** – from buckskin jackets and branding irons to Frederic Remington sculptures of turn-of-the-century Western life and the truth about the shoot-out at the OK Corral – is a serious and thoughtful examination of Western history and legends. The comprehensive collection of artifacts is organized into engaging sections on native peoples, European exploration, nineteenth-century pioneers, the Wild West, Asian immigrants and, of course, Hollywood's versions of all of the above. Catholic missionaries, gunslinging criminals, tribal medicine men, Romantic painters and Tinseltown directors are but a few of the colorful figures the museum honors, and sometimes criticizes. Less intriguing is the nostalgic **Travel Town Museum**, 5200 Zoo Drive (daily 10am–5pm; free), touted as a transportation museum but more a dumping ground for old trains and fire trucks, most of them presented without context or reason. Bounding Griffith Park's northwest rim, **Forest Lawn Hollywood Hills**, 6300 Forest Lawn Drive (daily 8am–5pm), is a cemetery of the stars that, while not quite as awe-inspiringly vulgar as its Glendale counterpart (see p.190), is no less pretentious, with showy gravestones and fancy memorials vying for attention. Luminaries like Buster Keaton, Stan Laurel, Ernie Kovacs, George Raft and Charles Laughton can all be found here in the Hollywood firmament, along with the likes of Andy Gibb and Liberace.

Hollywood Boulevard

From the 101 freeway to the edge of West Hollywood, **Hollywood Boulevard** is movie history incarnate, steeped in nostalgia and appealing in a way that no measure of commercialism is likely to diminish. The great majority of Hollywood's most popular and best-known attractions are located here, renovated movie palaces and noted watering holes among them, and crowds of tourists pore over the famous and infamous locales where legendary Tinseltown icons used to stroll, carouse and occasionally overdose.

Once you cross the freeway and reach Gower Street, you enter the most celebrated stretch of Hollywood Boulevard, which ends at La Brea Avenue. An unofficial dividing line between the east and west sides of this historic district is **Highland Avenue**.

East of Highland Avenue

Perhaps the most famous intersection in Los Angeles, the junction of **Hollywood and Vine** still tingles the spines of dedicated Hollywoodphiles. During the early years of film, the rumor spread that any budding star had only to parade around this junction to be "spotted" by big-name film directors, who nursed coffees behind the windows of neighboring restaurants, as the major studios were in those days all concentrated nearby. In typical Hollywood style, the whole tale was blown wildly out of proportion, and while many real stars like Tom Mix and Rudolph Valentino did pass by, it was only briefly on their way to and from work. The only thing marking the legend today, apart from disappointed visitors staring at the anonymous facades of old buildings, is a small plaque on the wall of a pizza joint.

The **Red Line** subway also stops here, so if you feel inclined to make a trip Downtown or up to North Hollywood in the San Fernando Valley, this is the

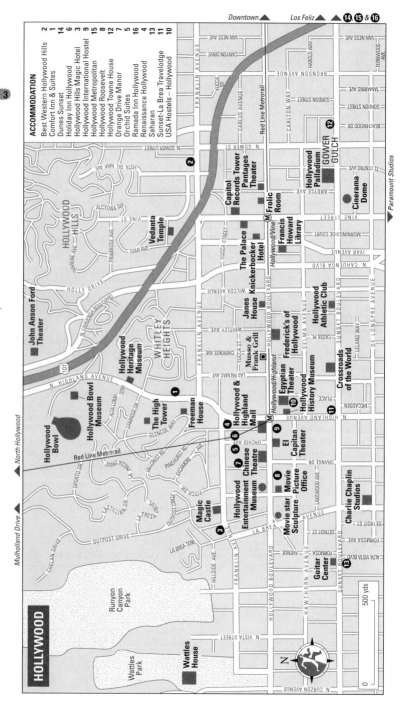

HOLLYWOOD

Mulholland Drive ◀

◀ *North Hollywood*

Downtown ▲   *Los Feliz* ▲   ▲ ⑭, ⑮ & ⑯

▼ *Paramount Studios*

Runyon Canyon Park

Wattles Park

Wattles House

Hollywood Bowl

Hollywood Bowl Museum

The High Tower

Freeman House

Magic Castle

Hollywood Entertainment Museum

Chinese Theatre

Movie star Sculpture

El Capitan Theater

Movie Picture Office

Guitar Center

Charlie Chaplin Studios

Hollywood & Highland Mall

Hollywood/Highland

Egyptian Theater

Hollywood History Museum

Crossroads of the World

Hollywood Athletic Club

Frederick's of Hollywood

Janes House

Musso & Frank Grill

John Anson Ford Theater

Hollywood Heritage Museum

WHITLEY HEIGHTS

HOLLYWOOD HILLS

Vedanta Temple

The Palace Knickerbocker Hotel

Francis Howard Library

Hollywood/Vine

Capitol Records Tower

Pantages Theater

Frolic Room

Hollywood Palladium

GOWER GULCH

Cinerama Dome

Red Line Metrorail

Red Line Metrorail

500 yds

N

spot – an underground station decorated with film reels and familiar cinematic imagery that is one of the few artistically interesting stops in LA's mass transit network. For a look at this and other subway-art highlights, the MTA transit system sponsors free two-hour tours of the most noteworthy and eye-catching installations (information at ☎213/922-2738 or ⓦwww.mta .net/metroart).

Nowadays, few aspiring stars loiter at Hollywood and Vine, but many visitors do come to trace the **Walk of Fame**, which officially begins here, a trail of brass stars set into the sidewalk and honoring various celebrities of the past and present. The laying of the stars began in 1960, instigated by the local Chamber of Commerce, which thought that by enshrining the big names in radio, television, movies, music and theater, it could somehow restore the boulevard's past glamour and boost tourism. However, dubious choices are often made; the Rolling Stones, for example, took decades to gain a star, long after they were past their prime, while such questionable picks as TV's *Rugrats* cartoon characters are enshrined frequently. Selected stars have to part with several thousand dollars for the privilege of being included: among them Marlon Brando (1717 Vine St), Marlene Dietrich (6400 Hollywood Blvd), Michael Jackson (6927 Hollywood Blvd), Elvis Presley (6777 Hollywood Blvd) and Ronald Reagan (6374 Hollywood Blvd). Almost every month there's a ceremony for some new luminary or curiosity to be "inducted" into the street; check the local newspapers for upcoming ceremonies.

Just north of Hollywood and Vine are a small cache of historic pop-culture buildings. The most familiar, the **Capitol Records Tower**, 1750 Vine St, resembles a stack of 45rpm records and continues to serve as the music company's headquarters, its dynamic 1950s design supposedly inspired by an off-hand remark by composer Johnny Mercer. Nearby, at 6233 Hollywood Blvd, the 1929 **Pantages Theater** has a bland facade but one of the city's greatest interiors, a melange of Baroque styling and ornate Art Deco friezes that mainly sees touring stage productions these days, but also served as the glossy site of the Academy Awards throughout the 1950s. Next door, the **Frolic Room** is an old-time watering hole (see p.280) that has appeared in countless movies, notable for its dynamic neon sign and interior mural of the stars drawn by the cartoonist Al Hirschfeld.

Around the corner, a bit of literary history can be found at 1817 Ivar Ave, the site of the fleabag rooming house where author and screenwriter **Nathanael West** lived during the 1930s after coming west in an unsuccessful attempt to revive his flagging finances. (The author vividly described Ivar Avenue as "Lysol Alley.") Gazing over the street's assortment of extras, hustlers and make-believe cowboys, he penned the classic satirical portrait of Hollywood, *The Day of the Locust*, whose apocalyptic finale was inspired by West's witnessing of the Hollywood Hills wildfires in the summer of 1935 (and which, oddly enough, includes a character named Homer Simpson). Across the street, the former **Knickerbocker Hotel**, 1714 Ivar Ave, now a retirement center, was where the widow of legendary magician Harry Houdini conducted a rooftop seance in an attempt to help her late spouse make the greatest escape of all. During the 1930s and 1940s, the hotel had a reputation for rooming some of Hollywood's more unstable characters, and a number of lesser names jumped from its high windows.

Further south on Ivar, between Sunset and Hollywood boulevards, the popular **Hollywood Farmers Market** has been doling out agrarian goodies for more than a decade, selling its wares on Saturdays to locals and tourists alike; while at 1623 Ivar Ave, the **Francis Howard Library**, a branch of LA's library system designed by Frank Gehry, is a depressingly successful attempt at fortress architecture, with blank walls, a faceless facade and maximum security above all else (famously profiled, and criticized, in Mike Davis's groundbreaking history of LA, *City of Quartz*). More inviting is the **Janes House**, back up on 6541 Hollywood Blvd, a 1903 Queen Anne dwelling that is now the home of the Hollywood **visitors' center** (Mon–Fri 9am–5pm; ☏ 323/689-8822).

At no. 6608 is the garish purple-and-pink **Frederick's of Hollywood**, a local landmark that sells racy lingerie and offers visitors a glimpse of famous undergarments from the 1940s to the present in its **lingerie museum** (Mon–Fri 10am–9pm, Sat 10am–7pm, Sun 11am–6pm; free), where the centerpiece of the collection is the **Celebrity Lingerie Hall of Fame**, showcasing underclothing donated by a host of famous wearers: Zsa Zsa Gabor's girdle, Cyd Charisse's leotard, Ava Gardner's skirt and Madonna's bustier, among many others. Across the street you can find the well-worn dining booths of the **Musso and Frank Grill**, no. 6667, a 1919 restaurant that has been a fixture since the days of silent cinema. Here, famous writers, actors and studio bosses would meet (and still do, occasionally) to slap backs, cut deals and drink potent lunches. It's no accident that this was the place where, in Tim Burton's *Ed Wood*, the title character – notorious B-movie director of *Plan 9 from Outer Space* – goes to drown his sorrows, only to encounter a loaded Orson Welles doing the same thing.

A little further on, at no. 6708, the very first Hollywood premiere (*Robin Hood*, an epic swashbuckler starring Douglas Fairbanks Sr), took place in 1922 at the **Egyptian Theatre**. Financed by impresario Sid Grauman, in its heyday the Egyptian was a glorious fantasy, modestly seeking to re-create the Temple of Thebes, with usherettes dressed as Cleopatra. This great old building was damaged in the 1994 earthquake, but has since been lovingly restored by the American Cinematheque film foundation, and now plays an assortment of Hollywood classics, avant-garde flicks and foreign films to small but appreciative crowds. Tourists, however, are encouraged to check out a short documentary, presented hourly, chronicling the rise of Hollywood as America's movie capital (Sat & Sun 2pm & 3.30pm; $7; ☏ 323/461-2020 ext 7, ⊛ www.americancinematheque.com). Alternatively, you can get the grand tour of the theater itself in hour-long, in-depth visits to sights like the backstage dressing rooms and projection booth, usually presented twice monthly in the middle of the month (10.30am only; $7; call for details at ☏ 323/461-2020 ext 115). Much less appealing, the eastern corners of the Hollywood and Highland intersection feature a handful of dreary tourist traps – wax museum, oddities gallery, world-record exhibit – that are worthwhile only if you're very easily amused.

Just to the north, the **Hollywood Heritage Museum**, 2100 N Highland Ave (Sat & Sun 10am–3.30pm; $3; ☏ 323/874-4005, ⊛ www.hollywoodheritage.org), formerly the Hollywood Studio Museum, occupies a historic horse barn that originally stood at the corner of Selma and Vine streets. In 1913, Cecil B. DeMille, Jesse Lasky and Sam Goldfish (later Goldwyn) rented one half of the structure while the barn's owner continued to stable horses in the other. From this base, the three collaborated to make *The Squaw Man*, Hollywood's first true feature film, whose success propelled them to move their operation – including the barn itself – to the current Paramount lot at Marathon Street and Van Ness Avenue. The barn was eventually brought to its present location as a monument to Hollywood history.

South of Hollywood and Highland, the now-shuttered Max Factor Museum, 1660 Highland Blvd, is set to reopen in 2003 as the **Hollywood**

History Museum, where four levels will exhibit the fashion, sets, make-up, special effects and art design of the Golden Age of movies. To see if it's finally open, call ☎323/464-7770 or check ⓦwww.hollywoodhistorymuseum .com.

West of Highland Avenue

Looming over the west side of its eponymous intersection, the long-awaited **Hollywood and Highland** complex must rank as one of LA's most frustrating attractions. After nearly a billion dollars of public and private investment, the commitment of a major hotel, boutiques and restaurants, and the relocation of the Oscars to the specially designed Kodak Theater on site, this towering beacon of commerce – which was supposed to revitalize Hollywood and give the district a cultural renaissance – is no better than your average suburban shopping mall. Loaded with big-name fashion chains and swank eateries, Hollywood and Highland still has the same tired feel as most any other shopping plaza, with fortress-like walls shielding consumers from the potential seediness of Hollywood Boulevard and private security keeping watch over "undesirable" elements. Perhaps the most ominous clue to the complex's ultimate fate may lie in its chosen theme: the Babylonian set from the 1916 D.W. Griffith film *Intolerance*, from which the mall borrows heavily in its super-sized columns, elephant statues and colossal archway. Unrivaled in film history for almost fifty years, the movie was Hollywood's first real financial disaster, helping to ruin the career of its director and making the movie studios permanently wary of taking any sort of creative risks.

One site that the mall has very nearly ruined already is Mann's **Chinese Theatre**, 6925 Hollywood Blvd, which has for no good reason been swallowed up by the complex, enveloped by a curving stucco wall and expanded into a multiplex (beyond the three theaters pre-dating the mall). As for what remains of the building, it's an odd version of a classical Chinese temple, replete with dubious Chinese motifs and upturned dragontail flanks, and the lobby's Art Deco splendor and the grand chinoiserie of the auditorium make for interesting viewing. Afterward, on the street outside the theater, you can hop aboard a tour bus for a look at the "homes of the stars," along with hundreds of other sightseers (see "Mainstream tours," p.35).

Hollywood impressions at the Chinese Theatre

Opened in 1927 as a lavish setting for premieres of swanky new productions, the **Chinese Theatre** was for many decades *the* spot for movie first nights, and the public crowded behind the rope barriers in the thousands to watch the movie aristocrats arriving for the screenings. The main draw, of course, has always been the assortment of **cement handprints** and **footprints** embedded in the theater's forecourt. The idea came about when actress Norma Talmadge accidentally (though some say it was a deliberate publicity stunt) trod in wet cement while visiting the construction site with owner Sid Grauman, a local P.T. Barnum of movie exhibitors who, with the Egyptian Theatre down the block and other such properties, established a reputation for creating movie palaces with gloriously vulgar designs based on exotic themes. The first formally to leave their marks were Mary Pickford and Douglas Fairbanks Sr, who ceremoniously dipped their hands when arriving for the opening of *King of Kings*, and the practice continues today. It's certainly fun to work out the actual dimensions of your favorite film stars, and to discover if your hands are smaller than Julie Andrews' or your feet are bigger than Rock Hudson's (or both).

Similarly, the **El Capitan Theater**, no. 6834, is a colorful 1926 movie palace, with Baroque and Moorish details and a wild South Seas-themed interior of sculpted angels and garlands, plus grotesque sculptures of strange faces and creatures. Restored to its full glory, the theater also has one of LA's great marquees, a multicolored profusion of flashing bulbs and neon tubes. The Disney-owned theater which mostly shows cartoons and comedies, is worth the price of a ticket to glimpse the eye-popping old Hollywood architecture.

A few doors down, at no. 7000, the **Hollywood Roosevelt** was movieland's first luxury hotel (see "Accommodation," p.227). Opened in the same year as the Chinese Theatre, it fast became the meeting place of top actors and screenwriters, its *Cinegrill* restaurant feeding and watering the likes of W.C. Fields, Ernest Hemingway and F. Scott Fitzgerald, not to mention legions of hangers-on. In 1929 the first Oscars were presented here, beginning the long tradition of Hollywood rewarding itself in the absence of honors from elsewhere. Look inside for a view of the splashing fountains and elegantly weighty wrought-iron chandeliers of its marble-floored lobby, and for the pictorial **History of Hollywood** on the second floor. The place is thick with legend: on the staircase from the lobby to the mezzanine, Bill "Bojangles" Robinson taught Shirley Temple to dance; and the ghost of Montgomery Clift (who stayed here while filming *From Here to Eternity*) reputedly haunts the place, announcing his presence by blowing a bugle. Surviving lounge divas like Eartha Kitt still put on the occasional show at the *Cinegrill* cabaret (see p.301).

Across the street, the **Hollywood Entertainment Museum**, 7021 Hollywood Blvd (Tues–Sun 11am–6pm; $8.75, students $4.50; Ⓣ323/465-7900, Ⓦwww.hollywoodmuseum.com), occupies a lower level of the crudely "futuristic" Hollywood Museum Center. While highlighted by the full set of the show *Cheers* and the bridge of the Enterprise from *Star Trek*, along with rotating exhibitions of antiques and curios from Hollywood history, the museum is a rather amateurish collection of odds and ends from old TV programs and movies, largely presented without context or any apparent purpose. Unfortunately, it's also the closest thing to an actual movie museum that Hollywood has at present. The museum's one jewel is the **Max Factor Collection**, which displays beauty artifacts from Hollywood's golden age, temporarily taken from the former Max Factor Museum (see p.98). Among the interesting and varied items are make-up samples from different historical eras; the kissing machine, used to test the endurance of Factor's potions; and the "beauty calibrator," a ghoulish-looking head cage with rows of pins designed to measure the wearer's face.

To catch a peek at a current Hollywood production, cross the road to the **Motion Picture Production Office**, 7038 Hollywood Blvd, 5th Floor (Mon–Fri 8am–6pm), which issues a "shoot sheet" every weekday ($1–2), detailing exactly what's being filmed around town that day. Most film shoots hire a couple of off-duty LAPD officers for security, but not all sets are impenetrable.

Hollywood Boulevard's historic stretch largely ends where it hits La Brea Avenue, on the corner of which stands Karl West's **Hollywood Gateway**. This iconic 1993 sculpture features a towering pylon and metallic Art Deco-styled roof supported by the arched figures of movie goddesses Dorothy Dandridge, Dolores del Rio, Anna May Wong and Mae West - supposedly an homage to diversity in Tinseltown history, though in reality something of a fabrication. The first three actresses had to struggle mightily for roles against the prevailing stereotypes of their eras, and even West herself was the target of small-minded censors with no patience for her "lascivious" antics.

One long block north, at 7001 Franklin Ave, the **Magic Castle** is a spooky Victorian mansion and private club that puts on magic shows and other spectacles; the only nonmembers allowed a look inside are guests at the adjacent *Hollywood Hills Magic Hotel* (see p.227).

Sunset and Santa Monica boulevards

Although Hollywood Boulevard is the undisputed hub of Hollywood legend, the area around **Sunset and Santa Monica boulevards** was the actual focus of the early film industry. At the start of the twentieth century, these streets hosted five of the seven major film studios, but by the 1930s, four had left for more spacious lots in cities like Burbank, which offered huge parcels of land to these studios, with lower taxes than LA. Ultimately, only **Paramount** stayed in its Hollywood location.

Today, both these streets are less touristy than Hollywood Boulevard, and their attractions are more modest and intermittent. Most of the interesting spots are grouped in pockets and should be explored by car, not on foot, as both strips can get dicey at night – drugs and prostitution being the major industries these days.

Sunset Boulevard

Famous as the title of the classic 1950 movie that featured Gloria Swanson as an aging, predatory movie star, **Sunset Boulevard** runs through Hollywood into West Hollywood, where it becomes the colorful Sunset Strip. Along with **RKO Studios** to the south, which went under in 1955, three film-making giants left sizeable holes in the landscape when they departed more than six decades ago. **Warner Bros** (1918–29), **Columbia** (1920–1934) and **William Fox Studios** (1924–35) were located within twelve blocks of each other, but all their studio buildings have been changed or destroyed – the former Warner Bros facility, 5858 Sunset Blvd, is now a TV station. Other, smaller, studios also occupied space along Sunset, and many actors would frequently try to get the attention of movie producers or casting directors by loitering around the corner of Sunset and Gower Street, the so-called **Gower Gulch**. Here, film extras in need of a few days' work would make appearances in the hope of being hired for the latest B-grade Western, as extras or emergency stuntmen. The gulch's air of desperation earned it the moniker "Poverty Row," which also collectively described the town's smaller studios, such as nearby Columbia, which Harry Cohn founded (along with Universal in Burbank), before it grew to become one of the majors – after it left the area.

Adjacent to the old Warner Brothers studios, the **Hollywood Palladium**, 6215 Sunset Blvd, was best known for hosting the big names in swing, jazz and big band music, notably Glenn Miller and Lawrence Welk, who played here for a solid fifteen years, and the place still puts on concerts today (see p.290). Down a few blocks, at no. 6360, the white concrete **Cinerama Dome** is an unmistakable sight, its hemispheric auditorium now part of a larger retail complex of theaters, shops and eateries. The dome was originally built to screen the three-projector films sweeping Hollywood at the end of the 1950s, but the movie fad faded even before the theater was completed; however, you can still see blockbusters in the dome on a large, curved screen – as fun and engaging a cinematic experience as any in LA. Nearby, the delectable Spanish Revival building at no. 6525, was, from the 1920s until the 1950s, known as the **Hollywood Athletic Club**, another of Hollywood's legendary watering holes, where the likes of Charlie Chaplin, Clark Gable, John Barrymore and Tarzan himself (Johnny Weismuller), lounged beside its Olympic-sized pool, while John Wayne threw pool balls at passing cars. After standing empty for 25 years, the building reopened in 1990 as a pool hall, bar and restaurant, only to close again at the end of the decade and remain shuttered, though opening for special parties and events.

Further west, **Crossroads of the World**, no. 6672, isn't much to look at these days, but when finished in 1936, it was a major LA tourist attraction and one of the city's very first local malls. The central plaza supposedly resembles a ship, surrounded by shops designed with Tudor, French, Italian and Spanish motifs – the idea being that the shops are the ports into which the shopper would sail. Oddly enough, time has been kind to this place, and considering the more recent and far brasher architecture found in the city, this has a definite, if muted, charm.

A few blocks east, the **Charlie Chaplin Studio**, 1416 N La Brea Ave, was built in 1918, a year before he teamed with other celebrities to create the United Artists studio. Now owned by Polygram Records, the complex preserves Chaplin's foot imprints near Stage 3. A few blocks to the west, the **Guitar Center**, a musical instrument store, does the same thing for rock stars, with handprints of your favorite guitar gods – Eddie Van Halen, Slash and so on. You might even see some of these virtuosos – with their axes in tow – at the so-called **"Rock'n'Roll" Denny's**, 7373 Sunset Blvd, which has long been a hangout for musicians who've just performed on the Sunset Strip the night before. It also served as the thinly veiled inspiration for "Winkie's" in David Lynch's film *Mulholland Drive*.

Santa Monica Boulevard

For a street with such a familiar name, **Santa Monica Boulevard** has relatively few noteworthy attractions, at least in Hollywood. A grungy strip plied by prostitutes and drug dealers, the boulevard is home to sizeable communities of Russian immigrants, pensioners and working-class gays. For excitement, you're better off heading further west into West Hollywood, where the street becomes a bit more lively – and safer. Still, despite its seediness, this stretch does have the distinction of bordering Hollywood's last remaining studio and most famous graveyard.

Not surprisingly for a town obsessed with marketing and PR, even the cemeteries in LA – and not only the actors – are renamed to draw the crowds. Thus the former Hollywood Memorial Park has been reincarnated as **Hollywood Forever** (daily 8am–5pm; free), though the graves have luckily been kept in the same places. Close to the junction of Santa Monica Boulevard and Gower Street and overlooked by the famous water tower of the neighboring Paramount Studios, the cemetery displays myriad resting places of dead celebrities, most notably in its southeastern corner, where a cathedral mausoleum includes, at no. 1205, the resting place of **Rudolph Valentino**. In 1926, 10,000 people packed the cemetery when the celebrated screen lover died aged just 31, and to this day on each anniversary of his passing (August 23), at least one "Lady in Black" will likely be found mourning – a tradition that started as a publicity stunt in 1931 (the first weeping damsel claimed to be a former paramour of Valentino's but was exposed as a hired actress) and has continued ever since. While here, spare a thought for the more contemporary screen star, Peter Finch, who died in 1977 before being awarded a Best Actor Oscar for his role in the film *Network* ("I'm as mad as hell, and I'm not going to take it any more!"). Unfortunately, his crypt is opposite Valentino's and tourists often lean against it while photographing Rudolph's marker.

Fittingly, outside the mausoleum, the most pompous grave belongs to **Douglas Fairbanks Sr**, who, with his wife Mary Pickford (herself buried at Forest Lawn Glendale), did much to introduce social snobbery to Hollywood. Even in death Fairbanks keeps a snooty distance from the pack, his ostentatious memorial (complete with sculptured pond), only reachable by a shrubbery-lined path from the mausoleum. If you revel in Tinseltown's postmortem pretensions, there are countless self-important obelisks and grandiose grave-markers throughout the park, under which LA's somebodies and nobodies finally, in death, mix. One of the cemetery's more animated arrivals was **Mel Blanc**, "the man of a thousand voices" – among them Bugs Bunny, Porky Pig, Tweety Pie and Sylvester – whose epitaph simply reads "That's All, Folks."

Despite its morbid glamour, the cemetery also has a contemporary function. As you enter, you will notice the many tightly packed rows of glossy black headstones with Orthodox crosses and Cyrillic lettering. These mark the resting places of **Russian and Armenian immigrants**, who increasingly populate the graveyard just as their living counterparts populate Central and West Hollywood.

South of the cemetery, at 5555 Melrose Ave, **Paramount Studios** used to provide a very limited trek around the sound stages and offices of its sizeable complex, though at present, tours are no longer offered, with the studio mysteriously citing "security concerns" for the suspension. Although you can still glimpse the studio's famed Melrose **gate**, comprising two great arches with metallic detailing, the original studio entrance – which Gloria Swanson rode through in *Sunset Boulevard* – is now inaccessible.

There are only two other interesting sights along this stretch of Santa Monica Boulevard, the first of which is the **Formosa Café**, no. 7156, where celebrities from Humphrey Bogart to Marilyn Monroe came to drown their sorrows. It's still open, and its colorful ambience, though faded, makes it an excellent spot to savour authentic Hollywood spirits. Nearby, at 1041 Formosa Ave, is **Warner Hollywood Studios**, owned by Warner Bros, though not the company's main studio lot (which is instead located in Burbank; see p.191). Built in 1919, this housed **United Artists Studios**, the production company of Charlie Chaplin (his second), Douglas Fairbanks Sr, Mary Pickford and D.W. Griffith, until 1975. With their studio as the symbol of the **star system** in the silent era, these four artists controlled their careers through the company, at least for a while, and helped craft the Hollywood marketing machine that sold movies by celebrity appeal, a system that endures to this day.

The Hollywood Hills

Once the exclusive domain of Hollywood's glitterati, and still a lofty location for the city's up-and-comers, the **HOLLYWOOD HILLS** are perhaps the best-known urban mountains in the US, and synonymous with the legendary LA image of celebrities enjoying the good life high above the urban sprawl. Roughly paralleling Hollywood itself, and forming the eastern end of the

Santa Monica Mountains chain, these canyons and slopes offer truly striking views of the basin at night, when LA spreads out like a huge illuminated grid in all directions, seemingly without end. Beyond the stunning views, most of the appealing sights in this area are located just north of Hollywood Boulevard, on narrow, snaking roads that are easy to get lost on. If you want to do serious exploring in these hills, bring a detailed map or prepare to be befuddled.

The eastern Hollywood Hills

On the eastern side of the area, Beachwood Drive heads into the hills north of Franklin Avenue and was the axis of the **Hollywoodland** residential development, a 1920s product of *Los Angeles Times* news baron **Harry Chandler**, who found ample time for real-estate speculation when he wasn't strong-arming city politicians. The pretentious **stone gates** of the development sit at Beachwood's intersection with Westshire and Belden drives; although the neighborhood is relaxing enough, the chief reason most people come to the area is for the view of the **Hollywood sign** at the top of Mount Lee above (see box). Unfortunately, there's no public road to the sign (Beachwood Drive comes nearest, but ends at a closed gate) and you'll incur minor cuts and bruises while scrambling to get anywhere near. In any case, infrared cameras and radar-activated zoom lenses have been installed to catch graffiti writers, and innocent tourists who can't resist a close look are also liable for a steep fine. For a much simpler look, you can check out the sign from your computer by visiting Ⓦ www.hollywoodsign.org, where the letters are visible day or night.

If you've seen the disaster epic *Earthquake*, you may remember **Lake Hollywood**'s dam bursting and flooding the LA basin; however, this manmade body of water is anything but dramatic – just a pleasantly rustic refuge in the heart of the city. The clear, calm waters, actually a reservoir intended for drought relief, are surrounded by clumps of pines in which squirrels, lizards and a few scurrying skunks and coyotes easily outnumber humans. You can't get too near the water, as metal fences protect it from the general public, but the footpaths

---

Tales of the Hollywood sign

The **Hollywood sign** began life in 1923 as little more than a billboard for the Hollywoodland development and originally contained its full name; however, in 1949 when a storm knocked down the "H" and damaged the rest of the sign, the "land" part was removed and the rest became the familiar symbol of the area and of the entertainment industry. Unfortunately, the current incarnation has literally lost its radiance: it once featured 4000 light bulbs that beamed the district's name as far away as LA harbor, but a lack of maintenance and frequent theft put an end to that practice.

The public's easy access to the sign is as distant a memory as the bright lights, for it has gained a reputation as a suicide spot, ever since would-be movie star Peg Entwhistle terminated her career and life here in 1932, aged 24. It was no mean feat: from the end of Beachwood Drive she picked a path slowly upward through the thick brush and climbed the fifty-foot-high "H," eventually leaping from it to her death. However, stories that this act led a line of failed starlets to make their final exit from Tinseltown's best-known marker are untrue – though many troubled souls may have nearly died of exhaustion while trying to get to it. Less fatal mischief has been practiced by students of nearby Cal Tech, who on one occasion took to renaming the sign for their school.

that encircle it make for a relaxed stroll, especially for a glimpse of the stone bear heads that decorate the reservoir's curving front wall. If you take such a walk, you'll encounter surprisingly few tourists, despite the lake's appearance in a number of films.

You can only reach the lake by car. Although opening and closing times vary widely throughout the year, the **lake access road** is generally open from 7am until noon and 2pm until 7pm on weekdays, and 7am till 7.30pm on weekends: to get to it, go north on Cahuenga Boulevard past Franklin Avenue, turn right onto Dix Street and left to Holly Drive and climb up to Deep Dell Place; from there it's a sharp left on Weidlake Drive. Follow the winding little street to the main gate.

Near Cahuenga Boulevard, pristine **Whitley Heights** is a small pocket of Spanish Colonial architecture, worth a look for its well-maintained houses and great city views. The district, accessible from Milner Road off Highland Avenue, was laid out in 1918 by business tycoon **Hobart J. Whitley**, an Owens Valley water conspirator who engineered, and profited from, the sale of San Fernando Valley real estate (under his aptly named corporation, "Suburban Homes"). He was also known as the "Father of Hollywood," as his Whitley Heights soon became a movie-star subdivision for such silent-screen greats as Marie Dressler, Gloria Swanson, Rudolph Valentino and one-time "Ben Hur" Francis X. Bushman. Another of LA's Historic Preservation Overlay Zones, the area still offers a revealing look at an elegant, ungated "Old Hollywood" neighborhood – a far cry from modern celebrity enclaves like the well-guarded Malibu Colony.

The Hollywood Bowl and around

Just north of Whitley Heights, and west of the Hollywood Freeway, sits the renowned **Hollywood Bowl**, 2301 N Highland Ave (☎323/850-2000, Ⓦ www.hollywoodbowl.org), an open-air auditorium that opened in 1921 and has since gained more fame than it deserves. The Beatles played here in the mid-1960s, but the Bowl's principal function is as home to the Los Angeles Philharmonic, which gives evening concerts from July to September. These tend to be far less highbrow than you might imagine, both for the type of music played (typically pops fare, including film and cartoon scores) and for the picnics that tend to continue throughout the show, often rendering the music barely audible above the crunching of popcorn and the clink of empty wine bottles rolling down the steps. If that racket alone doesn't bother you, there's also the constant drone of jumbo jets flying above the Bowl on their long final descent toward LAX. Although not a choice spot for lovers of fine music, the venue can still be fun, with ticket prices starting at $1. If you're really broke, come to the Bowl during summer mornings (Tues, Thurs & Fri 9am–noon) and listen to rehearsals for free. (For details on summer concerts here, see "Performing arts and film," p.295.)

More about the Bowl's history can be gleaned from the video show inside the **Hollywood Bowl Museum** (summer Tues–Sat 10am–8pm, Sun 4.30–7.30pm; rest of year Tues–Sat 10am–4.30pm; free) near the entrance, not an essential stop by any means, but worth a visit if you have any affection for the old concrete structure. With a collection of musical instruments from around the world, the museum also features recordings of notable symphonic moments in the Bowl's history and architectural drawings by Lloyd Wright, Frank's son (more famous for his Wayfarer's Chapel; see p.164), who contributed a design for one of the Bowl's many shells.

One of the elder Wright's memorable 1920s residences, the **Freeman House**, is just south of the Bowl at 1962 Glencoe Way (tours Sat 2pm & 4pm; $10, students $5; ☎213/851-0671): a squat, Mayan-modern hybrid made of concrete "knit-blocks," which doesn't actually seem like much from the outside, but inside you'll get an outstanding panoramic view of Hollywood, and a close-up look at Wright's geometric decorations and motifs. Make sure to call before arriving, as the house has been closed for long periods of time for repair from earthquake damage and acid rain decay. Another early-1920s design, the **High Tower**, is notable for a different reason. Inaccessible to the public, though viewable at the end of High Tower Drive, the Italian-styled campanile is the literary home of Raymond Chandler's **Philip Marlowe** – and Elliott Gould, playing Marlowe, lived in a dumpy apartment at the tower's apex in Robert Altman's 1973 film *The Long Goodbye* (see p.372).

The western Hollywood Hills

When he was directing *Chinatown*, Roman Polanski spent many hours in Jack Nicholson's house on **Mulholland Drive**, and later remarked of LA, "[t]here's no more beautiful city in the world … provided it's seen at night and from a distance." With its striking panorama after dark of the illuminated city-grid, stretching nearly to the horizon, Mulholland easily justifies the director's wry comment.

From its starting point near the 101 freeway to its terminus at LA County's beachside boundary, the road travels twenty-one miles through winding mountain passes and steep canyons, and offers a stunning overview of the region's size and character. The stretch between the 101 and 405 freeways is the best, especially at night, when alternating views of brightly lit LA and the San Fernando Valley, to the north, keep drivers dangerously distracted. Although nighttime parking is forbidden, as well as hazardous, daytime views are best experienced at a **roadside park**, at 7320 Mulholland Drive just west of Hillside Drive. Here, telescopes allow you to peek at Hollywood, Downtown and the many palatial homes.

Further west lies the northern edge of **Runyon Canyon Park**, which actually improves on the views from Mulholland's crest. Park your car in the dirt near its chained gate and wander inside to a rocky outcrop that overlooks the city. Below, a path winds down to closer views of Hollywood until it eventually reaches the base of the hills themselves. Here, the foundation of a **ruined estate** offers a certain decrepit charm amid the high canyon walls and low foliage. If you have the stamina, take the long hike back up the hill to Mulholland, and keep a look out for B-list celebrities walking their dogs or burning off a few pounds for their next roles; otherwise, leave the park at Fuller Street (the only southern exit) and call a cab to take you back up to the top. Follow Mulholland west past the Woodrow Wilson Drive entrance to the elite subdivision of **Mount Olympus**, a residential exercise in 1950s vulgarity that is to Neoclassical architecture what a toga party is to ancient drama, with faux palazzos, pseudo-Roman statuary, goofy marble urns and snarling stone lions added pell-mell to charmless stucco boxes. Much more appealing is the **Chemosphere**, 776 Torreyson Drive, quirky architect John Lautner's giant UFO-like house, balanced on a huge Space Age pedestal and overlooking the San Fernando Valley to the north.

Other architectural treats can be found with sufficient effort as well, notably the stunning **Case Study House #21**, 9038 Wonderland Park Ave, Pierre Koenig's hillside glass-and-steel box, part of the influential Case Study Program (see box below). Unfortunately, most of the area's other houses are hidden away, and there's no real way to explore in depth without your own car, a copy of the latest *Thomas Guide* map and, if possible, a detailed and updated guide to LA architecture. If you're more interested in peeking at the homes of the stars, check out one of the many tours designed expressly for celebrity gazing (see "Mainstream tours," p.35), or look up a master list on the Internet (ⓦwww.seeing-stars.com is a good place to start). Notable movie-star houses include Rudolph Valentino's extravagant **Falcon Lair** (1436 Bella Drive) and Errol Flynn's **Mulholland House** (7740 Mulholland Drive).

Mulholland Drive continues past a series of enjoyable parks, including **Fryman Canyon Overlook**, a good place for a hike in the Santa Monica Mountains, and **Coldwater Canyon Park**.

The Case Study Program

Of all the popular architectural images to appear in the decades after World War II, perhaps none has been as recognized or influential as the one of two women reclining in their evening gowns inside a glass-enclosed home overlooking the illuminated grid of Los Angeles. The photograph was of Case Study House #22, at 1635 Woods Drive in the Hollywood Hills, one of the 36 **Case Study Houses** planned in the LA area in the two decades after the war.

Created by the editor of the influential *Arts and Architecture* magazine, **John Entenza**, the Case Study Program was designed to show how industrial materials like glass and steel could be used for elegant, affordably modern homes, using "open-floor" plans to eliminate dining rooms and unnecessary walls – all revolutionary concepts at the time. Surprisingly, for a program that showcased what were then rather avant-garde structures, it was quite popular locally; selected homes were displayed for the public, and nearly 400,000 visitors took a walk through the first six of these open houses. Especially influential in design circles, the low-cost houses used construction materials that were often donated for free by various building-supply companies, with a free plug in the magazine as an incentive. However, despite its LA popularity and great influence in international design, the program never really came close to its goal of converting the broader American public to the modern mindset, though it did create some pretty impressive works (check out Elizabeth A.T. Smith's *Blueprints for Modern Living* for more details; see "Books," p.381).

With designs chosen by Entenza and his staff at the magazine, the houses were numbered in the order they were planned, irrespective of when, or if, they were ever built (23 eventually were, all but two in LA). The eighth house in the series was its first masterpiece, Charles and Ray Eames' colorful 1949 steel-and-glass complex of 1949, the **Eames House and Studio**, a colorful modular construction on the bluffs of Pacific Palisades (see p.199). Eventually, many of the biggest names in LA architecture – Richard Neutra, Raphael Soriano, Gregory Ain, among 27 others – took a stab at the program, with Craig Ellwood's #16 house, 1811 Bel Air Rd – a rigid exercise in steel, glass and stone – and Neutra's wood-and-brick **Bailey House**, near the Eames House at 219 Chautauqua Blvd, among the finest examples. Unfortunately, for a program that was designed to have a great public impact, almost all these houses are now closed to the public, so a drive-by look will have to suffice if you're interested in seeing them. The only exception is the prominent Eames House, which offers lectures and seminars and, on occasion, even tours.

West Hollywood

Between La Brea Avenue and Beverly Hills, **WEST HOLLYWOOD** is the newest of LA's constituent cities. For many years the vice capital of LA, with prostitution, gambling and drugs all occupying prominent places on the debauched **Sunset Strip**, a whole criminal subculture flourished in the absence of effective law-enforcement and with the tacit approval of lethargic locals. The area was incorporated in 1984, a move meant partly to clean up the place and partly to represent the interests of the gay community, elderly residents and property renters. West Hollywood has since gone on to become one of the most dynamic parts of the region, especially notable for its freewheeling bars and clubs. However, this success has not entirely eliminated strife, and the new waves of Russian and Armenian immigrants making their homes near Santa Monica Boulevard have made for an uneasy mix with the city's long-standing constituents. Not surprisingly, West Hollywood is in many ways more

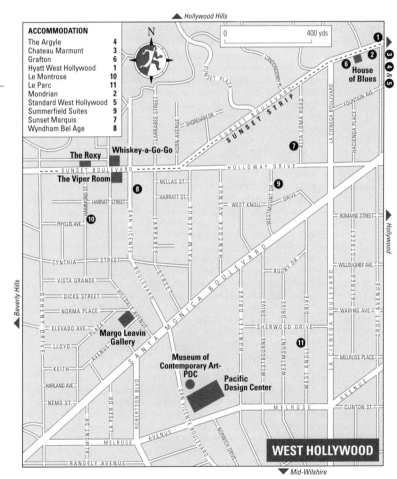

ACCOMMODATION

The Argyle	4
Chateau Marmont	3
Grafton	6
Hyatt West Hollywood	1
Le Montrose	10
Le Parc	11
Mondrian	2
Standard West Hollywood	5
Summerfield Suites	9
Sunset Marquis	7
Wyndham Bel Age	8

House of Blues

The Roxy
Whiskey-a-Go-Go
The Viper Room
Margo Leavin Gallery
Museum of Contemporary Art-PDC
Pacific Design Center

WEST HOLLYWOOD

akin to Hollywood, in its progressive character and attitudes, than it is to the prosaic wealth of Beverly Hills.

Except for the Sunset Strip – the well-known asphalt artery that features LA's best nightlife and billboards – West Hollywood's principal attractions lie west of **La Cienega Boulevard** around the colossal **Pacific Design Center**. The area to the east generally blends with the less inviting parts of lower Hollywood and has little appeal beyond a few clubs and restaurants.

The Sunset Strip

Sunset Boulevard from Crescent Heights Boulevard to Doheny Drive, long known as the **Sunset Strip**, is a roughly two-mile-long assortment of chic restaurants, plush hotels and swinging nightclubs. These establishments first appeared during the 1920s, along what was then a dirt road serving as the main route between the Hollywood movie studios and the early Westside "homes of the stars." F. Scott Fitzgerald and friends spent many leisurely afternoons over drinks here, around the swimming pool of the long-demolished *Garden of Allah* hotel, and the nearby *Ciro's* nightclub was *the* place to be seen in the 1940s, surviving today as the original *Comedy Store* (see p.300). With the demise of the studio system, the Strip declined, only reviving in the 1960s when a happening scene developed around the landmark *Whisky-a-Go-Go* club, which featured seminal rock bands such as Love and Buffalo Springfield. Since the incorporation of West Hollywood, the striptease clubs and "head shops" have been phased out and this fashionable area now rivals Beverly Hills for entertainment-industry executives per square foot.

Some tourists come to the strip just to see the enormous **billboards**, which take advantage of a very permissive, longstanding municipal policy that allows all kinds of gargantuan signs to pop up along the road. The ruddy-faced Marlboro Man is now gone, but there are many more along the strip to attract your eye: fantastic commercial murals animated with bright colors, movie ads with stars' names in massive letters, and self-promotions for mysterious actresses – note the amply bosomed "Angelyne" looming in Day-Glo splendor.

The Strip starts in earnest at the huge Norman castle of the **Chateau Marmont Hotel**, towering over the east end of Sunset Strip at no. 8221. Built in 1927 as luxury apartments, this stodgy block of concrete has long been a Hollywood favorite for its elegant private suites and bungalows (for review, see p.228). Howard Hughes used to rent the entire penthouse so he could keep an eye on the bathing beauties around the pool below, and the hotel made headlines in 1982 when comedian John Belushi died of a heroin overdose in the hotel bungalow that he used as his LA home. Across the street, the **House of Blues**, no. 8430, is a corrugated tin shack, with an imported dirt floor from the Deep South, that is one of the area's chief tourist attractions, although it pales in comparison with the more authentic scene found around the **Whisky-a-Go-Go**, no. 8901, and the **Roxy**, no. 9009, both famed for 1960s performers like Janis Joplin and The Doors. Although these clubs have flourished in recent decades with the emergence of punk and heavy metal, others have long since disappeared, like **Gazzarri's**, no. 9039, famous for hosting acts such as the Byrds, Van Halen and Guns N' Roses early on in their careers. Other spots, like the **Viper Room**, no. 8852, and the **Sunset Hyatt**, no. 8401, have also established their own notorious histories – Johnny Depp's trendy lair for rockers is the spot where River Phoenix overdosed, and the upscale hotel was the staging ground for the antics of The Who and Led Zeppelin – who took to racing motorcycles down its hallways.

La Cienega Boulevard

La Cienega Boulevard divides Hollywood roughly down the middle, separating the funky seediness to the east and West LA's snooty affluence to the west. The street holds a mixture of excellent hotels, clubs and restaurants, along with Cesar Pelli's **Pacific Design Center**, 8687 Melrose Ave, a hulking complex known as the "Blue Whale," loaded with interior design boutiques and furniture dealers. Completely out of scale to the low-scaled neighborhood around it, the entire Center is open to the public for viewing, but purchasing anything inside requires the assistance of a professional designer. Still, you're likely to be satisfied just snooping around, not so much in the octagonal **Center Green** – also called the "Green Apple," and largely vacant – but in **Center Blue**, a barn with a mix of showrooms and boutiques. Recently, the Center also added a branch of the **Museum of Contemporary Art** (Tues–Sun 11am–5pm, Thurs closes at 8pm; $3; ☏213/626-6222, Ⓦwww.moca.org/museum/moca_pdc.php), focusing on architecture and industrial and graphic design with a sleek, modern bent, and often part of multi-site exhibitions with the two Downtown branches (see pp.65 and 59).

Outside, a small **amphitheater** inset with stars honors architects and designers like Frank Gehry, Lawrence Halprin and Pelli himself, but the real highlight of the center is the annual spring unveiling of the **IdeaHouse**, where LA's collective status-craving is openly on display. Here, you'll find the residential lifestyle of the average, well-heeled Angeleno as the center imagines it: foyers with bronze paneling and marble-tiled floors, rec rooms with the latest high-tech electronic gizmos, kitchens stocked with expensive designer cookware and bedrooms with cashmere blankets.

Other architectural novelties exist on the surrounding streets, including the **Margo Leavin Gallery**, 817 N Hilldale Ave, notable for its striking facade: a giant Claes Oldenburg–designed knife cutting through the stucco. If you really have a taste for bizarre architecture, there's even more to be found on the streets around the area, which are home to any number of fancy designers, art galleries and trendy boutiques.

Back east of La Cienega Boulevard, the **Schindler House**, 835 N Kings Rd (Wed–Sun 11am–6pm, tours on the hour Sat & Sun 11.30am–2.30pm, and by appointment; $6), was for years the blueprint of California modernist architecture, with sliding canvas panels designed to be removed in summer, exposed roof rafters, and open-plan rooms facing onto outdoor terraces. Coming from his native Austria via Frank Lloyd Wright's studio to work on the Hollyhock House (see p.89), R.M. Schindler was so pleased with the California climate that he built this house without any bedrooms, romantically planning to sleep outdoors year-round in covered sleeping baskets on the roof. However, like other newcomers unfamiliar with the region's erratic climate, he misjudged the weather and soon moved inside. Now functioning as the **MAK Center for Art and Architecture**, the house plays host to a range of avant-garde music, art, film and design exhibitions, from the work of famous modernists like John Cage and Eric Owen Moss to lesser known photographers, artists and architects (program information at ☏323/651-1510, Ⓦwww.makcenter.com).

Beverly Hills and West LA

Although Downtown and Hollywood are richer in historic and cultural attractions, **BEVERLY HILLS** and **WEST LA** are where most tourists tend to spend most of their time. Along with neighboring West Hollywood, these areas boast the best hotels and restaurants, and relentlessly market themselves as the height of fashion – in this case little more than an ersatz European flair. Of course, with its diverse architecture and plentiful gardens, there's more to **Beverly Hills** than just the elite boutiques of Rodeo Drive, but for most visitors, the focal point lies within the three sides of the shopping zone known as the **Golden Triangle**. Above Beverly Hills, the canyon roads lead into the well-guarded enclaves of rich celebrities, while to the west, the bleak modern towers of **Century City** rise in the distance, with the district's main attraction being its large, eponymous mall.

As with the term "Westside," **West LA** has a somewhat amorphous definition, anything from a small neighborhood by the 405 freeway to everything west of Hollywood and Mid-Wilshire. Locals, however, recognize it as the area between Beverly Hills and Santa Monica, stretching south to the 10 freeway. One of West LA's main districts, **Westwood**, is somewhat unappealing along Wilshire Boulevard – in this part of town a sunless corridor of towering office blocks – but closer to **UCLA**, the area becomes pedestrian-friendly in the so-called "Village," and the university itself is full of resplendent buildings and peaceful gardens. To the west, along the **Sepulveda Pass**, the wooded wealth of **Bel Air** and **Brentwood** are split by the 405 freeway, which leads to the hilltop site of the **Getty Center**, a travertine icon of monumental proportions that many regard as LA's crown jewel, at least for its architecture. West LA's southern neighbor, **Culver City**, is far less conspicuous than other areas, even though it contains several movie studios and a trove of eye-catching deconstructivist buildings.

Beverly Hills

Without question, **BEVERLY HILLS** has become synonymous with images of suntanned Mercedes drivers, fur-clad poodle-walkers and outrageously priced consumer goods, illustrating how successful this city has been in marketing itself to the rest of the world – and in drawing visitors by the millions. Inevitably, this self-promotion doesn't quite match reality, but if you've come here to fawn over celebrities and press your nose against the display windows, you won't leave disappointed. Beverly Hills' sparkling image is also kept up in part by a formidable local police force – with more cops per capita than any other city in the world – that keeps the streets free of panhandlers. For the most part, the authorities won't bother tourists, though they have gained a nasty reputation for aggressive "racial profiling," questioning blacks and Hispanics on the basis of little or no evidence.

The heart of Beverly Hills is **Rodeo Drive**, which slices through Downtown with much pomp and circumstance. More picturesque sights are tucked away in the slopes and canyons north of Downtown, but even there you'll find gated-off mansions to match the area's super-exclusive stores.

The Academy and the Oscar

The **Academy of Motion Picture Arts and Sciences** was formed in 1927 by titans of the film industry such as Louis B. Mayer, Cecil B. DeMille, Mary Pickford and Douglas Fairbanks. Officially created to advance the cause of film-making, this organization was actually intended to combat trade-union expansion in Hollywood, which it tried to do, unsuccessfully, for ten years. After that, the Academy concentrated instead on standardizing the technical specifications of film-making – everything from streamlining script design to approving industry standards for sound and lighting. To expand its membership and appeal, the Academy began to include notable artists and craftworkers from most segments of the business and to promote its award show as an event of national significance.

This show was, of course, the **Academy Awards**, which began two years after the organization's creation and was designed to give the industry's stamp of approval to its own film product. Called the **Oscar**, an award with many dubious explanations for its name – everything from its being a forgotten acronym to the name of Academy librarian Margaret Herrick's uncle – the Academy's official blessing was a much sought-after honor even in its early years. From their infancy, however, the Oscars have generally recognized the best work produced by the **studio system**, not necessarily the best films overall, so as not to bite the hand that feeds it. This is why landmark works such as *Citizen Kane*, *Vertigo* and *Taxi Driver* have typically been ignored and event films like *The Greatest Show on Earth*, *Cavalcade* and *Out of Africa* have grabbed the accolades. Even in recent years, despite the renowned strength of independent studios (though most are subsidiaries of the majors), the top awards have gone to old-fashioned flicks like *Gladiator* and *A Beautiful Mind*, leaving the lower-budgeted films to clean up in "secondary" categories like screenwriting and cinematography.

The awards are not above the occasional upset, however. The appearance of a **streaker** during the 1974 show is the most notorious example, and actors Marlon Brando and George C. Scott publicly refused their awards in the early 1970s, with Scott describing the awards as a "meat parade." More recently, the awards ceremony has moved from its rotating residence at the Dorothy Chandler Pavilion and the Shrine Auditorium to a seemingly permanent home at the **Kodak Theater** inside the colossal Hollywood and Highland mall. Ironically, at a time when movie grosses seem to be breaking box-office records with each passing year, the TV ratings of the awards show itself have taken a nose-dive, and efforts to revamp the format and hasten the interminable ceremony have had little success.

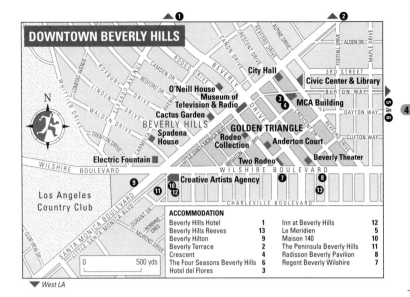

DOWNTOWN BEVERLY HILLS

City Hall
Civic Center & Library
O'Neill House
Museum of
Television & Radio
MCA Building
Cactus Garden
BEVERLY HILLS
Spadena
House
GOLDEN TRIANGLE
Rodeo
Collection
Anderton Court
Electric Fountain
Two Rodeo
Beverly Theater
Creative Artists Agency
Los Angeles
Country Club

ACCOMMODATION

Beverly Hills Hotel	1	Inn at Beverly Hills	12
Beverly Hills Reeves	13	Le Meridien	5
Beverly Hilton	9	Maison 140	10
Beverly Terrace	2	The Peninsula Beverly Hills	11
Crescent	4	Radisson Beverly Pavilion	8
The Four Seasons Beverly Hills	6	Regent Beverly Wilshire	7
Hotel del Flores	3		

0   500 yds

West LA

BEVERLY HILLS AND WEST LA | Beverly Hills

4

Wilshire Boulevard in Beverly Hills

From the east, a trip into Beverly Hills begins on **Wilshire Boulevard**, where you encounter the **Academy of Motion Picture Arts and Sciences (AMPAS)**, 8949 Wilshire Blvd, an unremarkable building that houses the headquarters of the organization that puts on the Oscars each year (see box). This film association also offers occasional public screenings in its excellent theater, along with regular exhibits in its **galleries** that showcase items from classic and contemporary American films, from scripts and storyboards to still photographs and animation cels (Tues–Fri 10am–5pm, Sat & Sun noon–6pm; free; ☎310/247-3000, ⓦwww.oscars.org). This stretch of Wilshire features other classic venues for movies, including the Zigzag Moderne **Wilshire Theater**, no. 8440, nowadays a home to traveling stage productions; the exuberant neon of the **Fine Arts Theater**, no. 8556, originally a theatrical stage built in 1936; and the once grand, now subdivided, **Music Hall Theater**, no. 9036.

Downtown Beverly Hills

Downtown Beverly Hills, successfully labeled the **Golden Triangle** by the city's PR department, is a ritzy wedge between Rexford Drive and Wilshire and Santa Monica boulevards, dotted with some of LA's top retailers, hotels and restaurants. Street parking is tough to come by in the area, though there are a few scattered public lots, the two best being those off Beverly Drive, north of Brighton Way and Dayton Way, respectively. Most people's chief reason for coming here is, of course, **Rodeo Drive**, which cuts right through a three-block area boasting the most exclusive names in international fashion. One store worth looking into is Ralph Lauren, 444 N Rodeo Drive, which caters to well-heeled WASPs who fancy themselves as canine-coddling English gentry. Besides the thousand-dollar suits and monogrammed Wellingtons, there are

113

exquisitely carved walking sticks, mounted game heads and an assortment of wooden and bronze dogs. At the foot of Rodeo Drive are LA's premier department stores, including Barney's, no. 9570, and Neiman-Marcus, no. 9700, which sell everything from $5 Swiss truffles to his'n'hers leopard skins. As yet, none of the stores charges for admission, though some do require an invitation. (For details on the various shops, see "Shopping," p.332.) Adjacent to Rodeo Drive and Wilshire Boulevard, **Two Rodeo**, the area's mock-European tourist route, is a rather unappealing consumer zone, where a cobblestoned street leads visitors into a curving shopping alley designed to resemble an Old World footpath, or at least a Disney version of one. Regardless, this "street" cannot escape its LA identity: the entire concourse is built on top of a multistory parking garage.

Just to the north of these snooty shops is Frank Lloyd Wright's decidedly unstodgy **Anderton Court**, 328 N Rodeo Drive, which resembles a boxy, miniature version of the Guggenheim museum crowned by a jagged horn, and is home to a few cramped retailers who must contend with Wright's awkward experiment in space and light. The attitude resumes at the **Rodeo Collection**, just up the street at no. 421, an uninspiring marbleized mall that nonetheless has much to interest upscale shoppers in its wide array of pretentious boutiques and high-end bauble merchants. For a complete overview of the shopping zone, including Rodeo Drive and beyond, take a trip on the **Beverly Hills Trolley** (summer & Dec daily noon–5pm; rest of year Sat noon–4pm; $5; ☎310/285-2438), which offers two worthwhile trips – a forty-minute glimpse of the town's highlights and a fifty-minute look at the city's art and architecture (Sat 11am only), both departing hourly from the corner of Rodeo and Dayton Way.

A few more interesting sights lie in and around Rodeo's elite commercial zone, most prominently the **Museum of Television and Radio**, 465 N Beverly Drive (Wed–Sun noon–5pm, Thurs until 9pm; $6, students $4; ☎310/786-1000, ⓦwww.mtr.org), which features a collection of more than 75,000 TV and radio programs, any of which you can watch or listen to. The museum, LA's first real attempt at providing a media museum of scholarly value, has a well-designed theater for public screenings of old and recent shows, including programs celebrating the golden age of 1950s TV and examining the role of the electronic media in reporting, and creating, the news. The building itself is immaculate white geometry from the leading practitioner of this style, Richard Meier – more famous for his Getty Center (see p.122) – whose other noteworthy Beverly Hills work is his spartan, garage-like **Gagosian Gallery**, just two blocks west at 456 N Camden Drive, where you're apt to see pricey contemporary painting and sculpture by the likes of Cindy Sherman, Eric Fischl, David Salle and Chris Burden.

A few blocks away at 360 Crescent Drive is the former **MCA Building**, architect Paul R. Williams' Georgian-style mansion with a central Florentine fountain and surrounding gardens – one of the few buildings in Beverly Hills that manages to convince you of its eighteenth-century heritage, despite being constructed in 1940. Another architectural triumph is the adjacent **Beverly Hills City Hall**, a 1932 concoction of Spanish Revival and Art Deco architecture that resembles a squat version of LA's City Hall, except for the ornate dome dripping with Baroque details and vivid colors. Within the complex, the new **Beverly Hills Municipal Art Gallery**, 450 N Crescent Drive (Mon–Fri 10am–4pm; free), occasionally offers programs of some interest, focusing on arts and crafts, furniture, antiques and photography. On Rexford Drive, the **Civic Center and Library** are built in Charles Moore's postmodern design with Art Deco elements, though remain much less appealing than City Hall.

Outside the triangle

Just west of the triangle is the **Electric Fountain**, created in 1930 by the Beverly Hills Women's Club, through the efforts of comedian Harold Lloyd's mother. Depicting the history of the West on a circular frieze running along its base, the fountain spews water from the hands of a nameless Native American sitting atop its central column, deep in a rain prayer.

Across from here, at the intersection of Wilshire and Santa Monica boulevards, sits the conspicuous headquarters of **Creative Artists Agency**, where powerbrokers, led by Mike Ovitz, made their company into one of the most feared institutions in town. With its white-marble curtain wall and curved glass, the I.M. Pei design befits the imperious mood of the company in the late 1980s, when it virtually ruled Hollywood and drove actors' salaries up into today's $20 million range.

Meanwhile, along Santa Monica Boulevard, the entire north side of the road in Beverly Hills is lined with a continuous strip of green known as **Beverly Gardens**. The most appealing stretch, between Camden and Bedford drives, is home to one of the largest municipal collections of cacti in the world, and a tranquil setting despite the abundance of prickly plants.

Further north is the residential side of Beverly Hills, with its winding, palm-lined streets and Mercedes-filled driveways. Although a number of lesser-known stars live on these streets, the real interest is the fanciful architecture. Without a doubt the most peculiar dwelling is the **Spadena House**, Carmelita Drive at Walden Avenue, whose sagging roof, gnarled windows and pointed wooden fence have earned it the nickname the "Witch's House." Built as the headquarters for a Culver City movie company in the early 1920s, the house was later moved to its present location. Another outlandish design, the **O'Neill House**, 507 N Rodeo Drive, looks like a melting birthday cake, with its undulating lines and lopsided shape.

The increasingly curvaceous roads head into the hills and become more upmarket, converging on the pink-plaster **Beverly Hills Hotel**, on Sunset and Rodeo (see "Accommodation," p.229), constructed in 1912 to attract wealthy settlers to what was then a town of just five hundred people. Much has changed in the intervening years, and the hotel's Mission style has been updated by a slew of renovations, though the core design of the building and its attendant gardens remain intact. Will Rogers, W.C. Fields and John Barrymore were but a few of the celebrities known to frequent the bar here, and the hotel's social cachet still makes its *Polo Lounge* a prime spot for movie execs to power-lunch.

The northern hills and canyons

Above the *Beverly Hills Hotel*, in the **northern hills and canyons**, a number of fairly well-concealed gardens and parks offer a respite from the shopping frenzy below. One such place, the wooded **Virginia Robinson Gardens**, 1008 Elden Way (tours Tues–Thurs 10am & 1pm, Fri 10am; $10, students $5; by appointment only at ☏310/276-5367), spreads across six acres of flora, with more than a thousand varieties, including some impressive Australian king palm trees. The land and the attached Mediterranean-style estate (not open to the public) were bequeathed to LA County by the heiress to the Robinson's department store chain. To the east, the grounds of the biggest house in Beverly Hills, **Greystone Mansion**, 905 Loma Vista Drive, are now maintained as a public **park** by the city (daily 10am–5pm; free), which uses it to disguise a massive underground reservoir. The fifty-thousand-square-foot manor was once the property of oil titan Edward Doheny, who was not only a huge figure in

4

The Beverly Hills oil baron

The 1920s were a busy time for millionaire oil magnate **Edward L. Doheny**. Not only did the former mining prospector build the mansion of his dreams, Greystone, at the end of the Beverly Hills street that would one day be named for him, but he was also granted the title of Knight of the Equestrian Order of the Holy Sepulchre in the Roman Catholic Church. Unfortunately, he was also involved in one of the biggest political scandals in US history.

Some three decades before, in 1892, Doheny and partner Charles Canfield struck black gold in the Temple-Beaudry district west of Downtown – a spot that quickly became the city's most lucrative terrain and which is now, ironically, one of its most desperate slums. But around 1909, petro-dollars made Doheny wealthy beyond all imagining, and he put some of his fortune into his elegant mansion in the Exposition Park district (which is still a marvel; see p.152) and invested even more into new wells throughout the city.

By 1921, the one-time miner was a formidable force in both the local and national economy, and he probably didn't need to offer a bribe to the newly installed Interior Secretary, **Albert Fall**, one of President Warren Harding's many corrupt subordinates, in exchange for preferential drilling leases in the Elk Hills region of Southern California. But he did just that, putting $100,000 in the secretary's wallet. Three years later, after Harding's untimely death, a national scandal was unearthed in Wyoming, where another bribery deal – this one engineered by oil titan Harry Sinclair – had been made over the lucrative **Teapot Dome** lease. Soon enough, the corrupt bargain for the Elk Hills property was uncovered, and Doheny was prosecuted. Over the next six years until 1930, the government tried to put him in prison, but two trials only resulted in acquittals on technicalities. Although the legal result was favorable for Doheny – though not for Fall, who served time – the damage was significant, and the scandal forever blackened his reputation. In a tragic coda to the story, Doheny's son, whom he had originally used to deliver Fall's bribe, died in a mysterious shooting in 1929.

LA history, but also a major player in the Teapot Dome scandal of the 1920s (see box). Although the house itself is rarely open (except for filming music videos and hosting political fundraisers), you can admire the limestone facade and intricately designed chimneys, then stroll through the sixteen-acre grounds, with their koi-filled fishponds, for excellent views of West LA.

Two miles northwest, **Franklin Canyon**, an isolated niche of the Santa Monica Mountains National Recreation Area, features two idyllic but fairly remote reservoirs and a ranch, and it routinely sees picnickers, joggers and even wedding parties. Although reaching the area may require a detailed LA map (or a visit to ⓦ ceres.ca.gov/smmc/franklin.htm), you can make the attempt by following Franklin Canyon Drive north into the parkland until you hit a fork in the road. The lake route, to the left, takes you to the upper reservoir, around which you can take a gentle walk amid ducks and old concrete abutments; the ranch route, to the right, leads to a series of hiking trails and a central lawn, popular with weekend vacationers throughout the year.

Further west, in the verdant canyons and foothills above Sunset Boulevard, a number of palatial estates lie hidden away behind security gates. **Benedict Canyon Drive** climbs from the *Beverly Hills Hotel* past many of them, including Harold Lloyd's 1928 **Green Acres**, 1040 Angelo Drive, where he lived for forty years. Although the secret passageways and a large private screening room are still intact (and off-limits to the public), the grounds, which once contained a waterfall and a nine-hole golf course, have since been broken up into smaller lots. Apart from the Period Revival houses that dominate the area, a smattering of other styles can be found off Benedict Canyon, best among them the **Anthony House**, 910 Bedford Drive, a terrific Craftsman work by Charles and Henry Greene designed for the head of Packard Automobiles. The house, with its rugged wooden frame and elegant garden, bears more than passing resemblance to the brothers' larger and better-known Gamble House in Pasadena (see p.183) – though this one isn't open to the public.

Century City

CENTURY CITY, along with Bunker Hill, is LA's most egregious example of building for the automobile, and one of its least pedestrian-friendly areas, overrun by giant boulevards and dominated by bland, boxy skyscrapers. It is, however, something of a landmark of West LA, its huge, triangular **Century Plaza Towers** visible from far across the Westside. Originally part of the 20th Century-Fox studio lot, Century City began taking shape in the early 1960s during the height of glass-and-steel corporate modernism and remains flash-frozen in that era. The only real reason to visit is the **Century City Shopping Center**, 10250 Santa Monica Blvd, a single-level, open-air mall loaded with pricey boutiques and department stores.

Perhaps due to its overall lack of charm, Century City has appeared in several Hollywood movies, most memorably in *Conquest of the Planet of the Apes* and in *Die Hard*, where Bruce Willis saved the day while holed up in the post-modern **Fox Plaza**, 2121 Avenue of the Stars. Just south at 10201 Pico Blvd, the current home of **20th Century-Fox** occupies much smaller digs than it used to, with much of its former 225 acres having been sold to make way for Century City. Now owned by Rupert Murdoch's News Corporation the company still has plenty of sound stages, offices and movie sets on the premises, but the public is kept firmly out.

Around Century City

East of Century City, below Beverly Hills, an unassuming building houses the **Simon Wiesenthal Center for Holocaust Studies**, 9786 Pico Blvd. The US headquarters of the organization dedicated to prosecuting former Nazis, the center has an extensive library of Holocaust-related documents and photographs. The main draw for visitors, however, is the affecting **Beit HaShoa Museum of Tolerance** (April–Oct Mon–Thurs 11.30am–6pm, Fri 11.30am–5pm, Sun 11am–7.30pm, Nov–March closes at 3pm on Fri; $9, students $5.50; ☏310/553-8403, ⓦ www.wiesenthal.com/mot), an extraordinary interactive resource center and the most technologically advanced institution of its kind, using videotaped interviews to provide LA's frankest examination of the 1992 riots, and leading the visitor through multimedia re-enactments outlining the rise of Nazism to a harrowing conclusion in a replica gas chamber. Equally unsettling is the **Museum of the Holocaust**, several miles to the east at 6006 Wilshire Blvd (Mon–Thurs 10am–5pm, Fri 10am–2pm, Sun noon–4pm; free), which recounts the history of anti-Semitism and serves as a memorial to those who died in the Holocaust, as well as an affecting presentation of survivors' thoughts and memories. Look for the intricate model of the Sobibor death camp, created by one of its survivors.

Apart from the **Westside Pavilion**, another of LA's multilevel shopping mall complexes west at Pico and Westwood boulevards, the area's only other sight of note is the colossal **Mormon Temple**, located on a hilltop some blocks to the north at 10777 Santa Monica Blvd. Visible throughout the mostly flat Westside, the local headquarters of the church is easily recognized by its 257-foot tower crowned by the angel Moroni. Although the main part of the building isn't open to non-Mormons, you can enter the **visitors' center** (daily 9am–9pm; free), and get a glimpse of a 12ft marble sculpture of Jesus.

Westwood and the UCLA campus

Just west of Beverly Hills and Century City along Wilshire Boulevard, **WEST-WOOD** is split into two main sections: the pleasantly low-rise neighborhood known as **Westwood Village**, crowded with students, shoppers and theater-goers, and the adjacent traffic corridor loaded with some of LA's tallest buildings. In earlier days, nearly all of Westwood resembled the Village, but during the 1970s and 1980s, the zone around Wilshire exploded with high-rises, where penthouse condos with private heliports sold for upwards of $12 million. Even now, after the boom has faded somewhat, the intersection of Wilshire and Westwood boulevards continues to be choked with overflowing traffic, with some of LA's longest waits for a green light.

At this corner, the **UCLA Hammer Museum**, 10899 Wilshire Blvd (Tues, Wed, Fri & Sat 11am–7pm, Thurs 11am–9pm, Sun 11am–5pm; $4.50, students $3, Thurs 6–9pm free; ☎310/443-7000, ⓦwww.hammer.ucla.edu) comprises a sizeable art stash amassed over seven decades by the flamboyant and ultra-wealthy boss of the Occidental Petroleum Corporation, Armand Hammer. Art critic Robert Hughes may have called the paintings here "a mishmash of second or third-rate works by famous names," but though the Rembrandts and Rubenses may be less than stunning, the nineteenth-century pieces like Van Gogh's intense and radiant *Hospital at Saint Remy* more than make amends, as do some American works, such as a Gilbert Stuart regal portrait of George Washington; Thomas Eakins' painting of *Sebastiano Cardinal Martinelli*, depicted with blunt, penetrating realism; and John Singer Sargent's *Dr Pozzi at Home*, another of the artist's skilled character studies. Now co-curated by the university, the museum has recently shifted gears to present more contemporary, avant-garde and multicultural exhibits.

Less well-known are the museum's occasional exhibitions drawn from the marvelous **Grunwald Center for the Graphic Arts**, which has some 35,000 drawings, photographs and prints from the Renaissance on, with some exceptional Expressionist works by Emil Nolde and Käthe Kollwitz, Impressionist etchings from Paul Cezanne, and more current drawings and prints by Jasper Johns.

Across from the museum, at the end of the driveway behind the Avco cinema, you'll find Armand Hammer's speckled marble tomb, sharing the tiny cemetery of **Westwood Memorial Park** with the likes of movie stars Peter Lorre and Natalie Wood, wildman jazz drummer Buddy Rich, and the alleged (unmarked) graves of Roy Orbison and Frank Zappa. To the left of the entrance in the far northeast corner, a lipstick-covered plaque marks the resting place of **Marilyn Monroe**. You can also spot some of these stars on the radiant mural inside the **Crest Theater**, 1262 Westwood Blvd, notable as well for its brash neon marquee.

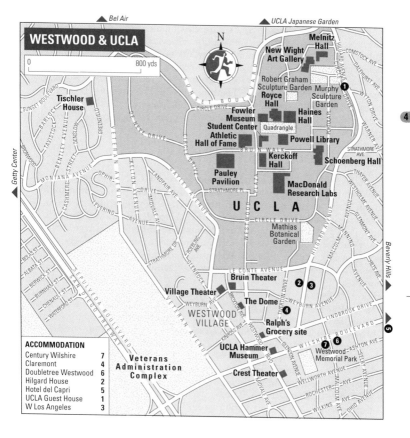

WESTWOOD & UCLA

0   800 yds

N

▲ Bel Air   ▲ UCLA Japanese Garden

Melnitz Hall

New Wight Art Gallery

Robert Graham Sculpture Garden

Royce Hall

Murphy Sculpture Garden

Tischler House

Fowler Museum

Haines Hall

Student Center

Quadrangle

Athletic Hall of Fame

Powell Library

Kerckoff Hall

Schoenberg Hall

Pauley Pavilion

MacDonald Research Labs

U C L A

Mathias Botanical Garden

Bruin Theater

Village Theater

The Dome

WESTWOOD VILLAGE

Ralph's Grocery site

UCLA Hammer Museum

Westwood-Memorial Park

Veterans Administration Complex

Crest Theater

Getty Center ▲

Beverly Hills ▶

ACCOMMODATION

Century Wilshire	7
Claremont	4
Doubletree Westwood	6
Hilgard House	2
Hotel del Capri	5
UCLA Guest House	1
W Los Angeles	3

Westwood Village

North of Wilshire Boulevard, **Westwood Village** is one of LA's more walkable neighborhoods, a cluster of low-slung brick buildings that went up in the late 1920s, along with the campus of UCLA, which had just relocated from its East Hollywood location. Much of the original Spanish Colonial Revival design has survived the intervening years, though most of the neighborhood businesses have been replaced by fancy boutiques and fast-food joints. It's an area that's easily explored on foot – street **parking** is nightmarish, so if you're driving, leave your car at one of the parking lots before beginning your wanderings.

Broxton Avenue, the Village's main strip, is crowded with record stores, moviehouses and diners, but its focal point is the great Zigzag spire atop the 1931 **Fox Westwood Village** at 961 Broxton Ave, which, together with the neon-signed **Bruin** across the street, showcases impressive Moderne designs. Both are sometimes used by movie studios for flashy movie premieres as well as sneak previews for test audiences. Another familiar Westwood image is **The Dome**, 1099 Westwood Blvd, now an upscale pan-Asian restaurant but formerly the offices of the Janss Investment Corporation, which created the surrounding Westwood real-estate development and many other districts. Nowhere is its design signature more evident than at the one-time **Ralph's Grocery Store**, 1150 Westwood Blvd, a Spanish Romanesque design with a red-tile roof and cylindrical corner tower that's now a Mexican restaurant. Among several historic structures west of UCLA, the best is R.M. Schindler's private **Tischler House**, 175 Greenfield Ave, which resembles a highly abstract boat: thick white rectangles jut out from the house's base, while the wooden-gabled living space on top recalls a ship's upper deck.

UCLA

The University of California at Los Angeles, or **UCLA**, is one of the country's most prominent academic and athletic institutions, and the dominant feature in Westwood, a group of lovely Romanesque buildings spread generously over well-landscaped grounds. It's worth a wander if you've time to kill, particularly for a couple of good exhibition spaces. The Student Union building, at the north end of Westwood Boulevard, half a mile north of Westwood, has a bowling alley, a good bookstore and a "rideboard" offering shared-expense car rides, and there's also a decent coffeehouse in Kerckhoff Hall, just behind.

Before embarking on your journey around UCLA, be sure to pick up a **map** at any of the various information kiosks scattered around the campus. A good place to start is at the **Mathias Botanical Garden**, 405 Hilgard Ave (daily 8am–4pm, summer Mon–Fri closes at 5pm; free; tour information at T310/206-6707, W www.botgard.ucla.edu), a bucolic glade on the east side of the university where you can pick your way along sloping paths through the redwoods and fern groves, past small waterfalls splashing into lily-covered ponds. Just north is the central **quadrangle**, a greenspace bordered by UCLA's most graceful buildings, where you'll find students throwing frisbees, eating lunch or just lolling around on the grass. The most visually appealing structures here include **Royce Hall**, modeled on Milan's Church of St Ambrosio, with high bell-towers, rib vaulting and grand archways; and the **Powell Library** (Mon–Sat 9am–5pm, Sun 1–5pm), featuring a spellbinding interior with lovely Romanesque arches, columns and stairwell, and an array of medieval ornaments. The highlight is the dome above the **reading room**, where Renaissance printers' marks are inscribed, among them icons representing pioneering publishers the likes of Johann Fust and William Caxton. (Ask at the reference desk for a guide to the art and architecture of the library.) Further south, one of UCLA's best contemporary structures, Robert Venturi's **MacDonald Research Labs**, is well worth seeking out for its postmodern take on the greatest hits of classical architecture.

Further north, the **Fowler Museum of Cultural History**, Bruin Walk at Westwood Plaza (Wed–Sun noon–5pm, Thurs open until 8pm; $5, free to kids and any students; T310/825-4361, W www.fmch.ucla.edu), exhibits an immense range of multicultural art – including ceramics, religious icons, paintings and musical instruments – with some political works thrown in for good measure. The museum's highlights include an intriguing selection of native masks from around the world, more than ten thousand textile pieces from different cultures, and an extensive collection of African and Polynesian art and various folk designs – including an arresting display of pre-Columbian headdresses that hint at the color and variety of the art of the Americas before

Cortés and Pizarro arrived. Not far away, in the center of campus near Rolfe Hall, the **Robert Graham Sculpture Garden** is a courtyard collection featuring the sculptor's array of miniature figures, many of them female nudes, with austere gazes and explicit anatomies posed on top of cylindrical pedestals.

To the northeast, the **Franklin Murphy Sculpture Garden** is LA's best outdoor display of modern sculpture, named for the UCLA chancellor during the 1960s who helped develop the LA County Museum of Art, and including pieces by such big names as Jean Arp, Henry Moore, Barbara Hepworth, Henri Matisse, Jacques Lipchitz and Isamu Noguchi. Other notable works include Auguste Rodin's *Walking Man*, a stark nude composed of only a torso and legs; Gaston Lachaise's Amazonian *Standing Woman*, a proud, if grotesque, 1932 sculpture; and George Tsutakawa's *OBOS-69*, a fountain resembling a stack of TV sets. Among the finest pieces are Joan Miró's amorphously birdlike *Mere Ubu*, north of the main lawn of the garden in its own space, and David Smith's *Cubi XX*, a striking collection of burnished steel boxes and columns; one of the few contemporary sculptures is Deborah Butterfield's *Pensive*, tree branches arranged in the shape of a horse. If you really like the pieces on display here, you can take an informative free tour of the garden as well (reserve at ☏310/443-7041).

Just north of the Murphy Garden, the **New Wight Art Gallery** (Mon–Fri 9am–4.30pm; free), part of the Eli Broad Art Center, has a less intriguing collection of contemporary art on display, but does house the **Center for Digital Arts**, which occasionally shows interesting multimedia works to the public. East of the Wight Gallery, in **Melnitz Hall**, UCLA's **film school** has produced offbeat film-makers like Francis Ford Coppola, Alison Anders and Alex Cox. Here, you'll also find the massive storehouse of the **UCLA Film and Television Archive**, a treasure trove of media that holds classic, foreign and art movies, and a wide range of old TV shows, state journalism footage, and even an assortment of Hearst newsreels from the turn of the twentieth century. The premises are open for research or simply viewing by making an appointment at 46 Powell Library, or by calling ☏310/206-5388 (hours Mon–Fri 9am–5pm). Melnitz Hall also presents regular screenings of new and old films in its **James Bridges Theater** (☏310/206-FILM, ⊛www.cinema.ucla.edu).

UCLA is also well known for its athletic prowess, winning more college basketball championships – eleven – than any other team in history. Some of this history is on display at the **Athletic Hall of Fame** (Mon–Fri 8am–5pm; free) near the center of campus, where you can check out the school's numerous awards in basketball, football and volleyball, among other sports. UCLA's basketball team plays just west of here, at **Pauley Pavilion**, along with its volleyball and gymnastics squads, while the football team has its home field at the Rose Bowl (see p.184).

For a more contemplative experience, travel just north of the UCLA campus to the **UCLA Hannah Carter Japanese Garden**, 10619 Bellagio Rd (Tues, Wed & Fri 10am–3pm; free; by appointment only at ☏310/825-4574 or ⊛www.japanesegarden.ucla.edu), a rather idyllic spot featuring magnolias and Japanese maples, and traditional structures and river rocks brought directly from Japan – though four hundred tons of dark-brown rocks were also hauled in from Ventura County to lend the right aesthetic touch. Adding to the calming Zen feel are a pagoda, teahouse, quaint bridges, and assorted gold and stone Buddhas.

Bel Air, Brentwood and the Getty Center

The gap through the Santa Monica Mountains known as the **Sepulveda Pass** runs alongside some of LA's most exclusive residential neighborhoods, as well as the **Getty Center**, and often gives tourists their first views of central LA as they travel south on the 405 freeway into town. The pass was, like the eponymous boulevard and district, named for Mexican soldier **Francisco Sepúlveda**, whose family controlled over fifty thousand acres of land in the LA region, and who gained ownership in 1839 of the Rancho San Vicente y Santa Monica, which once encompassed the surrounding area. The former rancho contains both the freeway and part of Sepulveda Boulevard – the longest road in LA County, leading from Long Beach into the north San Fernando Valley.

BEL AIR, just northwest of UCLA and east of the 405 freeway, is an elite subdivision – home to just under eight thousand swells – with opulent black gates fronting Sunset Boulevard and security guards driving about to catch loiterers and interlopers. Despite the area's famous name and reputation, very little goes on here, as the only business is the well-known, luxurious **Bel Air Hotel** and the residential architecture is near-impossible to see, typically hidden behind thick foliage.

For a closer look at the well-heeled, **BRENTWOOD** to the west is a much better bet. Known for its most famous resident, O.J. Simpson (his Tudor mansion has since been razed), Brentwood also has an upscale shopping strip along San Vicente Boulevard, with all the standard boutiques and restaurants. The neighborhood also contains several residences of architectural interest, such as Frank Gehry's **Schnabel House**, 526 N Carmelina Ave, a chunky collection of metal cubes connected to an incongruous Moorish dome, partially visible from the sidewalk; Eric Owen Moss's striking **Lawson–Westen House**, with its jagged gray facade, tilted windows and truly odd sense of proportion; and Frank Lloyd Wright's **Sturges House**, 449 Skyieway Rd, looking like a giant wooden shingle cantilevered off a hillside and hovering over the street below it, one of Wright's few LA experiments in contemporary, rather than pre-Columbian, housing design.

Back along Sepulveda Boulevard, near the crest of the Santa Monica Mountains, the **Skirball Cultural Center**, 2701 N Sepulveda Blvd (Tues–Sat noon–5pm, Sun 11am–5pm; $8, students $6), devotes its attention to the history, beliefs and rituals of Judaism. Concentrating on the more mystical elements of the faith, the fairly absorbing center hosts a range of exhibitions and lectures designed to illuminate the American Jewish experience, offering a broad overview of Judaic and popular history and culture, from Hanukkah lamps to a Holy Ark from a German synagogue to cels from the animated Exodus film, *The Prince of Egypt*. The center also looks at the American diaspora in stark photographs of c.1900 immigrants and written mementos of their arduous travel and assimilation, and among assorted other artifacts are an early copy of the Declaration of Independence and one of Abe Lincoln's stovepipe hats.

The Getty Center

Off Sepulveda and west of the 405 freeway, Getty Center Drive leads up to the monumental **Getty Center** (daily 10am–6pm, Sat & Sun closes at 9pm; free, parking $5; ⊕310/440-7300, ⓦ www.getty.edu), a gleaming 110-acre museum and research complex towering over the city, built over fifteen years at a cost of $1 billion to hold the vast art holdings of oil mogul J. Paul Getty. The Center's architect, Richard Meier, originally planned for the whole complex to be wrapped in white metallic panels – his signature style – but protests from the Brentwood neighbors over sun glare forced him to redesign part of the Center in travertine.

Getty started building his massive collection in the 1930s, storing much of it in his own house until the first museum opened in 1974 on an ocean bluff near Malibu. The site, which has been closed for years, is reopening as a showcase for the foundation's antiquities in 2004 (see p.201), while the museum itself has moved to the grounds of the Center, which also includes facilities for art research, conservation and acquisition, though none of these are open to the public. The museum itself provides more than enough interest to fill a day. Reservations for parking are required only on weekdays (call ⊕310/440-7300). For some, arriving by cab or bus (the #561 line, which you can pick up at LAX), provides a simpler alternative.

The Getty Museum

A good place to begin exploring the **Getty Museum** is outside in its **Central Garden**, a concentric array of leafy terraces designed by conceptual sculptor Robert Irwin. Occupying the middle ground of the complex, the garden is a stunning arrangement leading crowds along sloping paths through azaleas, bougainvilleas and other plants and flowers, while Meier's austere geometric pavilions loom imperiously in the background. More in the style of Meier, perhaps, is another dramatic piece of nature found on the south end of the complex – the **Desert Garden**, a low-scaled assortment of hardy plants that sits in tight, circular confinement above a precipice of the Santa Monica Mountains.

The museum itself consists of five two-story structures that are landscaped around open plazas and shallow fountains, with the collection spread throughout the buildings. No matter where you start, you'll find the artworks still heavily influenced by Getty's tastes, long after the oil baron's death. One of his greatest enthusiasms was his formidable array of ornate **furniture** and **decorative arts**, with clocks, chandeliers, tapestries and gilt-edged commodes, designed for the French nobility from the reign of Louis XIV, filling several overwhelmingly opulent rooms. These are all fascinating, perhaps more so to design historians, but it's the museum's paintings, sculpture and photographs that will really overwhelm you.

Painting

In **painting**, European art is principally represented from the post-Renaissance era, but there are a few notable exceptions, among them Andrea Mantegna's stoic *Adoration of the Magi*, Correggio's *Head of Christ*, an affecting portrait that rivals Rembrandt for the quality of the subject's emotional expression, and Titian's well-known *Venus and Adonis*, depicting in muted colors the last moments between the lovers before Adonis is gored by a wild boar. Notable **Mannerist** works include Pontormo's *Portrait of a Halberdier*, in which the subject's expression has been variously interpreted as arrogant, morose or contemplative, and Veronese's richly detailed *Portrait of a Man*, perhaps of the painter himself – a sword-bearing nobleman gazing proudly down at the viewer.

The finest works from the seventeenth century are **Flemish** and **Dutch**. Among the highlights are Rubens' *Entombment*, a pictorial essay supporting the

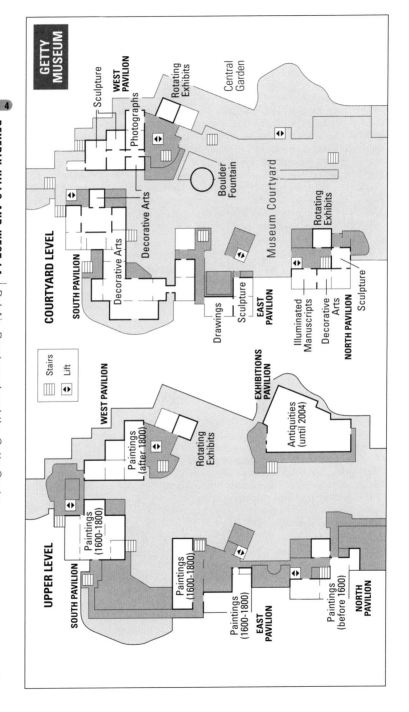

GETTY MUSEUM

COURTYARD LEVEL

Sculpture

WEST PAVILION

Rotating Exhibits

Photographs

Central Garden

Boulder Fountain

Decorative Arts

Decorative Arts

SOUTH PAVILION

Museum Courtyard

Drawings

Sculpture

EAST PAVILION

Sculpture

Rotating Exhibits

Illuminated Manuscripts

Decorative Arts

NORTH PAVILION

Sculpture

Stairs

Lift

UPPER LEVEL

WEST PAVILION

Paintings (after 1800)

Rotating Exhibits

Paintings (1600-1800)

SOUTH PAVILION

Paintings (1600-1800)

Paintings (1600-1800)

EAST PAVILION

EXHIBITIONS PAVILION

Antiquities (until 2004)

Paintings (before 1600)

NORTH PAVILION

Catholic doctrine of transubstantiation, Hendrik ter Brugghen's *Bacchante with an Ape*, showing a drunken libertine clutching a handful of grapes, an action mirrored by his pet monkey, and a trio of Rembrandts that emphasize the artist's interest in character and composition: *Daniel and Cyrus before the Idol Bel*, in which the Persian king tries foolishly to feed the bronze statue he worships; *An Old Man in Military Costume*, the exhausted, uncertain face of an old soldier; and the great portrait of *Saint Bartholomew*, wherein the martyred saint is shown to be a quiet, thoughtful Dutchman – the knife that will soon kill him barely visible in the corner of the frame.

While some lesser French Neoclassical works are included, notably David's overly slick and unaffecting *Farewell of Telemachus and Eucharis*, the best work from the general period is Gericault's later *Portrait Study*, a sensitive portrait of an African man – one of many that the artist created. The Getty Center is also known for bidding on **Impressionist works**; as such, these acquisitions read like a laundry list of late nineteenth-century French art: a portrait of *Albert Cahen d'Anvers* by Renoir, the inevitable Monet haystacks and one of Degas' ballet dancers. Van Gogh's *Irises* was the object of a bruising 1980s bidding war, in which an Australian financier beat out other competitors (at a price of more than $50 million), but later defaulted on his payments; the painting languished in legal limbo before the Getty Trust snatched it up for an unknown price.

Other significant works from the nineteenth century include *Bullfight* by Goya, in which the bull stares triumphantly at a group of unsuccessful matadors; J.M.W. Turner's frenzied *Ships a Sea, Getting a Good Wetting*, all hazy colors and soft lines that look surprisingly modern and abstract; and Caspar David Friedrich's elegant and understated *A Walk at Dusk*, a Romantic painting of a lone man bowing before a stone cairn during twilight. Not surprisingly, the museum's overall painting collection continues to expand, with the Getty Trust acquiring works by such figures as Cézanne, Poussin and Tiepolo.

Drawings and manuscripts

The museum also boasts a wide collection of **drawings**, though the permanent stash is never shown in full. Among the best are Albrecht Dürer's meticulous *Study of the Good Thief*, a portrait of the crucified criminal who was converted on the cross; his *Stag Beetle*, precise enough to look as if the bug were crawling on the page itself; Piranesi's dramatic image of a ruined, but still monumental, *Ancient Port*; and William Blake's bizarre watercolor of *Satan Exalting over Eve*, an expressionless devil hovering over his prone captive.

Also fascinating is the museum's excellent collection of medieval **illuminated manuscripts**, depicting Biblical scenes such as the Passion cycle, as well as notable saints. Exquisitely drawn letters introduce chapters from Scripture and maintain their radiance to this day. One of the most interesting volumes is the *Apocalypse with Commentary by Berengaudus*, an English Gothic tome that shows the Book of Revelation in all its fiery detail, including an image of the Four Horsemen of the Apocalypse looking more like medieval knights.

Sculpture, photography and other arts

As for **sculpture**, the best, or at least the most memorable, are Benvenuto Cellini's *Hercules Pendant*, a small, finely rendered piece of jewelry that shows the ancient hero in shock, mouth agape; Antonio Canova's gracefully Neoclassical rendering of the god *Apollo*; and Gian Lorenzo Bernini's much smaller *Boy with a Dragon* – done when he was only sixteen – depicting a plump toddler bending back the jaw of a dragon with surprising ease, either a playful putto or Jesus himself, depending on the interpretation.

Finally, some of the Getty's **photographs** include renowned works by Stieglitz, Strand, Weston, Adams, Arbus and others, but again, it's the museum's less familiar works that are the most intriguing: an 1849 *Portrait of Edgar Allan Poe*, by an unknown photographer, has the writer staring at the camera with manic intensity; Thomas Eakins' photo study *Students at the Site for "The Swimming Hole"*, which the painter used as a dry run for his famous painting, showing his pupils jumping naked from a flat rock into a muddy pond; Civil War photographer Timothy O'Sullivan's seemingly doomed wagon train grinding on through the *Desert Sand Hills*; and August Sander's feral *Frau Peter Abelen*, an androgynous woman with slicked-back hair, white culottes, business shirt and tie, holding an unlit cigarette between gritted teeth.

Beyond all this, the museum hosts periodic **exhibitions** of classical and modern work, everything from medieval tapestries and religious icons to old-fashioned lithographs and avant-garde photography. Unlike most of the Getty's permanent collection, the rotating exhibits are the places to see more contemporary pieces in a variety of media, with an acclaimed 2003 show by video-art pioneer Bill Viola offering hope that the museum may do more to shore up its spotty selection of modern art.

Culver City

Several miles south of Beverly Hills and Westwood, triangular **CULVER CITY** is one of the Westside's lesser-known gems, its past rich with movie lore and its current face shaped by groundbreaking architectural experiments. An extensive facelift in the last decade has resulted in more parks and footpaths, streets lined with historic lampposts and jacaranda trees, and fewer drab streets and buildings. Although wedged between unappealing Venice Boulevard and the 405 freeway, it's one of LA's most ethnically diverse cities, with a harmonious mix of whites, blacks, Hispanics and Asians.

The most impressive Culver City building is probably the **Ivy Substation**, at Culver and Venice boulevards, a 1907 power station for the old Red Car public transit line. Located in a palm tree-filled park, the Mission Revival building has been reborn as a 99-seat performing arts venue, though one that's irregularly open. Other major structures can be found nearby, including the **Helms Bakery**, 8800 Venice Blvd, a WPA landmark that is now home to local furniture dealers and craft shops, as well as the *Jazz Bakery* (a music venue reviewed on p.292). To the west, the **Culver Theater**, Washington Boulevard at Duquesne Avenue, is a striking 1947 moviehouse and occasional filming location (mostly for its streamlined marquee) that will re-emerge as the Kirk Douglas Theater in 2004.

Without a doubt, Culver City's most significant historic structures are its movie studios, many of which still function, though in different guises. The man responsible for creating the two greatest studio complexes was **Thomas Ince**, a film pioneer and producer who was a major film-industry figure until he was mysteriously killed on William Randolph Hearst's yacht (an event chronicled in the Peter Bogdanovich film, *The Cat's Meow*). Fans of *Gone with the Wind* may recognize the producer's former Ince Studios at 9336 Washington Blvd – predictably, this Colonial Revival "mansion" is no more than a facade.

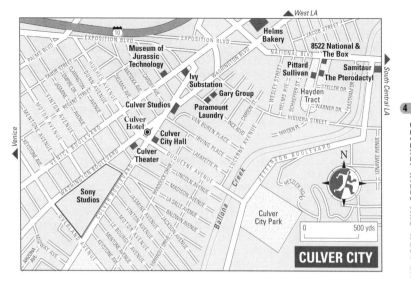

Eric Owen Moss and the Hayden Tract

Most small towns, even in LA, are known for their conservatism in design and attitude. Culver City is a major exception. With architect/artist **Eric Owen Moss**, this
city has not only welcomed his bizarre buildings, it has also helped subsidize the
business sites for many of his clients and prominently advertised his groundbreaking work. The **Hayden Tract**, one such city-subsidized business strip, has
excellent examples of contemporary architecture ranging from austere modernism
to cockeyed deconstructivism. Here, you can find a whole series of Moss's
designs, including the 1997 **Pittard Sullivan** building, 3535 Hayden Ave, a giant
gray box with massive wooden ribs poking out of its sides, not unlike flying but-
tresses. Thanks to its architect, the company even got around a Culver City building code – that one percent of any structure's budget must be used for public art
– when the building itself was declared art. Nearby, **8522 National**, also known as
the IRS Building (1990), featuring a jangled-up facade with a white staircase leading to nowhere. Adjacent to this is **The Box**, one of the works that first brought
Moss national recognition in 1994. This time, the familiar gray box, with a cubic
window riveted to one of its corners, looks ready to come off its hinges and tumble down onto the street below. One of the best Moss works in the Tract is the
1995 **Samitaur** building, 3457 S La Cienega Ave, massive, gray warehouse-like
offices with skewed lines, sharp points and a freakish sense of proportion. His
most recent marvel, **The Pterodactyl**, unfortunately lies hidden in a private parking lot.

A pocket of his earlier works, from 1987 to 1989, sits near Ince Boulevard and
Lindblade Street. The **Gary Group** building offers a fragmented white-and-red
sign with – again – a ladder leading to nowhere, while the side of the structure is
a concrete wall ornamented with jutting brick cubes and an array of metal chains.
The adjoining **Paramount Laundry** is no more conventional: a series of fat red
columns supports a metal awning, with one column sitting several feet out of
place.

Ince's later, bigger creation was **Triangle Pictures**, 10202 Washington Blvd, which he helped build with the financial aid of Harry Culver, a journalist and realtor who founded the city specifically for the movie business. The studio lot was the home of MGM during the Golden Years, and although the Triangle's original colonnade still sits along the boulevard, it's now part of the off-limits Sony lot.

A few blocks east, on a triangle of land formed by Duquesne Avenue and Culver and Washington boulevards, the early twentieth-century **Culver Hotel** has been restored to its original splendor, replete with checkered marble floor-ing, red-and-black interior and intricate iron railings. Plenty of Hollywood his-tory took place inside the hotel, which started as Harry Culver's office space and later became a place to stay for stars like Greta Garbo and Clark Gable. Not far away, **City Hall**, 9770 Culver Blvd, is notable for its huge detached facade – a re-creation of the entryway to the previous City Hall. Between the facade's freestanding archway and the actual building, you'll find a pleasant park with a peek-through movie camera detailing the city's film history. For more eye-catching architecture, head a mile east to the **Hayden Tract**, a stretch of Hayden Avenue that, apart from being a city business district, is also one of LA's most fertile spots for wild modern designs (see box overleaf).

If movie history and weird architecture aren't enough for you, top off your trip with a visit to the always bizarre **Museum of Jurassic Technology**, 9341 Venice Blvd (Thurs 2–8pm, Fri–Sun noon–6pm; $4; ⊕310/836-6131, ⓦwww.mjt.org), on the northern edge of Culver City. As much an art museum as a science center, this institution has little to do with distant histo-ry or roving dinosaurs. Rather, it features a great range of oddities from the pseudo-scientific to the paranormal to the just plain creepy, including trailer-park artworks, showing junk collections next to tiny model RVs and mobile homes about to be swallowed up by the earth; exhibitions of folk superstitions – most memorably the image of dead mice on toast used as a cure for bed-wetting; narrative rants by crank scientists; and displays of otherworldly insects, like an Amazonian bug that kills its prey using its giant head-spike. The ulti-mate effect is quite unnerving, as these vivid exhibits are shown in dark rooms without windows or sunlight. However, if you assume the museum is merely the work of a local crank, consider that its creator David Wilson was the win-ner of a MacArthur "Genius" Award in 2001, due largely to his enterprising work for this quirky institution.

5

Santa Monica and Venice

The epitome of Southern California's sun-and-surf culture, the adjacent beach cities of **SANTA MONICA** and **VENICE** represent two different sides of LA: Santa Monica, the trendy, well-heeled liberal enclave with its chic galleries, shops and coffeehouses; and Venice, the offbeat, anarchic focus of dive bars, junk emporia and fringe galleries. Of course, the beachside blocks of each city are much more similar, lined as they are with upscale condos and expensive hotels, and both places are colder than the rest of the basin, with average midsummer temperatures sitting comfortably around 66°F. Perhaps for this reason, these areas have become home to at least one-quarter of LA's population of British and Irish expatriates, many of whom can be spotted in the local Euro-friendly bars, nightclubs and restaurants.

Located on the western edge of LA, and next to the great crescent of Santa Monica Bay, the two cities contain some of the region's most enjoyable spots, with little of the pretension of Beverly Hills and West LA, and much in the way of laid-back attitudes and pleasantly low-scale development. Santa Monica's population is relatively stagnant due to the city's tight rent-control policies and the steep price of new housing and, like other parts of the Westside, is still fairly WASPy. Multiculturalism, however, has been long established in Venice, which was one of the few coastal cities not to use restrictive covenants to keep blacks from living there. The district continues to be home to a much wider range of classes and races than Santa Monica, plus everything from the latest architectural curiosities to ramshackle wooden heaps. Nowhere are these visual contrasts more apparent than near **Abbot Kinney Boulevard**, where upscale salons sit just a few short blocks from one of LA's bleakest ghettos, Oakwood.

Further south, the colorless real-estate development of **MARINA DEL REY** offers few spots of interest, but the adjacent Ballona Wetlands have much natural appeal and **PLAYA DEL REY** maintains a certain faded charm, which takes an eerie turn near the airport, around the site of LA's only urban ghost town.

Santa Monica

As one of the most sought-after places to live in LA, **Santa Monica** is one of the most difficult to move to – the city's rent-control policy, which had been in effect for nearly two decades, was undercut by a recent California state law allowing landlords to charge market rates for their units once they are vacated. Not only has this resulted in a spike in evictions, as landlords try to clear out the old tenants with controlled rents, it has also tripled the cost of many units on the market, making affordable living in this bayside city a pipe dream to all but the unevicted.

It's easy to understand why locals want to move here: the city has relatively low crime rates, cool ocean air throughout the year, and a generally unpretentious character, with much less snootiness than might be expected from a Westside district. While it has few main sights, Santa Monica most rewards casual wandering through its tree-lined neighborhoods or along its sandy beaches.

As little as a century ago, most of the land between Santa Monica and what was then Los Angeles was covered by ranch lands and citrus groves, interrupted by the occasional outposts of Hollywood and Beverly Hills. Like so much of the state, the land was owned by the Southern Pacific Railroad, whose chief Collis Huntington tried – and failed – to make Santa Monica into the port of Los Angeles, losing out to Phineas Banning and other interests who dredged the harbor at San Pedro – which was really a blessing in disguise for Santa Monica. The linking of the beachfront with the rest of Los Angeles by the suburban streetcar system, known as the Red Cars, meant the town instead grew into one of LA's premier getaways – a giant funfair city that was the inspiration for Raymond Chandler's anything-goes "Bay City," memorably described in *Farewell My Lovely*. While working- and middle-class residents flocked to the Santa Monica pier for its thrill-rides and freewheeling atmosphere, the town's elite sailed out to the gambling boats anchored offshore to indulge in a bit of illicit excitement beyond the reach of the local authorities. Today Chandler wouldn't recognize the place: changes in the gaming laws and the advent of private swimming pools have led to the removal of the offshore gambling ships and many of the popular bathing clubs, and Santa Monica is now among LA's more elegant seaside towns – an always-hip attraction that's not so commercialized as to be unbearable, as is the case with many other major California beach cities.

The city lies across Bundy Drive from West LA, and splits into three general areas: **oceanside Santa Monica**, holding a fair bit of Santa Monica's history and tourist attractions, sits on the coastal bluffs and includes the pier and beach; **Main Street**, running south from the pier towards Venice, is home to designer restaurants and quirky shops; and Santa Monica's interior, or **the rest of the city**, is split between exclusive neighborhoods and fine museums and galleries, to the north, and acres of grungy apartment blocks and quiet bungalows, to the south.

Oceanside Santa Monica

Although Santa Monica reaches fairly well inland, most visitors limit themselves to the city's **oceanside** amusements, with the main attraction being the **Santa Monica Pier**, a busy tourist zone jutting out into the bay at the foot of Colorado Avenue. The pier, constructed in 1874 and rebuilt many times since, was once one of LA's prime entertainments, offering nerve-jangling rides and a heady carnival atmosphere, while remaining fairly tame compared to the raucous Pacific Ocean Park that took shape a few decades later to the south (see p.135). Rebuilt and reconstructed several times, it was often threatened with demolition, narrowly averting this fate on several occasions in the 1970s

SANTA MONICA

Pacific Palisades

0   400 yds

Pacific Palisades

WILSHIRE BOULEVARD

ARIZONA AVENUE

SANTA MONICA BOULEVARD

Third Street Promenade

Bay City Guaranty Building

Visitor Center

Camera Obscura

BROADWAY

Bus Station

Santa Monica Place

Santa Monica Pier

UCLA Ocean Discovery Center

Angels Attic

COLORADO AVENUE

Pacific Park

International Chess Park

OLYMPIC BLVD

Workout Area

City Hall

SANTA MONICA FREEWAY

OLYMPIC PLACE

MICHIGAN AVENUE

Civic Auditorium

PICO BOULEVARD

Santa Monica State Beach

Bay Park

BAY STREET

BAY STREET

GRANT STREET

BICKNELL ST.

PACIFIC STREET

PACIFIC STREET

Horatio West Court

Hotchkiss Park

STRAND STREET

Joslyn Park

HOLLISTER AVENUE

KENSINGTON RD.

PEARL STREET

WADSWORTH AVE.

Edgemar complex

FRASER AVE.

Los Amigos Park

CEDAR STREET

Beach Park

OCEAN PARK BOULEVARD

PINE STREET

OCEAN PARK

MAPLE STREET

California Heritage Museum

HILL STREET

Ocean View Park

Jadis

RAYMOND AVE.

ASHLAND AVENUE

Parkhurst Building

PIER AVENUE

South Beach Park

MARINE STREET

N

MARINE CT.

NAVY ST.

NAVY CT.

DEWEY STREET

18th Street Arts Complex

West LA

Venice

ACCOMMODATION

Bayside	16
Cal Mar	3
Carmel	8
Fairmont Miramar	4
The Georgian	6
HI-LA/Santa Monica	7
Hotel California	10
Loew's Santa Monica Beach	11
Oceana	1
Ocean Park Hotel	15
Pico Blvd Travelodge	14
Radisson Huntley	2
Santa Monica Beach Travelodge	9
Shangri-La	5
Shutters on the Beach	12
Viceroy	13

(thanks largely to citizen advocacy groups). Other factors conspired against the pier, too, such as merciless storms in 1982 that nearly pounded the old pier into the sea and a growing reputation as a hangout for gangs and petty thugs from outside the area. Many visitors stayed away, especially at night when skirmishes between gangs and the police often took place, and business suffered accordingly. In recent years, the establishment of a substation of the Santa Monica Police Department has eliminated most of the violent crime, as has an uptick in the local economy, and nightly tourist traffic is once again visible, attracting everyone from local business workers to teens and families.

Although featuring an assortment of fast-food stands, video game parlors and watering holes, the pier's most obvious appeal is its restored 1922 wooden **carousel** (daily 9am–6pm; 50¢), with more than forty colorful hand-carved horses. Even more appealing is the **UCLA Ocean Discovery Center**, just below the pier near the carousel, at 1600 Ocean Front Walk (summer Tues–Fri 3–6pm, Sat 11am–6pm, Sun 11am–5pm; rest of year Sat & Sun 11am–5pm; $3; ☎310/393-6149, ⊛www.odc.ucla.edu), which presents engaging exhibits on local marine life and gives you the chance to touch sea anemones and starfish, though its aim is mainly to educate children in oceanography, as well as raise the public's consciousness about oceanic pollution – of which there is plenty in Santa Monica Bay (see box opposite).

To the south, kids can clamber about on the stone sculptures of a **children's park**. Further out on the pier itself, **Pacific Park** (daily 11am–11pm, Sat & Sun closes at 12.30am; $16, kids $9) offers only a hint of the freewheeling amusement park of old, its roller coaster and various other thrill rides part of a rather overpriced attempt to lure back the suburban families – you're better off saving your money for a real theme park. Near the end of the pier, anglers cast their lines into the murky depths of Santa Monica Bay, while below the pier, **Santa Monica State Beach** is a popular strip of sand, often tightly packed with visitors on summer weekends. Swimming here is a gamble due to contaminants from nearby storm drains, but the threat of water-borne infections doesn't keep some locals, or unknowing tourists, from venturing out into the waters.

Just south of the pier, Santa Monica has its own miniature version of Venice's muscle beach – though without the body-sculpting mania and corresponding contempt for the unpumped – a **workout area** loaded with rings, bars and other athletic equipment designed for would-be bodybuilders and fitness fans. If you'd rather match wits than compare biceps, visit the adjacent **International Chess Park**, a fancy name for a serviceable collection of chessboards that attracts a range of players from rank amateurs to slumming pros. An odd sidelight is the park's human-size chessboard, more of a novelty item than a place to spend your afternoon, unless you can find 32 "living pieces" to stand at rigid attention for a few hours. Finally, a **bike path** begins at the pier and heads twenty miles south to Palos Verdes, a stretch that ranks as one of the area's top choices for cycling. You can rent bicycles, surfboards or rollerblades at equipment-rental shacks by the pier, or just stroll along taking in the local color. While it's perfect for people-watching, the beach isn't so great for seclusion; there's hardly a deserted spot from Pacific Palisades to Redondo Beach.

Although you can't tell it these days, this general strip of sand around the pier was once the site of some of LA's swankiest hotels, none more impressive than the Queen Anne colossus of the **Arcadia**, named after the wife of sheep rancher and real-estate bigwig **Robert S. Baker**. He purchased much of the land that would become Santa Monica from the Sepulveda family, one of LA's old Spanish landowners (who also had dealings in West LA; see p.122). In the

Healing the bay

Although Los Angeles has a well-deserved reputation for having noxious air, its **water pollution** is less known, though in many ways worse: while the city's air pollution has actually tailed off considerably in recent decades, the **Santa Monica Bay** continues to suffer from all kinds of problems, only slowly getting better.

Cities and districts from Santa Monica to Palos Verdes have the bad luck of being trapped next to nearly all of LA's outlets for wastewater and sewage, with streetside **storm drains** emptying the runoff of a 5000-mile network of LA urban sprawl and a single treatment center – **Hyperion** – handling the task of cleaning up the collective filth. The periodic storms that LA receives, often driven by El Niño currents in the Pacific Ocean, make matters exponentially worse, forcing torrents of raw, untreated sewage directly into the bay and making any bodily contact with the seawater potentially hazardous, leading to anything from sinusitis to skin rashes.

You can see the pollution problem in full color just by walking past one of Santa Monica's storm drains, such as the ones near Pico Boulevard or Ashland Avenue, and seeing the rainbow slick of detritus floating along with the garbage. Just one look, or a sniff of the air, should be more than enough to keep you from bathing in Santa Monica Bay or from eating anything you might catch while fishing off the pier. Still, there have been improvements to the bay in the last fifteen years since **Heal the Bay** and other such environmental groups were formed: the EPA has gotten involved with the clean-up, Hyperion no longer freely dumps sewage as it once did, and chemical companies have stopped flushing DDT into the water. If you really feel the need to catch the California waves, make sure to do so well away from city piers – often the most polluted zones – and don't wade within one hundred yards of a beachside drain or venture into the water within three days after a storm, when runoff, sewage, bacteria and algae combine to form a repellent aquatic poison.

To check out the sands beforehand, visit the Heal the Bay website at ⓦwww.healthebay.org and click on the color-coded beach map detailing which areas are fine for swimming or fishing.

1880s, realtors tried to call the town the "Zenith City by the Sunset Sea," a clumsy moniker that never caught on. In later decades, the great beach houses just north of the pier were known as the "Gold Coast," because of the Hollywood personalities who lived there. The largest still standing, the **North Guest House**, 415 Palisades Beach Rd, was built as the servants' quarters of a massive 120-room house, now demolished, which William Randolph Hearst built for his mistress, actress Marion Davies. MGM boss Louis B. Mayer owned the adjacent Mediterranean-style villa, which was later rumored to be the place where the Kennedy brothers had their clandestine liaisons with Marilyn Monroe. Later rechristened as the Sand and Sea beach club, the old Hearst complex was closed after the 1994 Northridge earthquake, though there have been plans to rebuild the swimming pool, cabanas and other structures for use as a public facility.

North of the pier across Ocean Avenue, **Palisades Park** is a palm- and cypress-tree-lined strip overlooking the bay that affords stunning views stretching from Malibu to Palos Verdes – all the while sitting precariously atop high bluffs that are constantly being eroded. At least half of the **cliffside sidewalk** around the edge is usually fenced off, as it has a tendency to tumble down the bluffs. Inside the park, you may want to stop by the **visitors' information office** (daily 10am–4pm; ☏310/393-7593, ⓦwww.santamonica.com), in a kiosk just south of Santa Monica Boulevard at 1400 Ocean Ave, which gives out a handy free map of the town and the routes of the Santa Monica Big Blue

Bus transit system – a useful Westside complement to the MTA network (☎310/451-5444, ⓦwww.bigbluebus.com). Nearby, the **Camera Obscura**, 1450 Ocean Ave (Mon–Fri 9am–4pm, Sat & Sun 11am–4pm; free), provides unique entertainment by way of an old-fashioned device that prefigures modern photography. Inside a darkened room, you can view images of the outside world projected onto a circular screen by a rotating mirror on the roof – the sort of tool artists like Jan Vermeer once used as a visual aid for painting. On clear days, the clarity of the images can be startling. The camera is located within a social center for the elderly, so make sure to ask one of the senior citizens inside for a key to this upstairs room.

Two blocks east of Ocean Avenue, between Wilshire Boulevard and Broadway, the **Third Street Promenade** is a pedestrianized stretch that underwent a successful refurbishment in the early 1990s and now attracts a lively crowd of characters. It's fun simply to hang out in the cafés, pubs and nightclubs, or browse through the many secondhand and fine-art bookshops, though it's especially busy on weekends, when huge numbers of tourists and locals jostle for space with sidewalk poets, swinging jazz bands and bellowing evangelists, under the watchful eyes of water-spewing **dinosaur sculptures** draped in ivy. Unfortunately, the promenade is becoming a victim of its own success: independent businesses have become increasingly uncommon as chain retailers have muscled their way in, especially at the northern end of the strip between Wilshire Boulevard and Arizona Avenue.

Anchoring the mall's southern end is trendy **Santa Monica Place**, a white-stucco shopping precinct that is among architect Frank Gehry's less-inspired work. You'll find here the usual assortment of chain stores and a mandatory food court, all executed in an exhausted postmodern idiom, with faded pastel colors and gloomy chain-link fencing. Just to the north, towering over the shopping strip, is the landmark **Bay City Guaranty Building**, Third Street at Santa Monica Boulevard, a now-faded Zigzag Moderne marvel topped by a colorful clock that was for years Santa Monica's tallest building.

A little further north, the 1939 **Shangri-La apartments**, now a hotel at Ocean and Arizona avenues (see "Accommodation," p.233), is perhaps the city's finest example of the Streamline Moderne style, which used nautical motifs to great effect, making this structure look like a giant, landlocked ocean liner. Finally, just one block away on Ocean Avenue in Palisades Park, stands the austere white statue of the city's namesake, **Santa Monica**, the mother of St Augustine.

Main Street

The completion of the Santa Monica Freeway in 1965 bridged a deep urban arroyo and brought the city's beachfront homes within a fifteen-minute drive of Downtown, while isolating the north side of town from **Main Street**, five minutes' walk from the pier. Here, the collection of novelty shops, kite stores and classy restaurants makes it one of the most popular shopping districts on the Westside.

Although the big chain stores have arrived on the street, there are still enough quirky local operations to make a visit here worthwhile, notably **Jadis**, 2701 Main St, a prop-rental operation with LA's best display window: a collection of mannequins posed in various demented dioramas from 1930s horror films, such as a mad scientist's lab, and surrounded by all sorts of antiquated technical junk and contraptions. To make for a more comprehensive day of consumerism, you can travel between Main Street and the Santa Monica Promenade on the **Tide Shuttle** (daily noon–10pm, Sat & Sun until midnight), ponying up a mere quarter to hit all the shopping highlights, as well as travel along the sands south of the pier.

One of the few cultural sights, the **California Heritage Museum**, 2612 Main St (Wed–Sun 11am–4pm; $3), is the city's effort to preserve some of its architectural past in the face of ever-encroaching development. Two houses were moved here to escape demolition: one, the 1894 **Jones House**, hosts temporary displays on California cultural topics like old-time amusement parks and surfboard art, and has several rooms restored to variously evoke the years from 1890 to 1930. The second house, the 1903 **Trask House**, is known as the *Victorian Restaurant* and serves tea on its patio at weekends (reserve on ☎310/392-8537). There are also several noteworthy buildings on and around Main Street, including the angular gray volumes and strange geometry of Frank Gehry's **Edgemar** shopping development, no. 2415, a deliberately awkward construction that rewards closer inspection, especially on its second floor, where Gehry's chain-link fencing and sheet-metal design bring to mind an abstract sculpture or an industrial ruin. The more traditional **Parkhurst Building**, south on Main Street at Pier Avenue, is a 1927 Spanish Colonial Revival gem, while the cool white arches and simple boxlike shapes of Irving Gill's **Horatio West Court** (1919), north of Edgemar at 140 Hollister Ave, prefigured the rise of local modernism by about twenty years – it's also one of the few surviving works by the under-appreciated architect.

Not all of Santa Monica has been so lucky as to escape the wrecking ball. Ocean Park Boulevard was one of the main routes to the coast via the old streetcars of the Pacific Electric, and the entire beachfront between here and the Venice border, now overshadowed by massive gray condominiums, used to be the site of a resort community developed by Abbot Kinney, the man behind the design of Venice itself. Along with vacation bungalows, a wharf and a colorful boardwalk, the neighborhood also featured the largest and wildest of the old amusement piers: the fantastic **Pacific Ocean Park**, or "P-O-P" as it was known, which had a huge roller coaster, a giant funhouse and a boisterous midway arcade, which architectural historian Reyner Banham once described as a "fantasy in stucco and every known style of architecture and human ecology." Against the sanitized fun zones like Disneyland, though, the old piers began to look faded and depressing, and despite a late-1950s refurbishment, P-O-P went steadily downhill, languishing for a time as a makeshift obstacle course for daredevil surfers before being demolished in the mid-1970s.

The rest of the city

Although the interior of Santa Monica is generally marked by quiet, well-off neighborhoods, fast-food diners and entertainment-industry office parks, there are a handful of interesting attractions (mostly museums and galleries) that make a visit here worthwhile.

Wilshire Boulevard is the main commercial axis of this area, but further north, near the city border, **San Vicente Boulevard** is a more appealing diversion, a grassy tree-lined strip and a joggers' freeway that leads east to the wealthier confines of Brentwood. LA's true health-mania is visible just two blocks north of San Vicente, along Adelaide Drive between First and Seventh streets. Here an entire stair-climbing culture has evolved along the giant **stairways** that connect Santa Monica with Pacific Palisades. On any given morning, crowds of locals trot up and down the street, just waiting for a chance to descend down the bluffs and charge back up again, red-faced and gasping for air. You, too, may wish to descend the steps, to get a glimpse of the tonier confines of Pacific Palisades, Santa Monica's even more well-heeled neighbor (see p.198).

Two blocks south of San Vicente, the pricey restaurants and boutiques of **Montana Avenue** mark the upward mobility of the area. The area does have one example of world-class architecture in the wild **Gehry House**, 22nd Street at Washington Avenue, a fitting reflection of architect Frank Gehry's taste for the unusual. Now partially hidden by foliage and remodeled for the worse, the house shattered conventional notions of architecture upon its completion in 1978: not a unified design at all, but what appears to be random ideas thrown together helter-skelter and bundled up with concrete walls and metal fencing.

Back toward the 10 freeway is **Angels Attic**, 516 Colorado Ave (Thurs–Sun 12.30–4.30pm; $6.50, kids $3.50; ☏310/394-8331, ⓦwww.internetimpact .com/angelsattic), a slice of Victoriana in an elegant 1895 Queen Anne house that serves as a museum. Apart from the large collection of oversized dolls, c.1900 arts and crafts, and assorted wooden and tin toys, you'll find a number of finely detailed miniatures, all exquisitely rendered, particularly the dwarf palace of Versailles, though it's actually a more contemporary work. After peering inside the junior palaces and mini-houses, you can take a seat on the veranda for the museum's afternoon tea service.

Further east, **Side Street Projects**, 1629 18th St (Wed–Sat noon–6pm; free; ☏310/829-0779), is another of the town's ambitious art spaces – dedicated to both education and exhibition – forming part of the **18th Street Arts Complex**, 1639 18th St (ⓦwww.18thstreet.org), a hip and modern center for various types of art, much of it experimental. The performance space **Highways**, 1651 18th St (☏310/315-1459, ⓦwww.highwaysperformance.org), is one such example in the complex, showcasing edgy political and gender-based work.

Santa Monica has a number of fine galleries selling works by emerging local and international artists. Many of them are located at **Bergamot Station**, 2525 Michigan Ave, a collection of former tramcar sheds at 2525 Michigan Ave, near the intersection of 26th and Cloverfield (most galleries open Tues–Fri 10am–6pm; free; ☏310/828-4001, ⓦwww.bergamotstation.com). Many of LA's top artists – such as Lari Pittman, Manuel Ocampo, Robert Williams and Erika Rothenberg, to name a few – have shown here, and the highlight is, of course, the **Santa Monica Museum of Art**, in Bldg G-1 (Tues–Sat 11am–6pm; $3 donation; ☏310/586-6488, ⓦwww.smmoa.org). This is a good space to see some of the most engaging and novel work on the local scene, in temporary exhibits ranging from simple paintings to complex installation art. The museum also hosts Friday night **salons** (usually 7.30–9pm; $3), during which artists discuss their recent work and occasionally lead informal tours through their exhibits. Among the regular galleries in Bergamot Station, don't miss the **Gallery of Functional Art**, Bldg E-3 (free; ☏310/829-6990, ⓦwww.galleryoffunctionalart.com), for its array of mechanical gizmos and eccentric furniture like cubist lamps and neon chairs.

Venice

Immediately south of Santa Monica, **Venice** was laid out in the marshlands of Ballona Creek in 1905 by developer Abbot Kinney as a romantic replica of the north Italian city (see box, p.139). While most of the architecture and canals have long since disappeared, the lingering pseudo-European atmosphere has since proved just right for pulling in the artistic community he was aiming at, making Venice one of the coast's better spots to check out the underground arts scene and its grubby bohemian charm. Not only are artists' studios and galleries a vital part of town, even the mainstream commercial enterprises get into the spirit. Main Street, for instance, is home to the offices of advertising firm **Chiat/Day/Mojo**, just south of Rose Street. Marked by Claes Oldenburg's huge pair of binoculars that overshadow the entrance, the

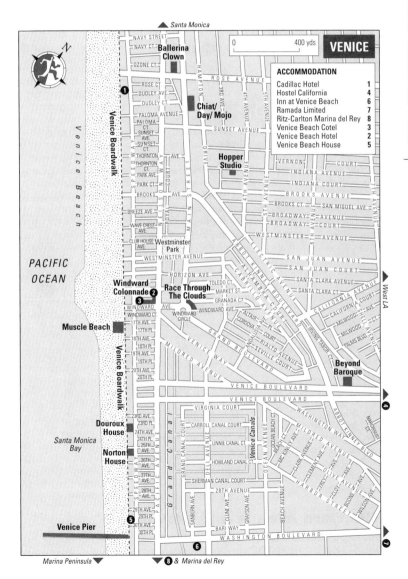

Frank Gehry–designed offices have no assigned desks, leaving employees to roam free with laptops and mobile phones through spartan rooms lined with modern art. A block north is the grotesque *Ballerina Clown*, an enormous sculpture by Jonathan Borofsky perched above the intersection of Rose Avenue and Main Street, its lithe body and stubbly clown head making for an unforgettably disturbing combination. Elsewhere, a strong alternative arts scene centers around the **Beyond Baroque** literary center and bookshop in the old City Hall, 681 Venice Blvd (Tues–Fri 10am–5pm, Sat noon–5pm; ☎310/822-3006, ⓦwww.beyondbaroque.org), which is a good place to get a flavor of the work of local artists and the city's latest cultural trends, or catch one of the regular book readings.

The beach and Boardwalk

Venice Beach draws most visitors to the district, and nowhere else does LA parade itself quite so conspicuously as it does along the **Venice Boardwalk**, a wide pathway tracking alongside the sands that's packed on weekends and all summer long with jugglers, fire-eaters, Hare Krishnas and roller-skating guitar players. City authorities, in their zeal for order, have tried to force the many street vendors to get licenses to sell their goods, but so far have failed to quell the anarchic spirit of the place. In any case, you'll have no difficulty picking up your choice of cheap sunglasses, T-shirts, personal stereos, sandals and whatever else you need for a day at the beach. South of Windward Avenue along the Boardwalk is **Muscle Beach**, a now-legendary outdoor weightlifting center where stern-looking, would-be Schwarzeneggers pump serious iron, and high-flying gymnasts swing on the adjacent rings and bars. If you'd like to check the place out yourself, contact the Venice Beach Recreation Center, 1800 Ocean Front Walk, for more information (☎310/399-2775), or if you're a real weightlifting enthusiast, you can visit in July, when the Bench Press Championships are held here, one of many such competitions taking place during the year.

Pumping iron is far from the only activity taking place amid the palm trees. Basketball players can join a pickup game on one of several concrete courts – ranked the third-best in the country by *Hoops* magazine – while rollerbladers, skateboarders, volleyball players and bicyclists are ubiquitous throughout the year. There are **rental shacks** along the beach for picking up skates, surfboards or bikes, and plenty of merchants selling Day-Glo tube tops and wraparound sunglasses – if you really want to fit in with the athletic locals.

Beyond the beach, what remains of the **Venice Pier** stretches into the ocean off of Washington Street, but don't expect much in the way of carnival fun or thrill rides – the pier doesn't offer a great deal of entertainment value these days, since it's used mostly for fishing in the often-polluted bay, and is a far cry from the wild amusement of old (see box opposite).

Incidentally, be warned that Venice Beach at night can be a dangerous place, taken over by street thugs, drug dealers and assorted psychos. Walking on the beach after dark is illegal, but you should have no problem supping at a beach-side café or browsing at a record store.

Windward Avenue and around

Windward Avenue is Venice's main artery, running from the beach into what was the Grand Circle of the canal system, now paved over and ringed by a

As with various other parts of LA, such as Beverly Hills and San Marino, the development of **Venice** owed much to the desire to emulate European models; however, if it weren't for a lucky coin flip, this Old World simulation would never have existed. When **Abbot Kinney**, winner of the fabled toss with his former real-estate partners, gained control of the area in 1904, he set about on a quixotic quest to build a paragon of learning, art and culture from scratch. After deciding to base his ideal burg on the great Renaissance city-state, and once this area was linked up to the rest of LA by the Red Car mass transit line, Kinney began construction of the town – then labeled "Venice-by-the-Sea" – by first draining the land's marshes and developing an extensive network of canals and roads, then creating theaters, performance venues and sites for restaurants and cafés, and even a think tank for the liberal arts. He put much of his own money into the effort, investing about $1.5 million, and the initial payoff seemed great. Visitors were smitten by the new arts center's bungalows and hotel rooms, its gondoliers (some from Italy) to navigate the waterways, and its pleasant pier for seaside relaxation.

Culture alone, however, did not pay the bills, and soon the crowds were demanding more amusement and less edification. In response, Venice shifted its focus to providing thrills to its seasonal vacationers and daily visitors, and Kinney oversaw the formation of what would become LA's greatest boardwalk. Minaret-topped palaces, roller coasters, a Ferris wheel, giant balloons, freak shows and all manner of carnival attractions were soon found along Venice's once-austere oceanfront, and by 1911, against competition from his Ocean Park neighbors to the north, Kinney engineered the town's incorporation, even though it scarcely resembled his original notion for the community (aside from certain visual motifs like the canals). The city thrived for about a decade, until the oil industry moved in next door: when the derricks started their crude production, water pollution became a major threat to the beloved canals, and before long the central lagoon and outlying channels became fetid sites for waste disposal and general filth. Although the boardwalk was still attracting tourists, the decaying canals sullied the town's image, leading to a significant fall-off in tourism. Without any solution in sight, Venice's city leaders (which at that point did not include Kinney, who died in 1920) allowed the growing metropolis of LA to take over. Before long, the larger city paved over most of the canals and the main lagoon around Windward Circle. Later decades would bring Depression-era economic convulsions, the demise of the boardwalk, and the severing of the Red Car line, all of which turned Venice into a shadow of its former self. The town's nadir may have come in 1958, when Orson Welles used it as a location in his film *Touch of Evil*, plausibly remaking it into a shabby Mexican border town rife with corruption and murder.

Over the years, Venice would see a renewed arts scene (with painters and poets moving into the cheaper apartments on Venice's oceanside blocks) and a redesigned boardwalk offering a hint of the old carnival atmosphere. Many of the old residents of the quaint seaside buildings have since been driven out by gentrification, and little remains of Kinney's original plan, although vestiges, such as the fading colonnade and five renovated canals, are still visible here and there.

number of galleries and the Venice **post office**, where you can peek at a mural of the early city layout. On the west side of the circle, the curvaceous roller-coaster facade of the 1987 **Race Through the Clouds** building pays tribute to the old theme park with a sweeping neon track and metal gridwork. Closer to the beach, colorful giant **murals** – depicting everything from a ruined freeway overpass cut short in midair to Botticelli's Venus in rollerskates – cover the walls of the original hotels; while a Renaissance-style

△ Ferris wheel, Santa Monica Pier

arcade, around Windward's intersection with Pacific Avenue, is alive with health-food shops, used-record stores and rollerblade-rental stands. Of the remaining classical columns, several are painted in Day-Glo colors that Kinney would no doubt have gasped at, while others retain their original black-and-white coloring.

This area has also become home to some of LA's most inventive architects, artists and designers, whose offices are scattered around Windward Avenue and the traffic circle. You'll see the fruits of their labors in the small boutiques and far-out houses throughout the district, but especially to the south, along Ocean Front Walk (see below). Just a few blocks south from Windward, the five remaining **canals** are still crossed by their original 1904 bridges – quaint wooden structures that are among LA's few touches of Americana – and you can also sit and watch ducks paddle around in the still waters. It's a great place to walk around, though if you're in a car and wish to avoid the tiny, mazelike streets between the canals, there's only one way to see the area. Head north on Dell Avenue between Washington and Venice boulevards – a route that often draws a procession of slow-moving motorized gawkers. Whether you walk or drive, you'll get an eyeful of eclectic residential styles, modernist cubes and Tudor piles mixed in with Colonial bungalows and postmodern sheds. Sadly, there's no organized way to take a boat trip through the canals.

To the north, diagonally between Venice Boulevard and Main Street, the shopping strip of **Abbot Kinney Boulevard** features a range of funky clothing stores and boutiques. However, wandering away from the strip at night is strongly discouraged, as this street is the southern border of Venice's notorious Oakwood ghetto. Even here, however, you can find the home of the odd celebrity – Dennis Hopper's **Hopper Studio**, 326 Indiana Ave, the ultimate in maximum-security architecture: a slanted, corrugated-steel box with no windows, incongruously surrounded by a quaint, white picket fence.

Ocean Front Walk

Between Marina del Rey and the ocean lies narrow Pacific Avenue, home to some of LA's finest contemporary architecture. Park either at the channel-side lot on the south side, near Via Marina street, or curbside on the north side, and follow **Ocean Front Walk** (actually the same route as the Venice Boardwalk further north) for a pleasant stroll by the sands and the colorful modern houses. From Venice Pier, the intersecting streets are named alphabetically – from Anchorage Street to Yawl Court – in keeping with a nautical theme.

From the north, you'll first hit Antoine Predock's groundbreaking **Douroux House**, 2315 Ocean Front Walk, frequently captured in TV commercials. Atop the heavy concrete frame are rooftop bleachers and a big red window that fully pivots toward the sea, allowing the ocean breezes to easily sweep through the geometric structure. Not far away is Frank Gehry's **Norton House**, 2509 Ocean Front Walk, a big yellow box with jagged wooden window-frames and a tiny metal staircase on the facade. Further south is the blue-and-white **Yacht House**, 3900 Pacific Ave, just a block east of Ocean Front Walk, an Art Deco–inspired "boat" whose bow is firmly stuck in the concrete sidewalk. Finally, the **Doumani House**, Ocean Front Walk at Yawl Court, is an angular white cube with stepped windows, metallic tracery and a vaguely exotic character.

Marina del Rey, the Ballona Wetlands and Playa del Rey

At its nadir in the 1950s and 1960s, Venice was confronted with a new and unwelcome neighbor to the south: **Marina del Rey**, a massive real-estate development that blotted out the old city's coastal views with high-rises. As with the colossal towers plunked down along Wilshire Boulevard in Westwood, investment capital proved irresistible to the indifferent county commissioners who controlled the unincorporated land, and Marina del Rey has since grown in big, ugly spasms without any restraint whatsoever. Unless you own a yacht and are free to tool around the area's upscale marina, you're unlikely to get too close to the water; the whole area is ringed by dreary chain restaurants, giant office complexes and ugly apartment superstructures – closer in look with the tenements of the East Coast than any notion of luxury living.

Still, despite its utter lack of charm, many visitors often find themselves in Marina del Rey for one reason or another: the nearness of LAX, the presence of several major hotels or just plain bad luck. Along the south end of the area, at the end of Fiji Way, **Fisherman's Village** is Marina del Rey's main visitor attraction, though it's difficult to see why, consisting as it does of low-end seafood joints and endless trinket and T-shirt shops. More appealing is the channel-side walking and biking **path** that stretches from the end of Fiji Way out to the end of the spit. Not only is this the place where the Christmastime regatta takes place, but it's also a good spot to watch everyday yachts and speedboats make a leisurely sail into the marina. The end of the spit is a short distance from the channel **bridge** over Ballona Creek, which allows you to leave Marina del Rey and cross the "creek," really a noxious storm drain, into the marginally more interesting district of Playa del Rey (see below).

Ballona Wetlands

Further south, down Lincoln Boulevard, Marina del Rey gives way suddenly to the wide expanse of the three-hundred-acre **Ballona** (pronounced *by-OH-na*) **Wetlands**, encompassing bodies of fresh and salt water that are home to two hundred major bird species and a host of other creatures, though their ecosystem has been disrupted in recent years by a rising number of foxes, which roam freely. Although off limits to humans, this natural preserve can be toured at a distance, starting by heading west on Jefferson Boulevard (off Lincoln) and taking a left onto Culver Boulevard. While you might not see conspicuous wildlife, you will get a sense of the uniqueness of this terrain in the heavily urbanized LA basin.

Before Abbot Kinney created what is now Venice, the wetlands of this mid-coastal area stretched all the way to the border of the community of Ocean Park, and was just one of several in the region. Since then, the old bogs have been filled in by development, and only the Ballona Wetlands remain, and for well over twenty years developers and environmentalists have battled for permanent control of this prime real estate – a conflict that shows no sign of abating.

Playa del Rey

To the west, Culver Boulevard leads to the former resort community of **Playa del Rey**, once an essential link in the Red Car transit line and the site of grand hotels, restaurants and a funicular railway, but since reduced to a faded collection of commercial shacks and unattractive condos.

The peaceful **lagoon**, nestled near the beach along Pacific Street, is a popular spot for children's activities and dog-walking, but you're better off heading up to a high bluff above the main part of Playa del Rey, to the neighborhood of **Palisades del Rey**, which makes for a pleasant, hilly hike past some fine views of the ocean. There used to be more to this neighborhood, and to Playa del Rey overall, but the need for a sound barrier between LAX and the ocean did much to ruin its idyllic setting. When the county condemned the property here, hundreds of homes were destroyed and an entire neighborhood all but disappeared. The result was one of LA's strangest attractions: a modern-day **ghost town** stretching for several miles from Waterview Street to Imperial Highway along Vista del Mar. Chain-link fences guard the empty streets, now lined by crumbling housing foundations and defunct street lights. The only residents these days are some 50,000 **butterflies** that have moved in since the area was turned into an ecological preserve. Head to Sandpiper Street to survey the surreal scene close up, at least until the next blaring takeoff of a jumbo jet makes you jump back in your car.

6

South Central and East LA

S outh Central and East LA are far removed from the tourist circuit, and are generally avoided by visitors and almost always by Westsiders, many of them believing any venture south of the I-10 freeway to be an open invitation to murder, mugging or some other unpleasantry.

In truth, while these places can be dicey and should be largely avoided at night, the ghetto stereotypes are blown out of proportion in many districts, and a number of interesting museums and historic-revival homes can be found here, especially on the northern side of South Central around Exposition Park. Contained mostly within the boundaries of the 405, 605 and 10 freeways, South Central and East LA make up a large portion of the metropolitan basin, encompassing diverse cultures, with neighboring communities often separated by major differences in language, ethnicity and religion. Hispanic population growth is a constant throughout these areas, as it is throughout the rest of LA, and sweeping racial categorizing is simply not possible for most of these parts.

South Central LA

Lacking the scenic splendor of the coast, the glamour of West LA or the movie history of Hollywood, **SOUTH CENTRAL LA** hardly ranks on the city's list of prime attractions – especially after it burst onto the world's TV screens as the focus of the April 1992 riots. However, it makes up a considerable part of the city: a big oval chunk bordered by Alameda Street and the 10 and 405 freeways.

Though once mostly black, the population is increasingly Hispanic and Asian, interspersed here and there with working-class whites. Mostly made up of detached bungalows enjoying their own patch of palm-shaded lawn, South Central has something of a communitarian spirit that long ago disappeared elsewhere in LA. Yet, this picture doesn't conceal for long the relative poverty of the area, which offers most residents little chance to move up the social ladder and fosters large, pervasive youth gangs as well. Not surprisingly, throughout much of the district, every block for miles looks much like the last, peppered with fast-food outlets, dingy liquor stores and abandoned factory sites, with the occasional Hispanic outdoor market to brighten the gloom. Most

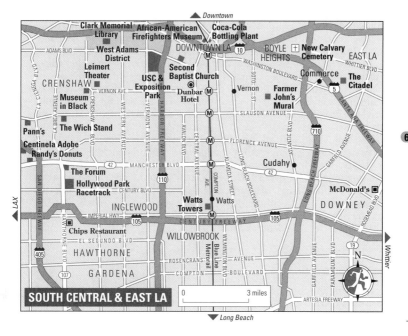

commuters drive blindly through the area on the Harbor Freeway (I-110), which is largely confined to its own walled-off channel. Nonetheless, there are compelling sights to be found, including the historic homes of the **West Adams** district, several museums in **Exposition Park** and the folk-art masterpiece of the **Watts Towers** – all best seen in daylight.

Some history

Like other parts of the city, much of South Central LA was settled in the nineteenth century by **Mexican immigrants** when the area was still governed by Mexico, and its large land tracts divided up as ranchos. Later, after the US took control of the land and California became the 31st state in 1850, **white American migrants** began arriving from the Midwest, drawn by the sunny weather, low cost of living and favorable job market, continuing into the early twentieth century.

Although LA had the largest African-American settlement on the West Coast in the 1930s, it was World War II that brought blacks in great numbers from the South and the East Coast to work in defense-related industries. Born or raised in LA were such notables as jazz musicians Dexter Gordon, Charles Mingus and Eric Dolphy, United Nations undersecretary Ralph Bunche, dance choreographer Alvin Ailey and Hollywood actress Dorothy Dandridge. (Even in the nineteenth century, when their population was significantly lower, black Angelenos were visible throughout the city, including such prominent figures as Robert Owens, a former slave who became the wealthiest and most prominent African American in Southern California in the 1850s.)

Most of the new residents were unpleasantly surprised to experience a taste of the Old South in new LA. The rampant, blatant discrimination of the time ensured the widespread presence of **color bars** and **restrictive covenants** – social codes and housing bylaws that kept blacks out of white neighborhoods. African Americans were hemmed in by avenues like Western and Slauson for their home-buying, and faced extreme hostility from whites whenever they ventured out of their neighborhoods to buy groceries, meet with friends or watch movies. Because of this, areas like Central Avenue and West Adams became segregated, though culturally rich, enclaves for blacks, with a thriving entertainment scene in the former and excellent architecture in the latter.

The Civil Rights Era and changing demographics put an official end to the old ways of segregation, and LA's southern neighborhoods have become a diverse blend of blacks, Hispanics and Asians, with many districts changing character in just a few decades. However, many problems persist, and what was formerly political and social apartheid has instead become de facto **economic segregation**. Poor and working-class blacks, even up to the middle class, are still stuck in South Central LA – largely to the western side – with Latinos increasingly settling in Watts and many other neighborhoods across the southern basin.

Inglewood

Bordered by the San Diego Freeway on the western edge of South Central, **INGLEWOOD** was once the world capital for chinchilla farming and the early site of LAX – then known as Mines Field – but is now better known for the **Hollywood Park Racetrack** (☎310/419-1500, ⓦwww.hollywoodpark .com), a landscaped track with lagoons and tropical vegetation, and a state-of-the-art wide screen that shows the otherwise obscured back straight. Next door are the white pillars that ring **The Forum**, the 17,000-seat stadium that was the former headquarters of both the LA Lakers (basketball) and the LA Kings (hockey), and is now mostly a concert venue.

Unless you're here to play the horses, Inglewood's best attraction is its pop architecture, starting with the **Loyola Theater**, at Sepulveda and Manchester boulevards, on the route to LAX – a late Streamline Moderne design with a sweeping, red goose-neck curve on its facade – that now serves as office space. Not far away at 805 Manchester Blvd, **Randy's Donuts** is one of LA's more surreal icons, a 1954 fast-food shack topped by a giant brown donut; while **Pann's**, a mile north at La Tijera Boulevard and Centinela Avenue, is perhaps the greatest "Googie" diner of all, still serving classic comfort food under its jaunty neon sign and low-slung pitched roof. Other famous diners are in fairly shopworn condition, except for the striking **Chips Restaurant**, a few miles south at 11908 Hawthorne Blvd, where three aquamarine columns support a sparkling set of letters, and the former **Wich Stand**, 4508 Slauson Ave, graced with a towering pastel pylon, though it no longer serves greasy burgers and fries – it's now a health-food store.

Just south of *Pann's*, the historic **Centinela Adobe**, 7636 Midfield Ave (Wed & Sun 2–4pm; free; private tours by appointment at ☎310/649-6272), was once home to Ignacio Machado, an heir to one of the Mexican founders of Los Angeles. It's the oldest building in the area, dating from 1834 and furnished with period antiques and replicas, including a good array of Victorian clothing and furniture, and offering details on Machado's life and his surrounding Aguaje de Centinela rancho, a 2200-acre land parcel granted him by the Mexican government. Also on the site is the **Daniel Freeman Land Office**, an 1887 structure that's now a center for historic preservation, a storehouse of information, curios and memorabilia of Inglewood city history and culture.

Crenshaw

Just to the north, **CRENSHAW** and adjacent **Leimert Park** form the contemporary center of African-American social activity in LA. Where once the nucleus of black culture was along Central Avenue, south of Downtown, it's now along **Crenshaw Boulevard**, a busy stretch of restaurants and book and record stores, as well as the Baldwin Hills Crenshaw Plaza, a multimillion-dollar shopping mall. The first of former Lakers star Magic Johnson's inner-city theater complexes is in the vicinity, too, as is the **Leimert Theater**, 3300 43rd Place, an Art Deco gem by architects Morgan, Walls and Clements (see p.80), recognizable by its soaring oil-derrick sign. The building lies in the heart of **Leimert Park Village**, several blocks of lively shops and decent restaurants.

The main cultural attraction here is the compelling **Museum in Black**, 4331 Degnan Blvd (Tues–Sat 11am–6pm; donation), which traces African and African-American art and history with roughly one thousand pieces in its collection, from knives, cooking utensils and totemic statuary of the Old World to racist advertising and political propaganda of the New. Particularly disturbing are the papers on display that document the purchase and transport of slaves from West Africa, some of which date back nearly three hundred years.

Above Crenshaw and Leimert Park, the black upper-middle class resides in pleasant **Baldwin Hills**, named after Wall Street gambler and Santa Anita race-track-builder E.J. "Lucky" Baldwin. Just before he died in 1909, Baldwin acquired the old Rancho La Cienega, which encompassed the hills. (He also built an estate east of Pasadena that's now home to the LA County Arboretum; see p.188.) Later, the area would host the Olympic Village for LA's 1932 summer games and become the site of a catastrophic 1963 dam burst and flood. This was due in no small part to environmental damage from oil drilling, which continues to this day and is most visible here along La Cienega Boulevard, giving a hint of what much of petroleum-obsessed LA looked like in the 1920s.

West Adams

The charming, but faded, **West Adams** neighborhood, along Adams Boulevard from Crenshaw Boulevard to Hoover Street, was one of LA's few racially mixed neighborhoods in the early part of the twentieth century. Here, the white and black upper-middle classes mingled and restrictive covenants were not as common as elsewhere in the city. It was also one of the spots where movie stars tended to live, known then as "Sugar Hill" and full of notable celebrities such as movie-musical director Busby Berkeley, Fatty Arbuckle and Theda Bara, among others.

Since then, many of these houses and mansions have become religious institutions. Berkeley's estate, the 1910 **Guasti Villa**, 3500 W Adams Blvd, is a graceful Renaissance Revival creation that might fit nicely in Italy but is now home to a New Age spiritual institute; the **Lindsay House**, no. 3424, a terracotta curiosity with a heavy stone facade, has become the Our Lady of Bright Mount Catholic church; and the **Walker House**, no. 3300, a mishmash of Craftsman half-timbering and a Mission tile roof, has turned into a Korean Seventh-Day Adventist church.

The finest building in the area is the French Renaissance **William Clark Memorial Library**, 2520 Cimarron St (Mon–Fri 9am–4.45pm; free; tours Mon–Fri 10am–2pm by reservation only, at ☎323/735-7605), with its tightly symmetrical composition, yellow-brick walls, formal gardens and grand entrance hall – a splash of Continental elegance in an unexpected LA setting. As millionaire heir to a copper fortune, founder of the LA Philharmonic and a US Senator from Montana, Clark amassed this great collection before donating it to UCLA, which continues to oversee it. Besides rare volumes by Pope, Fielding, Dryden, Swift and Milton, plus a huge set of letters and manuscripts by Oscar Wilde, the library includes four Shakespeare folios, a group of works by Chaucer and copies of key documents in American history, pertaining to the Louisiana Purchase and the like.

The USC Campus

The **USC** (University of Southern California) **Campus**, a few miles south of Downtown, is a wealthy enclave in one of the city's poorer neighborhoods. For many years a breeding ground for political and economic fat cats, the university was well known for hatching LA's shadow rulers for the secretive "Committee of 25," supplying Richard Nixon with advisers like H.R. Haldeman, and generally acting as the reactionary force in the local academic scene – while rival UCLA, under the progressive guidance of Franklin Murphy, occupied the other end of the political spectrum.

Today, USC, or the "University of Spoiled Children," is among the most expensive universities in the country, its undergraduates thought of as more likely to have rich parents than fertile brains. Indeed, the stereotype seems often borne out, both by their easygoing, suntanned, beach-bumming nature, and by USC's being more famous for its sporting prowess than its academic achievements: within fifteen years of the school's 1874 founding, it already had a football team, becoming the first university in Southern California to play the game. (Alumni include O.J. Simpson, who collected college football's highest honor, the Heisman Trophy, when he played here.)

Largely white, insular and conservative, the university hasn't escaped to the suburbs, as some of its alumni demanded after the Watts riots (and unlike its right-wing counterpart, Pepperdine), and there have even been a few small steps to integrate the campus population more closely with the local, predominantly black and Hispanic, community. This effort is further complicated by the fact that the **campus** resembles an armed camp, literally fenced off from the world around it (you can only enter by car through carefully monitored guard stations). Based on an Italian Romanesque style similar to that of UCLA, USC's 1920s buildings exhibit nice detail and ornamentation, but the lack of greenspace gives the campus the appearance of a concrete desert at times, and the severe arches and austere character of its modern buildings can, in places, look like something out of a de Chirico painting.

Though sizeable, the campus is reasonably easy to get around. You might find it easiest to take the free fifty-minute **walking tour** (Mon–Fri 10am–3pm; ☎213/740-6605, ⓦwww.usc.edu), leaving on the hour from the USC Admissions Center, near Gate 2. Without a guide, a good place to start is the **Doheny Library** (during academic year Mon–Thurs 8am–10pm, Fri 8am–5pm, Sat 9am–5pm, Sun 1–10pm; free), an inviting Romanesque structure named after the famous LA oil baron (see box, p.116), where you can pick up a campus map and investigate the large stock of overseas newspapers and magazines on the second floor. Another good place for general information is the **Student Union** building, just across from the library. Among the generally unremarkable eateries found here, a **café** under the Wolfgang Puck banner, featuring nouveau pizzas and salads, provides some respite.

Of things to see, USC's art collection is housed in the **Fisher Gallery**, 823 Exposition Blvd (open during exhibitions only, Tues–Sat noon–5pm; free), which stages several major international exhibitions each year and has a broad permanent collection, best for its nineteenth-century American works, including Thomas Cole's *The Woodchopper*, a Hudson River School painting, and Albert Bierstadt's landscape of *A Stream in the Rocky Mountains*, a grand Romantic vista. Elsewhere, you can see smaller shows of students' creative efforts in the **Helen Lindhurst Fine Arts Gallery**, inside Watt Hall (Mon–Fri 9am–4pm; free), and the **Helen Lindhurst Architecture Gallery and Library** (Mon–Fri 9am–5pm; free), in the USC School of Architecture, 850 W 37th St, a structure which itself is quite creative, with porch-level glass boxes doubling as skylights for the underground library.

Perhaps the only compelling public artwork on campus is Jenny Holzer's *First Amendment*, in the sculpture garden around Harris Hall – a work commemorating the fate of the Hollywood Ten, those writers and directors blacklisted for refusing to rat out their colleagues as Communists in the McCarthy era. A series of stair-stepping stone slabs lead to ten circular benches, all of which are inscribed with the names and writings of the persecuted film-makers.

Finally, the campus is also home to the **School of Cinema–Television**, a mainstream rival to the UCLA film school in Westwood. Ironically, **Steven Spielberg**, one of the biggest box-office directors in history, couldn't get in to USC when he applied, but nowadays his name is hallowed here, and writ large on the wall of the large and expensive sound-mixing center he later funded.

Between USC and Exposition Park, sports fans may want to stop at the **Coliseum** on Hoover Boulevard. The site of the 1932 and 1984 Olympic Games has fallen on hard times lately, with the LA Raiders football team long gone, and possible deals to land a new franchise repeatedly failing amid corporate infighting and lack of local interest. However, USC home games are still played here, and the imposing grand arch on the facade and muscular, headless commemorative statues create enough visual interest to make the place worth a look.

Exposition Park

Once known as Agricultural Park because of its produce vendors and farming exhibits, **Exposition Park** is, given the bleak nature of the surrounding area, one of the most appreciated parks in LA, incorporating lush landscaped gardens and several modest museums. Although this area just south of USC – along with the residential quarters north of the school – was once home to LA's elite, subsequent white flight and economic downturns have taken their toll, an effect visible in the countless low-end mini-malls and liquor stores that have set up shop here.

It's large by any standard, but the park has a close-knit feel – bolstered in part by its function as a favorite lunchtime picnic spot for school kids. After eating, they often head to the **California Science Center**, one of a cluster of **museums** off Figueroa Street at 700 State Drive (daily 10am–5pm; free, parking $6; ⓣ323/724-3623, ⓦwww.casciencectr.org). This nicely renovated, multimillion-dollar showcase for science education, with scores of working models and thousands of pressable buttons, has among its highlights a walk-in microscope, dizzying motion simulators and a giant talking robot that offers simple biology instruction. Although occasionally fun, the place is little more than lightweight, pop-science eye candy geared to the kids. There's also an **IMAX Theater** that plays short documentaries on a gigantic curved screen, including the occasional 3D presentation ($7.50, kids $4.50, $1 extra for 3D shows). Closer to Exposition Boulevard but still part of the Science Center, the recently reno-vated **Air and Space Gallery** is hard to miss, thanks to the sleek jet stuck to its facade. Besides the satellites and telescopes, and a slew of airplanes and rock-ets, you can also get up close to an LAPD helicopter "air ship" – as most visi-tors to LA soon discover, an almost constant presence in the skies above. The building itself, a white cubic mass, is something of a landmark, designed by Frank Gehry and prefiguring some of his later, better, work. The nearby **California African-American Museum**, 600 State Drive (Tues–Sun 10am–5pm; free; ☎213/744-7432, ⓦww.caam.ca.gov), has diverse temporary exhibitions on the history, art and culture of black people in the Americas, including a display of musical instruments from Africa and the Caribbean, shows devoted to the life and legacy of performers like Ella Fitzgerald, and painting and sculpture by local artists.

The **Natural History Museum of Los Angeles County** (Mon–Fri 9.30am–5pm, Sat & Sun 10am–5pm; $8; ☎213/763-3466, ⓦwww.nhm.org), an explosion of Spanish Revival architecture in the northwest corner of the park, has much appeal as the home to the park's most striking building and best museum overall. Foremost among the exhibits is a tremendous stock of dinosaur bones and fossils, and some imposing skeletons (usually casts), includ-ing the crested "duck-billed" dinosaur, the skull of a Tyrannosaurus rex and the astonishing frame of a Diatryma – a huge, flightless prehistoric bird. Exhibits on rare sharks, the combustible native plant chaparral and a spellbinding insect zoo – centered around a sizeable ant farm – add to the appeal, but there's a lot here beyond strict natural history, so you should allow several hours at least for a comprehensive look around. In the fascinating pre-Columbian Hall, you'll find Mayan pyramid murals and the complete, reconstructed contents of a Mexican tomb, while the Californian history sections document the early (white) settlement of the region during the Gold Rush era and after, with some stunning photos of LA in the 1920s. Topping everything off is the breath-taking gem collection: several roomfuls of crystals, and a tempting display of three hundred pounds of gold, safely behind glass.

On a sunny day, spare some time for a stroll through Exposition Park's **Rose Garden** (daily 10am–5pm; free). The flowers are at their most fragrant in April and May, which is when the bulk of the 45,000 annual visitors come by to admire the 16,000 rose bushes and the overall prettiness of their setting.

North of USC

Just to the north of USC and Exposition Park, around Adams Boulevard and Figueroa Street, is a fine collection of early twentieth-century architecture, much of which reflects the power of the district's most famous resident, oil magnate **Edward Doheny** (see box, p.116). The area around Adams and Figueroa has three of LA's best period-revival designs: the Italian Romanesque **St John's Episcopal Church**, 514 W Adams Blvd, which pays tribute to Martin Luther King Jr in stained glass; the grand **St Vincent de Paul Church**, catercorner to St John's, which was Doheny's high-cost donation to the faith – a wildly ornamental Mexican Baroque creation with a sparkling, tiled dome and richly detailed steeple; and the Romanesque **Stimson House**, 2421 S Figueroa St, a castle-like residence built of red sandstone. One long

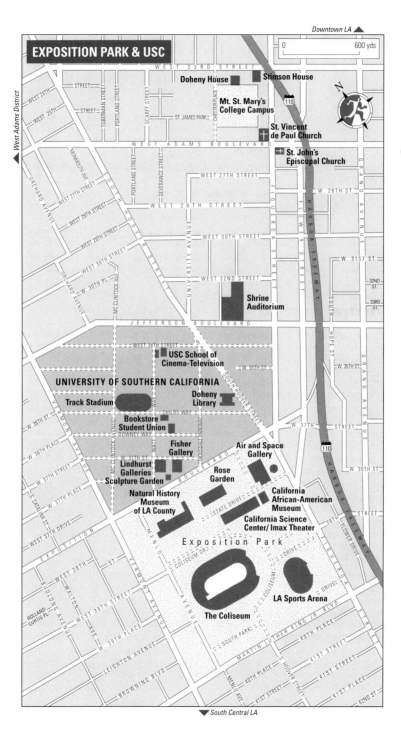

EXPOSITION PARK & USC

0   600 yds

N

West Adams District ▲

WEST 24TH STREET

WEST 25TH STREET

TOBERMAN STREET

PORTLAND STREET

SCARFF STREET

CHESTER PLACE

STREET

STREET

ST. JAMES PARK

Doheny House

Stimson House

Mt. St. Mary's College Campus

110

St. Vincent de Paul Church

W E S T   A D A M S   B O U L E V A R D

St. John's Episcopal Church

ORCHARD AVENUE

MONMOUTH AVE

PORTLAND STREET

SEVERANCE STREET

FIGUEROA STREET

FLOWER STREET

GRAND AVENUE

W. 28TH ST

WEST 27TH STREET

WEST 27TH STREET

WEST 28TH STREET

W E S T   2 8 T H   S T R E E T

WEST 29TH STREET

SOUTH HOOVER STREET

UNIVERSITY AVENUE

WEST 30TH STREET

WEST 30TH STREET

W. 30TH PL.

WEST 32ND STREET

W. 31ST ST.

HARBOR FREEWAY

SOUTH

32ND ST.

33RD ST.

Shrine Auditorium

MC CLINTOCK AVE

ORCHARD AVENUE

J E F F E R S O N   B O U L E V A R D

HOPE ST.

GRAND AVENUE

WEST 34TH STREET

W. 35TH ST.

W. 35TH ST.

USC School of Cinema-Television

UNIVERSITY OF SOUTHERN CALIFORNIA

SOUTH HOOVER STREET

Track Stadium

WATT WAY

Doheny Library

W. 36TH ST.

Bookstore Student Union

CHILDS WAY

DOWNEY WAY

W. 37TH STREET

110

W. 38TH ST

VERMONT AVENUE

MC CLINTOCK AVENUE

TROUSDALE PARKWAY

Fisher Gallery

Air and Space Gallery

W. 36TH PLACE

W. 37TH STREET

Lindhurst Galleries Sculpture Garden

W. 37TH ST.

Rose Garden

W. 37TH PLACE

S CATALINA ST.

Natural History Museum of LA County

MENLO AVENUE

BOULEVARD

STATE DRIVE

California African-American Museum

California Science Center/ Imax Theater

WEST 37TH DRIVE

EXPOSITION

WEST 38TH ST

BUDLONG AVENUE

WEST 39TH STREET

WALTON AVE

E x p o s i t i o n   P a r k

COLISEUM DR.

VERMONT AVENUE

COLISEUM

DRIVE

COLISEUM

DRIVE

38TH

FIGUEROA

TOWER DRIVE

STREET

S. HOOVER STREET

ROLLAND CURTIS PL.

39TH PLACE

The Coliseum

LA Sports Arena

SOUTH PARK DRIVE

MARTIN LUTHER KING JR BLVD

40TH PLACE

41ST STREET

LEIGHTON AVENUE

MENLO AVE

40TH PLACE

41ST STREET

41ST PLACE

BROWNING BLVD

41ST PLACE

42ND ST.

block to the west, **Chester Place** and **St James Park** are pedestrian-friendly zones loaded with officially declared "cultural heritage monuments," or more accurately, the opulent residences of some of LA's most prominent citizens of the early twentieth century. The area's centerpiece is the palatial **Doheny House**, 10 Chester Place, a triumph of the Spanish Gothic style, where you can dawdle in the palm conservatory and immense dining hall built to seat one hundred guests. After the 1958 death of Edward Doheny's wife Estelle, this and the surrounding property were given to Mount St Mary's College, and the house is now one of several elegant buildings on campus. Occasionally, the college hosts classical chamber music concerts under the mansion's beautiful, reverberant dome (Fri evenings at 8pm; $20–40; ☏213/477-2929, Ⓦwww .dacamera.org).

Just across the street from USC lies the most exotic piece of architecture in the area, the **Shrine Auditorium**, 665 W Jefferson Blvd, perhaps best known as the venue of the Oscars ceremony, which was presented here biannually from 1986 to 2001, before moving on to the Kodak Theater in Hollywood. Looking like a vestige of D.W. Griffith's *Intolerance* set in Hollywood, this 1920s Islamic-inspired fantasy, with its onion domes and streetside colonnade, is frequently a venue for traveling religious revival meetings and concerts by assorted pop stars.

Central Avenue

Once the focus of African-American commerce and culture during the interwar years, **Central Avenue** had a vigor that has never really been recaptured. Because pre-1960s segregation and restrictive housing covenants prohibited African Americans from living in large sections of LA, this avenue from Eighth Street to Vernon Avenue became the hub for numerous restaurants, nightclubs and jazz halls – including such hot spots as the *Down Beat Club* and *Last Word* – and attracted a broad mix of blacks, from blue-collar workers to celebrities, and occasionally white liberals from the Westside as well.

With the end of official segregation, Central Avenue inevitably declined, but there are still appealing sights to visit amid the abandoned lots and strip malls. A superb example of Streamline Moderne architecture lies at the north end of the street: the **Coca-Cola Bottling Plant**, 1334 S Central Ave, looking like a huge, landlocked ocean liner, complete with rounded corners, porthole windows and ships' doors. Besides being in excellent condition, the plant is still churning out bottles for the soft-drink giant. Built in 1937, this was the second groundbreaking building in LA created by Robert Derrah, after his Crossroads of the World (see p.102). Nearby at 1401 S Central Ave, the **African-American Firefighters Museum** (Tues–Thurs 10am–2pm; donation suggested; ☏213/744-1730, Ⓦwww.lafd.org/aafm.htm) is housed in Engine Company #30, LA's first all-black fire station, which protected the area from 1913 to 1980 during some of the city's worst segregation, and now displays a modest collection of historic equipment and memorabilia from the era. Eleven blocks south, pioneering black architect Paul R. Williams' **Second Baptist Church**, 2412 Griffith Ave, is a striking Romanesque church built in 1924; while further south, the **Dunbar Hotel**, 4225 S Central Ave, is the first US hotel built specifically for blacks (by a dentist, oddly enough) and patronized by many prominent African Americans – W.E.B. DuBois and Duke Ellington among them – during the 1930s through the 1950s. However, you can only see the hotel's restored lobby and facade, as it now serves as a home for the elderly (information through the OASIS senior center at ☏323/231-6220). In August, however, it hosts the Central Avenue Jazz Festival (details at ☎213/847-3169), which gives a hint of the area's swing and vigor in the old days.

LA's riots

The district of Watts achieved notoriety as the scene of the six-day **Watts Riot** of August 1965. The arrest of a 21-year-old African-American man, **Marquette Frye**, on suspicion of drunken driving, gave rise to charges of police brutality and led to bricks, bottles and slabs of concrete being hurled at police and passing motorists during the night of the 11th. The situation had calmed by the next morning, but by the following evening both young and old were on the streets, venting an anger generated by years of unfair treatment by the police and other white-dominated institutions. Weapons were looted from stores and many buildings set afire (though few residential buildings, black-owned businesses or community services, such as libraries and schools, were touched); street barricades were erected, and the events then took a more serious turn. By the fifth day the insurgents were approaching Downtown, which, along with the fear spreading through white LA, led to the call-out of the National Guard: 13,000 troops arrived, set up machine-gun placements and road blocks, and imposed an 8pm-to-dawn curfew, which caused the rebellion to subside. In the aftermath of the uprising, which left 36 dead, one German reporter said of Watts, "it looks like Germany during the last months of World War II."

Watts hit the headlines for a second time in 1975, when members of the **Symbionese Liberation Army** (SLA), who had kidnapped publishing heiress Patti Hearst, fought a lengthy – and televised – gun battle with police until the house they were trapped in burned to the ground. The site of the battle, at 1466 E 54th St, is now a vacant lot, though the surrounding houses are still riddled with bullet holes.

LA experienced even more **turmoil** in 1992 after the unexpected acquittal of five white Los Angeles police officers, charged with using excessive force after they were videotaped kicking and beating African-American motorist Rodney King. What few predicted was the scale and intensity of the response to the verdict, which was partly fueled, ironically enough, by the almost total lack of a police presence during the first evening's bloodshed. Beginning in South Central LA, where motorists were pulled from their cars and attacked, the situation quickly escalated into a tumult of arson, shooting and looting that spread from Long Beach to Hollywood. Downtown police headquarters were surrounded by a mixed crowd of blacks, Hispanics and whites, all chanting "No Justice, No Peace," and it took the imposition of a four-day dusk-to-dawn curfew, and the presence on LA's streets of several thousand well-armed National Guard troops, to restore calm – whereupon the full extent of the rioting became known. The worst urban violence seen in the US since the bloody, Civil War–era New York draft riots had left 58 dead, nearly 2000 injured, and caused an estimated $1 billion worth of damage. With much of the devastation concentrated in the city's poorest areas, a massive relief operation was mounted to feed and clothe those most severely affected by the carnage. A second trial, stemming from federal charges that the police had violated Mr King's civil rights, resulted in short prison sentences for two of the officers.

Prompted by the Rodney King case, the **Christopher Commission** was set up to investigate racial prejudice within the LAPD. Sadly, its recommendations had all too blatantly not been implemented by the time of the **Rampart police scandal** in 2000 (see box on p.70), when evidence of possible hit-squad tactics and other vigilante actions by members of the LAPD confirmed people's worst fears of the cops being beyond civilian control. While politicians and Westsiders expressed shock and dismay at such charges, and no doubt feared another riot in the scandal's wake, no one in South Central was very surprised – it's simply known as "business as usual" around here.

Watts and Compton

Few neighborhoods inspire more fear in white LA than Watts and Compton, known more for their street crime than anything else. It is true that these spots can be dangerous, especially at night, and are best explored by those familiar with the area or in the company of a local.

The abandoned Art Deco campus of **Pepperdine University**, Vermont Avenue and 80th Street, is one of LA's most visible emblems of white flight, marking the spot where the Church of Christ–affiliated school was located from 1937 to 1972, after which it left for a bluff in Malibu. While the only prominent structure that remains is the **Administration Building**, a graceful Streamline Moderne tower, some long-needed redevelopment money is helping to fund mixed-use housing and retail units. Beyond the former university, South Central becomes grittier and much more dicey. If areas like West Adams and Exposition Park are unfairly described as dangerous, places like **WATTS** and adjacent Willowbrook often justify the description. Now more Hispanic than African-American, Watts provides only one compelling reason to visit (and only during the day), the Gaudí-esque **Watts Towers**, sometimes called the Rodia Towers, at 1765 E 107th St, a half-mile off the 105 freeway on northbound Wilmington Avenue. Constructed from iron, stainless steel, old bedframes and cement, and adorned with bottle fragments and some 70,000 crushed seashells, these striking pieces of folk art are shrouded in mystery. Their maker, Italian immigrant Simon Rodia, had no artistic background or training at all, but labored over the towers' construction from 1921 to 1954, refusing offers of help and unable to explain either their meaning or why he was building them. Once finished, Rodia left the area, refused to talk about the towers and faded into obscurity. The towers, the tallest standing at almost 100 feet, managed to stave off bureaucratic hostility and structural condemnation for many decades, before finally being declared a cultural landmark. Because of lingering repair work from the 1994 Northridge earthquake, the site is open by appointment only; call the adjacent Watts Tower Arts Center, 1727 E 107th St (Tues–Sat 10am–4pm, Sun noon–4pm; free; ☏323/847-4646, Ⓦwww .artscenecal.com/WattsTowers.html), for more information.

Between Watts and the harbor area, the few districts are of passing interest. Despite its fame as the home of many of LA's rappers, as well as tennis champs Serena and Venus Williams, **COMPTON** is not a place where strangers should attempt to sniff out the local music scene. Oddly enough, the town's most famous resident was none other than former president George Bush (Sr), who lived here when the city was still known for its oil wells, and when whites were still in power. With the white flight of the 1950s and 1960s, though, investment capital dried up and Compton suffered greatly and still hasn't recovered. History buffs secure in their cars might chance a stop at the **Dominguez Ranch Adobe**, just off the 91 freeway at 18127 S Alameda St (Tues & Wed 1–4pm, second & third Sun of each month 1–4pm; free conducted tour ☏323/636-6030), which chronicles the social ascent of the adobe's founder, Juan Jose Dominguez, one of the soldiers who left Mexico with Padre Junípero Serra's expedition to found the California missions, and whose long military service was acknowledged in 1782 by the granting of these 75,000 acres of land. As the importance of the area grew, so too did the influence of Dominguez's descendants, who became powerful in local politics. The adobe's six rooms, filled with antiques and furnishings, offer a vivid glimpse of life during the Spanish and Mexican eras.

The gangs of LA

South Central LA is the heartland of the city's infamous **gangs**, said to number one hundred thousand members among them, which have existed for more than forty years and often encompass several generations of a family. The black gangs known as **Crips** and **Bloods** are the most famous, but there are also many burgeoning Hispanic gangs as well, most prominently the **18th Street Gang** who, despite their name, operate all over the LA basin and in the San Fernando Valley. The character-istic violence associated with these groups often stems from territorial fights over drug-dealing, with many gangs staking claim to certain neighborhoods through their monikers. The larger gangs employ rather sophisticated schemes involving protec-tion rackets, money laundering and expansion into legitimate businesses from small retail operations to, it is rumored, the music industry – all tactics reminiscent not of common street thugs, but of old-style Italian mobsters.

The old story of LA's gangs is increasingly becoming outdated, though, as social and demographic changes alter the landscape of crime. Gang life used to be fairly contained within the city, and could be broken down into simple black-on-black vio-lence, which occasionally spilled into other neighborhoods (such as Westwood in the 1980s), making white Westsiders increasingly paranoid and supportive of all manner of hamfisted police tactics, including SWAT teams and a paramilitary tank, in the pre-1992 riots era. Nowadays, though, local gangs are increasingly **interna-tional**, with chapters not only reaching other cities throughout the western US, but also strongly linked to Mexican gangs and organized-crime syndicates. Indeed, LA serves as a training ground for budding gangsters from Central America who, after their deportation, return to their home countries schooled in the high-tech ways of first-world killing, inflicting more misery on a region already awash in violence and poverty.

That said, with all the different ethnic (and multi-ethnic) gangs in the city, don't try to decipher the graffiti you see on the wall of an inner-city liquor store, or wrongly assume that a gang member must be an obvious hoodlum in the "bad part of town." This sort of crime is intrinsic to the city as a whole, from Downtown to the Westside, and is only at its most violent and visible in ghettos like South Central or Pico Union. By sticking to familiar areas in the day and well-policed districts at night, tourists should have few problems with gangs.

East LA

You can't visit LA without being made aware of the Hispanic influence on the city's demography and culture, whether through the thousands of Mexican restaurants, the innumerable street names in Español or, most obviously, the preponderance of Spanish spoken on the streets in dialects from Tijuana to Oaxaca, from Guatemala to Peru. Of the many Hispanic neighborhoods all over the city, the most long-standing is **EAST LA**, a Spanish-speaking enclave that begins two miles east of Downtown, across the concrete flood-control channel of the Los Angeles River. There was a Mexican population here long before the white settlers came, and from the late nineteenth century onward millions more arrived, chiefly to work as agricultural laborers in orchards and citrus groves. As the white inhabitants gradually moved west towards the coast, the Mexicans stayed, creating a vast Spanish-speaking community that's one of the most historic in the country, as well as one of the most insular and unfa-miliar to outsiders.

Activity in East LA (commonly abbreviated to "ELA" or "East Los") tends to be outdoors, in cluttered markets and busy shops. Non-Hispanic visitors are comparatively thin on the ground, but you are unlikely to meet any hostility on the streets during the day – though you should steer clear of the rough and very male-dominated bars, and avoid the whole area after dark. **Guadalupe**, the Mexican depiction of the Virgin Mary, appears in mural art all over East LA, nowhere more strikingly than at the junction of Mednik and Cesar Chavez avenues. When a housing project across the street was demolished in the early 1970s, one wall, bearing a particularly remarkable image of Mary surrounded by a rich band of rainbow colors, was saved from the wrecking ball and reinstated across the street. Lined with blue tile, the mural now serves as an unofficial shrine where worshippers place fresh flowers and candles.

Other than the street life and murals, there are few specific "sights" in East LA other than the mausoleum of **New Calvary Cemetery**, 4201 E Whittier Ave. Rivaling City Hall for sheer audacity, the monumental tomb piles on the

The heart of Southeast LA

Following the path of Interstate 5 between South Central and East LA, **Southeast LA** is generally made up of low-grade industrial sites – incinerators, salvage operations, auto wrecking yards – and their dingy bedroom communities, along with large expanses of deindustrialized concrete desert overflowing with weeds. In the years following World War II, Southeast LA was a center for auto manufacture and tire-making, but the subsequent loss of blue-collar jobs led to the disappearance of much of the white and African-American population. They were replaced by Mexican and Central American immigrant laborers, many of whom would work at or below the minimum wage in sweatshop conditions. Because this is one of the main US centers for new arrivals, population density in some places has become overwhelming – the tiny town of **Cudahy** packs nearly 25,000 people on one square mile of land, and not surprisingly has one of the country's highest poverty rates – while in other industrial towns, residential zones are practically forbidden, and sweatshops evade labor laws through lack of local oversight.

If, for some reason, you should wind up in this bleak area, there are a few things worth checking out, starting in **Vernon**, an inhospitable burg whose only highlight is the **Farmer John's Mural**, 3049 E Vernon Ave, a bucolic trompe l'oeil on a meat-packing plant, showing a team of little pigs scampering about a farm and managing to scale the building walls – an amusing scene that almost makes you forget the ugly business inside. Further east, in Commerce, is **The Citadel**, 5675 Telegraph Rd, modeled on the ancient architecture of Khorsabad in the Middle East; note the massive carvings of priests and warriors on the facade. Built by the architecture firm of Morgan, Walls and Clements (see box on p.80), this structure started life as the Samson Tyre and Rubber Company, before being abandoned and finally turned into a fashion outlet, in a convenient location near the 5 freeway (Ⓦ www.citadelfactory-stores.com).

To the south, the community of **Downey** is uneventful in itself, but does feature a true pop architecture icon – the country's original **McDonald's** fast-food restaurant, 10207 Lakewood Blvd, opened in 1953, a year before the chain officially started. Boasting a much more exuberant, colorful design than the mansard-roofed clones of today, this McDonald's also features big yellow-neon arches that stretch over, and into, the building itself, plus a winking chef named "Speedee" atop its 60-foot-high sign. More than just an old burger joint, the restaurant is also listed as a cultural monument by the National Trust for Historic Preservation and even has its own museum and gift shop.

styles, with Corinthian columns and pilasters, an Egyptian-pyramid roof and a few Byzantine domes, plus some sculpted angels thrown in for good measure. Beyond its exterior panache, the mausoleum is also the resting place of old-time Angelenos like Edward Doheny and movie stars like John and Ethel Barrymore, and Lou Costello.

For a more animated scene, stroll along **Cesar Chavez Avenue**, formerly Brooklyn Avenue, going eastward from Indiana Street and check out the wild-pet shops for their free-roaming parrots and cases of boa constrictors, and the **botanicas**, which cater to practitioners of Santería – a religion that is equal parts voodoo and Catholicism. Browse among the shark's teeth, dried devil fish and plastic statuettes of Catholic saints, or explain to the shopkeeper (in Spanish) what ails you, then pick out remedies from a wide selection of magical herbs, ointments and candles. Only slightly less exotic fare can be found in **El Mercado de Los Angeles**, 3425 E First St, a market not unlike Downtown's Olvera Street (see p.54) but much more authentic. Afterwards, drive through the sketchier, freeway-caged LA district of **Boyle Heights**, which through the 1940s was a center for Jewish culture but has since become a solidly Hispanic neighborhood, home to a large number of Central Americans from Guatemala, El Salvador and Honduras. Go to the junction of **Soto and Cesar Chavez**, where at 5pm each afternoon, Norteños combos (upright bass, accordion, guitar and banjo sexto) showcase their talents for free, hoping to be booked for weddings. Although this area can be relaxed and colorful during the day, it should be strictly avoided at night, when the local gangs make their presence felt.

Of the nearby districts, the only one of conceivable interest is **MONTEREY PARK**, northeast of East LA, a reasonably safe area that has the highest percentage of Asian residents of any city in the nation (40 percent) and is a major gateway for Taiwanese and mainland Chinese immigrants arriving in the US. It's also home to a number of excellent authentic Chinese restaurants, as well as many nightclubs, ethnic grocers and theaters, on its main drag, **Atlantic Boulevard**.

Whittier and around

Well to the south of East LA, and almost to the border of Orange County, the small town of **WHITTIER**, originally founded by Quakers and named after Quaker poet John Greenleaf Whittier, offers a handful of interesting sights. It was here that **Richard Nixon** – a Quaker himself – was raised, went to law school and started his first law office, a story which, if you don't already know it, many of the locals will be happy to recount for you in detail. (His birthplace and library is in the Orange County town of Yorba Linda; see p.214.) You can find out more at the engaging **Whittier Museum**, 6755 Newlin Ave (Tues–Fri 9am–4pm; $3; ☎562/945-3871, Ⓦwww.whittiermuseum.org), a treasure trove of historic city artifacts and assorted gizmos ranging from a working model of an oil derrick to replicas of a Pacific Electric Red Car and a stunt plane on display. Other highlights include an old-fashioned barn, a rebuilt version of a Quaker meeting hall, and the desk Nixon used in his first law office. For a look at another local politician who had an even harder time of it, there's the engaging **Pio Pico State Historic Park**, 6003 Pioneer Blvd (Wed–Sun 10am–5pm; free), centered around an adobe full of Victorian furnishings and artifacts tracing the life of **Pio Pico**, the last Mexican governor of California, who lived here for a period. Constructed in 1842, the house saw Pico lose his governorship, re-emerge on the LA City Council, make a fortune in real estate and finally go bankrupt, eventually dying penniless.

Several miles south, at 10211 S Pioneer Blvd, the **Clarke Estate** (Tues & Fri 11am–2pm; free; call ☎562/863-4896 for more details) is a popular wedding spot, with elegantly landscaped grounds. It's also another of Irving Gill's Mission Revival and early-modern melds, with Mediterranean balconies and Tuscan columns used to offset a number of pre-Columbian reliefs and icons – giving a hint of what LA would have looked like if it had been colonized by Italians and Mayans, instead of Spaniards. Neighboring **Heritage Park**, 12100 Mora Drive (daily 7am–10pm; free), is also worth a look for its collection of re-created, local historic buildings, including a windmill, aviary and carriage barn, accompanied by a pretty English garden. Less refined is the **LA County Sheriffs Museum**, 11515 S Colima Rd (Mon–Fri 9am–4pm; free), where you can examine a replica of an early jail and a sizeable set of law-enforcement antiques – from classic tommy guns to razor-sharp ice picks. Look, too, for the menacing meat hooks and crude knives that were popular tools in LA's mid-nineteenth-century "Hell Town" days. If you come during July, the sheriff's department also puts on quite an unusual show, taking the seized weapons of contemporary miscreants – knives, guns and the like – and destroying them before the eyes of spectators.

Finally, if you've already ventured this far for historic attractions, you might as well head north to the **Workman-Temple Homestead Museum**, 15415 E Don Julian Rd (Wed–Sun 1–4pm, weekends open at 10am; free; ☎626/968-8492, ⓦwww.homesteadmuseum.org), a historic estate that's the lone point of interest in the drab industrial **CITY OF INDUSTRY**. Here, an early emigrant party first staked a regional land claim and constructed this historic Spanish Colonial house around an 1840 adobe, complete with expansive grounds. There's a smokehouse and water tower, as well as a cemetery that contains the graves of many figures from regional history, including that of Pio Pico. The house itself is striking, full of carved wooden details, wrought-iron railings and tiled stairways, and the glimmering centerpiece – stained-glass windows depicting steadfast family members on their westward trek to Southern California.

7

The South Bay and LA Harbor

S tretching south of LAX to the edge of Orange County, the oceanside cities of the **South Bay** and **LA Harbor** share little in common except their proximity to the sea and insularity from the rest of the metropolis. While the streets around the beaches are the province of wealthy white Angelenos, poorer African Americans and Hispanics reside many miles inland, in middle-class suburbs like Carson and Hawthorne, and in bleak districts like North Long Beach. Overall, though, the area's balmy climate and windswept scenery make this one of the city's most visually appealing regions.

The South Bay begins south of the airport, with three **south beach cities** that are smaller and more suburban than LA's other seaside towns. Further south, and visible all along this stretch of the coast, the large, vegetated **Palos Verdes Peninsula** occupies a wild, craggy stretch of coastline, with some rustic parks and pricey real estate – much of it behind locked gates – while comparatively rough-hewn **San Pedro** is a gritty, working-class community that forms part of the site for the LA harbor. Its counterpart, **Long Beach**, is best known as the home of the *Queen Mary*, even though it is also the region's second-largest city, with nearly half a million people living here. Hardly a major draw for visitors, the **harbor** itself is a massive complex divided between San Pedro and Long Beach, consisting of so many ship passages, trucking routes and artificial islands that the huge Vincent Thomas Bridge had to be built to carry travelers over the entire works.

Perhaps the most enticing place in the area is **Santa Catalina Island**, twenty miles offshore and easily reached by ferry. Little visited, the island remains largely a wilderness, with many unique forms of plant and animal life, and just one significant center of population, **Avalon**, a city in which the only legal form of motorized transport is the golf cart.

South beach cities

Immediately south of LAX along the coast, you'll find few interesting sights, just the candy-striped stacks of the Scattergood steam plant, a few oil refineries and LA's only sewage treatment center – Hyperion, one of the villains responsible for polluting Santa Monica Bay (see box on p.133). Soon after,

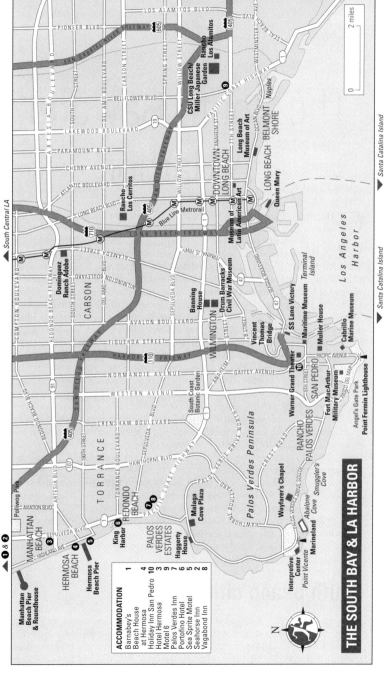

THE SOUTH BAY & LA HARBOR

Orange County

2 miles

0

Santa Catalina Island

Santa Catalina Island

Los Angeles Harbor

Terminal
Island

LONG BEACH   BELMONT SHORE

Naples

DOWNTOWN
LONG BEACH

Queen Mary

Long Beach
Museum of Art

Museum of
Latin American Art

CSU Long Beach/
Miller Japanese
Garden

Rancho
Los Alamitos

Rancho
Los Cerritos

Blue Line Metrorail

LONG BEACH FREEWAY

Dominguez
Ranch Adobe

CARSON

Banning
House

Drum Barracks
Civil War Museum

WILMINGTON

Vincent
Thomas
Bridge

SS Lane Victory

Maritime Museum

Muller House

Cabrillo
Marine Museum

SAN PEDRO

Warner Grand Theater

Fort MacArthur
Military Museum

South Coast
Botanic Garden

RANCHO
PALOS VERDES

Palos Verdes Peninsula

Angel's Gate Park

Point Fermin Lighthouse

Wayfarer's Chapel

Point Vicente

Marineland

*Abalone
Cove*   *Smuggler's
Cove*

Interpretive
Center

Malaga
Cove Plaza

PALOS
VERDES
ESTATES

Haggerty
House

REDONDO
BEACH

King
Harbor

Polliwog Park

MANHATTAN
BEACH

HERMOSA
BEACH

Hermosa
Beach Pier

Manhattan
Beach Pier &
Roundhouse

TORRANCE

South Central LA

ACCOMMODATION	
Barnabey's	1
Beach House	
at Hermosa	4
Holiday Inn San Pedro	10
Hotel Hermosa	3
Motel 6	9
Palos Verdes Inn	7
Portofino Hotel	6
Sea Sprite Motel	5
Seahorse Inn	2
Vagabond Inn	8

N

THE SOUTH BAY & LA HARBOR

though, the main access route, **Vista del Mar**, rises up a bluff as it hugs the coastline, and an eight-mile strip of beach towns begins. Sitting on small, gently sloped hills, these laid-back towns can make for a refreshing break if you like your beaches without trendy packaging. Along their shared beach boardwalk known as **The Strand** (which ends at Redondo Beach), the joggers and roller-skaters are more likely to be locals than outsiders, and each city has at least one municipal pier and a beckoning strip of white sand, with most oceanside locations equipped for surfing and beach volleyball. These little towns are also well connected to the rest of the city, within easy reach of LAX and linked by regular buses (#225, #232 and #439) to Downtown LA.

Manhattan Beach

Accessible along the bike path from Venice, or by car via Pacific Coast Highway or Vista del Mar, **MANHATTAN BEACH** is the most northern of the three, a likable place with a well-to-do air, home mainly to white-collar workers whose middle-class stucco houses sit near the beach, along the main drag of **Highland Avenue**. Like its counterparts to the south, Manhattan Beach was first linked to the rest of LA by the Pacific Electric Railway's Red Cars at the beginning of the twentieth century, and before long this stretch was a favorite spot for itinerant fishermen, boaters and pleasure-seekers of all types. While not as chaotic or thrilling as Venice and Santa Monica, these cities did provide a day's amusement along their sands and on their piers, though without many of the carnival games and working-class visitors of those more northerly towns. These days, there's not much to do on Manhattan Beach's **pier** besides stroll, though it's the site of the aptly named **Roundhouse**. The **aquarium** inside (Mon–Fri 3pm–dusk, Sat & Sun 10am–dusk; $2), is a mildly interesting spot where you can peer at sharks and lobsters, and fiddle around with the helpless creatures in a tide-pool "touch tank."

The **beach** itself is the main reason to visit, with generally cleaner water than at Santa Monica and Venice beaches (except around the piers); surfing is a major local pastime – a two-week international surf festival occurs each August – along with beach volleyball, evidenced by the profusion of nets across the sands. To play, just rent a ball at one of the many rental shacks found along the beach. The mildly diverting **Historical Center**, a mile from the beach in the post office at 1601 Manhattan Beach Blvd (Sat & Sun noon–3pm; free), exhibits locally crafted pottery from the early part of the twentieth century and an illuminating collection of photos, tracing the city's history, from when it was known as Shore Acres right up to the present. Nearby, the small **Manhattan Beach Art Center**, 1560 Manhattan Beach Blvd (Mon–Fri 2–6pm, Sat 1–4pm; free), presents more contemporary work from regional artisans working in media from glass to photography. The art center lies across from **Polliwog Park**, a pleasant greenspace, which in summer is one of several South Bay parks (including Point Fermin in San Pedro; see p.167) that host "**Shakespeare by the Sea**" (periodically Thurs–Sun 6 & 7pm; free; ⓦ www.shakespearebythesea.org), a festival of local performances of the Bard's work. Performances tend to vary in quality, but can make for a fun way to conclude a day spent on the waves or the sands.

Hermosa Beach and Redondo Beach

To the south, **HERMOSA BEACH**, across Longfellow Avenue, is more lower-income than Manhattan Beach, its houses smaller and less showy, but is in many ways more enjoyable, with a hint of a bohemian feel in certain spots. It also has a lively beachside strip, which is most energetic near the foot of the pier on Twelfth Street. Packed with restaurants and clubs (among them one of the South Bay's best-known nightspots, the *Lighthouse café*; see p.293), the area has long been a major hangout for revelers of all stripes, and is easily the most colorful spot in the South Bay before Long Beach. The **pier** itself is fairly low-key, though it is the site for the engaging **Beach Bash** in early June (see p.316). Apart from ocean-based activities, the town boasts a lush **green belt** – a long, grassy median running between Valley Drive and Ardmore Avenue, which connects to Manhattan Beach and makes a good place for a workout on any of several bike and jogging paths.

Further south, despite its familiar name, good strips of sand and fine views of Palos Verdes' stunning greenery, **REDONDO BEACH**, across Herondo Street, is less inviting than its relaxed neighbor, with hardly any noteworthy sights. You'll be treated to condos and large hotels lining the beachfront, and an unremarkable and touristy pier, while the exclusive eateries around the yacht-lined **King Harbor** are off-limits to curious interlopers.

The Palos Verdes Peninsula

South of the beach cities, the **PALOS VERDES PENINSULA**, a great green hump marking LA's southwest corner, is known for its rugged beaches and secluded coves, sweeping views of the coastline (from Malibu to Orange County), and some of the most expensive real estate in Southern California. Originally intended as a "millionaires' colony" by 1920s developers, Palos Verdes has more or less worked out according to plan, with several gated communities like **Rolling Hills**, numerous multimillion-dollar estates, and an armada of private security guards. Despite this, the Palos Verdes Peninsula is one of the best spots for experiencing nature in the area, with sea cliffs and tide pools, and its oceanside scenery is nothing less than awe-inspiring.

North Palos Verdes

The north section of the peninsula is largely ungated and accessible, with most attractions located near the coast of **PALOS VERDES ESTATES**, the first city founded on the peninsula, in 1939, and the one with by far the most significant architecture and public greenspace. The area was first laid out by **John Olmsted** and **Frederick Law Olmsted Jr** – sons of the famed designer of New York's Central Park – who both came here in the early twentieth century to design upscale neighborhoods and advise on the future direction of urban

---

Hiking tours of Palos Verdes

The Palos Verdes Peninsula Land Conservancy offers periodic monthly **hiking tours** of some of the most invigorating spots on Palos Verdes, from Abalone Cove to San Pedro's Sunken City. The treks are free and two-to-three hours in length, sometimes in rather rugged environs, and typically focus on the ecological, historical or cultural value of a given area – information you're not likely to discover very easily otherwise (information at ☎310/541-7613, ⓦwww.pvplc.com).

planning in LA (suggestions that were ahead of their time and were, predictably, ignored). Palos Verdes Estates amounts to a small-scaled version of what might have been had the Olmsted brothers had their way. Nearly one-third of its space is preserved as parkland (on which you may come across a roaming herd of peacocks), while the town itself has a pseudo-European air, threaded by circuitous streets that overlook the ocean, its commercial development tightly controlled. Indeed, the town's early overseers were so committed to the period-revival aesthetic that all new designs, housing or otherwise, had to be reviewed and approved by an officially sanctioned "art jury" – surely the only time this has ever happened in LA.

The best place to soak in this "Old World" atmosphere is at **Malaga Cove Plaza**, Palos Verdes Drive at Via Corta, a Spanish Colonial–style commercial center that the Olmsteds planned as a prototype for four other such areas in the city, none of which was ever built. Although the central plaza and arcaded buildings are attractive enough, the main draw is the **Neptune Fountain**, a smaller replica of a 1563 structure in Bologna, Italy, of the same name. Elsewhere, much of the city's seaside architecture has a strong Mediterranean flair, good examples of which are the **Olmsted House**, Paseo del Mar at Via Arroyo, an elegant Spanish Colonial estate with a walled garden that was built for Frederick Law Olmsted Jr, and the **Haggerty House**, 415 Paseo del Mar, an Italian-style villa that was built by the Olmsteds themselves, since reincarnated as the Neighborhood Church.

Inland on the north peninsula, there are few compelling sights save the **South Coast Botanic Garden**, 26300 Crenshaw Blvd (daily 9am–5pm; $5, kids $1; ☏310/544-6815, ⓦwww.palosverdes.com/botanicgardens), a relaxing spot that was first home to a diatomite mine for some 37 years and then to a giant landfill. In the 1950s and 1960s, LA dumped 3.5 million tons of its trash here, creating one of the bigger eyesores in the region, but since 1961, the turf has been covered by layers of soil and successfully reclaimed as a garden, filled with exotic bromeliads, an expansive cactus garden, various kinds of palm trees, ferns and flowering plants, and even a small French-style garden. The only sign of its former life is the terrain itself, which, thanks to the subsiding of the garbage below, has a weirdly undulating landscape, peppered here and there with "exhaust" pipes that allow for the release of carbon dioxide and methane from the chemical stew underground.

South of the garden you can follow Crenshaw Boulevard to some elite Palos Verdes neighborhoods, such as **ROLLING HILLS ESTATES**, and the similarly well-heeled **RANCHO PALOS VERDES**, a bit more open. In any case, amid the pricey architecture, you're afforded excellent vistas of the ocean.

South Palos Verdes

South of Palos Verdes Estates along Palos Verdes Drive, the beaches are more easily visited, and quite worthwhile for their significant natural attractions, one of which is the promontory of **Point Vicente**, sitting on high cliff walls above the Pacific Ocean. Here a **park** overlooks the sea, and although the **interpretive center** here is closed for renovation until 2004, you might catch sight of **whales** from here during their seasonal migrations (heaviest from December to January and March to April), which occasionally get close enough to photograph. Nearby, a **lighthouse** dating from 1926 towers nearly two hundred feet above sea level in a dramatic cliffside setting; however, you can't go inside, and probably don't want to get too close thanks to the steep drop-off below. A bit further south, at Long Point, the abandoned **Marineland** theme park used to be one of the prime draws to this part of the city. Like the northern piers, however, it's now just a part of LA's amusement-park history, and you can dimly see the old concrete sign, marine tanks and crumbling buildings from the park's still-accessible parking lot. More importantly for undersea explorers, Long Point offers some of LA's best **diving**, which you can get to from the park's lower gate near the parking lot (at least for now – a golf course and resort are planned for the site in coming years).

Continuing south on Palos Verdes Drive, **Abalone Cove**, reached from a parking lot on Barkentine Road or by a steep roadside stairway, boasts rock and tide pools and offshore kelp beds alive with sea urchins, rock scallops and the increasingly rare abalone. While you're in the area, don't miss **Wayfarer's Chapel**, across the street at 5755 Palos Verdes Drive, a masterpiece of pitched glass and wood that was designed by Frank Lloyd Wright's son, Lloyd. A tribute to the eighteenth-century Swedish scientist and mystic Emanuel Swedenborg, and funded by the Swedenborgian Church, the ultimate aim is for the redwood grove around the chapel to grow and entangle itself in the glass-framed structure – a fusing of human handiwork with the forces of nature in a symbolic union. Unsurprisingly, the place is one of LA's top choices for weddings. A half-mile south, the coast at **Portuguese Bend** provides another dramatic ocean vista (though it's also prone to landslides), and was once the place where Portuguese whalers hunted gray whales for their blubber, which was harvested for its oil. Strangely enough, their trade came to an end thanks to a simple lack of firewood to run their operation, and the only trace of their activity is the place name they inspired. Much more conspicuous is **Smugglers Cove**, at the end of a path off Peppertree Drive, which is a renowned nudist beach just around Portuguese Bend.

San Pedro

Forming part of the site of the LA harbor, scruffy **SAN PEDRO**, in contrast to Palos Verdes to the north, is a diverse blue-collar town settled by immigrants from the Mediterranean and Scandinavia, with a rich, often violent, history. As one of several places along the West Coast where labor strife erupted during the Depression, the city has a long tradition of populism and a nagging antipathy toward the city of Los Angeles, which annexed it in 1909, despite local opposition. That distaste remains and a drive for secession began in the 1990s, spurred on by complaints of under-representation at LA City Hall and bureaucratic incompetence in developing the area as a tourist attraction. For better or worse, everything about San Pedro, from its low-rise, old-time buildings to its maritime atmosphere, gives it little in common with any place else in the metropolis.

Downtown San Pedro

San Pedro's harbor abuts the city's **downtown** and forms part of the massive port of LA – the country's biggest, and the third biggest in the world outside of Hong Kong and Shanghai. The focus of all shipping activity is an industrial zone known as **Terminal Island**, a man-made island across the harbor's main channel that offers nothing but bleak industrial vistas. While you'll have to keep

△ Traffic on the Harbor Freeway

The Port of San Pedro

First called the "Bay of Smokes" for the many fires set by Tongva natives along its shoreline, this formerly Spanish-controlled city was named in 1603 after **St Peter** and consolidated in 1784 into the territory owned by Juan Domínguez, whose ranch house is still standing in Compton (see p.154). Later, around the time it was usurped by the US in the Mexican–American War, San Pedro became a major center for the maritime trade of animal skins and beef tallow and, by taking advantage of the Wilmington-to-Downtown LA **rail lines** of entrepreneur **Phineas Banning** (see p.386), later became linked to cities throughout the region in the 1870s. A decade later, the city was incorporated and began maturing as a port, with the action centered on **Timms Landing**, where animal hides were exported and seabound travelers embarked. Although little physical evidence remains, you can get a sense of the place during this period by reading Richard Henry Dana's classic maritime book *Two Years Before the Mast*.

Around this time, **Collis Huntington** of the Southern Pacific Railroad was threatening to make Santa Monica the chief harbor of the region, clashing with many LA bigwigs as he did so, especially Harrison Gray Otis of the *Los Angeles Times*, whose newspaper did much to excite passions for a "free" harbor. In the end, Huntington's battle was successful, and by the end of the century, construction on a massive two-mile breakwater had begun in San Pedro and was completed a decade later. Shortly thereafter, Los Angeles mounted its annexation drive and the military base **Fort MacArthur** (see p.168) was built next to the harbor. The world wars and a booming maritime economy further helped San Pedro to attract shipbuilding industries and commercial canneries, and by the 1950s, despite occasional labor conflicts, the district hit its peak.

The industrialization of the harbor took its toll on the environment, however, resulting on one occasion in smog so thick that the airport had to be shut down. As well, for many decades corporations pumped **DDT** directly into the sea near Palos Verdes, and today the contaminant sits in a giant deadly "bubble" offshore. Along with this, economic **recessions** and industrial retrenchment contributed to San Pedro's decline, and by the 1980s the city was decayed, full of boarded-up businesses and post-industrial eyesores. Although redevelopment money, some ecological clean-up and the opening of new museums have helped revitalize the city in recent years, most locals realize that if it weren't for the port, which is still busy, San Pedro would basically be dead.

your distance from the oceanside docks and machinery, there are some points along the channel worth investigating.

To get a better sense of the harbor's history, a good place to start is the **SS Lane Victory**, in Berth 94, off Swinford Street, across from the shipyard (daily 9am–4pm; $4; ℡310/519-9545, ⓦwww.lanevictoryship.com), a huge, ten-thousand-ton cargo ship that was built in the shipyard in 1945 for World War II, also operated in Korea and Vietnam, and today is maintained by the Merchant Marine. A tour will take you through its many cramped spaces, including the engine and radio rooms, crew quarters, galley and bridge. If you're after a ride, the ship offers elaborate, all-day summertime **cruises** to Santa Catalina Island (July & Aug Sat & Sun; $100, kids $60; information at ℡310/519-9545), involving onboard tours and meals, and historical re-enactments with captured stowaway spies, and dogfights with Japanese and American air squadrons. Overhead is the towering **Vincent Thomas Bridge**, California's third-longest suspension bridge, completed in 1963 to take over the work of transporting sailors and fishermen to and from Terminal Island.

There's more nautical history at the **Maritime Museum**, further south at Sampson Way at Sixth Street (Tues–Sun 10am–5pm; $1; ☎310/548-7618, Ⓦwww.lamaritimemuseum.org). Occupying the old ferry tower, the museum is a storehouse for art and artifacts from the glory days of San Pedro's fishing and whaling industries, focusing on everything from old-fashioned clipper-ship voyages to contemporary diving expeditions. Besides plenty of model ships, including Spanish galleons and British steamships (and the inevitable miniature replica of the *Titanic*), the museum also has interesting exhibits on Native American seacraft, navigation devices through the ages, and artful scrimshaw (intricately carved whale bones) from the whaling era. Behind the museum, you can find full-sized boats as well, including various tugs and fishing boats, an old-fashioned schooner and a racing yacht. Next door, at Berth 86, the museum houses **Fireboat 2** in its own large, red cylindrical building. Nearly one hundred feet long, this restored 1925 floating fire station has served the LA Fire Department for decades, spraying over ten thousand gallons a minute to put out naval fires around the harbor, and is viewable on museum tours. Just west of here, the austere **Bloody Thursday Monument**, Sixth Street at Beacon Street close to the City Hall, is another reminder of the city's gritty past. Marking the 1934 strike by local waterfront workers, many of them recently arrived immigrants, it commemorates the two who were killed when police and private guards opened fire.

Four blocks further west, the opulent **Warner Grand Theater**, 478 W Sixth St, is a terrific 1931 moviehouse, all dark Zigzag Moderne details and sunburst motifs. Now a repertory cinema and performing arts hall, the theater is the centerpiece of ongoing efforts to revive San Pedro's city center, which has lured back several clothing merchants and restaurants. Linking most of the city's major attractions is the **San Pedro Trolley** (Fri–Mon 10am–6pm; $1; actually three 1908 Pacific Electric red cars (two replicas, one restored) that run parallel to Harbor Boulevard and connect the SS *Lane Victory* with the Cabrillo Marina at 22nd Street.

A block west of the trolley route, another of San Pedro's historic sites, the **Muller House**, 1542 S Beacon St (first three Sundays of the month 1–4pm; donation), is the mildly attractive 1899 home of a shipbuilder that gives a taste of the city's glory days with its original 1920s decor and furnishings.

Although it's an easy walk from the trolley route, don't bother with the over-rated **Ports o' Call Village** – a dismal batch of wooden and corrugated iron huts supposedly capturing the flavor of seaports around the world by way of its T-shirt and junk-food vendors.

Point Fermin

At the tip of San Pedro, about a mile south of the trolley terminus, is **Point Fermin**, a cape that, at the end of the eighteenth century, explorer George Vancouver named for an early Franciscan missionary, Padre Fermín Lasuén. On the cape's far end, across Paseo del Mar, **Point Fermin Park** is a verdant strip of land sitting atop ocean bluffs that mark LA's southernmost point. Hidden on the seaward edge of the bluffs, blocked off by shoddy chain-link fences, sits what's left of an early twentieth-century resort known as **Sunken City**, where the crumbling streets and housing foundations are officially off-limits to the public. If you'd like to tour the area without trespassing and learn more about the history of the place, the Palos Verdes Peninsula Land Conservancy offers periodic **tours** of this and other interesting spots on the peninsula (see box, p.162).

Inland toward the middle of the park, **Point Fermin Lighthouse** once contained a 6600-candlepower light and beamed it 22 miles out to sea. Ending its service during World War II, the lighthouse fell into disrepair until it was renovated in the 1970s. The lighthouse isn't open to the public, but there is an outdoor whale-watching station where you can read up on the winter migrations. Bottle-nosed dolphins can often be seen during their fall departure and spring return as well, and there's also the less seasonally dependent thrill of spotting hang-gliders swooping down off the sea cliffs.

More aquatic wildlife can be sighted in **Angel's Gate Park**, just north at 3601 Gaffey St, on a hill overlooking the Pacific. Here, the **Marine Mammal Center** (daily 8am–4pm; free; ☎310/548-5677, ⓦwww.mar3ine.org/mmcc), which cares for sick and injured seals and sea lions, displays these animals during their recovery, and also has exhibits on marine biology. Not far away, a central pagoda contains the **Korean Bell of Friendship**, a 17-ton copper-and-tin gift to the city from South Korea. Inscribed with Korean characters and twelve lines representing the signs of the zodiac, the bell has no clapper; instead, a hefty log strikes the instrument only on three key days of the year: Korean and American independence days and New Year's Eve. Nearby, **Fort MacArthur Military Museum** (Tues, Thurs, Sat & Sun noon–5pm; free; ⓦwww.ftmac.org) is open to the public, on the old site of Battery Osgood, a gun emplacement at the original **Fort MacArthur**, a military post built in the late nineteenth century and named after General Arthur MacArthur – Douglas's dad (it has since been converted into private housing for service members). The fort became a nuclear-missile launch site during the Cold War, one of sixteen such sites in the LA area (however, the only one now open to the public can be found in the Santa Monica Mountains; see "San Vicente Mountain Park," p.206). Later retrofitted for surface-to-air missiles, the fort's museum displays a clutch of military outfits and old photographs, as well as assorted disarmed bombs, mines and missiles.

Below the bluffs, east of the fort, a beachside path winds around the cape and reaches the excellent **Cabrillo Marine Aquarium**, 3720 Stephen White Drive (Tues–Fri noon–5pm, Sat & Sun 10am–5pm; $2, parking $7; ☎310/548-7562, ⓦwww.cabrilloaq.org), where a diverse collection of marine life has been imaginatively assembled into 35 tanks and assorted displays: everything from predator snails and sea urchins to larger displays on otters, seals and whales, plus the rare "sarcastic fringehead" (a peculiar fish whose name makes sense once you see it). The building, designed by Frank Gehry, is not especially appealing, surrounded as it is with copious industrial chain-link fencing. Fully visible from the aquarium, a short jetty extends to a 1913 **breakwater** that is over 9000 feet long and marks the harbor entrance. At the end of the breakwater sits the **Angel's Gate Lighthouse**, a 75-foot-tall Romanesque monolith that blasts its automated foghorn twice per minute, using a rotating green light to direct ships into the protected harbor and helping them avoid the breakwater's three-million-ton rock seawall.

Wilmington

Due north of San Pedro, **WILMINGTON** is the center of LA's petroleum industry, and holds the third-largest oil field in the entire US. The city's stark industrial landscape, dotted with derricks and refineries, massive towers spurting jets of flame and cargo trucks barreling down the bleak Terminal Island

Expressway, was used to great effect as the dystopic backdrop for the *Terminator* movies.

It's startling that such a grim setting could be the home of several key structures from LA history. The first, the grand **Banning House**, 401 E Main St (guided tours hourly Tues–Thurs 12.30–2.30pm, Sat & Sun 12.30–3.30pm; $3; ☎310/548-7777, ⓦwww.banningmuseum.org), is an 1864 Greek Revival estate that was the residence of mid-nineteenth-century entrepreneur **Phineas Banning**, who made his fortune when the value of his land increased astronomically as the harbor was developed. Through his promotion of the rail link between Wilmington and Downtown LA, he also became known as "the father of Los Angeles transportation" (at a time when the local transit system was one of the best in the world), and helped push for the creation of a breakwater and lighthouse as well. However, in his final years, he argued against extending the rail line to San Pedro, which ultimately led to his own city's gradual decline, that was reversed only in the 1930s with the discovery of oil. The 23-room house remains an engaging spot to visit, full of opulent Victorian touches (chandeliers, elegant place settings and the like) and several restored carriages and stagecoaches kept in an outside barn.

Several blocks south is the **Drum Barracks Civil War Museum**, 1052 Banning Blvd (hourly tours Tues–Thurs 10am–1pm, Sat 11.30am–2.30pm, Sun 1.30–2.30pm; $3; ⓦwww.drumbarracks.org), originally part of a military base called Camp Drum and named for its commander, Richard Drum. Today, the only building remaining is the barracks, a rickety structure that now houses a hodgepodge of nineteenth-century military antiques and artifacts, notably a 34-star US flag and an early version of a machine gun. In the 1860s, this base was the Southwest headquarters for the US Army, which processed California volunteers here before sending them to fight in the battles in the East. It was also a staging point for attacks on nearby Confederate troops, who in the early years of the war had made territorial gains in neighboring Arizona and New Mexico, and in later decades became a base for federal soldiers fighting the native tribes of the Southwest.

Long Beach

Along with San Pedro, **LONG BEACH** is the home of the LA harbor, and a sizeable Southern California city in itself, with many acres of tract homes and flat, sprawling development. Not surprisingly, almost all of its interesting sights – including the *Queen Mary* – are grouped near the water, away from the port to the west, as are the tourist-oriented attractions around **Shoreline Drive** and the historic architecture of **downtown**.

Once the stomping ground of off-duty naval personnel, Long Beach's porn shops and sleazy bars lasted until the 1980s and 1990s, when a billion-dollar cash infusion into the town led – in the downtown at least – to a spate of glossy office buildings and hotels, as well as a convention center, shopping mall, and the restoration of some of the best c.1900 buildings on the coast. Inland from downtown, however, it's a different story – bleak housing projects on the perimeter of impoverished South Central LA – and the only real point of interest is **Rancho Los Cerritos**, 4600 Virginia Rd, northeast of the junction of the 405 and 710 freeways (Tues–Sat 1–5pm, tours Sat on the hour; free), the center of what was once a 27,000-acre Spanish land grant. This U-shaped adobe, built in the Monterey style, sits on five leafy acres with a delightful garden of roses, herbs and exotic plants, and even an antiquated water tower. Fortunately, it's easily accessible, via the 710, to Long Beach's more prominent attractions near the harbor.

Shoreline Drive and around

Since the early 1900s, Long Beach has sold itself as a resort community and, while it's difficult to imagine any romantic getaway nestled behind an industrial port basin, the city keeps trying. Its major seaside amusements now sit close to the curving strip of **Shoreline Drive**, an area that was much more of an entertainment center ninety years ago than it is today.

Around 1910, Long Beach developed its municipal pier, known as "**The Pike**" or the "Walk of a Thousand Lights," teeming with street vendors and throngs of tourists queuing up for such thrilling rides as the Cyclone Racer and Salt Water Plunge. The highlight was the legendary artwork of the **Looff Carousel**, designed in 1911 by master builder Charles Looff, who carved its finely decorated horses himself. After the carousel burned in 1943 and major theme parks like Disneyland arrived a decade later, the pier began its decline, and today it's long gone; these days, the focus of attention is **Shoreline Village**, just south of Shoreline Drive, a ragtag collection of middling shops and restaurants. The only real draw here is the **Tallship Californian**, a replica of a sleek 1848 cutter that takes tourists out for an afternoon spin or a multiple-day trip on the high seas (Sept–April only; half-day trips $75, multiple-day trips $140 per day; information at ⓣ1-800/432-2201).

North of Shoreline Village, along Ocean Boulevard, a row dominated by upscale corporate hotels has become the most visible symbol of Long Beach's renovation in the last few decades. Among the monoliths stands the appealing 1925 **Breakers Hotel**, 200 E Ocean Blvd, twelve pink stories of Spanish Revival design topped by a green copper roof. Although the hotel itself now serves as housing for senior citizens, the top-floor *Sky Room* bar and restaurant is still around, a good spot for a drink in 1930s-style surroundings. Two blocks south, Seaside Way connects with Shoreline Drive to create the circuit for the **Long Beach Grand Prix** (tickets at ⓣ1-888/82-SPEED, ⓦwww.longbeachgp.com), an Indy car race that attracts several hundred thousand spectators in mid-April for a three-day event, including a celebrity racing match. Just off the circuit, on the south side of Shoreline Drive in Marina Green Park, you can catch classic and current Hollywood films – part of the summertime **Outdoor Film Series** (Aug & Sept only, Friday nights; $6; ⓦwww.outdoorfilmseries.com) – on the park's expansive, grassy lawn near the marina.

Around a lagoon south of Shoreline Drive, the intriguing, if pricey, **Aquarium of the Pacific** (daily 9am–6pm; $18.75, kids $10; ⓣ562/590-3100, ⓦwww.aquariumofpacific.org) divides its marine life into regions – Southern California, the Micronesian island chain of Palau and the icy Bering Sea – in which you'll discover more than ten thousand species, from the familiar sea lions and otters, tide pool creatures and assorted ocean flora, to the more exotic leopard sharks and giant Japanese spider crabs.

Between November and March, more than fifteen thousand whales cruise the "**Whale Freeway**" past Long Beach on their annual migration to and return from winter breeding and berthing grounds in Baja California. Of several tour operators with bases in the area, Shoreline Village Cruises, 429 Shoreline Village Drive (ⓣ562/495-5884), and Star Party Cruises, 140 N Marina Drive (ⓣ562/799-7000), operate good whale-watching trips for around $15.

Along Ocean Boulevard, the four pastel "islands" visible offshore are not resort colonies, but rather oil-drilling platforms painted in soothing colors – Long Beach's attempt to beautify its harbor, which has over four hundred oil and gas wells operating in the region at any one time.

The Queen Mary and Scorpion submarine

Long Beach's most famous attraction is, of course, the mighty ocean liner **Queen Mary**, moored on Pier H at the end of Queens Highway South (daily 10am–6pm; $19 guided tours, kids $15; ☎562/435-3511, ⓦ www.queenmary .com), acquired by the city in 1964 with the sole aim of boosting tourism, which it has succeeded in doing, well beyond expectations. The ship lies across the bay, opposite Shoreline Village, and is accessible either by a lengthy walk or the free Long Beach Transit **shuttle** from downtown (information at ☎562/591-2301, ⓦ www.lbtransit.org). Once the flagship of the Cunard Line from the 1930s until the 1960s, the ship is now a luxury hotel with extravagantly furnished lounges and luxurious cabins, all carefully restored and kept sparkling. However, a glance at the spartan third-class cabins on the lower decks reveals something of the real story: the tough conditions experienced by the desperate migrants who left Europe on the ship hoping to start a new life in the US. The red British telephone kiosks around the decks and the hammy displays in the engine room and wheelhouse – closer to *Star Trek* than anything nautical – don't help, but it's nonetheless a marvelous ship, well worth a look. Apart from the wealth of gorgeous Art Deco details (glasswork, geometric decoration and streamlined edges), there are also stores and restaurants, and even a wedding chapel.

The latest addition to the *Queen Mary* site, the **Scorpion submarine** (daily 9am–9pm; $9), was until 1994 on active duty in the Soviet (and then Russian) navy, carrying a payload of 22 nuclear weapons and powered by diesel engines – a rather creaky means of locomotion for a craft built in 1972. It's worth a look for its cramped quarters, an especially bracing experience after a tour of the plush *Queen Mary*.

Downtown Long Beach

Running from Magnolia Avenue to Alamitos Boulevard and Ocean Boulevard to Tenth Street, **downtown Long Beach** can occupy a few hours of your time, with its boutiques, antique dealers and bookstores, many of them around a three-block strip known as **The Promenade**, lined with touristy restaurants and stores that can get quite busy on weekend nights. Two blocks west of the Promenade, at the terminus of the Blue Line light railway to Downtown LA, **Pine Avenue** has some of the city's best-preserved architecture. Highlights include the **First National Bank Building**, 115 Pine Ave, a 1900 Beaux Arts structure with a resplendent clock tower; the 1903 **Masonic Temple**, no. 230, a triple-gabled building with a brilliant sun mural inside on its second story; and, best of all, the **Rowan Building**, no. 201, a vibrant 1931 Art Deco creation with detailed terracotta decor. For a closer look, Long Beach Heritage runs a bimonthly architectural **tour** that begins at 315 W Third St, just a few blocks to the west (first & third Sat of month, 10am–12.30pm; $5; reserve at ☎562/493-7019, ⓦ www.lbheritage.org).

Further east is the striking **Villa Riviera**, 800 E Ocean Blvd, a fourteen-story Gothic Revival apartment block, recognizable by the high dormers on its pitched copper roof, pointed octagonal turret and narrow ground-level

Terminal Island, San Pedro

Belmont Shore, Naples

Santa Catalina Island

ACCOMMODATION

Long Beach Hilton **2**
Long Beach Travelodge **1**
Rodeway Inn **4**
Westin Long Beach **3**

archways. Curved to accommodate the bend in Ocean Boulevard, the Villa dominates the scenery in the immediate area and was the second-tallest building in all of LA when built in 1929. Just down the block, the 1905 **Tichenor House**, 852 E Ocean Blvd, a private Craftsman-style residence with Japanese touches, was designed by the firm of Greene & Greene (see Pasadena's Gamble House, p.183). Several blocks north from here, the **Museum of Latin American Art**, 628 Alamitos Ave (Tues–Fri 11.30am–7pm, Sat 11am–7pm, Sun 11am–6pm; $5; ℡562/437-1689, ⓦwww.molaa.com), is devoted to the increasingly broad subject of Hispanic art. Showcasing artists from Mexico to South America, the absorbing collection includes big names like Diego Rivera and José Orozco, as well as lesser-known newcomers working in styles that range from social criticism to magical realism. Four blocks west, at the corner of Seventh Street and Olive Avenue, **St Anthony Roman Catholic Church** is one of LA's most colorful churches, an appealing mishmash of historic styles constructed in 1933 and remodeled two decades later. Note the eye-catching neo-Gothic stained glass and hexagonal turrets, along with the facade's sizeable Byzantine golden mosaic, depicting the Virgin Mary amid flocks of angels.

East Long Beach

A mile east from the Villa Riviera, the **Long Beach Museum of Art**, 2300 E Ocean Blvd (Tues–Sun 11am–5pm; $5; ☎ 562/439-2119, ⊛ www.lbma.org), is housed in a 1912 Craftsman home, fringed by an abstract **sculpture garden** and featuring a modest collection of early modernism, folk art and contemporary Southern Californian art. The museum is notable for its horde of video art – one of the country's biggest collections – much of which is on display in the **video annex**, where you can stare at the thin white lines broadcast on Nam June Paik's television sets, or ponder the meaning of Bill Viola's enigmatic video projections. Another mile further, the affluent **Belmont Shore** district is full of designer shops and yuppified cafés, though there's not much to see.

From here, Second Street crosses man-made Alamitos Bay to reach the island community of **Naples**, supposedly designed after the Italian city, if that city was loaded with rows of T-shirt and trinket vendors. While the thin, circular **canal** may give you a romantic thrill during hour-long boat rides with picnic meals and serenading gondoliers (11am–11pm; $65 for two people; call Gondola Getaway for details ☎ 562/433-9595, ⊛ www.gondolagetawayinc. com), the place is still little more than a tacky aquatic suburb thronged with tourists.

Two miles north, **Rancho Los Alamitos**, 6400 Bixby Hill Rd (Wed–Sun 1–5pm, tours every half-hour; free), is a grand version of the typical nineteenth-century adobes found elsewhere in the region. Built in 1806, the renovated ranch house is noteworthy for its four acres of gardens, where you can wander amid herbs, roses, cacti, jacaranda and oleander planted along the terraces and landscaped walks. The house itself merits a look: you'll find twenty rooms filled with furniture, antiques, glassware and farm implements, as well as an on-site smithy. Nearby, the campus of California State University at Long Beach is perhaps best known for its towering pyramid-shaped athletic complex, but is really worth visiting for the **Earl Burns Miller Japanese Garden**, 1250 Bellflower Blvd (Tues–Fri 8am–3.30pm, Sun noon–4pm; $2; ☎ 562/985-8885, ⊛ www.csulb.edu/~jgarden), providing a peaceful spot amid weeping willows and bamboo. It's easy to spend an hour just wandering aimlessly around the immaculately landscaped grounds.

Santa Catalina Island

Though overlooked by many visitors, **SANTA CATALINA ISLAND** is an inviting mix of primitive beaches and wild hills twenty miles off the coast. Claimed by the Portuguese in 1542 as San Salvador, and renamed by the Spanish in 1602, it has stayed firmly outside the historical mainstream. Since 1811, when the indigenous Tongva Indians were forced to resettle on the mainland, the island has been privately owned, and has over the years grown to be something of a resort – a process hastened by businessman **William Wrigley Jr** (part of the Chicago chewing-gum dynasty), who financed the Art Deco *Avalon Casino*, the island's major landmark, in the 1920s. Wrigley also used the island as a spring training site for his baseball team, the Chicago Cubs, until the early 1950s.

Since 1975 the island has been almost entirely owned by the **Catalina Island Conservancy**, which maintains a sizeable nature preserve here, and in more recent years Catalina has become a popular destination for boaters and

Depending on the season, a round-trip **ferry** from San Pedro or Long Beach to Avalon costs from $30 to $40 and can take up to two hours or more. Catalina Cruises (☎1-800/228-2546) and Catalina Express (☎562/519-1212 or 1-800/481-3470, ⓦwww.catalinaexpress.com) run several services daily. From Newport Beach (see p.217) to Avalon, Catalina Passenger Service (☎949/673-5245) runs a daily round-trip for about $30. If you tend to get seasick, fifteen-minute **helicopter** trips to Avalon, costing $121 per person round-trip (with four to six people required for the flight), are offered by Island Express (☎310/510-2525, ⓦwww.islandexpress .com) from Long Beach and San Pedro.

Be warned that the price of hotel **accommodation** in Avalon hovers upwards of $90, and most beds are booked up throughout the summer and on weekends. The most evocative **hotels** are the *Zane Grey Pueblo Hotel* (☎310/510-0966 or 1-800/446-0271; ❺) and the six-room *Inn on Mount Ada* (☎310/510-2030, ⓦwww.catalina.com/mtada; ❾); but the cheapest spots are usually the *Atwater*, 125 Sumner Ave (☎310/510-2500 or 1-800/626-1496; ❸), or the *Catalina Bayview*, 124 Whittley Ave (☎310/510-7070; ❸). The only true budget option is **camping** ($12 per person, kids $6). Hermit Gulch (☎310/510-8368) is the closest site to Avalon and thus the busiest. Three other sites – Blackjack, Little Harbor and Two Harbors – in Catalina's interior (all bookable at ☎310/510-8368, ⓦwww.scico.com/camping) are usually roomier, though car travel is banned on Catalina Island and you'll have to plan an alternate way to reach these considerably more remote locations. For **eating**, *Catalina Cantina*, 313 Crescent Ave (☎310/510-0100), is the best, offering tasty and affordable Mexican staples washed down with margaritas, plus live music on weekends.

Unless you're a very good hiker, you'll most likely use buses or bicycles to get around the island. Catalina Safari Shuttle Bus (☎1-800/785-8425) runs between Avalon and Two Harbors for $40 round-trip, or $28 for kids. Catalina Island Company (☎1-800/343-4491) offers tours of the island, ranging from views of the casino ($12) to a fuller four-hour affair exploring the island's natural setting ($45) – the only way to see the interior of Catalina without hiking. **Golf carts**, for which you need a driver's license, and **bikes** (both banned from the rough roads outside Avalon) can be rented from stands throughout the island, including Catalina Golf Carts (☎310/510-1600, ⓦwww.catalinagolfcarts.com). Bikes run $10–25 per day, depending on the model, while golf carts are much steeper, at $30–40 per hour only.

As for **fishing**, the waters around Catalina are rich in yellowtail, calico bass, barracuda and sharks. Catalina Island Sportfishing, 114 Claressa St (☎310/510-2420), and Catalina Mako, 17 Cabrillo Drive (☎1-800/296-MAKO), operate **charter fishing trips** for around $100–120 an hour (though you can fish for free from the pier), and **snorkel** and **scuba** gear is available for rent at Catalina Divers Supply (☎310/510-0330 or 1-800/353-0330, ⓦwww.catalinadiverssupply.com). Lover's Cove, a marine preserve just east of Avalon, provides the best spot to view local sea life close-up, though only snorkeling is allowed.

nature lovers, and its small marina swells with luxury yachts and cruise ships in summer. Even so, the elegant hotels are unobtrusive among the whimsical architecture, and cars are rare – there's a ten-year waiting list to ferry one over. Consequently, most of the 3000 islanders walk, ride bikes or drive electrically powered golf carts.

Avalon and Two Harbors

The main city on the island, **AVALON**, can be fully explored on foot in two hours; pick up a map from the **Chamber of Commerce** at the foot of the ferry pier (☎310/510-1520, ⓦwww.visitcatalina.org). The town itself offers the usual assortment of T-shirt vendors, restaurants and boat operators – many of whom offer fishing trips or tours on glass-bottom boats. The undeniable highlight is the resplendent **Avalon Casino**, on a promontory north of downtown at 1 Casino Way. Built as a dance hall and moviehouse, this 1920s structure still features an Art Deco ballroom and lavishly decorated auditorium: painted wild horses and unicorns roam through a forest on the side wall, while an Art Deco superhero rides a wave on the front screen and, above it all, a waif-like Botticelli Venus stands atop a seashell over the heads of two thunderbolt-clutching gods. Perhaps not surprisingly, the muralist for the theater, John Beckman, also helped design the equally fanciful Chinese Theatre in Hollywood (see p.99), and you can still see Hollywood movies here as well on evenings throughout the year – an absolute must for any movie buffs who venture out this far. Much more subdued, a small **museum** (daily 10.30am–4pm, Jan–March closed Thurs; $2) on the same premises displays Native American artifacts from Catalina's past, as well as tiles from local potters, and old photographs and biology exhibits on the surrounding area.

To the south, the **Zane Grey Pueblo Hotel**, 199 Chimes Tower Rd, is the former home of the Western author, who visited Catalina with a film crew to shoot *The Vanishing American* and liked the place so much that he stayed, building for himself this "Hopi pueblo" house, complete with beamed ceiling, stark white walls and thick, wooden front door. The hotel rooms are themed after his books, and the pool is shaped like an arrowhead. As well, the grounds afford excellent views of Avalon and the bay below. Similarly, the **Inn on Mount Ada**, at 398 Wrigley Terrace Rd on the south hillside of Avalon, was the 1921 Colonial Revival home of William Wrigley and is now an elegant hotel (see opposite box for details), with sweeping ocean views and a fine garden of cacti and succulents native to the region. Also striking is the **Holly Hill House**, 718 Crescent Ave ($8 tours; call ☎310/510-2414 for details), one of the few tourable Victorian homes on Catalina, an 1890 Queen Anne cottage on a high bluff overlooking the bay, which on select Saturdays offers 45-minute tours of its elegant conical tower, restored rooms and wraparound verandas.

Several miles southwest of Avalon, the **Wrigley Botanical Garden**, 1400 Avalon Canyon Rd (daily 8am–5pm; $3), administered by the Catalina Island Conservancy, displays all manner of natural delights on nearly forty acres, but is especially strong on native, endangered plants, such as the local varieties of manzanita, ironwood and mahogany, and the wild tomato – a poisonous member of the nightshade family. Also fascinating is the **Wrigley Memorial Monument**, just beyond the garden, where a striking cenotaph, made from Georgia marble, blue flagstone and red roof-tiles, honors the chewing-gum baron. A grand tiled staircase leads to an imposing Art Deco mausoleum, where Wrigley was to have been interred (he's buried elsewhere).

Northwest of Avalon, the small, isolated resort town of **TWO HARBORS** sits on a small strip of land that connects Cherry Cove and Catalina Harbor. While there's little to see here, the presence of a large marina and campground make the area suitable for outdoor activities like kayaking, snorkeling and scuba diving.

The Santa Catalina interior

If you have the opportunity and a few days spare to explore it, venture into the rugged **Santa Catalina interior**, comprising 42,000 acres of largely untouched wilderness, home to many indigenous creatures and plants, and more than one hundred types of native birds. You can take a **bus tour** if time is short (see box, p.204); if it isn't, get a map and a free **wilderness permit**, which allows you to hike and camp, from the Chamber of Commerce or the Parks and Recreation Office (☏310/510-0688), both in Avalon. Mountain biking requires a $50 permit from the Catalina Island Conservancy, 125 Calressa Ave (☏310/510-1421, ⓦwww.catalinaconservancy.org), which controls and manages more than 80 percent of the island.

There are some unique **animals** roaming about the wildlands, among them the Catalina Shrew, so rare it's only been sighted twice, and the Catalina Mouse, bigger and healthier than its mainland counterpart thanks to abundant food and lack of natural enemies. There are also foxes, ground squirrels, pigs, bald eagles and quail, along with buffalo, descended from a dozen or so left behind by a Hollywood film crew and now a sizeable herd wandering about the island.

8

The San Gabriel and San Fernando valleys

long the eastern and northern limits of LA, the **SAN GABRIEL** and **SAN FERNANDO VALLEYS** are not as bland and homogenous as most people think. A broad range of classes and cultures dot the areas, from the old-money hauteur of San Marino to the slapdash vigor of media-fueled Burbank to the increasingly Hispanic sections of Van Nuys and Sherman Oaks.

In the San Gabriel Valley, on the east side of the Verdugo Mountains, **Pasadena** is not only a geographical junction between the relatively flat San Fernando Valley and the sloped foothills of the San Gabriel Valley, it's also a cultural counterweight of sorts to the city of LA – a small, patrician town full of great architecture and diligent historic preservation. The neighboring cities of **South Pasadena** and **San Marino** also have their charms, particularly the latter's Huntington Gardens, though the rest of the San Gabriel Valley holds more dispersed pleasures, worth a look only if you're staying in the LA region for at least a week.

North of the Hollywood Hills, the San Fernando Valley offers a more sprawling landscape, stitched together by seemingly endless ribbons of asphalt. The upper-middle-class suburb of **Glendale** is home to a famous cemetery; while **Burbank**, further west, is studio central, containing the likes of Disney, Warner Bros, and, in its own municipal enclave, Universal. Further west are the bulk of LA's secessionist-minded suburbs, known collectively as "the Valley," with historic attractions here and there, but mostly known for their sweltering temperatures and copious mini-malls. At the apex of the triangular Valley, places like **San Fernando** have a rich Spanish heritage, while further north, exciting **Magic Mountain** easily outdoes Disneyland for death-defying rides.

The San Gabriel Valley

Running between the Verdugo and San Gabriel mountains, the **San Gabriel Valley** largely escapes the derision that many Angelenos pile upon the San Fernando Valley. However, though it has genuine cultural cachet in many places, especially along its foothills, it contains just as many dreary spaces as

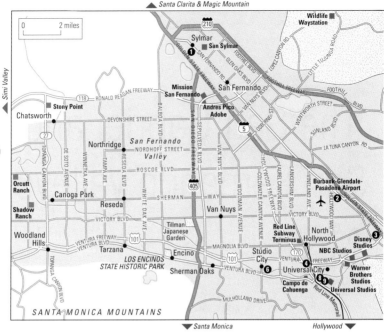

anywhere in the region – especially the eastern side, where you can breathe in some of the basin's worst smog.

After its early settlement by native Tongva tribes and the later arrival of Spanish soldiers and missionaries, the San Gabriel Valley had become by the beginning of the twentieth century a choice region for American agriculture, growing predominantly grapes and citrus crops. Railroads brought new migrants, and by the 1950s, the foothills of the San Gabriel Mountains developed into another populous arm of LA, with suburban ranch houses and swimming pools taking the place of ranches and orange groves. One thing that has not changed, however, is the torrential flooding. Thanks to its specific climate and geography, the Valley has always been a prime spot for **winter deluges**: great cascades of water sweep down the hillsides, turning into mudslides by the time they reach the foothills, and then charging through the canyons and destroying all in their wake – including encroaching suburban homes (memorably described by John McPhee in *Control of Nature*). This problem has been an occasional impediment to hillside growth, but with the creation of huge "catch basins" to contain the mudslides, real-estate developers have been able to push growth further up into the mountains.

Pasadena

At the western edge of the San Gabriel Valley, **PASADENA** is a mix of old-fashioned charms and contemporary popular appeal. Located ten miles northeast of Downtown LA, and connected to it by the rickety Pasadena Freeway (110 north), Pasadena was, like much of LA, settled by Midwesterners (in this case from Indiana) and even today retains a measure of its old style and genteel

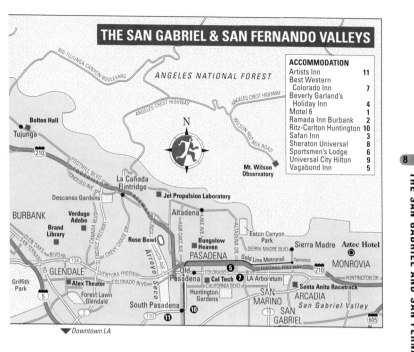

ACCOMMODATION

Artists Inn	11
Best Western Colorado Inn	7
Beverly Garland's Holiday Inn	4
Motel 6	1
Ramada Inn Burbank	2
Ritz-Carlton Huntington	10
Safari Inn	3
Sheraton Universal	8
Sportsmen's Lodge	6
Universal City Hilton	9
Vagabond Inn	5

habits. The **Rose Parade**, an event dating back to 1890 that takes place every New Year's Day, is one reflection of this heritage, as are the grand estates of the **Arroyo Seco** neighborhood and the Spanish Revival architecture of downtown Pasadena. In the 1970s and 1980s, Pasadena was in a slump, but once urban-renewal dollars began flowing in the last decade, tourists rediscovered the town, especially its **Old Pasadena** commercial strip and ever-popular architectural treasures like the **Gamble House**.

Downtown Pasadena

Bordered by Lake Avenue, California Boulevard, and the 210 and 710 freeways, **downtown Pasadena** is one of LA's few traditional downtowns, with fine municipal architecture, restaurants and shops, and it's easily navigable on foot as well; most places of interest are located near **Colorado Boulevard**, the city's commercial axis.

On and around this boulevard, between Fair Oaks and Euclid avenues, is **Old Pasadena**, a mix of antique sellers, used book and record stores, cafés, clothing boutiques and theaters that gets quite crowded on weekends. Some of these businesses are housed in elegant historic buildings, such as the Italianate **White Block**, Fair Oaks Avenue at Union Street, and the **Venetian Revival Building**, 17 S Raymond Ave, an 1894 Victorian design.

A short distance away is the fascinating **Castle Green**, also known as "Hotel Green," 99 S Raymond St, formerly a 1903 resort that centered around a now-demolished hotel across the street. Later additions included the apartments that remain today, plus a **bridge** that crossed Raymond Avenue to link the structures. Although the walkway, which was billed as the "Bridge of Sighs" after the Venetian version, has been sliced in half and now stops in mid-air, its design

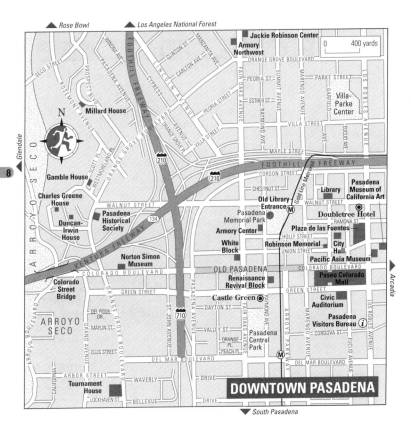

DOWNTOWN PASADENA

still fascinates, with everything from Spanish-tiled domes and turrets to curvaceous arches – a short, glorious trip to nowhere. The local preservation society, **Pasadena Heritage**, offers periodic tours of this and other area landmarks – including an excellent overview of Old Pasadena on the second Saturday of the month (Nov–June & Aug–Sept only; $5; reserve at ☎626/441-6333, ⓦwww.pasadenaheritage.org). Nearby, the **ruins** of the old Romanesque city library, located in what is now **Pasadena Memorial Park**, Walnut Street and Raymond Avenue, hint at the building's grandeur when it was open from the 1880s to the 1930s, before being demolished in 1954. (The current **Public Library**, three blocks away at 285 E Walnut St, is a Spanish Renaissance gem with Corinthian columns, arched windows, Spanish tiling, and an elegant courtyard and atrium.)

Across from the park, the **Armory Center** (Wed–Sun noon–5pm, Fri closes at 8pm; free), 145 N Raymond St, is a good place to get a glimpse of the local art scene in Pasadena, showing a mix of community folk art and professional avant-garde and modernist creations. More of the latter is on display in the center's annex, **Armory Northwest**, a mile north at 965 N Fair Oaks Ave (Fri–Sun noon–5pm; free), where edgier installation art and various other experiments are on display. Opposite, the **Jackie Robinson Center**, 1020 N Fair Oaks Ave (Mon–Thurs 8am–9pm, Fri 8am–5pm; free; information at ☎626/791-7647), is a social center named for the African-American baseball pioneer, which periodically hosts rotating exhibitions on the athlete, typically paintings and sculptures and, in one case, a small cake decorated to resemble Ebbets Field, where Robinson played for ten years for the Brooklyn Dodgers. You'll also find two nine-foot **bronze sculptures** of Jackie and his brother, Frank, winner of a silver medal at the 1936 summer Olympics in Berlin, just north of Old Pasadena, on Garfield Avenue at Union Street.

Pasadena's Old World trappings are evident in its early municipal buildings, such as the city's centerpiece, **Pasadena City Hall**, across from the Robinson sculptures at 100 N Garfield Ave, one of several city buildings in Mediterranean Revival styles – in this case Spanish Baroque. Set on a wide city plaza, the structure has a large, tiled dome and an imposing facade with grand arches and columns, and an elegant garden with a patio and fountain, all of which make it more impressive than LA's City Hall. Across Euclid Avenue from City Hall, **Plaza de las Fuentes** is Lawrence Halprin's postmodern public square, with colorful tile work and a blocky pastel design, that suffers in comparison to its elegant neighbor.

The engaging **Pacific Asia Museum**, diagonally southeast at 46 N Los Robles Ave (Wed–Sun 10am–5pm, Fri closes at 8pm; $5, students $3; ☏626/449-2742, ⊛www.pacificasiamuseum.org), is modeled after a Chinese imperial palace, with a sloping tiled roof topped with ceramic-dog decorations, inset balconies and dragon-emblazoned front gates. For twenty-five years, until 1948, this was the home of collector Grace Nicholson, who came to Pasadena around the beginning of the twentieth century and started amassing the expansive collection, which now includes thousands of historical treasures and everyday objects from Korea, China and Japan, including decorative jade and porcelain, hand-woven silk robes, various swords and spears, and a large cache of paintings and drawings. In the museum's peaceful **courtyard garden**, koi fish rest in pools beneath marble statues and a variety of trees native to the Far East. Just around the corner, at 490 E Union St, the three-story **Pasadena Museum of California Art** (Wed–Sun 10am–5pm, Fri closes at 8pm; $6, students & kids free; ⊛www.pmcaonline.org), despite its bland name, offers an eye-opening look at California-based art – in all kinds of media from painting to photography to digital art – since the state joined the US in 1850. On occasional Saturday evenings, the museum hosts live jazz, pop and dance music concerts on its rooftop terrace ($7, members free; information at ☏626/568-3665). If you'd like more information on this and other city attractions, the **Pasadena Visitors Bureau**, three blocks south at 171 S Los Robles Ave (Mon–Fri 8am–5pm, Sat 10am–4pm; ☏626/795-9311, ⊛www.pasadenacal .com), provides **maps** and booklets detailing self-guided tours of city architecture, history and museums.

The **Bungalow Heaven** historic district two miles northeast, bordered by Washington and Orange Grove boulevards and Hill and Catalina avenues, features a large number of quaint Craftsman bungalows that offer a glimpse of what much of the city looked like in the early 1900s. For Arts and Crafts enthusiasts, the neighborhood association puts on a yearly **tour** on the last Sunday in April ($12–15; information at ☏626/585-2172, ⊛home.earthlink.net/~bhna), peeking into eight of the classic structures. Further south, the commercial strip of **Lake Avenue** pulls in its share of visitors, but should be avoided unless you're in the mood for a cheek-to-jowl encounter with hordes of shoppers.

Much more appealing is the **California Institute of Technology**, or CalTech, campus, a few blocks east of Lake Avenue, best known for its "cool nerd" students and media-friendly seismologists who inevitably pop up on the local news every time a major temblor rumbles through the region. However, CalTech is worth visiting for its splendid assortment of pre-WWII architecture, notably the Spanish Baroque buildings of LA Central Library–designer Bertram Goodhue and the Islamic-styled work of Edward Stone; the campus makes for a fascinating jaunt if you have even the slightest interest in historic buildings; **architecture tours** are offered on the fourth Thursday of every month (except Nov, on the third Thurs) and depart from the Spanish Colonial–style Atheneum, 551 S Hill Ave (11am only; free; reserve at ☏626/395-6327, ⓦwww.caltech.edu), while regular **campus tours** are more frequent (Mon–Fri 1.45pm; free; ☏626/395-6327), leaving from the Visitors Center at 315 S Hill Ave.

|

The Norton Simon Museum

Just across the 710 freeway from downtown Pasadena, the **Norton Simon Museum**, 411 W Colorado Blvd (Wed–Mon noon–6pm, Fri closes at 9pm; $6, students $4; ☏626/449-6840, ⓦwww.nortonsimon.org), may not be a household name, but its collections are at least as good as those of the LA County or Getty museums. Established and overseen by the industrialist Norton Simon until his death in 1993, and since administered by his movie-star wife Jennifer Jones, the museum sidesteps the hype of the LA art world to concentrate on the quality of its presentation. You could easily spend a whole day wandering through the dark, intimate galleries, as well as a sculpture garden inspired by Monet's own Giverny.

The museum's focus is **Western European painting** from the Renaissance to early modernism. It's a massive collection, much of it rotated, but most of the major pieces are usually on view. Highlights include Dutch paintings of the seventeenth century – notably Rembrandt's vivacious *Titus, Portrait of a Boy* and Frans Hals' austerely aggressive *Portrait of a Man* – and Italian Renaissance work from the likes of Botticelli, Raphael, Giorgione and Bellini. There's a good sprinkling of French Impressionists and post-Impressionists: Monet's light-dappled *Mouth of the Seine at Honfleur*; Manet's plaintive *Ragpicker*; and Degas' *The Ironers*, capturing the extended yawn of a washerwoman; plus works by Cézanne, Gauguin and Van Gogh.

Unlike the Getty, the Norton Simon also boasts a solid collection of modernist greats, from Georges Braque and Pablo Picasso to Roy Lichtenstein and Andy Warhol. There are also some appealing, but less-heralded works from different eras, including Zurbaran's *Still Life with Lemons, Oranges and a Rose*; Jan Steen's *Wine is a Mocker*, an image of rural peasants assisting a drunken bourgeoise as she lies pitifully in the dirt; and Tiepolo's *The Triumph of Virtue and Nobility over Ignorance*, in which the winged, angelic victors gloat over their symbolic conquest of the wretched, troll-like figure of Ignorance. As a counterpoint to the Western art, the museum has a fine collection of **Asian art**, including many highly polished Buddhist and Hindu figures, some inlaid with precious stones, and many drawings and prints – the highlight being Hiroshige's masterful series of colored woodblock prints, showing nature in quiet, dusky hues.

The Arroyo Seco

The residential pocket northwest of the junction of the 134 and 210 freeways, known as **Arroyo Seco**, or "dry riverbed" in Spanish, is home to some of LA's best architecture. Orange Grove Avenue leads you into the neighborhood from central Pasadena and takes you to the **Pasadena Historical Society**, 470 W

Walnut St at Orange Grove (Wed–Sun noon–5pm; $6, kids free; ☎626/577-1660, ⓦwww.pasadenahistory.org), which has fine displays on Pasadena's history and tasteful surrounding gardens, but is most interesting for the on-site **Feynes Mansion** (Wed–Sun 1.30–3pm, tours hourly Thurs–Sun 1–3pm; free with admission), designed by Robert Farquhar, also famous for his Clark Memorial Library (see p.148) and California Club (see p.68). Decorated with its original 1905 furnishings and paintings, this elegant Beaux Arts mansion was once the home of the Finnish Consulate, and much of the folk art on display comes from Pasadena's "twin town" of Jarvenpää in Finland.

But it's the **Gamble House**, 4 Westmoreland Place (hour-long tours Thurs–Sun noon–3pm; $8, students $5; ☎626/793-3334, ⓦgamblehouse. usc.edu), that really brings people out here. Built in 1908 for David Gamble, of the consumer-products giant Proctor & Gamble, this masterpiece of Southern Californian Craftsman architecture helped give rise to a style that you'll see replicated all over the state, freely combining elements from Swiss chalets and Japanese temples in a romantically sprawling, shingled mansion. Broad eaves shelter outdoor sleeping porches, which in turn shade terraces on the ground floor, leading out to the spacious lawn. The interior was crafted with the same attention to detail, and all the carpets, cabinetry and lighting fixtures, designed specifically for the house, remain in excellent condition. The area around the Gamble House has at least eleven other private homes by the two brothers who designed it (the firm of Greene & Greene), including **Charles Greene's house**, 368 Arroyo Terrace, and the picturesque **Duncan-Irwin House**, around the corner at 240 N Grand Ave, a perfect two-story Craftsman with stone lanterns and a rustic stone wall out front.

A quarter of a mile north of here is Frank Lloyd Wright's "La Miniatura," also known as the **Millard House**, which you can only glimpse through the gate opposite 585 Rosemont Ave, a small, concrete-block house supposedly

Arroyo Culture

The neighborhood around the **Arroyo Seco** has shifted somewhat through the years, first by geography, later by culture. Orange Grove Boulevard, several blocks east of the Arroyo proper, was originally lined with a series of grand estates, tagged "Millionaire's Row," with the local gentry using the Arroyo itself as a source of wood and a place to picnic. The palaces went into decline in the early part of the twentieth century, to be replaced eventually by the apartment blocks visible today. Meanwhile, the Arroyo Seco was being built up by numerous Arts and Crafts–movement intellectuals, many from the East Coast and inspired by the English example of William Morris, and preaching a return-to-nature philosophy that reacted against the early-modern design aesthetic taking shape, along with industrialized culture in general. Built in the Arroyo's wooded lots amid craggy rocks and rugged cliffsides, the resulting Swiss chalets, Tudor mansions and Craftsman monuments were manifestations of a new **Arroyo Culture**, its artisan practitioners prized for working with wood, clay and stone. Not surprisingly, one of their heroes was Charles Lummis, famed for his eponymous boulder house in Highland Park (see p.71), and an equally prominent intellectual of the time, as well as an ardent propagandist for the new style, working as the first city editor of the *Los Angeles Times* when it was especially powerful in local affairs. Architects Charles and Henry Greene and Frank Lloyd Wright were all attracted by the Arroyo too, if not full believers in its attendant ideology. The culture faded, however, as much of the area was bought up by wealthy Angelenos, though fortunately, the architecture has been largely preserved – even as prices on the homes have predictably skyrocketed.

designed to look like a jungle ruin, with thick foliage growing over Mayan-style architecture. For information on touring the whole of this fascinating area, and tracking down the key Craftsman bungalows, call Pasadena Heritage at ☎626/441-6333 or visit ⓦwww.pasadenacal.com.

Somewhat incongruously, the 104,000-seat **Rose Bowl** is just to the north off of Arroyo Boulevard, out of use most of the year but home to a very popular **flea market** on the second Sunday of each month and, in the autumn, the place where the UCLA football team plays its home games (☎310/825-2101). Further south on Arroyo Boulevard, pass under the monumental spans of the **Colorado Street Bridge**, one of the area's structural wonders – a 1467-foot monolith of curving concrete, built in 1913 – to reach the **Tournament House**, 391 S Orange Grove Blvd (tours Feb–Aug 2–4pm; free; ☎626/449-4100, ⓦwww.tournamentofroses.com), the administrative headquarters of the annual Rose Parade, due to reopen in 2003 after a renovation that will restore the pink 1914 Renaissance Revival mansion – once owned by William Wrigley himself – back to its original splendor.

South Pasadena

For all its historic architecture and small-town appeal, the separate city of **SOUTH PASADENA**, due south of downtown Pasadena, finds itself in a precarious spot – in the path of the 710 freeway, which highway engineers have been trying to finish for thirty years, as the final link in their original plan to turn the metropolitan basin into a spider web of asphalt. The wrecking ball has not yet arrived for the seventy-odd historic sites in the city, or countless homes and trees, but it's hard to say how much longer the city can hold out against LA's insatiable desire for new freeway links.

The city's main strip, **Fair Oaks Avenue**, is where you'll find the landmark **Rialto Theater**, 1023 Fair Oaks Ave, a 1925 movie palace that also served as a theatrical stage and vaudeville venue. The faded splendor inside is a treat, adorned with Moorish organ screens, Egyptian columns, winged harpies and a central Medusa head, though it's viewable only during showtimes.

Meridian Avenue, which parallels Fair Oaks Avenue several blocks west of it, takes you through the quaint Victorian-era homes south of the 110 freeway and into the larger residences north of it – many of them doomed by the planned extension of the 710 freeway. On the southern end, the **Meridian Iron Works**, 913 Meridian Ave (Sat 1–4pm; free), houses the South Pasadena Preservation Foundation Museum, where exhibits and photographs cover the history of the ironworks (and its former lives as a hotel, blacksmith and bicycle dealer), as well as the city itself, including assorted curios from a local ostrich farm.

To the north, Meridian Avenue runs into posh **Buena Vista Street**, notable for two grand dwellings by Charles and Henry Greene: the **Garfield House**, no. 1001, a fairly well-preserved 1904 Swiss chalet with numerous Craftsman elements that was once the home of murdered US President James Garfield's widow; and the adjacent **Longley House**, no. 1005, the brothers' first commission, an eclectic 1897 mix of revival styles from Romanesque to Moorish to Georgian. A few blocks east, at the end of Oaklawn Avenue, the Greene's 1906 **Oaklawn Bridge**, a restored concrete relic draped in vines, spans the railway gully of the former Southern Pacific and Santa Fe line. In July 2003, the Metrorail **Gold Line** will link Pasadena with Downtown LA, and use the old railroad's path to connect with South Pasadena.

San Marino

East of South Pasadena, uneventful **SAN MARINO** is marked by some of LA's most privileged residents and widest neighborhood streets, with little of interest beyond the legacy of railway and real-estate magnate **Henry Huntington**, preserved in his museum and gardens.

Before hitting the museum, you may want to check out **El Molino Viejo**, 1120 Old Mill Rd (Tues–Sun 1–4pm; free), a weathered adobe built as a flour mill in 1816 by Spanish missionaries from Mission San Gabriel. After a replacement mill was built seven years later, the older mud-brick structure was allowed to rot until the 1920s, when restoration turned it into the clubhouse for Henry Huntington's golf course. Nowadays the old mill presents interesting historical exhibits and photographs, plus diagrams of how water generated the power to make flour. Just to the west, the towering **Ritz-Carlton Huntington Hotel**, atop a hill at 1401 S Oak Knoll Ave (see "Accommodation," p.235), began life as the *Wentworth Hotel* in 1906, later to be taken over by Huntington in 1913 and expanded considerably. The very definition of palatial accommodation, the hotel's Mediterranean-style main building boasts attractive gardens out back, and, further away, small bungalow-style residences for its swankiest guests – not surprisingly, the only part of the hotel off-limits to the general public.

The Huntington Library

San Marino's most (critics would say only) redeeming feature is the **Huntington Library, Art Collections and Botanical Gardens**, just off Huntington Drive at 1151 Oxford Rd (Tues–Fri noon–4.30pm, Sat & Sun 10am–4.30pm; $10, students $7; ☎626/405-2100, ⓦwww.huntington.org). Part of this is made up of the collections of Henry Huntington, the nephew of childless multimillionaire Collis P. Huntington, who owned and operated the Southern Pacific Railroad – which in the late nineteenth century had a virtual monopoly on transportation in California. Henry, groomed to take over the railroad from his uncle, was dethroned by the board of directors and took his sizeable inheritance to LA. Once there, he bought up the existing streetcar routes and combined them as the Pacific Electric Railway Company, which in turn controlled the Red Car line that soon became the largest transit network in the world, and helped make Huntington the largest landowner in the state. He retired in 1910, moving to the manor house he had built in San Marino, devoting himself full time to buying rare books and manuscripts, and marrying his uncle's widow Arabella and acquiring her collection of English portraits.

You can pick up a self-guided walking **tour** of each of the three main sections from the bookstore and information desk in the entry pavilion. The **library**, right off the main entrance, is a good first stop, its two-story exhibition hall containing numerous manuscripts and rare books, among them a Gutenberg Bible, a folio edition of Shakespeare's plays, Thoreau's manuscript for *Walden*, Thomas Jefferson's architectural plans, and the **Ellesmere Chaucer**, a c.1410 illuminated version of *The Canterbury Tales*. Displays around the walls trace the history of printing and of the English language from medieval manuscripts to a King James Bible, from Milton's *Paradise Lost* and Blake's *Songs of Innocence and Experience* to first editions of Swift, Coleridge, Dickens, Woolf and Joyce.

To decorate the **main house**, a grand mansion done out in Louis XIV carpets and later French tapestries, the Huntingtons traveled to England and returned with the finest art money could buy – most of it still hangs on the walls. Unless you're passionate about eighteenth-century English portraiture, head through to the back extension, which displays important works by Van Dyck and Constable, as well as the stars of the collection: Gainsborough's ever-popular *Blue Boy*, Lawrence's *Pinkie* and Reynolds' grandiose *Mrs Siddons as the Tragic Muse*. A bit less familiar, but perhaps more compelling, are colorful paintings from Turner, whose radiant *Grand Canal, Venice* is a vibrant, hazily sunlit image of gondolas on the water; and Blake, whose mystical *Satan Comes to the Gates of Hell* is the most stunning work in the collection, showing the ghostly, bearded figure of death facing off with spears against a very human Satan and a serpentine Eve. Nearby, the **Scott Gallery for American Art** displays paintings by Edward Hopper and Mary Cassatt, and Wild West drawings and sculpture, and also features work by the architects Greene & Greene – whose Craftsman houses are found in abundance in the nearby Arroyo Seco.

For all the art and literature, though, it's the grounds that make the Huntington truly worthwhile, and the acres of beautiful themed **gardens** surrounding the buildings include the Bonsai Court and Zen Rock Garden, complete with authentically constructed Buddhist temple and tea house; the Desert Garden, with the world's largest collection of desert plants, and twelve acres of cacti; two lush rose gardens; a sculpture garden full of Baroque statues; and a Japanese garden dotted with koi ponds, cherry trees and "moon bridges." While strolling through these botanical splendors, you might also visit the Huntingtons themselves, buried in a neo-Palladian **mausoleum** at the northwest corner of the estate, beyond the rows of an orange grove, built as a marble Greek temple and claimed to be the inspiration for the later 1930s Jefferson Memorial in Washington DC.

North of Pasadena

The neighborhoods north of Pasadena, Altadena and **LA CAÑADA FLINTRIDGE**, sit on hillsides that lead into the **Angeles National Forest**, a fifty-mile wilderness in the San Gabriel Mountains that is a favorite weekend spot for locals. Threatened by flood during heavy rains, these are also some of the more precarious places to live in LA, and you can see part of their elaborate flood-control system just off Oak Grove Drive, where the Hanamongna Watershed Park and Devils Gate Reservoir are dramatic testaments to the power of water: a huge green slope and massive catch basin designed specifically to contain water, mud, rocks, housing debris and assorted other elements in the event of catastrophic flooding.

Immediately north of the park and reservoir is one of the cornerstones of America's military-industrial complex: the **Jet Propulsion Laboratory**, 4800 Oak Grove Drive in La Cañada Flintridge (tours 9, 10am, 1 & 3pm; free; by reservation only at ☎818/354-9314, ⓦwww.jpl.nasa.gov), devoted to the research and development of all manner of high-tech, space-related machinery, including orbiting satellites, long-range missiles and rockets, and secretive government surveillance projects. For obvious public-relations reasons, the lab chooses instead to display replicas of the solar-system-exploring *Voyager* craft and the *Magellan* and *Galileo* vehicles that mapped Venus and Mars, and also has exhibits on the Hubble telescope, killer asteroids, and even Hollywood's treatment of space exploration.

Nearby, just a mile east of the reservoir, you can find one of LA's most unusual attractions, the **Mountain View Mausoleum and Art Gallery**, 2300 N Marengo Ave (daily 10am–4pm; free), which, along with serving as the final resting place for thousands of bodies, is also the unexpected home to a variety of contemporary artworks by local California artists. The undeniable highlight is the ethereal **Arbor of Light Radiance Corridor**, a dark room illuminated with stained-glass skylights, which cast radiant reflections of plants and flowers across the walls as the sun moves across the sky.

West off Foothill Boulevard, **Descanso Gardens**, 1418 Descanso Drive, La Cañada Flintridge (daily 9am–5pm; $5, kids $1; ☎818/949-4200, ⓦ www.descansogardens.org), squeezes all the plants you might see in the mountains into 155 acres of landscaped park, especially brilliant during the spring, when all the wildflowers are in bloom. The centerpiece is a live-oak forest loaded with camellias, and there's also a Japanese tea house and garden, with an accompanying narrow, red footbridge, and a tranquil bird sanctuary for migrating waterfowl.

Another of La Cañada's attractions is the historic **Lanterman House**, 4420 Encinas Drive (Sept–July Tues & Thurs and first and third Sun of month 1–4pm; $3, students $1; ☎818/790-1421, ⓦ www.lacanadaonline.com/lantermanhouse), an elegant two-story Craftsman structure that was the long-time home of politician Lloyd Lanterman, whose taste for dark-oak walls, French doors, and Arts and Crafts decor is on display throughout. The well-tended gardens are also worth a look for their native plants and bower of live-oak trees.

North from the 210 freeway, the **Angeles Crest Highway** (Hwy-2) heads into the mountains above Pasadena, through an area once dotted with resorts and wilderness camps. Today, a hike up any of the nearby canyons will bring you past the ruins of old lodges that either burned down or were washed away toward the end of the 1930s, when automobiles became popular. One of the most scenic of these trails, a rugged five-mile round trip, follows the route of the **Mount Lowe Scenic Railway**, once one of LA's biggest tourist attractions, a funicular that hauled tourists 1500 feet up to Echo Mountain, where the remains of "**White City**" are still visible. Formerly a mountaintop resort of two hotels, a zoo and an observatory, the complex burned down in 1900 but remained a popular destination on the Pacific Electric Railway, which maintained the route until 1937. To follow the old route of the railway, drive north on Lake Avenue until it ends at the intersection of Loma Alta Drive. Find a parking spot and head east along the trailhead. More fine hiking trails can be found further east in **Eaton Canyon Park**, 1750 N Altadena Drive, a natural refuge on 190 acres, the on-site **nature center** (daily 9am–5pm; free; ☎626/398-5420, ⓦ www.ecnca.org) providing more information on the region's geology, flora and fauna.

Further north, the Crest Highway passes through the **Angeles National Forest**, an increasingly crowded recreation zone where you can hike, camp most of the year and ski in winter, to Mount Wilson, high enough to be a major site for TV broadcast antennae. At the peak, the 1904 **Mount Wilson Observatory** has a small **museum** (daily 10am–4pm; $1; ⓦ www.mtwilson. edu) where you can browse various astronomical displays, including some detailing the work of Edwin Hubble, who, aside from having a famous telescope named after him, developed the now-dominant theory of cosmological expansion.

East of Pasadena

East of Pasadena, the San Gabriel Valley becomes a patchwork of small cities with a few appealing sights scattered across large distances. The one feature these places share is Foothill Boulevard, which, before it was displaced by the Foothill Freeway (Hwy-210), was famously known as **Route 66**. Formerly the main route across the US, "from Chicago to LA, more than three thousand miles all the way," the strip has declined in recent decades and can look a bit dreary, now that many of its classic buildings have been replaced by ugly mini-malls. However, the romance of the open road survives, and along its path you'll find numerous establishments advertising the route's nostalgia in bright neon letters.

If you follow Foothill Boulevard out of Pasadena, you'll come to **ARCADIA**, a colorless suburb whose **LA County Arboretum**, 310 N Baldwin Ave (daily 9am–5pm; $5, students $3; ☎626/821-3222, ⓦwww.arboretum.org), contains many impressive gardens and waterfalls, flocks of peacocks and, of course, a great assortment of trees, arranged by their native continents. This was the 127-acre home of Elias "Lucky" Baldwin, who made his millions in the silver mines of Nevada's Comstock in the 1870s, settled here in 1875 and built a fanciful white palace along a palm tree-lined lagoon (later used in the TV show *Fantasy Island*) on the site of the 1839 Rancho Santa Anita. He also bred horses and raced them on a neighboring track that has since grown into the **Santa Anita Racetrack** (racing Oct to early Nov & late Dec to late April Wed–Sun post time 12.30pm or 1pm; $5; ☎626/574-7223, ⓦwww.santaanita.com), still the most famous racetrack in California, with a Depression-era steel frieze along the grandstand.

The foothill district of **SIERRA MADRE**, on the northern edge of Arcadia, lies directly beneath Mount Wilson and is worth a visit if you're a hiker. A seven-mile round-trip trail up to the summit makes for an excellent, if tiring, trek; the trailhead is 150 yards up the private Mount Wilson Road. South of Sierra Madre stands the valley's original settlement, the church and grounds of **Mission San Gabriel Arcangel**, 428 S Mission Drive (daily 9am–4.30pm; $5; ☎626/457-3035, ⓦsangabrielmission.org), in the heart of the small town of **SAN GABRIEL**. The mission was established here in 1771 by Junípero Serra and the current building finished in 1812. Despite decades of damage by earthquakes and the elements, the church and grounds have been repaired and reopened, their antique-filled rooms, gardens and old winery giving some sense of mission-era life.

The attractions further east are even more isolated, in anonymous suburban towns, though still worth a look if you have the time and gas. The lone draw out in **MONROVIA**, east of Sierra Madre, is the zany **Aztec Hotel**, 311 W Foothill Blvd, a 1925 pre-Columbian creation from Mayan revivalist Robert Stacy-Judd that is still maintained as a boarding house, bar and restaurant. Its faux-ancient carvings and designs, monumental appearance and stunning facade encase a lobby that displays antiques like the original gas pumps found along Route 66, which runs just outside the front door. Beyond here, the only reason most Angelenos venture further east is to take a splash at **Raging Waters**, in the suburb of San Dimas at 111 Raging Waters Drive (open May Sat & Sun 10am–6pm; June–Aug Mon–Fri 10am–8pm, Sat & Sun 10am–9pm; $27, kids $15; ☎909/802-2200, ⓦwww.ragingwaters.com), a reasonably fun aquatic theme park with plenty of tubes and slides for cooling off from the summer heat, and plenty of summer smog as well – the area has some of LA's worst air pollution, thanks to unfavorable winds blowing in from central LA.

The San Fernando Valley

Home to acres of asphalt, countless mini-malls and nonstop tract housing, the **San Fernando Valley** is often derided by Westsiders as the apotheosis of dull,

LA's aqueducts

Just beyond Mission San Fernando, I-5 runs past two of LA's main reservoirs, the water carried by the **California Aqueduct**, traveling from the Sacramento Delta, and the **LA Aqueduct**, coming from the Owens Valley and Mono Lake on the eastern slopes of the Sierra Nevada Mountains.

How LA came into these water sources, however, is a shady matter indeed. Acting on behalf of William Mulholland, agents of the city, masquerading as rich cattle-barons interested in establishing ranches in the Owens Valley, bought up most of the land along the Owens River in the first years of the century before selling it, at great personal profit, to the City of Los Angeles. Tellingly, when the first rush of water was brought to the city with great fanfare, Mulholland publicly pronounced his triumph with the memorable command, "There it is! Take it!"

There is little doubt that the LA Aqueduct has served the interests of the city well, bringing water to two million people, but the legality of such a distant supply of water is still disputed. After much controversy, even the conservative state supreme court ruled that the endangered Mono Lake area – the salty home of fascinating tufa (gnarled limestone) columns – must finally be removed from the clutches of LA's water empire.

vacuous suburbia. While there's some truth to this, as of late the Valley has also become known for its rabid **secessionist movement**, which blames all difficulties – from crime to potholes to crummy schools – on Downtown LA bureaucrats, though so far little progress has been made.

The San Fernando Valley, whose 1769 Spanish discovery predated the settlement of Los Angeles, was first named after **St Catherine**, only later acquiring its present moniker with the development of Mission San Fernando at its northern tip. After the US took possession of California and the Southern Pacific Railroad cut through it, the Valley rapidly transformed, going from a nineteenth-century tract of wheat fields and ranchos to an early twentieth-century expanse of citrus groves to a post-World War II dynamo of industry, media and, above all, suburban housing. The spark that made all this development possible was the 1913 construction of the LA Aqueduct, which irrigated the land with water cleverly diverted from California's northern Owens Valley (see box, above).

While the Owens Valley farmers may have suffered, the San Fernando Valley landowners – including many Downtown LA businessmen, not least Harry Chandler of the *LA Times* – got rich, and they in turn sold their land at a premium to make way for even more residential development. Today, the agricultural ghosts are apparent only in streets with idyllic names like Orange Grove, Walnut and Magnolia.

Glendale

West of Pasadena, beyond the Verdugo Mountains, **GLENDALE** is a typical upper-middle-class suburb, unusual mostly for its size, in that it extends from Griffith Park all the way past the northern reaches of foothill communities like La Cañada Flintridge. At least its downtown is compact, south of the 134 freeway along Brand Boulevard, where, apart from a handful of restaurants and boutiques, you'll find the **Alex Theater**, 268 N Brand Blvd, a striking piece of green-and-yellow Art Deco with a towering pylon (and now serving as a performing arts center).

North of the 134, the city has a smattering of noteworthy buildings, such as the **Verdugo Adobe**, 2211 Bonita Drive (grounds daily dawn–dusk; free), displaying antiques and artifacts from the early nineteenth century; though the adobe itself is not open to the public, the gardens contain the **Oak of Peace**, a tree said to be more than five hundred years old, allegedly the place where in 1847 Mexican leaders decided to surrender to US troops in the Mexican–American War. Similarly, the **Casa Adobe de San Rafael**, 1330 Dorothy Drive (summer Sun 1–3pm; rest of year first Sun of each month 1–3pm; free), is a quaint, low-slung adobe set among birds of paradise, magnolias and eucalyptus trees, designed in 1871 for LA County's first sheriff. To the northwest, the **Brand Library**, or "El Miradero," 1601 W Mountain St (Tues & Thurs 1–9pm, Wed 1–6pm, Fri & Sat 1–5pm; free), is a white oddity from 1902, said to be modeled on the East India Pavilion at Chicago's 1893 Columbian Exposition, a striking Islamic design of domes and minarets containing art books from the main Glendale Library. Also located in Brand Park is the so-called **Doctors House** (tours Aug–June Sun 2–3pm; free), a charming Eastlake residence from 1888, named for three physicians who lived there successively, with period decor, a projecting roofline and dormers, and latticed white porches.

Seven miles north, **TUJUNGA** has a remarkable collection of boulder houses and bungalows built in the 1910s and 1920s, the inspiration of a small community of Socialists who, like the dwellers in Pasadena's Arroyo Seco (see box, p.183), believed earthy materials like wood and stone made for the best, and most moral, forms of construction. Their restored 1913 clubhouse, **Bolton Hall**, 10116 Commerce Ave (Tues & Sun 1–4pm; free), hints at their aims, with a rocky central tower and interior with exposed wooden beams, which were supposed to recall, according to the building's architect George Harris, "the dense foliage of a great tree to the blue sky." Not surprisingly, this striking creation was the second historic monument ever declared by LA, and displays a good selection of antiques from its rich and varied history – it has also doubled as the town's city hall, and its jail.

Forest Lawn Glendale

For most visitors, the main reason to come to the city is to visit the Glendale branch of **Forest Lawn Cemetery**, 1712 S Glendale Ave (daily 9am–5pm; free) – immortalized with biting satire by Evelyn Waugh in *The Loved One*, and at the vanguard of the American way of death for nearly a century. Founded in 1917 by one Dr Hubert Eaton, this soon became *the* place to be buried, its pompous landscaping and pious artworks attracting celebrities by the dozen to buy their own little piece of heaven. The graveyard's success has allowed it to expand throughout the LA region, notably with a branch near Griffith Park, in the Hollywood Hills (see p.95), though the others – in places like Covina Hills, Cypress Beach and Long Beach – are best avoided.

It's best to climb the hill and see the cemetery in reverse from the **Forest Lawn Museum** (open during park hours; free), whose hodgepodge of worldly artifacts includes coins from ancient Rome, Viking relics, medieval armor, and a mysterious, sculpted Easter Island figure, discovered being used as ballast in a fishing boat in the days when the statues could still be swiped from the island. How it ended up here is another mystery, but it is the only one on view in the US. Next door to the museum, the **Resurrection and Crucifixion Hall** houses the most colossal piece of religious art in the world, *The Crucifixion* by Jan Styka – an oil painting nearly 200 feet tall and 50 feet wide, showing Jesus standing by a fallen cross, not being crucified as the title

THE SAN GABRIEL AND SAN FERNANDO VALLEYS | The San Fernando Valley would suggest. In any case, you're only allowed to see it during the ceremonial unveiling every hour on the hour – and be charged $1 to boot. Besides this, Eaton owned a stained glass "re-creation" of Leonardo da Vinci's *Last Supper* and, realizing that he only needed one piece to complete his trio of "the three greatest moments in the life of Christ," he commissioned American artist Robert Clark to produce *The Resurrection* – which is unveiled every half-hour, appropriate since it's only half the size of the Styka. If you can't stick around for the ceremonial showings (with both, in any case, the size is the only aspect that's impressive), you can check out the scaled-down replicas just inside the entrance.

From the museum, walk down through the terrace gardens – loaded with sculptures modeled on the greats of classical European art, along with an ungainly 13-foot rendering of George Washington – to the **Freedom Mausoleum**, where you'll find a handful of the cemetery's better-known graves. Just outside the mausoleum's doors, Errol Flynn lies in an unspectacular plot (unmarked until 1979), rumored to have been buried with six bottles of whiskey at his side, while a few strides away is the grave of Walt Disney, who is not in the deep freeze as urban legend would have it. Inside the mausoleum you'll find Clara Bow, Nat King Cole, Jeanette MacDonald and Alan Ladd placed close to each other on the first floor. Downstairs are Chico Marx and his brother Gummo, the Marx Brothers' agent and business manager. Back down the hill, the **Great Mausoleum** is chiefly noted for the tombs of Clark Gable (next to Carole Lombard, who died in a plane crash just three years after marrying him), and Jean Harlow, in a marble-lined room that cost over $25,000, paid for by fiancé William Powell. Amid all this morbid glamour, the cemetery has actually been the site of thousands of **weddings**, not least being Ronald Reagan's star-crossed wedlock with Jane Wyman in 1940.

Burbank

Although Hollywood's name is synonymous with the movie industry, in reality many of the big studios moved out of Tinseltown long ago, and much of the business of actually making films (and TV shows) is located over the hills in otherwise boring **BURBANK**. Hot, smoggy and often downright ugly, Burbank nonetheless has a media district bustling with activity, thanks to the explosion in demand from overseas markets, cable TV and broadcast networks.

Disney is probably the most visible of the studios, with Robert A.M. Stern's starry wizard-hat building, visible from the 101 freeway, housing over seven hundred animators. Less appealing is Disney's other public face, its **Studio Office Building**, 500 S Buena Vista St, a clumsy effort from Michael Graves that has five of the Seven Dwarves propping up the building's roof. As for touring the studio, forget it – the secretive company would rather have you plunk down your cash in Disneyland.

Nearby, **NBC**, or the National Broadcasting Company, 3000 W Alameda St (box office open Mon–Fri 9am–4pm; $7; reserve at ☎818/840-3537), offers an engaging ninety-minute tour of the largest production facility in the US, even though only a handful of shows currently tape there. Apart from the tour, the studio gives you the chance to be in the audience for the taping of a TV program (phone ahead for free tickets), such as Jay Leno's *Tonight Show*. The **Warner Bros Studio**, 4000 Warner Blvd at Hollywood Way, offers tours of its facilities (May–Sept Mon–Fri 9am–3pm; Oct–April Mon–Fri 9am–4pm; $32; reservations only at ☎818/846-1403, ⓦwww.wbstudiotour.com) that take you past the big sound stages, around the production offices and through the

Map labels:
North Hollywood
Glendale
Studio Office Building
Disney Studios
NBC Studios
Johnny Carson Park
Buena Vista Park
Warner Brothers Studios
Forest Lawn Hollywood Hills
LA River
BURBANK STUDIOS
N
0   800 yards

▼ Universal Studios & Hollywood

outdoor sets for movies and TV shows. Ultimately, you won't get to see any actual filming, but if you want to see a major studio's actual working environment, the tour is worth the money.

Arguably Burbank's greatest attraction is the oldest **Bob's Big Boy** in existence, 4211 Riverside Drive, a nicely preserved Googie coffee shop from 1949, used for a host of Hollywood flicks, notably the first *Austin Powers*, and for good reason: the 70-foot-tall pink-and-white neon sign is a knockout. Occasionally on Friday nights, the restaurant hosts stylish hot-rod shows in the parking lot (6–10pm), and every Saturday and Sunday night, you can chow down on your burgers and fries with old-fashioned car-hop service (5–10pm).

Universal Studios

Just to the south along the 101 freeway, the largest of the backlots belongs to **Universal Studios** (summer daily 8am–10pm; rest of year daily 9am–7pm; $45; ☎818/508-9600, ⊛www.universalstudioshollywood.com), where the four-hour-long "tours" are more like a trip around an amusement park than a film studio, with the first half featuring a tram ride through a make-believe set where you can experience the fading magic of the Red Sea parting and a "collapsing" bridge, the second taking place inside the corny Entertainment Center, where unemployed actors engage in Wild West shootouts and stunt shows based on the studio's movies. The theme rides are based on the studio's more popular films, including *Back to the Future* (a jerky trip on a motion simulator), *Jurassic Park* (close encounters with prehistoric plastic), *Terminator 2* (a 3-D movie with robot stuntmen) and *Spiderman Rocks!* (a musical version of the blockbuster). You never actually get to see any filming, though.

Also part of the complex is **Universal Amphitheater**, a twenty-screen multiplex that hosts pop concerts in summer in an unincorporated LA County enclave known as Universal City. **Universal CityWalk**, also on the same lot, is an outdoor mall, free to all who pay the $7 parking (redeemable at the cinemas), a place where rock bands churn out MOR covers, street performers warble syrupy ballads, and giant TV screens run ads for the latest Universal releases.

The western San Fernando Valley

Beyond Burbank, the **western San Fernando Valley** suburbs of Los Angeles – some of the more well-known of which are **NORTH HOLLYWOOD**, **SHERMAN OAKS**, **VAN NUYS** and **RESEDA** – are often collectively called "the Valley," immediately bringing to mind strip malls, fast-food joints and endless asphalt, but also host a handful of interesting, though widely separated, sights. The Valley is also the capital of America's burgeoning **porn industry**, with home videotape sales and Internet demand making the low-rent video studios and distribution warehouses here an integral part of the local economy – cranking out more acres of photographed flesh than just about any spot on the planet. However, this is one aspect of the Valley's movie industry that, not surprisingly, is kept discreetly behind closed doors, and all you'll see are unmarked concrete warehouses and strip-mall office suites.

Along with porn, the Valley is also a hotspot for mutinous suburbanites. Strengthened by a law that allows them **secession** by plebiscite, the Valley's districts no longer have to get a green light from City Hall to go their own way, just approval by a majority of the voters of the city of LA (which they failed to do in a recent election). Their course is far from certain, with residents split on a need for total Balkanization of the area versus a San Fernando megacity that would be the nation's seventh largest. The first of the Valley's isolated points of interest is **Campo de Cahuenga**, across from Universal Studios – and a Red Line subway stop – at 3919 Lankershim Blvd, in North Hollywood (by appointment only; ☎818/763-7651). While not very well known locally, it is perhaps LA's most important historical site. Generals John Frémont and Andres Pico signed the 1847 Treaty of Cahuenga between the US and Mexico here – which led to the more famous Treaty of Guadalupe Hidalgo – thus ending the Mexican–American War and later allowing the US to officially acquire California and the rest of the Southwest, all of which is recounted here in fairly interesting detail. Unfortunately, the adobe on the grounds is only a replica of an original 1840s structure that was demolished at the beginning of the twentieth century.

Several miles north on Lankershim Boulevard, you'll find the buzzing commercial area of the **North Hollywood Arts District**, located around Magnolia Boulevard and accessible by a nearby Metrorail station, nicknamed "NoHo" by county bureaucrats as a play on New York's trendy SoHo. Although the similarities end there, it's still a lively enough spot that's well worth a trip if you're in the area, with no less than thirty live theaters and plenty of coffee shops, galleries, book stores, restaurants and odd little boutiques, which show unexpected flashes of a creative anarchic spirit.

About six miles west in Van Nuys, the **Tillman Japanese Garden**, 6100 Woodley Ave, near the 405 freeway (grounds Mon–Thurs & Sun noon–4pm, tours by reservation only Mon–Thurs; $3; ☎818/751-8166), is a pleasant spot – adorned with stone lanterns, bonsai trees, low bridges, a tea house, and artful streams and pools – which surprisingly uses reclaimed water from an adjacent treatment plant and sits in the giant flood plain of the Sepulveda Dam Recreation Area.

Due southwest, off Ventura Boulevard, the increasingly expensive hillside homes of **ENCINO** sit near **Los Encinos State Historic Park**, 16756 Moorpark St (Wed–Sun 10am–5pm, tours 1–4pm; grounds free, tours $2; ☎818/784-4849, ⓦwww.lahacal.org/losencinos.html), which includes all that remains of an original Native American settlement and later Mexican hacienda, along with an extensive cattle and sheep farm. In addition to a blacksmith's shop and lake fed by a natural spring, the main attraction is an 1849 adobe house, featuring high-ceilinged rooms that open out onto porches, shaded by oak trees (in Spanish, *encinos*) and kept cool by the two-foot-thick walls.

At the western end of the Valley, in **WEST HILLS**, are a few minor historic points of interest, including the **Shadow Ranch**, 22633 Vanowen St (Mon–Fri 10am–5pm, Sat 9am–5pm, Sun noon–5pm; free), the center of a 23,000-acre rancho that was controlled by land moguls I.N. Van Nuys and Isaac Lankershim. These days, it's mainly notable for its great stand of eucalyptus trees imported from Australia over 120 years ago, along with a main ranch home that retains its historic allure. To the northwest is the **Orcutt Ranch**, 23600 Roscoe Blvd (daily 8am–5pm, tours Sept–June on last Sun of month 2–5pm; free), also known as "Rancho Sombre del Roble," or Ranch Shaded by the Oak. Indeed, there's an impressive plot of ancient oaks here, and citrus trees and bamboo too, alongside a traditional Spanish Colonial ranch house with a romantic grotto and a large sundial. The ranch once belonged to William Orcutt, the oil geologist who first found fossils in the La Brea Tar Pits.

The northern San Fernando Valley

A few miles east of Orcutt Ranch, Topanga Canyon Boulevard heads into the far northwest reaches of the Valley to **Stony Point**, a bizarre sandstone outcrop that has been used for countless low-budget Westerns, and in recent years as a popular venue for LA's contingent of lycra-clad rock climbers. The area, though crossed by both Amtrak and Metrorail trains, has a desolate spookiness about it; it was used as a hideout by the legendary late-nineteenth-century bandit Joaquin Murrieta and, during the late 1960s, by the Charles Manson "family," who lived for a time at **Spahn Ranch**, just west at 22000 Santa Susana Pass Rd, though not much remains of the site these days.

West of Stony Point, at the end of Santa Susana Pass Road, the little town of **SIMI VALLEY** is the home of the **Ronald Reagan Presidential Library**, off Olsen Road at 40 Presidential Drive (daily 10am–5pm; $5, kids free; ☎800/410-8354, ⓦwww.reagan.utexas.edu). Unless you're a big fan of the Gipper, you're likely to find the affectionate portrayal of "Dutch" Reagan unbearable, though the stray graffiti-covered chunk of the Berlin Wall on display is worth a look. Far more captivating is the bizarre folk-art shrine of **Grandma Prisbrey's Bottle Village**, 4595 Cochran St (by appointment only; ☎805/583-1627, ⓦechomatic.home.mindspring.com/bv), where assorted buildings – from the Leaning Tower of Pisa to simple shacks – are constructed from colorful bits of junk. Auto parts, defunct lightbulbs, pencil shards, glass bottles and various other detritus all show up in the design of this miniature village – surprisingly listed on the National Register of Historic Places –

Earthquake central: The San Fernando Valley

The devastating 6.7 magnitude **earthquake** that shook LA on the morning of January 17, 1994, was one of the most destructive disasters in US history. Fifty-five people were killed, two hundred more suffered critical injuries and the economic cost is estimated at $8 billion. One can only guess how much higher these totals would have been had the quake hit during the day, when the many collapsed stores would have been crowded with shoppers, and the roads and freeways full of commuters. As it was, the tremor toppled chimneys and shattered windows all over Southern California, with the worst damage concentrated at the epicenter in the San Fernando Valley community of **Northridge**, where a dozen people were killed when an apartment building collapsed. At the northern edge of the valley, the I-5/Hwy-14 interchange was destroyed, killing just one motorist but snarling traffic for at least a year; while in West LA, the Santa Monica Freeway overpass collapsed onto La Cienega Boulevard at one of LA's busiest intersections. The Northridge event followed a quake in the eastern desert around **Landers** a few years earlier, and just eclipsed LA's previous worst earthquake in modern times, the 6.6 magnitude temblor of February 9, 1971, which had its epicenter in **Sylmar** – also in the Valley.

Small earthquakes happen all the time in LA, usually doing no more than rattling supermarket shelves and making dogs howl. In the unlikely event a sizeable earthquake strikes when you're in LA, protect yourself under something sturdy, such as a heavy table or a door frame, and well away from windows or anything made of glass. In theory, all the city's new buildings are "quake-safe"; the extent of the crisis in January 1994, however, forced the city to re-examine and reinforce buildings – though as the quake recedes in memory, the job seems to diminish in perceived importance. So when the inevitable "Big One," a quake in the 8+ range, arrives, no one knows exactly what will be left standing.

the highlight of which is undoubtedly the "Doll Head Shrine," a thoroughly disturbing array of antique plastic doll heads stuck on poles.

At the northern tip of the Valley, the San Diego, Golden State and Foothill freeways join together at I-5, the quickest route north to San Francisco. Standing near the junction, at 15151 San Fernando Mission Blvd in the small town of **SAN FERNANDO**, the church and many of the historic buildings of **Mission San Fernando Rey de España** (daily 9am–5pm; $5) had to be completely rebuilt following the 1971 Sylmar earthquake. It's hard to imagine now, walking through the nicely landscaped courtyards and gardens, but eighty-odd years ago, director D.W. Griffith used the then-dilapidated mission as a film site for *Our Silent Paths*, his tale of the Gold Rush. Nowadays, there's a good collection of pottery, furniture and saddles, along with an old-time blacksmith's shop.

Also in the vicinity, another key nineteenth-century site can be found at 10940 Sepulveda Blvd, the **Andres Pico Adobe** (Mon & third Sun of month 10am–3pm; free), the well-preserved estate and grounds of the Mexican general who fought off American troops, at least for a while, in the 1840s. This lovely, two-story brick adobe, built in 1834 and crammed with period furnishings and historical bric-a-brac, makes a good spot for a stroll in an idyllic setting.

Up the road in nearby **SYLMAR** – famous mainly as the site of the 1971 earthquake (see box, above) – the wondrous **San Sylmar**, 15180 Bledsoe St (Tues–Sat 10am & 1.30pm; free; reservations only at ☎818/367-2251), is a storehouse for all kinds of Wurlitzer organs, antique player pianos, cosmetic paraphernalia, Tiffany stained glass and classic French furniture, but the highlight is its **Nethercutt Collection**, a stunning showroom filled with the finest collectors' automobiles imaginable. Packard, Mercedes and Bugatti are all represented with classic models, but the eye-popping highlights are the Duesenbergs, splendid machines driven by movie stars in the Jazz Age, including a 1933 Arlington Torpedo model: a stunning silver roadster with curvaceous lines, sinuous bumpers, antique headlights and an array of exposed chrome pipes.

A few miles east of the city of San Fernando, nature lovers can take a winding journey into the Angeles National Forest to see the **Wildlife Waystation**, 14831 Little Tujunga Canyon Rd (hour-long tours first & third Sun of month; $12, kids $6; reserve at ☎818/899-5201, ⓦwww.waystation.org), which nurses and rehabilitates wild or exotic animals that have been injured in nature or abused in zoos, and you'll see everything from foxes and coyotes, to ocelots, orangutans, alligators and even lions.

North of the valleys

The thriving communities **north of the valleys** offer several compelling historical and cultural sights, along with one of LA's best theme parks. Most of these sights lie along or near the I-14 freeway, which leaves the San Fernando Valley to make a harsh trek into the periphery of the Mojave Desert – still part of the huge County of Los Angeles. To the far north of San Fernando, the ruins of the former company town of **Mentryville**, three miles west of I-5 at 27201 W Pico Canyon Rd (guided tours noon–4pm first & third Sun of month; $3; ⓦwww.mentryville.org), are where California's very first oil well was dug, in 1876. The boom only lasted a few decades and, despite the original well pumping on until 1990 (making it the longest-operating oil well in history, at 114 years), the site was virtually a ghost town for many years, until the Santa Monica Mountains Conservancy bought it from Chevron Oil. Saved from further deterioration, the preserved red-and-white barn, one-room 1880s schoolhouse, and Victorian house of town-founder Charles Alexander Mentry evoke some of the city's old character.

To the east, in the town of **SANTA CLARITA**, the **William S. Hart Ranch and Museum**, 24151 San Fernando Rd (Wed–Fri 10am–1pm, Sat & Sun 11am–4pm; free; ☎661/254-4584, ⓦwww.hartmuseum.org), holds a fine assemblage of Western history, filled with native artworks, Remington sculptures, displays of spurs, guns and lariats, Tinseltown costumes and authentic cowhand clothing, housed in a Spanish Colonial mansion. The estate was constructed by silent-movie star Hart, who made 65 westerns in the 1910s and 1920s, and is still considered one of the all-time cowboy greats – playing many more complex and often troubled characters than his main cinematic rival, the smiling, white-hatted Tom Mix.

Conveniently, a trip to the Hart Museum may be combined with a day at nearby **Magic Mountain**, Magic Mountain Parkway at I-5 (summer daily 10am–10pm; rest of year Sat & Sun only 10am–8pm; $43, kids $27, $6 parking; ☎661/255-4100, ⓦwww.sixflags.com), a three-hundred-acre complex that has some of the wildest roller coasters and rides in the world – a hundred times more thrilling than anything at Disneyland. Highlights include the Viper, a huge orange monster with seven loops; the Psyclone, a modern coaster modeled on the rickety wooden Cyclone in Coney Island; the Riddler's Revenge, a stand-up coaster that takes you over loops and twists at 65mph, many of them while you're upside down; the Goliath, full of harrowing 85mph dips; and Déjà Vu, twisting and jerking you in several different directions at once. The addition of an adjacent water park, **Hurricane Harbor** (same hours; $22, kids $15, or $53 for both parks; ☎661/255-4100, ⓦwww.sixflags.com), is another fun choice, providing plenty of aquatic fun if you don't mind getting splashed by throngs of giddy pre-adolescents.

The I-14 freeway, also called the Antelope Valley Freeway, branches off from I-5 into an extension of the Mojave Desert and takes you to **Vasquez Rocks Park**, off Agua Dulce Canyon Road, where acres of jagged, rocky outcroppings and an undulating terrain make for one of Hollywood's favorite film locations: everything from *The Flintstones* to *Dracula* to *Star Trek* has been shot here. Even more mythically, the illicit treasure of legendary bandit Tiburcio Vásquez is supposedly buried in the vicinity. Further up I-14, near the remote desert burg of **LANCASTER**, the awe-inspiring **Antelope Valley Poppy Reserve**, on Lancaster Drive, spreads over 1800 acres. Looking like an endless bright-orange sea of wild blossoms in spring, the reserve comes alive in April as the site of the annual California Poppy Festival (☎661/723-6077).

If you prefer the sound of screaming fighter jets up-close, continue well north on I-14 to Edwards Air Force Base, where pilot Chuck Yeager first broke the sound barrier in 1947. The **Air Force Flight Test Center Museum** (Tues–Sat 9am–5pm; free; call ahead at ☎805/277-8050, ⓦafftc.edwards .af.mil), displays small model planes that had their maiden flights at the base, as well as full-sized jets in its "Airpark," notably the sleekly menacing A-12 Blackbird spy plane, the prototype for the type of aircraft that conducted secret surveillance missions during the Vietnam War.

9

Malibu and the Santa Monica Mountains

Relatively free from smog, traffic and violent crime, **MALIBU** and the **SANTA MONICA MOUNTAINS** symbolize the good life in Southern California. Ironically, even as they hold some of LA's most expensive real estate, they are also under constant threat from natural dangers. Built on eroding cliffs forever sliding into the ocean, the area faces considerable trouble from summer hillside fires, which blacken the landscape and leave a slick residue of burnt chaparral – a perfect surface for the catastrophic floods and mudslides that come just a few months later. The periodic arrival of El Niño-driven wet weather only makes the situation more dire, with watery calamities a constant, inescapable threat.

Reached by way of a popular beachside motorway, the Pacific Coast Highway (otherwise known as "PCH" or Highway 1), Malibu and the mountains feature some of LA's most picturesque scenery, their canyons, valleys and forests making up a surprisingly large, pristine wilderness amid the surrounding urban development. From **Pacific Palisades**, a chic district just northwest of Santa Monica, to rustic **Topanga Canyon**, a wooded neighborhood with an artistic flair, to beautiful **Point Dume**, a whale-watching promontory, these seaside and mountainous areas are best navigated by car, unless you prefer to hike on their rigorous parkland trails, of which there are many. North of PCH, **Mulholland Highway** provides an alternative trip through the area, winding through the Santa Monica Mountains and skipping Malibu entirely, instead reaching the ocean less than a mile from LA County's distant northwest boundary – at one of its prime spots for surfing.

Pacific Palisades

Driving north on PCH beyond the bluffs of Santa Monica, you reach the sandy crescent of **Will Rogers State Beach** and, on the other side of the road, **PACIFIC PALISADES**, once an upper-crust community of artists and writers, but now the home of media-industry millionaires. No amount of wealth, however, has been able to keep the district's hillsides from slowly but surely falling into the ocean, most noticeably at the point above Chautauqua Boulevard and PCH. With each winter's storms, more of the place gets washed

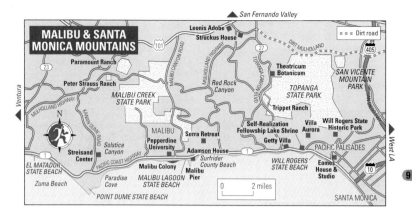

down to the street below by simple erosion or mudslides, blocking traffic on PCH and shrinking the backyards of the clifftop homes.

There are a few spots of interest among the suburban ranch houses, starting with the **Eames House**, just off PCH at 203 Chautauqua Blvd, perhaps the most influential building of post-war LA. Fashioned out of Prefabricated industrial parts in 1947 as part of the influential Case Study program (see box on p.107), the compound boasts a main residential unit and an adjacent studio building, both of which resemble large, colored metal-and-glass boxes – at the time perceived as a great step toward complete architectural modernity. Although the property is off-limits much of the time, and accessible only on a private drive, the grounds and exterior of the house are viewable, though strictly by appointment (call Mon–Fri 10am–4.30pm; ☎310/459-9663, ⓦwww.eamesoffice.com). The neighboring **Entenza House**, at no. 205, isn't quite up to the standard of the landmark next door, but this steel-framed structure was nonetheless built by the same architect, Charles Eames, with help from Eero Saarinen. Best of the more contemporary buildings in Pacific Palisades is the **Schwartz House**, 444 Sycamore Ave, designed in 1994 by Pierre Koenig, more famous for his late-1950s Case Study House #22 (see box, p.107). His unique design includes a black-steel frame and foundation pivoted at a 30-degree angle from the rest of the boxy gray house, making for an unusual Rubik's Cube effect, which also has the function of keeping the living room and bedrooms out of the full glare of the rising sun.

Unexpected among all the sleek designs is a collection of **log cabins**, along Haldeman Road east of Rustic Canyon Recreation Center, sitting in the wooded hills that rise from Chautauqua Boulevard. These self-consciously quaint houses were the product of the "Uplifters Club," a branch of the LA Athletic Club led by *Wizard of Oz* author L. Frank Baum, designed to "uplift art, promote good fellowship and build a closer acquaintance," but mainly serving as an excuse for having booze-soaked fun during Prohibition. The rural charms of the houses, too, are somewhat deceptive – like Hollywood sets, many of the "cabins" have log facades that are merely glued on.

To the north, Sunset Boulevard heads away from the ocean to **Will Rogers State Historic Park**, 14243 Sunset Blvd (summer daily 8am–dusk; rest of year daily 8am–6pm; free, parking $6), the home and ranch of the eponymous Depression-era cowboy philosopher, newspaper columnist and radio-show host, one of America's most popular figures of the time – after his death in a plane crash in 1935 (in a legendary, fatal Alaska journey with Wiley Post), there was a nationwide 35-minute silence. While he was renowned for his down-home, common-sense reasoning, famously remarking that he "never met a man he didn't like," Rogers was also a Socialist with a pointed wit who once served as mayor of Beverly Hills. Now an informal **museum** (daily 10am–5pm; free), his 31-room ranch house is filled with cowboy gear and Native American art, including ropes and lariats, sculptures by Frederic Remington, and the mounted head of a Texas longhorn. The 200-acre park has miles of foot and bridle paths, one of which leads up to the top of Topanga Canyon; on spring and summer weekends, professional **polo matches** take place on the park's main lawn – the only place in LA County with a regulation-size field – and attract a fair crowd of spectators (April–Oct Sat 2–4pm, Sun 10am–noon; free).

Castellammare

The western side of Pacific Palisades, **Castellammare** was named after a Latin port known as the "castle by the sea," its 1920s design mimicking Italian villas and Spanish Colonial estates. Although it's now just another rich suburb, it does hold some appeal, mainly in structures whose settings are just as dramatic as their architecture.

Just before the street reaches PCH, the Pacific end of Sunset Boulevard reaches the most conspicuous sight in the area: the **Self-Realization Fellowship Lake Shrine**, 17190 Sunset Blvd (Tues–Sat 9am–4.30pm, Sun 12.30–4.30pm; free; ☎310/454-4114, ⓦwww.yogananda-srf.org/temples/lakeshrine), a religious monument like no other, created in 1950 by Paramahansa Yogananda, whose life and works are recounted in an on-site **museum** (Sun 11am–4pm; free). Sitting below a giant, golden-domed temple, the ten-acre lake shrine is an ecumenical ode to world faiths, featuring symbols and credos of the major religions. Visitors are invited to circle the lake on a literal path of spiritual enlightenment, pausing to view such sights as the **Windmill Chapel** (Sun 1–4.30pm; free), a church built as a replica of a sixteenth-century Dutch windmill, along with a massive archway topped with copper lotus flowers, a houseboat that the shrine's Indian founder once used, a bird refuge, gardens with religious symbols, and numerous plaques and signs quoting the Bible, the Koran and such. The sparkling, hilltop temple, unfortunately, is strictly for monks.

Up the bluffs from Sunset, the **Villa Aurora**, 520 Paseo Miramar, is perhaps the best reason for visiting Pacific Palisades, an idyllic 1927 Spanish Colonial structure that was conceived as a public-relations project by the *LA Times*, which devoted a series of articles to the construction of the house and all its modern amenities – dishwasher, electric fridge, gas range – and stunning Mediterranean style, carried through in the Spanish tile, wrought-iron balconies and alluring gardens. Readers were encouraged to tour the house and, it was hoped, be inspired to buy their own suburban dream home (and thousands did). Later, as the home of writer Lion Feuchtwanger, it became the focus of German emigres, hosting salons attended by Bertolt Brecht, Thomas Mann, Kurt Weill, Arnold Schoenberg and Fritz Lang, and has since been reborn as the **Foundation for European American Relations**, which presents poetry readings, film screenings and music recitals of contemporary artists from the Continent (usually free; ☎310/454-4231, ⓦwww.usc.edu/isd/aurora). Closer to PCH, the area's most prominent house is the towering **Villa de Leon**, 17948 Porto Marina Way, a 1927 Italian Renaissance villa visible as you drive north on PCH and perched precariously near a cliff.

Just north of Sunset Boulevard's intersection with PCH, the imitation Roman estate of the **Getty Villa** sits on a picturesque bluff overlooking the ocean. Once the site of the Getty Museum (now in West LA; see p.123), the Villa is closed for renovation until 2004, when it will reopen with a focus on antiquities, its sizeable collection of sculptures, vases, amphorae and friezes displayed in galleries by theme, instead of chronology (call for an update at ☎310/440-7300 or visit ⓦwww.getty.edu/museum/villa.html).

Topanga Canyon

Around Topanga Canyon Boulevard north of PCH, **Topanga Canyon** is a stunning natural preserve. With hillsides covered in golden poppies and wildflowers, one hundred and fifty thousand acres of these mountains and adjacent seashore have been protected as the **Santa Monica Mountains National Recreation Area**. Boasting fine views and fresh air, the area is wilderness in many places, and you can still spot a variety of deer, coyotes and even the odd mountain lion. Like LA itself, the mountains are not without an element of danger, especially in winter and early spring, when mudslides threaten houses and waterfalls cascade down the cliffs. Most of the time, though, these hazards are of little concern to visitors, and park rangers offer free guided hikes throughout the mountains most weekends (information and reservations at ☎818/597-9192). There are also self-guided trails through the canyon's **Topanga State Park**, off Old Topanga Canyon Boulevard at the crest of the mountains, with spectacular views over the Pacific. A good starting point for visitors is **Trippet Ranch**, north off Entrada Road, where trails like the Musch Trail — an easygoing trek through prime wildflower country — thread through terrain less rugged than other parts of the park. The local Audubon Society offers periodic guided hikes through this and other LA-area nature zones ($3; reserve at ☎323/876-0202, ⓦwww.laaudubon.org). If you'd like to find out more, the Santa Monica Mountains **visitor center** in neighboring Thousand Oaks, 401 W Hillcrest Drive (Mon–Fri 8am–5pm, Sat & Sun 9am–5pm; ☎805/370-2301, ⓦwww.nps.gov/samo), has additional maps and information on hiking trails.

The nearby community of **TOPANGA**, further up Topanga Canyon Boulevard, was a proving ground for West Coast rock music in the 1960s, when Neil Young, the Byrds and other artists moved here and held all-night jam sessions in the sycamore groves along Topanga Creek. The neighborhood still has an air of this history, although few real bohemians are left. If you'd like to revisit a bit of the old musical spirit, the **Topanga Community House**, 1440 Topanga Canyon Blvd, hosts occasional classical and pop concerts, but is more typically used for children's puppet shows and storytelling hours. More enjoyable is the **Theatricum Botanicum**, close by at no. 1419, a wooded outdoor amphitheater known for its classical and modern plays, plus well-regarded summer performances of Shakespeare ($14–22, kids $8; ☎310/455-3723, ⓦwww.theatricum.com). Originally founded by Will Geer, known best as TV's Grandpa Walton, the theater is still very much a family affair, with daughter Ellen now directing the plays. Before leaving the area, don't miss **Red Rock Canyon**, off Old Topanga Canyon Road via Red Rock Road, a stunning red-banded sandstone gorge that was formerly a Boy Scout retreat. Now a California state park, the colorful rock formations, surrounding gardens and riparian wildlife give you a good reason to leave your car behind and go exploring on foot.

Malibu

Further up PCH, past a long stretch of gated beachfront properties, lies **MALIBU**, the very name of which conjures up images of beautiful people sun-bathing on palm-fringed beaches and lazily consuming cocktails. As you enter the small town, the succession of ramshackle surf shops and fast-food stands, scattered along both sides of the highway around the popular **Malibu Pier** (primarily a fishing pier, at 23000 PCH), don't exactly reek of money, but the secluded estates just inland are as valuable as any in the entire US, even though many are vulnerable to hillside wildfires that are notoriously difficult to control.

Adjacent to the pier, **Surfrider Beach** was the surfing capital of the world in the 1950s and early 1960s, popularized by the *Beach Blanket Bingo* movies filmed here, and starring the likes of Annette Funicello and Frankie Avalon. The waves are best in late summer, when storms off Mexico cause them to reach upwards of eight feet. Just to the west is **Malibu Lagoon State Beach** (daily 9am–7pm; parking $7), a nature reserve and bird refuge where bird-watching walks around the lagoon are offered on occasional weekends, along

Getting to the sands in Malibu

Visitors to Malibu commonly believe that all **beaches** in the area, aside from the offi-cially marked state or county variety, are off-limits to interlopers – not surprising con-sidering the sands are located in the very backyards of the gated communities that hug the Malibu shoreline. In reality, the sand along Santa Monica Bay is **open to visitors** below the high-tide mark, which means that as long as you stay off the pri-vate beachside territory above that mark (ie where the sand isn't wet and matted, but dry and hilly), you can go anywhere you please, peering into the guarded domains of the rich and famous – of which there are many, including Tom Hanks and Dustin Hoffman. The challenge, however, is in finding the **pedestrian rights-of-way** that give access to the beach. Space is at such a premium along PCH that there are hardly any public routes that lead to the public beaches. However, you can get around this situation with just a little effort. To begin with, there are no rights-of-way around the Malibu Colony, that gated and well-guarded celebrity province in the center of town, but if you don't mind walking a mile and a half along the ocean to get to the beaches behind these homes, you can park your car along the 22700 block of PCH (public parking lots are rare around here) and then take the unmarked stairway down to the sands. If for some reason you're thwarted at that entrance, or your *Map to the Stars' Oceanside Houses* simply directs you elsewhere, other access points can be found at 19900, 20300, 24300 and 25100 PCH – admittedly farther from where the glitzy action is.

While you may choose to head to the sands behind the Malibu Colony, there are almost as many celebs located to the east of Malibu Pier, around Carbon Beach. Even better, what decent works of architecture there are in Malibu can be spotted in full glory along this beach. There are few better than Richard Meier's stunning **Ackerberg House**, 22466 PCH, which looks like a nondescript wall of cement and white tile from the street, but from the beach looks exactly as its architect intended: a 1986 practice run for the Getty Center, rendered small, with the same rigidly geo-metric form clad in white-steel paneling and wraparound windows.

△ Malibu Creek State Park

with seasonal guided tours that showcase, among other things, the sea life in the marshes and tide pools. A small **museum**, 23200 PCH (tours Wed–Sat 11am–3pm; $3), gives you the historical rundown, from the Chumash era up to the arrival of Hollywood movie stars, with special emphasis on the long-running "Rindge saga" that informs much of Malibu's modern history.

The story involves one **May K. Rindge** (widow of the entrepreneur Frederick Rindge), who, up until the 1920s, owned all of Malibu – considered at the time to be the single most valuable real-estate parcel in the US. Employing armed guards and dynamiting roads to keep travelers from crossing her land on their way to and from Santa Monica, Rindge operated her own roads and private railroad and fought for years to prevent the Southern Pacific Railroad from laying down track through her property, as well as the state of California from building the Pacific Coast Highway across her land. She ultimately lost her legal battle in the state's supreme court and the highway was eventually finished.

Before Rindge lost her money in the Depression, Rindge's daughter, Rhoda, and her husband, Merritt Adamson, hired architect Stiles O. Clements, of the legendary firm of Morgan, Walls and Clements (see box on p.80), to design the magnificent **Adamson House** (grounds 8am–sunset, house Wed–Sat 11am–pm; $3; Ⓦ www.adamsonhouse.org), on the grounds of the Malibu Lagoon museum. One of LA's finest pieces of Spanish Colonial architecture, the house features Mission Revival and Moorish elements, such as individually carved teak doors, glazed ceramic tiles, detailed ironwork, and Spanish and Middle Eastern furnishings, as well as expansive gardens and a central pool and fountain.

After May Rindge's mischief finally ceased, her son took over the ranch and quickly sold much of the land, establishing the **Malibu Colony**, along Malibu Colony Drive off of Malibu Road, as a haven for movie stars. Unless you take a long oceanside trek (see box, p.202), there's very little to see here except the garage doors of the rich and famous; for a celluloid look inside, check out Robert Altman's *The Long Goodbye*, in which the colony plays home to washed-up artists and blasé murder suspects. If you're after a glimpse of the elite, visit the **Malibu Colony Plaza**, near the area's gated entrance, good for star-spotting and stocking up on food and drink before a day on the sands, or **Malibu Country Mart**, 3835 Cross Creek Rd, where celebrities can often be found munching on veggies or sipping espressos. Nearby, pure relaxation can be found at the **Serra Retreat**, 3401 Serra Rd (Ⓣ310/456-6631), a nondenominational religious haven named for Franciscan friar and missionary Junípero Serra, one of several such retreats operated by the friars throughout the West. You can enjoy a weekend getaway here in one of the 64 rooms, wander the flower gardens or get a fantastic hilltop view of the Pacific. The retreat was originally the site of the **Rindge Mansion**, but construction was mothballed during the Depression and the half-built property given over to the Franciscans, who finished the mansion and established their retreat here in 1943, only to see it burn down in 1970 and rebuilt after the missions of old.

Downtown Malibu, further north on PCH, doesn't have much to grab your attention other than the **Malibu Castle**, a bizarre mock-medieval Scottish castle – with arched windows, stone tower, and crenellated walls and battlements – that sits on a hilltop and is a frequent film and TV shooting location. Unless you're rich enough to come for a fundraiser or the opening-night party of the Malibu Film Festival ($250), it's strictly off-limits to the general public, and your best bet is seeing it from Civic Center Way, well below its battlements.

North of downtown, **Pepperdine University**, 24255 PCH, moved here after hastily abandoning its Art Deco digs in South Central LA in 1971, and is mainly notable for its sloping green lawns and gigantic white cross.

Across from Pepperdine, the hilltop **Malibu Bluffs State Park**, 24250 PCH, is a prime local spot for whale-watching in the winter months, when you may spot orcas or baleen whales, depending on the time and weather. Further up, the pleasantly uncrowded shoreline of **Dan Blocker County Beach** – dedicated to the actor who played Hoss in TV's *Bonanza* – is the most appealing sight before you get to Corral Canyon Road, which leads you into **Solstice Canyon Park**, one of LA's hidden treasures. The park can be accessed through the Sostomo Trail, a rugged mountaintop trek, or the International Trail, a tranquil forested walk. A mile down placid Solstice Canyon Creek is a rustic **cabin** from 1865 sitting in a state of arrested dilapidation – supposedly the oldest stone structure in Malibu still standing. Past the cabin are the atmospheric remains of a modern estate known as **Tropical Terrace**, built in 1952 by master architect Paul Williams (see also the MCA Building in Beverly Hills, p.114), which was once surrounded by an expansive ranch stocked with buffalo, camels, giraffes and deer imported from Africa. Burned down in a 1982 fire, the basic structure and foundation of this house are still standing, as are its surrounding brick steps, garden terraces and partially visible bomb shelter, overtaken by the natural setting, with trees sprouting through the concrete and vines covering the brickwork.

Point Dume and beyond

Four miles north of Malibu Pier, **Point Dume**, named after the Franciscan padre Francisco Dumetz in 1793, is the tip of a great seaward promontory built on lava extruded from an ancient volcano, offering stunning vistas of the entire Santa Monica Bay. Along with being a popular whale-watching spot from November to March, it also features some excellent strips of sand, including **Zuma Beach**, north at 30000 PCH (parking $7 for most area beaches), the largest of the LA County beaches; **Point Dume State Beach**, a relaxed spot below the bluffs; and **Pirate's Cove**, a nude beach up and over the rocks on the point's southern edge. Just to the east, **Paradise Cove** is a secluded stretch of land that makes for a fine walk, with superb views of fancy cliffside houses getting ready to fall into the surf from their high perches.

Given Malibu's walled-off security and privacy, the **Barbra Streisand Center**, north of Point Dume and PCH at 5750 Ramirez Canyon Rd (individual tours Wed 1–4pm, groups Tues & Thurs 1–4pm; free; by reservation only at ℡310/589-2850 ext 144, ⓦwww.ceres.ca.gov/smmc/sccs.htm), comes as a bit of a shock: a 22-acre complex of houses and gardens that the entertainer donated to the Santa Monica Mountains Conservancy in 1993. Amid extensive flower, herb and fruit gardens, you can get a glimpse into her former residences and properties: the stained-glass windows and river-rock fireplace of the quaint "Barn," the Mediterranean and Art Nouveau stylings of the "Peach House," the Craftsman splendor of the singer's one-time production company building, the "Barwood," and the finest building on the site, the "Deco House," with its red-and-black colors, geometric decor, and stainless-steel panels taken from Downtown's Richfield Building, before that Art Deco monument was destroyed in 1968.

Several miles north of Point Dume, at 32100 PCH, **El Matador State Beach** is as close as ordinary folk can get to the private-beach seclusion enjoyed by the stars, thanks mostly to its entrance being at an easily missable turn off PCH – look for it on the south side of the road about a half-mile east of the junction with Encinal Canyon Drive. Needless to say, its rocky-cove sands are a recluse's dream. Another five miles north, where Mulholland Drive reaches the ocean, **Leo Carrillo** ("ca-REE-oh") **State Beach Park**, 35000 PCH, marks the northwestern border of LA County and the end of the MTA bus system (on route #434). The mile-long sandy beach is divided by Sequit Point, a bluff with underwater caves and a tunnel you can pass through at low tide, and is also one of LA's best campgrounds (see p.240). The beach has also starred in quite a few Hollywood flicks, much like its namesake: Carrillo was an actor who appeared in nearly one hundred films and was best known as Pancho in the 1950s TV show *The Cisco Kid*.

Mulholland Highway

Most familiar as the road running along the crest of the Hollywood Hills, Mulholland Drive continues west of the 405 freeway and takes drivers through the heart of the Santa Monica Mountains, where it becomes **Mulholland Highway**, a lengthy, winding route that can easily take several hours to traverse because of its alternatively rutted terrain and hair-raising curves. Nonetheless, it's still an excellent introduction to LA's largely unheralded natural environment; just make sure to bring a sturdy car that can handle the initial leg of the trip. For most of its first seven miles westward, from Encino Hills Drive to Topanga Canyon Boulevard, Mulholland is a bumpy dirt road strewn with broken rocks, fallen trees and sizeable mudholes, truly earning its nickname, "**Dirt Mulholland**" – though the awe-inspiring vistas and abundant greenery are reward enough. While in the area, don't miss the towering ten-acre hilltop of **San Vicente Mountain Park**, about a mile and a half past Encino Hills Drive, a decommissioned nuclear-missile command center that was used between 1956 and 1968 as a radar site and launching pad for Nike thermonuclear missiles. This unusual state park offers you the chance to climb a zigzagging stairway up to a hexagonal viewing platform on top of the command tower, where you can ponder the Cold War while staring down at striking vistas of the San Fernando Valley.

The paved portion of Mulholland Highway can be picked up from either the end of Dirt Mulholland, roughly around Canoga Avenue in the suburb of Woodland Hills, or from the Mulholland Drive exit off the 101 freeway. Just to the north, the extraordinary **Struckus House**, Canoga Avenue at Saltillo Street, is a private residence designed by quirky architect Bruce Goff (see also LACMA's Pavilion for Japanese Art, p.84), consisting of a four-story redwood cylinder decorated with four vertically stacked, convex "eyes," a wooden roof with flywheel spokes, and a big square door that pivots on a single ball bearing. For a close-up look at another of the area's notable buildings, head north toward the 101, west of Mulholland Drive, to the **Leonis Adobe**, 23537 Calabasas Rd (Wed–Sun 1–4pm; $3; ☏818/222-6511, ⓦ www.leonisadobe-museum.org), an 1844 ranch and adobe. The grounds of this lovely (and reputedly haunted) Spanish estate include a blacksmith, windmill, barn and restored carriage, as well as the engaging **Plummer House**, another ranch house that was parked on the estate after being repeatedly vandalized at its former location, Rancho La Brea in West Hollywood. Inside, you can still see historic exhibits and artifacts on that rancho's history (same hours and included in admission).

To the south, Mulholland Highway takes you through the forest, brush and scattered dwellings of the Santa Monica Mountains, at times via dizzying switchbacks and narrow cliffside passages. The interesting diversions along the way are primarily movie-oriented, beginning at **Malibu Creek State Park**, just south of Mulholland Highway on Las Virgenes Road, a scenic 4000-acre park that once belonged to 20th Century-Fox studios, which filmed many Tarzan pictures here, as well as the original *Planet of the Apes*, and used the chaparral-covered hillsides to simulate South Korea for the TV show *M*A*S*H*. Pick up a map at the visitors center (Sat & Sun noon–4pm) to avoid getting lost on its nearly fifteen miles of hiking trails, or make a reservation beforehand to pitch your tent and camp (see p.240). Further west on Mulholland, **Paramount Ranch**, 2813 Cornell Rd (℡818/222-6511, ⓦwww.nps.gov/samo/maps/para.htm), is another old studio lot, with an intact Western movie set used in, among other things, films starring Gary Cooper, W.C. Fields and Hopalong Cassidy, and TV programs like *The Rifleman*, *The Cisco Kid* and *Dr. Quinn Medicine Woman*. Film and TV crews still occasionally shoot here on weekdays, though generally without public notice. Oddly, visitors often mistake the phony rail station and tracks behind the set and the dummy cemetery to the south for the real thing.

A few miles west of Cornell Road, the charming **Peter Strauss Ranch** was once the site of the **Lake Enchanto Resort**, a top LA amusement spot from the 1930s through the 1950s, until a nearby dam burst and washed it away. Resurrected variously as a resort and a nudist colony, the property passed into the hands of actor and producer Peter Strauss, who, after yet another dam burst, turned it over to its current caretakers, the Santa Monica Mountains Conservancy. Nowadays, the park is a low-key attraction, laced with plenty of rugged and easy hiking trails and hosting occasional outdoor sculpture exhibitions, as well as blues and classical concerts on Sunday afternoons in summer (call ℡805/370-2301 for details, ⓦwww.nps.gov/samo/maps/peter.htm). A few hints of the old resort do remain in the form of a disused swimming pool and swank terrazzo patio.

Mulholland continues westward until it reaches the Pacific Ocean near Leo Carrillo State Beach Park (see opposite), passing a number of excellent parks and striking vistas along the way, most of them controlled and protected by the Santa Monica Mountains Conservancy. Other than these natural delights, the last point of interest on Mulholland is the **Arch Oboler House**, one of Frank Lloyd Wright's lesser-known structures standing near Westlake Boulevard and the LA County line at 32436 Mulholland Hwy. The unfinished studio and gatehouse, angular modern curiosities built of wood and stone, were meant to be part of an expansive hillside complex for the now-forgotten film director Oboler, creator of such works as *Bwana Devil*, the first movie in 3-D, and *Five*, about the survivors of a nuclear holocaust – which the director filmed here at his own residence.

10

Orange County

Considered by many Angelenos to be the flip side of freewheeling, free-thinking Los Angeles, **ORANGE COUNTY** was for many decades the epitome of conservative suburban living in California, as well as the United States – an upper-middle-class, West Coast version of Levittown (the famous Long Island suburb) – where tract homes and asphalt stretched to the horizon and anyone not fitting into the rigid sense of bourgeois conformity was shunned, ridiculed or forced into exile in LA proper, just one county north.

These days, though, Orange County is no more bland, homogenous and white than any other part of LA. In fact, the county has in the last two decades become multicultural, with rising numbers of Latino immigrants transforming the character of cities like Santa Ana, and other newcomers from Southeast Asia, India and Eastern Europe developing their own urban communities as well. The fractured social landscape of libertarian beach cities, reactionary old-line suburbs, burgeoning immigrant districts, and hordes of itinerant tourists is bound together by the ubiquitous freeway system.

Although there is no simple way of splitting up the place, two general divisions are useful for your exploration. The original heart of the 1940s and 1950s suburbs, **inland Orange County** is the famous domain of Mickey Mouse and roller coasters – both Disneyland and Knott's Berry Farm were created here. The area's become just as notable, though, for its rapid cultural changes, as white-bread suburbia has become a salad bowl in a relatively short space of time. More appealing for visitors without a yen for theme parks, the **Orange County coast** is a collection of relaxed seaside towns with both easygoing "surfer-dude" attitudes and upscale, beach-condo snootiness. Keep in mind, though, that the coastal cities never really stop, but just blend into even more housing colonies as you head further south – a seemingly endless exurban stretch between LA and San Diego.

Inland Orange County

Located in the heart of **INLAND ORANGE COUNTY**, the first modern theme park, **Disneyland**, was opened in 1955 by Walt Disney, in anticipation of the acres of orange groves thirty miles southeast of downtown, in **Anaheim**, becoming the next center of population growth in Southern California. The famous illustrator and film-maker – as well as creator of such icons as Mickey Mouse and Donald Duck – was quite prescient in his guess, and Orange County soon became synonymous with white flight in the United States.

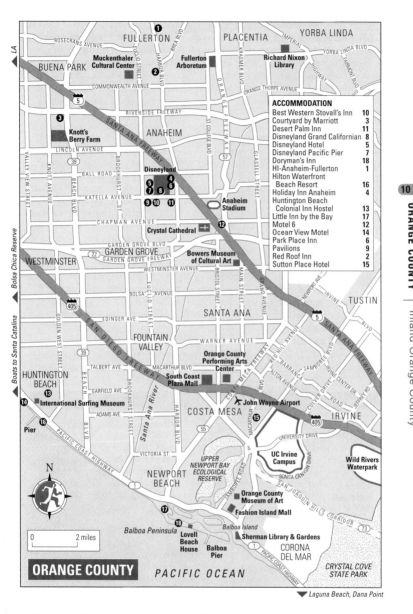

ACCOMMODATION

Best Western Stovall's Inn	10
Courtyard by Marriott	3
Desert Palm Inn	11
Disneyland Grand Californian	8
Disneyland Hotel	5
Disneyland Pacific Pier	7
Doryman's Inn	18
HI-Anaheim-Fullerton	1
Hilton Waterfront Beach Resort	16
Holiday Inn Anaheim	4
Huntington Beach Colonial Inn Hostel	13
Little Inn by the Bay	17
Motel 6	12
Ocean View Motel	14
Park Place Inn	6
Pavilions	9
Red Roof Inn	2
Sutton Place Hotel	15

▼ *Laguna Beach, Dana Point*

These suburbs continue to grow rapidly, but in a markedly different way than before. **Westminster**, for example, is now the home of Little Saigon, a center for Vietnamese expatriates, and is the most fervent bastion of anti-Communism in Southern California, long after the end of the Cold War.

One thing hasn't changed, though: Disneyland, or the allure of it, still dominates the area. As for diverting alternatives, **Knott's Berry Farm** features roller coasters that are more exciting than anything at Disneyland; the **Crystal Cathedral** is an imposing reminder of the potency of the evangelical movement; the **Richard Nixon Library and Birthplace** is a shrine to the old emblem of Orange County, reactionary and paranoid; and isolated spots of cultural and entertainment interest can even be found in places like **Santa Ana** and **Fullerton** – places usually well off the well-beaten tourist trail.

Disneyland

In the minds of many tourists, the sole reason to visit Orange County, if not LA in general, is to experience the colossal theme park of **Disneyland**, 1313 Harbor Blvd at Katella Avenue, Anaheim (summer daily 8am–1am; rest of year Mon–Fri 10am–6pm, Sat 9am–midnight, Sun 9am–10pm; $45 adults, $35 kids, parking $7; ☎714/781-4565, ⓦ disneyland.com), known the world over as one of the defining hallmarks of American culture (with some intellectual wags like Jean Baudrillard claiming *this* as the real America, and everything else as fake). Since its opening almost fifty years ago, Walt Disney's fun zone has long been the most famous, most carefully constructed, most influential theme park anywhere.

For such a culturally powerful place, Disneyland occupies less than one square mile of Anaheim (unlike Disney's Florida properties, which sit on 46 square miles of Disney-owned land near Orlando), and is increasingly hemmed in by the low-end developments surrounding it, making the park a hermetically sealed world unto itself. Even within such rigid boundaries, it remains corporate America's ultimate fantasy, with the emphasis strongly on family fun.

The main park

If you only have a one-day pass to Disneyland, you will not see everything in the park, no matter how hard you try: the lines are always lengthy and unavoidable.

Planning a trip to Disneyland

Depending on traffic, Disneyland is about 45 minutes by **car** from downtown LA using the Santa Ana Freeway. By **train** from downtown (ten daily), you can make the thirty-minute Amtrak journey to Fullerton, from where OCTD buses will drop you off at Disneyland or Knott's Berry Farm. By **bus**, use MTA #460 from downtown, which takes about ninety minutes, or the quicker Greyhound service, which runs thirteen times a day and takes 45 minutes to Anaheim, from which it's an easy walk to the theme park. You can also pick up the bus from Long Beach (eight daily, at 464 Third St), Pasadena (three daily, at 645 E Walnut St), and Hollywood (eight daily, at 1715 N Cahuenga Blvd).

As for **accommodation**, most people try to visit Disneyland just for the day and spend the night somewhere else. It's simply not the most appealing area, with dismal trinket stores and run-down diners everywhere, and most of the hotels and motels close to Disneyland costing well in excess of $80 per night. However, the park is least crowded immediately after opening, so one – perhaps the only – rationale for staying nearby is to get a jump on the morning crowds. If you choose to stay nearby, the *HI-Anaheim/Fullerton* hostel is by far the best bet (for this, and pricier options, see "Accommodation," p.238).

Finally, with regards to eating, Disneyland's massive central kitchen produces all the **food** for the park (you're not permitted to bring your own), unloading popcorn, hot dogs, hamburgers and other junk food by the ton. For anything healthier or more substantial, you'll need to leave the park and travel a good distance. The listings on pp.258 and 276 suggest some of the more palatable options.

As such, it's wisest to choose a few of the top rides – which during peak periods may have lines with two-hour waiting periods – alongside a larger range of less popular ones. The admission price includes them all, except for the new California Adventure, which will cost you quite a bit extra.

From the front gates, **Main Street** leads through a scaled-down, camped-up replica of a circa-1900 Midwestern town, filled with souvenir shops, food stand, and penny arcades, directly to **Sleeping Beauty's Castle**, a pseudo-Rhineland palace at the heart of the park that looks inviting, but in reality isn't much more than a prop – the official Disneyland logo, writ large.

Radiating out clockwise from Main Street, **Adventureland** was built near the height of the Tiki craze in the 1950s and 1960s, and could make for a swinging, retro-kitsch experience, if Disneyland ever bothered to update it. As it is, the old-time centerpiece, the Jungle Cruise, looks pretty antiquated these days, offering "tour guides" making crude puns about the fake animatronic beasts creaking amid the trees. Tarzan's Treehouse isn't much better, little more than a movie tie-in taking up the space once occupied by the Swiss Family Robinson Treehouse – catwalks in the branches, rustic rooms with assorted playthings and an eight-year-old target audience. Ultimately, if you're going to spend any time at all in this section of the park, you should get in the line for the **Indiana Jones Adventure**, which more than four hundred "imagineers" (the cutesy Disney term for ride engineers) worked to create. Two hours of waiting in line are built into the ride, with an interactive archeological dig and 1930s-style newsreel show leading up to the main feature – a speedy journey along 2500ft of skull-encrusted corridors, loosely based on the *Indiana Jones* trilogy, in which you face fireballs, burning rubble, venomous snakes and a rolling-boulder finale.

The nearby **New Orleans Square**, clockwise to the northwest, is the site of *Club 33*, Walt's ultra-exclusive dinner club for his friends in the corporate and political elite, which even today offers membership by invitation at a (last-reported) entry cost of $5000, and once featured microphones surreptitiously hidden in the chandeliers to record the comments of dinner guests. Although you definitely can't get in, you can spot the club's door, marked with a "33." The door is located next to the facade of the *Blue Bayou* restaurant, which, despite its jaw-dropping prices for steak and seafood, has some of the best dining ambience in Orange County: a darkly romantic waterfront scene with dim lighting, old-fashioned Southern decor and imitation crickets chirping in the distance. (Make sure to reserve early at ☎714/956-6755, the reservation line for all Disneyland restaurants; otherwise, you'll be waiting outside in yet another interminable line.) From your table, you'll be able to see crowds lining up to ride on what many feel is still the park's best ride, the **Pirates of the Caribbean**, a renowned boat trip through underground caverns, singing along with drunken pirates, laughing skeletons, and all manner of ruddy-cheeked yokels hooting and bellowing for your amusement. Nearby, another of Disneyland's legendary rides, the **Haunted Mansion**, features a riotous "doom buggy" tour in the company of the house ghouls, with a nightmarish elevator ride to start the trip off in skin-crawling fashion and plenty of creepy portraits to stare at along the way.

Less fun is **Frontierland**, the smallest of the various themelands, located further clockwise around the park. Supposedly the area takes its cues from the Wild West and the tales of Mark Twain, but any unsavory and complex elements have been carefully deleted. The centerpiece, Thunder Mountain Railroad, is a rather slow-moving roller coaster, which takes you through a rocky setting resembling a cartoony version of Hollywood Westerns. Nearby, the focus of **Critter Country** is Splash Mountain, a fun log-flume ride in which you can expect to get drenched.

Across the drawbridge from Main Street, **Fantasyland** shows off the cleverest but also the most sentimental aspects of the Disney imagination. The highlight, Mr Toad's Wild Ride, is a jerky funhouse trip through Victorian England. The other rides are much tamer, such as those involving Peter Pan flying over London and Snow White being tormented by the wicked witch. It's a Small World gets the most extreme reactions, with children delighting in this boat tour of the world's continents – in which animated dolls sing the same cloying song over and over again – and adults finding it a slow, gurgling torture test. Lastly, the sole Fantasyland roller coaster, the Matterhorn, is somewhat entertaining for its phony cement mountain and goofy abominable snowman appearing when you round a corner, though the dips and curves are rather bland compared with most coasters these days. On the park's northern end, **Toontown**, a cartoon village with goofy sound effects and Day-Glo colors, is aimed only for the under-10 set and generally unbearable for older, thrill-seeking visitors.

On the eastern side of the park, **Tomorrowland** is Disney's vision of the future, where the Space Mountain roller coaster zips through the pitch-blackness of "outer space," bumbling scientists dabble with 3-D trickery in Honey, I Shrunk the Audience, and a runaway space cruiser blasts through the Moon of Endor (home of the Ewoks) in George Lucas's Star Tours. This idea of the future occasionally looks like a hangover from the past – note rides such as Autopia, where you drive a miniature car at a glacial pace – but this fun zone has been updated somewhat in recent years, with new rides like the Jules Verne–inspired Astro Orbiter taking the place of old rides like the torpid PeopleMover and its failed replacement, Rocket Rods. One of the more interesting recent additions is Innoventions, which comes with a lot of futurist babble but is really little more than a fun opportunity to look at, and play with, the latest special effects. In addition to these attractions, **firework displays** explode every summer night at 9pm, and all manner of parades and special events celebrate important occasions – such as Mickey Mouse's birthday.

The California Adventure

The latest part of Disneyland, taking over a large chunk of its old parking lot, is the **California Adventure**, technically a separate park but wholly connected to the main one in architecture, style and spirit. It does for California's history and culture what Epcot Center in Florida does to the rest of the world's – namely, remove all the rough edges and make it digestible for even the youngest children. Aside from its more exciting roller coasters and slightly better food, the California Adventure is really just another "land" to visit, albeit a much more expensive one. You cannot get access to both parks with a single-day admission ticket, so if you want to visit, you'll instead have to shell out another $45 or plunk down $111 for a three-day pass that covers both (kids $90).

Despite all the hype about the new section, it's hard to justify spending the money when most of Disneyland's classic, and memorable, attractions are on the other side of the park. There are a handful of highlights if you do visit the new area, though: Grizzly River Run is a fun giant-inner-tube ride, splashing around through various plunges and "caverns"; Soarin' Over California is a fairly exciting trip on a mock-experimental aircraft that buzzes you through hairpin turns and steep dives; and the **Pacific Pier** zone has a slew of old-fashioned carnival rides that only faintly recall the wilder, harder-edged midways of California's past. There's also a rather tame zone devoted to Tinseltown, the **Hollywood Pictures Backlot** which, aside from a few theaters, special-effects displays and diners, is mainly notable for its loose borrowing of the set design from D.W. Griffith's 1916 film *Intolerance* – exotic columns, squatting elephants and all – while failing to mention that movie's unprecedented box-office failure. (This design is also used in the Hollywood & Highland mall; see p.99.)

Knott's Berry Farm

It's hard to escape the clutches of Disneyland even when you leave: everything in the surrounding area seems to have been designed to service the needs of its visitors. If you're a bit fazed by its excesses, you might prefer the more down-to-earth **Knott's Berry Farm**, four miles northwest, off the Santa Ana Freeway at 8039 Beach Blvd (summer Mon–Thurs & Sun 9am–11pm, Fri & Sat 9am–midnight; rest of year Mon–Fri 10am–6pm, Sat 10am–10pm, Sun 10am–7pm; $40, kids $30, or $20 for entry after 4pm; ☎714/220-5200, ⓦwww.knotts.com), a relaxed, though still pricey, park born during the Depression when people began lining up for the fried chicken dinners prepared by Mrs Knott, a local farmer's wife. To amuse the children while they waited for their food, Mr Knott reconstructed a Wild West ghost town and added amusements until the park had grown into the sprawling sideshow of roller coasters and carnival rides that stands today.

Unlike Disneyland, this park can easily be seen in one day, as long as you concentrate on the roller coasters, which now make Knott's second only to Magic Mountain (see p.196) for number of thrill rides per acre. Although there are ostensibly six themed lands here, several of them, namely the **Ghost Town** and **Indian Lands**, consist only of familiar carnival rides, fast-food stands and uneven historical interpretation. **Camp Snoopy** is the Knott's version of Disney's Toontown, and just as tiresome, while the **Wild Water Wilderness** isn't really a theme area at all, but simply the site of the moderately exciting Bigfoot Rapids giant-inner-tube ride.

Simply put, you should spend most or all of your time in just two areas: **Fiesta Village**, home to Montezooma's Revenge, the original one-loop coaster, and Jaguar, a high-flying coaster that spins you around the park concourse; and the **Boardwalk**, which is all about heart-thumping thrill rides. There's the Boomerang, a forward-and-back coaster that can easily induce nausea; WindJammer, two racing coasters looping and dipping around each other; Supreme Scream, a delightfully terrifying freefall drop; Hammerhead, featuring huge loops; and the new Perilous Plunge, a hellish drop at a 75-degree angle that's far more exciting than any old log-flume ride. Similarly, this Boardwalk, Knott's version of a carnival midway, with its death-defying rides and vomit-inducing thrills, easily puts Disney's Pacific Pier (see above) to shame. Knott's has recently added its own adjacent water park, **Soak City U.S.A.** (May–Sept only, hours vary but generally 10am–8pm; $23, kids $16, $13 for entry after 3pm; same contact details as Knott's Berry Farm), offering 21 rides of various heights and speeds, almost all of them involving the familiar water slides – either with or without an inner tube – that can really bring out the sweltering masses on a hot summer day.

Around Disneyland

To the south of Disneyland just off the Santa Ana Freeway, in the otherwise uneventful town of **GARDEN GROVE**, the giant **Crystal Cathedral**,

12141 Lewis St (tours Mon–Sat 9am–3.30pm; free; ☎714/971-4000, ⓦwww.crystalcathedral.org), is a hugely garish Philip Johnson design of tubular space frames and plate-glass walls that forms part of the vision of televangelist Robert Schuller. Not content with owning the world's first drive-in church (next door to the cathedral), Schuller commissioned this dramatic prop to boost the ratings of his nationally televised Sunday sermons, raising $1.5 million for its construction during one Sunday service alone. These sermon-shows reach their climax with the special Christmas production, using live animals in biblical roles and people disguised as angels suspended on ropes.

A more worthwhile attraction lies in the nearby burg of **SANTA ANA**, where the splendid **Bowers Museum of Cultural Art**, 2002 N Main St (Tues–Sun 10am–4pm; $12, kids $7; ☎714/567-3600, ⓦwww.bowers.org), features a great range of anthropological treasures from early Asian, African, Native American and pre-Columbian civilizations. Showcasing artifacts as diverse as ceramic Mayan icons, hand-crafted baskets from native Californians and highly detailed Chinese funerary sculpture, the museum is an essential stop for anyone interested in the art and history of non-Western civilizations. Same-day visitors can, for the same entry ticket, take their children to the adjacent **Kidseum** (Sat & Sun 10am–4pm), a less invigorating look at the same subject, made easily digestible for bored youngsters.

North of Disneyland, the unimposing town of **FULLERTON** also has a few interesting sights, among them the **Fullerton Arboretum**, in the northeast corner of the California State campus at 1900 Associated Rd (daily 8am–4.45pm; free), which provides relief from theme-park overload with its own themed garden spaces, including varieties of plants native to temperate, arid and tropical zones around the world. Much more surprising is the presence of an esteemed institution in such a little-known hamlet, the **Muckenthaler Cultural Center**, 1201 W Malvern Ave (Tues–Fri 10am–4pm, Sat & Sun noon–4pm; $5, kids free; ☎714/738-6595, ⓦwww.muckenthaler.org), located in an attractive 1924 Renaissance Revival mansion and hosting a wide range of cultural events and exhibits. The emphasis here is strongly on international multicultural art, with Native American art and textiles, African craftwork and jewelry, and contemporary Korean ceramics only a few of the highlights. There are also countless examples of decorative arts, drawings and textiles from around the world – not to mention periodic displays of local artists, and, this being Southern California, an annual display of "automotive art" in the spring, with many colorful car-related illustrations and designs.

The Richard Nixon Library and Birthplace

Mickey Mouse may be its most famous resident, but Orange County's favorite son was former US president Richard Milhous Nixon, born in 1913 in what is now freeway-caged **YORBA LINDA**, eight miles northeast of Disneyland. Here, the **Richard Nixon Library and Birthplace**, 18001 Yorba Linda Blvd (Mon–Sat 10am–5pm, Sun 11am–5pm; $6, kids $2; ☎714/993-5075, ⓦwww.nixonfoundation.org), is a relentlessly hagiographic library/museum that features oversized gifts from world leaders, amusing campaign memorabilia, and a collection of obsequious letters written by and to Nixon (including one he sent to the boss of *McDonald's* proclaiming the fast-food chain's hamburgers to be "one of the finest food buys in America"). However, it's in the constantly running archive of radio and TV recordings that the distinctive Nixon persona – shaking his head and glowering at cameras – really shines through.

Qualified as a lawyer and fresh from noncombat wartime service in the US Navy, **Richard Milhous Nixon** entered politics as a Republican congressman for the state of California in 1946, without a civilian suit to his name. A journalist of the time observed that Nixon employed "the half-truth, the misleading quotation, the loose-joined logic" to cast doubts on his rival Jerry Voorhees – traits he would perfect in the years to come.

Shortly after arriving in Washington, Nixon joined the **House Un-American Activities Committee (HUAC)**, a group of red-baiters led by the infamous Joseph McCarthy, which wrecked the lives and careers of many Americans. Although these hearings eventually backfired on McCarthy (he was later censured by Congress), they launched Nixon to national prominence, culminating in his becoming Dwight Eisenhower's **vice-president** in 1953, at only 39 years old. It almost didn't happen, though: just before the election, the discovery of undeclared income precipitated the "funds crisis," which cast doubts over Nixon's honesty. Incredibly, his **"Checkers speech"** convinced 58 million TV viewers of his integrity, his performance climaxing in the statement that, regardless of the damage it may do to his career, he would not be returning the cocker spaniel (Checkers) given to him as a gift and now a family pet.

Eight years later, Nixon was defeated in his own bid for the presidency by John F. Kennedy, due in no small part to his embarrassing performance during their 1960s live **TV debates**, in which Nixon refused to wear make-up and, with a visible growth of beard, perspired freely under the TV lights. This loss led him into his "wilderness years": staying out of the public spotlight, except to raise money for fellow Republicans, he took several lucrative corporate posts and wrote *Six Crises*, a book of deep introspection and, some believed, deep paranoia. Seeking a power base for the next presidential campaign, Nixon ran for the governorship of California in 1962. His humiliating defeat to Pat Brown, future governor Jerry's dad, ended with a memorable jibe at the press ("You won't have Nixon to kick around anymore") and prompted a short-lived "retirement," which did nothing to suggest that six years later he would beat Ronald Reagan to the Republican nomination and be **elected president** in 1968.

The country Nixon inherited was more divided than at any time since the Civil War. The **Vietnam War** was at its height, and in time his large-scale illegal bombing of Cambodia earned him worldwide opprobrium. Nixon was not, however, a conservative by modern standards. By breaking with his own party's right wing, he was able to re-establish diplomatic relations with China, begin arms reduction talks with the Soviet Union, create the Environmental Protection Agency, and reluctantly oversee the implementation of court-ordered busing to alleviate racial segregation. Nixon's actions surprised many and contributed to his decisive re-election in 1972.

Despite his victory, Nixon's second term ended prematurely over the **Watergate Scandal**. In January 1973, seven men were tried for breaking into and bugging the headquarters of the Democratic Party in Washington's Watergate building, an act discovered to have been financed with money allocated to the Committee to Re-elect the President (CREEP). Ironically, Nixon's insistence on taping all White House conversations in order to ease the future writing of his memoirs was to be the major stumbling block to his surviving the crisis. Upon the revelation of a "smoking gun" tape proving his complicity in obstructing justice, Nixon **resigned** in 1974 under immediate threat of impeachment.

The full **pardon** granted to Nixon by his successor, Gerald Ford, did little to arrest widespread public disillusionment with the country's political machine. Remarkably, Nixon's post-presidency saw him quietly seek to establish elder-statesman credentials, opining on world affairs through books and newspaper columns, and waging a seemingly endless legal battle to keep control of the notorious audiotapes (which have only recently become widely available to the public). He died in 1994 and was buried at Yorba Linda.

After viewing a few of these recordings, such as the famous "Checkers" speech (see box, overleaf), take a walk through the **World Leaders Gallery** of Nixon's heyday, with Mao, Brezhnev and de Gaulle among the bigwigs, cast in metal and arranged in rigid, pompous poses. Throughout the museum, Nixon's face leers down in Orwellian fashion from almost every wall, but only inside the **Presidential Auditorium** (at the end of the corridor packed with notes attesting to the president's innocence in Watergate) do you get the chance to ask him a question. Many possibilities spring to mind, but the choices are limited to those programmed into a computer, as are the stock answers.

On your way out, stop by the **gift shop** to see (and perhaps purchase) its most popular item, a picture of Nixon greeting a zonked-out Elvis in the Oval Office, on the occasion of the president's granting the King – ironically, considering how high Elvis was at the time – honorary status as a federal agent in the war on drugs.

The Orange County coast

A string of towns stretching from the edge of the LA Harbor to the border of San Diego County 35 miles south, the **ORANGE COUNTY COAST** is chic suburbia with a shoreline: swanky beachside houses line the sands, and the general ambience is easygoing, libertarian and affluent. As the names of the main towns suggest – **Huntington Beach**, **Newport Beach** and **Laguna Beach** – most of the good reasons to come here involve sea and sand, though a handful of museums and festivals can also make for an interesting excursion as well. To the far south, **San Juan Capistrano** merits a stop as the site of the best-kept of all the Californian missions, and **San Clemente** is a surfing hotspot and one-time stomping ground for Richard Nixon.

If you're in a rush to get from LA to San Diego, you can speed through Orange County on the inland San Diego Freeway (405). The coastal cities are linked by the more circuitous Pacific Coast Highway (PCH), which you can pick up in Long Beach (or from the end of Beach Boulevard, coming from Anaheim), though it's often busy in the summer. Amtrak is a good way to get from downtown LA (or Disneyland) to San Juan Capistrano, but you can travel all the way along the coast from LA to San Diego using local buses for about $5 – though you should allow a full day for the journey – or use the Metrorail train line to connect between downtown LA and San Clemente or down to Oceanside in San Diego County.

Huntington Beach

Starting on the north Orange County coast, **HUNTINGTON BEACH** is the most free-spirited of the beach communities and one that you don't need a fortune to enjoy. It's a compact little place composed of engagingly ramshackle single-story cafés and beach stores grouped around the foot of a long **pier**, off PCH at Main Street. Here, you can find the **Surfers Walk of Fame**, appropriately honoring the greats of the sport – this is where California **surfing** began in 1907, imported from Hawaii to encourage curious day-trippers to visit on the Pacific Electric Railway, whose chief, Henry Huntington, the town was named after (along with the grim industrial burg of Huntington Park in Southeast LA). Top surfers still flock here for the annual **Pro Surfing**

Championship, an internationally televised event held each June. Even more of this culture can be found at the **International Surfing Museum**, 411 Olive Ave (Wed–Sun noon–5pm; summer open daily; $3; ☎714/960-3483, ⓦwww.surfingmuseum.org), with exhibits on such legendary figures as Corky Carroll and Duke Kahanamoku, historic posters from various contests, and an array of traditional, contemporary and far-out boards, including one shaped like a Swiss Army knife.

In October, the largely blond and suntanned locals celebrate a plausible **Oktoberfest**, with German food and music. Otherwise, there's not much else to see, though it does have Orange County's cheapest beds in the **youth hostel** near the pier (see "Accommodation," p.239). Several miles north, nature lovers won't want to miss the **Bolsa Chica State Ecological Reserve**, PCH at Warner Avenue, a sizeable wetland preserve that's been kept out of the hands of local developers by state regulation. Taking a one-and-one-half-mile loop tour will get you acquainted with some of the current avian residents of this salt marsh, including a fair number of herons, egrets and grebes, and even a few peregrine falcons and endangered snowy plovers. Self-tours are free, and guided tours are available on the first Saturday of the month (9–10.30am; $2; groups by reservation at ☎714/840-1575, ⓦwww.amigosdebolsachica.org).

Newport Beach and around

Ten miles south from Huntington Beach, **NEWPORT BEACH** could hardly provide a greater contrast: an upmarket enclave with ten yacht clubs and ten thousand yachts, where the image-conscious residents work to acquire a deep tan they can show off on the long stretches of sand or in the singles bars nearby. You'll need a pocketful of credit cards and a presentable physique to join them properly, but the sheer exclusivity of the place may be an attraction in and of itself.

Newport Beach is spread around a natural bay that cuts several miles inland, and although there are hardly any conventional "sights" in town, the obvious place to hang out is on the thin **Balboa Peninsula**, located along Balboa Boulevard, which runs parallel to the three-mile-long beach. The most colorful and boisterous section is about halfway along, around **Newport Pier** at the end of 20th Street. To the north, beachfront homes restrict access; to the south, around **Balboa Pier** (the second of the city's piers), there's a marina from which you can go to Santa Catalina Island (see p.173) or take a boat ride on the *Pavilion Queen* (hourly cruises daily, summer 11am–dusk; rest of year 11am–3pm; $8) around Newport's own, much smaller, islands.

On the peninsula itself, the main highlight is the modernist **Lovell Beach House**, 1242 Ocean Ave, a private home designed by Rudolph Schindler and finished in 1926. Raised on five concrete legs, its living quarters jutting out toward the sidewalk, the house formed the basis of the architect's international reputation (though it has since been altered for the worse by errant renovations). Across the main harbor channel from the peninsula, the Newport Beach district of **Corona Del Mar** is a less ostentatious zone, worth a stop for the **Sherman Library and Gardens**, 2647 E Pacific Coast Highway (daily 10.30am–4pm; $3; gardens ☎949/673-2261, library ☎949/673-1880, ⓦwww.slgardens.org), for the vivid blooms of its botanical gardens, including lovely varieties of roses and a good selection of cacti and succulents.

Due north from the gardens, Newport Beach is home to the **Orange County Museum of Art**, 850 San Clemente Drive (Tues–Sun 11am–5pm; $5, free Tues; ☎949/759-1122, ⓦwww.ocma.net), a fine institution that focuses on contemporary work from local artists like Lari Pittman, Edward Ruscha and Ed Kienholz, and also periodically exhibits the work of video artists like Nancy Thater and Bill Viola. A short distance west, San Joaquin Hills Road leads you to Backbay Drive, which provides a marvelous trip around the edge of one of Orange County's natural wonders, the **Upper Newport Bay Ecological Reserve** (daily 7am–dusk; free; Ⓦwww.ocparks.com/uppernewportbay), an idyllic 750-acre preserve and renowned bird-watching spot, from which you can see a great range of birds, including falcons, pelicans, terns and rails, some of them endangered. The preserve – and its surrounding hills, wetlands and inlets – also presents excellent opportunities for hiking, kayaking, horseback riding and bicycling. Lastly, there's an **interpretive center**, 2301 University Drive (Tues–Sat 10am–4pm; free), which gives an overview of the area's ecology and geology.

On the eastern side of the north end of the reserve, University Drive crosses into the bland city of **IRVINE** (mostly owned by a single developer) to the University of California at Irvine, or **UC Irvine**, which is only interesting if you're a student or fan of contemporary architecture – the campus features a slew of buildings by such famous names as Frank Gehry, Robert Venturi, Charles Moore and Robert A.M. Stern. A one-hour **tour** may give you some sense of the campus and its assorted visual highlights (Mon–Fri noon; free; reserve by calling ☏949/824-4636, Ⓦwww.campustours.uci.edu).

Back along PCH, the area between Newport and Laguna beaches offers an inviting, unspoiled three-mile chunk of coastline, protected as **Crystal Cove State Park** – perfect to explore on foot, and far from the tourist crowds.

Laguna Beach

Six miles south of Crystal Cove, nestled among the crags around a small sandy beach, **LAGUNA BEACH** grew up late in the nineteenth century as a community of artists drawn by the beauty of the location. You need a few million dollars to live here nowadays, but there's a relaxed and tolerant feel among the inhabitants, who run from rich industrialists to upper-middle-class gays and lesbians to holdouts from the 1960s, when Laguna became a hippie haven – even Timothy Leary was known to hang out at the local *Taco Bell* on PCH. The scenery is still the prime attraction, and a flourishing arts scene remains in the many streetside galleries.

PCH passes through the center of Laguna, a few steps from the small main **beach**, which is less snooty than Newport Beach, and less crowded than the LA beaches. From the beach's north side, an elevated wooden walkway twists around the coastline above a protected **ecological area**, enabling you to peer down on the ocean and, when the tide's out, scamper over the rocks to observe the tide-pool activity. From the end of the walkway, make your way through the legions of posh beachside homes and head down the hill back to the center. You'll pass the **Laguna Beach Museum of Art**, 307 Cliff Drive (Tues–Sun 11am–5pm; $5; ☏949/494-8971, Ⓦlagunaartmuseum.org), which has changing exhibitions from its stock of Southern California art from the 1900s to the present day. A few miles south is less-touristy **South Laguna**, where the secluded **Victoria** and **Aliso beaches** are among several below the bluffs.

About two-and-a-half miles inland from downtown Laguna Beach is one sight not to be missed by lovers of sea life, the **Friends of the Sea Lion Marine Mammal Center**, 20612 Laguna Canyon Rd (10am–4pm; free; ☏949/494-3050, Ⓦwww.fslmmc.org), a rehabilitation center that allows you

Laguna Beach hosts a number of large summer **art festivals** over six weeks in July and August. The best-known, and most bizarre, is the **Pageant of the Masters**, in which the participants pose in front of a painted backdrop to portray a famous work of art. Prices are $15–65 per show (steep, but worth it – it's not as ridiculous as it may sound). The performances sell out months in advance, though you may be able to pick up cancellations on the night of the program (shows begin at 8.30pm; ☎1-800/487-3378, 949/494-1145 or ⓦwww.foapom.com for more information). The action takes place at the Irving Bowl, close to where Broadway meets Laguna Canyon Road, a walkable distance from the bus station. The pageant is combined with the **Festival of the Arts** (10am–11.30pm; $5; information as above) held at the same venue, showcasing the work of up to 150 local artists.

There's also the alternative **Sawdust Festival**, 935 Laguna Canyon Rd (June 28 to Sept 1, 10am–10pm; $6.50, season pass $12; ☎949/494-3030, ⓦwww.sawdustart-festival.org), which was created by hippies in the 1960s and subsequently stole some of the thunder from the other festivals. In this festival, local artists and crafts-people set up makeshift studios to demonstrate their skills; it's now just as estab-lished as the others, but still easier to get into.

to view the many underweight, injured or otherwise threatened seals and sea lions, as the organization slowly nurses them back to health. Like the Marine Mammal Center in San Pedro (see p.168), the institute has a habit of perhaps over-personalizing each of the aquatic animals, but this is a small concern when you get an up-close encounter with one of the friendly, barking scamps.

Dana Point

From South Laguna, it's possible to see **DANA POINT**, a town and promon-tory jutting into the ocean about four miles south. It was named after sailor and author Richard Henry Dana Jr, whose *Two Years Before the Mast* described (among other things) how cattle hides were flung over these cliffs to trading ships waiting below, and overall did much to romanticize the California coast while still viewing it with a wary eye. He ended his voyaging career here in 1830, and there's a statue of him and a replica of his vessel, *The Pilgrim*, at the edge of the harbor, on the grounds of the **Ocean Institute**, 24200 Dana Point Harbor Drive (Sat & Sun 10am–4.30pm; $5; ☎949/496-2274, ⓦwww.ocean-institute.org), which offers frequent marine-biology cruises and public visits during which you can view oceanic wildlife, from lobsters to anemones, in glass-enclosed tanks.

San Juan Capistrano and San Clemente

Three miles inland from Dana Point along the I-5 freeway, most of the small suburb of **SAN JUAN CAPISTRANO** is built in a Spanish Colonial style derived from the **Mission San Juan Capistrano**, right in the center of town at Ortega Highway and Camino Capistrano (daily 8.30am–5pm; $6; ☎949/234-1300, ⓦwww.missionsjc.com). The seventh in California's chain of missions, founded by Junípero Serra in 1776, the mission was so well populated within three years of its establishment that it outgrew the original chapel. Soon after, its **Stone Church** was erected, the ruins of which are the first thing you see as you walk in. The enormous structure had seven domes and a bell tower, but was destroyed by an earthquake soon after its completion in 1812, and now the ruins themselves are decaying rapidly, requiring up to $20 million in projected restoration. (For an idea of how it might have looked, visit the full-sized reconstruction – now a working church – just northwest of the mission.)

Meanwhile, the mission's **chapel** is small and narrow, decorated with Indian drawings and Spanish artifacts from its earliest days, and set off by a sixteenth-century altar from Barcelona. In a side room is the chapel of St Pereguin, a tiny room kept warm by the heat from the dozens of candles lit by hopeful pilgrims who arrive here from all over the US and Mexico.

The other restored buildings reflect the mission's practical role during the Indian period: the kitchen, the smelter and the workshops were used for dyeing, weaving and candle-making. There's also a rather dry **museum** (open during mission hours; free), which gives a broad historical outline of Spanish expansion throughout California and displays odds and ends from the mission's past. The complex is also noted for its **swallows**, popularly thought to return here from their winter migration on March 19. They sometimes do arrive on this day – along with large numbers of tourists – but the birds are much more likely to show up as soon as the weather is warm enough, and when there are enough insects on the ground to provide a decent homecoming banquet.

Five miles south of San Juan Capistrano down I-5, the sleepy town of **SAN CLEMENTE** is a pretty little place, its streets contoured around the hills, effecting an almost Mediterranean air. Because of its proximity to one of the largest military bases in the state, **Camp Pendleton**, it's a popular weekend retreat for military personnel. It's also home to some of Orange County's better surfing beaches, especially toward the south end of town, and a reasonable campground, too (see "Accommodation," p.240). It's here, around the city's southern tip, that San Clemente had a brief glimmer of fame when President Richard Nixon convened his **Western White House** from 1969 to 1974, regularly meeting with cronies and political allies. The 25-acre estate is visible from the beach, though off-limits to any closer look.

Listings

Listings

Accommodation

Since LA has 100,000-plus rooms, finding **accommodation** is easy, and whether you seek basic budget motels or world-class resorts, the city has something for everyone. However, finding somewhere that's low-priced *and* well-located can sometimes be difficult, though not impossible. If you're driving, of course, you needn't worry about staying in a less than ideal location – a freeway is never far away. Otherwise you'll need to be more choosy about the district you pick, as getting across town can be a time-consuming business.

Staying in LA has become a somewhat more affordable proposition in the last year or so, with a weak local economy mirroring that of the national scene. Hotel rates that in the late 1990s were reaching ridiculously high levels, even for unexceptional mid-range units, have come back down to earth, and you can often find worthwhile deals simply by shopping around or ordering from the Internet. Of course, the truly stratospheric resorts can charge whatever they please, so don't expect much trying to wring a deal from a five-star celebrity retreat.

Motels and low-end **hotels** start at $40–50 for a double, and though many are situated in seedy or distant areas, if you're comfortable in the familiar two-story, neon-lit 1960s motel built around a shallow swimming pool, you'll find many options. **Bed-and-breakfasts** are slowly becoming more common in LA (typically based on a Victorian-architecture or country-cottage theme), but the few that do exist tend to be quite expensive and frequently fully booked. (If you're traveling from the UK, try calling Colby International, who can book B&B rooms, as well as private apartments, in advance ☎0151/220 5848, ⓦ www.colbyintl.com).

For those on a tight budget, **hostels** are dotted all over the city, many in good locations with desirable amenities – though at some, stays are limited to a few nights. **Camping** is also an option – from the beach north of Malibu, throughout Orange County, and in the San Gabriel Mountains – but you'll need a car to get to the campgrounds. Clean, reasonably inexpensive **college rooms** are also sometimes available for rent during student vacation time: contact **UCLA**'s Interfraternity Council (☎310/825-7878) or **USC**'s off-campus housing office (☎1-800/USC-4632, ⓦ housing.usc.edu) for information.

LA is so big that if you want to see it all without constantly having to cross huge expanses, it makes sense to divide your stay between several districts. Prices – and options – vary by area. **Downtown** has many expensive and a few mid-range hotels, with cheaper accommodations west of Downtown, across the 110 freeway, in much dicier neighborhoods. **Hollywood** provides a good range of choices, a few of them historic hotels and many more retro-roadside motels, along Hollywood and Sunset boulevards, while **West Hollywood** has some of the most chic and trendy accommodations anywhere in town, with predictably high prices and smug attitudes. **West LA** and **Beverly Hills** are predominantly mid-to-upper-range territory, with expensive establishments in Century City and the relatively few bargains (other than dive motels) around the Westwood campus of UCLA. Staying in **Santa Monica** can be costly near the ocean and inexpensive further inland, while just south, **Venice** offers a cheaper alternative, with quite a few decent hostels and the occasional funky hotel.

Among options further out from central LA, the **South Bay** has an acceptable selection of low- to mid-range hotels strung along the Pacific Coast Highway, with higher-end corporate hotels sitting by the bay in **Long Beach**. The upscale choices in the **San Gabriel** and **San Fernando valleys** are around Universal City and Pasadena, although grungier alternatives can be found in North Hollywood and Burbank. The limited selections in **Malibu** are almost all upper-end resorts or inns, except for several roadside motels along Pacific Coast Highway – located well out of town. Finally, the dreariest accommodations in **Orange County** tend to be around Disneyland, where an array of faded motels competes for tourist dollars, while the county coast has many more appealing choices, from luxury hotels to quirky motels to inexpensive youth hostels.

Since there are few **booking agencies**, and visitor centers don't make accommodation reservations (though they will offer information and advice), you can only book a room through a travel agent, by phoning the hotel directly, through the hotel's online Web page – if it has one – or by using an Internet reservations site such as Yahoo! Travel. Ask if there are special weekend or midweek rates; remember, too, that hotels are generally less expensive if booked by the week than by the night.

Hotels and motels

Hotels and motels are listed below by neighborhood, with specific accommodation options for gay and lesbian travelers listed in a special section under "Gay and lesbian LA," p.306 – though most LA hotels are gay-friendly. If you're arriving on a late flight, or leaving on an early one, we've listed a few affordable places to stay near the airport (see box, p.231). Hotels near LAX are blandly similar and generally cost around $50–60 a night, but do offer complimentary shuttle service to and from the terminals. Prices increase at many tourist-oriented establishments during peak travel periods, typically over the summer and on weekends, especially those near major attractions like Disneyland and Universal Studios. However, weekday rates at business-oriented

---

Accommodation prices

All accommodation prices in this book have been coded using the symbols below, with prices quoted for the least-expensive double rooms in each establishment. Bear in mind that in Los Angeles all room rates are subject to a fourteen-percent **room tax** on top of your total bill. Individual rates rather than price codes are given for hostels and campgrounds.

❶ up to $40	❹ $70–90	❼ $150–200
❷ $40–55	❺ $90–120	❽ $200–250
❸ $55–70	❻ $120–150	❾ $250+

hotels, especially during conventions, can be just as expensive, or even more so, than weekend prices.

Listed **amenities** include features that are not always standard to hotel rooms in the area, such as balconies, Jacuzzis, kitchenettes and microwaves. More common amenities – the likes of ironing boards, hair-dryers, cable TV, free parking, etc – are not listed, except in truly low-end accommodations where their presence comes as a surprise.

Downtown

Biltmore 506 S Grand Ave at Fifth St ☎213/624-1011 or 1-800/222-8888, ⓦwww.thebiltmore.com. Renaissance Revival architecture from 1923, combined with modern luxury: a health club modeled on a Roman bathhouse, cherub and angel decor, and a view overlooking Pershing Square. The well-appointed rooms match the stateliness of the overall design. Now part of the *Millennium* chain. ❽

Downtown LA Standard 550 S Flower St ☎213/892-8080, ⓦwww.standardhotel.com. Located in a former oil-company building, the latest branch of LA's self-consciously trendy chain features sleek, modern furnishings and quirky decor, though is best for its rooftop bar (see p.279). Although billed as a "business hotel," the party scene is pretty much constant, with weekend drunken revelers carousing on the guest floors and screaming in the hallways. ❼

Figueroa 939 S Figueroa St at Olympic Blvd ☎213/627-8971 or 1-800/421-9092, ⓦwww.figueroahotel.com. Mid-range hotel on the southern side of Downtown, with a Southwestern flavor, cheery, sizeable pastel rooms, a Jacuzzi-equipped pool, 24-hour coffee shop, and even a few scattered statues of saints. ❹

Hyatt Regency 711 S Hope St ☎213/683-1234 or 1-800/233-1234, ⓦlosangelesregency .hyatt.com. A block from the Metrorail line, this chain hotel offers predictably unadventurous rooms just south of Bunker Hill, with a spa and health club on site. ❽

Kawada 200 S Hill St at Second St ☎213/621-4455 or 1-800/752-9232, ⓦwww.kawadahotel.com. Comfortable and clean rooms in a medium-sized hotel near the Civic Center; popular with value-oriented business travelers. ❹

Los Angeles Athletic Club 431 W Seventh St ☎213/625-2211, ⓦwww.laac.com. This brick-and-terracotta charmer is one of

Downtown's better Beaux Arts buildings. While still home to an exclusive club, the top three floors make up a hotel with 72 nicely furnished rooms and nine expensive suites; a real plus is free use of the club's track, pool, exercise equipment, and handball and basketball courts. ❼

Marriott Downtown 333 S Figueroa St ☎213/617-1133, ⓦwww.marriott.com. Palm tree-laden pool area, spacious rooms and health club add some charm to this chain hotel, centrally located near the 110 and 101 freeways. ❽

Miyako Inn and Spa 328 E First St ☎213/617-2000, ⓦwww.miyakoinn.com. Despite resembling a giant concrete box, this mid-price hotel remains a good bet in the heart of Little Tokyo. Modest but pleasant rooms include refrigerators, and hotel offers spa and karaoke bar as well. ❻

New Otani 120 S Los Angeles St ☎213/629-1200 or 1-800/421-8795, ⓦwww.newotani.com. Business hotel featuring spacious suites, a good restaurant with Asian cuisine (see p.260), and the small Japanese Garden in the Sky, which uses the traditional technique of "borrowed scenery" to incorporate existing views into the design. ❼

Omni Los Angeles 251 S Olive St at Fourth St ☎213/617-3300 or 1-800/327-0200, ⓦwww.omnilosangeles.com. Fancy Bunker Hill hotel with plush, elegant rooms, swimming pool and weight room. Adjacent to MOCA and the Music Center. ❽

Orchid 819 S Flower St at Eighth ☎213/624-5855 or 1-800/874-5855. The best deal in the heart of downtown, near the Seventh and Flower Red Line subway station. Comfortable and safe, even if the rooms are a bit plain. Weekly rates. ❷

Westin Bonaventure 404 S Figueroa St, between Fourth and Fifth sts ☎213/624-1000 or 1-800/228-3000, ⓦwww.westin.com. Modernist luxury hotel designed by John Portman, with five glass towers that resemble cocktail shakers, a six-story atrium with a "lake," and elegantly remodeled, conic-shaped rooms. Breathtaking exterior elevator ride – featured in the climax of the Clint Eastwood film *In the Line of Fire* – ascends to the rotating *Bona Vista* lounge. ❽

Wilshire Grand 930 Wilshire Blvd ⓣ213/688-7777 or 1-800/695-8284, ⓦwww.wilshiregrand.com. Large hotel on Bunker Hill with central access to many sights, health club and pool – though rather bland rooms. Mainly geared toward business travelers heading to the nearby convention center. ❼

Wyndham Checkers 535 S Grand ⓣ213/624-0000 or 1-800/WYNDHAM, ⓦwww.checkershotel.com. One of the great LA hotels, with sleek modern appointments in historic 1920s architecture, and nicely furnished rooms, rooftop pool and spa. Terrific Downtown views. ❾

Around Downtown

Best Western Mayfair 1256 W Seventh St ⓣ213/484-9789 or 1-800/528-1234, ⓦwww.mayfairla.com. Grand 1920s building with classical arches and pillars in the lobby and predictably clean, cookie-cutter rooms, with cable TV, sundeck and exercise room. ❻

City Center Motel 1135 W Seventh St at Lucas ⓣ213/628-7141. Bare but clean bargain accommodation with 1960s-style decor, free continental breakfast and airport shuttle bus. Walking not recommended in somewhat dicey surroundings. ❷

Guesthouse International 1904 W Olympic Blvd ⓣ213/380-9393, ⓦwww.guesthouse.net. Predictable lower-end chain motel with somewhat meager rooms and a swimming pool. Good value, though a somewhat risky location near Westlake. ❸

Holiday Inn Downtown 750 Garland Ave at Eighth ⓣ213/628-5242 or 1-800/628-5240, ⓦwww.holidayinnla.com. On the western fringe of downtown beside the Harbor Freeway, this *Holiday Inn* features a pool and cozy rooms with coffeemakers and cable TV. Good access to Downtown's major sights, including the LA Convention Center. As above, not in the most pedestrian-friendly neighborhood. ❺

Park Plaza 607 S Park View St, between Sixth St and Wilshire Blvd ⓣ213/384-5281, ⓦwww.theparkplazahotella.com. Facing MacArthur Park, a 1920s hotel with a marble floor, grand ballroom, a tasteful mix of Neoclassical and modern design, and sumptuous lobby popular with film-makers. Ongoing renovation promises to make for more appealing rooms. ❼

Vagabond Inn 3101 S Figueroa St ⓣ213/746-1531 or 1-800/522-1555, ⓦwww.vagabondinn.com. The best place to stay near USC and the Shrine Auditorium, a few miles south of Downtown. The chain-motel rooms are clean and spartan, and the pool is an added plus. ❹

Mid-Wilshire

Beverly Laurel 8018 Beverly Blvd at Laurel Ave ⓣ323/651-2441. The motel's coffee shop, *Swingers*, attracts the most attention here, primarily as a hangout for poseurs and inquisitive tourists (see p.251). The place has nice retro-1960s touches but rather mediocre rooms, though the location is good, not far from the Fairfax District and, to the west, Beverly Hills. ❹

Beverly Plaza 8384 W Third St ⓣ323/658-6600 or 1-800/624-9835. Elegant, nicely appointed rooms and the streetside *Cava* restaurant (see p.269) make this one of the area's better small-scale hotels, with swimming pool, hot tub and fitness center. Good location for accessing the monstrous Beverly Center mall. ❽

Bevonshire Lodge Motel 7575 Beverly Blvd at Curson Ave ⓣ323/936-6154. Well situated for both West LA and Hollywood, across from Pan Pacific Park and the black cube of CBS Studios. All the basic rooms come with a fridge; for a few dollars more you can have a kitchenette. ❸

Chancellor 3191 W Seventh St ⓣ213/383-1183. Cheap accommodation near Metrorail stop and Bullocks Wilshire building, with simple, tidy rooms – though the area can be dicey at night. ❷

Econo Lodge Wilshire 3400 W Third St ⓣ213/385-0061, ⓦwww.econolodge.com. Bargain-basement accommodation with clean, small, adequate rooms and complimentary breakfast. Located in a drab part of town, but five blocks from a Metrorail stop to the south. ❸

Farmer's Daughter 115 S Fairfax Ave ⓣ323/937-3930,

Ⓦ www.farmersdaughterhotel.com. A monument of motel kitsch conveniently located across from, naturally, the Farmers Market; the clean, sparse rooms offer limited amenities, but the no-frills swimming pool sometimes attracts slumming B-list celebs and bohemian poseurs. ❹

Oxford Palace 745 S Oxford Ave Ⓣ 213/389-8000, Ⓦ www.oxfordhotel.com. Solid choice for business travelers with nicely furnished lobby, 86 serviceable rooms and nine suites. Located near the heart of Koreatown, just around the corner from the Wiltern Theater. ❻

Radisson Wilshire Plaza 3515 Wilshire Blvd Ⓣ 213/381-7411 or 1-800/777-7800, Ⓦ www.radwilshire.com. Predictable chain accommodations, located in Koreatown, with modern Californian design, adequate rooms, pool, fitness center and complimentary breakfast. ❻

Wilshire Crest 6301 Orange St Ⓣ 323/936-5131, Ⓦ www.wilshirecrestinn.com. Small hotel with plain rooms in charming, period-revival residential area, conveniently located just north of Wilshire Blvd and west of Fairfax Ave and Museum Row. ❺

Wilshire Royale 2619 Wilshire Blvd Ⓣ 213/387-5311 or 1-800/421-8072, Ⓦ www.hojola.com. MacArthur Park hotel (and Howard Johnson franchise) with sleek Art Deco facade and classically elegant lobby, but rather predictable rooms. Located directly between two Red Line stops. ❻

Hollywood

Best Western Hollywood Hills 6141 Franklin Ave between Gower and Vine Ⓣ 323/464-5181, Ⓦ www.bestwesterncalifornia.com. Reliable chain hotel, with cable TV and heated pool, along with standard, clean rooms. At the foot of the Hollywood Hills. ❹

Comfort Inn and Suites 2010 N Highland Ave Ⓣ 323/874-4300, Ⓦ www.comfortinn.com. One of the best deals around, offering basic chain-motel rooms but with microwaves, fridges, DVD players, complimentary breakfast and heated pool. Just three blocks north of Hollywood Boulevard. ❹

Dunes Sunset 5625 Sunset Blvd Ⓣ 323/467-5171. On the dingier eastern side of Hollywood, but far enough away from the true grunginess even further east to feel

safe. Adequate motel rooms are decent and clean enough, given the location. ❸

Holiday Inn Hollywood 1755 N Highland Ave Ⓣ 323/462-7181 or 1-800/465-4329, Ⓦ www.holiday-inn.com. Massive and dull, but perfectly placed, near the heart of Hollywood Boulevard and the Chinese Theatre. Basic rooms, the price of which lowers with triple occupancy. The main highlight is the top-floor *Windows on Hollywood* revolving nightclub, which affords a great view of Tinseltown. ❻

Hollywood Hills Magic Hotel 7025 Franklin Ave Ⓣ 323/851-0800, Ⓦ www.MagicCastleHotel.com. One of the unheralded deals in these parts, an affordable suite-hotel with a kitchen, sofa and two TVs per room. An added plus is being able to buy tickets to the adjacent Magic Castle (see p.101) – otherwise off-limits to the general public. ❹

Hollywood Metropolitan 5825 Sunset Blvd Ⓣ 323/962-5800 or 1-800/962-5800, Ⓦ www.metropolitanhotel.com. Sleek high-rise in central Hollywood, featuring flashy exterior elevator, good views and somewhat spacious rooms. Good value for the area, though a bit east – and south – of major attractions. ❹

Hollywood Roosevelt 7000 Hollywood Blvd Ⓣ 323/466-7000, Ⓦ www.hollywoodroosevelt.com. The first hotel built for the movie greats in 1927, now in the *Clarion* chain. The rooms are unremarkable, but the Corinthian-columned lobby reeks of Hollywood atmosphere and the hotel features a Jacuzzi, fitness room, swimming pool decorated with a Hockney mural and a History of Hollywood exhibit on the second floor. The ever-popular *Cinegrill* cabaret (p.301) continues to entertain on the ground level. ❻

Hollywood Towne House 6055 Sunset Blvd at Gower St Ⓣ 323/462-3221. Motel with decayed exterior and 1920s-era phones that connect to the front desk only. Yet the place itself is comfortable enough, with decent rooms and spare furnishings. ❸

Orchid Suites 1753 Orchid Ave Ⓣ 323/874-9678 or 1-800/537-3052, Ⓦ www.orchidsuites.com. Roomy, if spartan, suites with cable TV, kitchenettes and heated pool; very close to the most popular parts of Hollywood – adjacent to the massive Hollywood & Highland mall. ❹

Ramada Inn Hollywood 1160 N Vermont Ave ☎ 323/660-1788, ⓦ www.ramadahollywood.com. Easily the best and safest place to stay in a somewhat dicey, though increasingly hip, part of East Hollywood, featuring comfortable rooms with microwaves and fridges, along with a pool, spa, bar, restaurant, fitness center and free continental breakfast. ❹

Renaissance Hollywood 1755 N Highland Blvd ☎ 323/856-1200, ⓦ www.renaissancehollywood.com. The hotel centerpiece of the new Hollywood & Highland mall complex, with upscale rooms and suites, and prime location in the heart of Tinseltown. ❼

Saharan 7212 Sunset Blvd at Poinsettia Place ☎ 323/874-6700, ⓦ www.saharanmotel.com. A classic 1950s-style motel: double-decker layout with standard rooms built around a pool, plus cheesy neon sign and brash color scheme. Comparatively good value, especially considering its central location. ❸

Sunset–La Brea Travelodge 7051 Sunset Blvd ☎ 323/462-0905, ⓦ www.travelodge.com. A safe, cheap bet just south of Hollywood's major sights, with adequate rooms (some of which are three-bed suites), sundeck and pool. There's another *Travelodge* at 1401 N Vermont St ☎ 323/665-5735, on the opposite side of the area in lower-rent East Hollywood, near Barnsdall Park and a Metrorail stop. Both ❸

West Hollywood

Argyle 8358 Sunset Blvd ☎ 323/654-7100, ⓦ www.argylehotel.com. An Art Deco landmark, once known as the Sunset Tower apartments, since converted into a luxury hotel, featuring automotive radiator-grill decor and well-preserved 1930s Zigzag Moderne style, but also modern amenities like stereos and VCRs, along with marble-floored bathrooms and prime views of the Sunset Strip. ❾

Chateau Marmont 8221 Sunset Blvd at Crescent Heights Blvd ☎ 323/626-1010, ⓦ www.chateaumarmont.com. Exclusive Norman Revival hotel, which resembles a dark castle or Hollywood fortress. The hotel has welcomed the likes of Boris Karloff, Greta Garbo, Errol Flynn, Jean Harlow, John Belushi (who died in one of its elite

bungalows) and Jim Morrison, who broke two ribs falling off a balcony. ❾

Elan Hotel Modern 8435 Beverly Blvd ☎ 323/658-6663, ⓦ www.elanhotel.com. The latest semi-upscale boutique hotel, located in a busy shopping zone just north of the Beverly Center mall. Rooms are nicely appointed, though a bit small; also with fitness center, spa and complimentary breakfast. ❼

Grafton 8462 Sunset Blvd ☎ 323/654-6470, ⓦ www.graftononsunset.com. A newly redesigned mid-level boutique hotel, with attractive furnishings, in-room stereos and VCRs, pool, fitness center, and complimentary shuttle to nearby malls and businesses. ❻

Hyatt West Hollywood 8401 Sunset Blvd ☎ 323/656-4101, ⓦ westhollywood.hyatt.com. Not too glamorous on the outside, this was the legendary site of outlandish rock-star antics, from Led Zeppelin to the Who to Guns N' Roses, but has been remodeled into a tastefully upscale business hotel, with nice, spacious rooms that offer Stripside balconies, but sadly without the same hip edge as before. ❼

Le Montrose 900 Hammond St ☎ 310/855-1115, ⓦ www.lemontrose.com. West Hollywood hotel with Art Nouveau stylings (including a terrific wood-latticed elevator), featuring upscale restaurant and rooftop tennis courts, pool and Jacuzzi. Most rooms are suites with full amenities such as stereos, sunken living rooms, dual televisions, refrigerators and expansive views. ❼

Le Parc 733 N West Knoll Drive ☎ 310/855-8888 or 1-800/578-4837, ⓦ www.leparcsuites.com. Graceful apartment hotel in a residential area, with simple studios, more spacious one- and two-bedroom suites, stereos, refrigerators, and rooftop pool and Jacuzzi with views of the hills. ❼

Mondrian 8440 Sunset Blvd ☎ 323/650-8999, ⓦ www.mondrianhotel.com. Like many other Strip hotels, this place oozes art and luxury from every orifice, though with a much heavier dose of pretension – especially in the celebrity-bootlicking *SkyBar* up top. Spacious rooms are well-decorated and acceptably chic, though not quite enough to justify the snooty attitudes. ❾

The Standard West Hollywood 8300 Sunset

Blvd ☏ 323/654-2800,
🌐 www.standardhotel.com. Amazing style, though not much substance, at this famed hipster "party hotel" offering extra-spartan rooms furnished with beanbags, swinging outdoor pool and bar, and a goofball design with Astroturf floors and other intentionally bizarre decor. **❼**

Summerfield Suites 1000 Westmount Drive ☏ 310/657-7400,
🌐 www.summerfieldsuites.com. Sumptuous hotel in a quiet, residential section of West Hollywood, within easy walking distance of major clubs and attractions, but just far enough away from the Strip's chaos and noise. Impressive, if small, suites with sunken living rooms, refrigerators and a pleasant courtyard. Now part of the *Wyndham* chain. **❻**

Sunset Marquis 1200 N Alta Loma Rd ☏ 310/657-1333 or 1-800/858-9758,
🌐 www.sunsetmarquishotel.com. A hangout for musicians (featuring an on-site recording studio), with two pools, Jacuzzi, sauna, weight room and outside gardens surrounding very pricey villas; most rooms are well-designed suites with kitchens, balconies and patios. Prices start at $320 and can top out over $1000. **❾**

Wyndham Bel Age 1020 N San Vicente Blvd ☏ 310/854-1111, 🌐 www.wyndham.com. Another of the Strip's top choices, overflowing with quality art (and some kitsch), plus lovely rooms with balconies and kitchens, and an exquisite lobby. Also with standard pool and health-club service. **❾**

Beverly Hills and Century City

Avalon 9400 W Olympic Blvd ☏ 310/277-5221, 🌐 www.avalon-hotel.com. Located in south Beverly Hills, three long blocks from the Golden Triangle, a hipster-oriented hotel with cozy rooms and cool, modern furnishings, along with in-room CD players, fax machines and VCRs, plus a fitness club. The poolside bar is where the young elite pose in their black – or whatever's the "new black" at the moment – threads. **❽**

Beverly Hills Hotel 9641 Sunset Blvd ☏ 310/276-2251 or 1-800/283-8885,
🌐 www.beverlyhillshotel.com. The classic Hollywood resort, with a bold pink-and-green color scheme and Mission-style design, and surrounded by its own exotic gardens. Rooms feature marbled bathrooms, VCRs, Jacuzzis, and other such luxuries, and the famed *Polo Lounge* restaurant is also on the premises. Along with W.C. Fields, John Barrymore and other countless celebrities, Marilyn Monroe also stayed here, and one of the select bungalows is decorated in her honor. **❾**

Beverly Hills Reeves 120 S Reeves Drive ☏ 310/271-3006, 🌐 www.bhreeves.com. Housed in a former apartment building just south of Wilshire Boulevard, this inexpensive hotel is an obvious choice if you're in LA on a tight budget. Simple and clean rooms include microwaves, refrigerators and complimentary breakfast, along with a rooftop sundeck. **❸**

Beverly Hilton 9876 Wilshire Blvd ☏ 310/274-7777 or 1-800/922-5432, 🌐 www.hilton.com. Prominent white, geometric hotel at the corner of Wilshire and Santa Monica boulevards, co-owned by Merv Griffin and site of the Golden Globe Awards, as well as famed *Trader Vic's* restaurant. Fairly nice rooms and decor, though not quite up to the other nearby luxury options. **❽**

Beverly Terrace 469 N Doheny Drive ☏ 310/274-8141,
🌐 ww.beverlyterracehotel.com. A good, clean, inexpensive motel with complimentary breakfast and some balconies. Central location on the border between Beverly Hills and West Hollywood. **❺**

Century Plaza Hotel and Tower 2025 Avenue of the Stars ☏ 310/277-2000 or 1-800/WESTIN-1, 🌐 www.centuryplazala.com. In the middle of Century City, a 1960s-era crescent-shaped hotel with elegant rooms with outstanding views from Beverly Hills to the ocean. Amenities include pool, health club, business center, rental car outlets and so on. A popular spot with celebrities and visiting politicians. **❾**

Crescent 403 N Crescent Drive ☏ 310/247-0505 or 1-800/451-1566,
🌐 www.beverlycrescenthotel.com. Adjacent to Beverly Hills City Hall and *Hotel del Flores*, with similarly inexpensive prices, the *Crescent* has plain rooms, but does offer complimentary breakfast and afternoon tea. **❺**

Four Seasons Beverly Hills 300 S Doheny Drive ☏ 310/273-2222 or 1-800/332-3442, 🌐 www.fourseasons.com. One of the most famous luxury hotels in Beverly Hills, featuring well-furnished rooms with balconies, elegant decor and decent artworks, along with pool and health-club facilities. Very high prices attract A-list celebs. ❾

Hotel del Flores 409 N Crescent Drive at Little Santa Monica Blvd ☎310/274-5115, ⓦ ww.hoteldelflores.com. Three blocks from Rodeo Drive. Modest, pleasant and surprisingly good value, with faded old period-revival look from 1926 and quaint rooms. Shared baths bring down the cost significantly. ❹

Inn at Beverly Hills 125 S Spalding Drive ☎310/278-0303, ⓦwww.innatbeverlyhills.com. A twice-renovated 1958 hotel, which now contains wood-and-marble decor, rooms with refrigerators, pool, sauna and fitness room, along with complimentary breakfast. Located near the Golden Triangle shopping zone, but far enough away to sit in its own quiet, leafy setting. ❼

Le Meridien 465 S La Cienega Blvd ☎310/247-0400, ⓦwww.lemeridien.com. Luxury hotel offers three hundred elegantly furnished rooms, swimming pool, spa and health club, with 55 ultra-chic suites providing boundless comfort for movie-industry players. ❾

Maison 140 140 S Lasky Drive ☎310/281-4000, ⓦwww.maison140.com. Recent, high-profile entry for swank hipsters, featuring rooms with CD players and nice appointments, plus salon, bar, fitness room and complimentary breakfast. ❼

Park Hyatt 2151 Avenue of the Stars ☎310/277-1234 or 1-800/233-1234, ⓦwww.hyatt.com. Century City stalwart with good access to sights in West LA and Beverly Hills. Decent rooms with balconies and on-site pool and spa. ❽

Peninsula Beverly Hills 9882 Little Santa Monica Blvd ☎310/551-2888 or 1-800/462-7899, ⓦwww.peninsula.com. Tucked away in a peaceful alcove near Wilshire and Santa Monica boulevards, a pricey luxury hotel featuring well-appointed rooms, suites and villas thick with graceful furnishings and decor, along with pool, sundeck, cabanas, rooftop gardens, whirlpool and weight room. ❾

Radisson Beverly Pavilion 9360 Wilshire Blvd ☎310/273-1400, ⓦwww.radissonbeverlyhills.com. A classic period-revival hotel with appealing little

rooms and good views, not far from posh Rodeo Drive. Slightly less pricey than surrounding luxury hotels. ❻

Regent Beverly Wilshire 9500 Wilshire Blvd ☎310/275-5200, ⓦwww.regenthotels.com. Located near the heart of Rodeo Drive, amid countless boutiques and chic department stores, this 1928 hotel has darkly furnished rooms, three restaurants, palatial designs and views overlooking Beverly Hills. Prices not for the timid, especially the immense Presidential Suite, which goes for $5000. ❾

West LA

Best Western Royal Palace 2528 S Sepulveda Blvd ☎310/477-9066, ⓦwww.bestwesternroyalpalace.com. The name overstates it more than a little, but if you want simple, cheap accommodation and don't mind staying near the junction of the 405 and 10 freeways, this is the place: with in-room microwaves, a pool, fitness center, and a shopping mall a mile away. Suites go for around $100. ❹

Carlyle Inn 1119 S Robertson Blvd ☎310/275-4445, ⓦwww.carlyle-inn.com. Just north of Pico Boulevard, a hotel close enough to Beverly Hills to make an affordable stay worthwhile; basic rooms include VCRs and there's also complimentary breakfast and a smallish gym. ❻

Culver Hotel 9400 Culver Blvd ☎310/838-7963 or 1-800/888-3-CULVER, ⓦwww.culverhotel.com. A lovely, restored historic landmark, once the offices of town founder Harry Culver and hotel of the midget cast during filming of *The Wizard of Oz*, today featuring red-and-black decor, checkered marble floors and old-time iron railings in the lobby, and cozy rooms with good views of the city. ❺

Econo Lodge 11933 W Washington Blvd ☎310/398-1651, ⓦwww.econolodge.com. Basic chain motel with small, clean rooms and complimentary breakfast; some rooms with microwaves and refrigerators. Located in somewhat dismal district of Mar Vista, but close enough to West LA and, further west, Venice. ❸

Holiday Inn Brentwood 170 N Church Lane at Sunset Blvd and 405 freeway ☎310/476-6411, ⓦwww.hibrentwood.com. Something of a cylindrical concrete eyesore that pokes out

Courtyard Marriott El Segundo/LAX 2000 E Mariposa Ave ⊤310/322-0700, ⊛www.courtyard .com/laxca. Given the surrounding area – industrial beachside suburbia best known for its oil refineries – this is one of the better options, a chain hotel offering rooms with microwaves and refrigerators, plus a spa, pool, weight room and airport shuttle. ❶

Days Inn 901 W Manchester Blvd ⊤310/649-0800 or 1-800/231-2508, ⊛www.daysinn.com. Modern hotel with clean rooms in a grubby neighborhood by the 405 freeway. Outdoor pool, free parking and free shuttle to LAX. ❸

Embassy Suites LAX North 9801 Airport Blvd ⊤310/215-1000 or 1-800/695-8284, ⊛www .embassysuites.com. Nice, predictable luxury from this chain-hotel giant, offering in-room wet bars, refrigerators and microwaves in spacious, two-room suites; also including spa, weight room, sauna, pool and airport shuttle. ❻. There's a

similar branch south of LAX at 1440 Imperial Ave ⊤310/640-3600. ❼

Quality Inn 5249 W Century Blvd ⊤310/645-2200 or 1-800/228-5151, ⊛www.qualityinn.com. Featuring ten floors of comfortable and well-equipped rooms, plus pool, weight room, two restaurants, a bar and free LAX shuttles every 15 minutes. ❸

Renaissance Hotel 9620 Airport Blvd ⊤310/337-2800 or 1-800/228-9898, ⊛www.renaissancehotels .com. If you feel compelled to splurge near the airport, this is the best of the LAX-area hotels: wood-and-marble decor, ample rooms and luxurious suites with free coffee and tasteful appointments, plus pool, spa and health club. ❻

Travelodge LAX–South 1804 E Sycamore Ave ⊤310/615-1073, ⊛www.travelodge.com. Five minutes south of LAX in the industrial burg of El Segundo, and convenient for the South Bay as well. Pool and free tea, coffee and breakfast, as well as kitchens and LAX shuttles. ❸

of a hillside below the Getty Center (and visually unavoidable from the 405 freeway), but with acceptable comfort and decent furnishings, plus pool, spa, weight room and rooftop restaurant with terrific views across the Westside. ❺

Holiday Inn Express West LA 10330 W Olympic Blvd ⊤310/553-1000, ⊛www.holiday-inn.com. Located between Century City and the Westside Pavilion mall, and offering adequate rooms with VCRs and fridges, and suites with lofts and spiral stairways. ❻

Hotel Bel Air 701 Stone Canyon Rd ⊤310/472-1211 or 1-800/648-1097, ⊛www.hotelbelair.com. Perhaps LA's nicest hotel, and the only commercial business in Bel Air, located in a thickly overgrown canyon, with lush gardens and waterfall. Go for a beautiful brunch by the Swan Pond if you can't afford the rooms, which will cost you at least $500 for their exquisite decor, spaciousness and the like. ❾

Luxe Summit Hotel Bel-Air 11461 Sunset Blvd

⊤310/476-6571 or 1-800/HOTEL-411, ⊛www.luxehotels.com. Not to be confused with the other *Hotel Bel Air*, this is not technically in Bel Air, but across the 405 freeway in Brentwood. Still, impeccable, smartly designed rooms with marble bathtubs and refrigerators, and two on-site pools, tennis courts, health club and free shuttle to nearby Getty Center. ❻

Westwood and UCLA

Century Wilshire 10776 Wilshire Blvd ⊤310/474-4506 or 1-800/421-7223, ⊛centurywilshirehotel.com. Renovated old hotel, located along a busy section of Wilshire near Westwood Village. Kitchens and complimentary breakfast are standard; some rooms have balconies. ❻

Claremont 1044 Tiverton Ave ⊤310/208-5957. An amazingly good deal for the area, this cheerful and inexpensive little hotel sits very close to UCLA and Westwood Village. Rooms are fairly basic, but the main difficulty is a lack of sufficient parking. **❸**

Doubletree Westwood 10740 Wilshire Blvd ☎ 310/475-8711, ⓦ www .doubletreelawestwood.com. Centrally located near Westwood Village, this big, blocky chain hotel offers the standard clean, unexciting rooms (and a handful of more expensive suites), with pool, sauna, gym and daily shuttle to the Getty Center. **❻**

Hilgard House 927 Hilgard Ave ☎ 310/208-3945 or 1-800/826-3934, ⓦ www.hilgardhouse.com. Positioned just beyond UCLA's southern boundary, this ivy-covered charmer draws the visiting-parent crowd for its nicely designed rooms, covered parking, continental breakfast, and some rooms with Jacuzzis and refrigerators. **❻**

Hotel del Capri 10587 Wilshire Blvd ☎ 310/474-3511 or 1-800/44-HOTEL, ⓦ www.hoteldelcapri.com. Within a mile of UCLA, this mid-range hotel provides passable rooms and suites with faded 1980s *Miami Vice*–style decor, pool, kitchenettes and complimentary breakfast; some suites also offer Jacuzzis. A squat building set in one of Wilshire Blvd's high-rise corporate canyons. **❺**

UCLA Guest House 330 Young Drive E ☎ 310/825-2923, ⓦ www.hotels.ucla.edu. Excellent choice for anyone visiting the UCLA campus, with affordable rooms offering basic amenities (including complimentary breakfast), use of nearby university recreation center, and kitchenettes available for only $5 extra. **❺**

W Los Angeles 930 Hilgard Ave ☎ 310/208-8765 or 1-800/421-2317, ⓦ www.whotels.com. The conspicuous height of luxury in Westwood, featuring well-decorated – though not huge – suites and pool, spa, health club and ample parking. Popular with the richest parents visiting kids at adjacent UCLA. **❽**

Santa Monica and Venice

Bayside 2001 Ocean Ave at Bay St ☎ 310/396-6000, ⓦ www.baysidehotel.com. Just a block from Santa Monica beach and Main Street. Outside of the colorful bathroom tiles, the rooms are fairly bland, as is the exterior. No phones, but generally comfortable, with ocean views from the more expensive rooms. **❹**

Cadillac 8 Dudley Ave at Rose Ave ☎ 310/399-

8876, ⓦ www.thecadillachotel.com. Stylish Art Deco hotel on the Venice Boardwalk. Although the suites are nice, some of the lower-end rooms are spartan and have few amenities; given the location and price, though, there are few better deals around. On-site sundeck, pool, gym and sauna. **❺**

Cal Mar 220 California St ☎ 310/395-5555, ⓦ www.calmarhotel.com. One of the more unheralded choices in Santa Monica, but excellent for its central location (two blocks from the beach, one from the Promenade), garden suites with dining rooms, heated kidney-shaped pool, fitness room and airport shuttle. **❺**

Carmel 201 Broadway at Second St ☎ 310/451-2469, ⓦ www.hotelcarmel.com. The best budget bet for lodging near Santa Monica beach and Third Street Promenade, with the ocean two blocks away. Good, basic accommodation with limited appeal, other than the location. **❻**

Fairmont Miramar 101 Wilshire Blvd ☎ 310/576-7777, ⓦ www.fairmont.com. Upscale even for this area, newly remodeled Santa Monica hotel features nicely appointed suites and quasi-tropical bungalows near the pool, with health club, salon, spa, fitness center, swimming pool and fine views over the Pacific. **❾**

Georgian 1415 Ocean Ave ☎ 310/395-9945 or 1-800/538-8147, ⓦ www.georgianhotel.com. A stunning blue-and-gold Art Deco gem, renovated with an airy Californian interior design. Rooms are elegant if a bit too small, though pricier suites offer more space and better views, from Malibu to Palos Verdes. The one downside: a single, excruciatingly slow elevator. **❽**

Hotel California 1670 Ocean Ave ☎ 310/393-2363, ⓦ www.hotelca.com. Near *Loew's*, below, but somewhat cheaper, with a central location not far from Third Street Promenade. Remodeled rooms are modest but elegant, with hardwood flooring and tasteful furnishings. **❼**

Inn at Venice Beach 327 Washington Blvd ☎ 310/821-2557 or 1-800/828-0688, ⓦ www.innatvenicebeach.com. A good choice for visiting the beach and the Venice canals, with simple, tasteful rooms with balconies and refrigerators. **❺**

Loew's Santa Monica Beach 1700 Ocean Ave at Pico Blvd ☎ 310/458-6700,

@www.loewshotels.com. One of Santa Monica's biggest hotels: a deluxe, salmon-colored edifice overlooking the ocean and the Santa Monica pier, and often in demand as a film set. The finest rooms top $450, with lesser rooms being adequate, if a bit cramped and overpriced. **❽**

Ocean Park Hotel 2680 32nd St ☎310/452-1469, @www.oceanparkhotel.com. Valuable alternative to the higher-priced accommodations nearby, with weekly rates only ($235–255) and clean, basic rooms with fridges, cable TV and shared bathrooms. Several miles from the beach, near the eastern edge of the city, not far from the Santa Monica Airport.

Oceana 849 Ocean Ave ☎310/393-0486 or 1-800/777-0758, @www.hoteloceana.com. An all-suite hotel with central courtyard, good oceanside views, pool, spa, fitness room, and in-room kitchens, CD players and video game units. Located at the base of trendy Montana Ave, giving some explanation for the overly steep prices. **❾**

Radisson Huntley 1111 Second St ☎310/394-5454 or 1-800/777-7800, @www.radisson /santamonicaca. Attractive, if overpriced, rooms, but the main draw here is the flashy exterior elevator that brings you up twenty stories to a lounge on top. Food is mediocre, but the views over Santa Monica and the rest of the city and ocean are worth the price of a drink or two. **❼**

Ramada Limited 3130 Washington Blvd ☎310/821-5086, @www.ramada.com. Located between Venice and Marina del Rey, a budget choice with basic, clean rooms and pool, spa, weight room and complimentary breakfast – a much better option than the grubby, low-end motels littering nearby Lincoln Blvd. **❹**

Ritz-Carlton Marina del Rey 4375 Admiralty Way ☎310/823-1700, @www.ritzcarlton.com. Perhaps the only good reason to come to this unappealing district, the *Ritz* is a luxury hotel with all the standard high-end accoutrements, including elegantly furnished rooms with balconies, swimming pool, spa, weight room, and garden terrace overlooking the marina. **❾**

Santa Monica Beach Travelodge 1525 Ocean Ave ☎310/451-0761, @www.travelodge.com. Predictably clean and basic chain lodging, excellent for its beach proximity. **❻**. To save a few bucks, try the less appealing units on

the eastern edge of town – one of the uglier motels you'll see in the area, resembling a stucco jail – at 3102 Pico Blvd ☎310/450-5766. **❹**

Shangri-La 1301 Ocean Ave ☎310/394-2791 or 1-800/345-STAY, @www.shangrila-hotel.com. Formerly the Shangri-La Apartments, a terrific, restored 1930s Art Deco structure with wraparound Streamline Moderne windows and railings, and alluring white-and-black design, with some original fixtures. Rooms are unexceptional but furnished with Deco motifs and art, and offer excellent, palm tree-level views of the ocean and nearby Third Street Promenade. **❽**

Shutters on the Beach 1 Pico Blvd at Appian Way ☎310/458-0030 or 1-800/334-9000, @www.shuttersonthebeach.com. The seafront home to the stars, a white-shuttered luxury resort south of the pier. Amenities include Jacuzzis (with shuttered screens), pool, spa, sundeck, ground-floor shopping and ocean views. No walk-ins – reservations only. **❾**

Venice Beach Hotel 1515 Pacific Ave ☎310/452-3052, @www.caprica.com/venice-beach-hostel. Built over one of the last remaining Venice colonnades, this hotel/hostel offers cheap and basic private rooms, cable TVs with VCRs, and close access to the beach. Shared hostel rooms start at $20; private rooms **❸**.

Venice Beach House 15 30th Ave ☎310/823-1966, @www.venicebeachhouse.com. A quaint bed-and-breakfast in a 1915 Craftsman house, with nine comfortable rooms and suites finished with period appointments and named for famous guests – Charlie Chaplin and Abbot Kinney, for example – and, true to the name, right next to the beach. **❻**

Viceroy 1819 Ocean Ave ☎310/451-8711, @www.viceroysantamonica.com. The old Pacific Shore Hotel, remodeled into a luxury item, with great bay views and nicely appointed rooms with CD players, on-site pool and lounge. The rooms start at $320 and top $2000. **❾**

The South Bay and LA Harbor

Barnabey's 3501 Sepulveda Blvd, Manhattan Beach ☎310/545-8466, @www.barnabeyshotel.com. Quaint Victorian inn, decorated with Belle Epoque touches, at the northern edge of Manhattan Beach; it's also adjacent to a lengthy green belt and about a mile from the beach. Offers 126 tasteful rooms with plush beds and old-time fixtures and detailing, with on-site pool, courtyard, gardens and Jacuzzi. **❻**

Beach House at Hermosa 1300 Strand, Hermosa Beach ☎310/374-3001, ⊛www.Beach-House.com. The height of casual luxury in the South Bay, offering two-room suites with fireplaces, wet bars, balconies, Jacuzzis, stereos and refrigerators, with many rooms overlooking the ocean – except for the cheapest. On the beachside concourse of the Strand. **❽**

Holiday Inn San Pedro 111 S Gaffey St, San Pedro ☎310/514-1414, ⊛www .holidayinnsanpedro.com. While not in a prime spot – several blocks from the end of the 110 freeway – the quaint decor, antique furnishings, and nicely appointed rooms and suites (all with fridges and some with kitchens) make this chain hotel worthwhile. **❺**

Hotel Hermosa 2515 PCH, Hermosa Beach ☎310/318-6000, ⊛www.hotelhermosa.com. In a busy part of town, between Hermosa and Manhattan beaches, a plush hotel with rooms starting at moderate prices and rising up to $350 suites. A short walk to the beach. **❹–❾**

Long Beach Hilton 2 World Trade Center, Long Beach ☎562/983-3400, ⊛www.longbeach .hilton.com. One of the better chain hotels in the area, with conventional rooms boasting wide harborside views overlooking Ocean Boulevard and downtown Long Beach. Within easy walking distance to many sights, with pool, spa and airport shuttle. **❼**

Long Beach Travelodge 80 Atlantic Ave, Long Beach ☎562/435-2471, ⊛www.travelodge.com. A decent bargain in a prime location, with the simple, spare rooms familiar to budget travelers, but also with refrigerators and coffeemakers and good access to major area sights. **❺**

Motel 6 5665 E 7th St, Long Beach ☎562/597-1311, ⊛www.motel6.com. Solid, basic rooms at cheap prices; good mainly for travelers on their way south to Orange County or San Diego. **❸**

Palos Verdes Inn 1700 S PCH, Redondo Beach ☎310/316-4211 or 1-800/421-9241, ⊛www.palosverdesinn.com. Affordable accommodation on the edge of Redondo

Beach, on a busy highway near Torrance and Palos Verdes, but just a half-mile from the beach. Clean but unexceptional rooms, pool, spa and weight room. **❺**

Portofino Hotel and Yacht Club 260 Portofino Way, Redondo Beach ☎310/379-8481, ⊛www.hotelportofino.com. One of the few good reasons to come to Redondo Beach is to stay at this elegant suite-hotel by the ocean. Although smaller single rooms are available, the best choices are the well-furnished, comfortable two-room suites, which look out over the elite playground of King Harbor. **❼**

Rodeway Inn 50 Atlantic Ave at Ocean Blvd, Long Beach ☎562/435-8369, ⊛www.rodewayinn.com. Inoffensive chain-motel accommodation, a block from the beach and a serviceable base for exploring Long Beach and its downtown and harbor area. Free in-room movies in rather lackluster rooms. **❹**

Sea Sprite Motel 1016 Strand, Hermosa Beach ☎310/376-6933, ⊛www.seaspritemotel.com. Right next to the beach along a popular strip. Several different room options come with varying prices, including weekly rates for longer stays. **❺**

Seahorse Inn 233 N Sepulveda Blvd, Manhattan Beach ☎310/376-7951 or 1-800/233-8050. Typical roadside motel with faded pastel exterior and clean rooms. Further from the beach than others, on a loud, busy stretch of road, but with a pool and adequate parking. **❸**

Vagabond Inn 6226 PCH, Redondo Beach ☎310/378-8555, ⊛www.vagabondinn.com. Clean and inexpensive lodging in a beachside tourist zone. Better value than comparable motels in the area. **❹**

Westin Long Beach 333 E Ocean Blvd, Long Beach ☎562/436-3000, ⊛www.westin.com. A solid bet for bayside luxury at surprisingly affordable prices (cheaper when ordered online), right by the convention center and providing all the standard high-end amenities: spa, fitness center, pool and nicely designed rooms. **❻**

The San Gabriel and San Fernando valleys

Artists Inn 1038 Magnolia St, South Pasadena ☎626/799-5668 or 1-888/799-5668, ⊛www.artistsinns.com. Easily the best place to stay in South Pasadena, a themed bed-and-breakfast inn with ten rooms and suites (some with spas) honoring famous painters and styles. Consider the stylish Fauve and Impressionist rooms – though best of all is the Italian Suite, with an antique tub and sun porch. **❼**

Best Western Colorado Inn 2156 E Colorado Blvd, Pasadena ☏626/793-9339, ⓦ www.bestwesterncalifornia.com. Comfortable chain accommodation with basic rooms just south of the Foothill Freeway and north of San Marino's Huntington Library and Gardens. **❺**

Beverly Garland's Holiday Inn 4222 Vineland Ave, North Hollywood ☏818/980-8000 or 1-800/BEVERLY, ⓦ www.beverlygarland.com. Two-tower complex with standard rooms, but also with pool, sauna and screening room, and close to Universal Studios CityWalk. The proprietor played maternal TV roles on *My Three Sons*, *Remington Steele* and *The New Adventures of Superman*. **❺**

Doubletree Pasadena 191 N Los Robles Ave, Pasadena ☏626/792-2727, ⓦ www.doubletreepasadena.com. Located in the cheesy, postmodern Plaza de las Fuentes, an imposing pastel creation with Spanish Revival touches like Mission-style arches and bright, fancy tiling. Luxury rooms have decent amenities, but location is the best feature, near Old Pasadena and grand municipal buildings like City Hall. **❼**

Motel 6 12775 Encinitas Ave, Sylmar ☏818/362-9491, ⓦ www.motel6.com. On the northern tip of the Valley near the 5 freeway, a budget chain motel with small, clean rooms, providing good access to sights near San Fernando and, further north, to Magic Mountain. **❷**

Ramada Inn Burbank 2900 N San Fernando Rd ☏818/843-5955, ⓦ www.ramada.com. An acceptable choice if you want somewhere to stay near the Burbank Airport, with bar, restaurant, free shuttle, clean rooms (some with microwaves) and a location that's within a reasonably short drive of the city's movie studios and, to the north, the Verdugo Mountains. **❺**

Ritz-Carlton Huntington 1401 S Oak Knoll Ave, Pasadena ☏626/568-3900, ⓦ www.ritzcarlton.com. Utterly luxurious and refurbished landmark 1906 hotel, built by master architect Charles Whittlesey and

located in residential Pasadena on an imposing hilltop. Palatial grounds, ponds and courtyards, three restaurants, expansive rear lawn and terrific San Gabriel Valley views. Rooms with marble and wood are a bit on the small side, but quite elegant, and suites can run well over $500. For even bigger bucks, inquire about the private bungalows. **❽**

Safari Inn 1911 W Olive St, Burbank ☏818/845-8586, ⓦ www.anabelle-safari.com. A classic mid-century motel, renovated but still loaded with Pop-architecture touches (tiki and googie styles). Features a pool, fitness room, Burbank airport shuttle and in-room fridges, with some suites also available. **❺**

Sheraton Universal 333 Universal Terrace, Universal City ☏818/980-1212 or 1-800/325-3535, ⓦ www.starwood.com. A large and luxurious high-rise hotel on the Universal Studios lot, with health club, spa, pool and good restaurant, and well-designed rooms with superior valley views. Easily visible and accessible off the 101 freeway. **❽**

Sportsmen's Lodge 12825 Ventura Blvd, Studio City ☏818/769-4700, ⓦ www.slhotel.com. As much of a retro-1960s experience as you're likely to get in LA, an old-time multistory motel built around a pool, with Jacuzzi, quaint gardens, exercise room, on-site restaurant and thirteen suites. True to the lodge's time-warp character, most of the 177 basic rooms are decorated with tacky, color-clashing decor. **❻**

Universal City Hilton 555 Universal Terrace, Universal City ☏818/506-2500, ⓦ www.hilton.com. A sleek high-rise neighbor to the *Sheraton Universal*, with similar appointments and amenities – pool, spa and health club – though a much better-looking steel-and-glass edifice. Rooms are nicely furnished and very close to CityWalk. **❽**

Vagabond Inn 1203 E Colorado Blvd at Michigan Ave, Pasadena ☏626/449-3170, ⓦ www.vagabondinn.com. Friendly budget chain motel, usefully placed for exploring Pasadena, with clean rooms and limited amenities. A similar *Vagabond Inn* is located at 120 W Colorado St in nearby Glendale ☏818/240-1700. Both **❹**

Malibu and the Santa Monica Mountains

Casa Malibu Inn 22752 PCH ☎310/456-2219. Located opposite Carbon Beach and featuring superb, well-appointed rooms – facing either the beach or a courtyard garden – with great modern design and some in-room fireplaces and balconies. ❺

Channel Road Inn 219 W Channel Rd at PCH ☎310/459-1920, ⓦwww.channelroadinn.com. The former house of oil baron Thomas McCall, built in 1910, offers fourteen rooms in a romantic getaway nestled in Pacific Palisades, in lower Santa Monica Canyon, with ocean views, a hot tub and free bike rental. Eat free grapes and sip champagne in the sumptuous rooms, each priced according to the view, size and amenities, from the simple Garden Room to a suite with four-poster bed and capacious living room. ❼–❾

Good Nite Inn 26557 Agoura Rd, Calabasas ☎818/880-6000 or 1-800/NITE-INN, ⓦwww.good-nite.com/calabasas.html. Double-decker chain motel with a pool and spa, offering clean rooms at affordable rates in a rustic suburb on the north side of the Santa Monica Mountains. A ten-minute drive to the ocean. ❷

Malibu Beach Inn 22878 PCH ☎310/456-6445 or 1-800/4-MALIBU, ⓦwww.malibubeachinn.com. Sunny pink Spanish Colonial resort by the Malibu Pier. With Southwest design, in-room fireplaces, tiled bathtubs, seaward balconies, VCRs, continental breakfast and oceanside hotel deck. Wooden ceilings and quaint period-revival touches add to the charm. ❽

Malibu Country Inn 6506 Westward Beach Rd ☎310/457-9622, ⓦwww.malibucountryinn.com. Just off PCH near Zuma Beach and Point Dume, a bed-and-breakfast with well-appointed rooms, Jacuzzis and refrigerators, with each unit having a different style and separate views of either the ocean, on-site gardens or Santa Monica Mountains. Ten garden-view rooms go for around $150, while five "mini-suites" cost more than $200. ❻

Malibu Riviera Motel 28920 PCH ☎310/457-9503. Quiet place outside town, less than a mile from the beach, with clean and basic rooms, a sundeck and Jacuzzi. Fairly isolated from the rest of the city. ❺

Malibu Surfer Motel 22541 PCH ☎310/456-6169, ⓦwww.malibusurfmo.qpg.com. Frightful interior decor, with eye-straining shag carpets and clashing colors, but just across from the beach and boasting king-sized beds, refrigerators and TVs. ❹

Topanga Ranch Motel 18711 PCH ☎310/456-5486, ⓦwww.topangaranchmotel.com. Thirty old-fashioned cottages painted red and white, with simple, no-frills decor; located a few blocks from the beach, not far from the intersection of PCH and Topanga Canyon Blvd. ❹

Anaheim around Disneyland

Best Western Stovall's Inn 1110 W Katella Ave ☎714/778-1880, ⓦwww.stovallshotels .com/stovall. Once heralded as the *Inn of Tomorrow* and featuring all manner of goofy, *Jetsons*-style decor, this motel has since been remodeled into elementary, no-frills accommodations, at fairly cheap prices for the area. ❸

Courtyard by Marriott 7621 Beach Blvd, Buena Park ☎714/670-6600, ⓦwww.courtyard.com/snabp. The best bet for visiting Knott's Berry Farm, and a good choice for its business-oriented accommodations, with refrigerators, pool and spa, on-site bar and restaurant, and comfortable overall setting. ❺

Desert Palm Inn and Suites 631 W Katella Ave ☎1-800/635-5423, ⓦwww.anaheimdesertpalm.com. Comfortable rooms with refrigerators, microwaves, VCRs and continental breakfast. Conventions in town make prices jump, but the *Inn* usually offers good amenities at agreeable rates. ❺

Disneyland Grand Californian 1600 S Disneyland Drive ☎714/956-6425, ⓦdisneyland.com/resort. Massive resort supposedly built in the spirit of Craftsman design, but mostly a lot of pseudo-rustic brown-and-green kitsch. Still, a pool, fitness room and day-care center offer some temptation to parents, along with the comfortable, well-furnished rooms (in rather tacky colors, though). ❽

Disneyland Hotel 1150 W Cerritos Ave at West St ☎714/956-6400, ⓦdisneyland.com/resort. The place to go for a pricey Disney-themed wedding with Mickey in attendance. Crude, cookie-cutter rooms in a huge, monolithic establishment, plus several pools, faux beach and interior shopping outlets. The Disneyland monorail stops right outside – though park admission is separate. **❽**

Disneyland Pacific Pier 1717 S Disneyland Drive ☏714/956-6425, ⊛disneyland.com/resort. Renovated concrete complex turned into overflow accommodation for park visitors; location is further from the main theme park than its counterpart on Cerritos Avenue, but shuttles are available and rooms are slightly cheaper, with the same general amenities and massive scale. **❼**

Holiday Inn Anaheim at the Park 1221 S Harbor Blvd ☏714/758-0900, ⊛www.holiday-inn.com. Safe, clean lodging not far from the Magic Kingdom, offering standard rooms with limited amenities. **❺**

Motel 6 2920 W Chapman Ave ☏714/634-2441, ⊛www.motel6.com. Unexciting chain-motel rooms, but given the surrounding options, the best bargain in the area. **❷**

Park Place Inn 1544 S Harbor Blvd ☏714/776-4800, ⊛www.stovallshotels.com/park_place. Reliable member of a nationwide chain, offering the *Best Western*'s typically clean rooms and adequate services. **❸**

Pavilions 1176 W Katella Ave ☏714/776-0140, ⊛www.stovallshotels.com/pavilion. Conveniently located and reasonable chain hotel, with basic rooms with refrigerators, plus pool, spa, sauna, and shuttle to Disneyland. **❸**

Red Roof Inn 1251 N Harbor Blvd ☏714/635-6461, ⊛www.redroof.com. One of the more worthwhile options in town, offering rooms with fridges and microwaves, pool, spa and free shuttle to Disneyland, about three miles away. **❸**

The Orange County coast

Doryman's Inn 2102 W Ocean Front, Newport Beach ☏714/675-7300, ⊛www.dorymansinn.com. Lovely historic B&B built in 1921 and located near the tip of Balboa Peninsula, overlooking the sands and offering eleven rooms with fireplaces, old-fashioned tubs (and a few Jacuzzis) and rooftop patio. **❽**

Hilton Waterfront Beach Resort 21100 PCH, Huntington Beach ☏714/960-7873, ⊛www.hilton.com. A towering high-rise with nicely furnished rooms and the added

attractions of private balconies, serpentine pool, spa and rentals of everything from surfboards to rollerblades. **❼**

Hotel Laguna 425 S Coast Hwy, Laguna Beach ☏949/494-1151, ⊛www.hotellaguna.com. In the center of Laguna Beach, near the throngs of tourist crowds. If you have the cash, this is the place to spend it. Nearly every comfortable room has an ocean view, though price of room depends on quality of view. **❺–❽**

Little Inn by the Bay 2627 Newport Blvd, Newport Beach ☏949/673-8800, ⊛www.littleinnbythebay.com. Eighteen nice, comfortable rooms near Newport Beach; the cheapest accommodation in the area, with in-room fridges, microwaves and complimentary breakfast. Close to Balboa Peninsula. **❹**

Mission Inn 26891 Ortega Hwy at I-5, San Juan Capistrano ☏949/493-1151. Rooms at this reasonably priced place come with use of Jacuzzi and pool. Located in a distant Orange County city, but close enough to the main draw, the old Spanish Mission. **❹**

Ocean View Motel 16196 PCH, Huntington Beach ☏562/592-2700. Family-run roadside establishment with tidy rooms off the main drag. As a bonus, get a jacuzzi in your room for an extra $15. **❸**

Ritz-Carlton Laguna Niguel PCH at Ritz Carlton Drive, Dana Point ☏949/240-2000 or 1-800/241-3333, ⊛www.ritzcarlton.com. Another of the palatial *Ritz-Carlton*s, with prime beach access and striking ocean views. Also with pool, racquet club, spa, surfing, boating, kayaking, and nicely refined suites with chic design and abundant space. Worth a stay if you have the money and don't mind driving halfway to San Diego. **❾**

Seacliff Motel 1661 S Coast Hwy, Laguna Beach ☏714/494-9717, ⊛www.seaclifflaguna.com. Unexceptional, rather dull accommodations, but right on the ocean and near an appealing section of Laguna Beach. Rates jump if you want a room with a sea view or a balcony. **❺–❼**

Seal Beach Inn and Gardens 212 Fifth St, Seal Beach ☏562/493-2416, ⊛www.sealbeachinn.com. Although located in a drab and uneventful burg, a fine bed-and-breakfast offering impressive furnishings two blocks from the sands. Rooms on lower level are interesting, with myriad appointments and antiques, but the best room, the exquisite Honeysuckle Suite, is up top overlooking the oceanside. **❼**

Surf and Sand Resort 1555 S Coast Hwy, Laguna Beach ☎949/497-4477 or 1-800/524-8621, ⓦwww.surfandsandresort.com. One of the best of the Orange County coast hotels, with terrific oceanside views, easy beach access, and numerous luxurious rooms and suites with many features, including balconies. Three penthouses are available to the true swells. **❾**

Sutton Place 4500 MacArthur Blvd, Newport Beach ☎949/476-2001 or 1-800/810-6888, ⓦwww.suttonplace.com/Newportbeach. Rather forbidding-looking hotel that features good amenities – pool, spa, tennis courts, restaurant, bar, shuttle to John Wayne Airport – and attractive, spacious rooms for a manageable price. **❻**

Hostels

As you might expect, **hostels** are found at the bottom of the price scale, offering sex-segregated dorm rooms and beds going for somewhere around $15–19. Many hostels also offer cut-rate single and double rooms. You can expect little more from your stay than a clean, safe bed, somewhere to lock your valuables, and a typically colorful crowd of visitors – this being Southern California. Some hostels also offer tours of surrounding areas (mostly tourist-friendly theme parks, shopping malls and stars' homes jaunts), while others organize social events – volleyball, pizza parties and the like. There's often a three-to-five night maximum stay, though this is generally enforced only when demand outstrips supply.

Adventure Hostel 527 Knickerbocker Rd, Big Bear Lake ☎1-866/866-5255, ⓦwww.adventurehostel.com. One of the region's best bets if you've got a car, a scenic mountainside locale with plenty of activities throughout the year, from skiing and snowboarding in winter to jet-skiing, hiking and parasailing in summer. Two-hour drive from LA; the only public buses run from San Bernardino (☎909/808-5465). Dorm rooms $20, private rooms $60 and up.

Banana Bungalow-Hollywood Hotel 2775 Cahuenga Blvd W, in the Cahuenga Pass ☎323/851-1129 or 1-800/446-7835, ⓦwww.bananabungalow.com. Popular, large hostel near Universal City and US-101, with free airport shuttles, tours to Venice Beach and Magic Mountain, and a relaxed, zoned-out atmosphere. Outdoor pool, free parking, and as much beer as you can drink every second night for $3. Dorms $18–21 and more expensive private doubles at $60 and up.

HI-Anaheim/Fullerton 1700 N Harbor Blvd at Brea, Fullerton ☎714/738-3721, ⓦwww.hostelweb.com/losangeles/fullerton .htm. Convenient and comfortable, five miles north of Disneyland on the site of a former dairy farm, with a rural, isolated feel. The hostel's numerous facilities include a grass volleyball court, golf driving range

and picnic area, along with fireplace, libraries and laundry facilities. Make reservations first – there are only 22 beds. Summer check-in from 5–11pm, rest of year 4–11pm. Mornings open 8am–noon. OCTA bus #43 stops outside. Members $15, nonmembers $18.

HI-LA/Santa Monica 1436 Second St, Santa Monica ☎310/393-9913, ⓦwww.hostelweb.com/losangeles/los_angeles .htm. A few blocks from the beach and pier, the building was LA's Town Hall from 1887 to 1889, and retains its historic charm, with inner courtyard, ivy-covered walls and a skylight. Members $25, nonmembers $28; private rooms for $66 and $72 – all prices include laundry machines and kitchen use. Smoking and drinking prohibited. Reservations essential in summer. Open 24 hours.

HI-LA/South Bay 3601 S Gaffey St, Bldg #613, San Pedro ☎310/831-8109, ⓦwww.hostelweb.com/losangeles/south_bay .htm. Sixty beds in an old US Army barracks, with panoramic view of the Pacific. Ideal for seeing San Pedro, Palos Verdes and the whole Harbor area, and directly adjacent to Angels Gate Park, Cabrillo Beach and Point Fermin. Open 7am–midnight. $15 members, $18 nonmembers; private rooms $37 and $40 per person. MTA bus #446 passes close by, but it's a two-hour journey from downtown. Can also take SuperShuttle from LAX.

Hollywood International Hostel 6820 Hollywood Blvd ☎323/463-0797 or 1-800/750-6561, ⓦ www.hollywoodhostels.com. One of three good-value locations in the area, this one in the heart of Hollywood, with free tea and coffee, game room, gymnasium, barbecues, patio garden, kitchen and laundry. Tours of Hollywood offered, as well as tours beyond the immediate area to theme parks, Las Vegas and Tijuana. Shared rooms start at $16 and reach $40 and over for private rooms.

Hostel California 2221 Lincoln Blvd at Venice Blvd, Venice ☎310/305-0250, ⓦ hostelcalifornia.hypermart.net. LA's first hostel, several miles from Venice Beach in a somewhat seedy commercial section of town. Twelve six-bed dorms with kitchens, pool table, big-screen TV, linen and parking. Free shuttle bus from LAX. $12 dorm rooms, private rooms $34.

Huntington Beach Colonial Inn Hostel 421 Eighth St at Pecan, Huntington Beach ☎714/536-3315, ⓦ www.huntingtonbeachhostel.com. Four blocks from the beach, mostly double rooms. Easy access to Disneyland and Knott's Berry Farm. Sleeping bags allowed. Open 8am–11pm. No curfew, but night key (available with $20 deposit) required for entrance after 11pm. Dorms $20, private rooms $22.50 per person.

Orange Drive Manor 1764 N Orange Drive, Hollywood ☎323/850-0350, ⓦ orangedrivehostel.com. Centrally located hostel (right behind the Chinese Theatre) offering tours of film studios, theme parks, and homes of the stars. Dorms $18, private rooms $36.

Orbit Hotel 7950 Melrose Ave ☎323/655-1510

or 1-877/ORBIT-US, ⓦ www.orbithotel.com. Assertively retro-1960s hotel and hostel with sleek Day-Glo furnishings and ultra-hip modern decor, offering complimentary breakfast, movie screening room, patio, café, private baths in all rooms, shuttle tours and $20-per-day car rental. Located just west of the most frenetic and colorful part of Melrose. Dorm rooms $19, private rooms $49.

Surf City Hostel 26 Pier Ave, Hermosa Beach ☎310/798-2323 or 1-800/305-2901, ⓦ www.lasurfcityhostel.com. Terrific location (though in a nondescript concrete building with a hard-to-find entrance) near popular beachside strip, the Strand, and near numerous restaurants, clubs and bars. Shared rooms from $17 or private double rooms from $45. Also with kitchen, laundry, beer parties, and shuttles to Disneyland and other major theme parks and shopping zones.

USA Hostels – Hollywood 1624 Schrader Ave ☎323/462-3777 or 1-800/LA-HOSTEL, ⓦ www.usahostels.com. A block south of the center of Hollywood Boulevard, near major attractions and with game room, private baths, main bar, Internet access, tours of region and garden patio, as well as airport and train shuttles. Shared rooms $16–19 and private rooms from $40.

Venice Beach Cotel 25 Windward Ave, Venice ☎310/399-7649, ⓦ www.venicebeachcotel .com. Occupying what's left of the old colonnade, with trompe l'oeil Venetian-style windows and painted-on people peering out, this is one of the stranger-looking hostels in LA. Directly near the Venice Boardwalk and Muscle Beach, with car-rental discounts, shared rooms at $15–18 and private rooms from $35–49. Also with door-to-door trips to major theme parks, homes of the stars, and Getty Center, plus complimentary boogie boards.

Campgrounds

A company called Reserve America (☎1-800/444-7275, ⓦ www.reserveamerica.com) processes reservations at many of the **campgrounds** listed below and can look for an alternative if your chosen site is full. It charges a $7 fee per reservation per night up to a maximum of eight people per site, including one vehicle. Campgrounds on Santa Catalina Island are processed through the Catalina Island Company (☎310/510-8368, ⓦ www.scico.com/camping), which charges $12 for adult use, $6 for kids, and usually requires reservations.

Island transportation by boat or bus is not included; see box on p.174 for more details on getting around the area.

Blackjack Campground Santa Catalina Island ☎310/510-8368. Not for the timid – an isolated site high in the trees near the island's center, a rugged nine-mile trek from the nearest town in Avalon (which has its own, much tamer *Hermit Gulch*, below), with limited facilities except for barbecues, fire pits, toilets and showers. $12.

Bolsa Chica Campground Huntington Beach ☎1-800/444-7275. Facing the ocean just north of Huntington Beach, near a wildlife sanctuary and bird-watchers' paradise (see p.217). $18 for campers with a self-contained vehicle. No tent camping.

Chilao Flat on Hwy-2 twenty miles northeast of Pasadena ☎626/574-1613. The only campground in the San Gabriel Mountains reachable by car, though there are many others accessible on foot. For more details contact the Angeles National Forest Ranger Station at 701 N Santa Anita Ave, Arcadia ☎626/574-1613. $18.

Crystal Cove State Park Orange County coast ☎1-800/444-7275. With two thousand woodland acres and nearly four miles of beach, a distant outpost in Orange County (between Laguna and Newport beaches) with much natural appeal; recreational activities include scuba diving, bicycling, swimming, and exploring the tide pools or craggy beachside coves throughout the park. $18.

Dockweiler Beach County Park Playa del Rey ☎310/305-9545. On a noisy stretch of Vista del Mar, almost at the western end of the LAX runways. Not a pretty beach and can be polluted at times, but good enough for watching waves and suntanning. Mainly for RVs; tent sites by reservation only for $18–24.

Doheny State Beach Campground Dana Point ☎949/496-6171 or 1-800/444-7275. Often packed with families, especially at weekends. Located at southern end of Orange County, not far from Dana Point Harbor. $12–24.

Hermit Gulch Campground Avalon ☎310/510-8368. Only a mile and a half from the boat launch at Avalon, a Santa Catalina Island campground popular and easy to access, with barbecues, picnic tables, and even a microwave and a few tepees. While not for the adventurous, it provides a good jumping-off point for exploring the island. $12.

Leo Carrillo State Beach Park northern Malibu ☎818/706-1310 or 1-800/444-7275. Near one of LA's best surfing beaches, 25 miles northwest of Santa Monica on Pacific Coast Highway, and served twice an hour in summer by MTA bus #434. Not far from the end of Mulholland Highway. $12–37.

Malibu Creek State Park 1925 Las Virgenes Rd, in the Santa Monica Mountains ☎818/706-8809 or 1-800/444-7275. A rustic campground in a park which can become crowded at times. Sixty sites in the shade of huge oak trees, almost all with fire pits, solar-heated showers and flush toilets. One-time filming location for *Planet of the Apes* and the TV show *M*A*S*H*. $12–45.

Parsons Landing Santa Catalina Island ☎310/510-8368. Remote site on the northern tip of the island; eight camp sites with no showers or fresh water, though offering fire rings, picnic tables and, for a fee from a lockbox, firewood and bottled water. Boating in is the obvious choice for arrival, although the site is accessible on foot, located seven miles from Two Harbors. $12.

San Clemente State Beach Campground 3030 Avenida del Presidente, two miles south of San Clemente ☎949/492-3156 or ☎1-800/444-7275. A prime spot for hiking, diving and surfing, around an area that was once home to Richard Nixon's "Western White House." $20 for hook-up sites, $12 for others.

Two Harbors Campground Santa Catalina Island ☎310/510-8368. Located on a lovely, rugged isthmus near the center of the island, this tourist-oriented campground offers the standard tent sites, along with "Catalina Cabins" for $30–35, which provide amenities like refrigerators and heaters. $12 a night for a standard tent site.

Restaurants and cafés

anging from the most exclusive supper clubs to the dingiest burger shacks, LA's countless **restaurants** and **cafés** cover every extreme. Whatever you want to eat and however much you want to spend, there are always plenty of choices, from trendy hybrids of international cuisines to good and cheap ethnic food. Besides the fast-food drive-ins that were invented here, LA is the birthplace of such enduring favorites as the cheeseburger, hot fudge sundae, French dip sandwich and Caesar salad, adding them to America's, and the world's, cuisine. As well, LA is littered with celebrity-owned outfits like *Planet Hollywood* and the *Hard Rock Café,* but the food is usually so unremarkable that we haven't listed them.

For many of the restaurants listed, you won't need to **reserve** ahead, though you should make the effort on weekends, during major holidays and at the most expensive or trendy places. For **dinner**, expect to pay $5–10 per person for simple fast food, $15–20 for most ethnic and old-fashioned American restaurants, and $30–60 for the latest hot spots of any sort. To sample great food without paying a bundle, go for **lunch** at those upscale eateries that offer it, where prices around $15–25 are common. Consider, too, the all-you-can-eat **buffets** at certain cafeteria-style restaurants that usually run $8–12. The price breaks do not, however, continue downward at those establishments that offer **breakfast**, and unless you're going for a rock-bottom meal at *Denny's* or at *Norm's* diners, you'll end up paying $10–15 for any sort of edible morning meal.

If you simply want to fill up quickly and cheaply, the options are nearly endless, and include free food (mostly bar fare like chicken wings and mozzarella sticks) available for the price of a drink during **happy hours**. However, you should also try to take at least a few meals in LA's top-notch restaurants, which serve superb food in self-consciously chic surroundings.

No matter where you choose to eat, though, don't reach for a cigarette – health-conscious LA banned **smoking** in 1993, and the state of California then followed with a blanket tobacco prohibition in restaurants and most bars.

Cuisines

Budget food is, of course, plentiful in LA, ranging from good sit-down meals in street-corner coffee shops to burger chains. Almost as common, and just as cheap, is **Mexican food**, the closest thing you'll get to an indigenous LA cuisine. Mexican burrito stands and lunch-counters are often the city's best deals, serving tasty, healthy and filling food for as little as $5 per person; they're at their most authentic in East LA, although there's a good selection of more Americanized examples all over the city. The cuisines of the rest of **Latin America** have made inroads, from the flavors of Honduras and Nicaragua and the blending of Peruvian cuisine with local seafood (aka "Peruvian seafood"), to the hot, garlicky platters of Argentine beef available throughout the Westside.

The city lacks a wide selection of **African** restaurants, other than those based on the cuisines of North Africa. Those that do exist are mainly found in Hollywood and Mid-Wilshire. **Moroccan** food is typically good, though not concentrated in any one neighborhood, and is sometimes served with a colorful floor show of belly dancing and the like, while the best **Ethiopian** restaurants are in a small pocket around Olympic Boulevard in Mid-Wilshire, and are fairly inexpensive. Aside from such singular cuisines, pan-African hybrids have made some headway on the menus of adventurous restaurants, mixing the grains, spices and vegetables of Africa with the foods of the Caribbean, Europe and the American South.

Old-fashioned **American** cuisine, with its steaks, ribs, baked potatoes and mountainous salads, has a deceptively low profile in faddish LA, although it's available almost everywhere, costing as little as $10 for a caloric blowout in a roadside diner, to well over $70 for a choice porterhouse served amid chandeliers and cherry-wood booths – typically in a luxury steakhouse chain. Much more conspicuous, and trendier, is the juggernaut of **California cuisine**, which not only adds new twists to American cooking, but often combines with other cuisines (Japanese, Indian, etc) to produce some unusual entrees. In its original form, "Cal-cuisine" uses fresh, locally available ingredients, more likely grilled than fried, and is stylishly presented with a nod to French *nouvelle cuisine*. Spicy **Cajun** food is affordable as well as enjoyable, and there are a number of fine establishments sprinkled throughout the region, as well as the token jambalaya that pops up on the occasional menu.

Unlike many ethnic cuisines in LA, those from the **Caribbean** – Jamaican, Cuban and the like – are more visible in West LA and Santa Monica than in Hollywood. With few exceptions, local Caribbean restaurants leave subtlety behind in exchange for sweat-inducing flavors and spices, added to staples like plantains, yucca root and jerked chicken.

LA's most fashionable districts offer many delicious **Chinese** and dim sum restaurants, favored by Far East immigrants and fast-lane yuppies alike, which can easily set you back $30. More authentic and less pricey outlets tend to be located Downtown, notably in Chinatown, where you can get a good-sized meal for $10–15. **Vietnamese** food is slowly catching on in LA restaurants, and is worth checking out when you can find it; your best bet, though, may be to venture into the Orange County suburbs of Santa Ana or Westminster, where growing numbers of Vietnamese immigrants operate inexpensive food stands and diners.

Predictably, **French** restaurants are among LA's fanciest and most expensive, with most blending traditional and *nouvelle* cuisines. On the other hand, LA's **Greek** restaurants provide rich, fairly traditional entrees for cheap prices, but are fairly thin on the ground, sometimes better known for their spirited nightly singing and dancing than for their menus.

Indian and **Sri Lankan** restaurants are growing in popularity – with restaurant menus embracing Californian dishes to create hybrids like curry polenta and duck tandoori, though more traditional meals are almost always offered as well. Most of the Indian restaurants in Hollywood or West LA charge $15–20 for a full meal, less for a vegetarian Indian dish. **Pakistani** variants on Indian cuisine can be equally delicious, though of course without pork ingredients, and are located in roughly the same areas as Indian eateries.

After decades of having nothing more exotic than takeout pizza chains, LA is now home to some of the country's best regional Italian restaurants, with those specializing in northern Italian food usually being the most expensive and trendy. That said, as common as it is, Italian food can also be quite variable in quality, often little more than bland, mealy piles of pasta, particularly at southern Italian places. A more appealing phenomenon is the **designer pizza**, invented at Hollywood's (now closed) *Spago* restaurant by celebrity chef Wolfgang Puck, and topped with duck, shiitake mushrooms, or whatever comes to mind. None of this comes cheap, however: the least elaborate designer pizza will set you back around $15. On the other hand, LA's **pizza** joints are generally good and affordable, even if some have given in and incorporated nouveau stylings into their menus.

Japanese cuisine is available throughout LA in a wide range of prices, styles and settings. Not surprisingly, Little Tokyo is a good place for sushi, with *udon* and *soba* spots more noticeable as you head further west, and more authentic fare concentrated in the immigrant center of Gardena. Along with French cooking, Japanese cuisine is one of the favorites used by California-cuisine chefs for their culinary experiments, making many "Japanese" restaurants more international in style, and good representatives of the city's latest cultural and gastronomic trends. But if you just want a simple bowl of noodles that isn't priced at a premium, there are plenty of those choices as well throughout the city.

Outside Koreatown, **Korean** cuisine tends to be limited to isolated pockets in the Westside and the northern suburbs. Spicy barbecued ribs and *kim chee* (pickled cabbage) are among the more traditional dishes, both worth a try; expect to pay under $20 per person for a good-sized meal.

The growing number of **Middle Eastern** restaurants can be affordably good. Aside from citywide falafel and pita chains, excellent examples of this cuisine are found in strip-mall ethnic eateries, and in health-food or vegetarian restaurants, where the old-style Levantine cooking becomes all but unrecognizable, containing ingredients such as avocado, bean sprouts, tofu and kasha.

Russian and **Eastern European** restaurants are uncommon in LA outside of isolated ethnic enclaves – particularly present in Mid-Wilshire and the eastern side of West Hollywood. For the most part, you can expect authentic dishes, though prices tend to vary, depending on the neighborhood and the type of restaurant.

Although **seafood** is offered throughout LA in a variety of styles, from Peruvian to nouveau American, there are plenty of worthwhile seafood-only restaurants in the city, predominantly along the coast, with a strong concentration near Malibu and Newport Beach. However, some oceanside restaurants (especially those decorated with a nautical theme) are better for their views than their food, and by venturing just a mile or so inland, you can find a better meal than you might at a restaurant located within sight of whales, seagulls and tourists.

Although it sometimes figures in California cuisine, **Spanish** cooking, along with **tapas bars**, hasn't made much of a dent in LA's culinary culture, and is often lumped in with a generalized pan-European cooking or, less often, with Latin American cuisine. Where they do exist, such restaurants are a good spot for a refreshing pitcher of sangría and good seafood and pork dishes.

Considering all of LA's options for East Asian cuisines, authentic **Thai** food might be the best deal, both for its succulent, spicy flavors and reasonable prices. The best restaurants are usually the least pretentious, found in the less trendy sections of town, such as mini-malls in Hollywood and run-down store-fronts in Mid-Wilshire. If you don't mind sacrificing atmosphere for delicious food, a trip to such ignoble environs is usually well rewarded.

Finally, mind- and body-fixated LA has a wide variety of **vegetarian** and **wholefood** restaurants, the bulk of them on the Westside and many along the

Restaurant directory

What follows is a list of all restaurants reviewed in this chapter, sorted by cuisine. To find the review, simply refer back to the relevant neighborhood section listed as a subheading underneath the cuisine.

African
Mid-Wilshire
Nyala 1076 S Fairfax Ave
Rosalind's 1044 S Fairfax Ave
Hollywood
Dar Maghreb 7651 Sunset Blvd
Moun of Tunis 7445 Sunset Blvd
Beverly Hills and West LA
Koutoubia 2116 Westwood Blvd, West LA
The San Gabriel and San Fernando valleys
Langano 14838 Burbank Blvd, Sherman Oaks
Marrakesh 13003 Ventura Blvd, Studio City

American, Californian and Cajun
Downtown
Checkers Restaurant 535 S Grand Ave
Engine Co. No. 28 644 S Figueroa St
L.A. Prime 404 S Figueroa St
New Moon 102 W Ninth St
Pacific Dining Car 1310 W Sixth St
Water Grill 544 S Grand Ave
Mid-Wilshire
Atlas 3760 Wilshire Blvd
Ca' Brea 346 S La Brea Ave
Flora Kitchen 460 S La Brea Ave
The Gumbo Pot 6333 W Third St
Patina 5955 Melrose Ave
Sabor Too 3221 Pico Blvd
Taylor's 3361 W Eighth St
Hollywood
Hollywood Canteen 1006 N Seward St
Musso and Frank Grill 6667

Hollywood Blvd
Off Vine 6263 Leland Way
Pig 'n Whistle 6714 Hollywood Blvd
Pinot Hollywood 1448 Gower St
vermont 1714 N Vermont Ave
Vida 1930 Hillhurst Ave, Los Feliz
West Hollywood
Café La Boheme 8400 Santa Monica Blvd
The Cajun Bistro 8301 Sunset Blvd
Jar 8225 Beverly Blvd
Beverly Hills and West LA
Arnie Morton's 435 N La Cienega Blvd
Café Blanc 9777 Little Santa Monica Blvd
The Cheesecake Factory 364 N Beverly Drive
The Daily Grill 11677 San Vicente Blvd
Maple Drive 345 N Maple Drive
Spago 176 N Cañon Drive
Santa Monica, Venice and Malibu
Crocodile Café 101 Santa Monica Blvd, Santa Monica
Flint's 3321 Pico Blvd, Santa Monica
Granita 23725 W Malibu Rd, Malibu
Hal's 1349 Abbot Kinney Blvd, Venice
Joe's 1023 Abbot Kinney Blvd, Venice
LA Farm 3000 W Olympic Blvd, Santa Monica
Michael's 1147 Third St, Santa Monica
17th Street Café 1610 Montana Ave, Santa Monica
South Central and East LA
Harold and Belle's 2920 Jefferson Blvd, South Central

coast as well. Some vegetarian places can be very good value ($5 or so), but watch out for those that flaunt themselves as a New Age experience and include soporific music and a gift shop selling crystals and pyramids – these can be three times as costly.

If you'd rather have a picnic than visit a restaurant, try the Trader Joe's chain – which started as a liquor store with a sideline in unusual food, but now sells imported cheeses, breads and canned foods – or the area's frequent **farmers markets**, loaded with organic produce and frequently advertised in the press.

The San Gabriel and San Fernando valleys
Monty's Steakhouse 595 S Fair Oaks Ave, Pasadena
Saddle Peak Lodge 419 Cold Canyon Rd, Calabasas
Orange County
Aubergine 508 29th St, Newport Beach
Bistro 201 3333 PCH, Newport Beach
The Cottage 308 N Coast Hwy, Laguna Beach
Five Crowns 3801 E Coast Hwy, Corona del Mar
Jack Shrimp 2400 W Coast Hwy, Newport Beach

Caribbean
Mid-Wilshire
Prado 244 N Larchmont Blvd
Hollywood
El Floridita 1253 N Vine St
Havana on Sunset 5825 Sunset Blvd
Beverly Hills and West LA
Bamboo 10835 Venice Blvd
Versailles 10319 Venice Blvd
Santa Monica, Venice and Malibu
Babalu 1002 Montana Ave, Santa Monica
The San Gabriel and San Fernando valleys
Kingston Café 333 S Fair Oaks Ave, Pasadena
Xiomara 69 N Raymond Ave, Pasadena
The South Bay and LA Harbor
Cha Cha Cha 762 Pacific Ave, Long Beach

Chinese and Vietnamese
Downtown
Grand Star Restaurant 934 Sun Mun Way

Mandarin Deli 727 N Broadway
Mon Kee 679 N Spring St
Ocean Seafood 750 N Hill St
Pho 79 727 N Broadway
Yang Chow 819 N Broadway
Mid-Wilshire
Genghis Cohen 740 N Fairfax Ave
Lucky Duck 672 S La Brea Ave
Hollywood
Little Hong Kong Deli 1645 N Cahuenga Blvd
Taipan 7075 Sunset Blvd
West Hollywood
Chin Chin 8618 Sunset Blvd
Joss 9255 Sunset Blvd
Beverly Hills and West LA
Chung King 11538 W Pico Blvd, West LA
Eurochow 1099 Westwood Blvd, Westwood
Mr Chow 344 N Camden Drive, Beverly Hills
Pho Bac Huynh 11819 Wilshire Blvd, West LA
Santa Monica, Venice and Malibu
Chinois on Main 2709 Main St, Santa Monica
P F Chang's 326 Wilshire Blvd, Santa Monica
The San Gabriel and San Fernando valleys
City Wok 10949 Ventura Blvd, Studio City
Sea Star 914 W Beacon St, Alhambra
Orange County
Anh Hong 10195 Westminster Ave, Garden Grove
Favori 3502 W First St, Santa Ana
Hue Rendezvous 15562 Brookhurst St, Westminster

continued overleaf

French
Downtown
Angelique Café 840 S Spring St
Café Pinot 700 W Fifth St
Mid-Wilshire
Alex 6703 Melrose Ave
Louis XIV 606 N La Brea Ave
Mimosa 8009 Beverly Blvd
Hollywood
Café des Artistes 1534 N
McCadden Place
West Hollywood
Fenix 8358 Sunset Blvd
L'Orangerie 903 N La Cienega Blvd
*The San Gabriel and San Fernando
valleys*
Café Bizou 14016 Ventura Blvd, San
Fernando Valley
Julienne 2649 Mission St, San
Marino
Paul's Café 13456 Ventura Blvd,
San Fernando Valley

Greek
Mid-Wilshire
Le Petit Greek 127 N Larchmont Blvd
Papa Cristos 2771 W Pico Blvd
Sofi 8030 W Third St
Beverly Hills and West LA
Delphi 1383 Westwood Blvd
The South Bay and LA Harbor
Mykonos 5374 E Second St, Long
Beach
*The San Gabriel and San Fernando
valleys*
Café Santorini 70 W Union St,
Pasadena
Great Greek 13362 Ventura Blvd,
Sherman Oaks

Indian and Sri Lankan
Mid-Wilshire
New East India Grill 345 N La Brea
Ave
India's Oven 7231 Beverly Blvd
Surya 8048 W Third St
Hollywood
Electric Lotus 4656 Franklin Ave
Beverly Hills and West LA
Bombay Café 12113 Santa Monica
Blvd
The Clay Pit 3465 W Sixth St
Nizam 10871 W Pico Blvd
Santa Monica, Venice and Malibu

Nawab 1621 Wilshire Blvd, Santa
Monica
*The San Gabriel and San Fernando
valleys*
Passage to India 14062 Burbank
Blvd, Van Nuys

Italian and pizza
Downtown
California Pizza Kitchen 330 S
Hope St
Ciao Trattoria 815 W Seventh St
Cicada 617 S Olive St
Mid-Wilshire
Angeli 7274 Melrose Ave
Campanile 624 S La Brea Ave
Chianti Cucina 7383 Melrose Ave
Hollywood
Louise's Trattoria 4500 Los Feliz
Blvd
Miceli's 1646 N Las Palmas St
Palermo 1858 N Vermont Ave
West Hollywood
**Frankie & Johnnie's New York
Pizza** 8947 Sunset Blvd
Beverly Hills and West LA
Barefoot 8722 W Third St
Jacopo's 490 N Beverly Drive
Locanda Veneta 8638 W Third St
Santa Monica, Venice and Malibu
Abbot's Pizza Company 1407
Abbot Kinney Blvd, Venice
Drago 2628 Wilshire Blvd, Santa
Monica
Valentino 3115 W Pico Blvd, Santa
Monica
Wildflour Pizza 2807 Main St, Santa
Monica
Wolfgang Puck Express 1315 Third
Street Promenade, Santa Monica
The South Bay and LA Harbor
L'Opera 101 Pine St, Long Beach
Mangiamo 128 Manhattan Beach
Blvd, Manhattan Beach
*The San Fernando and San Gabriel
valleys*
Market City Caffe 36 W Colorado
Blvd #300, Pasadena
Posto 14928 Ventura Blvd, Sherman
Oaks

Japanese
Downtown
Shibucho 3114 Beverly Blvd

A Thousand Cranes 120 S Los Angeles St
Mid-Wilshire
Mishima 8474 W Third St
Sushi Roku 8445 W Third St
Hollywood
Yamashiro 1999 N Sycamore Ave
West Hollywood
Miyagi's 8225 Sunset Blvd
Todai 8612 Beverly Blvd
Beverly Hills and West LA
Matsuhisa 129 N La Cienega Blvd, Beverly Hills
Mori Sushi 11500 W Pico Blvd, West LA
The Sushi House 12013 Pico Blvd, West LA
Santa Monica, Venice and Malibu
Chaya Venice 110 Navy St, Venice
Lighthouse Buffet 201 Arizona Ave, Santa Monica
The San Gabriel and San Fernando valleys
Genmai-Sushi 4454 Van Nuys Blvd, San Fernando Valley
Shiro 1505 Mission St, South Pasadena
Sushi Nozawa 11288 Ventura Blvd, Studio City

Korean

Mid-Wilshire
Busan 203 N Western Ave
Dong Il Jang 3455 W Eighth St
Woo Lae Oak 623 S Western Ave
Santa Monica, Venice and Malibu
Monsoon Café 1212 Third St, Santa Monica
The San Gabriel and San Fernando valleys
Arirang 114 W Union St, Pasadena
Orange County
In Chon Won 13321 Brookhurst St, Garden Grove

Mexican and Latin American

Downtown
El Taurino 1104 S Hoover St, Westlake
King Taco 2904 N Broadway
La Luz del Dia 107 Paseo de la Plaza
Mid-Wilshire
Casa Carnitas 4067 Beverly Blvd

El Cholo 1121 S Western Ave
El Coyote 7312 Beverly Blvd
Mario's Peruvian Seafood 5786 Melrose Ave
Hollywood
Burrito King 2109 W Sunset Blvd
Mexico City 2121 N Hillhurst Ave
Yuca's Hut 2056 N Hillhurst Ave
West Hollywood
Carlitos Gardel 7963 Melrose Ave
El Compadre 7408 W Sunset Blvd
Poquito Mas 8555 Sunset Blvd
Beverly Hills and West LA
Baja Fresh 475 N Beverly Drive
La Salsa 11075 W Pico Blvd at Sepulveda
Monte Alban 11927 Santa Monica Blvd
Santa Monica, Venice and Malibu
The Gaucho Grill 1251 Third St, Santa Monica
Mariasol 401 Santa Monica Pier, Santa Monica
Marix Tex-Mex Playa 118 Entrada Drive, Pacific Palisades
South Central and East LA
Ciro's 705 N Evergreen Ave, East LA
El Tepayac 812 N Evergreen Ave, East LA
Luminarias 3500 Ramona Blvd, Monterey Park
Paco's Tacos 6212 W Manchester Ave, Westchester
The South Bay and LA Harbor
By Brazil 1615 Cabrillo Ave, Torrance
El Pollo Inka 11000 PCH, Hermosa Beach
Pancho's 3615 Highland Ave, Manhattan Beach
Taco Surf 5316 1/2 E Second St, Long Beach
The San Gabriel and San Fernando valleys
Izalco 10729 Burbank Blvd, North Hollywood
Merida 20 E Colorado Blvd, Pasadena
Orange County
Las Brisas 361 Cliff Drive, Laguna Beach
Taco Mesa 647 W 19th St, Costa Mesa

continued overleaf

Middle Eastern
Mid-Wilshire
Eat A Pita 465 N Fairfax Ave
Hollywood
Marouch 4905 Santa Monica Blvd
Zankou Chicken 5065 Sunset Blvd
West Hollywood
Noura Café 8479 Melrose Ave
Beverly Hills and West LA
Falafel King 1059 Broxton Ave, Westwood
Magic Carpet 8566 W Pico Blvd
Shamshiry 1916 Westwood Blvd
The San Gabriel and San Fernando valleys
Burger Continental 535 S Lake Ave, Pasadena
Carousel 304 N Brand Ave, Glendale
Orange County
Zena's 294 N Tustin St, city of Orange

Russian and Eastern European
Mid-Wilshire
Csardas 5820 Melrose Ave
Hollywood
Uzbekistan 7077 Sunset Blvd
Santa Monica, Venice and Malibu
Warszawa 1414 Lincoln Blvd, Santa Monica
The South Bay and LA Harbor
Czech Point 1981 Artesia Blvd, Redondo Beach
The San Gabriel and San Fernando valleys
Hortobagy 11138 Ventura Blvd, Studio City

Seafood
Beverly Hills and West LA
McCormick and Schmick's 206 N Rodeo Drive
Santa Monica, Venice and Malibu
Geoffrey's 27400 PCH, Malibu
Gladstone's 4 Fish 17300 PCH, Pacific Palisades
Killer Shrimp 523 Washington St, Marina del Rey
Neptune's Net 42505 PCH, Malibu
The South Bay and LA Harbor
Beluga 1500 Morningside Drive, Manhattan Beach
King's Fish House 100 W Broadway, Long Beach

Orange County
Bluewater Grill 630 Lindo Park Drive, Newport Beach
Claes Seafood 425 S Coast Hwy, Laguna Beach
Crab Cooker 2200 Newport Ave, Newport Beach
Oysters 2515 E Coast Hwy, Corona del Mar

Spanish
Downtown
Ciudad 445 S Figueroa St
Mid-Wilshire
Cobras and Matadors 7615 Beverly Blvd
Beverly Hills and West LA
Cava 8384 W Third St
The South Bay and LA Harbor
Alegria Cocina Latina 115 Pine Ave, Long Beach
Soleil 1142 Manhattan Ave, Manhattan Beach
The San Gabriel and San Fernando valleys
La Luna Negra 44 W Green St, Pasadena

Thai
Mid-Wilshire
Tommy Tang's 7313 Melrose Ave
Vim 831 S Vermont Ave
Hollywood
Chan Dara 1511 N Cahuenga Blvd
Jitlada 5233 Sunset Blvd
Thai Seafood 5615 Hollywood Blvd
Beverly Hills and West LA
Talesai 9198 Olympic Blvd, Beverly Hills
Santa Monica, Venice and Malibu
Flower of Siam 2553 Lincoln Blvd, Venice
Thai Dishes 1910 Wilshire Blvd, Santa Monica
The San Gabriel and San Fernando valleys
Kuala Lumpur 69 W Green St, Pasadena
Saladang 363 S Fair Oaks Ave, Pasadena

Vegetarian and wholefood
Mid-Wilshire
Fountain of Health 3606 W Sixth St

Inaka Natural Foods 131 S La Brea Ave	Inn of the Seventh Ray 128 Old Topanga Rd, Topanga Canyon
West Hollywood	**Mäni's Bakery** 2507 Main St, Santa Monica
Real Food Daily 414 N La Cienega Blvd	**Shambala Café** 607 Colorado Ave, Santa Monica
Beverly Hills and West LA	*The South Bay and LA Harbor*
A Votre Sante 242 S Beverly Drive, Beverly Hills	**Good Stuff** 1300 Highland Ave, Manhattan Beach
Erewhon 7660 Beverly Blvd, West LA	**Papa Jon's** 5006 E Second St, Long Beach
Newsroom Café 120 N Robertson Blvd, Beverly Hills	**The Spot** 110 Second St, Hermosa Beach
Santa Monica, Venice and Malibu	
Figtree's Café 429 Ocean Front Walk, Venice	

Coffee shops, delis and diners

Budget food is everywhere in LA, at its best in the many small **coffee shops**, **delis** and **diners** that serve soups, omelets, sandwiches and a slew of comfort food. It's easy to eat this way and never have to spend much more than $6 for a full meal. There are, of course, the internationally franchised fast-food places on every street; better are the local chains of **hamburger stands**, most open 24 hours a day, providing filling meals as well as abundant local color. *Fatburger*, originally at San Vicente and La Cienega boulevards on the border of Beverly Hills, has branches everywhere selling deliciously greasy hamburgers; its chief competitor, *In-N-Out Burger*, doesn't rate too far behind.

Sadly, the best of the 1950s **drive-ins** have either been torn down, such as *Tiny Naylors* in Hollywood, or remodeled beyond recognition, such as *The Wich Stand*, now a health-food store.

Downtown and around

Clifton's Cafeteria 648 S Broadway ☎213/627-1673. Classic 1930s cafeteria, the last remaining in a chain of six quirky eateries, with plenty of bizarre decor: redwood trees, a waterfall, even a mini-chapel. The food is less daring – traditional meat-and-potatoes American – and cheap, too.

Cole's Pacific Electric Buffet 118 E Sixth St ☎213/622-4090. As the name suggests, this place has been here a very long time – since 1908, when the old Red Car transit fleet was still operating, making this LA's oldest surviving restaurant. The decor and food haven't changed much since then, with the dark-wood paneling, sawdust-covered floors and ancient-looking fixtures mirroring the rich, hearty French dip sandwiches loaded with steak, pastrami or brisket – a dish invented at this very spot.

Grand Central Market 317 S Broadway ☎213/624-9496. Selling plenty of tacos, deli

sandwiches and Chinese food, plus a few more exotic items, like pig's ears and lamb sweetbreads. A recent renovation makes this a fun, cheap place to eat.

Langer's Deli 704 S Alvarado St ☎213/483-8050. "When in doubt, eat hot pastrami" says the sign. Helpful, but you still have to choose from over twenty ways of eating what is easily LA's best pastrami sandwich. The MacArthur Park Metrorail subway stop nearby will help you escape the dicey neighborhood.

Mitsuru Café 117 Japanese Village Plaza ☎213/613-1028. On a hot day nothing beats the snow cones at *Mitsuru*, which come in such exotic flavors as *kintoki* (adzuki-bean paste) or *milk kintoki* (sweet custard). In colder weather, try the *imagawayaki* – adzuki beans baked in a bun. Located in a popular mall. Moderate.

Original Pantry 877 S Figueroa St ☎213/972-9279. There's always a line for the generous portions of meaty American cooking – chops and steaks, mostly – in

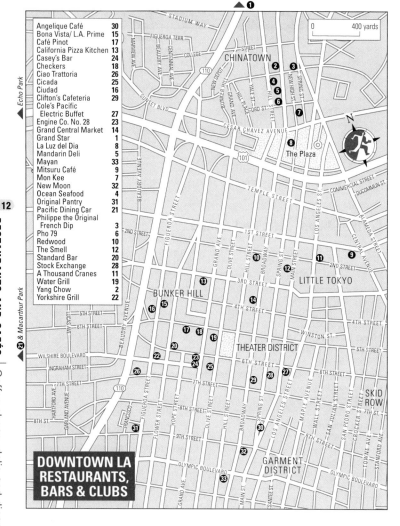

Angelique Café	30
Bona Vista/ L.A. Prime	15
Café Pinot	17
California Pizza Kitchen	13
Casey's Bar	24
Checkers	18
Ciao Trattoria	26
Cicada	25
Ciudad	16
Clifton's Cafeteria	29
Cole's Pacific Electric Buffet	27
Engine Co. No. 28	23
Grand Central Market	14
Grand Star	1
La Luz del Dia	8
Mandarin Deli	5
Mayan	33
Mitsuru Café	9
Mon Kee	7
New Moon	32
Ocean Seafood	4
Original Pantry	31
Pacific Dining Car	21
Philippe the Original French Dip	3
Pho 79	6
Redwood	10
The Smell	12
Standard Bar	20
Stock Exchange	28
A Thousand Cranes	11
Water Grill	19
Yang Chow	2
Yorkshire Grill	22

DOWNTOWN LA RESTAURANTS, BARS & CLUBS

this 24-hour diner owned by former mayor Richard Riordan. The quirky old-fashioned brochures are worth a look while you wait.

Philippe the Original French Dip 1001 N Alameda St, Chinatown ☎213/628-3781. Renowned sawdust café, a block north of Union Station, where you can tuck into juicy, artery-clogging French dips – loaded with turkey, pork, beef or lamb – at one of the long communal tables.

The Yorkshire Grill 610 W Sixth St ☎213/623-

3362. New York–style deli serving up big sandwiches and friendly service for under $10. Lunchtimes are crowded, so get there early.

Mid-Wilshire

Canter's Deli 419 N Fairfax Ave ☎323/651-2030. Iconic LA deli with huge sandwiches for around $7 and excellent kosher soups served by famously aggressive waitresses in pink uniforms and running shoes. Live music on Tuesday nights in *Canter's* adjoining "Kibitz Room." Open 24 hours.

Cassell's Hamburgers 3266 W Sixth St ☏213/480-8668. No-frills takeout hamburger stand that some swear by, serving up nearly two-thirds of a pound of beef per bun. Closes at 4pm.

Du-Par's 6333 W Third St, in the Farmers Market ☏323/933-8446. This LA institution draws grizzled old-timers with its greasy breakfasts and heavy-duty cheeseburgers. Make sure to sample the pies, which come in assorted bright colors and flavors. Also in West Hollywood at 8571 Santa Monica Blvd ☏310/659-7009, and two more branches in the Valley.

Hard Rock Café in the Beverly Center mall, Beverly Blvd at San Vicente Blvd ☏310/276-7605. Almost unavoidable for most visitors, and highlighted by rock'n'roll memorabilia, loud music and fancy merchandise; the bland, greasy food is an afterthought. Also at 1000 Universal Center Drive, Universal City ☏818/622-7626, and 451 Newport Center Drive, Newport Beach ☏949/640-8844, though all the branches are about the same.

Johnny Rockets 474 N Beverly Drive ☏310/271-2222. Chrome-and-glass, Fifties-style hamburger joint, open until 2am at weekends. One of many in a local chain.

KFC 340 N Western Ave ☏323/467-7421. The generic chain-restaurant-chicken meals are no different here than at any other *KFC*, but the Frank Gehry architecture is striking: a giant, 40-foot-high green "bucket" and a little white cube, featuring the colonel's face, balancing precariously on top. The towering interior ceiling and spiral staircases inside are well worth a look.

Maurice's Snack 'n' Chat 5549 W Pico Blvd ☏323/931-3877. Everything here is cooked to order: spoon bread or baked chicken requires a call two hours ahead, though you could just drop in for fried chicken, pork chops, grits or salmon croquettes. Don't even think about the calorie count; instead, look at the autographed pictures of celebrity diners – from Sammy Davis Jr to Ted Kennedy – that line the walls.

Oki Dog 5056 W Pico Blvd ☏323/938-4369. Along with *Pink's* (see below), this low-rent shack is an essential stop for lovers of "red hots" ($5), in this case wieners wrapped in tortillas and stuffed with all manner of

gooey, super-caloric ingredients – from cheese to chili.

Swingers in the *Beverly Laurel Motor Lodge*, 8018 Beverly Blvd at Laurel Ave ☏323/653-5858. Basic and cheap American food served in an unexpectedly trendy diner, luring a large crowd of hipsters and poseurs, as well as a few movie-star wannabes.

Hollywood

Back Door Bakery 1710 Silver Lake Blvd ☏323/662-7927. Popular for its healthy breakfasts of pancakes and French toast, this local favorite also serves standard lunch fare (soups, sandwiches), along with its unique variations on junk-food treats like cupcakes and Twinkies – served here home-made and doused in rich chocolate cream.

Fred 62 1854 N Vermont Ave, Los Feliz ☏323/667-0062. Vivid proof that California cuisine can invade any type of cooking – in this case, classic diner fare. This 1950s-inspired diner, complete with soda fountain, streamlined booths and 24-hour service – offers appetizing twists on staples like salads, burgers and fries, plus a tempting array of pancakes and omelets.

Hampton's 1342 N Highland Ave ☏323/469-1090. Longstanding comfort-food favorite, with hefty hamburgers served with a choice of over fifty toppings, plus an excellent salad bar.

Picholine 3360 W First St ☏213/252-8722. A good selection of sandwiches stuffed with gourmet ingredients – pesto, sun-dried tomato, etc – along with mouth-watering sides of pasta, all for under $8.

Pink's Hot Dogs 709 N La Brea Ave ☏323/931-4223. The quintessential chili dog, served with all kinds of messy toppings. Depending on your taste, these monsters are either gut bombs or lifesavers. Open til 2am, or 3am weekends.

Roscoe's Chicken and Waffles 1514 N Gower St ☏323/466-7453. An unlikely spot for Hollywood's elite, this diner attracts all sorts for its fried chicken, greens, goopy gravy and thick waffles. Listen to the ringing pagers and cell phones as you wait in line for breakfast with movie-industry big shots. One of four area locations.

Tommy's 2575 W Beverly Blvd, Echo Park ☏213/389-9060. One of the prime LA spots for big, greasy, mouthwatering burgers – and, many would say, the best. Just watch

RESTAURANTS AND CAFÉS | Coffee shops, delis and diners

Hollywood Memorial Cemetery & Paramount Studios ▼

All-Star Theatre Café	13	Deep	14	The Opium Den	27
American Legion Hall	1	Frolic Room	15	The Palace	5
Beauty Bar	25	Goldfingers	4	Papaz	8
Blue	21	Hampton's	39	Pig 'n Whistle	16
Boardners	20	Havana on Sunset	34	Pinot Hollywood	38
Bourgeois Pig	2	Highlands	7	The Power House	10
Café des Artistes	29	King King	12	The Room	26
Cat N' Fiddle	35	The Knitting Factory	36	Roscoe's Chicken and Waffles	33
Catalina Bar and Grill	22	Little Hong Kong Deli	23	The Ruby	17
Chan Dara	32	Miceli's	19	Sixteen-Fifty	24
Club Lingerie	31	Musso and Frank Grill	11	Taipan	30
Crush Bar	6	Off Vine	37	Uzbekistan	9
Cyber Java	18			Yamashiro	3

12

RESTAURANTS AND CAFÉS | Coffee shops, delis and diners

out for the Rampart neighborhood at night: one of the city's more dangerous drug-dealing zones. 24 hours.

West Hollywood

Astro Burger 7475 Santa Monica Blvd ☎323/874-8041. Not just burgers, but sandwiches and even veggie meals are the appeal of this lower-Hollywood diner – along with the late hours, until 3am weekdays, 4am weekends.

Barney's Beanery 8447 Santa Monica Blvd ☎323/654-2287. Two hundred bottled beers, along with hot dogs, hamburgers and bowls of chili, served in a hip, grungy environment. Open until 2am.

Duke's 8909 Sunset Blvd ☎310/652-3100. A favorite of visiting rock musicians (the *Roxy* and *Whisky-a-Go-Go* clubs are nearby), this

basic coffee shop also attracts a motley crew of night owls and bleary-eyed locals.

Hamburger Haven 8954 Santa Monica Blvd at Robertson Blvd ☎310/659-8796. Located in the frenetic heart of the city, a classic burger shack serving up rich, greasy fare in its cramped dining room and at outdoor patio tables (with a view of traffic whipping by at full volume). Especially busy on weekend nights.

Mel's Drive In 8585 Sunset Blvd ☎310/854-7200. Calorie-packing milkshakes, fries and, of course, burgers make this classic 24-hour diner a must if you've got the late-night munchies.

Tail o' the Pup 329 N San Vicente Blvd ☎310/652-4517. Worth a visit for the roadside Pop architecture alone (a thin wiener encased in a massive bun), though the hot dogs and hamburgers are also good.

Topz 8593 Santa Monica Blvd ☎310/659-8843.
A local chain of fast-food joints that
focuses, somehow, on the healthier side of
eating burgers, hot dogs and french fries,
with lo-calorie cooking oils and lean meats
on the culinary agenda. Six other locations,
the closest at 7514 Melrose Ave
☎323/852-0146.
Yukon Mining Co 7328 Santa Monica Blvd
☎323/851-8833. Excellent 24-hour coffee

shop with a diverse clientele – don't be
surprised to see a crowd of newly arrived
Russians, neighborhood pensioners and
glammed-up drag queens. Open til 2am.

Beverly Hills and West LA

The Apple Pan 10801 W Pico Blvd, West LA
☎310/475-3585. Grab a spot at the counter
and enjoy freshly baked apple pie and

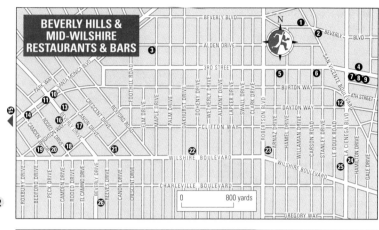

BEVERLY HILLS & MID-WILSHIRE RESTAURANTS & BARS

À Votre Santé	26	Cava	9	Locanda Veneta	6	Nate'n'Al's	13
Arnie Morton's	12	The Cheesecake Factory	17	Maple Drive	3	Newsroom	23
Backstage Café	16	Ed Debevic's	24	Matsuhisa	25	The Nosh of	
Baja Fresh	11	Hard Rock Café	2	McCormick		Beverly Hills	14
Barefoot	5	Jacopo's	10	& Schmick's	18	St Nick's	8
Brighton Coffee Shop	19	Jerry's Famous Deli	1	Mishima	7	Spago	21
Café Blanc	15	Kate Mantilini	22	Mr Chow	20	Sushi Roku	4

plump, juicy hamburgers – which some claim are LA's best – across from the imposing Westside Pavilion mall. An old-time joint that opened just after World War II.

Brighton Coffee Shop 9600 Brighton Way, Beverly Hills ☎310/276-7732. This simple coffee joint provides welcome relief from the smugness of the district – it's located right in the middle of the Golden Triangle – by offering solid diner food, with especially good sandwiches.

Ed Debevic's 134 N La Cienega Blvd, Beverly Hills ☎310/659-1952. The last four digits of the phone number give you a hint: a rollicking retro diner with brash singing waitresses, burgers'n'fries and beer. A bit overpriced, aimed more at tourists than locals.

In-N-Out Burger 922 Gayley Ave, Westwood ☎1-800/786-1000. The best-looking fast-food place in town, selling wonderfully greasy hamburgers in an award-winning Pop Art building – a red-and-white modern box with zingy yellow boomerang signs and an oversized interior logo looming behind the diners.

Jerry's Famous Deli 8701 Beverly Blvd, Beverly Hills ☎310/289-1811. The most appealing of the many *Jerry's* locations in LA, with a sizeable deli menu and open 24 hours. Occasionally, celebrities stop in to nosh.

John o' Groats 10516 W Pico Blvd, West LA ☎310/204-0692. Excellent cheap breakfasts and lunches (mostly staples like bacon and eggs), but come at an off-hour; the morning crowd can give you a headache.

Johnny's Pastrami 4017 S Sepulveda Blvd, Culver City ☎310/397-6654. A wonderful 1950s diner where fans line up for the gut-busting pastrami sandwiches, which cost around $6 and are prepared before your eyes in all their dripping, steaming glory.

Kate Mantilini 9101 Wilshire Blvd, Beverly Hills ☎310/278-3699. Appetizing, upscale versions of classic American diner food served up in a stylish interior designed by edgy architectural firm Morphosis. Open until 1am weekdays, 2am weekends.

Nate 'n' Al's 414 N Beverly Drive ☎310/274-0101. The best-known deli in Beverly Hills, popular with movie people and one of the few reasonable places for dining in the vicinity.

The Nosh of Beverly Hills 9689 Little Santa Monica Blvd, Beverly Hills ☎310/271-3730. Early-morning breakfasts and handmade

12

RESTAURANTS AND CAFÉS | Coffee shops, delis and diners

bagels, pies and deli fare are the favorites at this unassuming diner, a quiet hangout of movie-industry lawyers and producers.

Santa Monica, Venice and Malibu

Bagel Nosh 1629 Wilshire Blvd, Santa Monica ☎310/451-8771. Soak in the 1960s ambience at this neighborhood favorite, good for its sizeable omelets and bagel sandwiches, picked up from an old-fashioned short-order counter

Bicycle Shop Café 12217 Wilshire Blvd, Santa Monica ☎310/826-7831. Serves light meals, fish and salads, and also makes for a lively neighborhood place to drink. Take note of the plethora of bike decor: chains, frames and wheels are everywhere. Open until 2am weekends.

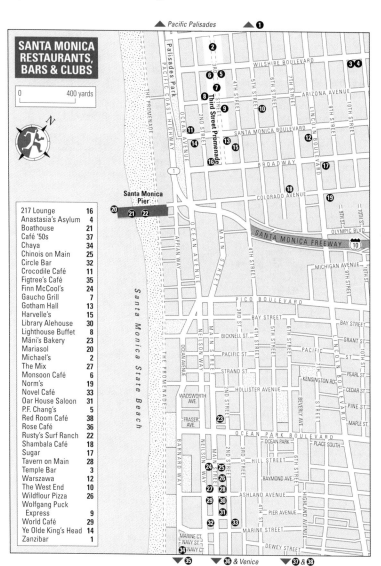

SANTA MONICA RESTAURANTS, BARS & CLUBS

0 ————— 400 yards

217 Lounge	16
Anastasia's Asylum	4
Boathouse	21
Café '50s	37
Chaya	34
Chinois on Main	25
Circle Bar	32
Crocodile Café	11
Figtree's Café	35
Finn McCool's	24
Gaucho Grill	7
Gotham Hall	13
Harvelle's	15
Library Alehouse	30
Lighthouse Buffet	8
Mäni's Bakery	23
Mariasol	20
Michael's	2
The Mix	27
Monsoon Café	6
Norm's	19
Novel Café	33
Oar House Saloon	31
P.F. Chang's	5
Red Room Café	38
Rose Café	36
Rusty's Surf Ranch	22
Shambala Café	18
Sugar	17
Tavern on Main	28
Temple Bar	3
Warszawa	12
The West End	10
Wildflour Pizza	26
Wolfgang Puck Express	9
World Café	29
Ye Olde King's Head	14
Zanzibar	1

Café 50's 838 Lincoln Blvd, Venice ☎310/399-1955. A favorite retro-styled diner with Ritchie Valens on the jukebox, and juicy burgers on the tables. One of several Westside locations.

Café Montana 1534 Montana Ave, Santa Monica ☎310/829-3990. The eclectic menu is highlighted by solid breakfasts, excellent salads and tasty grilled fish, in an upmarket section of Santa Monica.

Norm's 1601 Lincoln Blvd, Santa Monica ☎310/450-0074. One of the last remaining classic diner chains, this local joint has nine other LA branches and serves $3 breakfasts and similarly cheap lunches. Great Googie architecture, too.

Rae's Diner 2901 Pico Blvd, Santa Monica ☎310/828-7937. Small 1950s diner doling out heavy but tasty comfort food, and is especially popular with the late-night crowd. Its turquoise-blue facade and interior have been seen in many films, notably *True Romance*.

Reel Inn 18661 PCH, Malibu ☎310/456-8221. Seafood diner by the beach, with unsurprising food, but cheap prices and a fun atmosphere. Also at 1220 W Third St, Santa Monica ☎310/395-5538.

The Sidewalk Café 1401 Ocean Front Walk, Venice ☎310/399-5547. Though the interior is somewhat grim and the food only adequate, this café is a prime spot for watching the daily parade of beach people as you dine outside, especially during the morning hours. Open until midnight on weekends.

South Central and East LA

B & B Bar-B-Que Connection 1958 W Florence Ave, Huntington Park ☎323/671-8190 and 5403 S Vermont Ave, a mile and a half south of Exposition Park ☎323/778-6070. Barbecue aficionados may wish to venture into these dicey areas to sample slabs of LA's best ribs, smothered in barbecue sauce, and served with baked beans and a sweet-potato tart.

Chips 11908 Hawthorne Blvd, south of Inglewood ☎310/679-2947. A solid array of comfort food from sandwiches to burgers, served in a classic diner.

The Donut Hole 15300 Amar Rd, La Puente ☎626/968-2912. Pop architecture fans will definitely want to make the twenty-mile drive east from Downtown LA to see this eye-popping favorite which, like *Randy's Donuts* (see below), is shaped like a giant donut – except this one you can actually drive through, picking up a hot sack of fried, sugared dough from deep inside a tunnel of comfort food.

Pann's 6710 La Tijera Blvd, Inglewood ☎323/776-3770. One of the all-time great Googie diners (worth a stop for its design alone; see p.146), where you can't go wrong with the classic burgers or biscuits and gravy – and you can always jog off the calories in the nearby Baldwin Hills, just to the north.

Randy's Donuts 805 W Manchester Ave, Inglewood ☎310/645-4707. This Pop Art fixture (like *Pann's* just up the road) is hard to miss, thanks to the giant donut sitting on the roof. Excellent for its piping hot treats, which you can pick up at the drive-through on your way to or from LAX. One of four South Central locations, though the only one with an oversized donut on top.

The South Bay and LA Harbor

Blueberry Hill 5735 E PCH, Long Beach ☎562/986-4455. Hefty helpings of good, old-fashioned comfort food, a spot where the burgers are chunky and mouth-watering, the onion rings are stacked high, and the fries come coated in thick gravy. Located near the campus of Cal State Long Beach.

East Coast Bagels 5753 E PCH, Long Beach ☎562/985-0933. Located in a dreary mini-mall, but with an excellent selection of bagels, ranging from New York staples to California hybrids like the jalapeño-cheddar bagel stuffed with cream cheese.

Hof's Hut 4823 E Second St, Long Beach ☎562/439-4775. One bite of the *Hut*'s juicy Hofburger and you know you've found the real deal: succulent meat, plus fresh and tasty ingredients. Four other Long Beach locations, and five in Orange County.

Johnny Reb's 4663 N Long Beach Blvd ☎562/423-7327. The waft of barbecued ribs, catfish and hushpuppies alone may draw you to this prime Southern spot, where the portions are hefty and the price is cheap; it's also good for lunch after a trip to nearby Rancho Los Cerritos (see p.169).

The Local Yolk 3414 Highland Ave, Manhattan Beach ☎310/546-4407. As the name suggests, everything here is made with eggs, and there are airy muffins and pancakes, too. Breakfast and lunch only.

Ocean View Café 229 13th St, Manhattan Beach ☎310/545-6770. Enjoyably light

△ Mel's Drive In

breakfasts, and soup and baguettes for around $6, in a pleasant hillside setting on a quiet pedestrian path overlooking the Pacific Ocean. There's also outside seating for wave-watching.

Pier Bakery 100-M Fisherman's Wharf, Redondo Beach ☎310/376-9582. A small but satisfying menu with the jalapeño-cheese bread and cinnamon rolls. Probably the best food around in this touristy area.

Tony's Famous French Dip 701 Long Beach Blvd, Long Beach ☎562/435-6238. The name says it all, but alongside the delightful and affordable dips is a beckoning selection of soups and salads.

Art's Deli 12224 Ventura Blvd, Studio City ☎818/762-1221. Long-time film-industry favorite, with a good range of hefty, scrumptious sandwiches and soups.

Benita's Frites 1000 Universal Center Drive, Universal City ☎818/505-8834. Delicious french fries served in a paper cone, with a choice of multiple toppings, including mayonnaise. Located deep in the heart of CityWalk.

Bob's Big Boy 4211 W Riverside Drive, Burbank ☎818/843-9334. The classic chain diner, fronted by the plump burger lad, and a veritable Pop-architecture classic (see p.192). Open 24 hours.

Conrad's 820 N Central Ave, Glendale ☎818/246-6547. Best for its burgers and sandwiches, this old-time restaurant also throws in a little Italian and Mexican cooking into the mix.

Coral Café 3321 W Burbank Blvd ☎818/566-9725. A few miles north of Burbank's studios, this diner draws a mix of movie-crew workers and locals with its filling breakfasts and lunchtime burgers and steaks.

Dr Hogly-Wogly's Tyler Texas Bar-B-Q 8136 Sepulveda Blvd, Van Nuys ☎818/780-6701. Long lines snake out the door here for some of the best chicken, sausages, ribs and beans in LA, despite the depressing surroundings in the middle of nowhere.

Fair Oaks Pharmacy and Soda Fountain 1526 Mission St, South Pasadena ☎626/799-1414. A fabulously restored soda fountain, with many old-fashioned drinks, from lime rickeys to egg creams.

Goldstein's Bagel Bakery 86 W Colorado Blvd, Pasadena ☎626/792-2435. If money's tight,

feast here on day-old 15¢ bagels; otherwise enjoy what some call LA's best bagels, made in New York style. In the Old Pasadena shopping district.

The Hat 491 N Lake Ave, Pasadena ☎626/449-1844. Very popular roadside stand selling good burgers and French dip sandwiches at this and four other nearby locations.

Lamplighter 5043 Van Nuys Blvd, San Fernando Valley ☎818/788-5110. A funky, old-style diner serving tasty, good-sized portions that bring in assorted colorful characters. Two other locations in the Valley.

Pie 'n' Burger 913 E California Blvd, Pasadena ☎626/795-1123. Classic coffee shop near Cal Tech, with good burgers and excellent fresh pies.

Porto's Bakery 315 N Brand Blvd, Glendale ☎818/956-5996. Popular and cheap café serving flaky Cuban pastries, scrumptious sandwiches, cheesecakes soaked in rum, muffins, danishes, croissants, tarts and tortes, and cappuccino.

Rose Tree Cottage 395 E California Blvd, Pasadena ☎626/793-3337. Scones, shortbread and high tea in a country-home setting so thoroughly English that it's the West Coast headquarters of the British Tourist Board. Reservations are essential.

Wolfe Burger 46 N Lake St, Pasadena ☎626/792-7292. Mouthwatering burgers, chili and tamales, plus good gyros and break-fasts, including splendid huevos rancheros.

Angelo's 511 S State College Blvd, Anaheim ☎714/533-1401. Straight out of TV's *Happy Days*, a drive-in complete with roller-skating car-hops, neon signs, vintage cars and fairly good burgers. Open until 2am on weekends.

Café Zinc 350 Ocean Ave, Laguna Beach ☎949/494-2791. One of Laguna's best breakfast counters also serves simple soup-and-salad lunches and other light meals. Good for a day at the beach.

Duke's 317 PCH, Huntington Beach ☎714/374-6446. Steak and salad are the highlights at this frenetic beachside favorite, set in a prime location near the pier.

Harbor House Café 34157 PCH, Dana Point ☎949/496-9270. Worth seeking out for its excellent breakfasts, and particularly for its overstuffed, gut-busting omelets – a slew of them, with a veritable laundry list of options.

Heroes 305 N Harbor Blvd, Fullerton
☎714/738-4356. The place to come if you're
starving after hitting the theme parks.
Choose from countless beers and hearty
fare like hamburgers, beef stroganoff or
meatloaf.

Knott's Chicken Dinner Restaurant just
outside Knott's Berry Farm at 8039 Beach
Blvd, Buena Park ☎714/220-5080. Serving
cheap and tasty meals for over 65 years.
People have been flocking here for
delicious fried chicken dinners long before
Disneyland was around, and they still do.

Don't miss the delectable boysenberry
pies.

Mimi's Café 18342 Imperial Hwy, Yorba Linda
☎714/996-3650. Huge servings, low prices
and a relaxed atmosphere down the street
from the Nixon Library. Part of a sizeable
regional chain.

Ruby's 1 Balboa Pier, Newport Beach
☎949/675-RUBY. The first and finest of the
retro-Streamline 1940s diners that have
popped up all over LA – in a great location
at the end of Newport's pier. Mostly offers
the standard burgers, fries and soda fare.

Restaurants

The listings below generally follow the chapter divisions of our guide, grouping **restaurants** first by neighborhood, then by cuisine. A number of specialty
categories (late-night, expense-account, etc) appear in boxes.

Downtown

American, Californian and Cajun

Checkers Restaurant in the *Wyndham
Checkers Hotel*, 535 S Grand Ave ☎213/624-
0519. Elegant Downtown restaurant, serving
top-rated California cuisine, with the rack of
lamb and sashimi among the better
offerings. Very expensive.

Engine Co. No. 28 644 S Figueroa St
☎213/624-6996. All-American fare, featuring
grilled steaks and seafood, all served with
great fries in a renovated 1912 fire station.
An excellent wine list rounds out this
classic local eatery. Expensive.

L.A. Prime inside the *Westin Bonaventure* hotel,
404 S Figueroa St ☎213/612-4743. Plump
slabs of tender Midwestern beef are the
draw at this New York–style steakhouse, if
you can stomach the bill, while the side
orders and Strawberries Romanoff dessert
hold their own. Fine views from the hotel's
35th floor. Very expensive.

New Moon 102 W Ninth St ☎213/624-0186.
Good mainly for its location near the
Garment District and its reasonably priced
mix of American cooking – salads, soups,
steaks and the like – and Chinese dishes.
Inexpensive.

Pacific Dining Car 1310 W Sixth St ☎213/483-
6000. One of LA's oldest eateries, a would-
be English supper club housed inside an
old railroad carriage with excellent, though
highly expensive, steaks. Breakfast is better
value. Open 24 hours. Very expensive.

Water Grill 544 S Grand Ave ☎213/891-0900.
Although the fare is ostensibly seafood, the
style and preparation are pure California
cuisine – salmon with porcini mushrooms,
crab aioli and so on – making for a
memorably succulent, and pricey, visit.
Wear your silkiest power-tie to fit in with the
other diners. Very expensive.

Chinese and Vietnamese

Grand Star Restaurant 943 Sun Mun Way
☎213/626-2285. While the traditional soups

Restaurant prices

The restaurant reviews below are price-coded according to the following categories,
which are meant to give a general sense of the relative cost:

Inexpensive: Under $15   Expensive: $25–50
Moderate: $15–25   Very Expensive: Over $50

Prices average out the cost of a three-course meal, or the equivalent, and exclude
drinks, tax and tip.

Special restaurant categories

Celebrity-watching spots	p.268	Late-night eats	p.270
Expense-account		Restaurant directory	
restaurants	p.261	(by cuisine)	p.244

and meat dishes here are flavorful and authentic, the real appeal is the video karaoke – 8pm–1am on Sun, Tues and Wed. Also offers takeout. Moderate.

Mandarin Deli 727 N Broadway #109, ☎213/623-6054. Very tasty and very cheap noodles, pork and fish dumplings, and other hearty staples in the middle of Broadway's hustle and bustle. Also at 356 E Second St, Little Tokyo ☎213/617-0231. Inexpensive.

Mon Kee 679 N Spring St ☎213/628-6717. Longstanding favorite for fresh fish and rich, hearty seafood soups, in somewhat grubby surroundings. Moderate.

Ocean Seafood 750 N Hill St ☎213/687-3088. Cavernous but busy restaurant serving inexpensive and excellent food – abalone, crab, shrimp and duck are among many standout choices. Moderate.

Pho 79 727 N Broadway #120, ☎213/625-7026. Good, cheap Vietnamese fare – the standard rice dishes and noodle soups are quite filling. Inexpensive.

Yang Chow 819 N Broadway ☎213/625-0811. Solid Chinese restaurant, where you can't go wrong with the Szechuan beef or any shrimp dish. Moderate.

French

Angelique Café 840 S Spring St ☎213/623-8698. Marvelous Continental eatery in the middle of the Garment District, where you can sit on the quaint patio and dine on well-made pastries for breakfast or sandwiches, rich casseroles and a fine selection of salads for lunch. Moderate.

Café Pinot 700 W Fifth St ☎213/239-6500. Next to the LA Public Library, this elegant restaurant has a flair for French cooking, namely its grilled chicken and duck dishes, but its reputation rests on its standout nouvelle California cuisine. Expensive.

Italian and pizza

California Pizza Kitchen 330 S Hope St ☎213/626-2616. Mid-priced designer pizza at this national chain, with branches citywide. Nothing too adventurous, but

centrally located on Bunker Hill. Moderate.

Ciao Trattoria 815 W Seventh St ☎213/624-2244. Housed in a striking Romanesque building, full of lovely historic-revival decor, and a solid choice for upscale Northern Italian cuisine. Expensive.

Cicada 617 S Olive St ☎213/488-9488. Fine pasta for half the price of its fish and steak entrees in the stunning Art Deco Oviatt Building (see p.64). Very expensive.

Japanese

Shibucho 3114 Beverly Blvd ☎213/387-8498. Exceptional sushi bar just south of Silver Lake and popular with locals; go with someone who knows what to order, as most of the waiters don't speak English. Moderate.

A Thousand Cranes 120 S Los Angeles St, Little Tokyo ☎213/253-9255. Located beside the Japanese Garden in the Sky of the *New Otani Hotel* (see p.59), this is dining at its most refined, with pleasant views of the water and greenery, and multiple courses – notably tempura – served in an elegant setting. Expensive.

Mexican and Latin American

El Taurino 1104 S Hoover St, Westlake ☎213/738-9197. One of Downtown's top Mexican eateries, doling out stout portions of heavy, stomach-filling food to locals in the know – everything from fat beef ribs to succulent roasted lamb and spicy tostadas – all for an ultra-cheap price under the watchful eyes of giant steer heads. Weekends open 24 hours. Inexpensive.

King Taco 2904 N Broadway ☎323/222-8500. The most centrally located diner in a chain of the many around Downtown (this one a bit north of Chinatown), with many varieties of tacos – most of them quite savory. Inexpensive.

La Luz del Dia 107 Paseo de la Plaza ☎213/628-7495. Amid the throngs of trinket vendors on Olvera Street, this authentic Mexican eatery is worth seeking out for its fiery burritos, enchiladas and stews, served in sizeable portions. Inexpensive.

Spanish

Ciudad 445 S Figueroa St ☎ 213/486-5171. Roast chicken and quinoa fritters are some of the highlights at this colorful Mexican-influenced spot, where the live Latin music competes with the delicious food for your attention. Expensive.

Mid-Wilshire

African

Nyala 1076 S Fairfax Ave ☎ 323/936-5918. One of several Ethiopian favorites along Fairfax, serving staples like *doro wat* (marinated chicken) and *kitfo* (chopped beef with butter and cheese) with delightfully spongy *injera* bread. Moderate.

Rosalind's 1044 S Fairfax Ave ☎ 323/936-2486. Spicy goat meat and pepper chicken are among the highlights at this modest Ethiopian establishment. Moderate.

American, Californian and Cajun

Atlas 3760 Wilshire Blvd ☎ 213/380-8400. The food at this extremely stylish LA restaurant can be inconsistent, but the chicken and pasta dishes are good, and the eclectic music performances add much to the overall charm. Expensive.

Ca' Brea 346 S La Brea Ave ☎ 323/938-2863. One of LA's top choices for California and Italian cuisines – especially good for osso bucco and risotto – making this a difficult spot to get in to. Expensive.

Flora Kitchen 460 S La Brea Ave ☎ 323/931-9900. Connected to a flower shop, this eclectic, al fresco eatery is best for its California cuisine–style sandwiches, made with a host of deliciously fresh ingredients. Moderate.

Expense-account restaurants

At the following restaurants – good for business dinners or impressing your loved one – you'll definitely need to book ahead and, likely, dress up too. Meals can easily run about $100 per head, including drinks.

Alex 6703 Melrose Ave ☎ 323/933-5233; p.262.

Arnie Morton's 435 N La Cienega Blvd, Beverly Hills ☎ 310/246-1501; p.267.

Aubergine 508 29th St, Newport Beach ☎ 949/723-4150; p.276.

Café Blanc 9777 Little Santa Monica Blvd, Beverly Hills ☎ 310/888-0108; p.267.

Checkers Restaurant in the *Wyndham Checkers Hotel*, 535 S Grand Ave ☎ 213/624-0000; p.259.

Chinois on Main 2709 Main St, Santa Monica ☎ 310/392-9025; p.271.

Cicada 617 S Olive St, Downtown ☎ 213/488-9488; p.260.

Drago 2628 Wilshire Blvd, Santa Monica ☎ 310/828-1585; p.272.

Eurochow 1099 Westwood Blvd, Westwood ☎ 310/209-0066; p.267.

Fenix 8358 Sunset Blvd, West Hollywood ☎ 323/848-6677; p.266.

Granita 23725 W Malibu Rd, Malibu ☎ 310/456-0488; p.269.

L.A. Prime in the *Westin Bonaventure* hotel, 404 S Figueroa St ☎ 213/612-4743; p.259.

L'Orangerie 903 N La Cienega Blvd, West Hollywood ☎ 310/652-9770; p.266.

Maple Drive 345 N Maple Drive, Beverly Hills ☎ 310/274-9800; p.267.

Matsuhisa 129 N La Cienega Blvd, Beverly Hills ☎ 310/659-9639; p.267.

McCormick and Schmick's 206 N Rodeo Drive ☎ 213/629-1929; p.269.

Michael's 1147 Third St, Santa Monica ☎ 310/451-0843; p.270.

Mr Chow 344 N Camden Drive, Beverly Hills ☎ 310/278-9911; p.267.

Pacific Dining Car 1310 W Sixth St, Downtown ☎ 213/483-6000; p.259.

Patina 5955 Melrose Ave, Mid-Wilshire ☎ 323/467-1108; p.262.

Posto 14928 Ventura Blvd, Sherman Oaks ☎ 818/784-4400; p.275.

Saddle Peak Lodge 419 Cold Canyon Rd, Calabasas ☎ 818/222-3888; p.275.

Spago 176 N Cañon Drive, Beverly Hills ☎ 310/385-0880; p.267.

Valentino 3115 W Pico Blvd, Santa Monica ☎ 310/829-4313; p.272.

Water Grill 544 S Grand Ave, Downtown ☎ 213/891-0900; p.259.

The Gumbo Pot 6333 W Third St, in the Farmers Market ☎323/933-0358. Delicious and dirt-cheap Cajun cooking in a hive of greasy food stalls. Try the full-flavored *gumbo yaya* of chicken, shrimp and sausage, along with the fruit-and-potato salad. Inexpensive.

Patina 5955 Melrose Ave ☎323/467-1108. This dark, clubby and ultrachic place delivers exquisite California cuisine, taking duck, chicken and pheasant, adding exotic spices and herbs, and throwing in the occasional kidney or calf's foot – more appetizing than it sounds. Very expensive.

Sabor Too 3221 Pico Blvd ☎310/829-3781. California cuisine with the occasional nod to Cajun cooking, best for its molasses-and-ginger salmon, chili-spiced lamb chops and tart cactus salad. Moderate.

Taylor's 3361 W Eighth St ☎213/382-8449. Good old-fashioned American steaks and chops, priced a bit more reasonably than at similar Westside steakhouses. Expensive.

Caribbean

Prado 244 N Larchmont Blvd ☎323/467-3871. A crowded spot in the burgeoning Larchmont Village shopping zone, better than the standard Caribbean offerings in LA, using a wealth of tropical fruits and seafood – especially the pepper shrimp – to brighten up the cuisine. Moderate.

Chinese and Vietnamese

Genghis Cohen 740 N Fairfax Ave ☎323/653-0640. Familiar Chinese dishes with a Yiddish touch: the menu abounds with culinary puns, much like the restaurant's name. The Szechuan beef and *kung pao* chicken are good, as are the chicken wings served at lunchtime. Inexpensive.

Lucky Duck 672 S La Brea Ave ☎323/931-9660. Sitting in the shadow of a huge Asahi beer sign, this stylish restaurant serves excellent Chinese cooking mixed with a slew of East Asian cuisines, including Japanese, Laotian and Thai. Moderate.

French

Alex 6703 Melrose Ave ☎323/933-5233. Located between Hollywood and Mid-Wilshire, a Californian take on French cooking, emphasizing the usual culinary

experiments (eg, glazed duck in pear-walnut sauce), under dark decor and moody lighting. Very expensive.

Louis XIV 606 N La Brea Ave ☎323/934-5102. The prices may be a bit lower here than at comparable French restaurants, but the attitude is just as haughty. Still, the food is reliable and occasionally terrific, especially the steaks and seafood pasta, making this one of the few French spots that the expats don't sneer at. Expensive.

Mimosa 8009 Beverly Blvd ☎323/655-8895. French bistro cooking with an accent on pasta, with savory offerings like seafood risotto, beef bourguignon and tagliatelle, and macaroni with prosciutto au gratin. Expensive.

Greek

Le Petit Greek 127 N Larchmont Blvd ☎323/464-5160. Sizeable servings of Greek staples in a quiet Larchmont Village location. Stick to the lamb and fish dishes for maximum pleasure. Moderate.

Papa Cristos 2771 W Pico Blvd ☎323/737-2970. Consider venturing to this grim neighborhood near the 10 freeway to sample the authentic delights at this Greek joint, including delicious gyros and hefty portions of lamb chops or roast chicken for under $10. Inexpensive.

Sofi 8030 W Third St ☎323/651-0346. A pleasant, comfortable place near the Farmers Market, serving classic Greek like stuffed grape leaves and moussaka to a loyal crowd. Moderate.

Indian and Sri Lankan

New East India Grill 345 N La Brea Ave ☎323/936-8844. Southern Indian cuisine given the California treatment: impressive specialties include spinach curry, ginger chicken, curried noodles and adventurous "parmesan naan." Moderate.

India's Oven 7231 Beverly Blvd ☎323/936-1000. Bring your own bottle to this friendly Indian restaurant, where you'll get large, delicious portions of old favorites like stuffed naan, *vindaloo* and curry. Also at 11645 Wilshire Blvd ☎310/307-5522. Moderate.

Surya 8048 W Third St ☎323/653-5151. The menu, which features a scrumptious array of Indian flavors, borrows from Japanese and California cuisines, as well;

tandooris and *vindaloos* come with the familiar curry sauces and less predictable ingredients like duck and sashimi. Just west of the Farmers Market. Moderate.

Italian and pizza

Angeli 7274 Melrose Ave ☎ 323/936-9086. Refreshingly basic pizza styles – baked in a wood-burning oven – make this a worthwhile stop, as do its tasty frittatas and croquettes. Moderate.

Campanile 624 S La Brea Ave ☎ 323/938-1447. Rather pricey Northern Italian dishes, with good seafood, steak and rabbit. If you can't afford a full dinner, just try the dessert or pick up some of the city's best bread at *La Brea Bakery* nearby (see p.343). Expensive.

Chianti Cucina 7383 Melrose Ave ☎ 323/653-8333. Old-fashioned 1930s restaurant on Melrose's shopping strip south of Hollywood. Try the delicious raviolis or chicken and lamb entrees. Expensive.

Japanese

Mishima 8474 W Third St ☎ 323/782-0181. Great miso soup, and delicious *udon* and *soba* noodles, at very affordable prices at this chic, popular Westside eatery. Inexpensive.

Sushi Roku 8445 W Third St ☎ 323/655-6767. This upscale, and slightly stuffy, eatery is worth visiting for its fine Spanish mackerel sushi, octopus sashimi and crab rolls. Expensive.

Korean

Busan 203 N Western Ave ☎ 323/871-0703. Classy spot just north of Koreatown, with authentic and delicious spicy entrees and fresh fish that goes from the tank to your stomach in a jiffy. Expensive.

Dong Il Jang 3455 W Eighth St ☎ 213/383-5757. Cozy little restaurant where the meat is cooked at your table, with the added draw of tempura dishes and a sushi bar. Consistently good, the restaurant shines with its grilled chicken and beef. Moderate.

Woo Lae Oak 623 S Western Ave, Koreatown ☎ 213/384-2244. This well-known Korean barbecue spot is one of the best of its kind in town. Also a more crowded, pricier branch in Beverly Hills, 170 N La Cienega Blvd ☎ 310/652-4187. Expensive.

Mexican and Latin American

Casa Carnitas 4067 Beverly Blvd ☎ 323/667-9953. Delicious Mexican food from the Yucatán, inspired by Cuban and Caribbean cooking, and including lots of fine seafood, too.

El Cholo 1121 S Western Ave ☎ 323/734-2773. One of LA's first big Mexican restaurants and still among the best, offering solid staples like enchiladas and tamales, though popular with drunken frat-rats from USC. Also a branch at 1025 Wilshire Blvd, Santa Monica ☎ 310/899-1106. Moderate.

El Coyote 7312 Beverly Blvd ☎ 323/939-2255. Gloomy, labyrinthine restaurant serving heavy, greasy Mexican food, and lots of it; cheap and lethal margaritas are the real draw. Inexpensive.

Mario's Peruvian Seafood 5786 Melrose Ave ☎ 323/466-4181. Delicious and authentic Peruvian fare: supremely tender squid, rich and flavorful mussels, with a hint of soy sauce in some dishes. Inexpensive.

Middle Eastern

Eat A Pita 465 N Fairfax Ave ☎ 323/651-0188. Open-air stand serving cheap and sizeable falafel and hummus plates, as well as thirst-quenching vegetable-juice drinks. Inexpensive.

Russian and Eastern European

Csardas 5820 Melrose Ave ☎ 323/962-6434. Located a few blocks from the Paramount Studios gate, this funky little Hungarian restaurant serves up spicy Old World flavors, with its hearty stews, stuffed cabbage rolls, and roasted chicken and pork. Moderate.

Spanish

Cobras and Matadors 7615 Beverly Blvd ☎ 323/932-6178. A fine tapas restaurant just down the street from Pan Pacific Park, where you can sample all your favorite Castilian delights, like flavorful bites of spiced pork loin and game hen, in a hushed, intimate setting. Moderate.

Thai

Tommy Tang's 7313 Melrose Ave ☎ 323/937-5733. Terrific, very chic Thai restaurant in a hot shopping zone, and the incongruous setting for Tuesday drag nights, when the

male waiters can be seen "en femme."
Expensive.

Vim 831 S Vermont Ave ☎213/386-2338.
Authentic Thai and Chinese food at low
prices; the seafood soup and Pad Thai are
especially good. Inexpensive.

Vegetarian and wholefood

Fountain of Health 3606 W Sixth St
☎213/387-6621. Vegetarian chili and burgers
are the highlights at this affordable eatery
just south of Hollywood. Inexpensive.

Inaka Natural Foods 131 S La Brea Ave
☎323/936-9353. Located in the trendy La
Brea district and featuring vegetarian and
macrobiotic food with a strong Japanese
theme. Live music on weekends. Moderate.

Hollywood

African

Dar Maghreb 7651 Sunset Blvd ☎323/876-
7651. The rich Moroccan dishes, including
numerous chicken dishes as well as *b'stilla*
(a pastry stuffed with chicken, chickpeas
and spices), almost take a backseat to the
main entertainment here: belly dancing.
Expensive.

Moun of Tunis 7445 Sunset Blvd ☎323/874-
3333. Lemon chicken, spicy crepes and
other mouthwatering Tunisian dishes
presented in huge, multiple courses, heavy
on the spices and rich with exotic flavors.
Moderate.

American, Californian and Cajun

Hollywood Canteen 1006 N Seward St
☎323/465-0961. No-nonsense fish, steaks
and pastas, with some sushi for color, but
the old-fashioned club ambience is the
main attraction. Moderate.

Musso and Frank Grill 6667 Hollywood Blvd
☎323/467-7788. A 1919 classic, loaded
with authentic atmosphere and history in a
dark-paneled dining room. The drinks are
better than the pricey, mostly upscale diner
food. Expensive.

Off Vine 6263 Leland Way ☎323/962-1900. A
comfortably spacious bungalow somewhat
off the beaten Hollywood path, where the
eclectic California cuisine tends to be
outshined by the simpler steak and pasta
dishes. Expensive.

Pig 'n Whistle 6714 Hollywood Blvd
☎323/463-0000. Historic 1927 eatery

refurbished as a swank Cal-cuisine
restaurant, with the emphasis on all things
porcine, from ribs to pork roast to bacon.
Although much of the old spirit and decor
are the same, the prices are not: no diner
has food this pricey. Expensive.

Pinot Hollywood 1448 Gower St ☎323/461-
8800. Upmarket American food and
California/French nouvelle cuisine in a
spacious setting, plus 24 types of martinis
and Polish potato vodka. You may even
spot a celebrity or two, lurking in the
shadows. Expensive.

vermont 1714 N Vermont Ave ☎323/661-6163.
Pretentious lower-case letters aside, this is
one of the best Cal-cuisine spots to open in
recent years. The entrees may be
predictable – roasted chicken, crab cakes,
ravioli, etc – but the culinary presentation
can be inspired. Expensive.

Vida 1930 Hillhurst Ave, Los Feliz ☎213/660-
4446. Despite the cringe-inducing puns on
the menu – Thai Cobb Salad and the like –
this is ground zero for LA's culinary hipster
set, with a dark, Polynesian-style bar and
succulent Cal-cuisine like calamari (oddly
served in a paper bag) and organic,
hormone-free meat and chicken dishes.
Expensive.

Caribbean

El Floridita 1253 N Vine St ☎323/871-8612.
Lively Cuban restaurant where the dance
floor swings on the weekends. The menu
features solid standards like plantains,
croquetas and yucca, all affordably priced.
Moderate.

Havana on Sunset 5825 Sunset Blvd #105
☎323/464-1800. Like the name says,
everything is Cuban at this festive eatery,
from the lively music to the rich, authentic
meals of soups, seafood and garlic-heavy
entrees. Moderate.

Chinese and Vietnamese

Little Hong Kong Deli 1645 N Cahuenga Blvd
☎323/957-1998. Appealing for its traditional
Szechuan and Mandarin entrees, but also
worth trying for specials like succulent lemon
scallops and walnut shrimp. Moderate.

Taipan 7075 Sunset Blvd ☎323/464-2989. A
good neighborhood eatery offering
appetizing shrimp and chicken entrees,
plus a few surprises like black-bean catfish.
Moderate.

French

Café des Artistes 1534 N McCadden Place
☎323/469-7300. With a French chef at the
helm and French customers at the tables,
this is as authentically Gallic a spot as you'll
find in LA, highlighted by such treats as
plum-garnished pork roast, coq au vin and
an array of good seafood dishes.
Expensive.

Indian and Sri Lankan

Electric Lotus 4656 Franklin Ave, Los Feliz
☎323/953-0040. While somewhat cramped
and located in a mini-mall, an excellent
choice for traditional staples – *pakoras*,
vindaloo, curries, etc – at affordable prices.
Moderate.

Italian and pizza

Louise's Trattoria 4500 Los Feliz Blvd
☎323/667-0777. Everybody in LA knows this
chain: some love it for its good mid-priced
pizzas, while others hate it for its
overcooked, uninspired pasta. You decide.
Moderate.
Miceli's 1646 N Las Palmas St ☎323/466-
3438. Hefty, old-style pizzas that come
laden with gooey cheese and plenty of
tomato sauce. Moderate.
Palermo 1858 N Vermont Ave ☎323/663-1178.
As old as Hollywood itself, and with as
many devoted fans, who flock here for the
rich Southern Italian pizzas, cheesy decor
and gallons of affordable red wine. If you
like huge platefuls of spaghetti in chunky
red sauce, this is the place. Moderate.

Japanese

Yamashiro 1999 N Sycamore Ave ☎323/466-
5125. Although the food can occasionally
be a letdown, this place is still a must-see
for its outstanding gardens, koi ponds,
palatial design and outstanding view of LA
from the Hollywood Hills – making it a
perfectly romantic attraction. Expensive.

Mexican and Latin American

Burrito King 2109 W Sunset Blvd at Alvarado,
Echo Park ☎213/484-9859. Excellent burritos
and tasty tostadas from this small stand;
open until 2am. Also nearby at 2827
Hyperion Ave ☎323/663-9378.
Inexpensive.
Mexico City 2121 N Hillhurst Ave ☎323/661-

7227. Spinach enchiladas and other
California variations on Mexican standards,
served in a quiet corner of Los Feliz.
Moderate.
Yuca's Hut 2056 N Hillhurst Ave ☎323/662-
1214. A small hidden jewel serving good al
fresco burritos opposite the more popular
Mexico City (above). Inexpensive.

Middle Eastern

Marouch 4905 Santa Monica Blvd ☎323/662-
9325. Located in a nondescript part of
town, this excellent Lebanese restaurant
provides flavorful and very affordable
kebabs and shawarma. Moderate.
Zankou Chicken 5065 Sunset Blvd ☎323/665-
7845. Easily the best-value Middle Eastern
option in town (and part of a citywide
chain), with delicious, garlicky chicken
cooked on a rotisserie and tucked into a
delicious sandwich, plus all the traditional
salads – tabouli, hummus and the like.
Inexpensive.

Russian and Eastern European

Uzbekistan 7077 Sunset Blvd ☎323/464-3663.
Savory, though heavy, servings of mostly
lamb-based Uzbekistani food, especially
heavy on dumplings. Moderate.

Thai

Chan Dara 1511 N Cahuenga Blvd ☎323/464-
8585. Terrific Thai food, and the locals know
it, especially for the barbecued chicken and
Pad Thai. Also at 310 N Larchmont Blvd,
Mid-Wilshire ☎323/467-1052. Moderate.
Jitlada 5233 Sunset Blvd ☎323/667-9809. In a
dreary mini-mall, but the spicy chicken,
squid and seafood curries more than make
up for the setting. Affordable prices, too.
Moderate.
Thai Seafood 5615 Hollywood Blvd ☎323/461-
7053. Egg rolls, noodles and seafood are
the tasty, fairly authentic highlights of this
small joint in a busy section of Hollywood.
Moderate.

West Hollywood

American, Californian and Cajun

Café La Boheme 8400 Santa Monica Blvd
☎323/848-2360. Quintessential LA hot spot
whose dark, slightly spooky decor has
variously been compared to a film set,

theater and funhouse. The menu, an indulgent mix of Cal-cuisine and pan-Asian cooking, makes for a truly memorable experience. Expensive.

The Cajun Bistro 8301 Sunset Blvd ☏323/656-6388. Funky, unpretentious Cajun joint on a central part of the strip that dishes up lip-smacking Louisiana cooking – notably the jambalaya – without busting your wallet. Moderate.

Jar 8225 Beverly Blvd ☏323/655-6566. Just to the south of West Hollywood, this steakhouse features all the usual red-meat options – prime rib, T-bone, even a pot roast – with inspired Cal-cuisine touches. Expensive.

Chinese and Vietnamese

Chin Chin 8618 Sunset Blvd ☏310/652-1818. Flashy but affordable dim sum café, a longstanding favorite and one of several around town. Open until midnight. Moderate.

Joss 9255 Sunset Blvd ☏310/276-1886. Sitting at the west end of the Sunset Strip, the Westside's hip version of Chinese cuisine: pricey meals with rich, complex flavors and a minimum of color and style. Expensive.

French

Fenix 8358 Sunset Blvd, *Argyle Hotel* ☏323/848-6677. French cooking on the Sunset Strip, in an exclusive establishment popular with culinary trendsetters. *Fenix* offers up terrific steaks and seafood prepared with local and exotic ingredients. Very expensive.

L'Orangerie 903 N La Cienega Blvd ☏310/652-9770. The closest Francophiles can get to Escoffier in LA, though the stylish French food has more than a dash of California cuisine as well. If you haven't got the $150 it takes to sit down, or a fancy enough suit to wear, then enjoy the view from the bar. Very expensive.

Italian and pizza

Frankie & Johnnie's New York Pizza 8947 Sunset Blvd, West Hollywood ☏310/275-7770. Amid all the big rock clubs, an old favorite for its sizeable pies loaded with greasy and healthy ingredients alike. Check out the ink-scrawled messages on the walls, which include praise from famous regulars, from Don Knotts to Fred Durst.

Japanese

Miyagi's 8225 Sunset Blvd ☏323/650-3524. A hip sushi joint with a menu of traditional and hybrid raw-fish offerings, served on three floors to piped-in pop music. Moderate.

Todai 8612 Beverly Blvd #157 ☏310/659-1375. A tourist-friendly spot where the sushi and other Asian cuisine are more affordable than at comparable Japanese restaurants. One of eight LA-area branches. Moderate.

Mexican and Latin American

Carlitos Gardel 7963 Melrose Ave ☏323/655-0891. Rich and delectable Argentine cuisine – ie, heavy on the beef and spices – with sausages and garlic adding to the potent kick. Moderate.

El Compadre 7408 W Sunset Blvd ☏323/874-7924. Potent margaritas, live mariachi bands and cheap Mexican standards make this a music-loving gourmand's delight. Four other remote locations. Inexpensive.

Poquito Mas 8555 Sunset Blvd ☏310/652-7008. Grab a chicken enchilada or burrito, the top choices at this popular LA-wide chain. Inexpensive.

Middle Eastern

Noura Café 8479 Melrose Ave ☏323/651-4581. Moderately priced Middle Eastern specialties. For beginners, the "taster's delight"– hummus, baba ganoush, tabouli, falafel, fried eggplant zucchini and stuffed grape leaves – is a good, filling bet. Moderate.

Vegetarian and wholefood

Real Food Daily 414 N La Cienega Blvd ☏310/289-9910. Avocado rolls, beet bisque and salads draw a good crowd at this vegan restaurant, which also operates a branch at 514 Santa Monica Blvd in Santa Monica ☏310/451-7544. Moderate.

Beverly Hills and West LA

African

Koutoubia 2116 Westwood Blvd, West LA ☏310/475-0729. Good, authentic Moroccan lamb, couscous and seafood dishes, served in comfortable surroundings. Expensive.

American, Californian and Cajun

Arnie Morton's 435 N La Cienega Blvd, Beverly Hills ☎310/246-1501. A 1950s-style homage to the old days of American cuisine, where hefty steaks (go for the traditional porterhouse) and scrumptious sides of creamed spinach and baked potatoes pull in grizzled veterans of Tinseltown. Very expensive.

Café Blanc 9777 Little Santa Monica Blvd, Beverly Hills ☎310/888-0108. California cuisine that borrows freely from French and Asian cooking, resulting in a delicious hybrid of ever-changing flavors – the crab salad and lobster bisque are particularly good. The other constant here is the competition for tables, so reserve well in advance. Expensive.

The Cheesecake Factory 364 N Beverly Drive, Beverly Hills ☎310/278-7270. Beverly Hills' busiest restaurant, best experienced for its exceptional desserts, notably the wide variety of cheesecakes (chocolate-chip, peanut butter, key lime, etc). Come at an off-hour if you want a table. Moderate.

Daily Grill 11677 San Vicente Blvd, Brentwood ☎310/442-0044. Beef, chicken and fish are the main staples of this popular Westside chain, one of the few affordable restaurants around this upscale zone. Moderate.

Maple Drive 345 N Maple Drive, Beverly Hills ☎310/274-9800. Fine food drawn from a large culinary palette that includes foie gras, meatloaf and pork chops. If you're lucky, you might spot local celebs sneaking in for an oyster or two. Very expensive.

Spago 176 N Cañon Drive, Beverly Hills ☎310/385-0880. Now that the original Sunset Strip branch of LA's most famous restaurant has closed, you'll have to go to this stuffier Beverly Hills location to get a taste of über-chef Wolfgang Puck's latest Cal-cuisine concoctions, among them his famous designer pizzas. Very expensive.

Caribbean

Bamboo 10835 Venice Blvd, Culver City ☎310/287-0668. In a section of West LA full of enticing ethnic restaurants, *Bamboo* stands out for its chicken dishes and spicy Caribbean flavors, as well as its reasonable prices. Moderate.

Versailles 10319 Venice Blvd, West LA ☎310/558-3168. Bustling authentic Cuban restaurant with hearty dishes, including excellent fried plantains, paella, and black beans and rice. Several branches citywide. Inexpensive.

Chinese and Vietnamese

Chung King 11538 W Pico Blvd, West LA ☎310/477-4917. The best neighborhood Chinese restaurant in LA, serving spicy Szechuan food: don't miss out on the *bum-bum* chicken and other house specialties. Open until midnight. Moderate.

Eurochow 1099 Westwood Blvd, Westwood ☎310/209-0066. Located in the historic Dome building (see p.119), this stylish restaurant offers a melange of Chinese and European flavors, with a heavy dash of California cuisine: dumplings, pastas, shrimp rolls, seafood and even designer pizzas. The eye-catching decor and Spanish Colonial architecture are also a treat. Expensive.

Mr Chow 344 N Camden Drive, Beverly Hills ☎310/278-9911. Another of restaurateur Michael Chow's culinary experiments, an ultra-pricey hangout where delicious Chinese food comes in a wide variety of flavors and spices, extravagantly blended with a panoply of world cuisines. Very expensive.

Pho Bac Huynh 11819 Wilshire Blvd, West LA ☎310/477-9379. The authentic Vietnamese soup *pho* is the focus of this excellent Westside eatery, served as an entree with spices and exotic flavorings. Located in a strip mall like most other authentic eateries in the area. Moderate.

Greek

Delphi 1383 Westwood Blvd ☎310/478-2900. The place to come in West LA for authentic Greek cooking, from flavorful dolmas and tabouli to the hearty pitas and souvlaki – an unpretentious joint that offers plenty of food for a reasonable price. Moderate.

Indian and Sri Lankan

Bombay Café 12021 Pico Blvd, West LA ☎310/473-3388. One of LA's finest Indian restaurants, with terrific traditional and nouveau offerings and a helpful, friendly staff. Moderate.

Clay Pit 145 S Barrington Ave, West LA ☎310/476-4700. Another top choice, serving delights like lamb-stuffed *keema naan* and a fine tandoori chicken – all for around $15. Moderate.

If you're less interested in eating fine cuisine and would rather catch glimpses of your favorite film and TV stars, there are a number of places where you can watch **celebrities** go through their paces of alternately hiding from, and then mugging for, the public. While practically any upper-end eatery is a likely spot to find the stars – especially in Beverly Hills, Santa Monica and Malibu – some places have that special cachet. Note that the few restaurants listed below without page references are recommended for their star-spotting potential, not their food.

Buffalo Club 1520 Olympic Blvd, Santa Monica ☏310/450-8600.
Chinois on Main 2709 Main St, Santa Monica ☏310/392-9025; p.271.
Drago 2628 Wilshire Blvd, Santa Monica ☏310/828-1585; p.272.
Eurochow 1099 Westwood Blvd, Westwood ☏310/209-0066; p.267.
Frankie & Johnnie's New York Pizza 8947 Sunset Blvd, West Hollywood ☏310/275-7770; p.266.
Geoffrey's 27400 PCH, Malibu ☏310/457-1519; p.272.
Granita 23725 W Malibu Rd, Malibu ☏310/456-0488; p.269.
The Ivy 113 N Robertson Blvd, Beverly Hills ☏310/274-8303.
Jerry's Famous Deli 8701 Beverly Blvd, Beverly Hills ☏310/289-1811; p.254.
LA Farm 3000 W Olympic Blvd, Santa Monica ☏310/449-4000; p.270.
Le Dôme 8720 Sunset Blvd, West Hollywood ☏310/659-6919.
Maple Drive 345 N Maple Drive, Beverly Hills ☏310/274-9800; p.267.

Matsuhisa 129 N La Cienega Blvd, Beverly Hills ☏310/659-9639; p.268.
Mr Chow 344 N Camden Drive, Beverly Hills ☏310/278-9911; p.267.
Morton's 8764 Melrose Ave, West Hollywood ☏310/276-5205.
Musso and Frank Grill 6667 Hollywood Blvd ☏323/467-7788; p.264.
Nate 'n' Al's 414 N Beverly Drive ☏310/274-0101; p.254.
The Palm 9001 Santa Monica Blvd, Beverly Hills ☏310/550-8811.
Patina 5955 Melrose Ave ☏323/467-1108; p.262.
Patrick's Roadhouse 106 Entrada Drive, Pacific Palisades ☏310/459-4544.
Roscoe's Chicken and Waffles 1514 N Gower St ☏323/466-7453; p.251.
Spago 176 N Cañon Drive, Beverly Hills ☏310/385-0880; p.267.
Sunset Room 1430 N Cahuenga Blvd, Hollywood ☏323/463-0004.
Valentino 3115 W Pico Blvd, Santa Monica ☏310/829-4313; p.272.

Nizam 10871 W Pico Blvd, West LA ☏310/470-1441. Skip the food court in the mall across the street and instead visit this fine little Indian haunt, where hefty portions of curried lamb and tandoori chicken go for fairly cheap prices. Moderate.

Italian

Barefoot 8722 W Third St, Beverly Hills ☏310/276-6223. Good pastas, pizzas and seafood between Beverly Hills and the Beverly Center. Affordable prices, considering the upscale location. Moderate.
Jacopo's 490 N Beverly Drive, Beverly Hills ☏310/858-6446. Dumpy little brickhouse that surprisingly has some of LA's best pizzas, served piping hot and fairly cheap.

Also at 8166 Sunset Blvd, West Hollywood ☏323/650-8128. Inexpensive.
Locanda Veneta 8638 W Third St, Beverly Hills ☏310/274-1893. Whether it's the scrumptious ravioli, veal or the carpaccio, you can't go wrong at one of LA's previously quiet culinary joys (near the Beverly Center). Expensive.

Japanese

Matsuhisa 129 N La Cienega Blvd, Beverly Hills ☏310/659-9639. The biggest name in town for sushi, charging the highest prices. Essential if you're a raw-fish aficionado with a wad of cash; otherwise, you can dine two or three times at other fine, and much cheaper, Japanese restaurants. Very expensive.

Mori Sushi 11500 W Pico Blvd, West LA
☎323/479-3939. A subtly stylish spot that resists trendiness, offering up some of the city's finest sushi in spare and elegant arrangements, and almost always delicious. Moderate.

The Sushi House 12013 Pico Blvd, West LA
☎310/479-1507. Reggae and sushi coalesce in a hole-in-the-wall bar with limited seating. Try the "Superman," an appealing rainbow-colored roll of salmon, yellowtail, whitefish and avocado. Moderate.

Mexican and Latin American

Baja Fresh 475 N Beverly Drive, Beverly Hills ☎310/858-6690. Cheap and enjoyable Mexican food served to a hungry crowd of window-shoppers and movie-industry wannabes – thus the emphasis on "healthy" eating. Many other area locations. Inexpensive.

La Salsa 1154 Westwood Blvd ☎310/208-7083. The place to come for fresh, delicious soft tacos and burritos. One of several Westside branches. Inexpensive.

Monte Alban 11927 Santa Monica Blvd, West LA ☎310/444-7736. Forget the tacky mini-mall setting and focus on the fine selection of *mole* sauces and Mexican staples that make any trip here worthwhile. Inexpensive.

Middle Eastern

Falafel King 1059 Broxton Ave, Westwood
☎310/208-4444. Falafel is the house special here, and you can get a lot of it for only a few dollars. Inexpensive.

Magic Carpet 8566 W Pico Blvd, West LA
☎310/652-8507. Fried pancakes and falafel – both in generous portions – bring loyal crowds to this excellent Yemeni restaurant. Moderate.

Shamshiry 1916 Westwood Blvd, West LA
☎310/474-1410. Top Iranian restaurant in the area, offering delicious kebabs, pilafs and exotic sauces. Moderate.

Seafood

McCormick and Schmick's 206 N Rodeo Drive, Beverly Hills ☎213/629-1929. Swank joint with excellent fresh seafood, and known for its affordable weekend dinner specials. Expensive.

Spanish

Cava 8384 W Third St, West LA ☎323/ 658-8898. Fun dining spot where the Latin and Iberian dishes take a back seat to the delicious tapas, accompanied by shots of sherry. The sausage paella and roasted potatoes are a good start. Moderate.

Thai

Talesai 9198 Olympic Blvd, Beverly Hills
☎310/271-9345. Excellent curried seafood and Cal-cuisine–style noodle dishes served to in-the-know gourmets inside a drab strip mall. Expensive.

Vegetable and wholefood

A Votre Sante 242 S Beverly Drive, Beverly Hills ☎310/860-9441. Scrambled tofu and fried vegetables are on the menu – along with veggie and turkey burgers – at this Westside mini-chain. Open for breakfast and lunch. Moderate.

Erewhon 7660 Beverly Blvd ☎323/937-0777. A good old-fashioned juice bar and deli, where you can gulp down your choice of wheatgrass concoctions and bee-pollen smoothies. Moderate.

Newsroom Café 120 N Robertson Blvd, Beverly Hills ☎310/652-4444. A prime place to spot B-list celebrities with A-list attitudes scarfing down veggie burgers and tofu salads with wheatgrass "shooters." Especially popular for lunch. Also has magazine racks and Internet terminals. Moderate.

Santa Monica, Venice and Malibu

American, Californian and Cajun

Crocodile Café 101 Santa Monica Blvd, Santa Monica ☎310/394-4783. The calzones, pizzas and chicken dishes are all good at this local chain – a good budget choice if you're visiting the nearby Third Street Promenade (see p.134). A handful of branches in the valleys. Moderate.

Flint's 3321 Pico Blvd, Santa Monica
☎310/453-1331. Perhaps LA's most stylish steakhouse, tucked away in a grungy spot by the freeway, but loaded with dark, swinging charm. Rich and savory sides of beef feature on the menu, as do several odd but potent cocktails – notably the green-apple martini, garnished with a gummy worm. Very expensive.

Granita 23725 W Malibu Rd, Malibu ☎310/456-0488. Chef Wolfgang Puck's Malibu entry, an oceanside restaurant offering a heady

Late-night eats

The following restaurants serve all or a portion of their menus after 11pm at least twice a week, with many closing around 2am, and a handful staying open around the clock.

Downtown

El Taurino 1104 S Hoover St, Westlake ☎213/738-9197; weekends open 24 hours; p.260.
Original Pantry 877 S Figueroa St ☎213/972-9279; open 24 hours; p.249.
Pacific Dining Car 1310 W Sixth St ☎213/483-6000; open 24 hours; p.259.

Mid-Wilshire

Atlas 3760 Wilshire Blvd ☎213/380-8400; p.261.
Canter's Deli 419 N Fairfax Ave ☎323/651-2030; open 24 hours; p.250.
Du-Par's 6333 W Third St ☎323/933-8446; p.251.
Genghis Cohen 740 N Fairfax Ave ☎323/653-0640; p.262.
Hard Rock Café in the Beverly Center, Beverly Blvd at San Vicente Blvd ☎310/276-7605; p.251.
Louis XIV 606 N La Brea Ave ☎323/934-5102; p.262.
Pink's Hot Dogs 709 N La Brea Ave ☎323/931-4223; p.251.
Sushi Roku 8445 W Third St ☎323/655-6767; p.263.
Swingers Beverly Laurel Motor Lodge, 8018 Beverly Blvd at Laurel Ave ☎323/653-5858; p.251.

Tommy Tang's 7313 Melrose Ave ☎323/937-5733; open 24 hours; p.263.

Hollywood

Burrito King 2109 W Sunset Blvd at Alvarado ☎213/413-9444; p.265.
Café des Artistes 1534 N McCadden Place ☎323/469-7300; p.265.
Chan Dara 1511 N Cahuenga Blvd ☎323/464-8585; p.265.
Fred 62 1854 N Vermont Ave, Los Feliz ☎323/667-0062; open 24 hours; p.251.
Miceli's 1646 N Las Palmas St ☎323/466-3438; p.265.
Pinot Hollywood 1448 Gower St ☎323/461-8800; p.264.
Roscoe's Chicken and Waffles 1514 N Gower St ☎323/466-7453; p.251.
Shibucho 3114 Beverly Blvd, Silver Lake ☎213/387-8498; p.260.
Tommy's 2575 W Beverly Blvd, Silver Lake ☎213/389-9060; open 24 hours; p.251.

West Hollywood

Astro Burger 7475 Santa Monica Blvd ☎323/874-8041; p.252.
Barney's Beanery 8447 Santa Monica Blvd ☎323/654-2287; p.252.

---

mix of Cal-cuisine and Mediterranean flavors. While seafood stew, lobster, salmon and ravioli all rank high, most come to spot a Hollywood name or two. Very expensive.

Hal's 1349 Abbot Kinney Blvd, Venice ☎310/396-3105. Increasingly popular restaurant along a hip shopping stretch in Venice, where the well-prepared American standards include marinated steaks and salmon dishes. Expensive.

Joe's 1023 Abbot Kinney Blvd, Venice ☎310/399-5811. Offers appetizing Cal-cuisine dishes (mixed with a dash of French cookery) using grilled chicken, pork and salmon. Expensive.

LA Farm 3000 W Olympic Blvd, Santa Monica ☎310/449-4000. Delicious California cuisine, with an accent on seafood, though somewhat overpriced. The main draw, however, is the celebrity-watching: here the stars dine in peace, away from the flashier confines of places like Spago (see p.267). Expensive.

Michael's 1147 Third St, Santa Monica ☎310/451-0843. Longstanding favorite for California cuisine, served here amid modern art. This venerable establishment always attracts the crowds with its succulent steaks, pastas and game. Reservations are essential. Very expensive.

RESTAURANTS AND CAFÉS | Restaurants

Café La Boheme 8400 Santa Monica Blvd ☎323/848-2360; p.265.
Fenix 8358 Sunset Blvd, *Argyle Hotel* ☎323/848-6677; p.266.
Frankie & Johnnie's New York Pizza 8947 Sunset Blvd ☎310/275-7770; p.266.
Mel's Drive-In 8585 Sunset Blvd ☎310/854-7200; open 24 hours; p.252.
Yukon Mining Company 7328 Santa Monica Blvd ☎323/851-8833; open 24 hours; p.253.

Beverly Hills and West LA
The Apple Pan 10801 W Pico Blvd, West LA ☎310/475-3585; p.253.
Bamboo 10835 Venice Blvd, Culver City ☎310/287-0668; p.267.
Barefoot 8722 W Third St, Beverly Hills ☎310/276-6223; p.268.
Cava 8384 W Third St, West LA ☎323/658-8898; p.269.
Daily Grill 11677 San Vicente Blvd, Brentwood ☎310/442-0044; p.267.
Falafel King 1059 Broxton Ave, Westwood ☎310/208-4444; p.269.
In-N-Out Burger 922 Gayley Ave, Westwood ☎1-800/786-1000; p.254.
Jerry's Famous Deli 8701 Beverly Blvd, Beverly Hills ☎310/289-1811; open 24 hours; p.254.
Johnny's Pastrami 4017 S Sepulveda Blvd, Culver City ☎310/397-6654; p.254.

Kate Mantilini 9101 Wilshire Blvd, Beverly Hills ☎310/278-3699; p.254.
Locanda Veneta 8638 W Third St, Beverly Hills ☎310/274-1893; p.268.

Santa Monica, Venice and Malibu
Café 50's 838 Lincoln Blvd, Venice ☎310/399-1955; p.256.
Chaya Venice 110 Navy St, Venice ☎310/396-1179; p.272.
Crocodile Café 101 Santa Monica Blvd, Santa Monica ☎310/394-4783; p.269.
Gladstone's 4 Fish 17300 PCH, Pacific Palisades ☎310/454-3474; p.272.
Granita 23725 W Malibu Rd, Malibu ☎310/456-0488; p.269.
Hal's 1349 Abbot Kinney Blvd, Venice ☎310/396-3105; p.270.

The South Bay and LA Harbor
Alegria Cocina Latina 115 Pine Ave, Long Beach ☎562/436-3388; p.274.
Cha Cha Cha 762 Pacific Ave, Long Beach ☎562/436-3900; p.273.

The San Gabriel and San Fernando valleys
Bob's Big Boy 4211 W Riverside Drive, Burbank ☎818/843-9334; open 24 hours; p.258.

Orange County
The Harbor House Café 34157 PCH, Dana Point ☎949/496-9270; p.258.

17th Street Café 1610 Montana Ave, Santa Monica ☎310/453-2771. Good seafood, pasta and burgers at affordable prices in a chic part of town. Nicely casual atmosphere, unlike the flashy shopping zone around it. Also serves breakfast. Moderate.

Caribbean

Babalu 1002 Montana Ave, Santa Monica ☎310/395-2500. The pumpkin pancakes at this pan-ethnic, Caribbean-influenced restaurant are delightful, as are the fried Havana eggs – fried eggs in a salsa-and-bean tortilla – and the smiling image of Carmen Miranda above the front door. Moderate.

Chinese and Vietnamese

Chinois on Main 2709 Main St, Santa Monica ☎310/392-9025. Wolfgang Puck, creator of *Spago*'s designer pizza (see p.267), turns his sights across the Pacific to China, creating a mix of *nouvelle* French and Chinese cuisines designed to go with the green-and-black decor. Quite pricey, but worth it for a splurge, drawing a ravenous crowd of yuppie diners and self-appointed food critics. Very expensive.

P.F. Chang's 326 Wilshire Blvd, Santa Monica ☎310/395-1912. Known for its honey-shrimp and lettuce wraps, this chain specializes in serving rich, complex dishes at reasonable prices. Another Westside branch at 121 N

La Cienega Blvd, West LA ☎310/854-6467. Moderate.

Indian and Sri Lankan

Nawab 1621 Wilshire Blvd, Santa Monica ☎310/829-1106. Though there are few surprises on the menu, pleasing renditions of Indian standards like chicken *vindaloo* and *tikka masala* do the trick. Moderate.

Italian and pizza

Abbot's Pizza Company 1407 Abbot Kinney Blvd, Venice ☎310/396-7334. Named after the founder of the district, this home of the bagel-crust pizza allows your choice of seeds, tangy citrus sauce, or shiitake and wild mushroom sauce. Also at 1811 Pico Blvd, Santa Monica ☎310/314-2777. Inexpensive.

Drago 2628 Wilshire Blvd, Santa Monica ☎310/828-1585. Among LA's better superchic Italian eateries, serving various meats and pastas in an appropriately pretentious setting. Very expensive.

Valentino 3115 W Pico Blvd, Santa Monica ☎310/829-4313. Some call this the best Italian cuisine in the US, served up in classy surroundings with great flair. The listed specials, especially veal, duck and venison, are sure to please, though your pocketbook won't be quite so lucky. Very expensive.

Wildflour Pizza 2807 Main St, Santa Monica ☎310/392-3300. Serving up a great thin-crust pizza, this cozy little spot often draws the crowds. Inexpensive.

Wolfgang Puck Express 1315 Third Street Promenade, Santa Monica ☎310/576-4770. On the second floor of a food mall, watch Promenade tourists below while munching on great pizzas and salads. One of a national chain, which includes a branch on the USC campus. Moderate.

Japanese

Chaya Venice 110 Navy St, Venice ☎310/396-1179. Elegant mix of Japanese and Mediterranean foods in an arty sushi bar, with a suitably snazzy clientele. Expensive.

Lighthouse Buffet 201 Arizona Ave, Santa Monica ☎310/451-2076. All-you-can-eat sushi; indulge to your heart's content for under $10 at lunchtime or $20 in the evening. Inexpensive.

Korean

Monsoon Café 1212 Third St, Santa Monica ☎310/576-9996. Located on the popular Third Street Promenade, this stylish space offers a mix of Pacific Rim cuisines. Expect anything from sushi to Szechuan to Korean barbecued beef. Expensive.

Mexican and Latin American

Gaucho Grill 1251 Third St, Santa Monica ☎310/394-4966. One in a fine local chain of Argentine beef-houses, where the steaks come rich and garlicky, and the spices can bowl you over. Located along the Third Street Promenade. Moderate.

Mariasol 401 Santa Monica Pier, Santa Monica ☎310/917-5050. *Cervezas* with a view, hidden away at the end of the pier, with good, straightforward Mexican staples. On weekend afternoons, the small rooftop deck affords a sweeping panorama from Malibu to Venice. Moderate.

Marix Tex-Mex Playa 118 Entrada Drive, Pacific Palisades ☎310/459-8596. Flavorful fajitas and big margaritas in this rowdy beachfront cantina. Also at 1108 N Flores St, West Hollywood ☎323/656-8800. Moderate.

Russian and Eastern European

Warszawa 1414 Lincoln Blvd, Santa Monica ☎310/393-8831. Pleasant establishment with fine Polish cuisine. Don't miss the hearty potato pancakes, pierogi and borscht. Expensive.

Seafood

Geoffrey's 27400 PCH, Malibu ☎310/457-1519. One of Malibu's most upscale spots for seafood and sunset-watching. The Cal-cuisine–inspired menu is secondary to watching the Tinseltown luminaries drop in. Very expensive.

Gladstone's 4 Fish 17300 PCH, Pacific Palisades ☎310/454-3474. An inevitable tourist stop at the junction of Sunset Boulevard, known best for its prime beachfront location – not for its heavily fried and breaded seafood. Expensive.

Killer Shrimp 523 Washington St, Marina del Rey ☎310/578-2293. When all you want is shrimp, and lots of it, this popular, somewhat dreary-looking spot is the place to come. For a pretty cheap price, you can happily stuff your maw with fistfuls of crustaceans. Moderate.

Neptune's Net 42505 PCH, Malibu ☏310/457-3095. It's worth a trip to the far reaches of LA County's northwestern border to gorge on clams, shrimp, oysters and the like at grimy picnic tables in an otherwise pleasant setting. Inexpensive.

Thai

Flower of Siam 2553 Lincoln Blvd, Venice ☏310/827-0050. Some swear by this spicy but succulent, authentic Thai food, guaranteed to set your tastebuds on fire and your eyes watering. The chicken satay and noodles are highlights. Moderate.

Thai Dishes 1910 Wilshire Blvd, Santa Monica ☏310/828-5634. Very basic Thai meals geared toward diners unfamiliar with the spicier, more extreme versions of the cuisine. Part of a citywide chain. Inexpensive.

Vegetarian and wholefood

Figtree's Café 429 Ocean Front Walk, Venice ☏310/392-4937. Tasty veggie food and grilled fresh fish served on a sunny patio just off the Boardwalk. Health-conscious yuppies come in droves for breakfast. Moderate.

Inn of the Seventh Ray 128 Old Topanga Rd, Topanga Canyon ☏310/455-1311. The ultimate New Age restaurant in a supremely New Age area, serving vegetarian and other wholefood meals in a relatively secluded environment. Expensive.

Mäni's Bakery 2507 Main St, Santa Monica ☏310/396-7700. An array of culinarily correct treats – from sugarless brownies to meatless sandwiches – may draw you to this coffeehouse and bakery for breakfast or lunch. Look hard and you might even see a weight-obsessed celebrity darting in. Moderate.

Shambala Café 607 Colorado Ave, Santa Monica ☏310/395-2160. Apart from organic chicken, the menu is meat-free, with pasta, tofu, eggplant and some very unusual seaweed dishes. Moderate.

South Central and East LA

American, Californian and Cajun

Harold and Belle's 2920 Jefferson Blvd, South Central ☏323/735-9023. One of the best and most authentic of the Cajun-cuisine restaurants in town, with a rich gumbo and heaping portions of crayfish, catfish and shrimp, alongside standards like corn-on-the-cob. Moderate.

Mexican and Latin American

Ciro's 705 N Evergreen Ave, East LA ☏323/267-8637. A split-level cave of a dining room, serving enormous platters of shrimp and *mole* specials, while *flautas* – the main draw. They also offer takeout. Moderate.

El Tepayac 812 N Evergreen Ave, East LA ☏323/267-8668. Huge, scrumptious burritos and hot salsa – be prepared to wait in line. Also in Mid-Wilshire at 3400 W Third St ☏213/739-2239. Inexpensive.

Luminarias 3500 Ramona Blvd, Monterey Park ☏323/268-4177. Dance to salsa and merengue between bites of seafood-heavy Mexican food, surprisingly good for an area best known for its Chinese cuisine. Moderate.

Paco's Tacos 6212 W Manchester Ave, Westchester ☏310/645-8692. Potent margaritas and good, filling burritos are the highlights at this local chain. Inexpensive.

The South Bay and LA Harbor

Caribbean

Cha Cha Cha 762 Pacific Ave, Long Beach ☏562/436-3900. Paella, black-pepper shrimp and jerk chicken are all highly recommended here, one of Long Beach's better and more colorful restaurants. Moderate.

Greek

Mykonos 5374 E Second St, Long Beach ☏562/434-1856. Authentic dishes and spirited nightly dancing at this unpretentious Greek eatery, where the gyros, souvlaki and other favorites are served with a deft culinary flair. Moderate.

Italian and pizza

L'Opera 101 Pine Ave, Long Beach ☏562/491-0066. Hop off the Blue Line light rail and stop in at the former First National Bank building, where an upscale Italian eatery serves lip-smacking concoctions (with Cal-cuisine stylings) such as duck ravioli and stuffed blue prawns. Expensive.

Mangiamo 128 Manhattan Beach Blvd, Manhattan Beach ☎310/318-3434. Like the name says, "Let's eat!" Fairly pricey but worth it for the specialist Northern Italian seafood – and right off the beach, too. Expensive.

Mexican and Latin American

By Brazil 1615 Cabrillo Ave, Torrance ☎310/787-7520. Hearty Brazilian fare, mostly grilled chicken and beef dishes; worth a visit to inland Torrance for a taste. Moderate.

El Pollo Inka 1100 PCH, Hermosa Beach ☎310/372-1433. Peruvian seafood – fish cooked with a blend of Latin spices – is the specialty here, and it's quite good, especially considering the low prices. One in a chain of mostly South Bay restaurants, except for a branch at 11701 Wilshire Blvd, West LA ☎310/571-3334. Inexpensive.

Pancho's 3615 Highland Ave, Manhattan Beach ☎310/545-6670. Big portions, comparatively cheap for the area and one of the few decent Mexican establishments down this way. Moderate.

Taco Surf 5316 1/2 E Second St, Long Beach ☎562/434-8646. As you might guess, fish tacos are the main draw here, though the rest of the eatery's south-of-the-border offerings are also good. Inexpensive.

Russian and Eastern European

Czech Point 1981 Artesia Blvd, Redondo Beach ☎310/374-7791. One of the few good reasons to venture down to this pretentious beach town, a relaxed and unfussy diner presenting the cuisine of the Czech Republic, with tasty and filling goulash, schnitzel, dumplings and spicy, roasted meats. Inexpensive.

Seafood

Beluga 1500 Morningside Drive, Manhattan Beach ☎310/802-1160. Sample the savory roe available at this restaurant's appealing caviar bar, along with its excellent oyster, fish, steak and pasta dishes. Expensive.

King's Fish House 100 W Broadway, Long Beach ☎562/432-7463. In the middle of Long Beach's busy downtown, this esteemed seafood restaurant offers a full selection of predictable, but well-prepared, entrees – including salmon, tuna, oysters and sea bass – to an upscale crowd of locals and tourists. Expensive.

Spanish

Alegria Cocina Latina 115 Pine Ave, Long Beach ☎562/436-3388. Quality tapas and served with sangría on the patio, and to the beat of live flamenco at weekends, in a prime location in downtown Long Beach. Expensive.

Soleil 1142 Manhattan Ave, Manhattan Beach ☎310/545-8654. Spicy ceviche and a good range of tapas to tempt your palate at this unexpected Spanish spot in the South Bay. Expensive.

Vegetarian and wholefood

Good Stuff 1300 Highland Ave, Manhattan Beach ☎310/545-4775. Healthy eating, vegetarian or otherwise, is the goal at this popular spot, with a range of filling sandwiches and fruit plates. Moderate.

Papa Jon's 5006 E Second St, Long Beach ☎562/439-1059. Meatless Mexican entrees and garden burgers are the highlights at this quiet Belmont Shores eatery, which has totally vegan meals as well as an on-site market. Moderate.

The Spot 110 Second St, Hermosa Beach ☎310/376-2355. A staggering selection of vegetarian dishes, based on Mexican and other international cuisines and free of refined sugar or any animal products. Inexpensive.

The San Gabriel and San Fernando valleys

African

Langano 14838 Burbank Blvd, Sherman Oaks ☎818/786-2670. One of the few places in the Valley to fill up on Ethiopian food, but a solid choice nonetheless for its delicious *injera* bread and *wat* soups and stews. Moderate.

Marrakesh 13003 Ventura Blvd, Studio City ☎818/788-6354. Moroccan restaurant in the Valley, where good, filling couscous and lamb dishes are served amid lush furnishings and belly dancing. Expensive.

American, Californian and Cajun

Monty's Steakhouse 592 S Fair Oaks Ave, Pasadena ☎626/792-7776. Longstanding favorite where thick servings of juicy meat and hearty potatoes appeal to a loyal, graying crowd. Expensive.

Saddle Peak Lodge 419 Cold Canyon Rd,
Calabasas ☎818/222-3888. On the San
Fernando Valley side of the Santa Monica
Mountains, this is elite LA's nod to rustic
hunting lodges. Beneath mounted game
heads, you can elegantly devour exquisite
Cal-cuisine – from venison and boar to
antelope – prepared in ways the pioneers
couldn't have imagined. Very expensive.

Caribbean

Kingston Café 333 S Fair Oaks Ave, Pasadena
☎626/405-8080. All the Caribbean favorites
make an appearance here, including oxtail,
plantains, jerk chicken, beans and rice, and
other traditional specialties of Jamaica and
other islands. Moderate.

Xiomara 69 N Raymond Ave, Pasadena
☎626/796-2520. An upscale Old Pasadena
restaurant serving delicious Cuban and
Latin American meals, mainly beef, pork
and fish entrees, plus a solid range of
stews and colorful sauces. Expensive.

Chinese and Vietnamese

City Wok 10949 Ventura Blvd, Studio City
☎818/506-4050. A fine little establishment
selling Chinese food without frills or
attitude; the dishes are flavorful, the prices
are cheap. Inexpensive.

Sea Star 914 W Beacon St, Alhambra
☎626/282-8833. Dim sum at its best: pork
baos, potstickers and dumplings, along
with appealing sweets. Moderate.

French

Café Bizou 14016 Ventura Blvd, San Fernando
Valley ☎818/788-3536. Bringing affordable
French cuisine to the northern valleys is this
delightful, and always busy, restaurant,
serving succulent pork tenderloin and
salmon salads. Moderate.

Julienne 2649 Mission St, San Marino
☎626/441-2299. While the pâté and apricot
chicken are merely good, the chicken salad
and rich desserts are even better at this
excellent French restaurant. Not on the
menu are alcoholic spirits – forbidden in
teetotal San Marino. Moderate.

Paul's Café 13456 Ventura Blvd, San Fernando
Valley ☎818/789-3575. French cuisine with
California touches – note the sea bass in
crab marinade – with appetizing results and
surprisingly affordable. One of several
branches in the Valley. Moderate.

Greek

Café Santorini 70 W Union St, Pasadena
☎626/564-4200. A fine mix of Greek and
Italian food – capellini, souvlaki, risotto and
the like – with a little Armenian sausage
thrown in as well. Located in a relaxed
plaza and offering some patio dining.
Moderate.

Great Greek 13362 Ventura Blvd, Sherman
Oaks ☎818/905-5250. A required stop for
anyone with a taste for Greek food, this
busy enterprise serves delicious dolmas,
kebabs and moussaka to ethnic music
beats and fervent dancing. Moderate.

Indian and Sri Lankan

Passage to India 14062 Burbank Blvd, Van
Nuys ☎818/787-8488. Savory Indian cooking
with a British flair, covering a broad range of
South Asian staples like spicy *vindaloos*,
tandoori chicken, stuffed *naan*, and beef
and lamb kebabs. Moderate.

Italian and pizza

Market City Caffé 36 W Colorado Blvd #300,
Pasadena ☎626/568-2303. Excellent
Southern Italian pizzas and seafood, along
with a superb antipasto bar. Also at other
locations in the northern valleys. Moderate.

Posto 14928 Ventura Blvd, Sherman Oaks
☎818/784-4400. An offshoot of *Valentino* in
Santa Monica (see p.272), this Valley
variant also offers some of the best Italian
cuisine in LA, taking regional central Italian
dishes and adding a dash of Californian
creativity. Expensive.

Japanese

Genmai-Sushi 4454 Van Nuys Blvd, Sherman
Oaks ☎818/986-7060. *Genmai* is Japanese
for brown rice, which you can sample
alongside soft-shell crabs in *ponzu* sauce,
regular sushi and seasonal macrobiotic
dishes. Moderate.

Shiro 1505 Mission St, South Pasadena
☎626/799-4774. One of LA's few top-notch
restaurants in South Pasadena. The
seafood – particularly the grilled catfish and
smoked salmon – is best here, prepared in
rich, tangy flavors, such as *ponzu* sauce.
Expensive.

Sushi Nozawa 11288 Ventura Blvd, Studio City
☎818/508-7017. Traditional sushi dishes
served to trendy regulars who don't mind

being berated by the imperious chef: if you sit at the bar, he will decide what you'll eat. Period. Expensive.

Korean

Arirang 114 W Union St, Pasadena ☎626/577-8885. You can't go wrong at this scrumptious Old Pasadena eatery, where meat and seafood are barbecued before your eyes, and you'll have to split each sizeable platter with a companion. If you don't like barbecue, there's always sushi. Moderate.

Mexican and Latin American

Izalco 10729 Burbank Blvd, North Hollywood ☎818/760-0396. Salvadoran cuisine presented with style, from plantains and pork ribs to corn cakes and *pupusas* – a bit of a pleasant surprise for the area. Moderate.
Merida 20 E Colorado Blvd, Pasadena ☎626/792-7371. Unusual Mexican restaurant in the Old Pasadena shopping strip, featuring dishes from the Yucatán; try the spicy pork wrapped and steamed in banana leaves. Inexpensive.

Middle Eastern

Burger Continental 535 S Lake Ave, Pasadena ☎626/792-6634. Although it sounds like a fast-food joint, this is actually one of LA's better Middle Eastern restaurants, where you can get mounds of chicken and lamb kebabs for no more than a few dollars. Inexpensive.
Carousel 304 N Brand Ave, Glendale ☎818/246-7775. A Lebanese charmer in downtown Glendale, chock-full of Levantine cultural artifacts and dishing up deliciously authentic food, from roasted chicken and quail to several different kinds of kebabs. Moderate.

Russian and Eastern European

Hortobagy 11138 Ventura Blvd, Studio City ☎818/980-2273. Roasted pork and sausage, schnitzel and cabbage rolls are but a few of the appealing offerings available at this Hungarian restaurant in the Valley. Plenty of spicy, paprika-laden satisfaction for a fair price. Moderate.

Spanish

La Luna Negra 44 W Green St, Pasadena

☎626/844-4331. An affordable spot for mouthwatering tapas, including classic croquetas, paellas and spicy seafood dishes – prepared in mostly traditional fashion. Moderate.

Thai

Kuala Lumpur 69 W Green St, Pasadena ☎626/577-5175. Curried soups and tangy salads are a few of the highlights at this Malaysian eatery, along with coconut rice and spicy chicken, plus other delectable Southeast Asian dishes. Inexpensive.
Saladang 363 S Fair Oaks Ave, Pasadena ☎626/793-8123. Don't miss out on the Pad Thai, curry, salmon or spicy noodles at this chic spot. The restaurant's recent *Saladang Song* annex offers spicier, more traditional Thai dishes. Moderate.
Sanamluang Café 12980 Sherman Way, North Hollywood ☎818/764-1180. The cheap, plentiful noodles at this nearly-all-night Thai eatery are unbeatably good. Inexpensive.

Orange County

American, Californian and Cajun

Aubergine 508 29th St, Newport Beach ☎949/723-4150. Cal-cuisine versions of quail, pâté and other French delicacies, served with a noticeable lack of attitude. Very expensive.
Bistro 201 3333 W PCH, Newport Beach ☎949/631-1551. The salmon and lamb are among the better nouveau American cuisine offerings at this pleasant Orange County Coast restaurant. Expensive.
The Cottage 308 N Coast Hwy, Laguna Beach ☎949/494-3023. Hungry beachgoers can choose from filling American breakfasts, or else affordable seafood, pasta and chicken dishes at lunch and dinner. Moderate.
Five Crowns 3801 E Coast Hwy, Corona del Mar ☎949/760-0331. Ignoring the diverse menu, most locals come for the thick, juicy steaks, quality ribs and clubby English decor. Expensive.
Jack Shrimp 2400 W Coast Hwy, Newport Beach ☎949/650-5577. One in a chain of Cajun dinner establishments in various spots along the Orange County Coast, offering an appealing assortment of spicy seafoods and fairly authentic Louisiana staples. Moderate.

Chinese and Vietnamese

Anh Hong 10195 Westminster Ave, Garden Grove ☎714/537-5230. Despite the dumpy-looking exterior, a terrific Vietnamese restaurant known for its slew of traditional favorites (including broiled pork with vermicelli noodles) and "seven courses of beef," a multi-course meal that celebrates red meat in all its glory. Moderate.

Favori 3502 W First St, Santa Ana ☎714/531-6838. Worth the long drive out for what may be LA's best Vietnamese food, including delicious garlic shrimp, curried chicken with lemon grass and nicely flavored noodle dishes. Moderate.

Hue Rendezvous 15562 Brookhurst St, Westminster ☎714/775-7192. Authentic Vietnamese food in the heart of Little Saigon, the best of which are a simple chicken noodle soup (*pho*) and the slightly more exotic-sounding rice cakes with beef and pork stuffing. Moderate.

Korean

In Chon Won 13321 Brookhurst St, Garden Grove ☎714/539-8989. One of the best spots outside of LA's Koreatown for rich, succulent barbecue – from pork and chicken to wild boar – prepared before your very eyes. Moderate.

Mexican and Latin American

Las Brisas 361 Cliff Drive, Laguna Beach ☎949/497-5434. Enjoy sweeping ocean views while dining on the patio of this upscale eatery; the spicy Mexican seafood entrees are almost as good as the scenery. Expensive.

Taco Mesa 647 W 19th St, Costa Mesa ☎949/642-0629. Cheap, tasty, no-frills burritos and tacos at this always-reliable Orange County chain. Inexpensive.

Middle Eastern

Zena's 294 N Tustin St, city of Orange ☎714/279-9511. A friendly Lebanese spot offering a good selection of gyros, kebabs, stuffed grape leaves, shawarma and other traditional favorites. Inexpensive.

Seafood

Bluewater Grill 630 Lido Park Drive, Newport Beach ☎949/675-3474. Delectable and surprisingly affordable seafood standards – ahi tuna salmon and the like – accompanied by appealing ocean views from the patio. Moderate.

Claes Seafood in the *Hotel Laguna*, 425 S Coast Hwy, Laguna Beach ☎949/376-9283. Sample Cal-cuisine versions of delicious ahi tuna and halibut, with fine views of the Pacific from indoors. Expensive.

Crab Cooker 2200 Newport Blvd, Newport Beach ☎949/673-0100. The hefty plates of crab legs and steaming bowls of chowder make the long lines here a bit more bearable. Moderate.

Oysters 2515 E Coast Hwy, Corona del Mar ☎949/675-7411. Another Orange County stab at California cuisine-style seafood; not as expensive as *Claes Seafood* (see above), further up the road, but in taste and looks the food here is almost as good. Expensive.

Bars, coffeehouses and clubs

S ocial **drinking** in LA is less popular than it is in big cities like San Francisco or New York, with the **bars** here not so much destinations in their own right, but mainly places to pose while waiting to meet friends, before heading off to pose again somewhere more exotic. However, it is still possible to have a good time. For serious, uninterrupted drinking, there are bars and lounges on every other corner, especially in Hollywood, with many of the lower-end dives seeing a mixed crowd of grizzled old-timers and slumming hipsters. However, smoking is banned in most establishments under California law (though some proprietors and customers still manage to puff away furtively).

In any case, bar styles tend to go in and out of fashion quickly, changing from month to month, often according to music and showbiz trends. What follows are descriptions of some of the more established bars in LA, generally those that have been around for at least a year or two; the trendiest joints sometimes only last a few months, disappearing once they lose their buzz and their exorbitant overhead finally catches up with them.

If you want something of the bar atmosphere without the alcohol, visit one of LA's many **coffeehouses**, which carry a certain social cachet, given the West Coast's taste for expensive coffee concoctions. They can also make for a refreshing break from the usual bars, especially if you want some culture with your coffee – alternative music and performing art provide the entertainment at many java joints.

Also susceptible to trends and styles are the city's many lively **clubs,** the true focus of social activity. They're usually after-hours oriented, and feature scenes just as colorful as those at nonmusical watering holes. Even if you're not interested in listening to the latest dance or rock tunes, there are plenty of secluded spots to hole up with a boilermaker and let the evening slip quietly away.

Bars

The **bar** recommendations below reflect their locality: a clash of beatnik artists and financial whiz kids Downtown; leather-clad rock fans in Hollywood and movie brats in West Hollywood; cleaner-cut preppies and lawyers in West LA; a large contingent of British and Irish expats in the jukebox-and-dartboard bars of Santa Monica; and the less fashionable, more hedonistic characters of the South Bay. Ultimately, Central Hollywood is the undisputed center of the drinking scene, with most of LA's hippest bars around Hollywood and Sunset boulevards.

A few hard-bitten bars are open the legal **maximum hours** (from 6am until 2am daily), though you're likely to be drinking alone if you arrive for an early liquid breakfast: the busiest hours are between 10pm and midnight.

Downtown

Barragan Café 1538 W Sunset Blvd, Echo Park ☎213/250-4256. A fairly decent Mexican restaurant said to serve the most alcoholic margarita in LA – so drink up, if you dare.
Bona Vista at the *Westin Bonaventure* hotel, 404 S Figueroa St ☎213/624-1000. Thirty-five floors up, this constantly rotating cocktail lounge spins faster after a few of the expensive drinks, and offers an unparalleled view of the sun setting over the city.
Casey's Bar 613 S Grand Ave ☎213/629-2353. Classic lounge ambience with aging regulars, dark wood-paneled walls and nightly piano music – something of a local institution in entertainment-starved Downtown.
Mr T's Bowl 5621 N Figueroa Ave, Highland Park ☎323/960-5693. Formerly a bowling alley, this quirky bar draws a regular crowd of hipsters and local characters. On weekends, there's live music, with a strong punk-surfer bent.
Redwood 316 W Second St ☎213/617-2867. Not especially flashy or eventful, but a solid Downtown choice for serious drinking, attracting a mix of office workers, newspaper journalists and just a few outsiders.
Standard Hotel Bar 550 S Flower St ☎213/892-8080. The poseur pinnacle in Downtown LA, a rooftop, alcohol-fueled playpen where the black-leather-pants crowd goes to hang out in red metallic "pods" with waterbeds and sprawl out on an Astroturf lawn, against a backdrop of modern corporate towers. A velvet-rope scene with a $20 cover charge if you're not staying at the hotel.

Mid-Wilshire

El Adobe 5536 Melrose Ave ☎323/462-9421. Something of a celebrity hotspot in the 1970s, this Mexican restaurant serves only adequate food, but the house specialty is worth a try: lethal and cheap margaritas.
El Carmen 8138 W Third St ☎323/852-1552. Groovy faux dive-bar with a south-of-the-border theme pushed to the extreme: black-velvet pictures of Mexican wrestlers, steer horns, stuffed snakes and much more.
H.M.S. Bounty 3357 Wilshire Blvd, Mid-Wilshire ☎213/385-7275. Touting "Food and Grog," this grungy bar mostly attracts old-timers and slumming club-hoppers, who come for the dark ambience, lounge music and kitschy nautical motifs.
Martini Lounge 5657 Melrose Ave ☎323/467-4068. With two bars, a pool room and a dance floor, this is quite the bar experience, drawing a youthful, hip crowd. Also features good live rock. See also "Live music," p.290.
Molly Malone's Irish Pub 575 S Fairfax Ave ☎323/935-1577. Authentic, self-consciously Irish bar, with a crowd of regulars who look like they've been there for ages, plus nightly music, shamrock decor and the requisite pints of thick, foaming Guinness. See also "Live music," p.291.
St. Nick's 8450 W Third St ☎323/655-6917. A few blocks from the colossal Beverly Center mall sits this relaxed and unassuming neighborhood bar, with a decent selection of brews and a formidable jukebox.

Snake Pit 7529 Melrose Ave ☎ 323/852-9390. One of the better bars along the Melrose shopping strip, and not too showy, with a mix of jaded locals and inquisitive tourists.

Tom Bergin's 840 S Fairfax Ave ☎ 323/936-7151. Old-time drinking joint from 1936, a great place for Irish coffee, and less rough-and-ready than *Molly Malone's* down the road (see above). You can spot the regulars from the pictures on the walls.

Hollywood

Akbar 4356 Sunset Blvd ☎ 323/665-6810. A diverse crowd – manual laborers and bohemians, gays and straights, old-timers and newbies – frequents this cozy, unpretentious Silver Lake watering hole.

Beauty Bar 1638 N Cahuenga Blvd ☎ 323/464-7676. A seemingly ideal Southern California concept: a drinking spot devoted to hair, nails and cosmetics, featuring a welter of 1950s-style salon gadgets and retro-decor, and a cocktail list to match, emphasizing bright, colorful and well-groomed concoctions. See also "Shopping," p.339.

Boardners 1652 N Cherokee Ave ☎ 323/462-9621. A likably unkempt neighborhood bar in the middle of Hollywood's prime tourist territory, attracting salty old-timers and curious youngsters alike. Occasional guitarists provide the soundtrack.

Cat n' Fiddle Pub 6530 Sunset Blvd ☎ 323/468-3800. A boisterous though comfortable pub with darts, stout British food and expensive English beers on tap, and live jazz on Saturdays. See also "Live music," p.292.

Cheetah's 4600 Hollywood Blvd ☎ 323/660-6733. One of LA's biggest underground attractions, with strong drinks, topless entertainment and an appropriately grubby crowd of regulars.

Deep 1707 N Vine St ☎ 323/462-1144. Prime guilty-pleasure drinking in the middle of tourist central, a watering hole/dance club with elevated floors for dirty go-go dancing and an assertively sleazy style – not true Hollywood raunch, just an incredible simulation.

The Dresden Room 1760 N Vermont Ave ☎ 323/665-4298. Wednesday night is open-mike, otherwise the husband-and-wife lounge act takes requests from the crowd of old-timers and goatee-wearing hipsters. Seen in the movie *Swingers*.

Formosa Café 7156 Santa Monica Blvd ☎ 323/850-9050. Started during Prohibition, this tiny bar is said to be alive with the ghosts of Bogie and Marilyn. Indulge in the potent spirits (not the insipid food) and soak in a true Hollywood institution.

Frolic Room 6245 Hollywood Blvd ☎ 323/462-5890. Classic LA bar featured in the film *LA Confidential*, decorated with Hirschfeld celebrity cartoons and steeped in a dark, old-time ambience. Right by the Pantages Theater.

The Garage 4519 Santa Monica Blvd ☎ 323/683-3447. With a funky lounge and a pool room, this lively Silver Lake bar and club attracts a mix of scenesters and neighborhood boozers, and offers live music after 9pm. See also "Live music," p.290.

Goldfingers 6423 Yucca St, north of Hollywood Blvd ☎ 323/962-2913. Fascinating 1960s-kitsch decor, with striking black-and-gold lamé touches, plus a nightly selection of dance and acoustic sounds.

Good Luck Bar 1514 Hillhurst Ave ☎ 323/666-3524. A hip Los Feliz retro-dive, this hangout is popular for its cheesy Chinese decor and tropical drinks straight from the heyday of *Trader Vic's*. Located near the intersection of Sunset and Hollywood blvds.

Highlands 6801 Hollywood Blvd ☎ 323/461-9800. On the fourth floor of the Hollywood & Highland mall, this restaurant, bar and club mixes passable nouveau-American food, a solid range of cocktails and weekend dance beats, though the main attraction is the fine city view at night, yours for a steep Saturday-evening cover charge ($20).

Lava Lounge 1533 N La Brea Ave ☎ 323/876-6612. Still the height of LA kitschy chic, this intentionally seedy strip-mall bar retains an odd popularity among visiting hipsters. Come for a look and wallow in the lounge music and Brubeck-style jazz.

Musso and Frank Grill 6667 Hollywood Blvd ☎ 323/467-7788. Simply put, if you haven't had a drink in this landmark 1919 bar, you haven't been to Hollywood. You can also have a pricey bite to eat. For more details, see p.98.

Pinot Hollywood 1448 Gower St ☎ 323/461-8800. Nearly thirty types of martini and Polish potato vodka, served in airy surroundings with an upscale crowd. See also "Restaurants and cafés," p.264.

Power House 1714 N Highland Ave ☎ 323/463-9438. Enjoyable, longstanding hard-rockers' watering hole just off Hollywood Boulevard. Few people get here much before midnight.

The Room 1626 N Cahuenga Blvd ☏323/462-7196. Small, intense bar with acceptably stiff drinks and a decent nightly music selection, mostly funk and soul tunes.

Smog Cutter 864 N Virgil Ave 323/667-9832. A neighborhood joint that attracts a mix of boozers and jaded youth, who have slowly changed the character of this friendly old dive from grubby to (mildly) posey. Don't miss the Wednesday and Thursday karaoke, which, like the liquor, can be pleasantly mind-numbing.

Tiki Ti 4427 W Sunset Blvd ☏323/669-9381. Tiny grass-skirted cocktail bar straight out of TV's *Hawaii-Five-O*, packed with pseudo-Polynesian decor, on the edge of Hollywood. Powerful cocktails are around $7 a slug.

West Hollywood

Barney's Beanery 8447 Santa Monica Blvd ☏310/654-2287. Well-worn pool-room bar, stocking more than 200 beers, which used to be a haunt for rockers like Jim Morrison. It also serves food, of sorts (see "Restaurants and cafés," p.252).

Jones 7205 Santa Monica Blvd ☏323/850-1726. Trendy, youthful scene crowded with poseurs, serving good American cuisine, but the main draw is the head-spinning drinks named for rock stars.

The Palms 8572 Santa Monica Blvd ☏310/652-6188. Comfortable mixed scene, with pool tables and a patio making for a relaxed vibe; also has dance music most nights of the week.

Parlour Club 7702 Santa Monica Blvd ☏323/650-7968. Located in West Hollywood's somewhat grim eastern side, this strange and stylish bar has a widely eclectic musical selection (metal, rap, disco and electro) playing nightly and the occasional dose of creepy spoken-word performance art.

Red Rock 8782 Sunset Blvd ☏310/854-0710. British-oriented watering hole with a wide array of drafts on tap and a similarly broad assortment of customers, everyone from bleary-eyed club kids to slumming preppies.

Revolver 8851 Santa Monica Blvd ☏310/659-8851. A mostly gay spot featuring a sleek, comfortable bar and intimate lounge, with sizeable video screens that are used for karaoke, drag shows and TV-watching.

Santa Monica and Venice

Circle Bar 2926 Main St, Santa Monica ☏310/392-4898. A rather bleak, claustrophobic space, packed with bleary-eyed regulars, where the main purpose is getting bombed without spending a wad. Just a few blocks away, Venice is well within staggering distance.

Encounter 209 World Way, at LAX ☏310/215-5151. This space age–themed bar, inside architect Eero Saarinen's futuristic Theme Building, overlooking the LAX parking lot. Believe it or not, it's worth a visit to sample the potent Day-Glo drinks while watching the jets land.

Finn McCool's 2700 Main St, Santa Monica ☏310/452-1734. Despite the dubious-sounding name, this worthwhile Irish pub has a savory selection of Emerald Isle brews and Celtic artwork on the walls, plus hefty platters of traditional food (cabbage, liver, beef stew and the like) that require an accompanying pint of Guinness for proper consumption.

14 Below 1348 14th St, Santa Monica ☏310/451-5040. At this casual bar, pool tables and a fireplace compete for your attention with rock, folk and blues acts that perform nightly.

Gotham Hall 1431 Third St, Santa Monica ☏310/394-8865. The strong drinks and purple pool tables here appeal to a generally youthful set of drinkers, with a solid Hollywood contingent, plus the occasional tourists from the Promenade. See also p.287.

Library Alehouse 2911 Main St, Santa Monica ☏310/314-4855. Presenting the choicest brews from West Coast microbreweries and beyond, this is a good spot to select from a good range of well-known and obscure labels while munching on salty bar food.

Liquid Kitty 11780 Pico Blvd, West LA ☏310/473-3707. As its quirky name might suggest, this bar is aimed solidly at the tongue-in-cheek hipster contingent, with a fine selection of cocktails and periodic lounge and dance music to set the mood. A few blocks from the eastern border of Santa Monica.

Oar House Saloon 2941 Main St, Santa Monica ☏310/396-6658. Bar on the edge of Venice, but still on the Main Street shopping strip, and popular with students who get suitably rowdy on weekend nights.

O'Brien's 2226 Wilshire Blvd, Santa Monica ☎310/396-4725. A fun, tub-thumping scene serving Irish food and brews to a heady crowd of locals and Irish expats.

Tantra Bar 23 Windward Circle, Venice ☎310/452-2222. Inside the *St Mark's* club, a lively bar with dark and moody decor, salsa and jazz, and a central location not far from the boardwalk.

The Tavern on Main 2907 Main St, Santa Monica ☎310/392-2772. Dark and boisterous neighborhood joint off the Main Street shopping strip, with sports on TV and boisterous regulars on the bar stools.

217 Lounge 217 Broadway ☎310/394-6336. If the rest of the bars in Santa Monica aren't quite snooty enough for you, this place is the perfect antidote – a little slice of West LA by the bay, complete with upscale dress code, smart and simple decor, well-balanced cocktails and, of course, trendy regulars.

Ye Olde King's Head 116 Santa Monica Blvd, Santa Monica ☎310/451-1402. Anglophilic joint with a jukebox, dartboards and signed photos of all your favorite rock dinosaurs; don't miss the steak-and-kidney pie or the fish and chips. Popular with local British expats.

The San Gabriel and San Fernando valleys

Amazon 14649 Ventura Blvd, San Fernando Valley ☎818/986-7502. A small wonderland of kitsch, where you can knock back tropical cocktails – such as the potent "Amazombie" – in a self-consciously fake South American and Polynesian decor: waterfalls, ferns and so on.

Clearman's North Woods 7247 N Rosemead Blvd, San Gabriel ☎626/286-3579. A kitsch-lover's delight with fake snow on the outside

and mooseheads mounted on the walls inside; a great place to space out while listening to moody live torch singers and throwing your peanut shells on the floor.

The Colorado 2640 E Colorado Blvd, Pasadena ☎626/449-3485. A bright spot along an otherwise bleak Pasadena stretch of asphalt, where salty bartenders pour cheap drinks and patrons can shoot pool in hunting-themed decor.

Cozy's Bar & Grill 14048 Ventura Blvd, Sherman Oaks ☎818/986-6000. Listen to blues on the weekend, or come by any time to throw darts, shoot pool or knock back a few. A friendly, laid-back San Fernando Valley spot with a devoted clientele.

Gitana 260 E Magnolia Blvd, Burbank ☎818/846-4400. Giant entertainment complex in the shadow of a mall, with mixed drinks, pool tables, cigar bar and eclectic tunes on the dance floor. Pulls in a mixed crowd of tourists and locals.

Ireland's 32 13721 Burbank Blvd, Van Nuys ☎818/785-5200. One of the Valley's better spots for quaffing Irish drafts, scarfing down traditional stews and chops, and soaking in a fair amount of Emerald Island decor.

John Bull Pub 958 S Fair Oaks Ave, Pasadena ☎626/441-4353. Although shepherd's pie and fish and chips are still served, along with warm English beers, this classic pub's swanky facelift better suits the tourists than old-timers.

McMurphy's 72 N Fair Oaks Ave, Pasadena ☎626/666-1445. A fine little Irish pub in the Old Pasadena area, where you can get a taste of lively Celtic folk and foamy Guinness at the same time.

Red Chariot 14431 Burbank Blvd, Van Nuys ☎818/785-5200. Somewhat dismal-looking bar from the outside, but with a generally spirited atmosphere, affordable drinks, colorful customers and – most importantly – a notable karaoke scene, vigorously on display Wed–Sun.

Coffeehouses

You can find **coffeehouses** throughout LA, from hole-in-the-wall dives to sanitized yuppie magnets. Well-trafficked tourist routes like Melrose Avenue and Santa Monica's Third Street Promenade are loaded with traditional spots to grab a caffeinated jolt. The listings below, however, go beyond java, focusing on unique establishments that, while serving coffee (and perhaps tea, food and alcohol), also offer more cultured amusements like art, music, poetry or truly eye-popping decor. The areas to visit for these nouveau coffee joints are

Hollywood, Santa Monica and, surprisingly, the San Fernando Valley, which has more appealing coffeehouses than you might expect.

Hollywood and West Hollywood

All-Star Theatre Café 6675 Hollywood Blvd ☎323/962-8898. Antiques store/café with a 1920s feel and overstuffed armchairs, now inhabiting the historic Vogue moviehouse. Very sleek and hip. Open Sat & Sun 7pm–3am.

@Coffee 7200 Melrose Ave ☎323/930-1122. Potent coffee drinks like the "Albino Mocha," made with white chocolate, provide liquid sustenance for red-eyed Web warriors prowling the Internet at this appealing coffeehouse.

Bourgeois Pig 5931 Franklin Ave ☎323/962-6366. Hip environment and outrageously overpriced cappuccinos – you really pay for the atmosphere of mirrors, chandeliers and loveseats – but the tasty java, colorful clientele and inviting decor might make it worth your while.

Coffee Table 2930 Rowena Ave, Los Feliz ☎323/644-8111. Casual, unpretentious space with affordable coffees and relaxed surroundings – a nice antidote for *Bourgeois Pig* (see above), further west.

CyberJava 7080 Hollywood Blvd ☎323/466-5600, ⓦwww.cyberjava.com. Located near the corner of La Brea Avenue, this spot offers Internet access while selling Web surfers the usual smoothies, caffeinated drinks and assorted sweets.

Highland Grounds 742 N Highland Ave ☎323/466-1507. One of the poshest of LA's coffee bars, serving iced latte and pancakes. At night it's a club, with poetry readings, up-and-coming bands and even a bit of alcohol.

Insomnia 7286 Beverly Blvd ☎323/931-4943. A chic spot for chugging cappuccinos while sitting in comfortable sofas and admiring the vivid amateur art on the walls. A good refueling spot for exploring Beverly Boulevard.

King's Road Espresso House 8361 Beverly Blvd, West Hollywood ☎323/655-9044. Sidewalk café in the center of a busy shopping strip. Popular with the hipster crowd as well as a few interloping tourists.

Nova Express 426 N Fairfax Ave ☎323/658-7533. Hands down one of the grooviest coffee joints around, designed with retro-futuristic sci-fi decor, with weird colors and lighting, and additional curiosities like lava lamps and alien lounge, and dance music

on most nights.

Tsunami Coffee House 4019 Sunset Blvd ☎323/661-3476. Music and poetry midweek at this pleasant Silver Lake space, dressed in a lively and colorful decor.

Urth Caffé 8565 Melrose Ave ☎310/659-0628. As with all things on the image-obsessed western side of Melrose, the customers at this high-priced vendor tend toward navel-gazing and celebrity-watching, though the coffees here are certainly tasty enough, and the atmosphere is pleasant and fairly well-scrubbed.

Santa Monica and Venice

Anastasia's Asylum 1028 Wilshire Blvd, Santa Monica ☎310/394-7113. Comfortable place with quirky decor and customers, and strong coffee and tea. Also with nightly entertainment, of eclectic character and varying quality.

Novel Café 212 Pier Ave, Santa Monica ☎310/396-8566. Stacks of used books and high-backed wooden chairs set the tone, but this place also has good coffees, teas and pastries, and is usually packed with many self-consciously studious patrons. If crowded downstairs, head for the creaky old sofas on the upstairs level.

Red Room Café 1604 Pacific Ave, Venice ☎310/399-1785. A coffeehouse with acceptably good beverages and snacks, but best for its actual artworks displayed for your perusal, in forms ranging from painting to sculpture to multimedia installations.

Rose Café 220 Rose Ave, Venice ☎310/399-0711. A somewhat trendy, though not pretentious, place for coffee and pastries that also offers occasional blues and jazz music.

Un-Urban Coffee House 3301 Pico Blvd, Santa Monica ☎310/315-0056. A combination coffeehouse and performance space, worth a look for its mostly alternative music and comedy acts.

The World Café 2820 Main St, Santa Monica ☎310/392-1661. Surf the Net with other technophiles on the patio, or drag yourself away and drink in the dark café/bar. Crowded and touristy.

The South Bay and LA Harbor

Coffee Cartel 1820 S Catalina Ave, Redondo

Beach ☎310/316-6554. Somewhat unremarkable coffeehouse that nonetheless puts on interesting shows of acoustic music; worth a visit if you're in town.

Java Man 157 Pier Ave, Hermosa Beach ☎310/379-7209. Tables lit by halogen lamps, plus a rotating display of work from local artists, adorn this coffeehouse not far from the beach.

The Library 3418 E Broadway, Long Beach ☎562/433-2393. Like the *Novel Café* (see overleaf), this is a prime spot for reading and/or buying literature while gulping down hot and iced coffee drinks.

Portfolios 2400 E Fourth St, Long Beach ☎562/434-2486. The kind of place where you're encouraged to browse the artworks for sale as you knock back your demi-tasse.

Sacred Grounds 399 W Sixth St, San Pedro ☎310/514-0800. Coffeehouse/club where the sizeable stage hosts open-mike nights, music jams, and even some marginal comedy acts.

San Gabriel and San Fernando valleys

Aroma Coffee and Tea 4360 Tujunga Ave, Studio City ☎818/508-6505. Housed in a remodeled house in the Valley, this is an unfussy, mellow spot where you can enjoy beverages with cakes and scones, on the patio and in a redesigned living room with an old-fashioned fireplace.

Cobalt Café 22047 Sherman Way, Canoga Park ☎818/348-3789. A somewhat grungy but hip coffeehouse in the San Fernando Valley, with coffee, food and live music, and poetry readings, too.

Coffee Connection 4397 Tujunga Ave #D, Studio City ☎818/769-3622. Enjoyable java joint that presents nightly open-mike sessions around dinnertime, and weekend acoustic troubadours as well.

Coffee Gallery Backstage 2029 N Lake Ave, Altadena ☎626/398-7917. On the northern side of the San Gabriel Valley, an appealingly unpretentious spot to lounge on sofas, munch on pastries, browse regional artworks and various art and culture books while you sip your espresso. Periodically presents poetry and music in its spacious back room.

Coffee Junction 19221 Ventura Blvd, Tarzana ☎818/342-3405. If you end up trapped in this remote corner of the Valley, close to nothing particularly interesting, the tasty coffee and folk music here are worth a stop. Open-mike night on Sundays can also be entertaining.

Hallenbeck's General Store 5510 Cahuenga Blvd, North Hollywood ☎818/985-5916. A coffeehouse done up as an old-fashioned general store, serving treats like sarsaparilla along with the java, and presenting good nightly entertainment that leans toward spoken-word, folk and poetry.

Hotwired Café 11651 Riverside Drive, North Hollywood ☎818/753-9929. Ultra-caffeinated java in a Valley joint with diverse entertainment, from Monday night blues jams to comics and acoustic strummers several nights of the week.

iBrowse Coffee and Internet 11 W Main St, Alhambra ☎626/588-2233. Browse the Web to the sounds of dizzyingly eclectic music (especially big on alternative rock) while sipping supercharged coffee, at this spot off the main tourist path.

Kulak's Woodshed 5230 Laurel Canyon Blvd, North Hollywood ☎818/766-9913. Basic coffee vendor putting on nightly shows in a cramped but colorful space, ranging from acoustic and spoken-word to performance art and poetry.

Lulu's Beehive 13203 Ventura Blvd, Studio City ☎818/986-2233. This quirky coffee shop is good not only for a spot of java, but also for taking in some art work, along with regular performances of rock, folk and jazz – not to mention comedy and poetry.

Clubs and discos

Like most things in LA, **nightlife** is very style-conscious, and the city's clubs may be the wildest in the country, a celebration of Southern California hedonism that has few rivals anywhere. Ranging from poseur hangouts to industrial noise cellars, even the more image–conscious joints are like singles bars, with plenty of dressing up, sizing up and picking up going on, and everybody claiming to be either a rock musician or in the movies. Nowadays, many of the more interesting and unusual clubs are transient, especially those catering to the house, ambient and rave scene. As a result, the trendier side of the club scene is hard to pin down – so you should always check the *LA Weekly* before setting out.

Weekend nights are predictably the busiest, but during the week things are often cheaper, though rarely any less enjoyable. Everywhere, between 11pm and midnight is the best time to turn up. Most of the **cover charges** range widely, depending on the night and the "club" being presented (anywhere from $3 to $20; call ahead). The **minimum age** is 21, and it's normal for ID to be checked, so bring your passport or other photo ID. (Some establishments that don't serve alcohol or separate the bar from the rest of the club admit patrons ages 18–21.) You should obviously dress with some sensitivity to the club's style, but prohibitive dress codes are a rarity; only at those "velvet rope" clubs that supposedly cater to movie brats and starlets will you find much in the way of snooty attitudes.

Most of the top clubs are either in Hollywood or along a ten-block stretch of West Hollywood. Beverly Hills is a lifeless yuppie desert, Downtown is home to a handful of itinerant clubs operating above and below board, and the San Fernando Valley's more rough-and-ready scene is usually confined to the weekends.

Downtown

The Echo 1822 Sunset Blvd ☏213/413-8200. Like the name says, an Echo Park scene with scrappy rap and dance DJs performing nightly, spinning a range of old- and new-school favorites.

LA Entertainment Center 333 S Boylston St ☏213/989-7979. Salsa, rock and dance on weekend nights. One of the few Downtown clubs that adds a bit of spark to a formerly dead nocturnal scene.

Mayan 1038 S Hill St ☏213/746-4287. Latin rhythms and nonstop disco and house tunes on three dance floors, in the gorgeous and historic surroundings of a former moviehouse (see p.63). Fri and Sat only; no jeans or sneakers.

The Smell 247 S Main St ☏213/625-4325. Formerly the legendary *Al's Bar*, now a similar space with groovy art grunge, including strange decor, rock and punk music, and a notoriously bleak location.

Stock Exchange 618 S Spring St ☏213/489-3877. An attempt to broaden the Downtown club scene on a previously deserted stretch of road, spinning enough funk and disco tunes to make the yuppie crowd gyrate with abandon.

Mid-Wilshire

Atlas 3760 Wilshire Blvd ☏213/380-8400. Wednesday and weekend nights are the scene for uptempo house and hip-hop grooves, with a little reggae and R&B thrown into the mix. Stylish scene requires appropriate dress; the venue is in the classic Art Deco Wiltern complex.

Conga Room 5364 Wilshire Blvd ☏323/938-1696. A high-profile celebrity investment results in a surprisingly appealing feast of Cuban food and Latin music. Has expanded into an adjacent former camera shop, which is now called *La Boca del Conga Room*. See also "Live music," p.293.

El Rey Theater 5515 Wilshire Blvd ☏323/936-4790. On the third Sunday of the month, the club *Coven 13* materializes at the theater, with its eerie amusements, from tarot readings and seances to goth music from the last twenty years. Just don't forget to bring your fright wig. On the first Saturday, the theater hosts "Makeup," a monthly drag tribute to 1970s glam and disco.

Jewel's Catch One 4067 W Pico Blvd ☏323/734-8849. Sweaty barn catering to a mixed crowd of gays and straights, and covering two wild dance floors. A longstanding favorite for club-hoppers of all stripes.

Hollywood

A.D. 836 N Highland Blvd ☏323/460-6668. Spooky neo-Gothic and generally bizarre club that plays hosts to a range of interesting club nights, most notably the glam scene "Cherry" on Fridays.

Arena 6655 Santa Monica Blvd ☏323/462-0714. Work up a sweat to funk, hip-hop and house on a massive dance floor inside a former ice factory. The fervent crowd is diverse, but leans toward a mix of Hispanics and gays. Plays host to many different, ever-changing club nights.

Bar Sinister 1652 N Cherokee ☎323/769-7070. A collection of sprightly dance beats most nights of the week, then memorably spooky goth music drawing anemic-looking vampire types on Saturdays. Connected to *Boardners* bar (see p.280).

Blue 1642 N Las Palmas Ave ☎323/462-7442. Goth, industrial and some retro-1980s sounds draw the pallid and zombie contingent to this combo restaurant and club, nightly except Tuesdays and Thursdays.

Club Ghetto 5520 Santa Monica Blvd ☎323/966-9555. Trendy scene of the moment, with Wednesday night hip-hop and dance music, accompanied by quasi-strip shows and drag performers.

Club Lingerie 6507 Sunset Blvd 323/466-8557. Long-established dance club, recently remodelled and spinning hip-hop, dance, R&B music and more. See also "Live music," p.290.

Crush Bar & Club 1743 N Cahuenga Blvd ☎323/461-9017. Soul, reggae, R&B and assorted dance tracks play at this self-consciously retro-funky club just north of Hollywood Boulevard.

The Derby 4500 Los Feliz Blvd ☎323/663-8979. Restored supper club on Hollywood's east side, with gorgeous high wooden ceilings and round bar; one of the originators of the retro-swing craze, thanks to the movie *Swingers*.

Dragonfly 6510 Santa Monica Blvd ☎323/466-6111. Despite being located in a dismal stretch in Hollywood, this club is continually buzzing, thanks to its two large dance rooms and various club nights.

Florentine Gardens 5951 Hollywood Blvd ☎323/464-0706. Stuck between the Salvation Army and a porno theater, but very popular with the faddish LA crowd, especially the under-21 set.

The Palace 1735 N Vine St ☎323/462-3000. This massive club, housed in a landmark 1920s building, becomes a dance club on weekend nights, spinning a collection of house, funk, hip-hop and other bass-heavy sounds. With four bars and two main floors. See also "Live music," p.291.

The Ruby 7070 Hollywood Blvd ☎323/467-7070. A wide range of feverish dance clubs take turns nightly (except Mon and Tues),

covering everything from gothic and grinding industrial to perky house and garage.

Three Clubs 1123 N Vine St ☎323/462-6441. Dark, perennially trendy bar and club where the usual crowd of hipsters drops in for retro and funk music on Thursdays through Sundays, and gets pleasingly plastered the rest of the time. Colorless exterior and lack of good signage makes the joint even hipper.

West Hollywood

Barfly 8730 Sunset Blvd ☎310/360-9490. Reservations and a fancy outfit are required for this weekend dance club that leans strongly toward house, garage and tribal.

Coconut Teaszer 8117 Sunset Blvd ☎323/654-4773. Hipsters, rockers and voyeurs mingle on the two dance floors of this iconic Sunset Strip club and concert hall. The DJs play all night so you don't have to stop dancing until 6am. No cover before 9pm.

The Factory 652 N La Peer Drive ☎310/659-4551. A predominantly gay crowd grooving to DJs spinning house most nights of the week at a popular West Hollywood club.

The Gate 643 N La Cienega Blvd ☎310/289-8808. Retro and contemporary dance and pop sounds shake the walls of this elegant estate, where a crowded dance floor and two outdoor patios also add to the ambience. Not too pretentious, but just enough attitude to attract the swells.

Key Club 9039 Sunset Blvd ☎310/274-5800. A hot spot in the most lively section of the strip, attracting a young, hip group for its hip-hop, funk and house music spinning nightly.

7969 7969 Santa Monica Blvd ☎323/654-0280. Something of a landmark for its frenetic and wide-ranging assortment of gay-themed (but straight-friendly) entertainment, from go-go girls to male strippers and drag queens. One of LA's most colorful spots for dancing and grinding.

Tempest 7323 Santa Monica Blvd ☎323/850-5115. After 10pm, the eclectic grooves start to spin here, from retro-funk and disco to the latest hip-hop and 1960s *Austin Powers*-style sing-alongs.

Ultra Suede 661 N Robertson Blvd ☎310/659-4551. The spot for superior retro-dancing on Wednesday and weekend nights, heavy on '70s disco and '80s technopop. Neighboring *Factory* nightclub plays similar tunes, though with a touch of '60s pop as well.

BARS, COFFEEHOUSES AND CLUBS | Clubs and discos

The Viper Room 8852 Sunset Blvd ☎310/358-1880. Excellent live acts, with occasional DJs spinning an eclectic mix of dance and other styles. See also "Live music," p.291.

West LA

Backstage Café 9433 Brighton Way ☎310/777-0252. Epitomizing the best and worst of the bar scene on the Westside, a Cal-cuisine bar and restaurant where the nice decor and well-made cocktails are offset by pretentiousness, high prices and a corporate feel (most evident in the gift shop).

Café Muse 11301 W Olympic Blvd ☎310/268-7855. House beats from the Far East collide nightly with varying sounds – dub, trance, rap, reggae and more – at this electronica-friendly club.

Century Supper Club 10131 Constellation Blvd, Century City ☎310/553-6000. A rare Century City example of mildly spontaneous fun – an upscale dance club where a fine assortment of funk, hip-hop and pop tunes caters to a snooty clientele of entertainment-lawyer types, with high prices to match.

El Dorado Cantina 11777 San Vicente Blvd, Brentwood ☎310/207-0150. A decent Mexican restaurant and bar – one of the few adequate nightspots on the notoriously stiff Westside – providing serviceable spirits and regular dance music.

Osteria Romana Orsini 9575 W Pico Blvd ☎310/277-6050. Funk, rap and soul on weekends at this Italian restaurant, aka "Orsini's," where, despite the big beats, the crowd tends toward stuffy Beverly Hills attitudes.

Santa Monica and Venice

Gotham Hall 1431 Third St, Santa Monica ☎310/394-8865. Weekend soul, dance and rap tracks echo through the walls of this popular bar and pool hall along the Promenade.

Lush 2020 Wilshire Blvd, Santa Monica ☎310/829-1933. Resurrected dance beats are the top tunes at this swank favorite of the retro-poseur set, from tacky 1980s power pop to hip-hugging 1970s disco.

The Mix 2810 Main St, Santa Monica. ☎310/399-1953. Weekend dance music scene focusing on house, techno and jungle beats, and drawing a crowd of local scenesters and visiting interlopers.

Sugar 814 Broadway, Santa Monica ☎310/899-1989. Hard-hitting electronica, from big-beat to house, served up in a gorgeous glass-and-steel interior.

Temple Bar 1026 Wilshire Blvd, Santa Monica ☎310/392-1077. Club DJ nights encompass rap and R&B, plus heavy doses of world beat. Always an appealingly frenetic scene.

The West End 1301 Fifth St, Santa Monica ☎310/394-4647. As at *Lush*, DJs spin old 1970s and 1980s favorites, while bartenders serve up sugary, fern-bar cocktails; reggae, dance and house music sometimes feature as well.

Zanzibar 1301 Fifth St ☎310/451-2221. Wednesday and weekend dance music at this club favoring rap, house and funk beats, bringing some life to an area two blocks from the north end of the Promenade.

San Gabriel and San Fernando valleys

Bigfoot Lodge 3172 Los Feliz Blvd, Atwater Village ☎323/662-9227. Not far from Griffith Park to the east, a serious bar scene with rock, punk and funk tunes nightly from both live bands and DJs.

CIA 11334 Burbank Blvd, North Hollywood ☎818/506-6353. Unusual, eye-popping art installations are the vivid backdrop for sounds ranging from punk to electronic.

Gitana 260 E Magnolia Blvd, Burbank ☎818/846-4400. Giant dance-and-dining complex in the shadow of a mall, with pool tables, cigar bar and eclectic tunes on the dance floor. Mixed crowd of tourists and locals.

The Mix 2612 Honolulu Ave, Glendale ☎818/248-3040. Fairly safe sounds at this dance club and restaurant (located on the northern edge of Glendale), mainly country and middle-of-the-road tunes with plenty of retro-pop thrown in.

The Muse 54 E Colorado Blvd, Pasadena ☎626/793-0608. Old Town Pasadena is the site where funk and hip-hop tunes mingle in one tri-level club with a dozen or so pool tables. Thurs–Sun.

Sagebrush Cantina 23527 Calabasas Rd, Calabasas ☎818/222-6062. About as close as the western San Fernando Valley gets to having a live-music scene, this Mexican restaurant offers 1970s-leaning rock cover bands four nights of the week to an appreciative crowd.

14

Live music

Whether you're looking for a retro-1980s metal cover band, swinging jazz outfit or hybrid rap-punk group, LA has hundreds of excellent choices if you're in the mood for **live music**. New bands haven't broken through until they've won over an LA crowd, so there's seldom an evening without something exciting going on. Besides local acts, there are always plenty of big-name American, British and other international performers playing around, and there's an enormous choice of **venues** as well. Most clubs open at 8pm or 9pm, with headline bands usually onstage between 11pm and 1am. Cover ranges widely from $5 to $30, so phone ahead to check set times and whether the gig is sold out. You need to be 21 to get in and may be asked for ID.

The best sources of **listings** are the *LA Weekly* and the "Calendar" section of the Sunday *Los Angeles Times* (also online at ⓦ www.calendarlive.com), followed by the radio stations listed in Basics (see p.47), which carry details, previews and sometimes free tickets for forthcoming events.

You can buy tickets for concerts and sports events from Ticketmaster, which has branches in Tower Records stores, and charge-by-phone numbers (☎213/480-3232 or 714/740-2000), although it's cheaper just to pick up tickets from the venue's box office and skip the service charges. A quick way through the maze of LA's **theaters** is to phone *Theatre LA* (☎213/614-0556, ⓦ www.theatrela.org) and check the availability of discount tickets for a given show.

The music scene

Just about any musical form, along with various hybrids, can be heard in LA, whether on the biggest concert stages or in the dingiest bars. There's a proto-rock star on just about every corner, and the guitar case is in some districts (notably Hollywood) an almost de rigueur accessory. The current trends tend toward industrial noise, neo-punk and the vestiges of the grunge rock of the early 1990s, but you'll also find hip-hop in abundance in South Central, though it's best avoided if you're not familiar with the area; head to the dance clubs instead – usually found in Hollywood more than anywhere else – to catch rotating performers and styles.

Other types of music have established something of a foothold, too, notably **folk music**, which keeps alive the singer-songwriter tradition, and **country**, a surprisingly forceful presence on the Southern California music scene. Along with country music, the northern valleys are hotbeds of **bluegrass** and **swing**, and there are scattered **blues** and **jazz** venues, too, including a few authentic dives. The lively Latin dance music of **salsa**, immensely popular among LA's Hispanic population, has had some cross-over success in the mainstream, while a small live **reggae** scene plugs on.

Although LA has been a home to rock-and-roll music since its birth in the 1950s, in part due to such homegrown talent as Ritchie Valens and The Platters, it was only with the rise of 1960s pop culture that LA's **rock music** scene really took off. The style was first defined by **surf rock**, with the pleasant harmonies of the Beach Boys and Jan and Dean, and pop vocalists like Frankie Avalon pushing the Southern Californian dream of cool muscle cars, bikini-clad chicks and killer waves.

In the mid- to late-1960s, however, the mood darkened as **psychedelic rock** took over; bands like The Doors, Buffalo Springfield and Love made a heavy, tie-dyed splash, while lighter bands like the Mamas and the Papas added their own spin on "California Dreamin'." By the early 1970s, LA witnessed the advent of the laid-back, **country-rock** sound, defined by the Eagles, Jackson Browne and Linda Ronstadt, who sang about the city as a spaced-out pleasure zone filtered through a marijuana haze. This all came to an end around 1978, with the emergence of a thriving local **punk** scene, headed by groups like X, the Circle Jerks and Black Flag, which, along with their penchant for youthful rebellion, recaptured some of rock's earlier, more freewheeling days, before the dominance of slicked-down corporate rock. Perhaps the most popular movement of all, contemporary with both country-rock and punk, was **heavy metal**, its aggressive presence dating back to Led Zeppelin's first American tour at the dawn of the 1970s, and carried through the late 1970s and 1980s when Van Halen, Mötley Crüe, and Guns N' Roses leaped onto the national stage as soon as they hit it big on the Sunset Strip.

Alternative rock, to some extent a reaction against turgid arena rock and heavy metal, continues to make regular appearances on the local scene, with its introspective, downbeat lyrics and formal creativity, but for the most part LA has always been more of a follower on this musical trend, with most of the top acts imported from less sunny spots in the South and Pacific Northwest.

Far more influential in the last decade has been LA's own **hip-hop** or **rap music** scene, which in the 1990s was arguably the most vital force in popular music, though the style was, like alternative rock, largely imported from elsewhere – in this case, New York City. By the end of the 1980s, the city's rappers had created their own unique sound through the efforts of such risk-taking rappers and producers as N.W.A., Snoop Dogg, Ice Cube, Ice T, and especially Dr Dre, who almost single-handedly elevated the **West Coast sound** to prominence: laid-back beats, an undertone of funk and soul, and above all, a lyrical emphasis on violence and hedonism. This was the prototypical **gangsta rap**, a style that fueled an intercoastal rivalry (now played out) that allegedly resulted in the murders of the West Coast's Tupac Shakur and the East Coast's Notorious B.I.G.

Concert halls and performance spaces

LA's **concert halls** and **performance spaces** are spread throughout the region, though most major rock and alternative clubs are in Hollywood or West Hollywood, with many right on the Sunset Strip.

Major concert venues

Carpenter Performing Arts Center 6200 Atherton St, on the campus of Cal State Long Beach ☏ 562/985-7000, ⊛ www.carpenterarts.org. A major arts space in the South Bay, attracting mostly mid-level entertainers in pop, traditional rock, folk, jazz and country.

Cerritos Center for the Performing Arts 12700 Center Court Drive ☏ 1-800/300-4345, ⊛ www.cerritoscenter.com. Located to the north of Long Beach, a top draw for middle-of-the-road acts in country, gospel, lite rock, mainstream pop and jazz standards – usually nothing too loud, quirky or adventurous.

Greek Theatre 2700 N Vermont Ave, Griffith

Park ☎ 323/665-1927 ⊛ www.greektheatrela
.com. A broad range of mainstream rock
and pop acts stream through this outdoor,
summer-only venue, which has seating for
five thousand. Parking can be a mess, so
arrive early.

Grove of Anaheim 2200 E Katella Ave
☎ 714/712-2700, ⊛ www.thegroveofanaheim
.com. Orange County concert space
showcasing old-time performers and mid-
level entertainers in soul, country, pop and
jazz.

Hollywood Palladium 6215 Sunset Blvd,
Hollywood ☎ 323/962-7600, ⊛ www.hollywood-
palladium.com. This former dance hall for big
bands has kept its authentic 1940s interior,
but is now a home to all manner of hard
rock, punk and rap concerts.

Kodak Theatre 6801 Hollywood Blvd,
Hollywood ☎ 323/308-6363. Part of the
colossal Hollywood & Highland mall, this
state-of-the-art theater includes top-name
pop and rock acts on its roster and is the
venue for the Oscars, too.

Pantages Theater 6233 Hollywood Blvd,
Hollywood ☎ 323/468-1770. Atmospheric Art
Deco theater, with a stunning interior, deep
in the heart of historic Hollywood and once
the site of the Academy Awards.
Sometimes hosts rock concerts, but more
often traveling musicals. Stop by the *Frolic
Room* (see p.97), the classic LA bar next
door, for a drink before the show.

Staples Center 865 S Figueroa St, Downtown
☎ 213/624-3100, ⊛ www.staplescenter.com.
Glossy sports arena (home to the LA
Lakers) that serves as a good showcase for
Top 40 rock and pop acts.

Universal Amphitheater 100 Universal City
Plaza ☎ 818/622-4440, ⊛ www.hob.com/venues
/concerts/universal. A huge but acoustically
excellent auditorium putting on regular rock
shows by headline groups. Located on the
Universal Studios lot.

Wiltern Theater 3790 Wilshire Blvd, Mid-
Wilshire ☎ 323/388-1400. A striking Art Deco
movie palace, now a top performing space
for diverse acts including comedy, mainstream rock and pop, and edgy alternative
music.

Rock

American Legion Hall 2035 Highland Ave,
Hollywood ☎ 323-960-2035. One of the more
unexpected places to put on a punk

show, but still a good, popular venue that
draws plenty of authentic head-thrashers
and hard-rockers to its periodic performances.

Cat Club 8911 Sunset Blvd, West Hollywood
☎ 310/657-0888. Hard, meaty jams can be
heard here every night of the week, mainly
rock, punk and rockabilly – which should
come as no surprise since the owner's a
former Stray Cat.

Club Lingerie 6507 Sunset Blvd, Hollywood
☎ 323/466-3416. Wide-ranging venue that's
always at the forefront of new music, funk
and dance sounds. See also "Bars, coffeehouses and clubs," p.286.

Doug Weston's Troubadour 9081 Santa
Monica Blvd, West Hollywood ☎ 310/276-6168.
An old 1960s mainstay where the heavy
riffs and shaggy manes have been replaced
by more alternative and acoustic line-ups.

El Rey Theater 5515 Wilshire Blvd, Mid-Wilshire
☎ 323/936-4790. Although not as famous as
its Sunset Strip counterparts, this rock and
alternative venue is possibly the best spot
to see explosive new bands and enduring
oldsters. Also offers a variety of dance club
nights.

Gabah 4658 Melrose Ave, Hollywood ☎ 323/664-
8913. Eclectic, laid-back spot serving up a
mix of reggae, funk, dub and rock – even
flamenco. The dicey neighborhood leaves
much to be desired; always let the valet
take charge of your car.

The Garage 4519 Santa Monica Blvd, Silver
Lake ☎ 323/683-3447. A grim little venue that
adds a suitably gritty feel to its punk, alternative, hardcore and rock shows. Also features the occasional drag show. See also
"Bars, coffeehouses and clubs," p.280.

The Joint 8771 Pico Blvd, West LA ☎ 310/275-
2619. A dark, mirrored neighborhood venue
with assorted B-grade punk screamers and
occasionally decent rock and alternative
groups.

King King 6555 Hollywood Blvd ☎ 323/960-
5765. A solid Hollywood bet for midweek
concerts by chord-crunching rockers and
for live dance music on weekends, when
house, funk, rap and retro-pop are all on
the DJ docket.

Largo 432 N Fairfax Ave, Mid-Wilshire
☎ 323/852-1073. Cozy cabaret that features
some of LA's more unusual live bands, performing mostly jazz, rock and pop.

Martini Lounge 5657 Melrose Ave, Mid-Wilshire
☎ 323/467-4068. Something of a proving

ground for young rockers, with plenty of room for dancing (see also "Bars, coffeehouses and clubs", p.279).

The Mint 6010 Pico Blvd, Mid-Wilshire ☎323/954-9630. Right off Fairfax Avenue in a dreary part of town, this club is worth a look for its eclectic mix of rock, jazz and blues performers.

Opium Den 1605 1/2 N Ivar Ave, Hollywood ☎323/466-7800. A strip club turned nightclub, where up-and-coming rock and punk acts take turns on the overly small stage. May not look it, but considered a breaking ground for new thrash talent.

The Palace 1735 N Vine St, Hollywood ☎323/462-3000. Great old venue where you can catch solid rock and alternative acts during the week. See also "Bars, coffeehouses and clubs," p.279.

The Roxy 9009 Sunset Blvd, West Hollywood ☎310/276-2222. An intimate club showcasing the music industry's new signings and boasting a great sound system, too. On the western – but still frenetic – end of the strip.

Silver Lake Lounge 2906 Sunset Blvd ☎323/666-2407. A hole in the wall, popular for its energetic alternative and punk shows, while weekends are reserved for glam and drag fêtes.

Spaceland 1717 Silver Lake Blvd, Hollywood ☎213/833-2843. Good, longstanding option for catching up-and-coming local and national rockers and other acts.

Temple Bar 1026 Wilshire Blvd, Santa Monica ☎310/392-1077. A popular, if chaotic, mix of groove styles can be heard here, from funk and soul to rap and R&B, as well as occasional forays into rock, pop and world beat.

The Viper Room 8852 Sunset Blvd, West Hollywood ☎310/358-1880. Great live acts, plus a famous owner (Johnny Depp) and a headline-grabbing past have helped boost this club's hip aura. Expect almost any musician to show up onstage. See also "Bars and clubs," p.287.

Sixteen-Fifty 1650 N Schrader Blvd, Hollywood ☎323/465-7449. A massive club that has gone through a number of permutations, now defined by its mix of rock musicians and dance DJs.

Whisky-a-Go-Go 8901 Sunset Blvd, West Hollywood ☎310/652-4202. Legendary club (see p.109) and a hotspot for LA's rising music stars, mainly playing hard rock,

though you might catch an alternative act now and then.

Country and folk

Boulevard Music 4136 Sepulveda Blvd, Culver City ☎310/398-2583. This low-key music store hosts some worthwhile folk acts on weekends, from roots country to delta blues, with international groups added to the eclectic mix.

Celtic Arts Center 4843 Laurel Canyon Blvd, Studio City ☎818/760-8322, ⊛www.celticartscenter.com. A celebration of all things Celtic and Gaelic (and not just Irish, either), offering monthly concerts, dance lessons and, best of all, free Sunday night Céili dances followed by traditional-music jam sessions.

Cowboy Palace Saloon 21635 Devonshire St, Chatsworth ☎818/341-0166. Worth a trip to this distant corner of the San Fernando Valley for the spirited down-home country concerts and free Sunday BBQ fixings.

Crazy Jack's 4311 W Magnolia Blvd, Burbank ☎818/845-1121. Before the country music kicks into high gear at 9pm, this longstanding place offers free dance lessons Tues and Thurs–Sat. Don't miss their entertaining Dixieland nights.

CTMS Center 16953 Ventura Blvd, Encino ☎818/817-7756, ⊛www.ctmsfolkmusic.org. The home base for the California Traditional Music Society, which puts on ancient and modern folk music concerts throughout the year.

The Foothill Club 1922 Cherry Ave, Signal Hill ☎562/984-8349. In a bleak industrial city surrounded by Long Beach, this glorious dance hall dates back to the days when hillbilly was cool, complete with a mural showing life on the range and country legends. Don't be surprised to hear garage rock, and even dance music, at this diverse spot.

McCabe's 3103 W Pico Blvd, Santa Monica ☎310/828-4497. LA's premier acoustic guitar shop, long the scene of excellent and unusual folk and country shows, with the occasional alternative crooner thrown in, too.

Molly Malone's Irish Pub 575 S Fairfax Ave, Mid-Wilshire ☎323/935-1577. Local favorite for its colorful clientele, and mix of traditional Irish music, American folk, rock and R&B. See also "Bars, coffeehouses and clubs," p.279.

Oil Can Harry's 11502 Ventura Blvd, Studio City
☎818/760-9749. Unassuming joint with a
strong bent for country music, with occasional down-home performances, line-
dancing and a mildly cornpone atmosphere.

Rusty's Surf Ranch 256 Santa Monica Pier
☎310/393-7437. Offers not only surf music –
and displays of old-time long boards – but
also rock, pop, folk and even karaoke.
Always a popular spot for tourists, near the
end of the pier.

Viva Cantina 900 Riverside Drive, Burbank
☎818/845-2425. A Mexican restaurant on
the far side of Griffith Park, where you can
hear some of LA's most engaging country,
bluegrass and honky-tonk artists performing nightly. Free.

Jazz and blues

Babe and Ricky's Inn 4339 Leimert Blvd,
South Central ☎323/295-9112. Long a top
spot for blues on Central Ave, this premier
music hall continues to attract quality,
nationally known acts at its new Leimert
Park location.

The Baked Potato 3787 Cahuenga Blvd W,
North Hollywood ☎818/980-1615. A small but
near-legendary contemporary jazz spot,
where many jazz reputations have been
forged. Don't come looking for bland
lounge jazz/muzak – instead, expect to be
surprised.

BB King's Blues Club 1000 Universal Center
Drive, Universal City ☎818/6-BBKING. Ignore
the garish CityWalk exterior and head to
Lucille's, the club room (named after BB's
guitar), for good acoustic blues on weekends.

Blue Café 210 Promenade, Long Beach
☎562/983-7111. A range of nightly blues
near the harbor, plus a slew of pool tables
and an upstairs dance floor. No cover.

Café Boogaloo 1238 Hermosa Ave, Hermosa
Beach ☎310/318-2324. One of the better
spots in the South Bay for seeking out
nightly blues, with occasional New Orleans
jazz and swing.

Cat n' Fiddle Pub 6530 Sunset Blvd, Hollywood
☎323/468-3800. An English-style pub with
worthwhile jazz performers on Sundays
from 7pm until 11pm; no cover (see also
"Bars, coffeehouses and clubs," on p.280).

Catalina Bar and Grill 1640 N Cahuenga Blvd,
Hollywood ☎323/466-2210. This central

Hollywood jazz institution offers traditional
sounds and good acoustics, plus filling
meals and potent drinks.

Harvelle's 1432 Fourth St, Santa Monica
☎310/395-1676. Near the Third Street
Promenade, a stellar place for blues for
more than six decades, with different performers nightly and a popular band showcase on Tuesday nights.

House of Blues 8430 Sunset Blvd, West
Hollywood ☎323/848-5100. Over-commercialized mock sugar-shack, with good but pricey
live blues acts. Very popular with tourists,
there's also one at Disneyland (☎714/778-
2583). Covers can reach $30 or more.

Jax 339 N Brand Blvd, Glendale ☎818/500-
1604. A combination restaurant and performing stage where you can take in a
good assortment of jazz, from traditional to
contemporary. No cover.

Jazz Bakery 3233 Helms Ave, Culver City
☎310/271-9039. More performance space
than club, and the brainchild of singer Ruth
Price, where the best local musicians play
alongside big-name visitors in a former
bakery building.

Knitting Factory 7021 Hollywood Blvd
☎323/463-0204. West Coast branch of the
landmark New York club, featuring a wide
range of eclectic interpretation, much of it
avant-garde.

Lunaria 10351 Santa Monica Blvd, West LA
☎310/282-8870. This elegant French–Italian
restaurant comes alive each night, with jazz
performers playing everything from swing to
bebop in the intimate lounge. Free.

Spazio 14755 Ventura Blvd, 2nd Floor, Sherman
Oaks ☎818/728-8400. Swank Italian eatery
that's one of the bigger-name spots for
mainstream jazz, with regular nightly performances.

World Stage 4344 Degnan Blvd, South Central
LA ☎323/293-2451. Informal, bare-bones
rehearsal space that attracts top-name
players like drummers Billy Higgins and
Max Roach. Thursday jams, Friday and
Saturday gigs.

Latin and salsa

Boathouse 301 Santa Monica Pier ☎310/393-
6475. A good place for beginners and
tourists to get in on LA's salsa scene,
offering nightly lessons and a comfortable
atmosphere, plus a pleasant view of the
bay.

Club Samba 701 Long Beach Blvd, Long Beach ☎562/435-6238. A spirited joint with energy to spare, featuring Friday night Brazilian lessons followed by dancing, Saturday night samba lessons followed by live samba, and infectious bossa nova music on Sunday nights.

Conga Room 5364 Wilshire Blvd, Mid-Wilshire ☎323/938-1696. Live Cuban, salsa and South American music throughout the week at this hip, lively club on the Miracle Mile. See also "Bars, coffeehouses and clubs," p.285.

El Floridita 1253 N Vine St, Hollywood ☎323/871-8612. Decent Mexican and Cuban food (see "Bars, coffeehouses and clubs," p.264) complements a fine line-up of Cuban and salsa artists, who play on weekends and jam on other nights. Reservations required.

Luminarias 3500 Ramona Blvd, Monterey Park ☎323/268-4177. Hilltop restaurant (see "Bars, coffeehouses and clubs," p.273) with live salsa reckoned to be as good as its Mexican food. No cover.

Papaz 1716 N Cahuenga Blvd, Hollywood ☎323/850-1726. Not as brash or as colorful as some Latin clubs, but still appealing for its sleek modern decor and lively mix of dance beats and live music, leaning toward salsa, merengue, and Latin pop and rock.

Zabumba 10717 Venice Blvd, West LA ☎310/841-6525. In a colorful building amid drab surroundings, a venue that's worth a trip for its free-spirited groups performing bossa nova Brazilian.

Reggae

Club 49 49 S Pine Ave, Long Beach ☎562/493-9059. As with other clubs and restaurants featuring the music, reggae is not the sole focus here. Instead, a range of live music and DJs enlivens the surf'n'turf meals, often including Jamaican beats, depending on the night.

Domenico's 82 N Fair Oaks Ave, Pasadena ☎626/449-1948. This Old Pasadena restaurant has reggae offerings several nights a week; call first for the current schedule.

Golden Sails Hotel 6285 E PCH, Long Beach ☎562/596-1631. Some of the best reggae bands from LA and beyond show up at this hotel on Friday and Saturday nights.

Lighthouse Café 30 Pier Ave, Hermosa Beach ☎310/372-6911. Adjacent to the beach and the Strand, this club has a broad booking policy that spans reggae, rock, jazz and more.

14

LIVE MUSIC | Concert halls and performance spaces

Performing arts and film

D
espite the countless stereotypes about Southern California being a culture-free zone, populated only by Valley girls, skateboarders and surfer dudes, in truth the city offers a wealth of **performing arts** options scattered throughout the basin. While it's true that the city's range of highbrow cultural offerings was at one time quite limited, confined to arthouse cinemas and a handful of mainstream theaters, since then, LA has firmly established itself in the performing arts field thanks to a renewed push from old-money and corporate interests (most of them located Downtown), and the growth of underground and alternative arts venues (most of them located everywhere else).

LA boasts a world-class classical music orchestra and conductor, along with several less-familiar entities like chamber-music groups. The fields of **opera** and **dance** are also represented by several noteworthy companies. **Theater** is always a growth industry here, with more than a thousand shows annually (and more than one hundred running at any one time), plenty of actors to draw from, and a burgeoning audience for both mainstream and fringe productions. **Cabaret** caters to a select crowd of lounge-music fans, but **comedy** is always a big draw, and it comes as no surprise that this is one of the prime entertainment options that first-time visitors usually seek out. Not surprisingly, though, it's **film** that is still the chief cultural staple of the region, and there is no shortage of excellent theaters in which to catch a flick.

Classical music

LA's **classical music** scene is largely unknown to most visitors, despite the prominence of the LA Philharmonic's leader Esa-Pekka Salonen – one of the most esteemed and creative of contemporary US conductors. Even less well known, though still intriguing, are the city's smaller performing groups, which tend to float from art centers to universities to church venues, drawing a loyal, though limited, audience. Your best bet for following the cultural trends is to watch the press, especially the *LA Times*, for details. In any case, you can expect to pay from $10 to $70 for most concerts, and much more for really big names.

Classical music companies

Da Camera Society rotating venues throughout LA ☎ 213/477-2929, ⓦ www.dacamera.org. This organization's "Chamber Music in Historic Sites" series provides a great opportunity to hear classical, Romantic and modern chamber works in stunning settings, from grand churches to private homes, including such inspired sites as Doheny Mansion, the *Biltmore* and *Dunbar* hotels, and Robert Farquhar's beautiful Canfield-Moreno estate. Ticket prices vary widely, depending on the venue, and can run anywhere from $34 to $100.

Long Beach Symphony Terrace Theater, 300 E Ocean Blvd, Long Beach ☎ 562/436-3203, ⓦ www.lbso.org. A light alternative to LA's heavier repertoire, playing mainstream favorites like Tchaikovsky and Beethoven, interspersed with crowd-pleasing pops selections. $12–100.

Los Angeles Chamber Orchestra rotating local venues ☎ 213/622-7001 ext 215, ⓦ www.laco.org. Appearing at UCLA's Royce Hall and Glendale's Alex Theater on one weekend per month, the orchestra presents a range of chamber works, not all strictly canonical, from different historical eras. Concerts vary widely by price and seating choices. $15–63. (For a monumental interpretation of the orchestra's musicians, check out Kent Twitchell's colossal *Harbor Freeway Overture* mural in Downtown LA; see p.68.)

Los Angeles Master Chorale at the Music Center, 135 N Grand Ave, Downtown; also at rotating venues ☎ 1-800/787-LAMC, tickets through Ticketmaster at ☎ 213/365-3500, ⓦ www.lamc.org. Classic works, along with lighter madrigals and pops favorites, are showcased by this choral institution, which will move in the 2003–2004 season to the new Disney Hall (see below). $20–58.

Los Angeles Philharmonic at the Music Center, 135 N Grand Ave, Downtown ☎ 323/850-2000, ⓦ www.laphil.org. The one big name in the city performs regularly during the year, and conductor Esa-Pekka Salonen always provides a diverse, challenging program, from powerful Romantic works to craggy modern pieces. Slated to move in the 2003–2004 season to Disney Hall (see below). $14–100.

Pacific Symphony Orchestra Orange County Performing Arts Center, 600 Town Center Drive, Costa Mesa ☎ 714/755-5788 ⓦ www.pacificsymphony.org. Although not as groundbreaking or experimental as the LA Philharmonic, this suburban orchestra nonetheless draws big crowds for its excellent, stylish performances. Another attraction is that the symphony's ticket prices are lower than its LA counterpart. $20–60.

Pasadena Symphony at Pasadena Civic Auditorium, 300 E Green St ☎ 626/584-8833, ⓦ www.pasadenasymphony.org. Veering between the standard repertoire and more contemporary pieces, this esteemed symphony provides plenty of artistic sustenance for its audience. $22–64, $10 for students.

Classical music venues

Alfred Newman Recital Hall on the USC campus, South Central ☎ 213/740-2584, ⓦ www.usc.edu/music. As with Royce Hall at UCLA, this is a fine university venue for sonatas, concertos and other classical works, usually from September through May, with most tickets costing less than $20 (and even cheaper for students, around $12).

Bing Theater 5905 Wilshire Blvd, Mid-Wilshire ☎ 213/473-8493 or 213/473-0625, ⓦ www.lacma.org. When it isn't hosting movie revivals, this auditorium at the LA County Museum of Art provides a fine space for classical concerts, which occur periodically during the year.

Disney Hall First St at Grand Ave, Downtown ⓦ www.laphil.org/wdch. What is sure to be LA's most renowned cultural attraction (along with the Getty Center) when it opens for the 2003–2004 season of the LA Philharmonic. A striking Frank Gehry design (see p.58) that will host a range of officially-approved music and arts groups and, it is hoped, start drawing the tourists back to Downtown LA.

Dorothy Chandler Pavilion at the Music Center, 135 N Grand Ave, Downtown ☎ 213/972-7211, ⓦ www.musiccenter.org. This high-culture establishment hosts the LA Philharmonic only until the 2003 season, but will still be used by the LA Opera and other top names after that time.

The Hollywood Bowl 2301 N Highland Ave, Hollywood ☎ 323/850-2000, ⓦ www.hollywood-bowl.org. Surrounded by a hundred-acre park, the Bowl hosts the LA Philharmonic

PERFORMING ARTS AND FILM | Classical music

for open-air concerts, usually of the pops variety, Tuesday through Saturday evenings from July to September; unfortunately, the music can sometimes be drowned out by the noisy atmosphere (for more on the Bowl, see p.105).

Orange County Performing Arts Center 600 Town Center Drive, Costa Mesa ☎714/556-ARTS, ⓦwww.ocpac.org. Home of the Pacific Symphony Orchestra and Opera Pacific, and also showcasing traveling pop and jazz acts.

Pacific Amphitheater 100 Fair Drive, Costa Mesa ☎714/708-1870. A big open-air venue capable of drawing sizeable crowds for mainstream pop and rock shows. Orange County's answer to the Hollywood Bowl.

Royce Hall on the UCLA campus in Westwood ☎310/825-9261 or 825-2101, ⓦwww.performingarts.ucla.edu. Classical concerts,

often involving big names, occur at this splendid historic-revival structure throughout the college year (Sept–June, generally speaking).

The Shrine Auditorium 665 W Jefferson Blvd, South Central ☎213/749-5123; box office at 655 S Hill St. Huge 1926 Moorish-domed curiosity that hosts touring pop acts, choral gospel groups and countless award shows (but not the Oscars any more).

Topanga Community House 1440 Topanga Canyon Blvd, Santa Monica Mountains ☎818/999-5775, ⓦwww.topangasymphony .8k.com. This low-key concert venue – used also for rock and children's music performances – hosts symphonic and chamber works throughout the year by the Topanga Symphony, often for cheap prices or simply for free.

Opera and dance

Although far from being dominant cultural presences, **opera** and **dance** in LA can be quite compelling, and often reward your attention with risk-taking performances and creative interpretations. The few major opera companies in LA and Orange counties are divided between the old-line institutions that focus on the warhorses of the repertoire and newcomers that make more of an effort to cross artistic boundaries. Dance performances tend to be grouped around major events, so check cultural listings or call the venues listed below for seasonal information. Otherwise, check for performances at universities like UCLA (☎310/825-4401, ⓦwwww.performingarts.ucla.edu), where some of the most exciting names in dance have residencies.

Opera companies and venues

Casa Italiana Opera Company at St Peter's parish church, 1051 N Broadway, Downtown ☎310/451-6012, ⓦwww.casaitaliana.org. Several times during the year, this alternative company stages popular Romantic operas, from Puccini to Verdi and Mascagni, for very affordable prices. $30–40.

LA Opera at the Music Center, 135 N Grand Ave, Downtown ☎213/972-8001, ⓦwww.laopera.org. Stages productions between September and June, from heavy *opera seria* to lighter operettas. The mainstream heavyweight in town. $35–170.

Long Beach Opera at the Carpenter Center, 6200 Atherton St ☎562/439-2580, ⓦwww.lbopera.com. Despite being eight years older than the LA Opera, this alternative company presents the freshest and

edgiest work in town, from old pieces by Monteverdi to newer works by modernists like Bartok. Even canonical pieces by Puccini get radically reworked, driving purists to distraction and pleasing most everyone else. $30–100.

Opera Pacific Orange County Performing Arts Center, 600 Town Center Drive, Costa Mesa ☎949/474-4488 or 1-800/34-OPERA, ⓦwww.operapacific.org. Performs mostly mainstream grand opera and operettas. $20–80.

Dance companies and venues

Carpenter Performing Arts Center 6200 Atherton St, on the campus of Cal State Long Beach ☎562/985-7000, ⓦwww.carpenterarts.org. The South Bay's major arts space, hosting the Long Beach Opera and mainstream pop concerts, as well as periodic dance performances and touring arts groups.

Cerritos Center for the Performing Arts 12700 Center Court Drive, Southeast LA ☎ 1-800/300-4345, ⓦ www.cerritoscenter.com. Located in distant Cerritos on the Orange County border, this is one of LA's better-known and funded venues, home to classical and dance performances of all kinds, as well as mainstream pop and jazz performers.

Dance Kaleidoscope at John Anson Ford Theater, 2850 Cahuenga Blvd, Hollywood ☎ 323/343-5120, ⓦ www.fordamphitheatre.org. The year's major dance event is held over two weeks in July and is organized by the Los Angeles Area Dance Alliance (LAADA), a co-operative supported by LA's smaller dance companies that provides a central source of information on events. Prices vary.

Japan America Theater 244 S San Pedro St, Little Tokyo ☎ 213/680-3700, ⓦ www.jaccc.org. Presenting a range of intriguing dance and performance works drawn from Japan and the Far East.

John Anson Ford Theater 2850 Cahuenga Blvd, Hollywood ☎ 323/461-3673, ⓦ www.fordamphitheatre.org. Besides the summer "Dance Kaleidoscope," this open-air venue also presents eclectic productions by local groups.

Lankershim Arts Center 5108 Lankershim Blvd, North Hollywood ☎ 818/760-1278, ⓦ www.doversart.com/lag. Anchoring the North Hollywood arts zone, this San Fernando Valley institution puts on graceful dance programs during several periods of the year.

Pasadena Dance Theater 1985 Locust Ave, Pasadena ☎ 626/683-3459, ⓦ www.pasadenadance.org. One of the San Gabriel Valley's more prominent dance venues, hosting diverse groups throughout the year.

UCLA Center for the Performing Arts office at 10920 Wilshire Blvd, Westwood ☎ 310/825-4401, ⓦ www.performingarts.ucla.edu. Features a broad range of touring companies, and runs an "Art of Dance" series between September and June, with an experimental bent.

Theater

LA has a very active and energetic **theater** scene. You can expect to find most anything on any given night in one of the city's venues, including huge Broadway shows and traveling musical juggernauts, hole-in-the-wall and avant-garde productions, edgy political melodramas, and even revivals of classic works by the likes of Shaw and Ibsen. Aside from the nationally touring megahits, some of the productions to attract the most attention have been multicharacter one-person shows and irreverent stagings of canonical works, with Shakespeare often in the crosshairs.

Since the region is home to a wealth of **film actors**, most of them unemployed in the movie biz, there is always a good pool of thespians for local productions. Depending on the play, you may even find semi-popular TV actors or big celebrity names like Dustin Hoffman on stage, their presence occasionally impromptu and unannounced. While the bigger venues host a predictable array of shopworn musicals and hidebound classics, there are over a hundred "Equity waiver" theaters with fewer than a hundred seats, enabling non-Equity–cardholders to perform. This means a lot of fringe performances take place, for which prices can be very low and the quality can vary greatly – but you may catch an electrifying surprise now and again.

Tickets are less expensive than you might expect: a big show will set you back $30, or up to $80 for some blockbusters (matinees are cheaper), with smaller shows around $10 to $25. Regardless of size, you should always book ahead. For tickets, just phone **Theatre LA** (☎ 213/614-0556, ⓦ www.theatrela.org); be sure to ask about the availability of discount tickets for whichever show you're interested in.

Major theaters

Actors' Gang Theater 6209 Santa Monica Blvd, Hollywood ☎ 323/465-0566, ⓦ www.theactorsgang.com. Something of a cross between a major and an alternative theater; having less than a hundred seats keeps it cozy, though it does host occasionally spectacular productions that feature the odd big name from film or TV.

Ahmanson Theatre at the Music Center, 135 N Grand Ave, Downtown ☎ 213/628-2772, ⓦ www.taperahmanson.com. A two-thousand-seat theater hosting colossal traveling shows from Broadway. If you've seen a major production advertised on TV and on the sides of buses, it's probably playing here.

Alex Theater 216 N Brand Blvd, Glendale ☎ 818/243-ALEX, ⓦ www.alextheatre.org. A gloriously restored movie palace – with a great neon spike and quasi-Egyptian forecourt – that now hosts musical theater and one-person shows, along with occasional comedians and cinema revivals.

Coronet Theater 366 N La Cienega Blvd, West Hollywood ☎ 310/657-7377, ⓦ www.coronettheatre.com. Home of the LA Public Theater and the Youth Academy of Dramatic Arts, this venue is particularly notable as the spot where mid-level Hollywood actors come to test new material before crowds of supportive fans and curious onlookers.

Freud Playhouse in MacGowan Hall on the UCLA campus, Westwood ☎ 310/825-2101, ⓦ www.performingarts.ucla.edu. A nearly six-hundred-seat venue that features a mix of mainstream and contemporary pieces – plus the odd risk-taking experimental work – sometimes with Hollywood up-and-comers or familiar has-beens in the cast.

Geffen Playhouse 10886 Le Conte Ave, Westwood ☎ 310/208-5454, ⓦ www.geffenplayhouse.com. A five-hundred-seat, quaint Spanish Revival building that often hosts one-person shows. Named after movie and music impresario David Geffen, there's a decided Hollywood connection here, evident in the crowd-pleasing nature of many of the playhouse's productions.

International City Theatre 300 E Ocean Ave, Long Beach ☎ 562/436-4610, ⓦ www.ictlongbeach.com. Part of the Long Beach Performing Arts Center, this is an enjoyable, affordable spot for mainstream comedy and drama.

James Doolittle Theater 1615 N Vine St, Hollywood ☎ 323/462-6666. Administered by UCLA, this large, historic theater in the heart of Hollywood presents mainstream touring productions on a rather erratic schedule.

Mark Taper Forum at the Music Center, 135 N Grand Ave, Downtown ☎ 213/972-0700, ⓦ www.taperahmanson.com. Theater in the three-quarter round, with familiar classics and, less frequently, assorted new plays. Don't expect fringe-theater radicalism; this high-culture spot is mostly known for its conservatism and adherence to the mainstream repertoire.

Pantages Theater 6233 Hollywood Blvd, Hollywood ☎ 323/468-1770, ⓦ www.nederlander.com/pantages.html. Quite the stunner: an exquisite, atmospheric Art Deco theater, in the heart of historic Hollywood, hosting major touring Broadway productions.

Pasadena Playhouse 39 S El Molino Ave, Pasadena ☎ 626/792-8672 or 356-PLAY, ⓦ www.pasadenaplayhouse.org. A grand old space – also known as the State Theatre of California – that has been refurbished to provide enjoyable mainstream entertainment. Actors are often a mix of youthful professionals and aging TV and movie stars.

South Coast Repertory 655 Town Center Drive, Costa Mesa ☎ 714/708-5555, ⓦ www.scr.org. Orange County's major entry for theater, this is a recently refurbished venue where, on the main stage, you can watch standard, well-executed performances on the order of Shaw and Shakespeare, while edgier works by contemporary writers can be seen on the smaller, 150-seat second stage. Adjacent to the Orange County Performing Arts Center (see p.296).

Small and alternative theaters

A Noise Within 234 S Brand Blvd, Glendale ☎ 818/240-0910, ⓦ www.anoisewithin.org. A very mainstream performance space in downtown Glendale, focusing heavily on the classics, with a strong emphasis on Shakespeare.

Actors Forum Theater 10655 Magnolia Blvd, North Hollywood ☎ 818/506-0600, ⓦ www.actorsforumtheatre.org. Unpredictable venue that hosts a range of topical dramas, one-person shows, and the odd production from nontraditional actors like local weatherman Fritz Coleman. Dramatic workshops are also offered.

Cast-at-the-Circle 800 N El Centro Ave, Hollywood ☎ 323/466-0944. A small Hollywood theater hosting a variety of unpredictable plays and events, including edgy one-man and -woman shows. Emphasizes works by local playwrights, read by a cast of skilled up-and-comers.

The Complex 6476 Santa Monica Blvd, Hollywood ☎ 323/465-0383. A number of alternative theaters have sprung up in Hollywood west of Cahuenga Blvd, revolving around a group of six small theaters here at The Complex, where you're likely to see any number of dynamic productions.

Evidence Room 2220 Beverly Blvd, Mid-Wilshire ☎ 213/381-7118, ⓦ www.evidence-room.com. Edgy, startling works, alternated with more conventional modern dramas and comedies. The troupe has been somewhat itinerant recently, so call to confirm listings and venue space.

Gascon Center Theater 8737 Washington Blvd, Culver City ☎ 310/204-3126, ⓦ www.westside-fencing.com/theatre.html. Comedy and satire are frequently on the bill at this venue in the former Helms Bakery building; despite its location outside the Hollywood circuit, this theater offers as many interesting plays and skilled actors as most spots in LA.

Highways 1651 18th St, Santa Monica ☎ 310/453-3711, ⓦ www.18thstreet.org. Located in the 18th St Arts Complex, this is an adventurous performance space offering a range of topical drama and one-person shows, with a strong bent toward the angry, polemical and subversive.

Hudson Mainstage Theater 6539 Santa Monica Blvd, Hollywood ☎ 323/856-4252, ⓦ www.hudsontheatre.com. Socially conscious "message" plays alternate with more satiric, comedic works at this theater for upcoming actors.

Knightsbridge Theater 1944 Riverside Drive, Glendale ☎ 626/440-0821, ⓦ www.knightsbridgetheatre.com. On the edge of Griffith Park, Knightsbridge is a prime spot for classical theater, from Shakespeare to Molière. While you won't recognize most of the names in the cast, you'll likely enjoy the fresh spins on familiar standards.

Lee Strasberg Creative Center 7936 Santa Monica Blvd, West Hollywood ☎ 323/650-7777, ⓦ www.strasberg.com/hollywood. Although method acting as once taught by master instructor Strasberg is plentiful here – as well as a few stars in the crowd – all types of plays and styles are performed.

Lonnie Chapman Group Repertory 10900 Burbank Blvd, North Hollywood ☎ 818/769-PLAY. The Group Repertory troupe often tends toward plays involving dark and heavy social themes (though some musicals and comedies are staged, too).

Los Angeles Theatre Center 514 S Spring St, Downtown ☎ 213/485-1681. Despite the institutional name, this former bank is a fringe entity that has gone through numerous ups and downs. Currently, it offers irregular performances of modern works in its four theaters, ranging from one hundred to five hundred seats.

Matrix Theater 7657 Melrose Ave ☎ 323/852-1445. This Melrose theater offers excellent, uncompromising productions that often feature some of LA's better young actors and playwrights.

Odyssey Theater Ensemble 2055 S Sepulveda Blvd, West LA ☎ 310/477-2055, ⓦ www.odysseytheatre.com. Well-respected Westside theater company with a modernist bent, offering a range of quality productions on three stages for decent prices. Original plays come from a variety of theater groups, using mostly lesser-known actors.

Open Fist Theatre 1625 N La Brea Ave, Hollywood ☎ 323/882-6912, ⓦ www.openfist.org. As you might expect from the name, alternative and edgy works are often the focus at this small theater company, employing a limited cast of spirited unknowns – though sometimes with larger names dropping in.

Powerhouse Theater 3116 Second St, Santa Monica ☎ 310/396-3680. On the border of Venice, this alternative theater presents risk-taking experimental shows; perhaps the best of its kind in town. Located in a former electrical station for the old Red Car transit line.

Stages Theatre Center 1540 N McCadden Place, Hollywood ☎ 323/465-1010, ⓦ www.stagestheatrecenter.com. With three stages offering twenty to one hundred seats, an excellent place to catch a wide range of comedies and dramas, including re-stagings of canonical works and contemporary productions with either a mainstream or experimental bent.

Theatre West 3333 Cahuenga Blvd W, Hollywood ☎ 323/851-7977, ⊛ www.the-atrewest.org. A classic venue that's always a good spot to see inventive, sometimes odd, productions, with a troupe of excellent young up-and-comers.

Theatricum Botanicum 1419 N Topanga Canyon Blvd, Topanga Canyon ☎ 310/455-3723, ⊛ www.theatricum.com. Terrific spot showing a range of classic (often Shakespeare) and modern plays amid an idyllic outdoor setting. Founded by Will Geer – TV's Grandpa Walton.

Zephyr Theater 7456 Melrose Ave ☎ 323/653-4667. Although featuring a range of acting troupes and plays, shows here lean toward socially relevant, issue-related content, occasionally with a bit of irreverence.

Comedy

LA has a very wide range of **comedy clubs**. While rising stars and beginners can be spotted on the "underground" open-mike scene, most of the famous and soon-to-be-famous comics, both stand-up and improv, appear at the more established clubs, most of them in Hollywood, West LA or Mid-Wilshire. These venues usually have a bar, charge a $10–15 cover and put on two shows per evening, generally starting at 8pm and 10.30pm – the later one being more popular. The better-known places are open nightly, but are often solidly booked on Fridays and weekends.

Acme Comedy Theater 135 N La Brea Ave, Mid-Wilshire ☎ 323/525-0202, ⊛ www.acmecomedy.com. A fancy venue with mostly sketch and improv comedy, as well as variety shows. $10–15.

Bang Theater 457 N Fairfax Ave, Mid-Wilshire ☎ 323/653-6886. One-person shows and long-form improv are the specialties at this small theater/comedy club. Cheap cover, often $8.

Comedy & Magic Club 1018 Hermosa Ave, Hermosa Beach ☎ 310/372-1193. Strange couplings of magic and comedy; Jay Leno sometimes tests material here. Tickets can run $15–25.

Comedy Store 8433 W Sunset Blvd, West Hollywood ☎ 323/656-6225, ⊛ www.thecomedystore.com. LA's comedy showcase, and popular enough to be spread over three rooms – which means there's often space available, even on weekends, and usually a good line-up, too, with major names like Jerry Seinfeld and Drew Carey occasionally dropping by. Run, strangely enough, by Pauly Shore's mom. $5–10.

Empty Stage 2372 Veteran Ave, West LA ☎ 310/470-3560, ⊛ www.emptystage.com. Sometimes funny, sometimes irritating sketch comedy that draws upon long improv routines. Cast mainly with up-and-comers of varying hilarity. $5–10.

Groundlings Theater 7307 Melrose Ave ☎ 323/934-9700, ⊛ www.groundlings.com. Another pioneering improv venue; many promising comics make the effort, but only the gifted manage to survive the tough, fickle crowds and competitive atmosphere – among them, Pee Wee Herman. $12–20.

Ha Ha Café 5010 Lankershim Blvd, North Hollywood ☎ 818/508-4995, ⊛ www.hahacafe.com. Amateur and even a few professional comedians face off for your amusement on Thursday nights at this combination comedy club and café space. $5–10.

HBO Workspace 733 N Seward St, Hollywood ☎ 323/993-6099. If you're in the mood for experimental comedy, this is the place: HBO runs it as a proving ground for risky acts. Free.

The Ice House 24 N Mentor Ave, Pasadena ☎ 626/577-1894, ⊛ www.icehousecomedy.com. The undisputed comedy mainstay of the San Gabriel Valley, where Robin Williams and Steve Martin first came to prominence; often amusing, and still with the occasional big name. Two-drink minimum, plus $8–20 cover.

Improv Olympic West 6366 Santa Monica Blvd, Hollywood ☎ 323/962-7560, ⊛ www.iowest.com. Not to be confused with the other *Improv* (below), this intimate performance space presents lengthy routines involving significant participation from the audience, which sparks much of the humor. $5–10.

The Improvisation 8162 Melrose Ave, Mid-Wilshire ☎ 323/651-2583, ⊛ www.improv.com.

Longstanding brick-walled joint known for hosting some of the best acts working in the area, and one of LA's top comedy spots – so book ahead. Don't be surprised to find Billy Crystal or other celebs lurking in the background, and sometimes stepping on stage. $10.

LA Connection 13442 Ventura Blvd, Sherman Oaks ☎ 818/784-1868, ⓦ www.laconnection-comedy.com. Cozy space for sketch comedy, group antics and individual jokesters. Seldom less than memorable. $8–10.

LA TheaterSports 11050 Magnolia Blvd, North Hollywood ☎ 818/505-6406, ⓦ www.theatres-ports.com. As you might guess, comedy competitions here are arranged like sports contests, with plenty of feedback from the audience and all kinds of high-spirited theatrics.

The Laugh Factory 8001 Sunset Blvd, West Hollywood ☎ 323/656-1336, ⓦ www.laughfac-tory.com. Nightly stand-ups of varying standards and reputations, with the odd big name. Features a variable open-mike night. $10.

Cabaret

LA's **cabaret** scene is a favorite hangout for some SoCal hipsters, with the rediscovery of lounge music attracting a young, trendy crowd (as well as the requisite grizzled old-timers). The food at most of the venues leaves much to be desired, but it hardly matters to those who attend. Most of the best and biggest cabarets are in Hollywood.

Atlas 3760 Wilshire Blvd, Mid-Wilshire ☎ 213/380-8400. Along with dance music and pricey Cal-cuisine entrees (see "Restaurants and cafés," p.261), this spot offers regular cabaret shows, from fiery chanteuses to more experimental acts; it's located in the classic Art Deco Wiltern complex. Cover varies.

Canter's Kibitz Room 419 N Fairfax Ave, Mid-Wilshire ☎ 323/651-2030. Located next to *Canter's Deli*, this is one of the more bizarre versions of cabaret in LA, featuring an assortment of pop, rock and jazz artists – as well as audience members on open-mike nights – performing in a retro-1950s lounge space. Free.

Cinegrill 7000 Hollywood Blvd, Hollywood ☎ 323/466-7000, ⓦ www.hollywoodroosevelt.com. Housed in the beautifully restored landmark *Roosevelt Hotel* and still the biggest name in LA cabaret, offering an assortment of mostly mainstream jazz and cabaret acts. $10–25; two-drink minimum.

The Dresden Room 1760 N Vermont Ave, Hollywood ☎ 323/665-4294, ⓦ www.the-dresden.com. Little-known singers doing your favorite easy-listening covers from Wayne Newton to Tom Jones on Tuesday nights (see "Bars, coffeehouses and clubs," p.280), as well as a regular husband-and-wife lounge act the rest of the time. Another joint made popular by the film *Swingers*.

Free, except for two-drink minimum.

Gardenia Lounge 7066 Santa Monica Blvd, Hollywood ☎ 323/467-7444. No self-conscious irony here, only straight-up jazz and adult contemporary tunes presented to a gracious crowd nightly. The odd comedian provides some variation, but music is the real attraction. $10; two-drink minimum.

La Strada 3000 Los Feliz Blvd, Hollywood ☎ 323/664-2955. On weekend nights, big- and mid-level names in local opera drop in at this restaurant to belt out an aria or two, or just entertain the crowd with lighter tunes from operettas. No cover; two-drink minimum.

Largo 432 N Fairfax Ave, Mid-Wilshire ☎ 323/852-1073. Intimate cabaret venue that features a colorful range of singers and acts on periodic nights, along with some of LA's more unusual live bands (though mostly jazz, rock and pop).

Masquers Cabaret 8334 W Third St, Mid-Wilshire ☎ 323/653-4848, ⓦ www.masquer-scabaret.com. Zany comedies, slap-dash variety acts and energetic drag queens at this spirited nightly dinner theater near the Beverly Center mall. Although not always successful, the performers here rarely give up on trying to entertain the crowd. $5–15.

Queen Mary 12449 Ventura Blvd, Studio City ☎ 818/506-5619, ⓦ www.queenmaryshowlounge.com. Weekend drag shows and midweek karaoke torch-a-thons are the attraction at this longstanding San Fernando Valley venue. $5–10.

San Gennaro 9543 Culver Blvd, Culver City ⓣ310/836-0400. On weekends, prepare yourself for loving tributes to Ol' Blue Eyes at this swinging "cigar lounge." Along with hearing Sinatra covers, listen to slick crooners belting out favorites from Dean Martin, Tom Jones and other Vegas acts.

$10; two drinks included.

Vitello's 4349 Tujunga Ave, Studio City ⓣ818/769-0905. Broadway toe-tappers and operatic showstoppers are the norm in this cozy lounge with decent singers, passable Italian food, and just the right sort of funky, downmarket atmosphere. Wed & Fri–Sun; $10 minimum food and drink purchase.

Film

On many occasions, feature **films** are released in LA months (or years) before they play anywhere else in the world, sometimes only showing here and nowhere else. A huge number of cinemas focus on the new releases, though there are also plenty of venues for silver-screen classics, independent or art-house films and foreign movies. Tickets tend to be around $6–9, with cheaper prices for matinees and repertory screenings (around $5). **Drive-ins** are very rare these days; the ones that still exist are littered with weeds and offer dilapidated sound systems, and are located in distant burgs miles from anywhere you might want to find yourself.

For **cheap** or **free films**, the places to visit are the Bing Theater at the LA County Art Museum, 5905 Wilshire Blvd, Mid-Wilshire (ⓣ323/857-6010), which has afternoon screenings of Warner Bros classics and charges just $3; the USC campus, which often has interesting free screenings aimed at film students (announced on campus notice-boards); and UCLA's James Bridges Theater, which shows films drawn from the school's extensive archive (ⓣ310/206-FILM or ⓦwww.cinema.ucla.edu for details).

Countless venues for **mainstream cinema** exist, the most notable of which are in Westwood and Hollywood. For **art-houses** and **revival theaters**, there are a few worthwhile choices, some of them surprisingly sited in massive shopping complexes, but mostly scattered across the Westside. Finally, the grand **movie palaces** described elsewhere in this guide are here listed only as to their value as actual movie theaters, as many have been converted into performing-arts venues, music halls, churches or, depressingly, swap meets and flea markets.

Mainstream cinema

AMC Century 14 in the Century City mall, 10250 Santa Monica Blvd, Century City ⓣ310/553-8900. Never mind that it's in a mall – this is one of the best places to see new films in LA. The theaters are somewhat boxy, but if you're after crisp projection, booming sound, comfy seating and a rapt crowd – including camera-shy celebs sneaking about – there are few better choices.

Beverly Cineplex in the Beverly Center mall, Beverly and La Cienega blvds, Mid-Wilshire ⓣ310/777-FILM. An enterprisingly programmed venue with fourteen small screens which show a mix of artsy, independent film programs and first-run blockbusters.

Bruin 948 Broxton Ave, Westwood ⓣ310/208-8998. While smaller than it used to be, thanks to aggressive remodeling, this 1930s moviehouse remains a city landmark for its wraparound marquee and sleek Moderne styling.

Cinerama Dome 6360 Sunset Blvd, Hollywood ⓣ323/466-3401 or 464-4226. Built to cash in on the Cinerama craze, but completed after the fad went bust, this white hemisphere has the biggest screen in California, a giant curved panel with slight distortion at the corners. Now part of a larger retail complex of theaters, shops and eateries called ArcLight (ⓦwww.arclightcinemas.com).

Crest 1262 Westwood Blvd, Westwood
☎310/474-7866. A riot of neon and flashing lights outside, with glowing murals of Old Hollywood inside. Typically shows Disney flicks.

Fairfax 7907 Beverly Blvd, Mid-Wilshire
☎323/655-4010. A relative rarity in town, this is an independent moviehouse with cheap prices and great old decor; located in the middle of the Fairfax District.

Fine Arts 8556 Wilshire Blvd, Beverly Hills
☎310/652-1330. The simple exterior and lobby give way to a grandly opulent 1936 theater showing a mix of mainstream and art-house films.

IMAX Theater 600 State Drive, at the California Science Center in Exposition Park ☎213/744-2015. Six-story, hemispheric screen showing short, eye-popping documentaries, including the occasional 3-D presentation. Presents mostly science and nature films; though somewhat tedious, the monumental programs never fail to draw sizeable crowds of kids and tourists.

National 10925 Lindbrook Drive, Westwood
☎310/208-4366. In every way a period piece from the 1960s, this giant, curvaceous theater is another fine Westwood venue in the Mann theater chain.

Universal City 18 end of Universal City Drive, Burbank ☎818/508-0588. This eighteen-screen complex at Universal CityWalk is one of LA's better multiplexes, a plush complex that includes a pair of pseudo-Parisian cafés. Despite all the screens, though, only six or seven films are typically shown, with multiple theaters reserved for each.

Village 961 Broxton Ave, Westwood ☎310/208-5576. One of the most enjoyable places to watch a movie in LA, with a giant screen, fine seats, good balcony views and a modern sound system; it's a frequent spot for Hollywood premieres. Come early and take a look at the marvelous 1931 exterior, particularly the white spire on top.

Art-houses and revival theaters

Aero 1328 Montana Ave, Santa Monica
☎310/395-4990, ⓦ www.aerotheatre.com. Terrific little venue for art-house, classic and foreign films, located along the busy Montana Street shopping strip.

Charlie Chaplin Theater in the Raleigh Studios complex, 5300 Melrose Ave, Mid-Wilshire
☎323/466-FILM. Thanks to the American

Cinematheque film organization, you can watch classic movies in the historic surroundings of the old Raleigh movie studios. The fare is eclectic and intelligently programmed.

Directors Guild Theater 7920 Sunset Blvd, West Hollywood ☎310/206-8013. An excellent film venue that offers crisp images and booming sound; though mostly used for Directors Guild functions, the theater is also open sparingly throughout the year for special screenings and various film festivals (see ⓦ www.dga.org for more information).

Los Feliz 1822 N Vermont Ave, Hollywood
☎323/664-2169. Having successfully avoided a descent into the porn movie market in the 1960s, this theater's three small screens now show international and low-budget American independent fare.

New Beverly Cinema 7165 Beverly Blvd, Mid-Wilshire ☎323/938-4038. Not a particularly attractive theater, but a worthwhile one for its excellent art films and revival screenings, with some imaginative double bills.

Nuart 11272 Santa Monica Blvd, West LA
☎310/478-6379. Showing rarely seen classics, documentaries and foreign-language films, this is the main option for independent film-makers testing their work, and sometimes offers brief December previews of Oscar contenders long before they're released nationwide. Be prepared to wait outside the theater in a lengthy line near the 405 freeway, though.

NuWilshire 1314 Wilshire Blvd, Santa Monica
☎310/394-8099. With a solid booking policy, this is one of LA's better venues for art and foreign films, located a mile east of Palisades Park.

Old Town Music Hall 140 Richmond St, El Segundo ☎310/322-2592, ⓦ www.otmh.org. An old-fashioned spot to see historic movies, with accompanying organ or piano music on some nights, this quaint theater is unfortunately sited in a grim industrial location south of LAX.

Royal 11523 Santa Monica Blvd, West LA
☎310/477-5581. Though it doesn't quite live up to its regal name, this is still a prime spot for independent fare, with a spacious, classically ornamented theater.

Silent Movie 611 N Fairfax Ave, Mid-Wilshire
☎323/655-2520, ⓦ www.silentmovietheatre .com. Offers an enjoyable mix of silent comedies and adventure flicks – Douglas Fairbanks swashbucklers and the like –

along with darker fare like Fritz Lang's *Metropolis* and even the occasional "talkie."

Sunset 5 8000 Sunset Blvd, West Hollywood ☎323/848-3500. This art-house complex sits on the second floor of the Sunset Plaza outdoor mall and shows a good assortment of edgy independent flicks.

Vista 4473 Sunset Drive, Hollywood ☎323/660-6639. A nicely renovated moviehouse with very eclectic offerings – from mindless action flicks to micro-budget indie productions – located near the intersection of Sunset and Hollywood boulevards.

Westside Pavilion Cinemas in the Westside Pavilion mall, 10800 Pico Blvd, West LA ☎310/475-0202. Something of a surprise: one of the city's better art-houses located on the third floor of a huge mall. Multiple screens, plus free parking.

Movie palaces

Avalon 1 Casino Way, Santa Catalina Island ☎310/510-0179. Located in the stunning Casino building, this great old moviehouse is a riot of mermaid murals, gold-leaf motifs, and an overall design sometimes called "Aquarium Deco." Also presents a yearly silent-film fest.

Chinese 6925 Hollywood Blvd, Hollywood ☎323/464-8111, ⓦmann.moviefone.com. With its large main screen, six-track stereo sound and wild chinoiserie design, this Hollywood icon shows relentlessly mainstream films – but the first-night audience's loud participation is entertainment in itself. Has recently and unfortunately been expanded and incorporated into the design of a giant adjacent shopping mall.

Egyptian 6712 Hollywood Blvd, Hollywood ☎323/466-FILM, ⓦwww.americancinematheque.com. Thanks to the American Cinematheque film group, this historic moviehouse has nightly showings of revival, experimental and art films, and has been lovingly restored as a kitschy masterpiece of the Egyptian Revival – all grand columns, winged scarabs and mythological gods. During the day, a PR film about Hollywood is shown to tourists.

El Capitan 6834 Hollywood Blvd, Hollywood ☎323/467-7674. Whether or not you enjoy the typically kiddie-oriented fare offered here – thanks to its Disney ownership – the restored splendor of this classic Hollywood movie palace is bound to impress you.

Los Angeles 615 S Broadway, Downtown ☎213/623-CITY. Boasting an exquisite French Second Empire lobby, with triumphal arches lined by marble columns supporting an intricate mosaic ceiling, and an 1800-seat auditorium enveloped by trompe l'oeil murals. One of the all-time great moviehouses in the country, though only periodically open to the public. You can get a glimpse inside on Los Angeles Conservancy tours (see "City tours," p.35) or during the Last Remaining Seats film festival in June (tickets $18 per film; call ☎213/623-CITY for details).

Orpheum 842 S Broadway, Downtown ☎213/239-0939. A spellbinding mix of French Renaissance and Baroque decor, with a pipe organ, leafy and brazen chandeliers, ornamental facial grotesques, a few nude nymphs, and grand arches in gold-leaf. Sadly, the action flicks presented here just don't do the place justice.

Palace 630 S Broadway, Downtown ☎213/688-6166, ⓦwww.downtownpalace.com. Not to be confused with the music venue in Hollywood, this actual movie palace sports mock-Venetian architecture galore, with gilded Corinthian columns, splendid Baroque arches and ornament, and an imitation Tiepolo hanging near the movie screen. Slated for renovation back to its former glory.

Rialto 1023 Fair Oaks Ave, South Pasadena ☎626/799-9567. A 1925 movie palace that also served as a theatrical stage and vaudeville locale, with Moorish organ screens, Egyptian columns, winged harpies and a central Medusa head. Having survived numerous demolition threats over the years, the theater is now a historic landmark, designed to be the focus of the city's proposed Theater and Arts District.

State 703 S Broadway, Downtown ☎213/239-0962. Once the jewel of MGM's LA theaters, the State is a colossus with nearly 2400 seats and a staggering display of Spanish Renaissance and Baroque designs with copious mythological ornament, intricate friezes, and two prominent pseudo-opera boxes on the sides. Grime and decay have discolored the old glamour, but when the moody blue-and-orange house lights are on and the eager crowd sits waiting, you can almost envision the theater's golden age, when it showed grand epics and musicals.

Warner Grand 478 W Sixth St, San Pedro

☎ 310/548-7672, Ⓦ www.warnergrand.org.
Definitely worth a trip down to the LA harbor to see the glory of this restored 1931 Zigzag Moderne masterpiece, with its dark geometric details, majestic columns and sunburst motifs – a style that almost looks pre-Columbian. Having fallen into disuse for many years, the theater is now a repertory cinema and performing arts hall.

Gay and lesbian LA

A lthough nowhere near as prominent as San Francisco's, LA's **gay and lesbian scene** is similarly well-established. The best known gay-friendly area is the city of **West Hollywood**, which has become synonymous with the (affluent, white) gay lifestyle, not just in LA but all over California. Santa Monica Boulevard, east of Doheny Drive, in particular has a wide range of restaurants, shops and bars aimed at gay men, though less flashy lesbian-oriented businesses can also be found throughout the city. West Hollywood is also the site of the exuberant **Gay Pride Parade** (☎323/860-0701), held annually in late June. Another well-established gay and lesbian community is **Silver Lake**, home to the gay-oriented bars and restaurants of Hyperion Boulevard, and with more of a Hispanic feel along Sunset Boulevard.

Gay couples will find themselves readily accepted at most LA **hotels**, but there are a few that cater especially to gay travelers and can also be useful sources of information on the scene in general. Listed below, too, are **restaurants**, **bars** and **clubs** that cater specifically to gay men and lesbians. Of course, you shouldn't have too much of a problem wherever you go – attitudes in LA are usually quite tolerant.

The most-read local publication, though it's also distributed nationally, is *The Advocate* (ⓦ www.advocate.com), a bimonthly gay news magazine with features, general information and classified ads. Other gay-oriented publications feature weekly club and event listings, community information and topical articles, and can be found at eateries and retailers around LA – often for free.

Accommodation

Coral Sand Motel 1730 N Western Ave, Hollywood ☎1-800/467-5141, ⓦwww.coral-sands-la.com. A cruisey spot exclusively geared towards gay men. All rooms face the inner courtyard pool. ❹

Holloway Motel 8465 Santa Monica Blvd, West Hollywood ☎323/654-2454, ⓦwww.holloway-motel.com. Typical roadside motel that's a bit pricey and somewhat dreary looking, though clean and well-kept. Comes with complimentary breakfast. ❺

Hollywood Metropolitan 5825 Sunset Blvd ☎323/962-5800, ⓦwww.metropolitanhotel.com. Spanish-style hotel with a mix of small, comfortable rooms and larger suites, fea-

turing the *Havana on Sunset* restaurant on site (see "Restaurants and cafés," p.264). Just off the 101 freeway. ❹

Ramada Inn 8585 Santa Monica Blvd, West Hollywood ☎310/652-6400 or 1-800/845-8585. The self-styled "Gay Hotel," a modern place with clean and comfortable rooms, in the center of the community. ❺

San Vicente Inn 854 N San Vicente Blvd, West Hollywood ☎310/854-6915, ⓦwww.gayresort.com. Small and comfortable bed-and-breakfast located just north of Santa Monica Blvd. Aimed primarily at gay men. ❺

Restaurants and cafés

For an explanation of the price codes in the reviews, see p.259.

Cobalt Cantina 616 N Robertson Blvd, West Hollywood ☎310/659-8691. Rich, filling Cal-cuisine, leaning toward Mexican fare, served in an appropriately stylish setting. Another branch in Silver Lake at 4326 Sunset Blvd ☎323/953-9991. Moderate.

Coffee Table 2930 Rowena Ave, Los Feliz ☎323/644-8111. A neighborhood coffee-house with low-fat sandwiches and health food, mixed with a smattering of tasty desserts. Inexpensive.

French Quarter 7985 Santa Monica Blvd, West Hollywood ☎310/654-0898. Inside the French Market Place, a New-Orleans theme restaurant that can be at least as much fun as Disneyland, with food that's more tasty than it is authentic. Moderate.

Golden Bull 170 W Channel Rd, Pacific Palisades ☎310/230-0402. Enjoyable steak-and-seafood restaurant and bar that makes for a relaxed atmosphere near the ocean, not far from Santa Monica. Expensive.

Marix Tex-Mex Playa 118 Entrada Drive, Pacific Palisades ☎310/459-8596. Flavorful fajitas and big margaritas in this rowdy beachfront cantina, which attracts mixed gay and straight crowds. An even livelier branch at 1108 N Flores St, West Hollywood ☎323/656-8800. Moderate.

Mark's 861 N La Cienega Blvd, West Hollywood ☎310/652-5252. High-end establishment serving Cal-cuisine, with especially good crab cakes, *osso bucco* and Australian lamb chops. Expensive.

Numbers 8741 Santa Monica Blvd, West Hollywood ☎323/652-7700. Second-story bar and restaurant with Continental and Cal-cuisine, with a nice view overlooking the city. Moderate.

Woody's at the Beach 1305 S Coast Hwy, Laguna Beach ☎949/376-8809. Upscale bar and restaurant in Orange County serving quality California cuisine to a fairly well-heeled clientele. Expensive.

Yukon Mining Company 7328 Santa Monica Blvd, West Hollywood ☎323/851-8833. Slightly seedy but fun 24-hour joint with a wide mix of customers, gay and straight. Widely known in the scene for its colorful clientele. Inexpensive.

Bars and clubs

Mid-Wilshire

Faultline 4216 Melrose Ave ☎323/660-0889. Fairly hardcore denim-and-leather scene with all kinds of frenetic activity inside, including plenty of driving house beats and testosterone-fueled mayhem.

Jewel's Catch One 4067 W Pico Blvd ☎323/734-8849. Longtime favorite on the local club scene, a sweaty barn catering to a mixed crowd and covering two wild dance floors.

The Plaza 739 N La Brea Ave ☎323/939-0703.
Nondescript joint hosts wild, mind-blowing
drag shows to a multiethnic, mostly gay
crowd.

Silver Lake

Akbar 4356 Sunset Blvd ☎323/665-6810. A
mellow and unpretentious Silver Lake
watering hole that draws a diverse,
bohemian crowd, including a loyal coterie of
gay visitors. No cover.

Cobalt 4326 Sunset Blvd ☎323/953-9991. A
low-key, elegant bar and restaurant where
the arty, stylish interior contrasts dramatically with the grungy neighborhood outside.
Two-for-one drinks are available during the
5–7pm happy hour.

Le Bar 2375 Glendale Blvd ☎323/660-7595.
Quiet and welcoming bar in a bland section
of Silver Lake. Not as much attitude as with
some West Hollywood spots. No cover.

Rudolpho's 2500 Riverside Drive ☎323/669-1226.
Every second Saturday of the month, it's time
to "dress up, drag down" to "Dragstrip 66"
night at this Mexican restaurant located
around Griffith Park; other nights are reserved
for salsa, rockabilly and dance music.

Woody's Hyperion 2810 Hyperion Ave
☎323/660-1503. Although you can simply
drink beer or shoot pool at this neighborhood hangout, you might also want to
catch some of the eclectic entertainment:
anything from dance beats to drag revues
to strip shows to karaoke sing-alongs,
depending on the night.

Hollywood and West Hollywood

Arena 6655 Santa Monica Blvd ☎323/462-0714.
A longtime gay hangout for its funk, trance
and house grooves, as well as the occasional
live band. Also at the same address, *Circus*
(☎323/462-1291) has electronica dance
nights and eye-opening weekend drag
shows. (See also "Bars, coffeehouses and
clubs," p.285.) Cover can reach $20 or more.

The Factory 652 N La Peer Drive ☎310/659-
4551. DJs spin house music most nights of
the week at what is one of West
Hollywood's more popular clubs.

Micky's 8857 Santa Monica Blvd ☎310/657-
1176. Lively, pulsating scene with a full range
of club nights, including the usual retro-70s
and -80s dance-pop, thundering house and

hip-hop beats, twice-weekly drag shows,
and even monthly swing and Dixieland
bands, performing on Sunday afternoons.

Mother Lode 8944 Santa Monica Blvd
☎310/659-9700. Strong drinks, wild dancing
to house and hi-NRG music, and periodic
drag antics make this one of the more
colorful and frenetic area clubs.

The Palms 8572 Santa Monica Blvd ☎310/652-
6188. Mostly house and pop music dance
nights at West Hollywood's most established lesbian bar, which increasingly caters
to a mixed crowd.

Rage 8911 Santa Monica Blvd ☎310/652-7055.
Very flashy gay men's club playing the latest
hi-NRG and house. Also with drag comedy.
Drinks are fairly cheap.

Revolver 8851 Santa Monica Blvd ☎310/659-
8851. With its sleek bar and intimate lounge,
this popular club usually attracts a crowd of
mostly gay men. Sizeable video screens are
used for karaoke, drag shows and TV-
watching.

7969 7969 Santa Monica Blvd, West Hollywood
☎323/654-0280. Legendary club back in
business after closing due to fire, and
offering Hi-NRG dance tunes on weekend
and Tuesday nights.

Ultra Suede 661 N Robertson Blvd ☎310/659-
4551. Featuring various clubs where a mixed
gay and straight crowd gyrates to new
wave, rock, house and retro-pop music.

The valleys and Orange County

Boom Boom Room 1401 S Coast Hwy, Laguna
Beach ☎949/494-7588. The pulse-pounding
name says it all: house and disco tunes
spun by local DJs on weekends, male strip
shows on Thursdays, and vibrant drag displays on Wednesdays.

Ozz Supper Club 6231 Manchester Blvd, Buena
Park ☎714/522-1542. If you're searching for a
gay scene in Orange County, you'll have to
look pretty hard outside of Laguna Beach;
still, *Ozz* does stand out – a lively dance
club with booming house, disco and salsa
music on the weekends and assorted drag
shows, cabaret music and lounge performers as well.

Queen Mary 12449 Ventura Blvd, Studio City
☎818/506-5619. Weekend drag shows and
midweek karaoke attract mixed crowds at
this longstanding San Fernando Valley
venue, though the gay scene is mainly in
the bar at the back of the club.

Sports and outdoor activities

R enowned for its sun and surf, Los Angeles has plenty of **sports** and **outdoor activities** to keep you occupied, wherever your interests may lie. While LA doesn't have the same die-hard enthusiasm for its **spectator sports** as does, say, New York or Chicago, Angelenos still often make a good showing at basketball, baseball and hockey games, especially if the home squad is having a good year. If seeing games in person isn't your idea of fun, there are always **sports bars** where you can catch your favorite team on television.

Regardless of the local level of interest in these team sports, it's obvious that **participatory sports** like surfing and hang-gliding are what most often define LA to the rest of the world, along with more self-conscious pursuits like **body-building**. Much of the stereotype of Southern California as a body-fixated culture can be depressingly accurate at times, but with the right pastime, you can usually enjoy yourself without concern for having the right clothes, attitude or abs.

Water and **beach sports** are still the city's main claims to fame, be they swimming or surfing in the Santa Monica Bay, snorkeling or scuba diving along the further reaches of the coast, or even kayaking and jet-skiing. If you'd rather not get wet, you can always try a bit of in-line skating, skateboarding or bicycling along strips like the Venice Boardwalk, or simply suntanning at the beach – always a good choice for making an impression in the land of well-bronzed movie stars and celebrities. For less earthbound thrills, **airborne activities** include ballooning above the LA basin, hang-gliding off precarious seaside cliffs, or just traveling safely in a helicopter tour. For more of a physical jump-start, there are many **fitness sports** to make you gasp and sweat, including jogging, rock climbing and hiking – not to mention hanging out in one of the city's many fitness clubs. Just as strenuous, **skiing** and **snowboarding** are available in the mountains east of LA, especially around the Big Bear region, a favorite weekend getaway for many locals. If all this sounds like too much work, there are plenty of other **leisure activities**, like horseback riding, fishing and bowling, to keep you amused.

Spectator sports

In this section, we've included details of each of the main **spectator sports** and the teams that represent LA.

Baseball

LA has two area major-league **baseball teams**: the **LA Dodgers** (☏323/224-1-HIT, ⓦwww.dodgers.com), who play at Dodger Stadium in Chavez Ravine, north of Downtown, and the **Anaheim Angels** (☏1-888/796-4256 or 714/663-9000, ⓦwww.angelsbaseball.com), who play at Anaheim Stadium out in Orange County. The Dodgers are historically the more triumphant and beloved franchise, having relocated from Brooklyn in the late 1950s, though they've taken some hits in recent years, both for being purchased by media mogul Rupert Murdoch and for being consistently overpaid and underachieving. The Angels had their best season in 2002, winning the World Series for the first time. Tickets for Dodger games run $6–21; for the Angels, $7–30.

Basketball

Basketball's flashy **LA Lakers** (☏213/480-3232, ⓦwww.lakers.com) have boasted such luminaries through the years as Kareem Abdul-Jabbar, Magic Johnson and, currently, Shaquille O'Neal and Kobe Bryant, and have won a total of thirteen championships, including three in a row through 2002. They play at the Staples Center in Downtown LA; tickets run from $22 to over $165, but can be somewhat hard to come by. The far lesser light in LA's basketball galaxy, the **LA Clippers** (☏213/742-7430, ⓦwww.clippers.com), have a history of shocking ineptitude; games are also held at the Staples Center, with seats running $10–120, and you should have no problem getting a ticket.

Los Angeles currently has no professional **football** teams – the Raiders moved back to Oakland and the Rams departed for St Louis. However, collegiate ball is a good alternative; Pasadena's 102,000-seat **Rose Bowl** (☏626/577-3100, ⓦwww.rosebowl-stadium.com) hosts the annual New Year's Day championship game, and is also the home field for UCLA's football team (tickets $12–35; ☏310/UCLA-WIN, ⓦuclabruins.ocsn.com). Rival USC also plays in historic digs, at the LA Coliseum in South Central (tickets $30–55; ☏213/740-GOSC, ⓦusctrojans.ocsn.com), site of the 1932 Olympics and former home of the Raiders.

Hockey

Hockey in LA didn't mean much until the late 1980s, when the **LA Kings** (☏1-888/KINGS-LA, ⓦwww.lakings.com) bought superstar Wayne Gretzky from the champion Edmonton Oilers. Gretzky's long gone from these parts, and the Kings have since moved from the Forum to the Staples Center; seats are $20–100. The **Anaheim Mighty Ducks**, in Orange County, are owned by Disney and play at Arrowhead Pond in Anaheim (☏714/704-2500, ⓦwww.mighty-ducks.com); tickets $15–175.

Soccer

One of the newer teams in town, the **LA Galaxy** (☏1-877/3-GALAXY, ⓦwww.lagalaxy.com) plays **soccer** in the MLS (Major League Soccer), and games take place at the National Training Center (opening June 2003) on the college campus of Cal State Dominguez Hills, in the city of Carson in the South Bay. The season runs much of the year, save winter; tickets $12–35.

Horse racing

Horse racing is a fairly popular spectator sport in the LA area, which has two main tracks. **Santa Anita**, in the San Gabriel Valley town of Arcadia at 285 W Huntington Drive, has a winter and spring season (☏626/574-7223, ⓦwww.santaanita.com); while **Hollywood Park**, 1050 S Prairie Ave in Inglewood, has a spring-to-autumn season (☏310/419-1500, ⓦwww.hollywoodpark.com).

Water and beach sports

Visitors to LA usually head straight for the ocean. Along the sands from Malibu to Orange County, you can find any number of **water** and **beach sports** to keep you busy. However, for more passive pleasures at the seaside, **suntanning** with crowds of other locals and visitors is always a popular option.

Swimming, snorkeling and scuba diving

Although you'd never believe it from watching TV, **swimming** in many coastal areas is definitely not recommended. As a rule, the further you go from most city piers, the better off you are. Piers, along with run-off pipes and channels, are often sources for water-borne contamination, thanks to heavy-metal and chemical offshore dumping, and the nasty, unfiltered overflow from the city's streetside drains. The authorities, however, will only inform you of dangerous conditions when heavy rains make it absolutely off-limits for human activity. (For more on the state of LA's waters, see box on p.133.)

The beaches closer to Malibu, Palos Verdes and Orange County are usually less crowded and much safer than those around Santa Monica and Venice, though of course any spots near the harbor are to be avoided. **Parking** at major strips of sand will cost you upwards of $7, even for a short time, but there are usually sufficient roadside spots to deposit your car if want to take a dip along the rockier coves and crags.

Similarly, **snorkeling** and **scuba diving** are better experienced well away from LA in places like Santa Catalina Island. Prices for excursions to see Catalina's astounding undersea life, kelp forest and shipwrecks can vary widely, but expect to pay at least $80–100 for any trip. Some of the better operators are Catalina Divers Supply in Avalon (☏1-800/353-0330 or 310/510-0330, ⓦwww.catalinadiverssupply.com), which leads undersea tours of Santa Catalina and rents scuba and snorkeling equipment; Catalina Island Kayak Expeditions, PO Box 386, Avalon 90704 (☏310/510-1226, ⓦwww.kayakcatalinaisland.com), offering kayaking and snorkeling trips and hourly, half-day or two-day packages; Scuba Luv, 126 Catalina Ave, Avalon (☏1-800/262-DIVE or 310/510-2350, ⓦwww.scubaluv.com), good for introductory dives for beginners; and Sundiver, 106 N Marina Drive, Long Beach (☏562/493-0951 or 1-800/955-9446, ⓦwww.sundiver.net), whose popular package deals include boating trips to area islands for one or two days of scuba diving. Lover's Cove, a marine preserve just east of Avalon, is the best spot to view the local sea life close-up, though only snorkeling is allowed. One operator at the site, Catalina Ocean Explorer (☏1-877/SNORKEL, ⓦwww.catalinaoceanexplorer.com), has ecological tours, snorkeling equipment for rent (generally $24 per day for a decent package) and underwater cameras for sale.

Surfing, windsurfing, kayaking and jet-skiing

Since railroad magnate Henry Huntington first began importing Hawaiian talent to publicize his Red Car route to the South Bay, **surfing** has been big business in LA, while having no small impact on the city's culture and image.

If you want to give the sport a try, head to where the surfers are: mostly along the Malibu section of the Pacific Coast Highway from **Surfrider** to **Leo Carrillo** beaches and around the great promontory of Point Dume. Although South Bay and Orange County surfers also have

△ Snowboarder, Bear Mountain

their favorite turf – including **Huntington Beach**, which is also home to the International Surfing Museum (see p.217) – surf culture in its purest form is best seen at the beaches in Malibu. Don't worry about buying equipment, though: **surfboards** are available for rent by the hour ($20–25, and $10 for a wet-suit in winter months) from rental shacks up and down the coast, such as Zuma Jay Surfboards, 22775 Pacific Coast Hwy, Malibu (☎310/456-8044).

If you've never been **windsurfing**, a trip to LA might not be the ideal time to start, the success of the experience depending on your overall dexterity and the velocity of the wind. But if you feel confident, several coastal outlets rent windsurfers by the hour or day, for upwards of $20–30 per hour. One such place to check out is Long Beach Windsurf Center, 3850 E Ocean Blvd, Long Beach (☎562/433-1014), near the Belmont Pier, which also rents in-line skates and kayaks.

Somewhat easier for novices is **kayaking**, with ocean-going kayaks ($10–20 per hour) being more basic and manageable than river kayaks, as you simply sit atop the sea-going boat and row with another person. Alfredo's Beach Rentals, 5411 Ocean Blvd, Long Beach (☎562/434-6121), rents kayaks, as well as small boats. On Santa Catalina Island, the West End Dive Center, at Two Harbors (☎1-800/785-8425 or 310/510-0303, ext 272), specializes in kayaking trips and instruction; and Catalina Ocean Rafting, 103 Pebbly Beach Rd, Avalon (☎1-800/990-RAFT or 310/510-0211, ⓦwww.catalinaoceanrafting.com), takes groups out in a small, flat boat to tour the oceanside terrain.

Finally, there's **jet-skiing**, a popular choice that will cost you around $100 to rent a machine for a half-day of splashing around Santa Monica Bay or elsewhere. Two well-established places for rentals (by appointment only) are Jet Ski Fun, in Santa Monica at 1753 Ninth St, Suite 201 (☎310/822-1868), and So-Cal Watercraft, in Huntington Beach at 15561 Computer Lane #A (☎1-800/908-8976, ⓦwww.socal-rentals.com), which also rents boats and water-skis.

In-line skating and bicycling

The popularity of **in-line skating**, or rollerblading, cannot be overesti-mated along the Venice Boardwalk and other beachside paths, or in cer-tain urban parks and recreation zones. These linear skates are found on the feet of countless locals and visitors traveling along the **cycling path** from Santa Monica to Palos Verdes, a terrific route for exploring the seaside edge of the metropolis. If you're walking, you should avoid this crowded path, as skaters and cyclists race down the asphalt lanes like automobiles, giving little respect to the painted yellow lines. You can rent skates from one of the seaside vendors like Perry's Café and Rentals, 2400 & 2600 Ocean Front Walk, Venice (☎310/452-2399, ⓦwww.perryscafe.com), and 930 Pacific Coast Hwy, Santa Monica (☎310/394-0086), where the skates go for $18 per day or $6 per hour.

The oceanside path along this area is also the main choice for **bicycling** in LA, even though there are myriad bike paths throughout the region, from the peaceful, leafy setting of the Arroyo Seco to the post-apocalyptic landscape of the LA River. Contact the AAA (American Automobile Association), 2601 S Figueroa St (Mon–Fri 9am–5pm; ☎213/741-3686, ⓦwww.aaa-calif.com), the LA office of the state Department of Transportation, known as CalTrans, 120 S Spring St (Mon–Fri 8am–5pm; ☎213/897-3656, ⓦwww.dot.ca.gov), or the California Association of Bicycling Organizations (☎310/639-9348, ⓦwww.cabobike.org) for maps and information. However, the beachfront is the only place with a good selection of dealers, who charge $10–15 an hour for skates or bikes, depending on the location and equipment.

Some of the better spots to rent blades or bikes include Sea Mist, 1619 Ocean Front Walk, Venice (☎310/395-7076); Bikestation, 105 Promenade North, Long Beach (☎562/436-BIKE, ⓦ www.bikestation.org), which offers bicycle rental, repair and storage, and even valet bike parking; and Spokes 'n' Stuff, 4175 Admiralty Way, Marina del Rey (☎310/306-3332), and also at 1700 Ocean Ave, Santa Monica (☎310/395-4748), just two of many similar dealers along the sands, while in Griffith Park, the outfit has a branch near the LA Zoo, at 4400 Crystal Springs Drive (weekends during daylight hours; $6 per hour; ☎323/662-6573).

Airborne activities

If you want to get above the smog, LA has several worthwhile **airborne activities** that may interest you. The most affordable is **hang-gliding**, using a simple glider to drift down from a hill, mountain or cliff on air currents and slowly coming to a safe landing. Of the equipment-rental outlets throughout town, Windsports Soaring Center, 16145 Victory Blvd, Van Nuys (☎818/988-0111, ⓦ www.windsports.com), is one of the more prominent; for around $120, they will give you the basic experience, but if you want a greater challenge, more expensive package deals are also available for $200. If you've come to LA as a hang-gliding pro, bring your glider to the bluffs overlooking the Pacific near Point Fermin for a strikingly picturesque trip over the seacliffs and toward the beach.

An appealing alternative for air enthusiasts is **soaring** in enclosed gliders. Again using air currents to rise and fall, these simple craft provide a memorable experience, if not quite as awe-inspiring as that of hang-gliding. North of LA in the Antelope Valley, Great Western Soaring, 32810 165th St E, Llano (☎1-800/801-GLIDE or 805/944-3341, ⓦ www.greatwesternsoaring.com), provides planes and lessons, at a cost of $82 for a basic lesson, up to $169 for a more involved ride. While most of your time will doubtless be spent watching from the back seat of the glider, you'll have a vivid experience that you, and your stomach, will not soon forget.

If the above ideas don't sound appealing, a **helicopter ride** may provide all the airborne excitement you need, allowing you to view some of LA's premier sights, like the Hollywood sign, from thousands of feet above the ground. There are a number of different packages and tours available, all at fairly steep prices, from such companies as Bravo Aviation, 401 World Way at LAX (☎310/337-6701, ⓦ www.bravoair.com), which offers short excursions to the South Bay for around $100 and hour-long overhead tours of LA's top sights for $289, or $150 for a half-hour tour; and Group 3 Aviation, 16425 Hart St, Van Nuys Airport, San Fernando Valley (☎818/994-9376, ⓦ www.group3aviation.com), which takes movie-oriented trips from central LA to various points along the coast (from $120–210).

Finally, the most conventional mode of flying is also available - an **airplane trip** in a single- or twin-engine craft. Blue Skies Aviation, 7535 Valjean Ave #4, Van Nuys (☎818/901-1489, ⓦ www.blueskiesaviation.com), offers charter flights for $290 per hour or, for those already in possession of at least a student pilot's license, prop-plane rentals for $70–100 per hour.

Fitness activities and extreme sports

LA's preoccupation with tanned, muscular and silicone-boosted bodies is most evident in the city's vigorous pursuit of **fitness activities**, which can veer from simply keeping one's body in shape to zealously worshipping it to testing the body's physical limits with **extreme sports**.

Fitness activities

For a taste of LA's health mania, **working out** at a fitness club or along the beach is an obvious place to start. Whether you've come to pump iron yourself or watch the weightlifters go through their paces, there are few better spots than **Muscle Beach** near the Venice Boardwalk – although having the right abs and biceps is essential if you're in the mood to show off your physique before flexing bodybuilders and gaping tourists. Contact the Venice Beach Recreation Center, 1800 Ocean Front Walk (℡310/399-2775), for more information on bench-pressing with the local iron-pumpers. If you're not quite there yet, the exercise and training equipment just south of the **Santa Monica Pier** should start you on your way to being sufficiently buff and trim. For less conspicuous body-building and training, LA's numerous **health clubs** are everywhere, with Gold's Gym being the most prominent.

For less social workouts, **jogging** is a popular choice, though you should stick to the safer Westside, and avoid anywhere Downtown or in Mid-Wilshire. Although Hollywood would at first seem like a dubious choice for exercising, the steeply inclined paths and fine views of Runyon Canyon Park make for an excellent workout (enter off Mulholland Drive or Fuller Avenue), as does the circuitous route around Lake Hollywood (see p.104). Elsewhere, the best paths for joggers include the green median strip of San Vicente Boulevard from Brentwood to Santa Monica; Sunset Boulevard through Beverly Hills and West LA (but not Hollywood); the Arroyo Seco in Pasadena; and most stretches along the beach – except for the busy, chaotic bike path and anywhere near the harbor.

Also along the beach, you may be able to join a **volleyball** game at any of the sandy courts from Santa Monica to Marina del Rey. Hermosa Beach is another good choice for volleyball (the city famously hosts competitions in the sport throughout the year), as are seaside towns in Orange County, like Huntington and Laguna beaches. **Tennis** is also played at courts across LA, with space available for visitors at city parks and universities. Call the city's Department of Recreation and Parks for more information on reserving a court (℡213/485-5555).

The best workout in town is also one of the cheapest. **Hiking** in LA doesn't have the same reputation as it does in other parts of the country, but under no circumstances is it an inferior, token pursuit. Rather, the Santa Monica Mountains – a huge natural preserve west of LA and north of Malibu – have many different trails and routes for exploration, most of which feature jaw-dropping scenery, copious wildlife and interesting rustic sights. You can order information and maps for locations throughout LA by contacting the state Department of Parks (℡818/880-0350, ⓦwww.parks.ca.gov), the Santa Monica Mountains Conservancy (℡310/589-3200, ⓦceres.ca.gov/smmc), the Sierra Club (℡213/387-4287, ⓦangeleschapter.org) or Hiking in LA (℡818/501-1005), a private group that offers treks through the Santa Monica Mountains in several foreign languages, as well as English.

The local Audubon Society also provides periodic guided hikes through this and other LA-area nature zones ($3; reserve at ☏323/876-0202, Ⓦwww.laaudubon.org), and the official Santa Monica Mountains **visitor center** is located in neighboring Thousand Oaks, 401 W Hillcrest Drive (Mon–Fri 8am–5pm, Sat & Sun 9am–5pm; ☏805/370-2301, Ⓦwww.nps.gov/samo), offering additional maps and information on hiking trails.

Extreme sports

As elsewhere in the country, **extreme sports** have gained a strong following in Los Angeles, with many such pursuits originating in the city itself; if you're already an acolyte, there are few better ways to spend your vacation here.

Of course, any of the previously listed sports, such as hang-gliding or kayaking, can with the right intensity level and risk-taking behavior be converted into an extreme activity. Beyond those pursuits, however, there are some edgy sports and activities that are also popular.

The original "extreme sport" was arguably **skateboarding**, and LA quickly became a trailblazer for the high-flying version of this sport, establishing its dominance worldwide. The most well-known official event here is the colorful **Beach Bash** (Ⓦwww.hermosawave.net), held in early June in Hermosa Beach, during which hundreds of extreme-sports athletes compete in events like skateboarding, freestyle biking and the more daredevil variety of in-line skating. (For a list of above-board skateboard parks in LA, visit Ⓦskateboardparks.com/California.)

Slightly more sedate, though potentially just as thrilling, **rock climbing** has gained in renown in recent years, and private rock "clubs" or "gyms" allow you to scale vertical surfaces to your heart's content, and equipment can also be rented for an additional fee. The Rock Gym, 600 Long Beach Blvd, Long Beach ($15, kids $12; ☏562/983-5500, Ⓦwww.therockgym .com), is one of several LA-area climbing venues. For a close-up look at the sport without paying a dime, turn up at Stony Point near Chatsworth, in the San Fernando Valley, to watch crowds of hardcore rock enthusiasts dangling perilously by their fingertips.

For sheer terror, **bungee jumping** is hard to beat. One of the best, and most longstanding, operators is Bungee America (☏310/322-8892, Ⓦwww.bungeeamerica.com), which usually supplies equipment to amusement parks and Hollywood, but also offers thrilling weekend jumps from the so-called "Bridge to Nowhere" in the Angeles National Forest, an abandoned span; package deals start from $69 for one leap to $165 for five.

If that isn't extreme enough for you, there's always **skydiving**, which you can experience in the desert north of Los Angeles at a cost of $159 a jump. Although you'll be tethered to an expert and won't be truly freefalling (five training jumps at $125 a pop will get you that privilege), only a half-hour introductory session is required before you make your ten-thousand-foot airborne journey to the desert floor. Contact California City Skydive, 22521 Airport Way, in California City near Edwards Air Force Base (☏1-800/2-JUMPHI, Ⓦwww.calcityskydive.com), to reserve your jump.

Skiing and snowboarding

Although the LA area is not well-known for winter sports, it does boast some prime territory for **skiing** and **snowboarding** in the mountainside lake and hamlet of **Big Bear**, located about two hours east of Downtown LA, north of

San Bernardino. Along with Mount Baldy and other such places in the general vicinity of the San Bernardino Mountains, Big Bear is deservedly a top winter draw for thousands of Angelenos, who drive out here (there are hardly any public transit options, except from San Bernardino itself) to experience the excellent ski and snowboard conditions from November through April, and similarly fine opportunities for hiking, boating, fishing and jet-skiing in the summer. Located near state highways 18 and 38, Big Bear has several appealing resorts that provide plenty of outdoor activities, winter or summer, while the fine *Adventure Hostel* (see p.238) is an inexpensive alternative.

One of the best ski areas is **Snow Summit**, 880 Summit Blvd, Big Bear Lake (lift tickets $40, kids $12; ℡909/866-5766, ⓦwww.snowsummit.com), which has twelve chairlifts that operate in summer for hikers and mountain bikers. The other major ski area, **Bear Mountain**, 43101 Goldmine Drive, Big Bear Lake (lift tickets $39, kids $12; ℡909/585-2519), offers twelve chairlifts and has the added attraction of four parks for freestyle snowboarding, as well as all the summer activities found elsewhere.

Further out from Big Bear Lake, one good choice is **Snow Valley**, 35100 Hwy-18 near Running Springs (lift tickets $38; ℡909/867-2751, ⓦwww.snow-valley.com), where besides the usual snow sports, you'll find a "terrain park" for creative snowboarding, along with twelve chairlifts. Several more of these terrain parks can be found at **Mountain High**, closer to Wrightwood at 24512 Hwy-2 (lift tickets $43, kids $15; ℡760/249-5803, ⓦwww.mthigh.com), which caters to more assertive winter athletes with two high-speed chairlifts (out of ten), plus night skiing every day of the week until 10pm. Finally, back on the fringe of LA County, the ski zone at **Mount Baldy**, off Mountain Avenue in the Angeles National Forest ($40, kids $10; ℡909/981-3344, ⓦwww.mtbaldy.com) offers a nice assortment of straightforward skiing trails and routes, along with decent snowboarding opportunities.

Leisure activities

If you're interested in activities that don't require a lot of grunting and sweating, LA has numerous **leisure activities**, beyond simply watching TV in your hotel room.

Fishing

Fishing is encouraged at a few locations, like some of the northern beaches around Malibu. Elsewhere, however – especially the Santa Monica and Venice piers – you risk ingesting a lifetime's worth of mercury and cadmium from any fish you bite into. A better, though more costly, alternative is to charter a **sport-fishing cruise** out to sea and cast your line there, for one to two thousand dollars for a six-hour trip on a winter weekday, or three thousand sand or more for an eight-hour cruise during a summer weekend.

A California State fishing license is required for anything from pier casting to ocean fishing, and costs nonresidents $6, $11 or $30, for one, two or ten days of fishing, with annual licenses running $82 ($30 for residents). Salmon, bass and abalone fishing require special permits for $3–13 more. Many cruise operators and fishing-supply dealers provide short-term fishing licenses. For more information, check ⓦwww.dfg.ca.gov/licensing.

Catalina Island Sportfishing 114 Claressa St,
Avalon ☎310/510-2420. Runs charter fishing
trips for $100–120 an hour in the waters off
Santa Catalina Island.

LA Harbor Sportfishing 1150 Nagoya Way,
Berth 79, San Pedro ☎310/547-9916,
ⓦwww.laharborsportfishing.com. Partial or full-
day trips to offshore waters are offered,
along with seasonal whale-watching cruises
and harbor tours.

Long Beach Sportfishing 555 Pico Ave, Berth
55, Long Beach ☎562/432-8993, ⓦwww.long-
beachsportfishing.com. Organizing overnight
and half-day fishing expeditions to deep-
sea waters, as well as whale-watching
trips.

Marina del Rey Sportfishing 13759 Fiji Way,
Marina del Rey ☎310/822-3625. Somewhat
more touristy than the other operators,
though the tour packages are much the
same (rental equipment, licenses, day or
half-day trips, etc).

Redondo Sportfishing 233 N Harbor Drive,
Redondo Beach ☎310/372-2111, ⓦwww.redon-
dosportfishing.com. Half-, full- and multiple-
day trips are offered, sailing to waters near
Palos Verdes all the way out to more distant islands off the California coast. Also
offers whale-watching cruises.

Bowling

Bowling attracts a diehard crowd of
local enthusiasts, and you can find
bowling alleys at many spots in LA,
from old linoleum-and-formica lanes
to newer bowl-o-ramas where flashy
bowling nights feature glow-in-the-
dark lanes and bowling balls. Costs
start around $5 per game, with shoe
rental a few dollars extra.

All Star Lanes 4459 Eagle Rock Blvd
☎323/254-2579. Located between Glendale
and Pasadena in the little burg of Eagle
Rock, this retro-styled alley features a bar,
dance floor, video games and pool tables to
keep you busy when you're not prowling
the lanes. Rockabilly bands provide the live
soundtrack, and you can bowl the whole
night away for just $12.

Brunswick West Covina 675 S Glendora Ave,
West Covina, San Gabriel Valley ☎626/960-3636.
Lovers of Googie pop architecture will not
want to miss this colorful, Polynesian-styled
alley – with its own coffee shop and cock-

tail lounge – though it's located out in the
middle of nowhere.

Jewel City Bowl 135 S Glendale Ave, Glendale
☎818/243-1188. Bowling zealots may hate it,
but casual fans will enjoy a trek out to this
popular Valley spot, where glowing balls,
heavy metal music, artificial fog and
headache-inducing lights all serve to dis-
tract you from hitting strikes.

Mar Vista Lanes 12125 Venice Blvd, West LA
☎310/391-5288. A set of funky old alleys
east of Venice, which also features Mexican
food and weekend karaoke. Appeals to the
more hardcore league bowlers.

Pickwick Bowling 921 W Riverside Drive,
Burbank ☎818/842-7188. With twenty-four
lanes and a mixed crowd of young and old,
this colorful Valley spot has gimmicks like
Friday dance-music nights and Saturday's
"Electric Fog" bowling, featuring copious
amounts of dry ice and wild lighting.

Regal Lanes Tustin St, city of Orange
☎714/997-9901. Located in Orange County
and supposedly the biggest bowling center
on the West Coast, with an astounding 72
lanes, plus an accompanying German bar
and restaurant.

Sports Center Bowl Ventura Blvd, Studio City
☎818/769-7600. Although not as wild as
other youth-oriented bowling alleys, this
place draws a crowd for its celebrity-
friendly location and rock'n'roll atmosphere.
Don't be surprised to see a B-list TV actor
or recent Hollywood has-been in the lane
next to you.

Horseback riding

You can experience **horseback riding** at several ranches and stables
throughout the greater LA region,
principally around the Santa Monica
Mountains and the hills of Griffith
Park. Most businesses give you a
choice of packages that may include
evening journeys, individual or group
rides, easy or difficult routes, and
various added amenities like dinners
or barbecues. Costs can be anywhere
from $15 to $50 per hour, depending
on the location and package.

Bar S Stables 1850 Riverside Drive, Glendale
☎818/242-8443. A Griffith Park–area
operator that provides guided equine tours
during the daylight or evening hours, and

occasionally under moonlight, for around $20 per hour.

Catalina Stables 600 Avalon Canyon Rd, Avalon ☏ 310/510-0478, ⓦ www.bdaservices.com/catalinastables. Offers guided tours of gorgeous Santa Catalina Island, with simple half-hour tours starting around $30, two-hour treks for $65, and five-hour journeys costing $150.

Circle K Riding Stables 910 S Mariposa St, Burbank ☏ 818/843-9890. Located near the LA Equestrian Center, the Circle K provides affordable rides for $15–20 per person per hour.

Griffith Park Horse Rental 480 Riverside Drive, Burbank ☏ 818/840-8401, ⓦ www.la-equestriancenter.com. Located in the Los Angeles Equestrian Center, across the LA

River from Griffith Park, this outfit offers horse rentals for $20 an hour or evening rides for $40, with a tasty barbecue to boot.

Sunset Ranch 3400 N Beachwood Drive, Hollywood ☏ 323/469-5450, ⓦ www.sunse-tranchhollywood.com. A Griffith Park operation that provides evening horse rides through the surrounding area, for $40 by reservation only, up to a Mexican restaurant for dinner and some live country and honky-tonk music.

Will Rogers Trails 1501 Will Rogers State Park Rd, Pacific Palisades ☏ 310/455-2900. Watch a polo match on the park's front lawn (April–Oct Sat 2–4pm, Sun 10am–noon; free) before enjoying a horseback ride in the vicinity for $45.

Festivals and events

L A has a great number of **parades** and **festivals** to celebrate throughout the year. No matter when you come, you'll likely find some sort of street fair or celebration, especially in summer, when beach culture is in full bloom. This selective list concentrates on some of the more notable observances, along with smaller, local events that provide unusual or nontraditional festivities. For a list of **national public holiday** observances in LA, see Basics, p.37.

January

Japanese New Year (1st) Art displays, ethnic cuisine, cultural exhibits and more at this annual Little Tokyo festival, centered around the Japanese American Community and Cultural Center. ☎213/628-2725, ⓦwww.jaccc.org.

Tournament of Roses Parade (1st) Pasadena's famous procession of floral floats and marching bands along a five-mile stretch of Colorado Blvd, coinciding with the annual Rose Bowl game. ☎626/795-9311 or 449-ROSE, ⓦwww.tournamentofroses.com.

Martin Luther King Parade and Celebration (mid-month) The civil rights hero is honored with activities at King Park, Baldwin Hills, Crenshaw and many other city locations. ☎310/314-2188 in LA, ☎562/570-6816 in Long Beach.

Golden Globe Awards (mid- to late Jan) As the annual run-up to the Oscars, this preliminary awards show is held by the Hollywood Foreign Press Association at the *Beverly Hilton*, and attracts ever-increasing (some say undeserved) attention. Tourists are encouraged to watch the stars arrive, and gape accordingly. ☎310/657-1731, ⓦwww.hfpa.org.

February

Chinese New Year (early to mid-Feb) Three days of dragon-float street parades, tasty food and various cultural programs, based in Chinatown, Alhambra and Monterey Park. ☎213/617-0396.

Mardi Gras (mid-month) Floats, parades, costumes, and lots of singing and dancing at this Brazilian fun fest, but nowhere as colorfully as in West Hollywood. Throughout LA at ☎323/634-7811 or 310/289-2525.

Bob Marley Reggae Festival (mid- to late Feb) A two-day event that exalts the reggae legend with food, music and plenty of spirit.

At the Long Beach Convention and Entertainment Center. ☎562/436-3661, ⓦwww.bobmarleydayfestival.com.

Queen Mary Scottish Festival (mid- to late Feb) All the haggis you can stand at this two-day Long Beach celebration, along with peppy Highland dancing and bagpipes. ☎562/435-3511.

Camellia Festival (late Feb) In Descanso Gardens in La Cañada-Flintridge, many different varieties of camellias are on display to the public. ☎818/952-4401, ⓦwww.descansogardens.org.

The Academy Awards (end Feb) The top movie awards, presented at the Kodak Theatre at the Hollywood & Highland mall. Bleacher seats are available to watch the limousines draw up and the stars emerge for the ceremony. ☎310/247-3000, ⊛www.oscars.org.

March

LA City Marathon (early March) Cheer on the runners all around town, or sign up to participate in this fun 26-mile run. ☎310/444-5544.

Los Angeles Bach Festival (mid-month) Revel in the Baroque master's music at the First Congregational Church, just north of Lafayette Park in Westlake. ☎213/385-1345, ⊛www.fccla.org.

St Patrick's Day (mid-month) No parade in LA, but freely flowing green beer in the "Irish" bars along Fairfax Ave in Mid-Wilshire. Parades along Colorado Blvd in Old Town Pasadena (☎626/796-5049), and in Hermosa Beach ☎310/374-4972, ⊛www.stpatricksday.org.

Spring Festival of Flowers (late March) A floral explosion of color at Descanso Gardens, including different types of tulips, lilies and daffodils, among many others. ☎818/952-4401, ⊛www.descansogardens.org.

Cowboy Poetry and Music Festival (end March) Folk music from the Old West and accompanying cowboy poems – some excellent, some cornpone – are the highlights of this three-day Santa Clarita celebration, just north of LA. ☎661/286-4078 or 1-800/305-0755.

April

California Poppy Festival (early April) Lancaster's 180-acre poppy reserve draws big crowds with its blinding orange colors each spring, while the town festival presents local foodstuffs, folk art and crafts to go with the blooms. ☎661/723-6077, ⊛www.poppyfestival.com.

Blessing of the Animals (Sat before Easter) A long-established ceremony, Mexican in origin, in which locals arrive on Olvera Street to have their pets blessed, then watch an accompanying parade. ☎213/625-5045.

Songkran Festival (Thai New Year) (weekend nearest 13th) The Wat Thai Temple in North Hollywood is the focus for this cultural event, with spicy food and authentic music. ☎818/997-9657.

Long Beach Grand Prix (mid-month) Some of auto-racing's best drivers and souped-up vehicles zoom around Shoreline Drive south of Downtown in the city's biggest annual event, taking place over three days and drawing thousands of spectators. ☎562/752-9524 or 1-888/82-SPEED, ⊛www.longbeachgp.com.

Antique Street Fair (mid- to late April) Dig out those treasured family heirlooms and see how much they're worth at this Whittier antique show, where nearly a hundred appraisers are available to assist you. ☎562/696-2662.

Fiesta Broadway (late April) Lively Hispanic pop singers and delicious Mexican food are the highlights of this street fair along Broadway in Downtown. ☎310/914-0015.

May

Cinco de Mayo (5th) A day-long party to commemorate the Mexican victory at the Battle of Puebla. Besides a spirited parade along Olvera Street, several blocks Downtown are blocked off for Latino music performances. There are also celebrations in most LA parks. ☎213/625-5045.

LA Modernism (mid-month) This annual show, at Santa Monica Civic Auditorium, is a fine opportunity to see a wealth of modernist art and design from the twentieth century. ☎310/455-2886, ⊛www.caskeylees.com/modernism.

NoHo Theater and Arts Festival (mid-month)

Music, food, poetry, theater and dance fill the streets of the artsy district of North Hollywood in the San Fernando Valley. ☎818/508-5155.

Venice Art Walk (mid-month) A great chance to peer into the private art studios in town, where you can see the work of big-name local artists and lesser-known talents. ☎310/664-7911.

UCLA Jazz and Reggae Festival (late May) Two days of jazz and reggae concerts, plus heaps of food, on the UCLA campus. ☎310/825-9912.

Renaissance Pleasure Faire (weekends in May & June, plus Memorial Day) Dress up in your Tudor best for this old-fashioned celebration, which includes dancing, theater, food, and the inevitable jousting. Held at distant Glen Helen Park in San Bernardino. ☎909/880-0122, ⊛recfair.com/socal.

June

Beach Bash (early June) Extreme-sports athletes descend on the South Bay town of Hermosa Beach to compete in events like skateboarding, freestyle biking and in-line skating, while everyone else plays beach volleyball. ☎310/376-0951, ⊛www .hermosawave.net.

Long Beach Chili Cook-off (early June) Rock, reggae and blues bands, and an appropriately huge chili cook-off, are just some of the high points of this annual South Bay party, formerly called "Beach Fest." ☎562/434-5408, ⊛www.longbeachchili-cookoff.com.

Valley Jewish Festival (early June) The largest event of its kind west of the Mississippi, featuring food, entertainment and stalls staffed by organizations of all stripes. Activities begin at Pierce College, in the San Fernando Valley district of Woodland Hills. ☎818/587-3205.

Irish Fair and Music Festival (2nd weekend) Sizeable Irish music, food and culture celebration held at Woodley Park in Encino, in the San Fernando Valley. ☎626/503-2511, ⊛www.irishfair.org.

Playboy Jazz Festival (mid-month) Renowned event held at the Hollywood Bowl, with master of ceremonies Bill Cosby introducing a line-up of traditional and not-so-traditional musicians. ☎213/480-3232 (tickets), ⊛www.playboy.com/arts-entertainment/jazzfest2003.

Bayou Festival (late June) Rainbow Lagoon in Long Beach comes alive with the sound of Cajun and zydeco bands, dance lessons and lots of tasty, spicy cooking. ☎562/427-3713, ⊛www.longbeachfestival.com.

Gay Pride Celebration (late June) Raucous parade along Santa Monica Blvd in West Hollywood, with hundreds of vendors, an all-male drag football cheerleading team and a heady, carnival atmosphere. ☎323/860-0701, ⊛www.lapride.org.

July

Festival of the Arts/Pageant of the Masters (early July to late Aug) Laguna Beach's signature street festival, featuring the standard displays of food, arts and dancing, but most memorable for its living tableaux, which re-create classic paintings – a unique Southern California spectacle (see box, p.219). ☎949/494-1145, ⊛www.foapom.com.

Independence Day (4th) The *Queen Mary* in Long Beach hosts a particularly large fireworks display, as well as colorful entertainment (☎562/435-3511). Other fireworks displays throughout LA, including West Hollywood's Plummer Park (☎323/848-6530).

Lotus Festival (first weekend after 4th) An Echo Park celebration featuring dragon boats, ethnic food, pan-Pacific music and, of course, the resplendent lotus blooms around the lake. ☎213/485-1310.

Old Pasadena Jazz Festival (early to mid-July) In the historic Old Pasadena zone, a nice mix of mainstream jazz and appetizing foodstuffs. ☎818/771-5544, ⊛www.omegaevents.com.

Greek Festival (mid-month) Three days of food and music at St Katherine Greek Orthodox Church in Redondo Beach, with arts and crafts displays and energetic dancing adding to the festivities.

△ Rose Parade float

☎310/540-2434,
🌐www.sbgreekfestival.com.
Central Avenue Jazz Festival (late July) Jazz and blues concerts by big names and lesser-known performers, held in front of the historic *Dunbar Hotel* in South Central. ☎213/847-3169.

August

Festival of the Chariots (early Aug) A unique LA phenomenon: three giant chariots, brightly painted and decorated with flowers, parade down Venice Boardwalk to the sound of lively music and the smell of ethnic food. Sponsored by the International Society for Krishna Consciousness. ☎310/839-1572, 🌐www.festivalofchariots.com.

International Surf Festival (early Aug) Newcomers and old-time fans alike will find this surfing tournament and festival in the South Bay an exciting three-day spectacle. Also includes volleyball, fishing and sandcastle design. ☎310/305-9546, 🌐www.surffestival.org.

Festa Italia (mid-month) An enticing display of food, music and culture in the otherwise dreary confines of Santa Monica's Civic Auditorium. ☎310/535-2416.

Long Beach Jazz Festival (mid-month) Relax and enjoy famous and local performers at the Rainbow Lagoon park in downtown Long Beach. ☎562/436-7794, 🌐www.longbeachjazzfestival.com.

Nisei Week (mid-month) Eight-day festival in Little Tokyo, with martial arts demonstrations, karaoke, Japanese brush painting, baby shows and various performances. ☎213/687-7193, 🌐www.niseiweek.org.

African Marketplace and Cultural Faire (late Aug) Hundreds of arts and crafts booths and many different entertainers make up this annual celebration at Exposition Park in South Central LA. ☎323/734-1164, 🌐www.AfricanMarketplace.org.

Sunset Junction Street Fair (late Aug) A spirited neighborhood party, and one of LA's most enjoyable fêtes, along Sunset Boulevard in Silver Lake. The live music, ethnic food and carnivalesque atmosphere draws a big crowd of locals in the know. ☎323/661-7771, 🌐www.sunsetjunction .org.

September

Festival of Philippine Arts and Culture (early Sept) Good food, music, dancing, theater and film at this annual Point Fermin event in San Pedro. ☎213/389-3050, 🌐www.fila-marts.org.

Long Beach Blues Festival (early Sept) Hear the region's and the country's top blues performers at this annual event at Cal State University. ☎562/985-1686.

Manhattan Beach Arts Festival (early Sept) Colorful arts and crafts are on display at this South Bay event, along with food and music. ☎310/545-5621 or 802-5000.

LA's birthday (5th) A civic ceremony and assorted street entertainment around El Pueblo de Los Angeles to mark the founding of the original pueblo in 1781. ☎213/625-5045.

Koreatown Multicultural Festival (mid-month) Dancing, parading and tae kwon do exhibitions are the main events at this Mid-Wilshire event ☎213/730-1495. (A similar event takes place in Pasadena around the same time. ☎626/449-2742.)

Los Angeles County Fair (last two weeks) In the San Gabriel Valley, Pomona hosts the biggest county fair in the US, with livestock shows, pie-eating contests, rodeos and fairground rides. ☎909/623-3111, 🌐www.fairplex.com.

Aloha Concert Jam (late Sept) You can string fragrant leis, race outrigger canoes, indulge in island cuisine and listen to ethnic music at this celebration of Hawaiian culture in Queen Mary park. ☎909/628-9797.

Oktoberfest (late Sept through Oct) Venture into Alpine Village, in the South Bay suburb of Torrance, to revel in Teutonic culture, from the hearty German food to music and dancing. ☎310/327-4384, 🌐www.alpinevillage.net. Also a spirited event in Huntington Beach, Orange County. ☎714/895-8020, www.oldworld.ws.

Watts Towers Day of the Drum/Jazz Festival (late Sept) Two days of community spirit and free music – African, Asian, Cuban and Brazilian – with the towers as the striking backdrop, while in the same location, the venerable Jazz Festival attracts a formidable line-up of performers. ☎213/847-4646.

October

Catalina Island Jazz Trax (first three weekends) A huge line-up of major and rising jazz stars performs in the beautiful Art Deco ballroom of the historic *Avalon Casino* (see p.175). ☎1-888/330-5252, www.jazztrax.com.

Lithuanian Fair (early Oct) Traditional music and food, and Easter egg painting, are some of the highlights of this Los Feliz fair, held at St Casimir's Church. ☎323/664-4660.

LA Street Fair and Carnival (second weekend) Free rock music, arts and crafts, and carnival rides on the streets of Sherman Oaks in the San Fernando Valley. (At the same time as the West Hollywood Street Festival, a display of handmade arts and crafts. ☎310/781-2020.)

Eagle Rock Music Festival (mid-month) This funky district, due north of Downtown LA near Glendale, hosts a freewheeling festival of food, crafts and a widely eclectic assortment of music – classical to karaoke, Cajun to cabaret. ☎323/226-1617, www.erccc.org.

Scandinavian Festival (mid-month) Folk dancing with assorted foods and art, along with vivid displays of ethnic costumes. Held at Grand Hope Park in Downtown LA. ☎213/661-4273, asfla.org.

Halloween (31st) A wild procession in West Hollywood, featuring all manner of bizarre and splashy outfits and characters (☎310/289-2525). There's also the Halloween Shipwreck on the *Queen Mary*, which spends one day as a "haunted" ocean liner filled with ghouls and demons. ☎562/435-3511.

November

Dia de Los Muertos (2nd) The "Day of the Dead," celebrated authentically throughout East LA and more blandly for tourists on Olvera Street and elsewhere. Mexican traditions, such as picnicking on the family burial spot and making skeleton puppets, are faithfully upheld. ☎213/625-5045.

Intertribal Marketplace (early Nov) Jewelry, baskets, pottery, beads and more presented by Native American artists at Highland Park's Southwest Museum. ☎323/933-4510, www.southwestmuseum.org.

LA Mariachi Festival (mid- to late Nov) Munch on Mexican food or take a mariachi workshop, all to the sounds of nonstop mariachi bands in Boyle Heights. ☎213/485-2437.

Doo-dah Parade (Sat after Thanksgiving) Absurdly costumed characters marching through Pasadena are the main attraction at this immensely popular LA event, which began as a spoof of the Tournament of Roses parade. ☎626/440-7379, www.pasadenadoodahparade.com.

Griffith Park Light Festival (late Nov) Hugely popular spectacle stretching a mile along Crystal Springs Road, complete with drive-through tunnels of light, thematic displays and representations of familiar LA sights like the Hollywood sign. ☎213/485-8743.

December

Hollywood Christmas Parade (1st) The biggest of LA's many Yuletide events, with a procession of mind-bogglingly elaborate floats, marching bands, and famous and semi-famous names from film and TV. ☎323/469-2337, www.hollywoodchristmas.com.

Belmont Shore Christmas Parade (early Dec)
Home-made floats and marching bands
kick off the holiday season in the area at
this East Long Beach event. ☎562/434-
3066.

Christmas Boat Parade (mid-month) Marina
del Rey is the site for this annual, ocean-
going procession of brightly lit watercraft,
supposedly the largest of its kind on the
West Coast. ☎310/821-7614. A similar
event takes place along Shoreline Village in
Long Beach. ☎562/435-4093.

Las Posadas (mid- to late Dec) An Olvera St
event that re-enacts the biblical tale of Mary
and Joseph looking for a spot to rest on
Christmas Eve, culminating with a piñata-
breaking. ☎213/625-5045.

LA County Holiday Celebration (Christmas
Eve) Thousands of people pack the Dorothy
Chandler Pavilion in Downtown LA to catch
this juggernaut of multicultural entertainment, including everything from Japanese
dance to Jamaican reggae. ☎213/974-
1396.

19

Kids' LA

A lthough most of LA's attractions are geared for adults, the city does hold some appeal for **kids**, from popular **museums** and numerous **aquariums** to the natural attractions of the region's excellent **parks and beaches**. If these don't hold the kids' interest, there are always a number of **shops** in town where you can pick up something bright and shining that will. And many, if not most, kids will doubtless want to experience the thrills of major theme parks like **Disneyland** (p.210), **Knott's Berry Farm** (p.213) and **Magic Mountain** (p.196), but it only takes a couple of days – or even hours – of being jostled by massive crowds, waiting in interminable lines and eating lackluster theme-park food for kids to grow tired of the experience. As such, it always helps to have contingency plans available, which may involve some of the selections below.

Museums

Perhaps the most obvious choice for children is the city's many **museums**, some of which feature kid-friendly exhibits and hands-on, interactive displays with lots of flashing lights and bright colors. Although the Children's Museum of Los Angeles is moving to locations in Mid-Wilshire and the San Fernando Valley (set to open in 2004), youngsters can have a similar experience at several worthwhile museums. **Exposition Park** (p.149), south of Downtown, has two such places where you can let the kids loose for a while: the **California Science Center** (p.149) and the neighboring **Air and Space Gallery** (p.150). Starry-eyed youngsters will also be enchanted by the aeronautical displays further afield at the **Jet Propulsion Laboratory** (p.186) near Pasadena, and the **Air Force Flight Test Center Museum** (p.197), in the northern desert near Edwards Air Force Base.

All age groups should find the **Natural History Museum of Los Angeles County** (p.150) to be a worthwhile experience; like the **George C. Page Museum** in Mid-Wilshire (p.81), it's a fine place to view the colossal dinosaur bones of extinct creatures. The Page Museum itself features mammoths, sloths, wolves and saber-toothed cats dredged up from the adjacent La Brea Tar Pits.

For Western-tinged fun, the **Will Rogers State Historic Park** (p.199) has a great ranch house loaded with lariats, cowboy gear and even the mounted head of a Texas Longhorn. Kids with a taste for roping and riding may also warm to the **William S. Hart Ranch and Museum** (p.196), for its wide range of Western duds, cowboy equipment and Tinseltown memorabilia, as well as the more meatier exhibits at the **Gene Autry Western Heritage Museum** (p.93).

If all else fails, there are also a good number of offbeat museums in LA that may intrigue children. The least odd of these is **Angels Attic** (p.136), devoted to dolls and dollhouses of the Victorian and other eras. More unusual are the **Fantasy Foundation** (p.91), one of LA's best bets for inquisitive kids with a penchant for old monster movies and sci-fi paraphernalia; and the **Museum of Neon Art** (p.68), crammed with flashy road signs of yesteryear. Older kids with a taste for the surreal may enjoy the **Museum of Jurassic Technology** (p.128), an institutional haunted house of sorts filled with all manner of bizarre displays, including obscure bugs.

Aquatic attractions

The region's biggest and most comprehensive collection of marine life is kept at the **Aquarium of the Pacific** (p.170) in Long Beach, where there are plenty of sharks, tide-pool creatures, jellyfish and many other specimens to tantalize kids. Less crowded is the smaller **Cabrillo Marine Aquarium** (p.168) in San Pedro, which is also the site of two rehabilitation centers – the **Marine Mammal Center** (p.168) and the **Friends of the Sea Lion** (p.218) – where kids can watch injured animals being nursed back to life.

Just a few miles north, along the beautiful and rugged coastline of Palos Verdes, the **Point Vicente Interpretive Center** has simple exhibits on local marine life (closed until 2004; p.163), but is best for its whale-watching potential during the winter months. These massive creatures can also be spotted from other promontories along the Santa Monica Bay, but if you wish to take a **whale-watching cruise**, there are plenty of tour-boat operators to assist you on Santa Catalina Island and in Long Beach (p.170).

Further north from Point Vicente, Manhattan Beach's **Roundhouse and Aquarium** (p.161) offers an inexpensive look at the region's ocean flora and fauna, but for a much more in-depth view, the **UCLA Ocean Discovery Center** (p.132) is another good choice, second only to the Aquarium of the Pacific. Here, at the base of the Santa Monica Pier, kids can get good views of a multitude of sea creatures and receive a good dose of marine-biology education while they're at it.

Finally, if you're on your way south toward San Diego, bring the kids to the **Ocean Institute** (p.219) in Dana Point, where the highlight isn't any sea creature, but a full-sized replica of a tall ship anchored just offshore.

Parks

The most prominent of LA's natural attractions is **Griffith Park** (p.91), just north of Hollywood. Here you can find an excellent network of hiking, biking and horse-riding trails, amid the rustic charm of a large, mountainous greenspace, not to mention prime views of the LA basin and even a glimpse of the Hollywood sign. The park has numerous attractions to pique children's interest, including a pleasant **bird sanctuary** and a peaceful **Fern Dell**, as well as the imposing profile of the **Griffith Observatory**, which is closed for renovation until 2005.

The observatory, and its attendant displays, will probably appeal to older children more than the **LA Zoo** (p.92) on the other side of the park, where a standard array of animals is shown before the public in mostly outdated displays and cramped environments. Younger kids may enjoy the zoo's central pens for reptiles and koalas, though everyone else may be tempted to make for the exits. Much more revealing is the **Wildlife Waystation** (p.196) in the northern San Fernando Valley, a rehabilitation center for abused animals where the public can get a close-up look at familiar and exotic species. Back in Griffith Park around the zoo, **Travel Town** (p.95) is geared to smaller tots, who will appreciate walking around the disused old trains sitting near the LA River.

If you're not planning a stop at Griffith Park but still want a rustic experience for the kids, the **Santa Monica Mountains** are a good place to visit for its many hiking trails and buzzing wildlife. One sight in the mountains, **San Vicente Mountain Park** (p.206), a decommissioned missile base, is a fascinating excursion for older kids, who can get great views of LA by clambering atop a tower that used to cover a launch center.

Paramount Ranch (p.207) is equally interesting for kids and adults as the site of numerous Hollywood Westerns, just as the nearby **Peter Strauss Ranch** (p.207) is an idyllic natural landscape that was once the site of a colorful resort. Not far away, **Malibu Creek State Park** (p.207) is a good choice for a half-day family outing into some of LA's more rugged, unspoiled terrain, while **Tropical Terrace** (p.205) is a ruin of a modern estate that kids can easily explore.

Both parents and kids may enjoy spending time in the city's **ecological reserves**, which offer fine opportunities for hiking, bird-watching and sometimes horseback riding and bicycling. Although LA's own Ballona Wetlands are not readily explored, much of Santa Catalina Island (p.173) makes for a rewarding experience, whether hiking, camping or taking a bus tour around the island's rugged, unspoiled interior. Orange County, too, has several worthwhile options, including **Crystal Cove State Park** (p.218) along the coast, and the **Bolsa Chica** (p.217) and **Upper Newport Bay** (p.218) ecological reserves, both worthwhile if the children have any interest in seeing nature in its sublime, undeveloped state.

Beaches and water parks

Finally, LA has, of course, a number of popular **beaches**, most of which will be fine for a supervised day of splashing around. The best, and least polluted, can be found around **Malibu** (p.202) and along the **Orange County Coast** (p.216). One beach area that's no good for swimming, but has a better slice of social activity for children (at least during the daytime), is the **Santa Monica Pier** (p.130), a fine place for cotton candy, video games and carnival rides.

For fresh-water amusement, the region has a quartet of **water parks** that are sure to delight kids with a yen for hydrotubes and splash pools. These include the excellent, and sometimes expensive, rides at Magic Mountain's **Hurricane Harbor** (p.197), Knott's Berry Farm's **Soak City U.S.A.** (p.213), **Raging Waters** in the eastern San Gabriel Valley (p.188), and **Wild Rivers** in the Orange County city of Irvine, at 8770 Irvine Center Drive (June–Aug: hours vary, generally daily 10am–8pm; May & Sept: Sat & Sun 10am–5pm; $25, kids $18; ☏949/788-0808, ⊛www.wildrivers.com), loaded with forty water tubes, pools and flumes, and a short distance from the 405 freeway.

Bright, motivated children with a taste for **culture** will not be disappointed by LA. Though the **Getty Center** (p.122) and **Los Angeles County Museum of Art** (p.81) are not specifically geared toward children, they both offer headphones and "listening tours" for kids on occasion, and also sell children's guidebooks to fine art in their bookstores. The Getty's **Central Garden** has attractive foliage and concentric paths for kids to walk off some of their excess energy.

One museum in the region, the **Bowers Museum of Cultural Art**, features a separate institution – the **Kidseum** (p.214) – geared for the little ones, with simplified displays on native and world cultures. Better, perhaps, is the **Muckenthaler Cultural Center** (p.214) in nearby Fullerton, a whole mansion loaded with international cultural treasures.

Children may find **functional art** to be of particular interest in several of the city's galleries. Bizarre clocks, chairs and televisions are but a few of the novelties to look at, and perhaps even touch and tinker with, at places like the **Gallery of Functional Art** (p.136) in Santa Monica's Bergamot Station, or **Artscape**, 2226 E Fourth St, Long Beach (℡562/434-3224, www.Artscape-Gallery.com), with decorative and wearable art.

For art out in the open, away from confining museums and galleries, the **Franklin Murphy Sculpture Garden** is without peer (p.121). Not even the LA County Museum's **Cantor Sculpture Garden** (with its many Rodins; p.82) can beat UCLA's treasure trove of twentieth-century abstract sculpture for its visual appeal, all set amid bright sunshine and grassy lawns.

Finally, for a bit of musical edification, the **LA Philharmonic** (p.295) offers seasonal "youth symphonies" either at the Music Center or the Hollywood Bowl, playing child-oriented staples like Prokofiev's *Peter and the Wolf*, Saint-Saëns' *Carnival of the Animals* and accessible works from Bach, Mozart and Vivaldi. Call ℡213/850-2000 for information on this year's offerings.

While you're in the neighborhood, a trip to the Music Center can be combined with a visit to the **Bob Baker Marionette Theater**, 1345 W First St (shows Tues–Fri 10.30am, Sat & Sun 2.30pm; $10, toddlers free; by reservation only at ℡323/250-9995, www.bobbakermarionettes.com), one of LA's best puppet shows for forty years running, performed by a classic puppeteer. The only downside is the theater's dicey location on the west side of the 110 freeway – don't linger in the area after dark. An alternative puppet experience in a more hospitable location is the tiny **Santa Monica Puppet and Magic Center**, 1255 Second St, which has displays of historic puppets and a performance space for the long-running spectacle of *Puppetolio!* (shows Wed 1pm, Sat & Sun 1pm & 3pm; $6.50; ℡310/656-0483, www.puppetmagic.com), a one-man production featuring whimsical characters.

Shops

FAO Schwarz in the Glendale Galleria mall, Central Ave at Colorado St, Glendale ℡818/547-5900. The place to go if you're looking for the latest, flashiest and most expensive toys, from Barbie collector sets to huge stuffed animals to assorted high-tech gizmos. Also in the Orange County town of Costa Mesa at 3333 Bristol St, #1824 ℡714/751-6000.

Gregory's Toys and Adventures 16101 Ventura Blvd #135, Encino ℡818/906-2212. This San Fernando Valley retailer stocks a fine selection of action figures, puzzles, electric trains, old-fashioned blocks and more – all at competitive prices, typically lower than the big names.

Hollywood Toys and Costumes 6600 Hollywood Blvd, Hollywood ℡323/464-4444 or 1-888/760-3330. A one-of-a-kind LA business, with not only an array of dolls and action figurines, but also dress-up treats – wigs, Halloween outfits, costume jewelry and all kinds of colorful trinkets.

Imperial Toy 2060 E Seventh St #CB, Downtown ☎213/489-2100. Despite its location on a decrepit strip by the LA River, this toy dealer offers some of the best prices in town on frisbees, dolls, action figures and especially marbles. One of several well-priced wholesalers in the vicinity.

Robotoys 12025 Ventura Blvd, Studio City ☎818/769-5563. You guessed it: nothing but robots to suit every taste, ranging from cheesy tin toys to slick Transformers-types, and even kit-sets that allow you to build your own mechanical man.

San Marino Toy and Book Shoppe 2424 Huntington Drive, San Marino ☎626/309-0222 or 1-888/895-0111. Excellent, but pricey, selection of puppets, dollhouses and building blocks, along with more unusual items such as woolly-mammoth skeleton puzzles and children's "mood lamps."

Would You Believe? 1118 Fair Oaks Ave, South Pasadena ☎626/799-3828. A terrific spot for magic supplies, novelty gifts, balloons and juggling equipment, as well as toys. Kids and adults can also rent costumes and go around town dressed as a moose, monk or Darth Vader.

Wound & Wound Toy Company 7374 Melrose Ave ☎1-800/937-0561. Something of a shop-ping institution, packed with all kinds of wind-up toys, from goofy aliens and tin trucks to burgers with feet. The display cases full of rare collectibles – Star Wars dolls prominently among them – are worth a look.

KIDS' LA | Shops

Shopping

S hopping in LA is an art, and the city is packed with practicing virtuosos. The level of disposable income in the wealthy parts of the city is
astronomical, and touring the more outrageous stores can offer some
insight into LA life – revealing who's got the money and what they're
capable of blowing it on. Whether you want to shop for a new dress or a pair
of socks, lay waste to a wad, or simply be a voyeur in the orgy of acquisition,
there are, besides the run-of-the-mill chain retailers, big **department stores**
and mega-sized **malls** where most of the serious shopping goes on. Not to be
missed are LA's countless **clothing** stores, which sell everything from ritzy
designer apparel to moth-eaten thriftwear, and its **hair** and **make-up salons**,
which give the fanciest dos and looks to the city's fashion elite, and anyone else
who can afford them.

LA also has a good assortment of **book** and **record stores**, and whether
you're in search of a cozy secondhand shop or a megastore with all the new
releases, plus a café to boot, you won't have a hard time finding it, especially in
the trendiest shopping zones. There's an equally diverse array of **food stores**,
from corner delis and supermarkets to exquisite cake stores and gourmet markets. You'll also find several **specialty stores** selling perfectly weird LA souvenirs, from colorful wind-up toys to macabre beach towels.

If you have bags of money to spend, LA provides plenty of cultural shopping
as well, in the form of trendy **galleries**, where you can spot the latest works
from the city's hottest artists offered at jaw-dropping prices.

Shopping categories

Shopping districts

While you can find souvenirs and touristy merchandise in most consumer zones, there are a few stellar **shopping districts** worth noting. In Downtown, the main shopping area is the **Garment District**, where you can pick up a variety of fabrics and clothes, including designer knockoffs and markdowns, for some of the lowest prices anywhere on the West Coast. Mid-Wilshire has no less than four major shopping areas: **La Brea Avenue**, just north of Wilshire, a stretch of clothing, furniture and antique stores along a busy thoroughfare; **Third Street**, a short strip of boutiques and restaurants east of the Beverly Center mall; **Larchmont Village**, a mix of small retailers and chain stores on the edge of Hancock Park; and the irrepressible **Melrose Avenue**, between Mid-Wilshire and Hollywood, LA's most conspicuously hip area, where quirky shops mingle with high-priced boutiques.

To the north, **Hollywood Boulevard** is one big shopping zone, especially for movie memorabilia and discount T-shirts, with merchandisers concentrated between La Brea Avenue and Gower Street, and the giant Hollywood & Highland mall anchoring the whole scene. More appealing, perhaps, is the **north Vermont Avenue** strip in Los Feliz, which attracts the city's alternative-minded buyers with its subversive bookstores, idiosyncratic boutiques and good restaurants. By contrast, West Hollywood is more self-consciously chic, and you can expect to find small boutiques along **Santa Monica Boulevard**, and numerous music and book stores (and more than a few sex shops) along the **Sunset Strip**. Beverly Hills is, of course, the pinnacle of upscale shopping, especially in the downtown core known as the **Golden Triangle**, highlighted by the stratospheric retailers of **Rodeo Drive**. West LA has fewer attractions for tourists, except perhaps for Brentwood's **San Vicente Boulevard**, another ritzy zone, and **Westwood Village**, a student haven full of inexpensive bookstores, clothing outlets and used record stores. Out in Santa Monica, the **Third Street Promenade** is one of LA's most trafficked strips, with a mix of small retailers and, increasingly, mega-chain stores; linked from the Promenade by a free bus (in summer), Santa Monica's **Main Street** is popular for its book dealers, clothing stores and trinket shops. The same types of retailers are also visible further south, around Venice's **Windward Arcade**, though of a funkier and more downmarket character.

In the outlying areas, there are countless malls, mini-malls and chain-store outlets, but only fewer truly interesting places to shop or browse. **Downtown Long Beach**, especially around Pine Avenue, is appealing for its used-book stores and scattered clothing shops; **Old Pasadena** – notably Colorado Boulevard – offers music stores, apparel merchandisers and used-book sellers; **Ventura Boulevard**, running through Studio City in the San Fernando Valley, is a good place to buy new and used music, assorted souvenirs, colorful trinkets and cheap clothing; the so-called **NoHo Arts District** in North Hollywood in the Valley has a clutch of eclectic boutiques and arty souvenir stores; and along Newport Beach's **Balboa Peninsula**, along the Orange County Coast, you can pick up expensive designer duds and similarly pricey outfits at numerous boutiques. Oddly enough, the high-profile city of Malibu has relatively few unique shopping attractions that are open to the general public.

Department stores and shopping malls

You won't have to travel far to find LA's flagship **department stores**. Bloomingdale's, Macy's, Neiman-Marcus, Nordstrom, Robinsons-May and

Saks Fifth Avenue are all located in malls throughout the region. For mall addresses, refer to "Shopping malls" below.

Department stores

Barneys 9570 Wilshire Blvd, Beverly Hills ☎310/276-4400. At the base of the Golden Triangle, this high-end retailer offers five levels of dapper shoes and clothing – and food, on the fifth floor; if you don't have the right look, expect the sales clerks to ignore you.

Bloomingdale's 10250 Santa Monica Blvd, in the Century City Marketplace, Century City ☎310/772-2100. This major chain features all the standard men's and women's apparel, kitchen items, and assorted jewelry and kidswear. Also in the Beverly Center, Sherman Oaks Fashion Square and Newport Beach Fashion Island.

Macy's 8500 Beverly Blvd, in the Beverly Center mall ☎310/854-6655. A familiar figure in the LA department store scene, offering a broad selection of clothing and personal effects. Also at the Century City Marketplace ☎310/556-1611; 750 W Seventh St, Downtown ☎213/628-9311; 10861 Weyburn Ave, Westwood ☎310/208-4211; the Santa Monica Place mall ☎310/628-9311; Sherman Oaks Fashion Square ☎818/783-0550; Paseo Colorado mall ☎626/796-0411; 401 S Lake Ave, Pasadena ☎626/792-0211; Del Amo Fashion Center ☎310/542-8525; Glendale Galleria ☎818/240-8411; Burbank Media Center, 201 E Magnolia Blvd, Burbank ☎818/566-8617; and Newport Beach Fashion Island ☎714/640-8333.

Neiman-Marcus 9700 Wilshire Blvd, Beverly Hills ☎310/550-5900. With three fancy restaurants, opulent displays of jewelry and a plethora of fur coats, this store is quintessential Beverly Hills, located at the base of the Golden Triangle. Also in Orange County at Newport Beach Fashion Island ☎949/759-1900.

Nordstrom 10830 Pico Blvd, in the Westside Pavilion mall, West LA ☎310/470-6155. Mostly clothing and accessories at this Westside department store. If you can't decide on the right party dress or power tie, a "personal shopper" can help you – for a steep price. Also at Glendale Galleria ☎818/502-9922; 6602 Topanga Canyon Blvd, Canoga Park ☎818/884-7900; and South Coast Plaza ☎714/549-8300. A much cheaper option is the Nordstrom Rack at 901 S

Coast Drive, Costa Mesa ☎714/751-5901; and 227 N Glendale Ave, Glendale ☎818/240-2404.

Robinsons-May 103 Santa Monica Place, in the Santa Monica Place mall ☎310/451-2411. Offers better prices than some of its competitors, along with a wide selection of clothing and housewares. Also at 725 S Figueroa St, Downtown ☎213/683-1144; 10730 W Pico Blvd, West LA ☎310/475-4911; 6050 Sepulveda Blvd, Culver City ☎310/390-8811; Glendale Galleria ☎818/247-2600; Del Amo Fashion Center ☎310/542-5941; South Coast Plaza ☎714/546-9321; Newport Beach Fashion Island ☎949/644-2800.

Saks Fifth Avenue 9600 Wilshire Blvd, Beverly Hills ☎310/275-4211. A high-end chain with expensive perfume, eye-popping jewelry and high fashion – everything you need for a day strolling around Rodeo Drive and looking like you belong there. Also at South Coast Plaza ☎714/540-3233; 35 N De Lacey Ave, Pasadena ☎626/396-7100; and in the South Bay at 550 Silver Spur Rd, Rancho Palos Verdes ☎310/265-2600.

Shopping malls

Beverly Center 8500 Beverly Blvd, between Mid-Wilshire and West Hollywood ☎310/854-0070. Chic shopping for the masses: seven acres of boutiques, Macy's and Bloomingdale's department stores, a multiplex cinema and a ground-level *Hard Rock Café*.

Century City Marketplace 10250 Santa Monica Blvd, Century City ☎310/553-5300. An outdoor mall with one hundred upscale shops and a good food court. The place to see stars do their shopping or catch a first-run movie at the excellent AMC Century 14 Theater (see p.302).

Del Amo Fashion Center Hawthorne Blvd at Carson St, Torrance ☎310/542-8525. A huge mall in the South Bay, with a Macy's, Robinsons-May and Sears, plus a convenient location just south of the 405 freeway.

Fashion Island 401 Newport Center Drive, Newport Beach ☎949/721-2000. A reasonable alternative to Orange County's South Coast Plaza, though not as large, with an appealing outdoor setting. The mall, anchored by Bloomingdale's, Macy's,

Robinsons-May and Neiman Marcus, is close to the Orange County Museum of Art.

Glendale Galleria Central Ave at Colorado St, Glendale ☎818/240-9481. A sprawling down-town complex with five major stores, including Robinsons-May, Nordstrom and Macy's, and a broad selection of clothiers.

The Grove 6301 W Third St, Mid-Wilshire ☎323/571-8830. Stylish, open-air complex in the vicinity of the Farmers Market, with all the usual chain retailers and restaurants, and movie theaters.

Hollywood & Highland at the same intersection in Hollywood ☎323/960-2331. A mega-mall modeled after an elaborate silent-film set, but offering the usual corporate boutiques and trendy shops, and a multiplex connected to the Chinese Theatre.

Media City Center 201 E Magnolia Blvd at N San Fernando Rd, Burbank ☎818/566-8617. Branches of Sears, Mervyn's and the low-cost furniture retailer IKEA occupy this complex of buildings just outside the heart of old Burbank, right beside the I-5 freeway.

Paseo Colorado E Colorado Blvd at S Los Robles Ave, Pasadena ☎626/795-8891. Two levels of (mostly chain) stores beneath several levels of housing, with street-front entrances and an open-air design that invites strolling.

Santa Monica Place Broadway at Second Street, Santa Monica ☎310/394-5451. Sunny, skylit mall with three tiers of major chain stores and outdated pastel decor.

Sherman Oaks Fashion Square 14006 Riverside Drive, San Fernando Valley ☎818/783-0550. The famed Galleria – the original

Sherman Oaks home to the notorious "Valley girls" – no longer exists, so this nearby mall now suffices for Valley denizens. Macy's and Bloomingdale's are the anchors, with around 120 other chain stores vying for your attention.

Sherman Oaks Galleria 15301 Ventura Blvd, Sherman Oaks ☎818/990-4060. Sleek mall with a handful of restaurants and shops, plus a multiplex – mildly worthwhile if you're in the neighborhood.

South Coast Plaza 3333 Bristol St, north of 405 freeway, Costa Mesa ☎714/435-2000. Orange County's main super-mall, where you'll get a good workout navigating around the nearly three hundred shops and huge crowds of locals and tourists. Includes seven anchor stores – among them Robinsons-May, Saks Fifth Avenue and Nordstrom – as well as a good mix of low- and high-end retailers.

Third Street Promenade Third St between Broadway and Wilshire Blvd, Santa Monica. A rare successful attempt to lure back consumers to the heart of the city, packed on weekend evenings with mobs scurrying about the bookstores, fashion outlets, restaurants and cinemas amid throngs of itinerant musicians, homeless people and street lunatics. Chain retailers have replaced the smaller shops in recent years, and dominate the area north of Arizona Avenue.

Westside Pavilion Pico and Westwood blvds, West LA ☎310/474-6255. The obligatory chain stores at this postmodern shopping complex centered on the Nordstrom department store.

Clothes and fashion

LA's **clothing** stores are some of its most important cultural phenomena – where you're given the chance to pick out a new personality to go with a freshly bought Hermes bag, velvet cape or gold lamé dog collar. Apart from the slew of chain clothing stores across the city, you'll find hordes of haughty designer boutiques along Rodeo Drive, on the western side of West Hollywood and increasingly along Melrose Avenue. Much more relaxed are the funky clothing stores for which LA is famous, many of them located along La Brea and north Vermont avenues and Santa Monica and Sunset boulevards. If you're just looking for cheap duds, however, LA has a good selection of secondhand clothiers and vintage clothing dealers to choose from.

Upscale chain stores

Bernini Sport 131 S La Cienega Blvd, in the Beverly Center mall ☎310/659-0228. Any

money you haven't spent elsewhere in the mall will quickly evaporate at this pricey Italian shop, which offers chic men's and women's clothing, notably fancy suits and tuxedos, plus colognes and perfumes. Also at 362 N Rodeo Drive, Beverly Hills ☎310/278-6287; 10401 Venice Blvd, West LA ☎310/815-1786; and in the Century City Marketplace ☎310/553-5300.

Chanel 400 N Rodeo Drive, Beverly Hills ☎**310/278-5500.** As you'd expect, a pricey selection of clothes and perfumes from Paris. You'll get a healthy dose of attitude, too, if you've only come to browse. For Chanel clothes on consignment, try visiting 11306 Ventura Blvd, Studio City in the San Fernando Valley ☎818/980-9990.

Ermenegildo Zegna 301 N Rodeo Drive, Beverly Hills ☎**310/247-8827.** Exclusive lines of menswear and the high-end men's ZegnaSport collection make this a popular spot for brash young celebrities and even old-money types. Also at South Coast Plaza ☎714/444-1534.

Façonnable 9680 Wilshire Blvd, Beverly Hills ☎**310/247-8277.** An upper-income clothing merchant at the base of the Golden Triangle, selling sleek casual and dress wear, and an assortment of colognes and fragrances; a shade less pretentious than some of its bigger-name neighbors. Also at South Coast Plaza ☎714/966-1140.

Giorgio Armani 436 N Rodeo Drive, Beverly Hills ☎**310/271-5555.** One of LA's most elite fashion dealers, featuring sleek, well-cut suits that are standard issue to movie agents, lawyers and other self-anointed big shots. For cheaper, though still very expensive, clothing, try Emporio Armani just down the road at 9533 Brighton Way ☎310/271-7790, while affordable sportswear and women's clothes can be found at Armani Exchange, at 8700 Sunset Blvd, West Hollywood ☎310/659-0171; and 29 W Colorado Blvd, Pasadena ☎626/795-7527.

Gucci 347 N Rodeo Drive, Beverly Hills ☎**310/278-3451.** Aside from the outlandishly priced shoes, wallets and accessories that you can find here, there's also a fair assortment of men's and women's clothing.

Hugo Boss 414 N Rodeo Drive, Beverly Hills ☎**310/859-2888.** The place to go if you're looking for a thousand-dollar suit. Also at 8625 Sunset Blvd, West Hollywood ☎310/360-6935; in the Beverly Center mall ☎310/659-6676; and in the Century City Marketplace ☎310/553-5300.

Kenneth Cole Broadway at Second St, in the Santa Monica Place mall ☎**310/458-6633.** Leather jackets, tapered boots, sleek ear-

rings and hip-hugging pants – all in black – to help you get into the chic nightclubs in town. Also a branch in the Century City Marketplace ☎310/553-5300.

Louis Vuitton 295 N Rodeo Drive, Beverly Hills ☎**310/859-0457.** Designer wallets and luggage, with plenty of expensive styles from which to choose. Also at the Beverly Center mall ☎310/360-1506; and in Macy's at the San Fernando Valley's Sherman Oaks Fashion Square ☎818/986-7908. For buying Vuitton on consignment, visit 11306 Ventura Blvd, Studio City ☎818/980-9990.

Prada 343 N Rodeo Drive, Beverly Hills ☎**310/385-5959.** The best place to gape at the stars: an incomparable clothier whose clients don't bat an eyelash at paying thousands for a shirt. Somewhat less stuffy is the branch at South Coast Plaza ☎714/979-3003, and there's a wholesale version in Downtown, 1125 Maple Ave ☎213/749-9696.

Ralph Lauren 444 N Rodeo Drive, Beverly Hills ☎**310/281-7200.** An incomparable place to get yourself outfitted as a member of the English gentry. Pick up a gilded walking cane, finely tailored suit and a smart tweed cap, all for a small fortune.

Designer boutiques

Betsey Johnson 8050 Melrose Ave ☎**323/852-1534.** An upscale boutique where stiletto heels, micro-miniskirts and fashionably dingy attire are all part of a funky look, for which you'll pay plenty. Other branches in the Sherman Oaks Fashion Square, 14006 Riverside Drive ☎818/783-0550; Beverly Center Mall, 8500 Beverly Blvd ☎310/854-0070; plus a wholesaler at 127 E 9th St, Downtown LA ☎213/489-2326.

Diavolina 334 S La Brea Ave, Mid-Wilshire ☎**323/936-3000.** Shoes you can really strike a pose with: killer stilettos, modest mules and funky boots, priced anywhere from around $100 to well over $500.

Fred Segal 8118 Melrose Ave ☎**323/655-3734.** For those poseurs and party-hoppers who wouldn't be spotted dead in Beverly Hills, this Melrose complex of four Segal outlets – selling everything from stylish shoes and duds to hair products and makeup – provides just the right mix of designer gloss and funky edge. Also located in Santa Monica at 500 Broadway ☎310/458-3557, with many other citywide branches.

Frederick's of Hollywood 6606 Hollywood Blvd, Hollywood ☎323/637-7770. The pink-and-purple tower of Frederick's houses a panoply of frilly, lacy and leathery lingerie (prices vary), as well as a Hall of Fame devoted to famous celebrity undergarments (see p.98). Eight other branches in LA, though none with the style and pizzazz of this one.

Giselle 1306 Montana Ave, Santa Monica ☎310/451-2140. Well-made designer women's clothing in a variety of styles, but with a strong emphasis on wispy, pre-Raphaelite designs aimed for size-2 waifs. Tourists don't often make a beeline to see the fashions in this chic Montana Ave store, which is why crowd-shy starlets often do. Also at 3835 Cross Creek Rd, Malibu ☎310/456-0142.

Jimmy Choo 469 N Canon Drive, Beverly Hills ☎310/860-9453. Even if you're just looking, and can't afford the exorbitant prices, there are enough glam stilettos, silky slingbacks and stylish leather boots to give you warm memories on your trip home.

Kbond 7257 Beverly Blvd, Mid-Wilshire ☎323/939-8866. On the cutting edge of contemporary trendiness on the Westside, a cheeky high-end clothing merchant selling rotating labels (depending on the month) amid artworks of varying quality and coffee-table books on upscale art and design.

Maxfield 8825 Melrose Ave, West Hollywood ☎310/274-8800. One of LA's most exclusive (and haughty) boutiques, selling big-name and lesser-known labels and displaying pricey classic and modern antiques, expensive baubles and an eye-popping array of jewelry.

Paper Bag Princess 8700 Santa Monica Blvd, West Hollywood ☎310/358-1985. A cross between an elite boutique and a second-hand store: an upscale dealer in gently worn vintage designer fashions – from Chanel to Versace. Some items on the racks are on consignment from actual celebrities (who allegedly frequent the place).

Scala 153 S La Brea Ave, Mid-Wilshire ☎323/954-8204. Quirky but smart women's attire that's actually made by the owner herself. This trendy little boutique has lower prices than comparable stores to the west, though it's still far from cheap.

Don't Panic! 802 N San Vicente Blvd, West Hollywood ☎310/652-9689. The racy counterpart to the many bland T-shirt shops in LA, stocking more than a hundred styles bearing shocking, crude or off-color slogans. Also at 1738 Cordova St, just off the I-10 freeway in Mid-Wilshire ☎323/373-1965.

Dream Dresser 8444 Santa Monica Blvd, West Hollywood ☎323/848-3480. Something of a fetish-wear institution, with a selection of corsets, dresses and lingerie made from rubber, leather and vinyl, plus matching whips and harnesses for the S&M set. Custom-designed outfits can be tailored for women or men.

Ipso Facto 517 N Harbor Blvd, Fullerton ☎714/525-7865. Piercing supplies, goth clothing and a full range of skull-emblazoned belts, rings and boots at this retailer in, of all places, Orange County.

Necromance 7220 Melrose Ave ☎323/934-8684. A skeleton in the window invites you in to try on the latest ghoulish clothing at this morbidly themed shop, which sells outfits suitable for black-clad goth kids.

Plastica 8405 W Third St, Mid-Wilshire ☎323/655-1051. A one-of-a-kind LA shrine to all things plastic: shoes, boots, shirts, tank-tops, spectacles and accessories, along with jewelry, furniture, handbags, pillows and countless other cheap knick-knacks.

Retail Slut 7308 Melrose Ave, Mid-Wilshire ☎323/934-1339. An essential Melrose stop for decades, where you can pick up all the vinyl dresses, skull necklaces, leather dog collars, bondage gear and spiked wristbands you'll ever need.

Trashy Lingerie 402 N La Cienega Blvd, West Hollywood ☎310/659-4550. Not only can you find the sort of undergarments suggested by this store's name, you can also browse through a wide selection of more traditional satin and silk bras, teddies and bustiers. All of the revealing items are handmade, and you'll have to pay $2 for an annual "membership fee" to get in.

Uncle Jer's 4459 Sunset Blvd, Silver Lake ☎323/662-6710. Quirky shop crammed with colorful and inexpensive clothing from developing countries, much of it handmade, along with soaps and fragrances, incense and "magic potions," and assorted trinkets.

20

SHOPPING | Clothes and fashion

Vampire Technology 401 W Washington Blvd, Downtown ☎213-745-5521. Just south of the Convention Center, this shrine to all things dark and spooky carries assorted black goth-wear, skirts made of recycled tire-rubber, strap-on leather dresses and corsets, studded bikinis and spiky dog collars. Each item is a handcrafted, one-of-a-kind item and is priced accordingly.

Secondhand and vintage clothing

Aardvark's Odd Ark 21434 Sherman Way, Canoga Park ☎818/999-3211. One of LA's best spots for buying used garments, whether wild psychedelic shirts, old leisure suits, goofy ball caps and frumpy pants, or more recent – and more fashionable – shirts, skirts, dresses and suits. Also at 7579 Melrose Ave ☎323/655-6769.

American Rag 150 S La Brea Ave, Mid-Wilshire ☎323/935-3154. Not your typical second-hand clothing store; the beaten-up denim jackets, floral-print dresses and retro shoes for sale here are often high-end designer material, sometimes restyled into brand-new forms. Another branch at 5724 W Third St, Mid-Wilshire ☎323/965-8339.

Cheap Vintage 705 S Pacific Ave, San Pedro ☎310/547-1000. Worth a trip down to the harbor area for its bargain-basement coats, dresses, shoes and skirts ($3–$15). The secondhand garments vary in quality, but some are in surprisingly good condition.

Decades Two 8214 Melrose Ave, West Hollywood ☎323/655-0223. A reseller of elegant designer wear, but concentrating on mod retro-clothes from the 1960s, with occasional detours into stylish 1950s apparel and ungainly 1970s jumpsuits.

Golyester 136 S La Brea Ave, Mid-Wilshire ☎323/931-1339. Very vintage stuff, with clothes dating as far back as the nineteenth century, in every sort of fabric imaginable. Also sells antiques from roughly the same eras.

Jet Rag 825 N La Brea Ave, Hollywood ☎323/939-0528. If you're headed to the classic retro-lounge *Formosa Café* just a few blocks away (see p.103), drop in first at this vintage dealer to pick up a stylish club jacket from the old Hollywood days, or sample any other attire from the early 1900s to the present. Another branch in the South Central district of Florence, at 1001 E 62nd St ☎323/232-1191.

Julian's 8366 W Third St, Mid-Wilshire ☎323/655-3011. No retro-kitsch here, only ultra-chic vintage clothing from the 1950s and earlier, including hats, furs, dinner jackets, dresses and scarves, at somewhat higher prices than elsewhere.

Junk for Joy 3314 W Magnolia Blvd, Burbank ☎818/569-4903. A suburban vintage dealer whose old-time clothing from the 1950s through the 1970s not only looks great, it's also never been worn. The attire on display consists of ancient, discontinued items that have been overlooked by various fashion trends.

Muskrat 1248 Third St Promenade, Santa Monica ☎310/394-1713. The best place to look if you're hankering for a comfortable, old Hawaiian shirt. Also has a good collection of jackets, dresses and outfits from the 1940s, mostly in sleek, enduring styles.

Ozzie Dots 4637 Hollywood Blvd, Los Feliz ☎323/663-2867. A vintage store that offers a fine selection of 1930s-through-1970s attire – but since this is East Hollywood, the place also has assorted offbeat theatrical costumes, props and accessories like feather boas and peacock feathers.

Polkadots and Moonbeams 8367 Third St, Mid-Wilshire ☎323/651-1746. Dresses, swimsuits and sweaters from the pre-1970s era, most in fine condition and some quite affordable. If it's more modern clothing you crave, drift down to the pricier contemporary outlet at 8379 Third St ☎323/655-3880.

Reel Clothes 5525 Cahuenga Blvd, North Hollywood ☎818/508-7762. A San Fernando store that sells all types of used clothing and props from movie and TV-show sets. Buy the scarf, hat or dress – or even a complete outfit – of a lead character in a recent movie of your fancy, with 40–90 percent off retail.

Re-Mix 7605 1/2 Beverly Blvd, Mid-Wilshire ☎323/936-6210. Stylish men's and women's shoes from the Art Deco 1930s up to the disco 1970s, all of them authentic and none of them ever worn before.

Star Wares 5341 Derry Ave, Agoura Hills ☎818/881-9077. If you desperately want something previously owned by a movie or TV celebrity, this store on the western edge of LA County, just off the 101 freeway, sells old junk from the closets of the stars. As with Reel Clothes, the prices are far below retail.

SHOPPING | Clothes and fashion

Hair, make-up and nails

As the capital of self-worship and personal transformation, LA has a large array of **hair** and **make–up salons** where you can be teased, sprayed and made up. While cheap spots for a haircut are everywhere, if you're really looking to get a fancy makeover, or a **manicure** or **pedicure**, there are a few top–notch salons around, as well as some that charge affordable prices.

Ball Beauty Supply 416 N Fairfax Ave, Mid-Wilshire ☎323/655-2330. A great storehouse for inexpensive make-up, wigs and other adornments, where the clientele is a mix of youthful male and female club-hoppers and old-timers who've been coming here for ages.

Beauty Bar 1638 N Cahuenga Blvd ☎323/464-7676. A fun watering hole where you can choose from an array of beauty services at affordable prices. See also "Bars and clubs," p.280.

Goodform 727 N Fairfax Ave, West Hollywood ☎323/658-8585. Whether you're going clubbing or to a power lunch, this colorful parlor will do the trick for around $50–100, using a variety of hair styling and makeover techniques, along with more straightforward skin care and manicures.

Jessica's Nail Clinic 8627 Sunset Blvd, West Hollywood ☎310/659-9292. The place where the stars get their manicures, and you can too, often for around $35 – a bargain for clients like Julia Roberts and Nancy Reagan.

Larchmont Beauty Center 208 N Larchmont Blvd, Mid-Wilshire ☎323/466-6859. Features a comprehensive, and pricey, assortment of beauty-care treatments, from hair styling, manicures and pedicures, makeovers and skin care to Swedish massage and aromatherapy.

Raphaël 9020 Burton Way, Beverly Hills ☎310/275-5810. Watch this hair-care wizard do masterful things to your tangles and split ends; in the process, you might even glimpse a celebrity or two.

Robinson's Beautilities 12320 Venice Blvd, West LA ☎310/398-5757. A fun spot to get supplies for your own hair-and-facial design. Along with a good selection of hair-care products and make-up, this supply house stocks a fascinating assortment of designer and fright wigs, facial glitter and special-effects make-up for the movie biz.

Rudy's Barber Shop 4451 W Sunset Blvd, Los Feliz ☎323/661-6535. Idiosyncratic LA salon, a super-hip joint in a converted East Hollywood garage that draws the local rocker and actor crowd. Expect a long, but worthwhile, wait to re-imagine yourself in a spiked mohawk, feathered 1970s look or a trendy goatee, or something a bit more conventional.

Umberto 452 N Camden Drive, Beverly Hills ☎310/274-0393. Another celebrity-friendly locale, with rather steep prices, but not quite as much pretension as some of its neighbors. While you wait, eat a sandwich or sip a cappuccino from the in-house food service. Also at 416 N Canon Drive, Beverly Hills ☎310/274-6395.

Vidal Sassoon 9403 Little Santa Monica Blvd, Beverly Hills ☎310/274-8791. While the full-price haircuts may seem out of reach, assistants in training charge roughly half the cost ($50–60) – a very good deal considering the pricey area. Cosmetology students can also tinker with your looks for even less at Vidal Sassoon's own "hair academy," located at 321 Santa Monica Blvd, Santa Monica ☎310/255-0011.

Wax Poetic 3208 W Magnolia Blvd, Burbank ☎818/843-9469. A good choice for those who want to be pampered with a full range of treatments (waxings, hair styling, tints, chemical peels) in a welcoming atmosphere.

Drugstores and pharmacies

Horton & Converse 11600 Wilshire Blvd, West LA ☎310/478-0801. Open 24 hours. Other locations are open regular business hours: 2001 Santa Monica Blvd, Santa Monica ☎310/829-1834; 9201 Sunset Blvd, West Hollywood ☎310/272-0488; 735 S Figueroa St, Downtown ☎213/623-2838; and 1127 Wilshire Blvd, Downtown ☎213/481-7030. Open seven days at 325 N Larchmont Blvd, Mid-Wilshire ☎323/

466-7606; and 10250 Santa Monica Blvd, West LA ☎310/557-2332.

Kaiser Permanente in the LA Medical Center, 4867 Sunset Blvd, Hollywood ☎323/667-8301.

Longs Drugs 8490 Beverly Blvd, Mid-Wilshire ☎323/653-0880. Also at 9618 Pico Blvd, West LA ☎310/858-1070; and 11941 San Vicente Blvd, West LA ☎310/440-4160.

Rite-Aid 226 N Larchmont Blvd, Mid-Wilshire ☎323/467-1397. Also at 463 N Bedford Drive, Beverly Hills ☎310/247-0838; 300 N Canon Drive, Beverly Hills ☎310/273-3561; 7900 Sunset Blvd, Hollywood ☎323/876-4466; 6130 Sunset Blvd, Hollywood ☎323/467-8608; 1132 N La Brea Ave, Hollywood ☎323/461-4295; 1533 N Vermont Ave, Hollywood ☎323/664-9854; 7900 W Sunset Blvd, West Hollywood ☎323/876-4466; 501 S Broadway, Downtown ☎213/626-0947; 1101

Westwood Blvd, West LA ☎310/209-0708; 1843 S La Cienega Blvd, West LA ☎310/559-1402.

Sav-On 201 N Los Angeles St, Downtown ☎213/620-1491. Also at 861 N Vine St, Hollywood ☎323/466-7300; 5570 Wilshire Blvd, Mid-Wilshire ☎323/936-6121; 5510 Sunset Blvd, Hollywood ☎323/464-2169; 7302 Santa Monica Blvd, Hollywood ☎323/850-6839; 8491 Santa Monica Blvd, West Hollywood ☎310/360-7303; 12315 Venice Blvd, West LA ☎310/390-6296; 12015 Wilshire Blvd, West LA ☎310/479-6500; 2505 Wilshire Blvd, Santa Monica ☎310/828-6056; 13171 Mindanao Way, Marina del Rey ☎310/821-8908.

West LA Medical Center Pharmacy 6041 Cadillac Ave, West LA ☎323/857-2151. Open 24 hours.

Food and drink

Since eating out in LA is so common, you may never have to shop for **food** and **drink** at all. But if you're preparing a picnic, or can indulge in a bit of home cooking, there are plenty of places to stock up. Delis and groceries, many open around the clock, can be found on many street corners, and supermarkets are almost as common, with some open 24 hours or at least until 10pm – try Albertson's, Gelson's, Vons, Pavilions, Ralph's and Trader Joe's. There are also a number of good ethnic groceries and health-food stores, as well as various outlets for baked and dairy goods, mainly clustered in West LA.

Delis and groceries

Art's Deli 12224 Ventura Blvd, Studio City ☎818/762-1221. Long-standing film-industry favorite, providing a good range of sandwiches, soups, meats and breads.

Bristol Farms 7880 W Sunset Blvd, Hollywood ☎323/874-6301. One of the region's best grocers, with delicious meats, cheeses, wine and caviar, but prices can be rather high. Also at 9039 Beverly Blvd, West Hollywood ☎310/248-2804; 1515 Westwood Blvd, West LA ☎310/481-0100; 606 Fair Oaks Ave, South Pasadena ☎626/441-5450; and 1570 Rosecrans Ave, Manhattan Beach ☎310/643-5229.

Brent's Deli 19565 Parthenia Ave, Northridge ☎818/886-5679. This New York–style deli, in a remote corner of the San Fernando Valley, features a huge takeout selection of meat, fish, desserts, salads and sandwiches. Easily the best of its kind in the Valley, if not LA itself.

Canter's Deli 419 N Fairfax Ave, Mid-Wilshire ☎323/651-2030. An LA institution, next to its own unusual cabaret (see p.301), with sandwiches, kosher soups, a good selection of meat and fish, and assorted sweets. Open 24 hours.

Izzy's Deli 1433 Wilshire Blvd, Santa Monica ☎310/394-1131. Long-standing favorite for straightforward deli fare, and one of the few good bets for authentic deli sandwiches along the coast.

Jerry's Famous Deli 8017 Beverly Blvd, West Hollywood ☎310/289-1811. This local institution has the standard array of takeout soups, sandwiches and meats, but is best for its wide array of tempting cakes and pies. This particular branch is open 24 hours, as is the one in Studio City at 12655 Ventura Blvd ☎818/766-8311. Also at 13181 Mindanao Way, Marina Del Rey ☎310/821-6626; and 16650 Ventura Blvd, Encino ☎818/906-1800.

Junior's 2379 Westwood Blvd, West LA

☎310/475-5771. This fine Westside deli and restaurant features a good bakery and deli counter that stocks all of the usual favorites – including lox and egg dishes. An appetizing alternative to the insipid food court at the nearby Westside Pavilion mall.

Langer's 704 S Alvarado St, Mid-Wilshire ☎213/483-8050. In the middle of the high-crime Westlake district, this is nevertheless one of LA's finest delis, with an excellent selection of takeout meats and baked goods, and twenty variations on LA's best pastrami sandwich. Open daylight hours only; curbside pickup available.

Nate 'n' Al's 414 N Beverly Drive, Beverly Hills ☎310/274-0101. This superior deli, in the middle of Beverly Hills' Golden Triangle, has a good array of meat and bread offerings – not to mention terrific blintzes, lox and matzo-ball soup.

Smart and Final 7220 Melrose Ave, Mid-Wilshire ☎323/655-2211. This bulk retail chain packs its stores with big, industrial-sized boxes of cereal, paper towels, fruit juice and just about anything else you might need in massive quantities. Many locations around town.

Stan's Produce 9307 W Pico Blvd, West LA ☎310/274-1865. A popular neighborhood grocer with a fine selection of fruits, vegetables and exotic produce. Just south of Beverly Hills.

Vicente Foods 12027 San Vicente Blvd, Brentwood ☎310/472-5215. If you're in this upscale neighborhood, this is a good place to stop for a terrific selection of quality foods, with breads, cheeses and meats to suit your fancy and worth the high prices.

Ethnic groceries

Alpine Village 833 W Torrance Blvd, Torrance ☎310/323-6520. Though quite a hike, and in a rather drab South Bay area, this place has all the bratwurst and schnitzel you'll ever need, and plays host to one of LA's more spirited Oktoberfest celebrations (see p.324).

Bang Luck Market 5170 Hollywood Blvd, Hollywood ☎323/660-8000. Thai grocer in Los Feliz, with meat, fish, sauces and noodles to help you cook a Southeast Asian feast, or provide a simple snack.

Bay Cities 1517 Lincoln Blvd, Santa Monica ☎310/395-8279. An excellent, centrally located deli and retailer that offers piles of fresh pasta, along with spices, meats, sauces, and many French and Middle Eastern imports.

Bharat Bazaar 11510 Washington Blvd, Culver City ☎310/398-6766. One of several excellent Indian grocers in this section of Culver City, providing all the goods for making your own curries and *vindaloo*.

Cañon Liquor and Deli 1586 E Chevy Chase Drive, Glendale ☎818/547-1764. Pick up a bottle of wine or a pound of Italian meat at this excellent grocer.

Claro's Italian Market 1095 E Main St, Tustin ☎714/832-3081. This compact but well-stocked spot has everything from Italian wines, chocolate and crackers to store-brand frozen meals, plus a deli and a bakery offering some forty varieties of cookies. Worth the drive out to this distant section of Orange County.

Domingo's Italian Grocery 17548 Ventura Blvd, Encino ☎818/981-4466. A good reason for traveling to the San Fernando Valley: authentic Italian meats, pastas and cheeses.

Elat Meat Market 8730 Pico Blvd, West LA ☎310/659-7070. Mainly Middle Eastern staples at this colorful market, located near other ethnic grocers on Pico Blvd, just southeast of Beverly Hills.

Gastronom 7859 Santa Monica Blvd, West Hollywood ☎323/654-9456. Smoked fish and caviar are the highlights at this bustling market, a fixture in the area's burgeoning Russian community.

La Canasta in El Mercado 1737 W Sixth St, Westlake ☎213/484-6159. If you don't mind venturing to the dicey Westlake area, you'll find a good assortment of authentic Mexican and Central American food – chilis, *chayotes* and tasty desserts – at this inexpensive grocery.

Mandarin Deli 727 N Broadway ☎213/623-6054. Very tasty and cheap noodles, pork and fish dumplings and other hearty staples in the middle of Chinatown. Also at 356 E Second St, Little Tokyo ☎213/617-0231.

Market World 3030 W Sepulveda Blvd, Torrance ☎310/539-8899. A good selection of pre-pared Asian meat, vegetable and noodle dishes at this South Bay grocery. Located just off Crenshaw Blvd.

Nijiya Market 2130 Sawtelle Blvd, West LA ☎310/575-3300. *Bento*s – simple rice-and-meat combinations served in a bowl – are some of the succulent takeout items available at this Japanese grocer. Also a branch in the South Bay at 2121 W 182nd St, Torrance ☎310/366-7200.

Olson's Deli 5560 Pico Blvd, Mid-Wilshire ☎323/938-0742. Herring, meatballs and assorted sausages at this Swedish grocer, one of the few Scandinavian food stores in LA and definitely worth a try.

Portos Cuban Bakery 315 N Brand Blvd, Glendale ☎818/956-5996. Tasty baked goods and desserts, along with flaky Cuban pastries, cheesecakes soaked in rum, muffins and tortes.

Standard Sweets and Snacks 18600 Pioneer Blvd, Artesia ☎562/860-6364. Good Indian finger-food joint selling vegetarian *dosas* (pancakes) and delicious desserts, along with other traditional fare. North of Long Beach.

Thailand Plaza 5321 Hollywood Blvd, Hollywood ☎323/993-9000. This Thai supermarket and eatery has an impressive selection of Southeast Asian dishes and delicacies for very cheap prices.

Tsarina Russian Gourmet Deli 14445 Ventura Blvd, Tarzana ☎818/986-8889. A small, authentic spot in the San Fernando Valley with excellent food and cheap prices on such Slavic staples as caviar, stuffed cabbage rolls, borscht, blintzes, dumplings and lamb soup.

United Poultry 736 N Broadway, Downtown LA ☎213/624-3788. This Chinatown food retailer stocks not only chicken, but an array of familiar and exotic meats, from pork to boar.

Health-food stores

Co-Opportunity 1525 Broadway, Santa Monica ☎310/451-8902. A very popular neighborhood store selling organic and vegetarian foods, which are unfortunately arranged in overly cramped spaces, making shopping here a nerve-wracking experience during peak hours.

Erewhon 7660 Beverly Blvd, Mid-Wilshire ☎323/937-0777. The epitome of health-obsessed LA, selling pricey health food and all the wheat grass you can swallow. Close to the CBS studios.

Full o' Life 2515 W Magnolia Blvd, Burbank ☎818/845-8343. This mother of all health-food stores dates back to 1959 and offers an organic market, deli, dairy, restaurant and book department, and there are

nutritionists and a naturopath on the premises daily.

Mother's Market 225 E 17th St, Costa Mesa ☎949/631-4741. A large health-food retailer in Orange County, the perfect place to stock up on bulk supplies of juice, vitamins, veggie cuisine and even animal-friendly beauty supplies and books on maintaining a nutritionally correct lifestyle. Also at 19770 Beach Blvd, Huntington Beach ☎714/963-6667, and 2963 Michelson Drive, Irvine ☎949/752-6667.

Nature Mart 2080 Hillhurst Ave, Hollywood ☎323/667-1677. A Los Feliz storehouse for organic produce, nonsugary sweets and a wealth of vitamins and herbs. Somewhat cheaper than comparable Westside retailers.

Papa Jon's 5006 E Second St, Long Beach ☎562/439-1059. Long-standing restaurant and market catering to vegetarians and vegans, with a range of affordable breads and juices as well as meatless entrees and garden burgers.

VP Discount Health Food 11665 Santa Monica Blvd, West LA ☎310/444-7949. A chain retailer that has a following of hard-core acolytes and vegans willing to pay a bit more for clean, sanctified food. Also at 3002 S Sepulveda Blvd, West LA ☎310/478-9798, and ten other branches in the San Gabriel and San Fernando valleys.

Whole Foods Market 239 N Crescent Drive, Beverly Hills ☎310/274-3360. One in a nation-wide chain of health-food megastores, this rather small branch is located in the exclusive Golden Triangle shopping zone, and offers scrumptious vegetarian offerings and a good assortment of deli food. Other central LA branches at 11666 National Blvd, West LA ☎310/996-8840; 11737 San Vicente Blvd, Brentwood ☎310/826-4433; and 7871 Santa Monica Blvd, West Hollywood ☎323/848-4200.

Wild Oats Community Market 3474 S Centinela Ave, West LA ☎310/636-1800. An excellent organic wine store and deli that mixes fresh fruit drinks at its smoothie bar. Also at 603 S Lake Ave, Pasadena ☎626/792-1778; 1425 Montana Ave, Santa Monica ☎310/576-4707; and 500 Wilshire Blvd, Santa Monica ☎310/395-4510.

Baked and dairy goods

Al Gelato 806 S Robertson Blvd, West LA ☎310/659-8069. That delectable Italian version of ice cream – gelato – is served here with American panache: delicious flavors doled out in sizeable helpings. The espresso gelato is particularly mouth-watering.

Beverlywood Bakery 9128 Pico Blvd, West LA ☏310/278-0122. Old World desserts and baked goods, from heavy strudels to chewy, thick-crusted breads are on offer, along with premium prices that reflect the store's proximity to Beverly Hills, a block north.

The Cheese Store 419 N Beverly Drive, Beverly Hills ☏1-800/547-1515 or 310/278-2855. More than four hundred types of cheese from all over the world, including every kind produced in the US – many of them suspended invitingly over your head, plus typically high prices to match.

Cobbler Factory 33 N Catalina Ave, Pasadena ☏626/449-2152. Boasting a range of fruity desserts and a faithful local following, this place sits in a prime spot near Old Pasadena, where you can snack on these tempting sweets as you wander about the grand architecture of this buzzing shopping precinct.

Cold Stone Creamery 132 S Brand Blvd, Glendale ☏818/547-2663. Ever-popular dessert spot, often packed with shoppers and tourists, where the gimmick is to pick your own ice-cream ingredients and watch them being stirred on a "cold stone" tablet, with plenty of candy bars and flavored syrups mixed in. A citywide chain with a dozen other branches.

Diamond Bakery 335 N Fairfax Ave, Mid-Wilshire ☏323/655-0534. In the heart of the Fairfax District, this great old Jewish bakery provides traditional favorites, including cheesecakes, breads and rugelach.

Doughboys Café and Bakery 8136 W Third St, Mid-Wilshire ☏323/651-4202. Tasty and filling pizzas and sandwiches are available for midday meals, but the real highlight of this Westside bakery is the bread: rich, hearty loaves with interesting ingredients like walnuts, olives and various cheeses.

Eiger Ice Cream 124 S Barrington Place, Brentwood ☏310/471-6955. Whether in cones, dishes or pies, the ice cream at this Westside favorite is always good and rich.

Fosselman's 1824 W Main St, Alhambra ☏626/282-6533. For delicious frozen dairy treats, this long-standing spot in Gabriel Valley has few equals, serving up ice cream and sorbets in fifty tempting flavors.

Hansen Cakes 193 S Beverly Drive, Beverly Hills ☏310/273-3759. A local institution that sells resplendently decorated, and rather tasty, cakes – though not by the slice.

La Brea Bakery 624 S La Brea Ave, Mid-Wilshire ☏323/939-6813. This bakery (adjacent to the upscale *Campanile* restaurant; see p.263) is a serious treat for anyone with an interest in fine breads, from traditional sourdough offerings to fancier olive- and cherry-laden loaves.

LA Desserts 113 N Robertson Blvd, Beverly Hills ☏310/273-5537. If you don't mind a few snide looks from the Hollywood swells, step into this terrific bakery inside the swank *Ivy* restaurant and try the delicious cakes and tarts, all available for absurdly high prices.

Mäni's Bakery 2507 Main St, Santa Monica ☏310/396-7700. This vegetarian- and vegan-oriented bakery provides sugarless brownies and meatless sandwiches to local bohemians and slackers. Also at 519 S Fairfax Ave, Mid-Wilshire ☏323/938-8800.

Mousse Fantasy 2130 Sawtelle Blvd, West LA ☏310/479-6665. A Japanese version of a French patisserie, located in a crowded strip mall, where the range of tasty tarts and pastries includes the noteworthy Green Tea Mousse cake – an unusual-tasting concoction.

Mrs Field's Cookies 907 Westwood Blvd, Westwood ☏310/208-0096. Chewy, sweet cookies, made to a "secret recipe" that has plenty of devoted fans – nationwide branches include nine others in LA.

Röckenwagner 2435 Main St, Santa Monica ☏310/399-6504. A Westside culinary delight serving up a fine mix of California cuisine and nouveau German food, including chocolate desserts, rich pastries and scones, and hearty breads. Located in the Edgemar shopping complex. A sister restaurant, *Röck*, has more decadent offerings at 13445 Maxella Ave, Marina del Rey ☏310/822-8979.

Say Cheese 2800 Hyperion Ave, Silver Lake ☏323/665-0545. A distinctive array of French and other international cheeses, priced from moderate to expensive. The delicious sandwiches may be your best bet.

Viktor Benes Continental Pastries 8718 W Third St, West LA ☏310/276-0488. The place to go for freshly baked bread, coffee cakes, Danish pastries and various chocolate-flavored treats, and appreciative local fans know it. Five other area locations as well.

Wine and liquor

Greenblatt's Fine Wine 8017 Sunset Blvd, West Hollywood ☎323/656-0606. A Sunset Strip deli and liquor mart that's a neighborhood favorite, and is most well known for its wide assortment of wine, brandy, Champagne and Scotch. Open until 2am.

Red Carpet Wine 400 E Glenoaks Blvd, Glendale ☎818/247-5544 or 1-800/339-0609. Besides having an in-store wine bar and a sizeable stock of wine and beer, this store is also a fine spot to purchase spirits, cigars, Champagne, and even Godiva chocolates.

Valley Beverage Company 14901 Ventura Blvd, Sherman Oaks ☎818/981-1566. Offering an excellent selection of local and international wines, many at discounted prices, with a special emphasis on kosher wines, Scotch, tequila and brandy.

Wally's 2107 Westwood Blvd, West LA ☎310/475-0606. A gourmet grocery that has a good assortment of caviar, cheeses and other fancy treats, and sells hard liquor and cigars, too.

Wine and Liquor Depot 16938 Saticoy St, Van Nuys ☎818/996-1414. Promising the lowest area prices on blended and single malt Scotch, this Valley dealer is also worth a look for its international wines, port, sherry, bourbon and beer.

Bookstores

At times, it can seem like LA has almost as many **bookstores** as people, with enough variety to suit every taste, whether you want flagship superstores, cozy local bookstores, or specialist and secondhand places that may reward several hours' browsing along the miles of dusty shelves. Also, while not so common, there are a few good travel bookstores worth noting, too.

Chains and superstores

Barnes and Noble 1201 Third St, Santa Monica ☎310/260-9110. High-volume bookstore with three floors of general and specialty books overlooking the end of the Third Street Promenade. Branches all over Southern California.

Bookstar 12136 Ventura Blvd, Studio City ☎818/505-9528. Discount chain bookstore with plenty of space for browsing and a nice selection of books. A decent Westside branch at 100 N La Cienega Blvd, West Hollywood ☎310/289-1734, directly across from the Beverly Center mall.

Borders 1360 Westwood Blvd, West LA ☎310/475-3444. Easily the top LA branch of this omnipresent retailer, and at one time the biggest Borders in the US, with two sprawling floors, an upper-level café with outside seating, an expansive music area with listening stations, and as many new books on general topics as you're likely to find on the Westside. Also located just east of Beverly Hills, at 330 S La Cienega Blvd ☎310/659-4045.

Dutton's 11975 San Vicente Blvd, Brentwood ☎310/476-6263. LA chain bookstore, part of an ungainly complex, where the aisles tend to be cluttered, and the category sections scattered awkwardly throughout the store, but the selection is good; just try to visit during the less-crowded weekdays. Also in the San Fernando Valley at 5146 Laurel Canyon Blvd, North Hollywood ☎818/769-3866, and 3806 W Magnolia Blvd, Burbank ☎818/840-8003.

Rizzoli Bookstore 332 Santa Monica Blvd, Santa Monica ☎310/278-2247. Located around the corner from the Third Street Promenade, this upscale bookseller is always crowded and features a sizeable range of art books and literature, all sold at full price. Also at 9501 Wilshire Blvd, Beverly Hills ☎310/278-2247.

Tower Books 8844 W Sunset Blvd, West Hollywood ☎310/657-3344. Hip chain merchant across the street from the massive Tower Records on the Sunset Strip, with a broad selection of titles centered on youth culture, rock music, sexuality and leftist politics.

General interest and new books

Book Baron 1236 S Magnolia Ave, Anaheim ☎714/527-7022. Large independent bookseller with stacks upon stacks of new and used books. Part of a complex that includes Magazine Baron and Music Baron, both selling recent and secondhand material at affordable prices.

Book Soup 8818 W Sunset Blvd, West Hollywood ☎310/659-3110. Great selection, right on the Sunset Strip, and open daily until midnight. Narrow, winding aisles are packed with books on every subject, but with an emphasis on entertainment, travel and photography.

Either/Or 950 Aviation Blvd, Hermosa Beach ☎310/374-2060. A voluminous fiction selection and a wide variety of New Age tomes, with free publications in abundance. Open until 11pm.

Midnight Special 1318 Third St, Santa Monica ☎310/393-2923. A large general bookstore on the Promenade, with high bookcases, eccentrically arranged shelves, and a focus on leftist politics and social sciences.

Skylight Books 1818 N Vermont Ave, Hollywood ☎323/660-1175. Just north of Barnsdall Park in a trendy shopping zone, this Los Feliz bookseller has a broad range of mainstream and alternative literature, plus a fine selection of film books.

Small World Books 1407 Ocean Front Walk, Venice ☎310/399-2360. A modest neighborhood dealer by the beach that has many good choices for mystery novels and literature from local and national authors.

Vroman's 695 E Colorado Blvd, Pasadena ☎1-800/769-2665 or 626/449-5320. One of the San Gabriel Valley's largest retailers for new books, and a good place to browse, but don't expect to find any bargains. Also includes an in-store café.

Secondhand books

Acres of Books 240 Long Beach Blvd, Long Beach ☎526/437-6980. Worth a trip down the Blue Line Metrorail just to wallow in LA's largest, and most disorganized, secondhand bookstore. You may not be able to find the exact title you're looking for, but chances are you'll stumble across something good.

Aladdin Books 122 W Commonwealth Ave, Fullerton ☎714/738-6115. Despite having what may be the region's finest assortment of film and fantasy titles, both new and used, this shop is a little-known commodity to most Angelenos, but shouldn't be missed by visitors willing to drive to this distant Orange County burg.

Atlantis Book Shop 144 S San Fernando Rd, Burbank ☎818/845-6467. Just down the street from the huge Media City Center mall, and adjacent to the 5 freeway, Atlantis specializes in history, fiction, politics and – as the name might suggest – the speculative and the paranormal.

Berkelouw Books 830 N Highland Ave, Hollywood ☎323/466-3321. An easy-to-miss dealer with voluminous stacks of titles and notable sections in fiction, biography, entertainment and history – plus a knowledgeable owner who'll be glad to help you sift through his well-chosen collection.

Book Alley 611 E Colorado Blvd, Pasadena ☎626/683-8083. A handsomely designed bookstore with a large stock of affordable used books on a wide variety of subjects. You'll find a similar selection at the store's annex, Book Alley Too!, nearby at 696 E Colorado Blvd ☎626/795-0818.

Brand Book Shop 231 N Brand Blvd, Glendale ☎818/507-5943. A San Fernando Valley used-book seller with a broad range of titles, but particularly strong in entertainment, history and politics. Located in the heart of downtown Glendale.

Cliff's Books 630 E Colorado Blvd, Pasadena ☎626/449-9541. This longstanding used bookseller, with narrow aisles stacked with titles on a wide assortment of subjects, has a bigger selection than some other bookstores in the vicinity, with slightly higher prices as well.

Cosmopolitan Book Shop 7017 Melrose Ave ☎323/938-7119. A cozy Westside dealer loaded with thousands of titles stacked high on oversized bookcases, spanning a variety of subjects but especially strong on film and media. Although the prices are good, the selection is disorganized, so plan on taking enough time to hunt through the shelves.

House of Fiction 1559 N Hill Ave, Pasadena ☎626/449-9861. You'll find not only fiction, but assorted scholarly titles as well at this bookseller located on the northern edge of Pasadena.

Wilshire Books 3018 Wilshire Blvd, Santa Monica ☎310/828-3115. An excellent used bookstore for its size, which is quite small and cramped. Features a well-chosen collection of tomes on art, politics, religion and music – all of them coherently organized and accessible.

Specialist bookstores

Bodhi Tree 8585 Melrose Ave, West Hollywood ☎310/659-1733. Ultra-trendy Melrose book retailer stocking a range of New Age, occult and self-help titles, and the healing power of crystals, pyramids and the like.

Circus of Books 4001 Sunset Blvd, Silver Lake ☎323/666-1304. Take a trip through LA's seamier side at this well-known dealer in weird murder tales, serial-killer exposés, S&M diaries and assorted pornography. Although the place attracts a mix of the sane and the creepy, visitors should beware: it's also something of a pick-up joint. Also at 1639 N Las Palmas Ave, Hollywood ☎323/467-3850, and 8230 Santa Monica Blvd, West Hollywood ☎323/656-6533.

A Different Light 8853 Santa Monica Blvd, West Hollywood ☎310/854-6601. The city's best-known gay and lesbian bookstore, in the heart of the city's gay district, with monthly art shows, readings and women's music events. See also "Gay and lesbian LA," p.307.

Hennessey and Ingalls 1254 Third St, Santa Monica ☎310/458-9074. An impressive range of coffee-table art and architecture books makes this Promenade bookstore among the best of its kind in LA. Rare posters, catalogs and hard-to-find books are also in stock. However, while there are many displays of cut-rate remainders, the books you'll likely want will be priced at premium.

Koma Books 548 S Spring St, Downtown ☎323/239-0030. An edgy alternative dealer selling books on true crime, paranoid conspiracy rants and a host of underground topics through its small store and large mail-order base.

Larry Edmunds Book Shop 6644 Hollywood Blvd, Hollywood ☎323/463-3273. Many stacks of books, a large number of them out of print, are offered on every aspect of film and theater, with movie stills and posters. Located at the center of tourist-oriented Hollywood.

Mitchell Books 1395 E Washington Blvd, Pasadena ☎626/798-4438. A favorite San Gabriel Valley dealer in detective and mystery novels, where you can grab a copy of Raymond Chandler, Walter Moseley or James Ellroy to use as a fiction travel-guide to LA's dark side.

Mysterious Bookshop 1036 Broxton Ave, Westwood ☎310/659-2959. Browse the shelves for Dashiell Hammett, or more contemporary crime novelists like Ross MacDonald, at this terrific seller of old and new mysteries and thrillers. Has a nice cache of rare titles and first editions.

Norton Simon Museum Bookstore 411 W Colorado Blvd, Pasadena ☎626/449-6840. Prices in this museum store are lower than in any other art bookstore in LA, and the stock is, not surprisingly, superb. Includes numerous titles on museum specialties like Impressionism and early modern art, and biographies and monographs of the artists in the institution's collections.

Samuel French Theatre & Film Bookshop 7623 Sunset Blvd, Hollywood ☎323/876-0570. LA's broadest selection of theater books is found in this local institution, along with a good collection of movie and media-related titles. In the back room, you can sometimes find discounted or used titles.

Sisterhood Bookstore 1351 Westwood Blvd, West LA ☎310/477-7300. Westside landmark with music, cards, books and literature pertaining to the national and international women's movements.

Taschen 354 N Beverly Drive, Beverly Hills ⊛www.taschen.com. Fun and edifying titles that cover everything from Renaissance art to Americana kitsch, all inexpensively priced – even the coffee-table books are occasionally affordable. Also features an art gallery, café and performance space. Opening spring 2003.

Travel bookstores

California Map and Travel Center 3312 Pico Blvd, Santa Monica ☎310/396-6277. You'll find atlases, maps and books about outdoor activities and local adventures at this bookshop near the 10 freeway, on the eastern edge of Santa Monica.

Distant Lands 56 S Raymond Ave, Pasadena ☎626/449-3220. Well-stocked travel bookstore in Old Pasadena, with some fairly hard-to-find titles, as well as maps and travel gear. Also hosts the occasional public speaker.

Literate Traveller 8306 Wilshire Blvd ☎310/398-8781 or 1-800/850-2665. Guidebooks aren't the focus here, but rather high literature and personal essays with a travel bent.

Nations Travel Mall 500 Pier Ave, Hermosa Beach ☎310/318-9915. A South Bay travel-guide retailer that sells all the familiar publishers at reasonable prices, along with a decent selection of maps and travel accessories.

Rand McNally in the Century City Marketplace, 10250 Santa Monica Blvd, Century City ☎310/556-2202 or 1-800/333-0136. A cramped little store loaded with tourists and shoppers, featuring a wide range of travel books and maps, and even a good selection of globes. One of several regional branches, with most in Orange County.

Thomas Brothers Maps 521 W Sixth St, Downtown ☎213/627-4018 or 1-888/277-6277. The well-known mapmakers who produce highly detailed, spiral-bound city maps operate this Downtown store, which also carries a good assortment of travel publications. Also in a distant corner of Orange County at 17731 Cowan St, Irvine ☎949/863-1984.

Traveler's Bookcase 8375 W Third St, Mid-Wilshire ☎323/655-0575. Located along the trendy Third Street shopping strip, a bookseller overflowing with travel guides, maps and publications, along with a fine array of literary travel stories and personal essays.

Music stores

Music lovers will be spoiled for choice when it comes to shopping for **music** in LA. The selection below leans toward the city's more one-of-a-kind stores, many of which still carry used LPs.

A-1 Record Finders 5639 Melrose Ave, Mid-Wilshire ☎213/732-6737. One of the West Coast's top spots for tracking down classic and (not-so-classic) vinyl. The staff can assist you in hunting for forgotten platters, whether it's an obscure 1960s garage-rock band or a legendary blues singer of the 1940s.

Amoeba Music 6400 W Sunset Blvd, Hollywood ☎323/245-6400. Immensely popular record store with a vast selection of titles on CD, tape and vinyl, which you can sample at listening carrels throughout the store.

Aron's Records 1150 N Highland Ave, Hollywood ☎323/469-4700. A sizeable stock of used discs in all musical styles and at all prices, though nothing too out of the ordinary. Getting help can be a problem, as the place is often packed.

Destroy All Music 3818 Sunset Blvd, Silver Lake ☎323/663-9300. The punk-rock antidote to the chain stores, selling recordings new and old from Southern California to Europe. Located next door to the You've Got Bad Taste music store and punk-rock museum (☎213/669-1718), where you can browse nostalgic reminders of local punk faves X and Black Flag.

DMC Records 7619 Melrose Ave ☎323/651-3520. A prime spot to buy used dance CDs and, especially, vinyl, popular with local club-hoppers and DJs. The selection is good, but prices could be better.

Fingerprints 4612 E Second St, Long Beach ☎562/433-4996. A formidable indie outfit in the South Bay, offering alternative-leaning CD and vinyl, plus in-store performances from local rockers, and a mellow, soft-sell attitude. Located in the Belmont Shore district.

Heavy Rotation 12354 Ventura Blvd, Studio City ☎818/769-8882. Cheap prices for used CDs, cassettes, laserdiscs and video games are a big draw at this San Fernando Valley dealer; another is the interesting assortment of music-industry promotional records scattered through the stock.

Penny Lane 12 W Colorado Blvd, Pasadena ☎626/564-0161. New and used records at reasonable prices. Always crowded, this local chain features listening stations where you can sample dozens of eclectic discs. Also at 7563 Melrose Ave (☎323/651-3000) and 10914 Kinross Ave, Westwood (☎310/208-5611).

Poo-Bah Records 1101 E Walnut Ave, Pasadena ☎626/449-3359. Plenty of American and imported New Wave sounds, along with 1980s technopop and various other genres.

Record Surplus 11609 W Pico Blvd, West LA ☎310/478-4217. A massive LP collection of surf music, early rock'n'roll, 1960s soundtracks and unintentionally hilarious spoken-word recordings. Prices are excellent, with many CDs and cassettes offered at ridiculously low prices. Anyone with an interest in classic, alternative or offbeat music knows this place.

Rhino Records 1720 Westwood Blvd, West LA ☎310/474-8685. A great selection of international independent releases at this terrific retailer that features a fine assortment of new and used CDs – including rock, punk, funk and everything else – as well as the entire stock of recordings produced on its own label.

Rockaway Records 2395 Glendale Blvd, Silver Lake ☎323/664-3232. Great place to come for both used CDs and LPs, as well as laserdiscs. Also offers old magazines, posters and memorabilia. Located just east of the Silver Lake reservoir.

Tower Records 14621 Ventura Blvd, Sherman Oaks ☎818/789-0500. The San Fernando Valley branch of this big chain (opposite a

regular, high-priced Tower store) features discontinued or deleted CDs and cassettes from major labels at low prices – often around $8. Also at 8801 W Sunset Blvd, West Hollywood ☎310/657-7300, one of the Sunset Strip's busiest retailers.

Vinyl Fetish 7305 Melrose Ave, Mid-Wilshire ☎323/935-1300. Besides the punk and post-punk merchandise, a good place to discover what's new on the ever-changing LA music scene and even to buy a cheesy T-shirt or two.

Virgin Megastore 8000 Sunset Blvd, West Hollywood ☎323/650-8666. A Sunset Strip corporate-music giant with steep retail prices, but well worth a look for the extensive selection spread over two levels, including CDs, DVDs, books and video games.

Specialty stores

The **specialty stores** below are some of the more colorful you'll find in LA.

Condomania 647 N Poinsettia Place, Hollywood ☎323/933-7865. A huge assortment of prophylactics in a variety of colors, textures and sizes, all inflated on a central rack, so you can see what they potentially look like when in use.

Forbidden Fruit 9960 Glenoaks Blvd, Sun Valley ☎818/504-1871 or 1-800/258-1999. Take a trip back in time when you visit this novelty store in the eastern San Fernando Valley, which sells incense, clove cigarettes, lava lamps, water pipes and even black-light lamps.

Le Sex Shoppe 6315 Hollywood Blvd, Hollywood ☎323/464-9435. Hollywood's prime sex-paraphernalia dealer, with everything from magazines and videos to handcuffs and lingerie, catering to a mix of curious Westsiders and seedy regulars. Also at 5507 Hollywood Blvd, Los Feliz ☎323/462-2460, and 3147 N San Fernando Rd, north of Silver Lake in Atwater Village ☎323/258-2867.

Noisy Toys 8728 S Sepulveda Blvd, Westchester, just north of LAX ☎310/678-9957 or 1-800/874-8223. A cacophonous shrine to percussion, loaded with drums and other instruments from around the world, not least among them zithers, rain sticks, bongos, maracas, castanets, kazoos, wooden whistles, tambourines and even

didgeridoos. Best of all, you can sample each instrument at your leisure.

Off the Wall 7325 Melrose Ave ☎323/360-1080. Appealing mid-twentieth-century antiques cleaned up and sold as high-priced goods, from Bakelite jewelry to Fiestaware dishes, as well as faded consumer items like outdated board games and old telephones.

Skeletons in the Closet 1104 N Mission Rd, Downtown ☎213/343-0760. Believe it or not, this is the LA County Coroner Gift Shop, selling everything from skeleton-adorned beach towels and T-shirts to toe-tag key chains – a great place to buy unique LA merchandise.

Vidiots 302 Pico Blvd, Santa Monica ☎310/392-8508. Easily one of LA's best video stores, providing an excellent selection of classics and current flicks, but also a good range of cult and bizarre films, strange government propaganda and experimental art movies.

Wacko 4633 Hollywood Blvd, Hollywood ☎323/663-0122. The name says it all – freakish alternative comic books, odd-smelling candles, funky posters and toys, and various underground magazines. Part of a complex that includes the Soap Plant, where, along with soap, you can find body creams, fragrant oils and bubble baths.

Galleries

The Westside is the province of LA's top art **galleries** for painting, mixed-media, sculpture and, especially, photography. Indeed, snapping pictures is what a city based on the movie industry does best, and you're likely to find terrific retrospectives of long-departed artists like Weston and Stieglitz among the breakout shows of up-and-coming local shutterbugs. Keep in mind that the galleries listed below – mainly in Santa Monica, Hollywood, the La Brea district, Beverly Hills and the Wilshire corridor – represent only established arthouses in LA, and that by wandering through the right parts of Venice, Silver Lake and Downtown's northeast fringe, you can often find art that's just as interesting and much cheaper. The only challenges are that many of the lower-rent galleries have irregular operating hours, are closed for erratic periods and tend to appear and disappear overnight. However, by taking a **tour** of such areas (on, say, the Venice Art Walk, p.322, or the Discovery Tour of the Arroyo Arts Collective, p.72) you can see what grass-roots artists are currently up to – long before they reach the walls of the big-name galleries below.

Armory Center for the Arts 145 N Raymond Ave, Pasadena ☎626/792-5101. Shows by young artists and retrospectives of local painters and photographers make this an enjoyable, fairly unpretentious spot.

Beyond Baroque 681 Venice Blvd, Venice ☎310/822-3006. A gallery and art center that's as interesting and unpredictable as any place else in town, with a wide spectrum of performance art, fiction and poetry readings, assemblage and mixed-media, painting, drawing, photography and more.

Center for Land Use Interpretation 9331 Venice Blvd, Culver City ☎310/839-5722, ⓦ www.clui.org. Narrowly focused but often fascinating museum/gallery that looks at land use from various angles, notably time-lapse photography, satellite images, and even field trips to mudslide catch basins, aviation graveyards and windswept eastern deserts.

Fahey-Klein 148 N La Brea Ave, Mid-Wilshire ☎323/934-2250. This institutional heavyweight features contemporary work, especially local photography, much of it in black-and-white. Don't be deterred by the forbidding, windowless exterior – the gallery is open and accessible most days of the week.

Gagosian Gallery 456 N Camden Drive, Beverly Hills ☎310/271-9400. A major name in LA art that occasionally shows big names like Lichtenstein, Miró and Twombly. With prices in the stratosphere, you're better off window-shopping here.

Gallery 825 825 N La Cienega Blvd, West Hollywood ☎310/652-8272. Affiliated with the Los Angeles Art Association, a longstanding spot devoted to groundbreaking exhibits by emerging artists and thoughtful career retrospectives.

Gallery of Functional Art 2525 Michigan Ave, Santa Monica ☎310/829-6990. Noise-emitting clocks, ornamental wooden furniture, and funky, Space Age wall sconces are for sale at this Bergamot Station gallery, where form and function mix with intriguing results.

Iturralde Gallery 116 S La Brea Ave, Mid-Wilshire ☎323/937-4267. Established and emerging Latino artists are usually on display here, with shows often alternating between the work of talented locals and international figures.

Jan Kesner Gallery 164 N La Brea Ave, Mid-Wilshire ☎323/938-6834. This stylish gallery features retrospectives of noted artists – many of them photographers – as well as openings by up-and-comers. Sits among numerous other galleries on La Brea.

Judson Gallery 200 S Ave 66, Highland Park ☎323/255-0131, ⓦ www.judsonstudios.com. A good place for checking out what's going on in Downtown's artsy northeastern fringe, heavy on contemporary stained glass as well as periodic exhibitions in a variety of media.

Koplin Gallery 464 N Robertson Blvd, West Hollywood ☎310/657-9843. Elite art dealer specializing in etchings, paintings and drawings, with an eye toward contemporary art from LA and elsewhere. One of many high-priced galleries scattered around this upscale section of town.

Los Angeles Contemporary Exhibitions 6522 Hollywood Blvd, Hollywood ☎323/957-1777. Also known as LACE, this regional institution hosts a wide-ranging selection of mixed-media, painting, drawing and video work, while its various community outreach programs bring art to the masses.

Margo Leavin Gallery 812 N Robertson Blvd, West Hollywood ☎310/273-0603. This eclectic gallery is worth a look for what's new and trendy on the West Hollywood gallery scene (see p.110).

New Alchemy 6909 Melrose Ave ☎323/933-6912. A hip Melrose gallery that offers dark, edgy work that's slightly less expensive than some galleries on the Westside. Painting, mixed-media and photography are often on display.

Rosamund Felsen Gallery 2525 Michigan Ave, Santa Monica ☎310/828-8488. A noteworthy gallery in Bergamot Station, featuring estab-lished Southern California artists and more recent arrivals. The eclectic selection is often striking, but you can forget about buying anything: the prices here are always high.

Susanne Vielmetter/Los Angeles Projects 5363 Wilshire Blvd, Mid-Wilshire ☎323/933-2117. Miracle Mile gallery showing contemporary artists, particularly those working in untraditional media, with a strong Southern Californian bent.

Track 16 2525 Michigan Ave, Santa Monica ☎310/264-4678. Politically oriented artworks tending toward mixed-media and assemblage, though you can also find traditional painted and sculpted works, with one message or another boldly attached.

Directory

Airports Burbank/Glendale/Pasadena ☏818/840-8840; John Wayne/Orange County ☏949/252-5200; LAX ☏310/646-5252; Long Beach ☏562/570-2600; Ontario ☏909/937-2700; Van Nuys ☏818/785-8838

Beach information Coastal weather conditions for Malibu ☏310/457-9701, Santa Monica ☏310/578-0478, South Bay ☏310/379-8471

Coast guard Search-and-rescue, Los Angeles/Long Beach ☏562/980-4444, Orange County/Newport Beach ☏949/834-3800

Consulates Australia, Century Plaza Towers, 19th floor, 2049 Century Park East, Century City ☏323/229-4800; **Canada**, 500 S Hope St, 9th Floor, Downtown ☏213/346-2700; **New Zealand**, 12400 Wilshire Blvd #1150, Westwood ☏310/207-1605; **United Kingdom**, 11766 Wilshire Blvd, Suite 400, West LA ☏310/477-3322

Currency exchange Outside of banking hours, exchange offices are scattered inconveniently throughout town. Most reliable are those at LAX; hours vary by terminal (often daily until 11pm ☏310/649-2801).

Dental referral service The cheapest place is USC School of Dentistry, 925 W 34th St, South Central (☏1-888/USC-DENT, ⓦwww.usc.edu/hsc/dental/patient_care) on the USC campus, costing $50–200. Turn up and be prepared to wait all day. You can also get emergency treatment at the LA Dental Society, 3660 Wilshire Blvd #1152 ☏213/380-7669, ⓦwww.ladentalsociety.com.

Directory assistance Local ☏411 (a free call at pay phones); long distance ☏1 + area code + 555-1212.

Electricity 110V AC. European appliances typically require two-pin plug adapters for lower US voltages.

Emergencies Dial ☏911. For less urgent needs: fire ☏323/890-4194; civil defense and disaster services ☏213/974-1120; police ☏213/625-3311; sheriff ☏213/526-5541; poison control center ☏1-800/777-6476; food poisoning reports ☏213/240-7821; earthquake tips ☏818/787-3737.

Internet access Available from cyber-oriented coffee shops (see "Coffeehouses," p.30), the *Newsroom Café* (p.269), many city libraries, and sit-down terminals near flight gates at LAX. Outside of libraries, expect to pay around 25¢ per minute to browse the Web.

Laundry Most hotels do laundry, but they charge quite a bit for the service. You're better off going to a laundromat or a dry cleaner (see *Yellow Pages* under "Laundries").

Left luggage All Greyhound bus stations have left-luggage lockers for around $1 a day, $2.50 for larger lockers. See p.27 for station locations.

Libraries Downtown's Central Library is the city's best (see p.68), with branches throughout LA. Other cities also have good main libraries, notably Beverly Hills (see p.114) and Santa Monica, 1343 Sixth St. Specialist libraries are quite common and well-funded, such as the Margaret Herrick Library (p.85) for film-related materials, and the One Institute (see box, p.307) for gay and lesbian publications.

Measurements and sizes Measurements of length are in inches, feet, yards and miles; weight in ounces, pounds and tons. American pints and gallons are about four-fifths of imperial ones. Clothing sizes are two figures less than they would be in Britain (a British size 12 is an American size 10). To calculate your American shoe size, simply add one to your British size.

Medical care The following have 24-hour emergency departments: Cedars-Sinai Medical Center, 8700 Beverly Blvd, Beverly Hills ☎310/855-6517 or 423-8780; Good Samaritan Hospital, 1225 Wilshire Blvd, Downtown ☎213/977-2121; Kaiser Permanente, 6041 Cadillac Ave, Mid-Wilshire ☎323/857-2000; and UCLA Medical Center, Tiverton Drive at Le Conte Place, Westwood ☎310/825-2111.

Mexican tourist office and consulate 2401 W Sixth St, 5th Floor, Downtown ☎1-800/44-MEXICO or 213/351-2069, ⊛www.visitmexico.com. Call for general information or pick up a tourist card – necessary if you're crossing the border. Mon–Fri 9am–5pm.

Newspapers Newsstands are scattered throughout the region, and both USC's Doheny and UCLA's Powell libraries have recent overseas publications. Day-old English and European papers are on sale in Hollywood at Universal News Agency, 1645 N Las Palmas Ave (daily 7am–midnight), and World Book and News, 1652 N Cahuenga Blvd (24 hours). See "The media," p.45, for a rundown of LA's papers.

Pharmacies 24-hour pharmacy at Horton & Converse, 11600 Wilshire Blvd, West LA (☎310/478-0801) and at Kaiser's West LA hospital, 6041 Cadillac Ave (☎323/857-2151).

Post office The main Downtown post office, Alameda Station, is located at 760 N Main St (☎213/617-4405), next to Union Station. Open Mon–Fri 8am–7pm, Sat 8am–4pm; mail pick-up Mon–Fri 8am–3pm.

Public toilets Uncommon outside of hotels and restaurants, though sometimes found at larger retailers. Street toilets are a rarity – and rarely clean.

Smog LA air quality can often be very poor and, especially in the valleys in late summer, sometimes quite dangerous. An air-quality index is published daily in the *Los Angeles Times* and if the air is really bad, warnings are issued on TV and radio. For more information contact the South Coast Air Quality Management District (☎1-800/CUT-SMOG, ⊛www.aqmd.gov).

Taxes LA sales tax is 8.25 percent; hotel tax variable, generally 14 percent.

Time Pacific Standard Time (PST), 3 hours behind US Eastern Standard Time and 8 or 9 hours behind GMT, depending on seasonal observance of Daylight Savings Time.

Tipping Generally 15 percent for restaurants, though upscale eateries may expect closer to 20 percent (still, it's up to you) and many restaurants will slap a flat 18 percent charge on parties of six or more. Generally $1 per carried bag at hotels and $1 per day for maid service (both with a minimum $2 tip).

Traffic Check AM radio news channels for frequent updates on which freeways are suffering from gridlock or congestion; if a highway section is particularly immobile, a "Sig-Alert" will be issued, meaning "avoid at all costs." Radio stations emphasizing traffic reports include KNX 1070 AM and KFWB 980 AM; also try ⊛www.sigalert.com on the Internet.

Contexts

Contexts

A brief history of Los Angeles

To casual observers, Los Angeles is a place with no sense of **history**, an ultramodern urban sprawl that lives up to its vapid stereotypes: the land of sunny skies, carefree surfers and Hollywood movie stars. However, since the founding of modern-day LA some two hundred years ago, a potent countermyth has emerged of dystopic LA, in which violent outbreaks and scandals are commonplace, and lying beneath the city's sunny surface is a dark and dangerous underbelly. Although both of these myths have some validity, what they most reveal is LA's sense of drama in viewing itself, and not just the Hollywood variety, either. Whether they see their city as a paradise of oranges and sunshine or a necropolis, Angelenos tend to agree that their chosen metropolis is a harbinger of things to come for the rest of America.

For a list of figures who helped shape the city, see p.386.

Native peoples

For thousands of years prior to the arrival of Europeans, **native peoples** subsisted in different parts of the Los Angeles basin without too much difficulty. The dominant groups in the area were **Tataviam**, **Chumash** and **Tongva** (whom the Spanish called Gabrieleño) peoples. Of these, the dominant tribes were the Chumash, who lived along the coast around modern-day Malibu and Ventura, and the Tongva, who occupied much of the central LA basin. These tribes, however, had little in common, and were an easy target for the **Spanish** conquerors and missionaries – although it's also true that they were wiped out by European-borne epidemics as much as by outright Spanish aggression.

Today, although you'll find few reservations here, LA County is home to the greatest number of native peoples of any county in the US – up to two hundred thousand by some estimates, many migrating from other parts of the US. Indeed, most Native Americans in these parts are now Navajo, and little remains to mark the existence of the early tribes.

European discovery and Spanish colonization

The first explorer to use the name California was **Juan Cabrillo**, who sighted San Diego harbor in 1542, and continued north along the coast to Santa Catalina Island and the Channel Islands off Santa Barbara. He bestowed a number of other place names that survive, including, in the LA area, Santa Monica and San Pedro Bay, named for the first Bishop of Rome.

Other European explorers followed, charting the California coast and naming more of the islands, bays and coastal towns, but it was the **Spanish**, moving up from their base in Mexico, who were to colonize Southern California and map out the future city of Los Angeles.

The Spanish occupation of California began in earnest in 1769 as a combination of military expediency (to prevent other powers from gaining a foothold) and Catholic missionary zeal (to convert the heathen Native Americans). Padre **Junípero Serra** began the missions, setting off from Mexico and going all the way up to Monterey; assisting him was **Gaspar de Portola**, a soldier who led the expedition into LA.

The first mission sited in Los Angeles was **Mission San Gabriel**, in 1771; from that beginning, Spanish military garrisons served to hold the natives, subject to the demands of Franciscan friars who ordered them to abandon their religious beliefs, cultural rituals and languages. The penalties for disobedience were stiff: flogging with twenty to forty lashes was standard practice. Needless to say, while the Spanish were trying to "convert the savages," they were also decimating the native population, reducing their ranks by 95 percent over the course of 150 years. By World War I, fewer than 17,000 natives remained.

The Spanish era

Aside from abusing the natives, the Spanish who colonized Southern California effected the first crude designs for LA, which they established in 1781 at a site northwest of the current Plaza. The city's original **pobladores**, or settlers, of which there were less than fifty, set a multicultural precedent for the region, as they were made up of a majority of black, mestizo, mixed-race and native peoples, with the white Spanish being a distinct, though powerful, minority. The early **pueblo** (town), designed by California's governor **Felipe de Neve**, grew in short spurts, aided by the creation of the *zanja madre*, or "mother ditch," that brought water into town. Despite half-hearted efforts by the Spanish to make the settlement grow, it took a devastating 1815 flood for large-scale development to begin, starting with the construction of the current Plaza and its Plaza Church – La Placita – and Avila Adobe buildings.

As the town grew from remote outpost to regional centerpiece, the power of the Spanish crown began to fade. While the military and missions exercised official power, the functional operation of the little burg was increasingly the province of a small group of mestizo families whose names are still reflected in LA's street names – Sepulveda, Pico and so on – along with a few white American expatriates who for various reasons found the region to their liking. By the early 1800s, the Spanish were playing only a de jure role in city administration; soon after, they would be forcibly removed from power.

Mexican rule

Mexico gained independence in 1821, calling itself the United States of Mexico, and over the next four years, the Mexican residents of Southern California evicted the Spanish and made the region into a territory of Mexico itself – Alta California.

The 24 subsequent years of Mexican rule were marked by some dramatic changes in governance and the social order – and the destruction and looting of many missions – but no end to the oppression of native peoples. The Tongva and others now found themselves at the bottom level of a new hierarchy, where rich land barons controlled huge parcels of land known as **ranchos** and reduced the natives to a state of near-serfdom. Due to widespread social oppression and frequent clashes between the wealthy land bosses (often linked to internal politics in southern Mexico), the period was largely a chaotic one, well described by Richard Henry Dana, Jr in his book *Two Years before the Mast*. By the time Governor **Pio Pico** successfully established his Alta California capital in Los Angeles (long his preferred spot for governance), the period of Mexican rule was almost at an end, its demise assured by the factional struggles and laggardly ways of the ranch owners.

The Mexican–American War

From the 1830s onward, driven by the concept of **Manifest Destiny**, the popular, almost religious, belief that Americans had a divine or moral charge to occupy the country from coast to coast, the US government's stated policy regarding California was to buy all of Mexico's land north of the Rio Grande, the river that now divides the US and Mexico. When President James Polk went ahead and annexed Texas – still claimed by Mexico – war broke out. Most of the fighting in the **Mexican–American War** took place in Texas, though a few skirmishes occurred in Southern California.

By the summer of 1846, after the American capture of Monterey and San Diego, Pico and his colleagues had difficulty even finding significant numbers of loyal Mexicans to defend LA against the US. A truce was signed to avoid bloodshed and American troops walked into the city virtually unopposed. However, despite this relatively pacific start, the military chieftains left local government in the hands of the incompetent **Archibald Gillespie**, who promptly instituted martial law and just as quickly turned the populace against the American presence. The situation further degenerated, with outbreaks of local hostilities, and by the time Mexican general Andreas Pico and American "pathfinder" John C. Fremont signed the final **peace treaty** in January 1847 at Campo de Cahuenga, after several battles and much bloodshed, the chasm between the Mexican residents and their new American conquerors had grown considerably.

Early American rule

California was admitted to the US as the 31st state in 1850, a move quickly followed by the **1851 Land Act**, through which the new white settlers targeted the rancho owners, forcing them to legally prove their right to the land they had been granted. The countless legal battles that ensued left many of the owners destitute, and while the rancho boundaries and some of their elemental chunks continued to linger for up to a century or more, the central goal of the new settlers had been accomplished: the old-line Mexicans were driven out and replaced by a gringo elite. However, even as this process was taking place, and the latest real-estate magnates were consolidating their power, the city's social structure continued its slide into chaos.

For many good reasons, LA was called "**Hell Town**" in the middle of the nineteenth century. The lives of the native peoples got even worse, as they were subject to all manner of mob aggression and legal disenfranchisement. Because the city had no effective municipal authority, and because it was crowded with hordes of aggressive fortune-hunters who had failed in the northern gold rush, it became a magnet for violent criminals and other ne'er-do-wells, and was peppered with gambling halls, saloons and brothels – a Wild West town decades before such a thing existed. The bellicose citizenry usually focused their rage against the groups at the bottom of the social hierarchy, tactics that eventually backfired when roving groups of Mexican bandidos, such as Tiburcio Vasquez, emerged to counter the threats.

The local situation got so bloody that "**vigilance committees**" were created to deal with the crime, which had reached the same levels as San Francisco even though LA only had a tenth as many people. The vigilantes summarily executed 32 people, and gave rise to even more extreme groups who would hunt down lawbreakers, real or imagined, and severely maim or kill them. The El Monte Rangers, an imported gang of Texas thugs, was perhaps the most notorious, though there were many others, and LA remained a city solidly under the thumb of mob rule until after the Civil War.

During the height of its social strife, the area managed to sketch the outlines of what would later become the metropolitan area. Post offices, banks, newspapers and churches were a few of the emblems of encroaching civilization, and the activity of such pioneering entrepreneurs as **Phineas Banning** – the developer of the Wilmington harbor plan – also brought early growth to the city.

In 1860, LA's citizens chose the wrong side in the **Civil War**, casting only a meager 18 percent of their ballots for Abraham Lincoln, and soon became possessed by secessionist rage and racial hatred. Adding to the rancor, many in the city and region were clamoring to split from northern California and create their own autonomous enclave, where they wouldn't be subject to state or federal power. Thirteen thousand soldiers were stationed in Wilmington's Drum Barracks to ensure domestic order and also act against Southwest rebel activity and, later, quash native uprisings. Just as tellingly, a crowd of revelers gathered in LA after hearing news of Lincoln's assassination. Their celebration was broken up – but only with the aid of the federal soldiers.

Late nineteenth-century growth

The last three decades of the nineteenth century were an era of **rapid growth** and **technological change** in LA, principally because of three key factors: periodic real-estate booms that often involved the subdivision of the old ranchos into smaller, more profitable chunks; the building of railroad lines externally, to places like San Francisco, and internally, from Downtown to the port at San Pedro; and the most important factor, the mass arrival of Midwesterners.

From the 1870s, LA gained a reputation as a bastion of healthy living. While eastern American cities were notorious for sooty air and water pollution, LA was touted as a sunny, clean-air paradise where the infirm could recover from their illnesses and everyone could enjoy the fruits of the invigorating desert lifestyle. The **orange** was the perfect symbol of this new arcadia, and trees and citrus groves were planted by the thousands, ultimately leading to towns being named for oranges and walnuts, and streets for magnolias and white oaks. Huge numbers of Iowans and Kansans moved to the city in the Victorian era, spurred on as well by cheap one-way railroad tickets: thanks to a price war between the Santa Fe and Southern Pacific railroads, fares from Kansas City to LA dropped to a mere dollar; before long, the passenger cars were full of church-going Protestants seeking desert salvation.

The Midwesterners of the 1880s did much to displace lingering Hispanic influences, meanwhile exacerbating racial tensions, which flared up in such instances as the **anti-Chinese riot of 1871**. After a disagreement left a white man dead at the hands of a Chinese shopkeeper, a mob assembled and quickly set about attacking and murdering what Chinese residents it could get its hands on. While there were only about two hundred Chinese in LA at the time, the mob managed to strangle, shoot, stab and hang 22 of them. In an ominous portent of LA-style justice, few of the perpetrators faced jail time, and those that did only served a year or so.

Beyond its racial animus and Midwestern migrations, LA was becoming an attraction of sorts for a few of the nation's more colorful characters. **Charles Fletcher Lummis** was the first of these, a fervent supporter of the rights of native peoples, yet also an isolationist who saw a looming threat from foreign immigration. Aside from that, Lummis was a bit of a crank who was so committed to his own notion of healthy living that he created a boulder house, "El Alisal," which still stands in Highland Park, and he took the unusual step of coming to LA from Cincinnati **on foot** – a distance of nearly three thousand miles. Lummis would be just one of many individualists to inhabit the LA region, including others like the Pasadena artisans who created "**Arroyo culture**" just after the turn of the century (an arts-and-crafts philosophy that owed much to Lummis; see box, p.183), and left-wing political activists like **Job Harriman**, whose commune in the northern desert town of Llano del Rio was intended to be the blueprint for a socialist utopia.

While the dreamers and artists experimented with alternative living, the politicians and businessmen were busy expanding the city by every means possible: the **harbor** was developed at San Pedro by Collis Huntington of the Southern Pacific Railroad, **railway lines** were added throughout the region by Collis's nephew Henry, through his electric Red Car transit system, and other entrepreneurs like Edward Doheny grew rich drilling for **oil** throughout the region.

The early twentieth century – water and power

Around the turn of the century, LA's population reached 100,000; perhaps more important to the city's development, however, **William Mulholland** was put in charge of the city's water department. Mulholland was the catalyst for a water-stealing scheme that even now remains legendary: various bankers, publishers and railway bosses purchased large land holdings in the San Fernando Valley, and shortly thereafter, a small cadre of city bankers secretly began buying up land in California's distant Owens Valley 250 miles away. By the time the northern farmers realized what had happened, the bankers had consolidated control over the valley watershed and were making plans to bring the bulk of the region's water to the seemingly drought-stricken citizens of

LA. Seemingly is the key word, for modern evidence suggests that massive amounts of water were being deposited into the city sewers so area dams and reservoirs could drop precipitously, thus making it look like the region was on the verge of a severe drought.

Following the land grab, Mulholland built a **giant canal system** – one of the country's biggest public works projects (see box, p.189) – that carried the stolen water to Southern California, but not LA proper. Instead, the aqueduct mysteriously ended in the San Fernando Valley and city politicians had little choice but to **annex** the valley, thus wiping out thousands of acres of fertile agricultural land and making the real-estate interests there – actually Downtown bankers and political powerbrokers who secretly bought up the land – wealthy beyond imagination. The entire enterprise surely ranks as one of the country's biggest municipal swindles, and one that the Owens Valley farmers did not soon forget. In the 1920s, when Mulholland and company set about acquiring more property for the canal system, the farmers responded by destroying sections of the system with carefully placed dynamite charges. This violence, coupled with the unrelated bursting of the St Francis dam north of LA – a catastrophe that killed more than four hundred people – destroyed Mulholland's reputation. However, by that time, his main work had already been accomplished: the aqueduct helped turn LA into a metropolis.

Accompanying the development of the modernizing city was the growth of **organized labor**. In 1910, a series of strikes at breweries and foundries crippled the city, and local labor was also responsible for nearly bringing socialist Job Harriman to power. However, when the main building of the *Los Angeles Times* – the right-wing organ of labor's archenemy **Harrison Gray Otis** – was bombed, a slow erosion of leftist support took place and ultimately led to defeat for Harriman, who then retreated to his northern desert commune.

World War I to the Great Depression

Metropolis or not, LA continued to display its regressive, provincial character in many ways, especially in its treatment of **minorities**. Chinese residents were still subject to all manner of exclusionary laws, as were the Japanese, and both were among the Asian immigrants targeted by the **1913 Alien Land Bill**, which kept them from purchasing further land tracts and limited their lease tenures. Finally, even though industrial production during World War I doubled the black population of the city, the total number of **African Americans** was still fairly small (less than three percent of the population).

Despite its lack of progressive ideas, rapid growth continued, and after World War I, LA became quite a **tourist magnet** – long before the arrival of Disneyland. Sights like Abbot Kinney's pseudo-European Venice and the carnival midways in Santa Monica and Long Beach all drew good numbers of seasonal visitors, as did Santa Catalina Island and the Mount Lowe Railroad in the San Gabriel Mountains.

Soon, another great **wave of newcomers** began arriving, from all across America. By the 1920s, LA was gaining residents by one hundred thousand per year, most coming by car and flocking to spots that were then and still are **suburbs**: Glendale, Long Beach, Pasadena and so on. **Petroleum** was adding to the boom, from places like Signal Hill to Venice, with oil wells popping up all over the region, usually without regard to aesthetics or environmental pollution. Naturally, the wells helped fuel the explosive growth of the local **car culture**, which even in the 1920s had become a potent force, eventually displacing the Red Car mass-transit system. The quintessential symbol of the dynamic, forward-looking atmosphere of the time was **City Hall**, built as a mix of classical and contemporary elements, and topped by none other than a small replica of one of the long-lost ancient wonders of the world – the Mausoleum at Halicarnassus. This was civic ego on a grand scale, a fitting reflection of the attitudes of the time, but also a symbolic portent of the 1930s.

Into this highly charged environment also came the first **movie pioneers**, whose typically Jewish backgrounds, and origins in the Eastern garment industry, were looked down on by the Downtown elite. Because of exclusionary housing laws, film titans like Adolph Zukor and Samuel Goldwyn developed the Westside as their base of operations, an action that had long-lasting effects. Even today, West Hollywood, Beverly Hills and West LA remain the cultural focus of the city, with Downtown far behind, despite the constant financial efforts of the remaining Downtown elite to remedy the situation.

The boom years ended with the onset of the **Great Depression**. Banks collapsed, businesses went bankrupt, and Midwestern drought brought a new round of immigrants to Southern California, much poorer and significantly more desperate than their forebears. These hard times spawned a number of movements. Led by fiery evangelists like Aimee Semple McPherson, religious **cults** gained adherents by the thousands, Communist and Fascist organizations trawled for members among the city's more frustrated or simple-minded ranks, and the muckraker **Upton Sinclair** emerged as the greatest threat to LA's ruling hierarchy since Job Harriman.

With his **End Poverty in California (EPIC)** campaign, Sinclair frightened the upper crust across the region, and was countered not only by the usual Downtown stalwarts, but also by their Westside adversaries, the Hollywood movie bosses, who rightly perceived a danger in Sinclair's message to their control over the film industry and film-crew labor. Fraudulent newsreel propaganda (showing hordes of homeless men and various halfwits testifying their allegiance to Sinclair) helped speed Sinclair's demise in the gubernatorial contest, but no one could stop the tide of reform, which brought down LA's corrupt mayor **Frank Shaw** and his attendant cronies. The entire political and social mess was reflected in the most famous literary works of the time: Nathanael West's *Day of the Locust* and Raymond Chandler's entire corpus of detective fiction, all of which portrayed a morally decayed society on the verge of collapse.

World War II and after

The misery of the continuing Depression and the dark, paranoid atmosphere in the early part of the war exacerbated the underlying social tensions and unleashed new rounds of violence and oppression against the perceived enemies of white Protestants. Although Chinese citizens had suffered after Union Station was plunked on top of the destroyed, former site of Chinatown, it was the city's Japanese population who now received the full brunt of the region's, as well as the nation's, racial animus. One of Franklin Roosevelt's executive orders gave the green light to mass deportations of Japanese-American citizens, who were forcibly relocated to bleak desert internment camps for the duration of the war. Minorities who hadn't been shipped away made for fat targets as well, especially Mexican Americans.

The **Sleepy Lagoon Murder case** – in which seventeen Hispanics were rounded up and sent to jail for a single murder, only to be later released by a disgusted appellate court – was but a prelude to the turmoil that would come to be known as the **Zoot Suit Riots**, named for the popular apparel Hispanic youth wore at the time, with wide stripes, broad shoulders and accessories like dangling watch chains. Over the course of several days in early June 1943, two hundred sailors on leave attacked and beat up a large number of Mexican Americans – with the assistance of local police, who made sure that the black-and-blue victims were promptly arrested on trumped-up charges. The violence continued until it became a federal issue, causing a rift in international relations between the US and Mexico. After the chaos ended, the LA City Council responded aggressively to the ugly events – by banning the wearing of zoot suits.

Although anti-Asian and -Hispanic feelings still remained, the end of the war brought a shift in hostilities. A growing contingent of **black migrants**, drawn by the climate and defense-related jobs, became the focus of white wrath, and the reason was clear: from 1940 to 1965, the number of blacks in LA increased from 75,000 to 600,000. The white elite did what it could to marginalize the new residents – keeping blacks confined to eastern sections of town around Central Avenue and "redlining" them out of personal loans and business financing – but these tactics only served to heighten the hostility that would later erupt in mass violence.

In the meantime, LA was becoming one of the USA's largest cities almost overnight, with the nonstop arrival of newcomers from across the country, the rebirth of the local economy and the construction of a **vast freeway network** to replace the old Red Cars – due principally to a decline in public transit users and active subversion by oil, gas and automotive interests. Defense industries, notably in aerospace, began a decades-long dominion over the local economy, superseding, most notably, the movie industry, which experienced a sharp decline in the 1950s because of television's impact and governmental antitrust actions (see "The rise of Hollywood," p.365). Not surprisingly, with the rise of the military-industrial complex, the LA region became a focus of Cold War defense as many hilltop sites, from San Pedro to the Santa Monica Mountains, were converted into command centers for launching nuclear weapons, and installations like the Jet Propulsion Laboratory and Edwards Air Force Base became the focus of a local economy still on a war footing.

Concurrently, suburbs like Orange County drew old-time residents from the heart of the city into expanding towns like Garden Grove, Huntington Beach and Anaheim – where **Disneyland** also acted as a pop-culture beacon. The northern valleys traded orange groves for subdivisions and asphalt, and before long, the entire LA basin was swelling with people in every conceivable direction. In contrast, much of the wealth in the Hollywood and Mid-Wilshire sections of town, areas that had first been developed by middle-class automotive travel in the 1920s and 1930s, left with the "white flight" of bourgeois residents to the outlying suburbs, and the old commuter suburbs west of Downtown increasingly became part of the inner city and the new home of working-poor minorities.

The 1960s to the 1980s

The type of right-wing leadership evident in LA's postwar politicians, such as the race-baiting mayor Sam Yorty, and the city's so-called **Committee of 25**, a business cabal that acted as a sort of shadow government from its California Club headquarters, got its comeuppance with 1965's **Watts Riots**. The riots – which started with the arrest of one Marquette Frye for speeding, lasted a week and ended with the arrival of 36,000 police and National Guard troops – caused $40 million worth of property damage and permanently dismantled white LA's beliefs about the perceived laziness of minorities and willingness to accept overt subjugation. While many blacks did not see, and still have not seen, a diminution in poverty levels, the old municipal overlords couldn't help but take notice at the potent brew of anger and frustration they had helped create.

Along with this, the late 1960s **protests** by student radicals, mostly against the involvement in Vietnam, and the emergence of flower power and hippie counterculture caused a dramatic break between generations – the staid Orange County parents versus their rebellious, pot-smoking kids.

After much effort, the progressive forces in LA politics finally began to undermine the corrupt power structure that had ruled LA for nearly a century. Eight years after the riots, LA's first black mayor, **Tom Bradley**, was elected by a coalition of black, Hispanic and Westside Jewish voters. The political success of these groups galvanized others into action on the LA political scene, notably women and gays. Accordingly, the *LA Times*, long a paragon of reactionary yellow journalism, underwent a historic change through the efforts of **Otis Chandler**, son of archconservative former publisher Harry Chandler, who turned the paper into a liberal icon with a range of world-class writers and critics.

Bradley's twenty-year tenure was also marked, less fortuitously, by the disappearance of LA's manufacturing base. South Central and Southeast LA ceased to be centers for oil, rubber and automotive production, the San Fernando Valley saw its car plants close, and heavy industries like Kaiser's mammoth steel-making operation in Fontana shut down. Though this was somewhat tempered in the 1980s by the infusion of foreign money, heavily invested in Downtown real estate, the decade ended hard with the **demise of aerospace jobs**, which had provided the region with its military-industrial meal ticket since the early Cold War era.

Modern LA: The 1990s to the present

The early Nineties continued the hard times, which only got bleaker when black motorist **Rodney King** was videotaped being beaten by uniformed officers of the LA Police Department. The officers' subsequent acquittal by jurors in conservative Simi Valley sparked the April 1992 **riots**, which highlighted the economic disparities between rich and poor, along with the more obvious abuses of police power and privilege. Ten years on, the aftermath of the riots (which involved all races in mass chaos from South Central to

Koreatown and were not simply black versus white) has not yet been fully realized or understood, and new initiatives promised by local and federal authorities to combat LA's endemic violence and poverty never materialized. Meanwhile, episodes like the **O.J. Simpson trial** have only served to further confuse matters. In 1995, Simpson, a black former football star, was acquitted of killing his wife and her friend, in what was termed the "Trial of the Century," an ugly and protracted affair in which public opinion was split along racial lines.

All these factors combined to make the first five years of the 1990s perhaps the bleakest since the Great Depression, and **natural calamities** – regional flooding, Malibu fires and mudslides, and two dramatic earthquakes – only added to the general malaise.

The rest of the decade was not nearly as dramatic. **Richard Riordan**, a multimillionaire technocrat, was mayor for eight years in the mid- to late-1990s and presided over a major **revival** in the city's economic fortunes and a **restructuring** of its economic base – aerospace and automotive industries giving way to tourism, real estate and, as always, Hollywood. New property developments attempted to revitalize blighted sections of town, and even crime and violence tailed off marginally. However, the city's old demons continued to stir. The shocking debacle of the **Belmont Learning Complex** – in which a much-needed school for inner-city youth was carelessly sited over a polluted former oil field and not mothballed until $170 million had been poured in from city coffers – soured many residents on the unaccountable behavior of LA's bureaucrats, but more than anything else, the allegations behind the **Rampart police scandal** (see p.70) – where a group of corrupt police officers acted worse than the gangs they were trying to shut down – made people realize what truly awful elements still lurked under LA's glossy surfaces.

The 2001 mayoral election of bland, uninspiring bureaucrat James Hahn didn't help matters, but his appointment of New York police reformer **William Bratton** to head the LAPD surprised many, giving hope that an outsider with no connection to the department's entrenched ways might be just the person to reform it.

The rise of Hollywood

To this day, the word **Hollywood** remains synonymous with the motion picture industry, even if the reality of that association has not always held true. What follows is a brief history of the movie business in Los Angeles and how the studio system took root in Hollywood, from its genesis to the beginning of its decline.

Westward migration

While we now think of Hollywood's emergence as a simple matter of abundant sun, low taxes and cheap labor – all important factors, to be sure – the original reason the first film-makers established themselves here was due to something much simpler: **fear**. But for the strong-arm tactics of Thomas Edison and company, the movie business might never have come to Southern California.

Edison and his competitors (companies like Biograph, Vitagraph and Pathé, among many others) had by 1909 consolidated their various patents on film technology and processing to form what was known as "**the Trust**": the Motion Picture Patents Company (the MPPC). Although it didn't even last a decade (thanks to bad business practices and a federal antitrust suit), the MPPC did manage to scare off many directors and producers in the first years of its existence, including producer William Selig and director Francis Boggs, both of whom wanted to get as far away from the MPPC's seat of power, New York City, as they possibly could. Southern California was their choice, and more prominent film-industry figures soon followed, finding the taxes, labor costs and abundant shooting locations much to their liking.

Early Hollywood

Thomas Ince, **Mack Sennett** and **D.W. Griffith** were the early film legends who helped to establish Hollywood as the focus of the American movie business. Ince, with his studios in Culver City and Edendale, and his coastal "Inceville" north of Santa Monica, founded the elemental model of the studio system that was to hold sway for many decades: writers would prepare detailed scripts in collaboration with directors and Ince himself, after which a tightly budgeted production would be filmed at pre-arranged locations, and a final cut of the movie would be carefully edited. This sort of precise planning minimized the possibility of surprises during shooting, as well as groundbreaking or idiosyncratic storytelling, and contributed to the factory-like character of Ince's operation.

By comparison, Sennett's **Keystone Film Company** in Edendale, in East Hollywood, produced Keystone Kops comedies in less rigorous fashion. However, with production needs mounting, Sennett adopted his former colleague's model (both had worked for Triangle Films in Culver City) and went on to a two-decades-long career making his signature brand of wacky entertainment.

The largest creative presence in early Hollywood was, however, D.W. Griffith, who began as a theatrical actor and director of one-reel shorts and reached the peak of his fame with *Birth of a Nation*, a runaway hit in 1914 – despite its glamorization of the Ku Klux Klan, its epic length (2hr 40min) and its unprecedented $2 admission fee. Woodrow Wilson praised the film for "writing history with lightning," overlooking that its source was not actual history, but the bigoted ramblings of Southern preacher Thomas Dixon, on whose book, *The Clansman*, the movie had been based.

Generating a firestorm of controversy with the film, Griffith fired back at his critics with his next film, *Intolerance* – a bloated historical epic – but only succeeded at shooting himself in the foot. With its preachy moralizing and colossal sets loaded with Babylonian columns and squatting elephants, *Intolerance* became a buzzword for box-office failure and directorial narcissism. Long before this, Griffith would make a slow slide into obscurity in the 1920s, but not before he perfected the essential aesthetic components he developed with *Birth of a Nation*: close-ups, flashbacks, cross-cutting and the like.

The birth of the big studios

In 1913, **Cecil B. DeMille**, an itinerant theatrical actor and director, came west to rent a horse barn for a movie. From this simple act, DeMille and his partners, glove-maker Sam Goldfish (soon to be renamed Goldwyn) and vaudeville producer Jesse Lasky, established the basis for the big studios that would follow. The film made in the barn (even as there were horses still in it) was *The Squaw Man*, which became a huge commercial triumph; DeMille became one of the early industry's most bankable directors of historical and biblical epics, and Lasky and Goldwyn later teamed with Adolph Zukor to create the colossus known as **Paramount Studios**.

Like other studios in the coming decades, Paramount used a number of tactics to push its product, including "block booking" (in which film packages, rather than individual films, were sold to exhibitors, thus maximizing studio revenue) and buying up theater chains across the country (to ensure exhibition spaces for its films). These influential practices served to consolidate the industry. By the end of World War I, three major studios had risen to dominance: Paramount, **Loew's** and **First National** – though only Paramount would survive in name during the height of the studio system.

The 1919 creation of **United Artists (UA)** looked promising for actors and directors. This studio, formed by Douglas Fairbanks Jr, Mary Pickford, D.W. Griffith and Charlie Chaplin, seemed to suggest a greater role might be in store for the creative individuals who actually made the films, instead of just the studio bosses and executive producers. Things didn't quite work out that way, and the next decade saw UA in the role of bit player, along with Columbia and Universal, principally because it didn't own its own theaters and had to rely on one of the major studios for booking its films. The one major development UA prefigured was the dominance of the **star system**, by which big-name actors (such as Fairbanks and Pickford), rather than writers, directors or the story itself, would drive the production and marketing of studio product – a scheme that has barely changed in more than eighty years.

The golden age

The five largest studios from the 1920s to the 1940s were **Paramount**, the **Fox Film Corporation** (later 20th Century-Fox), **Warner Bros**, **Radio-Keith-Orpheum** (known later as RKO), and the biggest of them all, **Metro-Goldwyn-Mayer**, or MGM, which was controlled by the still-powerful Loew's corporation in New York. The majors used every method they could to rigidly control their operations, and they did much to industrialize the business, breaking down the stages of production and using specialists (editors, cinematographers and so on) to create the product. The arrival of **sound** in the late 1920s further specialized the industry, and the possibility of a lone professional with a camera shooting a nationally released film vanished.

Ince's original system had been perfected into rigorous, clinical efficiency. Even the content of the movies was controlled, in this case because of **Will Hays**, who was hired away from the corrupt Harding administration, where he was Postmaster General, when a series of 1920s scandals (not least, Fatty Arbuckle's three trials for the murder-rape of actress Virginia Rappe) tarnished the industry and raised the specter of government censorship. Hays' major claim to fame was as the developer of the 1930 "**Hays Code**," a series of official proscriptions and taboos that the studios were supposed to follow, involving intimations of sex, miscegenation, blasphemy and so on. Although Hays is often credited with enforcing movie-industry censorship, it was actually **Joseph Breen** who wielded the real censorial power starting in the mid-1930s, when the Code first began to be rigidly enforced. With Breen and the Catholic organization the Legion of Decency looking over its shoulder, Hollywood produced a brand of entertainment that was safe, fun and mostly noncontroversial. That film-makers like John Ford, Orson Welles, Howard Hawks and Preston Sturges were able to make classic films in such a stifling environment says much about the degree of talent the studios were employing during this time – although the industry also produced many tepid, cloying melodramas and tiresome serials that followed the Code precisely and today remain almost unwatchable.

Although Hollywood was, as an industrial system, unmatched by any other production complex in the world, it was, even at its height, something of an illusory power. For while the most visible and glamorous of the movie industry's stars and bosses smiled for the paparazzi in Hollywood, the real financial muscle continued to come from New York City. Companies like Loew's, which were based there, had the power – infrequently used until the 1950s – to command studios like MGM to change their policies and even films, simply by applying pressure in the corporate boardroom. It was only the financial discipline of the Southern California tycoons, their ability to turn a handsome profit and their fear of the Wall Street honchos that kept Hollywood with a reasonable degree of autonomy. And when times turned bad, New York took over – firing even the all-powerful Louis B. Mayer in 1951.

The demise of the studios

The emergence of the **film noir** style at the end of World War II should have sounded a warning to the old studio system. With bleak storylines, chiaroscuro photography, morally questionable antiheroes and dark endings, film noir was an abrupt departure from many of Hollywood's previous aesthetic conventions. This stylistic change, and the postwar disillusion it reflected, preceded several major transformations that permanently altered the way the studios did business.

The greatest threat to the system, the **federal government**, in its antitrust prosecution of Paramount, was beginning to dismantle the practices of block booking and theatrical ownership that had kept the majors in firm control over the exhibition of their films. The increasing power of independent producers, helped by this and other structural changes, also removed some of the majors' control over the industry, as did the increasing ability of actors to finally use the star system to their advantage by not allowing the studios to lock up their careers for interminable lengths of time (starting with Olivia de Havilland, who sued Warner Bros to get out of her contract and won in California's supreme court after a three-year legal battle). Along with these changes, television reduced film viewership by great numbers and the studio bosses had to resort to desperate devices like 3-D, widescreen and Cinerama to try to lure back their audiences.

Furthermore, the institution that the Hays Code had censored, with the blessing of Congress, began to come under direct attack from McCarthyite politicians. The House Un-American Activities Committee (HUAC) dredged up information on the alleged presence of Communist and left-leaning groups in Hollywood, and many screenwriters, actors and directors were either humiliated into testifying or found themselves on an internal **blacklist** that kept them from working.

After the HUAC proceedings, Hollywood was creatively damaged, but the government's activities didn't keep directors like Otto Preminger from challenging the Hays Code. Through a series of legendary battles, on films like *The Moon is Blue* and others, Preminger and other film-makers succeeded in throwing off the yoke of the Code, which had been in place for more than thirty years. This change, combined with the diminishment of pressure groups like the Legion of Decency, further loosened the control of the studio bosses over movie content and later led to the establishment of the **ratings system** in place today.

The aftermath

By the end of the 1950s, the studio system, at least as it had been known, was finished, and it took many years for the majors to regain much of the ground they had lost. However, while the industry eventually **rebounded** – through greater international sales and the development of ancillary markets like cable TV and home video – and moviemaking has become profitable once more to the studios (if not necessarily for their investors), it's unlikely that the industry will see a return to Depression-era days, when each studio churned out hundreds of films per year.

Currently, Hollywood only manages to pump out a few big-budget spectacles and a declining number of medium-budget flicks – often cumulatively less than twenty annual films per studio. Modern American film-making, driven by exorbitant **talent costs**, is quite different from the old mechanized industry between the wars. Television–film studio mergers, videotape sales and multimedia production have only served to highlight the differences from the old way of doing business. In one way, though, the studios have reasserted their dominance: by bringing innovative independent companies like Miramax under their wing, they have ensured that risky, lower-budget productions come under their direct control, to their direct benefit – just like the old days.

LA on film

Since its birth in the 1910s, Hollywood has often searched its own back-yard for compelling scenes and interesting stories. While not always successful in conveying the truth of LA to a film audience, Hollywood **films** have nevertheless helped define the city for domestic and foreign audiences alike. The list below focuses on films that best use their LA backdrop as well as key works in Hollywood film history, and films tagged with a ✴ are particularly recommended.

Hollywood does Hollywood

Barton Fink (Joel Coen 1991). Tinseltown in the 1940s is depicted by the Coen brothers as a dark world of greedy movie bosses, belligerent screenwriters and murderers disguised as traveling salesmen. Allegedly based on the experience of playwright Clifford Odets.

The Big Knife (Robert Aldrich 1955). An incisive portrayal of Hollywood politics, in which a weak-willed actor can't get free from the tentacles of a hack director, despite the pleas of his wife. Based on a play by Clifford Odets and filmed like one as well.

Day of the Locust (John Schlesinger 1975). Somewhat awkward realization of the classic satire by Nathanael West. The author's vivid colors are rendered here as bland pastels. See "Books," p.378, for a review of the source.

Ed Wood (Tim Burton 1994). The ragged low-budget fringes of Fifties Hollywood are beautifully re-created in this loving tribute to the much-derided auteur of *Plan 9 from Outer Space* and *Glen or Glenda*. Gorgeously shot in black and white, with a magnificent performance by Martin Landau as an ailing Bela Lugosi.

Gods and Monsters (Bill Condon 1998). An interesting, fact-based tale of the final days of 1930s horror-film director James Whale, ignored by the moviemaking elite and slowly dying of malaise by his poolside in Hollywood. The title refers to a memorable Ernest Thesiger line from Whale's classic *Bride of Frankenstein*.

Good Morning, Babylon (Paolo and Vittorio Taviani 1987). Two restorers of European cathedrals find themselves in 1910s Hollywood, working to build the monstrous Babylonian set for D.W. Griffith's *Intolerance*, in this Italian story of the contribution of immigrants in early Tinseltown. Oddly enough, that same set has now been rebuilt in Hollywood – as part of a mall (see p.99).

Hollywood Canteen (Delmer Daves 1944). Based on an actual, eponymous Hollywood establishment where popular movie stars from the World War II era sang and danced to a bevy of toe-tapping tunes. Most of Warner Bros' stars were featured in the picture – those that wouldn't appear were labeled "unpatriotic."

Hollywood on Trial (David Helpern Jr 1976). This interesting documentary examines the early 1950s witch-hunts in Hollywood and the blacklisted screenwriters, actors and directors.

Hollywood Shuffle (Robert Townsend 1987). Ultra-low-budget, scattershot satire on movie hiring practices and racial bias. When it's on target, though, it's scathingly funny.

Hurlyburly (Anthony Drazan 1998). David Rabe's acidic play about Hollywood players and hucksters is rendered in celluloid as a prattling pathos-fest, with much angst for Sean Penn and Chazz Palminteri and much ironic detachment for Kevin Spacey and Garry Shandling.

LA Story (Mick Jackson 1991). LA in-jokes and movie allusions abound in this low-key comedy starring Steve Martin as a lovelorn TV weatherman.

The Last Tycoon (Elia Kazan 1976). F. Scott Fitzgerald's unfinished, would-be masterpiece is here rendered as an interesting failure: a rich, opulent world of Hollywood gloss that translates into slow, clumsy storytelling.

★ **The Player** (Robert Altman 1992). Tim Robbins is a studio shark who thinks a disgruntled screenwriter is out to get him; he kills the writer (at South Pasadena's *Rialto* theater; see p.184), steals his girlfriend and waits for the cops to unravel it. A wickedly sharp satire about contemporary Hollywood, with some great celebrity cameos.

Postcards from the Edge (Mike Nichols 1990). Written by Carrie Fisher, an insider's look at behind-the-scenes Hollywood, with Meryl Streep as the drug-addicted daughter of pushy glamour-queen Shirley MacLaine – thinly veiled versions of Fisher and her mother, Debbie Reynolds.

Singin' in the Rain (Stanley Donen/Gene Kelly 1952). A merry trip through Hollywood set during the birth of the sound era. Gene Kelly, Donald O'Connor and Debbie Reynolds sing and dance to many classic tunes, including "Good Morning," "Moses," "Broadway Melody" and countless others.

A Star Is Born (William Wellman 1937; George Cukor 1954). Based on the film *What Price Hollywood?* (see below), these adaptations tell the story of the rise of a starlet mirroring the demise of her Svengali. Janet Gaynor and Fredric March star in the 1930s version, Judy Garland and James Mason in the later. Both are worthwhile, while a 1977 remake with Barbra Streisand and Kris Kristofferson runs a distant third.

The State of Things (Wim Wenders 1982). A European filmmaker sees his financing disappear while stranded in LA and is beset by boredom in his mobile home. Essential if you're a fan of Wenders or of music by the punk band X – then near their peak.

Sullivan's Travels (Preston Sturges 1941). A high-spirited comedy about a director who wants to stop making schlock pictures and instead create gritty portrayals of what he thinks real life to be. The first two-thirds are great, though the film ends in mawkish fashion.

★ **Sunset Boulevard** (Billy Wilder 1950). Award-winning film about a screenwriter falling into the clutches of a long-faded silent-movie star. William Holden was near the beginning of his career, Gloria Swanson well past the end of hers. Erich von Stroheim fills in nicely as Swanson's butler, and even Cecil B. DeMille makes a cameo appearance.

Swimming with Sharks (George Huang 1994). Movie producer Kevin Spacey spits venom at assistant/whipping boy Frank Whaley, with predictably vengeful results.

The Way We Were (Sydney Pollack 1973). Aside from the Barbra Streisand–Robert Redford pairing and cloyingly memorable songs, a worthwhile portrait of the dark days of the Red Scare and Hollywood blacklist of the 1950s.

What Price Hollywood? (George Cukor 1932). The template for the *A Star Is Born* movies that followed:

Constance Bennett is the starlet, an ambitious waitress, and Lowell Sherman is the drunken director.

Whatever Happened to Baby Jane (Robert Aldrich 1962). Bette Davis and Joan Crawford are former child stars who plot against one another in a rotting Malibu house. A fine slice of modern horror.

Who Framed Roger Rabbit? (Robert Zemeckis 1988). Despite being a live-action/cartoon hybrid, a revealing film about 1940s LA, where cartoon characters suffer abuse like everyone else and the big corporations seek to destroy the Red Car transit system.

LA crime stories

Beverly Hills Cop (Martin Brest 1984). Still-amusing Eddie Murphy flick, in which the actor plays an unorthodox, fast-talking Detroit detective who takes LA by storm while trying to solve a murder case.

The Big Sleep (Howard Hawks 1946). One of the key film noirs of the 1940s, with Humphrey Bogart playing Philip Marlowe, and featuring a wildly confused plot – even screenwriter Raymond Chandler admitted he didn't know who killed a particular character – that ends up being subordinate to the crackling chemistry between Bogie and Lauren Bacall.

Chinatown (Roman Polanski 1974). One of the essential films about the city. Jack Nicholson hunts down corruption in this dark criticism of the forces that animate the town: venal politicians, black-hearted land barons, crooked cops and a morally bankrupt populace. Great use of locations, from Echo Park to the San Fernando Valley.

Dead Again (Kenneth Branagh 1991). The director's take on LA is a creative adaptation of film noir, and features plenty of plot twists, humor, and a gallery of notable American and British actors.

Devil in a Blue Dress (Carl Franklin 1995). Terrific modern noir, in which South Central detective Easy Rawlins (Denzel Washington) navigates the ethical squalor of elite 1940s white LA and uncovers a few ugly truths about the city's leaders.

Double Indemnity (Billy Wilder 1944). The prototypical noir film. Greedy insurance salesman Fred MacMurray collaborates with harpy wife Barbara Stanwyck to murder her husband and cash in on the settlement. Edward G. Robinson lurks on the sidelines as MacMurray's boss.

Get Shorty (Barry Sonnenfeld 1995). Slick Miami gangster Chili Palmer, played by John Travolta, takes up residence in Tinseltown and decides he wants to become a movie producer, in this amusing adaptation of an Elmore Leonard novel.

The Glass Shield (Charles Burnett 1995). Institutionalized racism in the LAPD is brought under the harsh glare of director Burnett, one of the great chroniclers of LA's black urban underclass.

The Grifters (Stephen Frears 1990). A memorable film with Annette Bening, John Cusack and Anjelica Huston playing the title characters, con artists hunting through the LA underworld for their next victims.

He Walked by Night (Alfred Werker 1948). This vérité-style crime story set in "the fastest growing city in the nation" starts with a random cop-killing in Santa Monica and ends with a manhunt through the 700-mile subterranean city storm-drain system, stunningly shot by torch-light by peerless noir cinematographer John Alton.

Heat (Michael Mann 1995). Stars big names like De Niro and Pacino, but this crime drama, which does include some stunning set-pieces (eg a Downtown LA shootout), is ultimately less than the sum of its parts, with a frustratingly predictable ending.

In a Lonely Place (Nicholas Ray 1950). One of the all-time great noirs, and an unconventional one at that. Humphrey Bogart is a disturbed, violent screenwriter who causes trouble for those around him, particularly girlfriend Gloria Grahame – at the time, the director's real-life ex-wife.

Jackie Brown (Quentin Tarantino 1997). A glorious return to form for Pam Grier, who, as a tough airline stewardess, plays the perfect foil for Samuel Jackson's smooth gangster. LA provides the dark, menacing backdrop.

LA Confidential (Curtis Hanson 1997). Easily the best of the contemporary noir films, a perfectly realized adaptation of James Ellroy's novel about brutal cops, victimized prostitutes and scheming politicians in 1950s LA. Even the good guys, Russell Crowe and Guy Pearce, are morally questionable.

The Long Goodbye (Robert Altman 1973). Altman intentionally mangles noir conventions in this Chandler adaptation. Elliott Gould plays Marlowe as a droning schlep who wanders across a sun-drenched landscape of casual corruption, encountering bizarre characters like nerdy mobster Marty Augustine, played with relish by movie director Mark Rydell, and Sterling Hayden as a hulking alcoholic writer. Old-time screenwriter Leigh Brackett freely changes Chandler's original ending.

Murder My Sweet (Edward Dmytryk 1944). One-time Busby Berkeley crooner Dick Powell changed his tune and became a grim tough-guy detective in the best work from this director, who was briefly blacklisted for his former communist ties, then ratted on his colleagues once he was released.

One False Move (Carl Franklin 1991). A disturbing early role for Billy Bob Thornton, as a murderous hick who kills some people in an LA bungalow with his girlfriend and a psychotic, nerdy colleague, then gets pursued by the LAPD and a small-town Arkansas sheriff.

Point Blank (John Boorman 1967). Engaging, somewhat pretentious art-house flick with Lee Marvin as a hit man out for revenge. Begins and ends in Alcatraz, but in between successfully imagines LA as an impenetrable fortress of concrete and glass. Remade as the 1999 Mel Gibson vehicle *Payback*.

The Postman Always Rings Twice (Tay Garnett 1946). Lana Turner and John Garfield star in this seamy – and excellent – adaptation of the James M. Cain novel, first brought to the screen as *Ossessione*, an Italian adaptation by Luchino Visconti. Awkwardly remade by Bob Rafelson in 1981 with Jessica Lange and Jack Nicholson.

Touch of Evil (Orson Welles 1958). Supposedly set at a Mexican border town, this noir classic was actually shot in a seedy, decrepit Venice. A bizarre, baroque masterpiece with Charlton Heston playing a Mexican official, Janet Leigh as his beleaguered wife, and Welles himself as a bloated, corrupt cop addicted to candy bars.

True Romance (Tony Scott 1993). With a Quentin Tarantino plot to guide them, Patricia Arquette and Christian Slater battle creeps and gangsters amid wonderful LA locations, from seedy motels to the classic *Rae's Diner* in Santa Monica.

Apocalyptic LA

Blade Runner (Ridley Scott 1982). The first theatrical version may have flopped, but the recut director's version confirms the film's stature as a sci-fi classic, in which dangerous "replicants" roam the streets of a dystopic future LA and soulless corporations rule from pyramidal towers.

Earthquake (Mark Robson 1974). Watch the Lake Hollywood dam collapse, people run for their lives and chaos hold sway in the City of Angels. Originally presented in "Sensurround!"

Falling Down (Joel Schumacher 1993). Fired defense-worker Michael Douglas tires of the traffic jams on the freeways and goes on a rampage through some of the city's less picturesque neighborhoods, railing at petty injustices and wreaking havoc at every turn.

Kiss Me Deadly (Robert Aldrich 1955). Perhaps the bleakest of all noirs, starring Ralph Meeker as brutal detective Mike Hammer, who tramples on friends and enemies alike in his search for the great "whatsit" – a mysterious and deadly suitcase.

Lost Highway (David Lynch 1997). A lurid, frightening take on the city by director Lynch, using nonlinear storytelling and actors playing dual roles, and which had critics screaming for the exits, but if you like Lynch, this is essential viewing.

Strange Days (Kathryn Bigelow 1995). In a chaotic, nightmarish vision of LA, Ralph Fiennes, Angela Bassett and Juliette Lewis run around the city screaming-in the new millennium. More interesting as a reflection of mid-1990s LA angst than as compelling cinema.

The Terminator (James Cameron 1984). Modern sci-fi classic, with Arnold Schwarzenegger as a robot from the future sent to kill the mother of an unborn rebel leader. Bravura special effects and amazing set-pieces here were successfully followed up with the director's 1989 sequel, *T2: Judgment Day*, in which Arnold becomes a good robot.

Volcano (Mick Jackson 1997). A memorably cheesy disaster flick in which a volcano pops up near the La Brea Tar Pits, and Tommy Lee Jones and Anne Heche fight the lava with gusto.

Contemporary life in LA

Anywhere but Here (Wayne Wang 1999). Susan Sarandon pursues stardom for daughter Natalie Portman in the City of Angels. Based on the novel by Mona Simpson.

Bob & Carol & Ted & Alice (Paul Mazursky 1969). Once-daring, but still funny zeitgeist satire about wife-swapping and bed-hopping in hedonistic Southern California, starring Natalie Wood, Robert Culp, Elliott Gould and Dyan Cannon as the titular foursome.

Boyz N the Hood (John Singleton 1991). An excellent period piece that cemented the LA stereotype as a land of gangs and guns, starring Cuba Gooding Jr in his first big role, and Laurence Fishburne as his dad.

Clueless (Amy Heckerling 1995). Jane Austen's *Emma* transplanted to a rich Southern California high school, with a fine performance by Alicia Silverstone as a frustrated matchmaker.

Dogtown & Z-Boys (Stacy Peralta 2002). Even if you have no interest in skateboarding, this is a fun, high-spirited look at the glory days of the sport, when a daring group of LA kids took to using the empty swimming pools of the elite as their own private skate-parks.

Ghost World (Terry Zwigoff 2001). Sardonic portrait of alienated high-schooler Thora Birch trying to find her place in a grim LA world of strip malls, pointless jobs and adult lies. Based on an equally effective and groundbreaking comic strip.

Go (Doug Liman 1999). A kinetic joyride through LA's rave subculture told from three perspectives, including Sarah Polley's botching of an aspirin-for-Ecstasy drug sale, and Jay Mohr and Scott Wolf – as two TV soap stars – stuck in a police sting operation.

Grand Canyon (Paul Mazursky 1992). An overly sentimental flick that many movie fans love anyway, made at the nadir of LA's self-loathing of the early 1990s, involving folks from various races and classes trying to get chummy and rediscover their humanity.

The Limey (Steven Soderbergh 1999). Gangster Terence Stamp wanders into a morally adrift LA looking for his daughter's killer, and finds the burned-out husk of former hippie Peter Fonda. Arguably this director's best work.

The Loved One (Tony Richardson 1965). An effective adaptation of Evelyn Waugh's pointed satire about the dubious practices of the funeral industry, inspired by a trip to Forest Lawn.

Magnolia (Paul Thomas Anderson 1999). A darkly affecting travelogue of human misery starring Jason Robards and Tom Cruise, among many others. The San Fernando Valley serves as an emotional inferno of abusive parents, victimized children, haunted memories and a mysterious plague of frogs.

Mi Familia (Gregory Nava 1994). The saga of the Sanchez family, featuring fine performances by a range of Hollywood's best Hispanic actors, including Jimmy Smits, Edward James Olmos and Esai Morales. Overly earnest and sentimental in places, though.

Mi Vida Loca (Alison Anders 1993). Depressing ensemble piece about the hard lives of Latinas in Echo Park girl-gangs and the central reason the director won a prestigious MacArthur Fellowship.

Pulp Fiction (Quentin Tarantino 1994). A successful collection of underworld stories by then-hot director Tarantino. Set against a backdrop of downtrodden LA streets, bars, diners and makeshift torture chambers.

The Rapture (Michael Tolkin 1991). Mimi Rogers plays an LA telephone operator who abandons her hedonistic lifestyle after hearing a fundamentalist group talking about the impending "Rapture," and becomes born again, ultimately heading into the desert to await Armageddon. Michael Tolkin's wonderfully literal film takes his premise just as far as it can go, and then some.

Safe (Todd Haynes 1995). In Haynes' brilliant tale of millennial unease and corporeal paranoia, Julianne Moore plays a San Fernando Valley homemaker with seemingly little inner-life and an opulent outer one, who is diagnosed with environmental sickness and finds refuge at a New Age desert retreat.

Short Cuts (Robert Altman 1993). Vaguely linked vignettes tracing the lives of LA suburbanites, from a trailer-park couple in Downey to an elite doctor in the Santa Monica Mountains. Strong ensemble cast bolsters the intentionally fractured narrative.

Slums of Beverly Hills (Tamara Jenkins 1998). Troubled teen Natasha

Lyonne deals with growing pains in a less-than-glamorous section of town, where a pill-popping cousin, manic uncle, weird neighbors and her own expanding bustline are but a few of her worries.

Speed (Jan de Bont 1994). Ultimate LA action flick, in which a bus careens through the freeways and boulevards of the city – and will blow up if it slows below 50mph. Much better than its sequels.

Star Maps (Miguel Arteta 1997). Melodrama of immigrant life on the fringes of Hollywood. Carlos, who has grandiose dreams of movie stardom, is doing time in his father's prostitution ring, standing on street corners ostensibly selling maps to stars' homes, in reality selling his body for cash.

Swingers (Doug Liman 1996). Cocktail culture gets skewered in this flick about a couple of dudes who flit from club to club to eye "beautiful babies" and shoot the breeze like Rat Pack–era Sinatras. Many LA locales shown, including the *Dresden Room* and *The Derby*.

"Way-out" West

Barfly (Barbet Schroeder 1987). Mickey Rourke channeling writer Charles Bukowski in this liquor-soaked romp through LA's seedy world of low-lifes, fistfights and general depravity.

Beach Blanket Bingo (William Asher 1965). A cult favorite – the epitome of sun-and-surf movies, with Frankie Avalon and Annette Funicello singing and cavorting amid hordes of wild-eyed teenagers.

The Big Lebowski (Joel Coen 1998). A bizarre Coen foray into LA, exploring the lower-class underbelly of the city – Jeff Bridges' "The Dude" and his pal John Goodman uncover mysteries, meet peculiar characters, and do lots and lots of bowling.

Boogie Nights (Paul Thomas Anderson 1997). A suburban kid from Torrance hits the big time in LA – as a porn star. Mark Wahlberg, Julianne Moore and Burt Reynolds tread through a sex-drenched San Fernando Valley landscape of the disco years.

Car Wash (Michael Schultz 1976). Laid-back party flick about laboring in LA during the de-romanticized 1970s, set to a fun disco soundtrack.

Down and Out in Beverly Hills (Paul Mazursky 1986). A West Coast adaptation of Jean Renoir's classic *Boudu Saved from Drowning*, with homeless Nick Nolte salving the nerves of nouveau riche neurotics.

Escape from LA (John Carpenter 1996). In John Carpenter's alternative vision of the future, LA is cut off from the mainland by an earthquake and has been turned into a deportation zone for undesirables. Sent in to uproot insurrection, Kurt Russell battles psychotic plastic surgeons and surfs a *tsunami* to a showdown in a netherworld Disneyland.

House on Haunted Hill (William Castle 1958). Not the clumsy remake, but the glorious Vincent Price original, with the King of Horror as master of ceremonies for a ghoulish party thrown at his Hollywood Hills estate – actually, Frank Lloyd Wright's Ennis-Brown house (see p.91).

★ **Mulholland Drive** (David Lynch 2001). Told in the director's inimitable style, a nightmarish tale of love, death, glamour and doom in LA – in which elfin cowboys mutter cryptic threats, elegant chanteuses lip-sync to phantom melodies, and a blue key can unlock a shocking double identity.

Permanent Midnight (David Veloz 1998). A grim tour through the city's drug subculture, with Ben Stiller as your heroin-addicted guide. Based on the autobiographical novel by former sitcom-writer Jerry Stahl, who was responsible for *Alf*.

Repo Man (Alex Cox 1984). Emilio Estevez is a surly young punk who repossesses cars for Harry Dean Stanton. Very imaginative and fun, and darkly comic.

Seconds (John Frankenheimer 1966). One of Rock Hudson's better performances, as a bored suburbanite who gets a second chance at life transplanted in the body of a younger man. Bleak in its treatment

of Southern California's swinging Sixties.

Shampoo (Hal Ashby 1975). Using LA as his private playground, priapic hairdresser Warren Beatty freely acts on his formidable, though nonchalant, libido. A period piece memorable for its 1970s look.

They Live (John Carpenter 1988). Ludicrous but entertaining horror flick, in which a drifter living on the outskirts of LA discovers that aliens are subliminally encouraging the city's rampant consumerism.

Valley Girl (Martha Coolidge 1983). Early Nicolas Cage flick, in which the actor winningly plays a new-wave freak trying to woo the title character (Debra Foreman) in a clash of LA cultures. Good soundtrack, too.

Drama and history

Colors (Dennis Hopper 1988). Early chronicle of gang warfare in LA, directed with flash and vigor by Hopper.

The Doors (Oliver Stone 1991). Val Kilmer plays the great Jim Morrison at the height of his 1960s debauchery, under the frenetic direction of Oliver Stone.

Fat City (John Huston 1972). Great late-Huston film starring Stacy Keach as a washed-up boxer and Jeff Bridges as his young, incompetent charge. Quietly and effectively depressing.

The Killing of a Chinese Bookie (John Cassavetes 1976). Strange and self-indulgent, but perfectly evoking the sleazy charms of the Sunset Strip, Cassavetes' behavioral crime story about a club-owner (Ben Gazzara) in hock to the mob is just one of his many great LA-based character studies.

La Bamba (Luis Valdez 1987). The fictionalized story of Ritchie Valens,

the LA rocker who died in an untimely plane crash with Buddy Holly. Lou Diamond Phillips gives a compelling performance, despite looking nothing like Valens.

Less Than Zero (Marek Kanievska 1987). More valuable as a period piece than as inspired cinema, a depiction of the drug habits of fatuous LA youth. The book wasn't much better.

Nixon (Oliver Stone 1996). A long, dark look at the first president from Southern California (played by Anthony Hopkins), as well as the old-time LA suburbs where he grew up.

 Rebel without a Cause (Nicholas Ray 1955). Troubled-youth film, starring, of course, James Dean. A Hollywood classic with many memorable images, notably the use of the Griffith Park Observatory as a shooting location.

Stand and Deliver (Ramon

Menendez 1988). Inspired by the story of East LA's miracle-working teacher Jaime Escalante, played effectively by Edward James Olmos. A somewhat moving film better suited for TV than the big screen.

They Shoot Horses, Don't They? (Sydney Pollack 1969). Gloomy story set during the Depression, in which contestants desperately try to win money in an exhausting dance marathon. Aptly reflects the fatalistic attitudes of the late 1960s.

To Sleep with Anger (Charles Burnett 1990). An interesting view of LA's overlooked black middle-class, directed with polish by a very underrated African-American filmmaker.

Tupac and Biggie (Nick Broomfield 2002). In-your-face documentary about the murders of rappers Tupac Shakur and Notorious B.I.G., implicating hip-hop producer Suge Knight and rogue elements of the LAPD.

Zabriskie Point (Michelangelo Antonioni 1970). Muddled, pretentious misfire from the director that nonetheless features some promising early work by Jack Nicholson and visually interesting shots of the LA basin.

Zoot Suit (Luis Valdez 1981). A simplified overview of the Sleepy Lagoon Murder case and resultant anti-Hispanic violence, told as a musical.

Books

n the reviews below, publishers are listed in the format US/UK, unless the title is available only in one country, in which case the country has been specified. Highly recommended titles are signified by 🗖 . Out-of-print titles are indicated by o/p.

Travel and general

Mike Davis *Ecology of Fear* (Metropolitan Books). Despite containing certain factual errors, a compelling read about LA's apocalyptic style, focusing on gloom and doom in movies and literary fiction, the danger of earthquakes and fires, mountain-lion attacks and even tornadoes.

Robert Koenig *Mouse Tales* (Bonaventure Press). All the Disneyland dirt that's fit to print: a behind-the-scenes look at the ugly little secrets – from disenchanted workers to vermin infestations – that lurk behind the happy walls of the Magic Kingdom.

Anthony Lovett and Matt Maranian *LA Bizarro* (St Martin's Press). Without a doubt the best alternative, off-kilter guide to the city: indispensable reading if you're touring LA's dingiest motels, grungiest bars, goofiest architecture and most infamous death sites.

Jan Morris *Destinations* (Oxford University Press UK). A collection of essays that appeared in *Rolling Stone*, only one of which is about LA, but as Joan Didion said in response to the piece, "She got it."

 Leonard Pitt and Dale Pitt *Los Angeles A to Z* (University of California Press US). If you're truly enthralled by the city, this is the tome for you: six hundred pages of encyclopedic references covering everything from conquistadors to movie stars.

Kevin Roderick *The San Fernando Valley: America's Suburb* (Los Angeles Times Publishing). A surprising and occasionally intriguing view of the history, geography and culture of "The Valley," provided by one of its former denizens.

Alexander Vertikoff and Robert Winter *Hidden LA* (Gibbs-Smith). An architecture photographer and writer present their favorite unheralded sights in the metropolis, using glossy photos to highlight such spots as the Monrovia's *Aztec Hotel* and the tomb of Henry Huntington.

John Waters *Crackpot* (Random House; Fourth Estate). The irreverent director of cult classics like *Pink Flamingos* and *Hairspray* takes you on a personalized tour of the city's seamy underside.

Paul Young *LA Exposed: Strange Myths and Curious Legends in the City of Angels* (Griffin). Lurid Hollywood mysteries and sordid urban lore from the last century revealed in a fast-paced and readable style.

History and politics

Oscar Zeta Acosta *Revolt of the Cockroach People* (Vintage). The legendary model for Hunter S. Thompson's bloated "Dr. Gonzo," the author was in reality a trailblazing Hispanic lawyer who used all manner of colorful tactics to defend oppressed and indigent defendants. A striking, semi-autobiographical portrait of 1970s East LA, written just before the author's mysterious disappearance.

Lou Cannon *Official Negligence* (Times Press US). One man's version of the 1992 riots, which lets the Rodney King–beating cops off easy while concentrating its attack against LA's political leadership and the upper brass of the LAPD.

Gordon DeMarco *A Short History of Los Angeles* (Lexicos US o/p). A 180-page summary of the major events and phenomena that have shaped the city, with particular regard to class and racial struggles. Excellent reading.

Robert Fogelson *The Fragmented Metropolis: Los Angeles 1850–1930* (University of California Press US). Deftly covers a hefty chunk of local history, with significant insight. A sweeping story from the early "Hell Town" to the go-go days of the 1920s.

Lynell George *No Crystal Stair* (Anchor; Verso). A depressing account of the struggles of LA's African-American community, rendered in precise, painful detail.

Robert Gottlieb and Irene Wolt *Thinking Big: The Story of the Los Angeles Times* (Putnam US). An insightful look at the way the city's biggest and most important newspaper has reported and manipulated the news through the years.

Paul Greenstein et al *Bread and Hyacinths: The Rise and Fall of Utopian Los Angeles* (Classic Books US). A chronicle of efforts to create communal living by some city activists, particularly the socialist and near-mayor Job Harriman.

Norman Klein *A History of Forgetting* (Verso). A good companion to Mike Davis's *City of Quartz* (above), uncovering some of the political ugliness and minority oppression that have characterized LA's past.

Carey McWilliams *Southern California: An Island on the Land* (Gibbs-Smith US). Still one of the most important books about the city ever written, detailing the social clashes and intrigues that rocked LA in the first half of the twentieth century. McWilliams brings special insight as the lead defense attorney in LA's shameful prosecution of the Sleepy Lagoon Murder case.

Harris Newmark *Sixty Years in Southern California: 1853–1913* (Houghton Mifflin US). One of the great nineteenth-century leaders of the Jewish community offers an insider's take on the region's politics as well as various secrets of the time.

Don Normark *Chavez Ravine, 1949* (Chronicle). Black-and-white photographs and a compelling narrative provide a vivid look at life in a rural Hispanic community on the fringes of Downtown LA, just before the area was paved over to make way for Dodger Stadium.

★ **Mark Reisner** *Cadillac Desert* (Penguin). An essential guide to water problems in the American West, with special emphasis on LA's schemes to bring upstate California water to the metropolis. One of the best renderings of this sordid tale.

Jack Smith *Jack Smith's LA* (McGraw-Hill US). A collection of the author's wry, incisive columns for the *Los Angeles Times*, which details the daily life of the city and its many assorted urban characters.

Kevin Starr *Material Dreams: Southern California through the 1920s* (Oxford University Press). The third of the author's five-volume series on the history of LA, from the late rancho period to the years after World War II, and perhaps the most interesting, covering the city's boom years and its attendant scandals and colorful celebrities.

Urban theory

Jean Baudrillard *America* (Verso). A sacred text for some academics (arrogant ramblings to others), posing such profundities as Disneyland being the real America and everything else being fake.

★ **Mike Davis** *City of Quartz: Excavating the Future in Los Angeles* (Vintage; Pimlico). A leftist counterpoint to Kevin Starr's mainstream history (see below). Written in the early 1990s, Davis's descriptions of racial hatred, security-system architecture, shifty politicians and industrial decay have dated somewhat, and his fact-finding methods have been questioned, but there's still plenty here worth reading.

Umberto Eco *Travels in Hyperreality* (Harcourt Brace US). A pointed examination of "simulacra," and a nice literary time capsule of Southern California life several decades ago, discussing such things as a now-closed museum in Orange County that re-created the great works of art as wax figurines.

William Fulton *The Reluctant Metropolis: The Politics of Urban Growth in Los Angeles* (Solano Press US). A highly readable account of political and economic conflicts in contemporary LA, with notable sections on modern Chinatown and the aftermath of the 1992 riots.

Blake Gumprecht *The Los Angeles River: Its Life, Death and Possible Rebirth* (Johns Hopkins University Press). The downhill history of the LA River, from its early days as a meandering stream to its concrete paving to its final transformation into a bleak, lifeless flood channel.

Merry Ovnick *Los Angeles: The End of the Rainbow* (Balcony Press). A riveting account of the city's political and social struggles, as seen through its institutions and architecture.

W.W. Robinson *Ranchos Become Cities* (San Pasqual Press US). A chronicle of the changes that turned the old Mexican rancho system into subdivided plots of land fit for real-estate speculation, urban growth and massive profit-taking.

Architecture

★ **Reyner Banham** *Los Angeles: The Architecture of Four Ecologies* (Penguin). The book that made architectural historians take LA seriously, and still an enjoyable read. Valuable insights on the city's freeways, vernacular buildings and cultural attitudes circa 1971.

Federal Writers Project *The WPA Guide to California* (Pantheon US). A 1939 guide that serves as a remarkable handbook to the architecture and neighborhoods of the time.

David Gebhard and Harriette Von Breton *Los Angeles in the Thirties: 1931–1941* (Hennessey & Ingalls US). Great old black-and-white photos documenting LA's Streamline Moderne architecture.

David Gebhard and Robert Winter *Los Angeles: An Architectural Guide* (Gibbs-Smith US). Still the definitive guide to the city's architecture, covering a full range of structures from programmatic to Art Deco to modern, despite being published in 1994.

Philip Jodidio *Contemporary California Architects* (Taschen). An overview of the city's most vibrant and influential architects, including Frank Israel, Eric Owen Moss and Frank Gehry. Somewhat lacking in analysis, but filled with splendid color images.

Sam Hall Kaplan *LA Lost and Found* (o/p). Of interest for the excellent pictures that accompany this former newspaper critic's lament for the good old days of local architecture.

Esther McCoy *Five California Architects* (Hennessey & Ingalls US). This still-relevant 1960s book was the first to draw attention to LA's Irving Gill, an early twentieth-century forerunner of the modern style, as well as other important architects who practiced in Southern California.

Robert McGrew and Robert Julian *Landmarks of Los Angeles* (Abrams). A large-format guide, with numerous large, glossy photos, listing LA's historic sights and structures.

Richard Meier *Building the Getty* (Knopf). Highly readable account of the conception and creation of the Getty Center, as told by its architect,

the prince of modernism.

Charles Moore *The City Observed: Los Angeles* (Random House US). Twenty-year-old volume that's still worth a look for its maps, pictures and anecdotes, plus recommendations to set you on your way to exploring the old-time nooks and crannies of LA.

Elizabeth A.T. Smith *Blueprints for Modern Living: History and Legacy of the Case Study Houses* (MIT Press US). An excellent compendium of essays and articles about the built and unbuilt homes of the Case Study Program (see box on p.107), with descriptions, diagrams and photographs of each.

Robert Winter *The Hollywood Bungalow* (Hennessey & Ingalls US). A discussion of the vernacular housing style that can be found throughout the city, and a good companion to an informal tour of such homes.

Music

Clora Bryant et al *Central Avenue Sounds: Jazz in Los Angeles* (University of California Press US). Vividly re-creating the bouncy, kinetic scene on Central Avenue in the mid-twentieth century, and telling a long-overdue story in LA's, and the nation's, musical history.

Don Snowden *Make the Music Go Bang: The Early LA Punk Scene* (St Martin's Press). One of the few volumes on a critical stage in local music history, this book is most valuable for its striking pictures from the 1970s, highlighting such bands as

Black Flag, the Germs and X.

Mark Spitz and Brendan Mullen *We Got the Neutron Bomb: The Untold Story of LA Punk* (Three Rivers Press US). Long-overdue recollection of the glory days of the local punk and thrash scene in the 1970s.

Danny Sugarman *Wonderland Avenue* (Sphere; Abacus). The former Doors' publicist gives a mind-bending tour of the local rock scene from the late 1960s on, providing lurid accounts of famous and infamous figures.

Hollywood and the movies

Kenneth Anger *Hollywood Babylon* (Bantam; Arrow). Deliciously dark and lurid stories of sex scandals, bad behavior and murder in Tinseltown, written by the *enfant terrible* of 1960s

experimental films. Not especially well written, but it holds your attention throughout.

Robert Berger *The Last Remaining Seats* (Balcony Press; Princeton

Architectural Press). An excellent photo guide to the extant movie palaces of Los Angeles, including many shots of theaters that are now closed to the public.

Peter Bogdanovich *Who the Devil Made It* (Random House US). Acclaimed book of conversations with great old Hollywood film-makers, including Alfred Hitchcock, Fritz Lang and Howard Hawks.

David Bordwell, Janet Staiger and Kristin Thompson *The Classical Hollywood Cinema* (Columbia University Press; Routledge). Learn all about the techniques used by film-makers and studios up to the 1960s: cross-cutting, eyeline-matches, the shooting axis and other devices that you may not know by name, but have seen in countless movies.

Kevin Brownlow and John Kobal *Hollywood: The Pioneers* (Knopf US). An intriguing look at the founders of American cinema in the silent era, told from the points of view of an esteemed film historian and preser-vationist, and a prolific writer on movie topics.

Carrie Fisher *Postcards from the Edge* (Pan/Picador UK; currently o/p in US). The real-life Princess Leia had serious problems: a mother from hell, the pressures of teenage stardom and the unstoppable force of the Hollywood Movie Machine. After caving in to chemical comfort, she cleaned up her act, rebuilt her rela-tionship with Mom and wrote this memorable book - a *Heart of Darkness* for 1980s Hollywood.

Otto Friedrich *City of Nets: A Portrait of Hollywood in the 1940s* (University of California Press; Headline). Descriptions of the major actors, directors and studio bosses of the last good years of the studio sys-tem, before TV, antitrust actions and Joe McCarthy ruined it all.

Ian Hamilton *Writers in Hollywood: 1915–1951* (Carroll & Graf US). A revealing look at screenwriters from the early days of the studio system up to its decline, with special focus on literary heavyweights like F. Scott Fitzgerald and William Faulkner, who also wrote for the movies.

Charles Higham *Hollywood Cameramen* (o/p). A discussion of seven of the great masters of cine-matography, whose work in lighting movie classics has been all too fre-quently overlooked by the general public. A classic read, with a few copies still floating around.

Gerald Horne *Class Struggle in Hollywood: 1930–1950* (University of Texas Press US). Excellent exploration of a commonly overlooked aspect of Tinseltown – the ongoing strife between labor unions and the studios, which culminates here with a dramatic strike and subsequent violence.

★ **Ephraim Katz** *The Film Encyclopedia* (Harper). The essential reference guide for anyone interested in the movies, providing valuable information on the old movie companies and countless studio-system bit players, along with more contemporary figures. The first, 1980, edition is the best.

Sidney Kirkpatrick *Cast of Killers* (GK Hall o/p). Fascinating account of the death of director William Desmond Taylor in the early 1920s, and the bizarre circumstances sur-rounding it. Based on the previously unpublished research of old-time film-maker King Vidor.

Colin McArthur *Underworld USA* (Viking US o/p). One of the best analyses of the Hollywood gangster film, as realized by directors from Fritz Lang to Don Siegel.

Corey Mitchell *Hollywood Death Scenes* (Olmstead Press US). A valu-able guide to the seamy side of movieland, covering all the famous murders – from the Black Dahlia to Charles Manson – with pictures of the morbid sites, then and now.

Julia Phillips *You'll Never Eat Lunch in This Town Again* (Signet; Mandarin). Amusing, if somewhat self-serving, portrayal of the drugs and violence behind the Hollywood gloss.

Thomas Schatz *The Genius of the System* (Henry Holt; Faber & Faber). A laudatory account of the big studios and bosses of the golden age of movies, covering the structure of the industry and detailing the major and minor players. A bit overbroad in its praise, but still a very worthwhile read.

Alain Silver and Julia Ward *Film Noir: An Encyclopedic Reference to the American Style* (Overlook). A large-format guide to the bleak films of the 1940s to the present, and an essential title that has gone through many editions.

Jerry Stahl *Permanent Midnight* (Warner). When his employers on TV's *Alf* heard that star writer Stahl was spending more than his already-huge paycheck to support his heroin and other habits, they gave him a raise to cover the difference and keep him on the job. The result is another gritty descent into (and miraculous recovery from) Tinseltown drug hell.

Fiction

T.C. Boyle *Tortilla Curtain* (Penguin; Bloomsbury). Set in LA, this book boldly borrows its premise – a privileged white man running down a member of the city's ethnic underclass – from Tom Wolfe's *Bonfire of the Vanities*, but carries it off to great satiric effect.

Kate Braverman *Palm Latitudes* (Penguin US o/p) Vivid tales of three women experiencing their own idiosyncratic struggles in hard-knocks LA. Worth looking for, though it's long been out of print.

Charles Bukowski *Post Office* (Black Sparrow). An alcohol- and sex-soaked romp through some of LA's festering back alleys, with a mailman surrogate for Bukowski as your guide. One of several books by the author exploring his encounters with the city's dark side.

James M. Cain *Double Indemnity, The Postman Always Rings Twice, Mildred Pierce* (Vintage; Picador). With Raymond Chandler, the ultimate writer of dark, tough-guy novels. His entire oeuvre is excellent reading, but these three are the best explorations of LA.

Raymond Chandler *Farewell, My Lovely, The Long Goodbye, The Lady in the Lake* (Random House; Penguin). All of these books, and several more, have been adapted into movies, but Chandler's prose is inimitable: terse, pointed and vivid. More than just detective stories (centered on gumshoe detective Philip Marlowe), these are masterpieces of fiction.

Susan Compo *Life After Death and Other Stories* (Faber). The club life of the black-clad members of the local goth-rock scene is the subject here, and the author's prose brings it to life in sordid detail.

Joan Didion *Play It as It Lays* (Vintage US). Hollywood rendered in booze-guzzling, pill-popping, sex-craving detail. Oddly, the author went on to write the uninspired script for a third adaptation of *A Star is Born*.

Steve Erickson *Amnesiascope* and *Arc d'X* (Henry Holt US o/p). The two best of the author's wildly florid, postmodern novels about the city, featuring bizarre characters in surreal settings.

John Gregory Dunne *True Confessions* (Dutton o/p; No Exit Press). The tale of an LA cop and his priestly brother, based in part on the city's notorious Black Dahlia Murder case. A first-rate book, made into a second-rate movie.

Bret Easton Ellis *Less Than Zero* (Vintage; Picador). Whining, drug-addicted LA youth criticized and glorified in a prototypical 1980s novel.

James Ellroy *The Black Dahlia, The Big Nowhere, LA Confidential, White Jazz* (Warner; Arrow). The LA Quartet: an excellent saga of city cops from the postwar era to the 1960s, with each novel becoming progressively more complex and elliptical in style.

John Fante *Ask the Dust* (Black Sparrow; Rebel Inc.). The first and still the best of the author's stories of itinerant poet Arturo Bandini, whose wanderings during the Depression highlight the city's faded glory and struggling residents.

Robert Ferrigno *The Horse Latitudes* (Avon; Pocket Books o/p). A drug-dealer-turned-academic begins a descent into a bizarre LA world when he encounters a corpse at his home, possibly left by his missing ex-wife.

David M. Fine *Imagining Los Angeles: A City in Fiction* (University of New Mexico Press US). Excellent overview of fiction set in LA, from early historic romances to detective novels to apocalyptic tales.

F. Scott Fitzgerald *The Last Tycoon* (Macmillan; Penguin). The legendary author's unfinished final work, a major novel on the power and glory of Hollywood. Intriguing reading that gives a view of the studio system at its height.

Chester Himes *If He Hollers Let Him Go* (Thunder's Mouth Press; Serpent's Tail). A fine literary introduction to mid-twentieth-century race relations in LA, narrated by one Bob Jones, whose struggles mirror those of author Himes, who eventually ended up living in Spain.

Aldous Huxley *Ape and Essence*

(I.R. Dee; Flamingo). Imaginative depiction of post-nuclear LA, in which books are burned in Pershing Square for warmth and the *Biltmore* hotel is the site of an annual orgy.

Christopher Isherwood *Down There on a Visit* (Noonday Press; Minerva). Incisive, involving read by a British expatriate, who penned much of his later fiction in and on Southern California.

Helen Hunt Jackson *Ramona* (New American Library; Fisher Press). Ultraromanticized depiction of mission life that rightfully criticizes the American government's treatment of Indians while showing the natives to be noble savages and glorifying the Spanish exploiters. Not particularly good reading, but a valuable period piece – and perhaps the most influential piece of fiction ever written about LA.

Gavin Lambert *The Slide Area* (Serpents Tail US). Seven short tales focusing on the dark side of Hollywood and LA's beachside towns, first published over forty years ago but still absorbing for its urban insights and lurid details.

Elmore Leonard *Get Shorty* (Bantam; Penguin). Ice-cool mobster Chili Palmer is a Miami debt collector who follows a client to Hollywood, and finds that the increasing intricacies of his own situation are translating themselves into a movie script.

Ross MacDonald *Black Money* (Vintage; Allison & Busby). Private detective Lew Archer pilots himself through the nasty underworld of LA society, both high and low. A captivating read.

Walter Mosley *Devil in a Blue Dress, A Red Death, White Butterfly, Black Betty, A Little Yellow Dog, Bad Boy Brawly Brown* (Pocket Books; Pan). Six excellent modern noir novels featuring black private detective Easy Rawlins, who "does favors" from his South Central base. Mosley compellingly brings to life Watts and, later, Compton.

Kem Nunn *Tapping the Source* (Four Walls Eight Windows Press). One of the most unexpected novels to emerge from California beach culture, this eerie murder-mystery is set amid the surfing scene of Orange County's Huntington Beach.

Thomas Pynchon *The Crying of Lot 49* (HarperPerennial; Vintage). The hilarious adventures of techno-freaks and potheads in Sixties California, revealing among other things the sexy side of stamp collecting.

John Ridley *Love is a Racket* (Knopf; Bantam). A delightful slice of Hollywood hell, in which protagonist Jeffty Kittridge, slumming through the dregs of local society and being abused by countless predators, leads us on a darkly comic journey through LA's many bleak corners.

Geoff Ryman *Was* (Penguin). A pop-lit masterpiece that bizarrely updates and twists the *Wizard of Oz* for more contemporary times, creating a fascinating work of Southern Californian magical realism.

Danny Santiago *Famous All Over Town* (NAL US). A compelling portrayal of life in a struggling Hispanic community, set in the barrio of East LA, and featuring a cast of street gangs.

Budd Schulberg *What Makes Sammy Run?* (Vintage). Classic anti-Hollywood vitriol by one of its insiders, a novelist and screenwriter whose acidic portrait of the movie business is unmatched.

Mona Simpson *Anywhere but Here* (Vintage; Faber). Engaging story of a mother's desire to put her daughter on the fast track to Hollywood stardom. Recently made into a less inspired movie (see p.373).

Upton Sinclair *The Brass Check* (Ayer Press o/p). The failed California gubernatorial candidate and activist author's vigorous critique of LA's yellow journalism and the underhanded practices of its main figures. Sinclair also wrote *Oil!*, about the city's 1920s oil rush, and *The Goose Step*, concerning collegiate life at USC.

Terry Southern *Blue Movie* (Grove Press). Sordid, frequently hilarious take on the overlap between high-budget moviemaking and pornography, with the author's vulgar themes and characters cheerfully slashing through politically correct literary conventions.

Michael Tolkin *The Player* (Grove Atlantic; Faber). A convincing look at the depravity and cut-throat dealings of the film-making community, with special scorn reserved for venal movie execs. Made into a classic flick by Robert Altman (see p.370).

Gore Vidal *Hollywood* (Modern Library). The fifth volume in the author's "Empire" series about emerging US power on the world stage, this one focusing on the movie industry, its interaction with Washington bigwigs and boundless capacity for propaganda.

Joseph Wambaugh *The Onion Field* (Dell US). One in a group of crime novels by a former LAPD cop. The most worthwhile in the author's series of LA tales, all of them gripping, popular reading, even if none is up to the rarefied levels of Cain and Chandler.

Evelyn Waugh *The Loved One* (Little Brown). The essential literary companion to take with you on a trip to Forest Lawn – here rendered as Whispering Glades, the pinnacle of funerary pretension and a telling symbol of LA's status-obsessed ways.

★ **Nathanael West** *The Day of the Locust* (Signet; Picador UK o/p). The best book about LA not involving detectives; an apocalyptic story of the characters on the fringes of the film industry, culminating in a glorious riot and utter chaos.

Glossaries

LA people

AUTRY Gene The "singing cowboy" who starred in a string of successful Westerns, reaching the height of his popularity in the years before World War II. Wrote *Here Comes Santa Claus*; also owned baseball's Anaheim Angels.

BALDWIN Lucky Wealthy mining investor who developed the Santa Anita racetrack in 1873, also founding and becoming the mayor of Arcadia, where the track is located. In 1909, he acquired the future site of the 1932 summer Olympics, now known as "Baldwin Hills."

BANNING Phineas The "Father of the LA Harbor," Banning founded the town of Wilmington, though it never actually became the harbor site. He also built the first rail line in Southern California, connecting Downtown LA with the ocean.

BOWRON Fletcher From 1938 to 1953, the reform mayor who streamlined city services, abolished the LAPD's underhanded "Red Squad," and brought the city back from the utter corruption of his criminal predecessor, Frank Shaw. One of the few public figures to quickly, and publicly, recant his support for Japanese internment during World War II.

BRADLEY Tom A former police officer who became LA's first black mayor in 1973, Bradley was instrumental in building up Downtown and in staging the 1984 Olympics.

CABRILLO Juan Portuguese explorer who claimed the coast of Southern California for his employer, Spain. More associated with San Diego than LA, though he did name several local geographic points such as San

Pedro Bay, and now has an aquarium there named for him.

CALL Asa Insurance executive who exercised inordinate control over LA politics and affairs of the 1950s and 1960s, including electing mayors and spurring Downtown investment. As a prime mover in the elite, secretive "Committee of 25," Call was nicknamed "Mr Big."

CHANDLER Harry Publisher of the *Los Angeles Times* from 1917 to 1941 and son-in-law of Harrison Gray Otis. The classic right-wing conservative, Chandler and his paper fought against unions, socialism and the like. Son Otis turned the paper on its head in 1960, bringing it a liberal bent and, finally, quality journalism.

CHAPLIN Charlie Seminal comedy actor/director whose Little Tramp character is known to audiences worldwide. He was also the co-founder of United Artists and a prime force behind the emergence of the star system.

DEMILLE Cecil B. Larger-than-life director of biblical epics like *The Ten Commandments*, but also one of the creators of the silent-movie success *The Squaw Man*, which helped lead to the creation of Paramount Studios.

DISNEY Walt Legendary creator of Mickey Mouse, Disney Studios and a bevy of theme parks, of which Disneyland was only the first, in 1955. Guarded, sometimes paranoid, personality who was not nearly as animated as his films – though contrary to popular belief, was buried, not frozen, at Forest Lawn.

DOHENY Edward Wildly successful oil entrepreneur who was implicated as the man who bribed Interior

Secretary Albert Fall in the 1923 Teapot Dome scandal.

DOMINGUEZ Juan Jose Spanish soldier and cattle rancher who owned the 76,000 acres of Rancho Palos Verdes and Rancho San Pedro.

EISNER Michael Disney CEO and still one of the most powerful executives in Hollywood, running a multimedia empire of music, movies, theme parks and television.

FAIRBANKS Douglas Popular Hollywood swashbuckler and husband to Mary Pickford, both of whom helped found the United Artists studios. One of the few stars to successfully make the transition from silent to sound films.

GATES Daryl Controversial LA police chief from 1978 to 1992, popular with politicians and fellow cops, but blamed by residents for helping create the hostile climate that led to the riots of 1992, which cost him his job. Famous for the line, spoken at a Congressional hearing, "Casual drug users should be taken out and shot. Smoke a joint, lose your life."

GEHRY Frank Perhaps LA's most famous architect – creator of the Geffen Contemporary museum and his own bizarre Santa Monica house, as well as the Vitra Design Museum in Germany, the Guggenheim Museum in Spain and LA's Disney Hall (p.58), scheduled to be unveiled in fall 2003.

GETTY J. Paul LA oil baron turned art collector. His holdings, originally contained in his small oceanside residence, now reside in the hilltop Getty Center.

GILL Irving Once nearly forgotten local architect whose Mission/modern hybrids helped chart the course for much of LA's later modernist buildings. His best work, the Dodge House, was sadly demolished in the 1960s.

GOLDWYN Samuel One-time glove manufacturer (and formerly Sam Goldfish) who helped create the film *The Squaw Man* in a horse barn with Cecil B. DeMille and Jesse Lasky. Despite his prominence in the industry, Goldwyn left his various partnerships before they became the legendary studios (Paramount and MGM) of Hollywood.

GREENE Charles and Henry Architects and brothers whose firm built many local examples of Craftsman houses, notably Pasadena's Gamble House (p.183) – which, like other of their works, also includes a number of Japanese influences.

GRIFFITH David Wark Known by his initials "D.W.," one of Hollywood's most prominent early directors and a co-founder of United Artists. Made his name with *Birth of a Nation*; undid much of his success with the bomb *Intolerance*.

GRIFFITH Griffith J. Mining millionaire who gave LA the land for a large, centrally located park on the crest of the Hollywood Hills. Also known for shooting his wife in the eye in a drunken rage, and spending two years in San Quentin Prison for attempted murder.

HAHN Kenneth One of the most powerful county supervisors in LA history, who engineered the funding of hospitals, mass transit and emergency freeway call-boxes, and helped steer baseball's Dodgers away from Brooklyn.

HAMMER Armand Oil-industry executive who founded Occidental Petroleum and greatly helped business relations between the US and Soviet Union. Also an intrepid art collector who relocated his stash of paintings from the LACMA to his own eponymous museum in Westwood.

HARRIMAN Job Utopian socialist who ran for LA mayor in 1911, though his candidacy was undone by his association with confessed bombers of the *LA Times* building. Defeated again in the next election, Harriman withdrew to his social colony of Llano del Rio in the Antelope Valley (p.197).

HEARST William Randolph Though not an Angeleno per se, had inordinate influence on LA politics and culture through his ownership of the *Los Angeles Examiner* (later *Herald-Examiner*), the more liberal rival to the *LA Times*. Also known for his extramarital courtship of actress Marion Davies and possible involvement in the death of producer Thomas Ince.

HUGHES Howard Tool-dynasty heir behind Hughes Aircraft who later controlled TWA as well. As a movie producer, he scored big with *The Outlaw*, a Jane Russell vehicle that dared to show cleavage. Lived his last years in a Las Vegas hotel suite as a paranoid recluse surrounded by Mormon manservants.

HUNTINGTON Henry Nephew of railroad magnate Collis Huntington and developer of the Pacific Electric Railway. As the largest landowner in California, Huntington was able to bring his "Red Cars" to cities across the basin; after selling out to the Southern Pacific Railroad in 1910, he developed philanthropic enterprises like the Huntington Library and Gardens in San Marino.

INCE Thomas Early movie producer whose studios, in Culver City and the San Ynez Canyon (nicknamed "Inceville"), helped standardize and streamline the film-making process. Died near the height of his success in 1924 – rumored to have been accidentally shot by William Randolph Hearst while aboard Hearst's yacht.

KING Rodney Black motorist whose beating at the hands of LA cops was captured on videotape and replayed for the nation to see; the

1992 riots ensued after the cops were acquitted. Amid the violence, he famously remarked "Can't we all just get along?"

KINNEY Abbot Wide-ranging entrepreneur who devised Venice of America, a city of quasi-quattrocento buildings and canals near the sea that was meant as a beacon for cultural activity, but which turned into a carnival zone and, later, a polluted oil-well site.

LUMMIS Charles City editor of the *Los Angeles Times*, early historic preservationist, city librarian and founder of the Southwest Museum. Lummis created El Alisal, a boulder house in Highland Park that served as the model for many other local wood-and-stone structures.

MAHONY Roger Current cardinal of Los Angeles, and major player in American Catholic politics, whose liberal outlook on immigrants were first seen in his moving the official seat of ecclesiastical power from the Westside to Downtown. Oversaw the building of a $50 million cathedral – Our Lady of the Angels (see p.58) – atop Bunker Hill.

MANSON Charles Head of his own "family" of societal dropouts, who lived out at Spahn Ranch and occasionally came down to visit LA's Westside and plan the murders of Sharon Tate and others. Convicted and condemned to die in a major 1970 trial at the Hall of Justice, then let off the hook when the US Supreme Court temporarily overturned the death penalty.

MASON Biddy Former slave, nurse and midwife who gained freedom and wealth. Moving to LA, she became a major property-owner Downtown. Best known for co-founding the seminal First African Methodist Zion Church, one of LA's most prominent African-American institutions.

MAYER Louis B. In a town known for bigger-than-life Hollywood studio bosses with colossal powers and egos, Mayer was perhaps the exemplar: the head of MGM who ran the company with an iron fist and oversaw its dominance of the golden age. Was unceremoniously fired in 1951 when times turned sour.

McINTYRE James Francis Far-right Catholic cardinal, the first ever from the western US, who ruled from his St Basil's headquarters from 1953 to 1970. Prominent in local politics as an avid McCarthyite and red-baiter, he went on to become a major proponent of the LAPD's paramilitary tactics and, later, of the Vietnam War.

McPHERSON Aimee Semple Legendary, vivacious preacher who founded the Foursquare Gospel Church in Echo Park, which was famed for its circus-like religious spectacles and fiery orators. Briefly disappeared under suspicious circumstances, then resurfaced in a public scandal when her vanishing act was linked to a Hollywood tryst.

MORRISON Jim Lead singer of legendary 1960s rock group The Doors, which often performed on the Sunset Strip. Had artistic pretensions, occasionally obscene stage antics and, perhaps inevitably, an unseemly death in a Paris hotel.

MULHOLLAND William Engineer who constructed the LA Aqueduct from Northern California, commenting on the public arrival of the water, "There it is! Take it!" Later defamed for shoddy building methods in the St Francis dam collapse that killed 450 people, though exonerated after his death.

MURPHY Franklin Huge figure in LA's civic affairs, one who helped build the Music Center and LA County Museum of Arts, along with teaching medicine and acting as chancellor at UCLA (where an excellent sculpture garden is named for him). One of the few liberal members of the shadowy Committee of 25.

MURRAY Cecil Leader of the First AME Church in South Central LA and one of the city's more visible and respected ministers, whose calls for calm in the days after the 1992 riots were somewhat heeded.

NEUTRA Richard Along with fellow Austrian ex-pat Rudolf Schindler, a prominent advocate for architectural modernism and builder of a slew of clean, white geometric homes, the most famous of which is the Lovell House.

NIXON Richard The 37th US president, with a checkered political career that includes starting the Cambodian bombing campaign, opening ties with China and the Soviet Union, and engaging in a variety of "high crimes and misdemeanors" that led to his 1974 resignation. His birthplace and library are at Yorba Linda in Orange County.

O'MALLEY Walter Owner and president of the Dodgers baseball team, who moved the club to LA from Brooklyn in 1958 – an action still held in contempt by old-time New Yorkers. O'Malley quickly stirred up local controversy by siting the new Dodger stadium on land slated for low-income housing in Chavez Ravine.

ORCUTT William Early oil geologist who uncovered many fossil finds from the La Brea Tar Pits and whose San Fernando Valley ranch is still an appealing place to visit.

OTIS Harrison Gray Brigadier general and real-estate magnate who owned and edited the *Los Angeles Times*, a newspaper he shaped into a paragon of right-wing, anti-labor ideology.

OVITZ Mike The head of the Creative Artists Agency in the 1980s and early 1990s, the most powerful group of Hollywood agents in Tinseltown history, which drove up actor salaries and made the film business less profitable for the major studios.

PARKER William LA supercop from 1950 to 1966, who fought corruption in the force, which had reached staggering levels under some of his predecessors. Unfortunately, he also allowed minorities to be brutally treated, which led in no small part to the Watts Riots in 1965.

PICKFORD Mary Queen of the silent screen, known as "America's Sweetheart," and best remembered for starring in films like *Rebecca of Sunnybrook Farm*. Also co-founded United Artists studios with husband Douglas Fairbanks in 1919, and built the lavish – now demolished – Pickfair mansion in the Hollywood Hills.

PICO Pío The last Mexican governor of California, who fled after the Mexican–American War but later returned to LA to own several sizeable ranchos and properties. Unfortunately, bad luck and poor judgment led to the collapse of his finances, and he died in poverty in 1894.

PORTOLA Gaspar de Leader of the first Spanish exploratory mission into what is today LA, in 1769, trekking around the basin near the current Plaza and Sepulveda Pass. A soldier and governor of Baja California, Portola later became Alta California's first governor.

PUCK Wolfgang Master chef and culinary celebrity, the man who made the restaurant *Spago* synonymous with chic California eating.

REAGAN Ronald Fortieth US president, head of the Screen Actors Guild, fervent right-winger and anti-Communist, and B-list movie actor who starred in such flicks as *Bedtime for Bonzo* and *The Killers* (his creative high point). His

presidential library is located in Simi Valley.

RIORDAN Richard Multimillionaire powerbroker and former mayor of Los Angeles. A staunchly Catholic Republican, Riordan was actually a fairly moderate figure, promoting business investment in LA and trying to streamline city bureaucracy.

ROGERS Will Cowboy philosopher and entertainer, mayor of Beverly Hills, political commentator and Depression-era movie star, Rogers met a tragic end in a 1935 plane crash in Alaska.

SCHINDLER Rudolf Trailblazing modernist architect and Austrian expatriate who first arrived in LA to work on Frank Lloyd Wright's Hollyhock House, then built his own influential home in West Hollywood and many other important local residences.

SHULER Bob Notorious 1920s preacher of hate and intolerance, also known as "Fighting Bob," whose dramatic sermons targeted Catholics, blacks, Communists and various other groups for derision and contempt.

SENNETT Mack Actor, director and producer whose Keystone Studios launched the careers of entertainers like Fatty Arbuckle, Charlie Chaplin and the bumbling Keystone Kops.

SEPULVEDA Francisco Mexican leader and landowner whose claim to Rancho San Vicente y Santa Monica gave him title to over 30,000 acres in what is today LA's Westside.

SERRA Junípero Franciscan missionary who somewhat coercively established a chain of twenty-one missions in Alta California, including Mission San Gabriel and San Fernando.

SHAW Frank Corrupt mayor of the 1930s who was convicted of doling out public jobs for bribes and various favors. The longtime darling of the right-wing *LA Times* was finally toppled and sent to jail in 1938.

SIMON Norton Business titan, controlling major food and publishing companies, and failed politician, but most familiar as an art collector, especially of seventeenth-century Dutch art and Impressionism, shown at his eponymous Pasadena art museum.

SIMPSON Orenthal James Known to all as O.J. – star running-back for the NFL's Bulls and 49ers franchises, as well as a fixture in a series of Hollywood B-movies, who was accused – and acquitted – of murdering his ex-wife Nicole and her friend in 1994.

SMITH Jack Columnist for the *Los Angeles Times* whose insightful, piquant observations did much to define the city as a colorful, chaotic metropolis. His attempt to nickname LA the "Big Orange," however, never really caught on.

STERLING Christine Amateur historic preservationist who helped engineer the rebirth of Olvera Street in the Plaza. Sterling also tried to create pseudo-cultural zones, like "China City," complete with rickshaws and kitsch chinoiserie, with mixed results.

STREISAND Barbra Singer, actress, director and producer. A primal force in Hollywood, Streisand has also donated her Malibu estate to create a nature preserve and a walk-in movie-star habitat.

VASQUEZ Tiburcio Legendary Mexican bandit, and to some a folk hero, who fought Yankee migrants and cops. Wanted for a string of robberies and murders with other members of his gang, he was eventually captured and hanged in 1875.

WARNER Jack Movie executive who, with his three siblings, founded the Warner Bros film studio in 1918 – which made its name with the release of the first sound pic, *The Jazz Singer*.

WHITLEY Hobart J. Known as the "Father of Hollywood" for founding the early movie-star colony Whitley Heights. Also conspired to buy up San Fernando Valley real estate in advance of the arrival of Owens Valley water, then sell it for huge profits.

WILSHIRE Gaylord Oil entrepreneur who founded the Orange County town of Fullerton and widely promoted his own brand of utopian socialism. Named, modernized and developed Wilshire Boulevard.

WRIGHT Lloyd Son of Frank and a long-time LA architect who designed scores of memorable buildings, best of all the Wayfarer's Chapel in Palos Verdes.

YORTY Sam Notorious race-baiting mayor from 1961 to 1973, a right-wing populist in the George Wallace tradition, who rejected federal poverty assistance and tried to blame the Watts Riots on Martin Luther King Jr. Finally beaten by Tom Bradley after three exhausting terms.

ZUKOR Adolph New Yorker who established Hollywood film-production company Zukor's Famous Players, which merged with Jesse Lasky's company in 1916 to become Paramount. Zukor was active head of the new company for twenty years and remained Chairman Emeritus until his death – at age 103.

Architectural terms

Art Deco Catch-all term for Zigzag Moderne, Streamline Moderne, governmental WPA and other styles, often identified by geometric motifs, sharp lines and sleek ornamentation. See the Miracle Mile, pp.78–80.

Beaux Arts Turn-of-the-century

movement imported from New York and Europe emphasizing Neoclassical symmetry, imposing dimensions, grand columns and stairways, and other features now associated with old-time banks. Few authentic examples remain locally, except for the monumental Hall of Justice, p.57.

Brutalist Late-modern extreme architectural style first popularized in Britain and poorly executed in LA, emphasizing concrete, box-like construction and utter lack of ornament and aesthetic interest. See Downtown's Our Lady of the Angels church, p.58.

Bungalow Prototypical style of home design in the early twentieth century, originating in the Far East but finding popularity in LA for its use of shingles, porches and sloped roofs, and compact design. Although it was most often linked to the Arts and Crafts movement, many varieties can be spotted with Spanish Colonial, Mission, Continental and even Moderne influences. See Bungalow Heaven in Pasadena, p.181.

Case Study Program Postwar design project initiated by *Arts and Architecture* magazine, which planned and sometimes constructed modern, affordable homes made principally of steel and glass. See box on p.107 for more details, or the Eames House in Pacific Palisades, p.199.

Corporate Modern Bland reduction of the original modern aesthetic, with glass curtain walls, boxy geometry and an inhuman scale. Usually found with towering office blocks Downtown or in Century City, though sometimes inventive, as with the Library Tower, p.67.

Craftsman Early twentieth-century style, using exposed wood beams, overhanging rooflines, large shingles, cobblestones and prominent fireplaces to create a rough-hewn look. See the Gamble House, p.183.

Deconstructivist Architecture that looks like it's falling apart or incomplete, characterized by irregular shapes, aggressive asymmetry and lack of formal coherence. See box on the work of Eric Owen Moss, p.127.

Folk Architecture Home-made structures created by untrained, self-taught builders, the Watts Towers being a glorious example, p.154.

Googie Free-spirited coffee-shop architecture, with bright colors, sharp curves and boomerang shapes, pitched roofs and neon trim. See *Pann's* in South Central, p.146, or *Bob's Big Boy* in Burbank, p.192.

High-Tech 1970s and 1980s variant on the machine aesthetic, characterized by exposed pipes and ducts and industrial decor. Few good examples survive locally, although the post-industrial Carlson-Reges Residence, p.72, comes close.

Historic-Revival The early twentieth-century use of various older architectural styles – notably Spanish Colonial in the 1920s. See box on the architectural firm of Morgan, Walls and Clements, p.80.

Mission Originally the unimposing, ranch-style buildings put up by the Spanish in the eighteenth and early nineteenth centuries, such as Mission San Fernando, p.195. Later a period-revival style that reached its height with 1920s housing; see Union Station, p.56, for its most monumental form.

Modern Clean, geometric design aesthetic, beginning in the 1920s and 1930s with houses built by R.M. Schindler and Richard Neutra, such as the Lovell House, p.91, and continuing on to today's exemplars like the Getty Center, p.122.

Moderne A popular architectural style that used Art Deco ornamentation and sleek lines to convey quiet elegance. See any glossy movie set from the 1930s, or Crossroads of the World, p.102.

Period-Revival See "Historic-Revival."

Postmodern Contemporary rehash of Neoclassical architecture, often in pastel colors. See Charles Moore's Civic Center in Beverly Hills, p.114.

Pre-Columbian Quirky 1920s architecture, employing blocky sunbursts, abstract floral motifs and stylized faces to create an ancient look for the modern city. See the *Aztec Hotel*, p.188, or almost any LA work by Frank Lloyd Wright.

Programmatic Buildings taking a particular, nonarchitectural shape, such as dogs, boots, rockets and hats. See *Tail o' the Pup*, p.252, or *The Donut Hole*, p.256, for good examples.

Ranch Quintessential style of Southern California design, typically found in suburban homes with low-slung, single-story plans, open layouts with few interior walls, and abundant windows. Best seen in its grandest form at the ranch at Will Rogers State Historic Park, p.199.

Sculptural Architecture as art, often "molded" by the architect using computer-assisted design to create structures that would not be possible at a drafting table. Quite striking when successful, as in much of the work of Frank Gehry, especially the new Disney Hall, p.58.

Spanish Colonial Perhaps the quintessential style for housing architecture in LA, especially in the period-revival 1920s, emphasizing tiled roofs, wrought-ironwork, whitewashed walls and romantic landscaping. See Villa Aurora, p.200.

Streamline Moderne Buildings resembling ocean liners and sometimes airplanes, borne of a 1930s worship of all things mechanical. See the Coca-Cola Bottling Plant, p.152.

Victorian General term for late 1800s housing styles – Eastlake, Queen Anne, Stick – few of which remain in the city. See Angelino Heights, p.70, or Heritage Square, p.71.

Zigzag Moderne A late-1920s version of Art Deco that had particular popularity in LA, with strong verticality, narrow windows, geometric ornamentation and occasional use of pre-Columbian or Egyptian motifs. See Bullocks Wilshire, p.75.

Index

and small print

Index

Map entries are in color

F

INDEX

Twenty years of Rough Guides

In the summer of 1981, Mark Ellingham, Rough Guides' founder, knocked out the first guide on a typewriter, with a group of friends. Mark had been traveling in Greece after university, and couldn't find a guidebook that really answered his needs.There were heavyweight cultural guides on the one hand – good on museums and classical sites but not on beaches and tavernas – and on the other hand student manuals that were so caught up with how to save money that they lost sight of the country's significance beyond its role as a place for a cool vacation. None of the guides began to address Greece as a country, with its natural and human environment, its politics and its contemporary life.

Having no urgent reason to return home, Mark decided to write his own guide. It was a guide to Greece that tried to combine some erudition and insight with a thoroughly practical approach to travelers' needs. Scrupulously researched listings of places to stay, eat, and drink were matched by careful attention to detail on everything from Homer to Greek music, from classical sites to national parks and from nude beaches to monasteries. Back in London, Mark and his friends got their Rough Guide accepted by a farsighted commissioning editor at the publisher Routledge and it came out in 1982.

The *Rough Guide to Greece* was a student scheme that became a publishing phenomenon. The immediate success of the book – shortlisted for the Thomas Cook Award – spawned a series that rapidly covered dozens of countries. The Rough Guides found a ready market among backpackers and budget travelers, but soon acquired a much broader readership that included older and less impecunious visitors. Readers relished the guides' wit and inquisitiveness as much as the enthusiastic, critical approach that acknowledges everyone wants value for money – but not at any price.

Rough Guides soon began supplementing the "rougher" information – the hostel and low-budget listings – with the kind of detail that independent-minded travelers on any budget might expect. These days, the guides – distributed worldwide by the Penguin Group – include recommendations spanning the range from shoestring to luxury, and cover more than two hundred destinations around the globe. Our growing team of authors, many of whom come to Rough Guides initially as outstandingly good letter-writers telling us about their travels, are spread all over the world, particularly in Europe, the USA, and Australia. As well as the travel guides, Rough Guides publishes a series of dictionary phrasebooks covering two dozen major languages, an acclaimed series of music guides running the gamut from Classical to World Music, a series of music CDs in association with World Music Network, and a range of reference books on topics as diverse as the Internet, Pregnancy, and Unexplained Phenomena. Visit **www.roughguides.com** to see what's cooking.

Rough Guide credits

Text editor: Yuki Takagaki
Managing director: Kevin Fitzgerald
Series editor: Mark Ellingham
Editorial: Martin Dunford, Jonathan Buckley,
Kate Berens, Ann-Marie Shaw, Helena Smith,
Olivia Swift, Ruth Blackmore, Geoff Howard,
Claire Saunders, Gavin Thomas, Alexander
Mark Rogers, Polly Thomas, Joe Staines,
Richard Lim, Duncan Clark, Peter Buckley,
Lucy Ratcliffe, Clifton Wilkinson, Alison
Murchie, Matthew Teller, Andrew Dickson,
Fran Sandham, Sally Schafer, Matthew
Milton, Karoline Densley (UK); Andrew
Rosenberg, Richard Koss, Hunter Slaton,
Chris Barsanti (US)
Design & Layout: Link Hall, Helen Prior, Julia
Bovis, Katie Pringle, Rachel Holmes, Andy
Turner, Dan May, Tanya Hall, John McKay,
Sophie Hewat (UK); Madhulita Mohapatra,
Umesh Aggarwal, Sunil Sharma (India)
Cartography: Maxine Repath, Ed Wright,
Katie Lloyd-Jones (UK); Manish Chandra,
Rajesh Chhibber, Jai Prakesh Mishra (India)
Cover art direction: Louise Boulton
Picture research: Sharon Martins, Mark
Thomas
Online: Kelly Martinez, Anja Mutic-Blessing,
Jennifer Gold, Audra Epstein, Suzanne
Welles, Cree Lawson (US); Manik Chauhan,
Amarjyoti Dutta, Narender Kumar (India)
Finance: Gary Singh
Marketing & Publicity: Richard Trillo, Niki
Smith, David Wearn, Chloë Roberts, Demelza
Dallow, Claire Southern (UK); David Wechsler,
Megan Kennedy (US)
Administration: Julie Sanderson
RG India: Punita Singh

Publishing information

This 3rd edition published July 2003 by **Rough
Guides Ltd**,
80 Strand, London WC2R 0RL
345 Hudson Street, 4th Floor,
New York, NY 10014, USA
Distributed by the Penguin Group
Penguin Books Ltd,
80 Strand, London WC2R 0RL
Penguin Putnam, Inc.
375 Hudson Street, NY 10014, USA
Penguin Books Australia Ltd,
487 Maroondah Highway, PO Box 257,
Ringwood, Victoria 3134, Australia
Penguin Books Canada Ltd,
10 Alcorn Avenue, Toronto, Ontario
M4V 1E4 Canada
Penguin Books (NZ) Ltd,
182–190 Wairau Road, Auckland 10,
New Zealand
Typeset in Bembo and Helvetica to an original
design by Henry Iles.
Printed in Italy by LegoPrint S.p.A.

416pp includes index
A catalogue record for this book is available from
the British Library

ISBN 1-84353-058-9

The publishers and authors have done their best
to ensure the accuracy and currency of all the
information in **The Rough Guide to Los
Angeles**, however, they can accept no
responsibility for any loss, injury, or
inconvenience sustained by any traveller as a
result of information or advice contained in the
guide.

1   3   5   7   9   8   6   4   2

SMALL PRINT

Help us update

We've gone to a lot of effort to ensure that the
3rd edition of the **Rough Guide to Los
Angeles** is accurate and up to date. However,
things change – places get "discovered",
opening hours are notoriously fickle,
restaurants and rooms raise prices or lower
standards. If you feel we've got it wrong or left
something out, we'd like to know, and if you
can remember the address, the price, the
time, the phone number, so much the better.
We'll credit all contributions, and send a
copy of the next edition (or any other Rough
Guide if you prefer) for the best letters.
Everyone who writes to us and isn't already a
subscriber will receive a copy of our full-color
thrice-yearly newsletter. Please mark letters:
"**Rough Guide Los Angeles Update**" and
send to: Rough Guides, 80 Strand, London
WC2R 0RL, or Rough Guides, 4th Floor, 345
Hudson St, New York, NY 10014. Or send an
email to **mail@roughguides.com**.
Have your questions answered and tell
others about your trip at
www.roughguides.atinfopop.com.

Acknowledgements

JD would like to thank his wife.

The editor would like to thank Katie Pringle, Andy Turner and Julia Bovis for seamless production work, Melissa Baker for fine mapmaking, Stephen Lipuma for resourceful picture research, Diane Margolis for diligent proofreading, and Hunter Slaton and Andrew Rosenberg for their valuable editorial support.

Photo credits

Cover credits
Hollywood Boulevard © Axiom
Small front top picture Century city © Robert Harding
Small front lower picture Walk of Fame © Robert Harding
Back top picture Downtown skyline © Getty
Back lower picture mural © Robert Harding

Color introduction
Heavy traffic on the freeway © Larry Brownstein/Getty Images
Venice skateboarder ©Michael Brands/Network Aspen
Hollywood sign © Jeffery Aaronson/Network Aspen
Palm trees © Network/Aspen
Randy's Donuts © Todd Cheney
Main Street King Kong, Universal Studios © Trip/C. Rennie
Starstruck fans © Queen WireImage.com
Kodak Center © Michael Brands/Network Aspen
Freeway traffic © Network Aspen
Fox Westwood Theater Hollywood © Jeff Aaronson/Network Aspen
Zuma Beach © Todd Cheney

Things not to miss
1. Third Steet Promenade ©David Butow/Corbis SABA
2. Getty Center ©Trip/Amanda Edwards
3. Venice Boardwalk © Claus Guglberger
4. Gamble House © Courtesy of the Gamble House
5. Griffith Park © Griffith Observatory

6. Bradbury Building © www.greatbuildings.com
7. Melrose Avenue ©Draughtsman Ltd 2003
8. The Viper Room ©2003 The Viper Room
9. Musso and Frank Grill © Claus Guglberger
10. Greystone Mansion © Courtesy of Greystone Mansion
11. Queen Mary © RMS Foundation/The Queen Mary
12. Chinese Theatre © Claus Guglberger
13. Watts Towers © Draughtsman Ltd 2003
14. Museum of Contemporary Art, Downtown © Owen McGoldrick
15. Canter's Deli © Todd Cheney
16. Sunset Boulevard © Dorling Kindersley
17. Rodeo Drive sign © Bill Bachmann/Network Aspen
18. Disneyland Castle © Disney Enterprises
19. Malibu Creek State Park © Courtesy of Malibu Creek State Park

Black and white chapter photos
Angels Flight Railway © Jeff Dickey (p.66)
Hand- and footprints, Chinese Theatre © Claus Guglberger (p.94)
Santa Monica Pier © Draughtsman Ltd 2003 (p.140)
Traffic on the Harbor Freeway © Trip/S. Grant (p.165)
Malibu Creek State Park © Draughtsman Ltd 2003 (p.203)
Mel's Drive In © Network Aspen (p.257)
Snowboarder © 2003 Big Bear Mountain Resorts (p.312)
Rose Parade © 2003 Corbis (p.323)

SMALL PRINT

Rough Guides travel

Rough Guides travel

Rough guides music, reference & CDs

check www.roughguides.com for the latest news

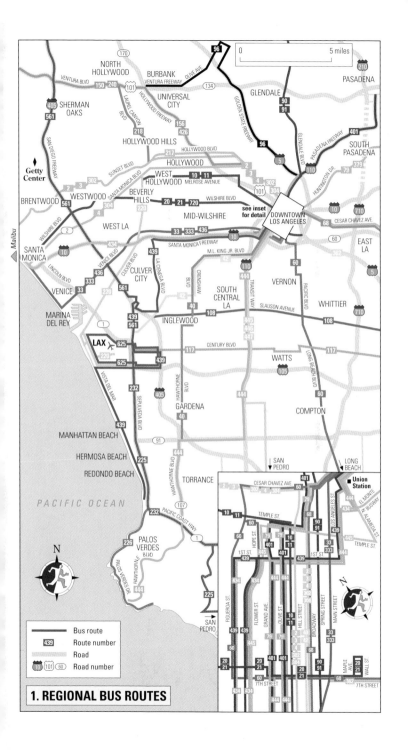

1. REGIONAL BUS ROUTES

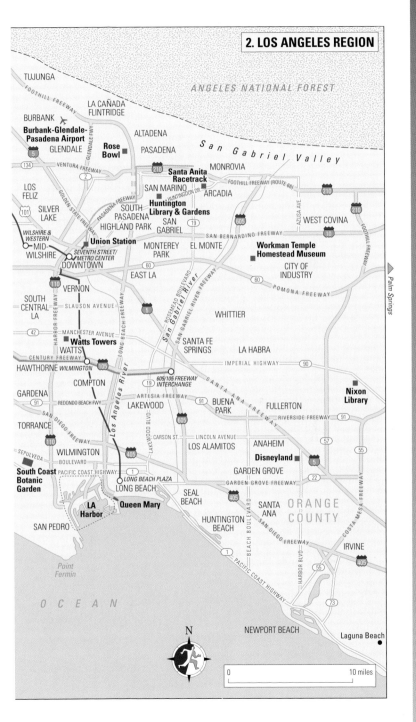

2. LOS ANGELES REGION

TUJUNGA

Foothill Freeway

LA CAÑADA FLINTRIDGE

ANGELES NATIONAL FOREST

BURBANK

Burbank-Glendale-Pasadena Airport

GLENDALE

ALTADENA

Rose Bowl

PASADENA

San Gabriel Valley

134 *Ventura Freeway*

2

MONROVIA

210

Santa Anita Racetrack

Foothill Freeway (Route 66)

210

LOS FELIZ

101 SILVER LAKE

Golden State Freeway

Pasadena Freeway

SAN MARINO

Huntingdon Dr.

ARCADIA

WEST COVINA

210

Huntington Library & Gardens

SOUTH PASADENA

Azusa Ave

110

Foothill Freeway

WILSHIRE & WESTERN

HIGHLAND PARK

SAN GABRIEL

19

San Bernardino Freeway

MID-WILSHIRE

Union Station

MONTEREY PARK

EL MONTE

Workman Temple Homestead Museum

SEVENTH STREET/METRO CENTER

DOWNTOWN

60

CITY OF INDUSTRY

110

VERNON

EAST LA

60

Pomona Freeway

SOUTH CENTRAL LA

Slauson Avenue

5

WHITTIER

42

Manchester Avenue

Watts Towers

WATTS

SANTA FE SPRINGS

LA HABRA

HAWTHORNE *WILMINGTON*

Century Freeway

105

Imperial Highway

90

Nixon Library

GARDENA

91

COMPTON

605/105 Freeway Interchange

19

Artesia Freeway

FULLERTON

Riverside Freeway 91

Redondo Beach Fwy

LAKEWOOD

91 BUENA PARK

TORRANCE

110

San Diego Freeway

605

Lakewood Blvd

Carson St.

Lincoln Avenue

LOS ALAMITOS

ANAHEIM

57

55

Sepulveda

WILMINGTON

405

Disneyland

5

Boulevard

South Coast Botanic Garden

Pacific Coast Highway

1

GARDEN GROVE

22

Garden Grove Freeway

Long Beach Plaza

LONG BEACH

SEAL BEACH

SANTA ANA

ORANGE COUNTY

LA Harbor

Queen Mary

405

Beach Boulevard

San Diego Freeway

SAN PEDRO

HUNTINGTON BEACH

55

Costa Mesa Freeway

Point Fermin

1

Pacific Coast Highway

IRVINE

405

OCEAN

N

NEWPORT BEACH

Laguna Beach

73

0 — 10 miles

▷ Palm Springs

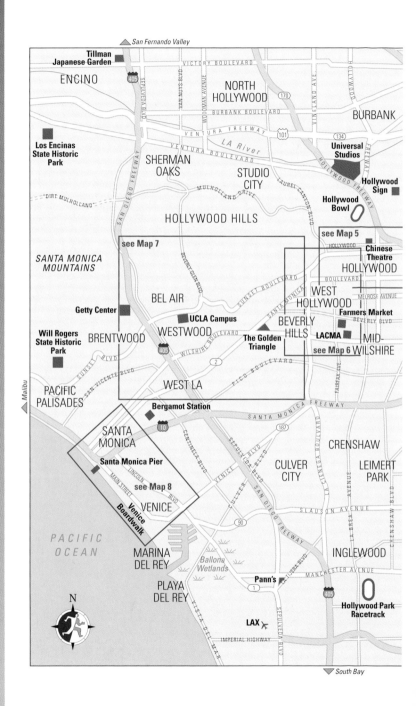

San Fernando Valley

VICTORY BOULEVARD

Tillman
Japanese Garden

ENCINO

405

NORTH
HOLLYWOOD

170

BURBANK

BURBANK BOULEVARD

VENTURA FREEWAY

101

134

Universal
Studios

Los Encinas
State Historic
Park

VENTURA BOULEVARD

LA River

SHERMAN
OAKS

STUDIO
CITY

Hollywood
Sign

MULHOLLAND DRIVE

LAUREL CANYON BLVD

HOLLYWOOD FREEWAY

"DIRT MULHOLLAND"

SAN DIEGO FREEWAY

HOLLYWOOD HILLS

Hollywood
Bowl

SANTA MONICA
MOUNTAINS

see Map 7

HOLLYWOOD

see Map 5

Chinese
Theatre

HOLLYWOOD

BEVERLY GLEN BLVD

SUNSET BOULEVARD

SANTA MONICA

BOULEVARD

HOLLYWOOD

WEST
HOLLYWOOD

MELROSE AVENUE

BEL AIR

Getty Center

UCLA Campus

Farmers Market

BEVERLY BLVD

BEVERLY
HILLS

LACMA

Will Rogers
State Historic
Park

BRENTWOOD

WESTWOOD

WILSHIRE BOULEVARD

405

The Golden
Triangle

2

MID-
WILSHIRE

see Map 6

SUNSET BLVD

PICO BOULEVARD

SAN VICENTE BLVD

WEST LA

PACIFIC
PALISADES

Malibu

Bergamot Station

10

SANTA MONICA FREEWAY

187

SANTA
MONICA

CENTINELA BOULEVARD

VENICE

SEPULVEDA BLVD

CULVER
CITY

LA CIENEGA BOULEVARD

CRENSHAW

LEIMERT
PARK

CRENSHAW BLVD

Santa Monica Pier

LINCOLN

MAIN STREET

BLVD

see Map 8

VENICE

Venice
Boardwalk

CULVER BLVD

SAN DIEGO FREEWAY

SLAUSON AVENUE

PACIFIC
OCEAN

MARINA
DEL REY

90

Ballona
Wetlands

Pann's

1

INGLEWOOD

LA TIJERA BLVD

MANCHESTER AVENUE

PLAYA
DEL REY

405

Hollywood Park
Racetrack

VISTA DEL MAR

LAX

SEPULVEDA BLVD

N

IMPERIAL HIGHWAY

South Bay

Angeles National Forest

0   5 miles

LA CAÑADA-FLINTRIDGE

GLENDALE

ALTADENA

Rose Bowl

Gamble House

PASADENA

134

VENTURA FREEWAY

COLORADO BLVD

OLIVE AVENUE

GLENDALE BLVD

BRAND BLVD

COLORADO ST

GOLDEN STATE FREEWAY

SAN FERNANDO ROAD

Griffith Park

Eagle Rock

OLD PASADENA

Griffith Observatory

HIGHLAND PARK

Huntington Library and Gardens

SAN MARINO

2

Southwest Museum

SOUTH PASADENA

PASADENA FREEWAY

LOS FELIZ BLVD

BLVD

LOS FELIZ

SILVER LAKE

SUNSET BLVD

GLENDALE FREEWAY

5

Heritage Square

110

HUNTINGTON DRIVE

HYPERION AVE

VALLEY BOULEVARD

101

ECHO PARK   see Map 4

WESTLAKE   CHINATOWN

SAN BERNARDINO FREEWAY

10

WILSHIRE BOULEVARD

KOREA TOWN   Bullocks Wilshire Building

Union Station

PICO BLVD

LA City Hall

DOWNTOWN

BOYLE HEIGHTS

EAST LA

710

ATLANTIC BOULEVARD

GARFIELD AVENUE

10

POMONA FREEWAY

60

WEST ADAMS

USC Campus

WHITTIER BOULEVARD

Exposition Park

M.L. KING JR BLVD

SANTA ANA FREEWAY

The Citadel

110

VERNON

LA River

5

WESTERN AVENUE

VERNON AVENUE

HARBOR FREEWAY

CENTRAL AVENUE

ALAMEDA STREET

PACIFIC BLVD

SLAUSON AVENUE

SOUTHEAST LA

GARFIELD AVENUE

FLORENCE AVENUE

SOUTH CENTRAL LA

FLORENCE AVENUE

710

42

WILMINGTON BLVD

FIRESTONE BOULEVARD

CENTURY BOULEVARD

WATTS

Watts Towers

LONG BEACH ROAD

ATLANTIC AVENUE

IMPERIAL HIGHWAY

105

3. CENTRAL LA

San Gabriel Valley

Whittier

Orange County

210

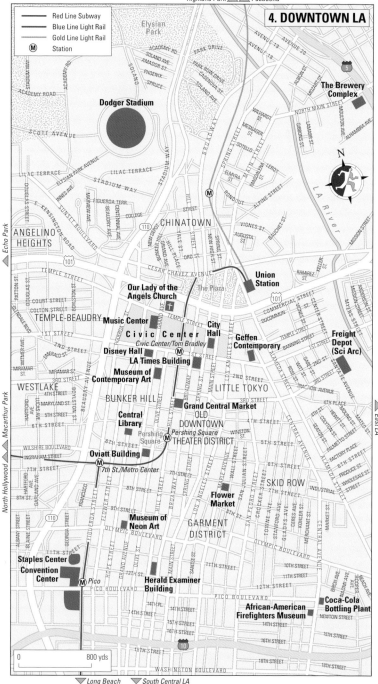

4. DOWNTOWN LA

Red Line Subway
Blue Line Light Rail
Gold Line Light Rail
Ⓜ Station

Elysian
Park

ACADEMY RD.
SOLANO AVE
AMADOR ST
PHOENIX
SPRUCE

PARK DRIVE
PARK ROW DRIVE
CASENZA ST
SOLANO AVE

AVENUE 19
AVENUE 20
AVENUE 18

The Brewery
Complex

MOZART ST
NORTH MAIN STREET
MIDDLETON AVE
ALHAMBRA AVE

ACADEMY ROAD

Dodger Stadium

WILHARDT ST
MESNAGER ST
ELMYRA ST
SOTELLO ST
LEROY
MAGDALENA ST
LAMAR ST
GIBBONS ST

SCOTT AVENUE

LILAC TERRACE
ELYSIAN PARK AVENUE
KENSINGTON ROAD
LILAC TERRACE
STADIUM WAY
STADIUM WAY

BROADWAY
SPRING STREET
MAIN STREET

ALPINE STREET
RONDOUT ST
BAUCHET ST.

LA River

ANGELINO
HEIGHTS

FIGUEROA TERR.
BEAUDRY AVE
CENTENNIAL ST
COLLEGE
HILL STREET

CHINATOWN

VIGNES ST
AUGUSTA ST

N

ECHO PARK
SUNSET BOULEVARD
DOUGLAS ST
KENSINGTON ROAD
INNES AVE
MARVIEW AVE

NEW DEPOT ST
SUNSHINE ST
HILL PLACE
GRAND AVE
YALE ST
ORD ST.
NEW HIGH ST
SPRING ST
NEW DEPOT ST

RAMIREZ ST
KELLER ST

TEMPLE STREET

CESAR CHAVEZ AVENUE

The Plaza

**Union
Station**

COMMERCIAL STREET
DUCOMMUN

MISSION ROAD

**Our Lady of the
Angels Church**

TEMPLE-BEAUDRY
Music Center

C i v i c   C e n t e r
Civic Center/Tom Bradley Ⓜ

TEMPLE STREET
**City
Hall**
**Geffen
Contemporary**

TEMPLE STREET
BANNING STREET

**Freight
Depot
(Sci Arc)**

PATTON ST
DOUGLAS ST
COURT STREET
COLTON STREET

1ST STREET
2ND STREET
WITMER ST
EMERALD ST

FIGUEROA ST
GRAND AVE
HILL STREET
BROADWAY
SPRING ST

CENTER STREET
CENTER STREET
VIGNES ST

Disney Hall
LA Times Building
1ST STREET
Ⓜ

LOS ANGELES ST
2ND STREET
3RD STREET

ALAMEDA STREET
SANTA FE AVENUE
SANTA FE AVENUE
TRACTION AVENUE
HEWITT ST

MIRAMAR ST
3RD STREET
MIRAMAR ST

**Museum of
Contemporary Art**

2ND STREET

LITTLE TOKYO

4TH PLACE
4TH STREET

WESTLAKE
4TH STREET
MARYLAND ST

BUNKER HILL

Grand Central Market
OLD
DOWNTOWN

3RD STREET
CENTRAL AVENUE
COTTON ST
SEATON ST
PALMETTO STREET
FACTORY PLACE

MACARTHUR PARK
HARTFORD AVE
5TH STREET

**Central
Library**

4TH STREET

WINSTON ST
5TH STREET

PRODUCE ST
WHOLESALE ST

WILSHIRE BOULEVARD
INGRAHAM STREET

Pershing
Square Ⓜ
**Pershing
Square**
THEATER DISTRICT

6TH STREET

NORTH HOLLYWOOD
7TH STREET
HARTFORD AVE
GARLAND AVE
8TH STREET

Oviatt Building

Ⓜ 7th St./Metro Center
FRANCISCO ST
FLOWER STREET
HOPE STREET
GRAND AVE
OLIVE STREET

7TH STREET
8TH STREET

SKID ROW

INDUSTRIAL STREET

MAPLE AVENUE
SAN JULIAN STREET
SAN PEDRO STREET
CROCKER STREET
TOWNE AVENUE

**Flower
Market**

**Museum of
Neon Art**

OLYMPIC BOULEVARD

GARMENT
DISTRICT

8TH STREET
STANFORD AVE
GLADYS AVE
CERES AVE
KOHLER ST
MERCHANT ST

OLYMPIC BOULEVARD

ALBANY STREET
BLAINE STREET
GEORGIA ST

FIGUEROA ST
FLOWER ST

11TH STREET
12TH ST

9TH STREET

MAIN STREET
SANTEE ST

11TH STREET
11TH STREET
12TH STREET

MARKET
HOOPER AVE

Staples Center
**Convention
Center**

Ⓜ Pico
PICO BOULEVARD

**Herald Examiner
Building**

PICO BOULEVARD
10TH STREET

Coca-Cola
Bottling Plant

14TH PL.
14TH STREET
14TH STREET

15TH STREET
16TH STREET

PICO BOULEVARD

**African-American
Firefighters Museum**

14TH STREET

NEWTON STREET

15TH STREET

0   800 yds

18TH STREET

WASHINGTON BOULEVARD

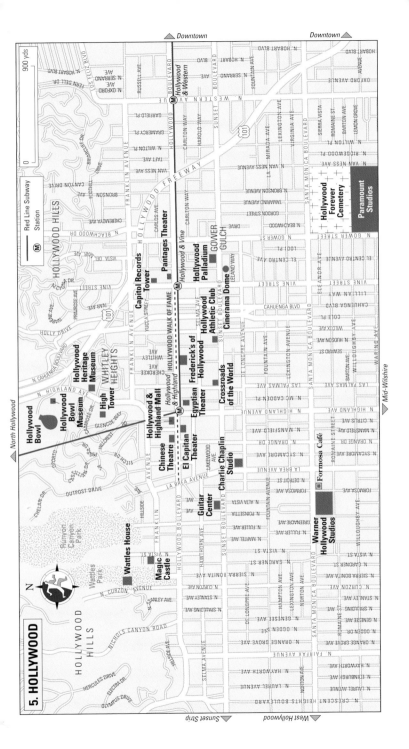

5. HOLLYWOOD

Red Line Subway
Ⓜ Station

900 yds
0

N

Downtown △△ *Downtown* △

△ *North Hollywood*

HOLLYWOOD HILLS

Runyon Canyon Park

Wattles Park

Hollywood Bowl
Hollywood Bowl Museum
Hollywood Heritage Museum
High Tower House
WHITLEY HEIGHTS

Wattles House
Magic Castle
Guitar Center
Chinese Theatre
El Capitan Theater
Charlie Chaplin Studio
Hollywood & Highland Mall
Ⓜ Hollywood & Highland
Egyptian Theater
Frederick's of Hollywood
Crossroads of the World
Formosa Café
Warner Hollywood Studios

Capitol Records Tower
Pantages Theater
Ⓜ Hollywood & Vine
Hollywood Palladium
Hollywood Athletic Club
Cinerama Dome
GOWER GULCH

Ⓜ Hollywood & Western

Paramount Studios
Hollywood Forever Cemetery

HOLLYWOOD WALK OF FAME

HOLLYWOOD FREEWAY

△ *Sunset Strip*
▽ *West Hollywood*
▽ *Mid-Wilshire*

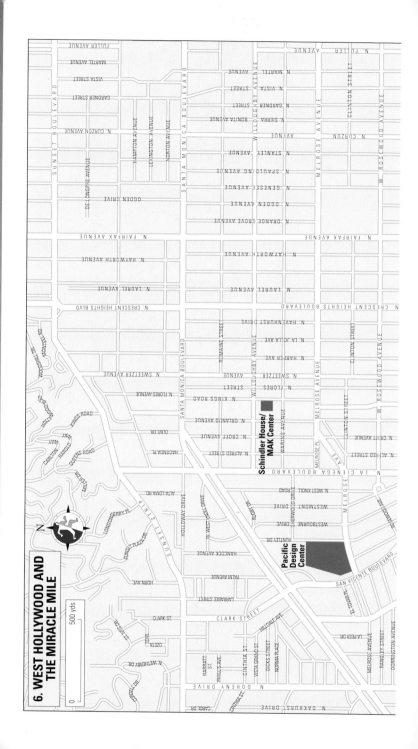

6. WEST HOLLYWOOD AND THE MIRACLE MILE

N

0   500 yds

Schindler House/
MAK Center

Pacific
Design
Center